COLLECTED PAPERS, VOLUME 2

Collected Papers, Volume 2

KNOWLEDGE, RATIONALITY, AND MORALITY, 1978–2010

Stephen Stich

OXFORD
UNIVERSITY PRESS

OXFORD
UNIVERSITY PRESS

Oxford University Press is a department of the University of Oxford.
It furthers the University's objective of excellence in research,
scholarship, and education by publishing worldwide.

Oxford   New York
Auckland   Cape Town   Dar es Salaam   Hong Kong   Karachi
Kuala Lumpur   Madrid   Melbourne   Mexico City   Nairobi
New Delhi   Shanghai   Taipei   Toronto

With offices in
Argentina   Austria   Brazil   Chile   Czech Republic   France   Greece
Guatemala   Hungary   Italy   Japan   Poland   Portugal   Singapore
South Korea   Switzerland   Thailand   Turkey   Ukraine   Vietnam

Published in the United States of America by Oxford University Press
198 Madison Avenue, New York, NY 10016

www.oup.com

Oxford is a registered trade mark of Oxford University Press in the UK and certain other countries.

Library of Congress Cataloging-in-Publication Data
Stich, Stephen P.
[Selections. 2011]
Collected papers / by Stephen Stich.
    v.   cm.
Includes bibliographical references.
Contents: v. 1. Mind and language, 1972–2010
ISBN 978-0-19-973410-8 (v. 1 : alk. paper)
I. Title.
B945.S7551   2011
191—dc22   2010013600

9 8 7 6 5 4 3 2 1

Printed in the United States of America
on acid-free paper

To Dick Nisbett

Contents

COLLECTED PAPERS, VOLUME 2

INTRODUCTION

THE ESSAYS IN this second volume of my *Collected Papers*, like those in the first, are arranged chronologically, and the similarity between the volumes does not stop there. In both books, the essays span more than three decades and cover a wide variety of topics. Also, apart from correcting minor errors and updating the references where this was required, the papers in both volumes appear as they were published. The focus of the earlier volume was on issues in the philosophy of mind and the philosophy of language. Here the focus shifts to knowledge, rationality, and morality. There is one respect in which the essays collected here are more unified. In the first volume, as I noted in its introduction, there were two unifying themes: the debate over eliminative materialism, which challenges the viability of the commonsense conception of the mind, and the exploration of the philosophical implications of research in cognitive science. In this volume, that first theme has all but disappeared; all the essays, except for the first, are concerned in one way or another with the ways in which findings and theories in the cognitive sciences can contribute to, and sometimes reshape, traditional philosophical conversations and debates.

1. Knowledge and Rationality

Though the work of many cognitive scientists is discussed in the pages that follow, no one has played a greater role in shaping my thinking than my friend and former colleague Richard Nisbett. The story of how these essays unfolded begins with him. From 1968 to 1978, I was on the faculty at the University of Michigan in Ann Arbor, and sometime during my last two or three years at Michigan, Alvin Goldman, a Philosophy Department colleague, told me that an acquaintance of his in the Psychology Department had completed a draft of a book on human judgment and human reasoning, which, the psychologist felt, would benefit from the feedback of philosophers. Would I, Goldman asked, be willing to participate in a group, meeting every few weeks, in which he and I would discuss the manuscript with the author and one of his graduate students? Though I have acquired many intellectual debts to Goldman over the decades, none of them is more important than the debt I owe him for that invitation. The Psychology Department colleague was Dick Nisbett, whom I hadn't met prior to the start of the discussion group, and the manuscript we were discussing was a draft of *Human Inference*, co-authored with Stanford psychologist Lee Ross. The graduate student, who rounded out the group, was Tim Wilson, who went on to a stellar career at the University of Virginia. *Human Inference* was the first book-length overview of research in what soon became known as the "heuristics and biases" tradition, begun a few years earlier by Amos Tversky and Danny Kahneman. To the best of my notoriously fallible memory, I knew nothing about the research on heuristics and biases until I read the Nisbett and Ross manuscript. And it is no exaggeration at all to say that when I began reading the manuscript, it blew me away. It had, and continues to have, a profound effect on my approach to philosophy. A brief explanation of why I was so deeply influenced by work in the heuristics and biases tradition will provide some useful context for the essays on knowledge and rationality.

Aristotle, as all philosophy majors know, thought that man is a rational animal, and much of the philosophical tradition for the last 2,400 years has concurred. Philosophers are aware, of course, that people often do and say irrational things. But, prior to the emergence of the heuristics and biases tradition, this irrationality was thought of as noise—an unfortunate aberration that could be explained by the influence of factors such as fatigue, unruly emotions, distracted attention, or strong drink. In the admittedly anachronistic jargon of contemporary cognitive science, the view was that normal humans have an underlying rational competence, and that instances of irrational reasoning and decision making are performance errors. The work that Nisbett and Ross were reviewing, and contributing to, in *Human Inference* seemed to pose a head-on challenge to this venerable view. Yes, some instances of irrational thought and judgment, or perhaps many, are performance errors that do not reflect the agent's underlying competence. But in lots of other cases people are irrational because that's the way the human mind works. The only resources they have available for many important reasoning tasks is a set of heuristics and biases—reasoning strategies that sometimes end up with the normatively sanctioned result, and sometimes don't. The take-home message of *Human Inference* was that humans aren't really rational animals, and that their departures from rationality are systematic and can be empirically explored.

Though I thought that this research had important implications for a wide range of philosophical projects, the first connection that came into focus was the challenge it posed for Nelson Goodman's enormously influential work on the justification of induction, in *Fact,*

Fiction and Forecast (Goodman 1965). It was no accident that this link to the philosophical literature was the one that seemed clearest to me, since as an undergraduate I had been a student of Goodman's. In what was by far the most impressive and influential course in my undergraduate career, Goodman used the Socratic method to lead a small class through the arguments in *Fact, Fiction and Forecast*. In my probably somewhat idealized memory, Goodman did nothing but ask questions and raise objections to the answers that students proposed. He never seemed to *tell* us anything. Yet by the end of the course, we had re-created all the arguments in *Fact, Fiction and Forecast*, and, having re-created them on our own, or so it seemed, many of us embraced them. I certainly did. But the results recounted by Nisbett and Ross in *Human Inference* seemed to pose a serious problem for one of the most important parts of *Fact, Fiction and Forecast*. In chapter 3, Goodman asks what is required to show that a rule of inference, either deductive or inductive, is *justified*. His answer, which you will find quoted more than once in the essays to follow, was that rules of inference

> are justified by their conformity with accepted deductive practice. Their validity depends on accordance with the particular . . . inferences we actually make and sanction. . . . [R]ules and inferences alike are justified by being brought into agreement with each other. *A rule is amended if it yields an inference we are unwilling to accept; an inference is rejected if it violates a rule we are unwilling to amend.* The process of justification is the delicate one of making mutual adjustments between rules and accepted inferences; and in the agreement achieved lies the only justification for either. (Goodman 1965, 64; emphasis in the original)

In *A Theory of Justice*, Rawls (1971) introduced the term "reflective equilibrium" for the endpoint of the process of mutual adjustment that Goodman describes. Though Goodman does not tell us *why* rules of inference that are in reflective equilibrium are justified, a natural reading is that the reflective equilibrium process provides an analysis (or a "conservative explication") of what we *mean* when we say that a rule is justified.

Nisbett and I thought that a growing body of findings in the heuristics and biases literature made this more than a bit implausible. For in the domain of probabilistic reasoning most notably, the inferences that many people "actually make" are, to put it mildly, normatively problematic. People ignore base rates; they judge that the probability of a conjunction is greater than the probability of the individual conjuncts; they take no account of regression to the mean; the list goes on and on. Moreover, in some cases at least, it is plausible to suppose that if a person who makes inferences of this sort was presented with a rule of inference that allows such inferences, he would accept them both. So the rule would pass Goodman's reflective equilibrium test. But despite this, we had no inclination at all to say that such a rule of inference is justified. And that, we argued in "Justification and the Psychology of Human Reasoning" (chapter 2), suggests that Goodman's reflective equilibrium analysis fails to capture our concept of justification. Nisbett and I went on to propose an alternative analysis of justification that focused on the reflective equilibrium of experts, though in "Reflective Equilibrium, Analytic Epistemology and the Problem of Cognitive Diversity" I argue that that one does not work, either.

The critique of Goodman that Nisbett and I developed depends crucially on the empirical claim that human reasoning competence is, in some areas at least, far from rational. Many philosophers were skeptical of that claim, and they backed their skepticism with a variety of arguments. Dan Dennett had developed a very influential account of how people go about ascribing intentional states to agents which entailed that the intentional states we attribute, and the behavior explained by those intentional states, must be rational. So for Dennett, intentional ascription and rationality are a package deal. If an agent is not rational, we can't attribute beliefs to him at all. And if that's right, Dennett pointed out, then there must be something very wrong about the claims made by researchers in the heuristics and biases tradition, since they are attributing beliefs and other intentional states to their experimental subjects, and going on to claim that these subjects draw irrational inferences from these beliefs. I was not much impressed by that argument since, for reasons set out in "Dennett on Intentional Systems" (vol. 1, chapter 5), I think Dennett's rationality-based "intentional systems" account of intentional ascription is mistaken. In "Could Man Be an Irrational Animal?" (chapter 3), my critique of Dennett relies on an alternative account of intentional ascription that I first developed in a paper called "On the Ascription of Content" (Stich 1982). That paper is not included in this collection because I no longer endorse either the account or the method used to support it. My current view is that giving an account of how people actually go about attributing intentional states is a job for cognitive science, not for armchair philosophy. And while the jury is still out, I think it is pretty clear that Dennett's rationality-based theory isn't in the running.[1] A second influential argument that Dennett offered for the conclusion that normal humans must be rational was based on evolutionary considerations. But, as I argue in "Could Man Be an Irrational Animal?," that one doesn't work, either.[2]

The third argument considered in "Could Man Be an Irrational Animal?" was developed by the Oxford philosopher L. Jonathan Cohen, and it takes a very different tack. Cohen adopts Goodman's reflective equilibrium account of what is required to give a normative justification for a set of inferential rules. Then, borrowing an idea from Chomsky, Cohen argues that a *descriptive* theory of reasoning competence, like a descriptive theory of grammatical competence, will be an idealized theory aimed at capturing intuitions—grammatical intuitions in the case of grammar, and intuitions about the correctness or incorrectness of inferences in the case of reasoning. The conclusion Cohen draws is that a correct theory of reasoning competence must be identical with a normative theory of reasoning, since they use the same data and idealize it in the same way. Intriguingly, Cohen says much the same about a descriptive theory of moral competence and a normative theory in ethics. When I first heard Cohen present this argument, I was struck by the

1. My reasons are set out in Nichols and Stich 2003, 142–48.
2. For a more detailed version of my argument see Stich 1990, ch. 3.

fact that if we take the analogy with grammar seriously, we should expect that there are lots of very different reasoning competences to be found in the world, just as there are lots of very different grammatical competences. And if that's right, Cohen's view leads to a florid relativism in the normative theory of reasoning, since each of these reasoning competences would, according to Cohen, be normatively impeccable. To avoid this sort of extreme relativism, Cohen might (and occasionally does) suggest that our reasoning competence is innate.[3] But, as I note in "Could Man Be an Irrational Animal?," this is an *empirical* claim for which Cohen offers no evidence at all. The conclusion I drew from all of this is that Cohen had given the wrong account of what is required for an inferential system to be rational or justified.

While Cohen clearly had no evidence to support the assumption that reasoning competence is innate and does not vary from individual to individual or from culture to culture, I didn't have a lot of evidence indicating that it does. The heuristics and biases literature could be read as offering a bit of support for the idea that reasoning competence varies, since in these experiments it is not the case that *all* subjects neglect base rates, commit the conjunction fallacy, etc.[4] Also, the analogies with grammar and morality suggest that there should be lots of cross-cultural variability. However, I didn't think my critique of Goodman's reflective equilibrium account of justification required that reasoning competence actually does vary from culture to culture. All I needed, or so I thought, is that it was logically possible that it *could* vary. That, I thought (and continue to think), is obviously true. Still, the analogies between grammar, reasoning, and morality led to a suspicion that has played a major role in my thinking for the last three decades. If Chomsky is right, all grammars share lots of important features. But there are also some very important culturally determined differences, as we discover very quickly when we try to learn a foreign language. If reasoning and morality are similar to grammar in this respect, then culture is profoundly philosophically important because it affects features of the mind that are of central concern to philosophers. And if culture shapes both reasoning and moral judgment, this will likely lead to a cascade of ways in which culture affects our mental lives. Put succinctly, the suspicion that has helped shape my thinking for the last thirty years is that *the impact of culture runs deep*.

Since that was *only* a suspicion, however, I had to make do with the fact that it *might* be true, and I focused my attention on exploring what would follow if it is. In "Justification and the Psychology of Human Reasoning," Nisbett and I argued that Goodman's reflective equilibrium account of justification fails to capture our concept of justification, and offered an alternative that focused on the reflective equilibrium of experts. But it didn't take long for me to realize that our alternative account failed for much the same

---

3. Actually, though neither Cohen nor I made note of it at the time, the innateness of reasoning competence is not enough to avoid relativism, since there are *lots* of innate human traits, ranging from sex to blood type to hair color, that are far from universal.

4. Nor is it the case that when a subject gets the right answer, it is just a lucky guess. Stanovich 1999 shows that some subjects get the right answer much more often than others.

reason that Goodman's had. As I note in "Reflective Equilibrium, Analytic Epistemology, and the Problem of Cognitive Diversity" (chapter 4), "it seems entirely possible for the expert community, under the influence of ideology, recreational chemistry, or evil demons, to end up endorsing some quite nutty set of [inferential] rules." My first reaction to this realization was to look for a better account. But while at work on that project, I gradually realized that if the impact of culture runs deep, then the project itself is deeply problematic. For if there can be cultural variation in reasoning strategies and other cognitive processes, there can also be cultural variation in the evaluative concepts used to assess reasoning. So it might well be the case that some culture, real or imagined, differs from ours in two ways. Both their reasoning processes *and* the concepts they use to evaluate reasoning are very different from ours. Moreover, it is entirely possible that while our evaluative concepts (concepts such as justification, rationality, and the like) rank our reasoning processes far above theirs, their evaluative concepts rank *their* reasoning processes far above *ours*. Now suppose that we are trying to decide whether to stick with our reasoning processes or to adopt those of the alien culture. Would it help at all to know that *our* evaluative concepts decree that our reasoning processes are better? The answer urged in chapter 4 is that without some reason to think that our evaluative concepts are better than theirs, it would be of no help at all. Though it took me a while to realize it, the argument I've just sketched is a close cousin of an argument Wesley Salmon used, back in 1957, to criticize Peter Strawson's proposed justification of induction (Salmon 1957). Justifying induction is easy, Strawson argued, since being supported by inductive evidence is part of what *we mean* when we say an empirical belief is *reasonable*. But if that's the end of the story, Salmon replied, it doesn't help at all, since it doesn't tell us why anyone should *want* to be reasonable.

So it looked like conceptual analysis wasn't going to be of much help in deciding among alternative ways of going about the business of reasoning. What's the alternative? Quine, who had long been one of my intellectual heroes, had proposed that epistemology could be "naturalized" by studying how the process of belief formation actually works.

> The stimulation of his sensory receptors is all the evidence anybody has had to go on, ultimately, in arriving at his picture of the world. Why not see how this construction really proceeds? Why not settle for psychology? (Quine 1969, 75)

But, as I argue in "Naturalizing Epistemology: Quine, Simon, and the Prospects for Pragmatism" (chapter 6), the heuristics and biases literature makes it clear that this won't work, since in building their picture of the world, many people use epistemically problematic strategies. A much better idea is to focus on people who are doing a *good* job at reasoning and theory building, and try to figure out how *they* do it. Once we understand their reasoning processes, we might even be able to find ways to improve them. Whose reasoning processes should we study? Leading scientists are an obvious choice, and in chapter 6 I sketch some of the fascinating work done by Herbert Simon and his associates, aimed at understanding, simulating, and perhaps improving upon the reasoning of good scientists. Of course, scientists are not the only group whose cognitive processes could be studied in this way. We could also study the reasoning of leading historians or literary critics or theologians or entrepreneurs. And it might well turn out that leading figures in these fields reason in importantly different ways. If it does, then the sort of naturalized pragmatic epistemology that I endorse will offer an array of "hypothetical imperatives": If you want to do widely admired physics, use reasoning strategy A. If you want to do widely admired literary criticism, use reasoning strategy B. If you want to do widely admired theology, use reasoning strategy C. It is not the job of this sort of epistemology to tell you which of these goals you should want. That, I believe, requires something rather like an existential choice.

In a paper published in 1975, Nisbett and Borgida drew the widely quoted conclusion that research in the heuristics and biases tradition has "bleak implications" for the rationality of ordinary people. What the research shows, according to Slovic, Fischhoff, and Lichtenstein (1976), is that "people lack the correct programs for many important judgmental tasks. . . . We have not had the opportunity to evolve an intellect capable of dealing conceptually with uncertainty." The challenges to this conclusion posed by Dennett and Cohen, in the late 1970s and early 1980s, were philosophical challenges rooted in philosophical accounts of intentional ascription and the justification of inferential rules. Toward the end of the 1980s, a very different sort of challenge emerged. Evolutionary psychologists, led by Leda Cosmides, John Tooby, Gerd Gigerenzer, and Steven Pinker, argued that from an evolutionary perspective it is singularly implausible that our species would have evolved with no "instinct for probability" or that we would be "blind to chance" (Pinker 1997, 351). Since probabilistic information is widespread and enormously useful in a wide range of tasks, genes that led to improved probabilistic reasoning would likely have been favored by natural selection. But natural selection typically does not build mechanisms to solve problems that the species does not confront. So we should expect that the mental mechanisms subserving probabilistic reasoning would be built to handle the sorts of problems that confronted our Pleistocene forebears, not the sorts of problems typically presented in heuristics and biases experiments. This line of reasoning led evolutionary psychologists to design reasoning experiments in which the probabilistic problems posed were claimed to be more similar to problems that would have been encountered by our hunter-gatherer ancestors, and in many cases subjects' performance improved dramatically. In the wake of these results, a number of writers began to flirt with a view that sounded rather similar to the one Cohen had defended. Perhaps all the reasoning errors reported in the heuristics and biases literature are just performance errors. Perhaps, as Cosmides and Tooby provocatively suggested, "humans [are] good intuitive statisticians after all" (1996). In "Rethinking Rationality: From Bleak Implications to Darwinian Modules" (chapter 7), Richard Samuels, Patrice Tremoulet, and I dubbed this the "Panglossian interpretation" of research on human reasoning. Our goal in that paper was to set out the case on both sides and then explore whether the bleak interpretation or the Panglossian interpretation was closer to the truth. What we concluded is that if the account of the mind defended by evolutionary psychologists is on the right track, then *neither* interpretation is satisfactory. If the mind really is chockablock with "Darwinian modules," as the evolutionary psychologists maintain, then in many cases errors in reasoning will be neither performance errors nor a result of a defective reasoning competence. A richer taxonomy of the causes of error is required. The familiar reliabilist account of how a reasoning mechanism is assessed will also need to be rebuilt.[5]

Samuels and I were rather pleased with ourselves for having sorted all of this out. But the cacophonous debate between evolutionary psychologists and researchers in the heuristics and biases tradition raged on. We were convinced that there was more heat than light in this dispute, so we teamed up with Mike Bishop to write "Ending the Rationality Wars: How to Make Disputes About Human Reasoning Disappear" (chapter 9). What we argue in that paper is that the claims about human rationality urged by the two camps could, in a fairly principled way, be divided into core claims and rhetorical flourishes. The rhetorical flourishes include claims that are not supported by experimental evidence and claims that get withdrawn when challenged. While each side adamantly rejects the other's rhetorical flourishes, neither research program denies the core claims made by the other side, and in many cases they clearly do, or could, accept them. This is not to say that there are no real disputes between evolutionary psychologists and heuristics and biases researchers. There are. But these deal with issues like the proper interpretation of probability and whether a theory of reasoning must include a process model. On questions about the scope and limits of human rationality, we argue, there is far more consensus than discord. At my insistence, we began the "Rationality Wars" paper with a biblical quote: "Blessed are the peacemakers; for they shall be called the children of God." I don't know if anyone called us the children of God, though I do know that we were called lots of other things. Many researchers made it clear that they were not happy with our paper. But since the criticisms came from both sides, I am inclined to think we got it just about right.

As I noted earlier, I have long suspected that the impact of culture runs deep, and that cultural differences in the way we reason and make moral judgments would have important implications for a host of philosophical issues. But in the mid-1980s, when I wrote "Reflective Equilibrium, Analytic Epistemology, and the Problem of Cognitive Diversity," I didn't have much evidence for my suspicion. So I did what philosophers often do: I described a hypothetical case of cultural diversity—a culture that reasoned quite differently from us and also used quite different evaluative concepts when evaluating reasoning—and I asked what conclusions could be drawn from the fact that a culture like that *might* exist. My answer, you will recall, is that it made the entire project of using conceptual analysis as a central tool in assessing reasoning look problematic. And while I thought this was quite a powerful and persuasive argument, it found remarkably little

---

5. In another paper, not included in this collection, Samuels, Luc Faucher, and I explore the issues further (Samuels, Stich, and Faucher 2004).

traction. One reason for this, I gradually came to realize, is that philosophers didn't see anything really new in the argument. Of course it is (logically) possible that a culture could reason and evaluate reasoning in ways that we find odd and unfamiliar. And perhaps this can be used in an argument for skepticism about Goodman's reflective equilibrium strategy for justifying inferential rules. However, it is also (logically) possible that people embedded in identical environments could have radically different perceptual experiences. And perhaps that can be used in an argument for skepticism about beliefs in the external world. But we've known that since Descartes! So, a number of philosophers told me, there is really nothing new in your argument about cultural diversity in reasoning. It is just (yawn!) a special case of Cartesian skepticism. It certainly didn't help that I had myself invoked an evil demon at one point in my "Reflective Equilibrium" paper.

At this juncture in the story of how these essays came to be, Dick Nisbett makes another crucial appearance. As the previous century was drawing to a close, our paths crossed at a conference in Davis, California, and he urged that we steal away and talk for a few hours, because he was doing some work that he wanted to tell me about. At an outdoor coffee shop, in the cool California sun, he began to describe his new line of research, exploring cultural differences in cognitive possesses. Focusing on East Asians from China, Japan, and Korea and on Americans whose cultural background was European, Nisbett and his students had been finding an astounding array of difference in memory, attention, perception, explanatory strategies, categorization, and patterns of belief revision. My jaw dropped. I was completely astonished. And, truth be told, I'm not sure I believed it. Certainly, had I heard this from anyone but Nisbett, who I knew to be a scrupulously careful scientist, I would have been flat-out skeptical. Though I had long suspected that the effects of culture run deep, it had never occurred to me that they run *that* deep.[6] I asked Dick to send me as many drafts of papers as he could, and as soon as I returned to Rutgers, I set up a discussion group to talk about this extraordinary work. Apart from its paradigm-shattering scientific importance, it was of course not lost on me that Nisbett's new work provided a superb way to respond to those who dismissed the argument in "Reflective Equilibrium" (and the longer version of the argument in my book *The Fragmentation of Reason*) as just a special case of Cartesian skepticism.[7] We don't have to *imagine* a group of people who reason very differently from us. The existence of such people is not just *possible*, it is *actual*. They are called East Asians, there are more than a billion of them, and they are doing quite well, thank you.

This, however, only showed that half of what I had conjured in my thought experiment actually existed. What about the other half—cultures that invoke different evaluative concepts? As luck would have it, Chris Knapp, then a graduate student at Rutgers, had drawn

---

6. And there was a lot more to come. For an exciting and provocative update, see Henrich, Heine, and Norenzayan 2010.

7. Stich 1990.

my attention to some recent work by Jonathan Haidt. Jon, who was in the vanguard of the new wave of moral psychology that I'll discuss in the second part of this introduction, was interested in cultural variation in the application of moral evaluative terms. While hunting for differences between Brazilians and Americans, he made an unexpected discovery. Though the differences between these two groups were small, there were much larger differences between high- and low-socioeconomic-status (SES) individuals within each of these groups. When asked about such actions as eating the family dog after it had been accidentally run over by a motorist, or having sex with a dead chicken before cooking and eating it, just about everyone thought they were quite disgusting. But low-SES subjects also thought they were morally wrong; high-SES subjects didn't. So there was some experimental evidence for important differences in how people in different groups applied evaluative terms. To the best of my knowledge, though, there were no comparable studies of epistemic evaluative terms. However, at Rutgers and nearby institutions, these were heady times for people with a naturalistic and interdisciplinary approach to philosophy. The Rutgers Cognitive Science Center was flourishing, there was an established tradition of inviting empirical people to take over sessions of philosophy graduate seminars, and Ethics 2000 (of which more anon) was being planned. Also, though I'm not sure I knew it at the time, Joshua Knobe, who was then a graduate student down the road at Princeton, was gearing up to run the famous experiments that first demonstrated the "Knobe effect," and Joshua Green, another Princeton graduate student, was beginning to think about putting people in brain scanners to study the mechanisms underlying their moral judgments. So rather than lamenting the absence of empirical studies of the sort we needed, Jonathan Weinberg, Shaun Nichols, and I decided to run the experiments ourselves. Arguably, that project, along with the work of Knobe and Greene, were the launching pads for the experimental philosophy movement.

With Nisbett as both inspiration and consultant, Weinberg, Nichols, and I decided to look first at possible differences between Rutgers students with East Asian cultural backgrounds and those with Western cultural backgrounds. Our choice of which concept of epistemic evaluation to focus on was easy enough—we'd start with knowledge. The results were fascinating. As we reported in "Normativity and Epistemic Intuitions" (chapter 8), our subjects' intuitive judgments on "True-Temp" cases varied in just the way that Nisbett's work predicted. More surprisingly, our East Asian and Western subjects had dramatically different intuitions about the sort of Gettier cases that had brought about a sea change in philosophical epistemology when Gettier first proposed them almost four decades earlier. I now had the evidence I needed to recast the argument of "Reflective Equilibrium" without appealing to evil demons, imagined cultures, or other hypothetical possibilities. Both reasoning strategies and concepts of epistemic evaluation really do vary by culture. And that, Weinberg, Nichols, and I argued, poses a serious problem for epistemic projects like Goodman's (or Cohen's or Goldman's) that try to extract normative epistemic principles from evidence about people's intuitions. In a second paper, "Meta-Skepticism: Meditations in Ethno-Epistemology" (chapter 10), Nichols, Weinberg, and I presented some additional data about group differences in epistemic intuition and argued that these data posed a new sort of problem for some traditional skeptical arguments, since crucial premises in those arguments are supported only by appeal to intuition, and those intuitions appear to vary by culture, SES, and years of philosophical training.

After Weinberg, Nichols, and I completed "Meta-Skepticism," the focus of my work in experimental philosophy moved from epistemology to morality, discussed in the section to follow, and the theory of reference, discussed in the introduction to volume 1. But recently, in collaboration with Wesley Buckwalter, and with Joe Henrich and others affiliated with the Culture and the Mind Project, I have once again been involved in the empirical exploration of epistemic intuitions and epistemic norms. I'll say a bit about that work at the end of this introduction.

2. Morality

My interest in moral psychology and moral theory has a rather curious history. It grew out of a passion for undergraduate teaching. As a graduate student at Princeton in the middle years of the 1960s, I hadn't thought much about teaching; there was no need. There were no graduate student TAs, and in the few large lecture courses the Philosophy Department taught, the discussion sections—called "precepts" at Princeton—were taught by faculty. So when I arrived at the University of Michigan as an assistant professor, in 1968, I was horrified to learn that in my second semester I would be expected to teach the large Introduction to Philosophy course. The class had three or four hundred students and a small army of TAs, and the lectures were given in a huge auditorium with a main floor and a balcony! Though I had spent many hours preparing, I was petrified when I first stepped out on the stage. However, fifteen or twenty minutes into that initial lecture, I recall pausing to catch my breath and saying to myself, "Damn! This is fun!" It still is. I teach the large Intro course at Rutgers almost every year.

A few years after I arrived at Michigan, the Philosophy Department was looking for ways to increase undergraduate enrollment. As an experiment, I designed a new lecture course, Science and Society, aimed at teaching the basics of the philosophy of science and spicing it up with some controversial social issues engendered by scientific research. The students were clearly more interested in the social issues than in the philosophy of science, so over the next few years that course gradually morphed into one of the early versions of the now ubiquitous courses on contemporary moral issues.

One of the controversial issues in the mid-1970s, particularly in Ann Arbor and other leading research centers, was the newly emerging science and technology of genetic engineering, which many people thought should be banned. It was an ideal topic for Science and Society. But since neither the students nor I had a clue about the relevant science, I invited a molecular biologist colleague, David Jackson, to come to my class and bring us up to speed. One thing led to another, and I soon found myself collaborating with Dave and his wife, Ethel, also a molecular biologist, on presentations at public meetings, organizing a conference, and editing a volume of essays on the debate.[8] At one point, I was invited to testify at a congressional hearing on human genetic engineering chaired by a very impressive and remarkably well-informed young congressman named Al Gore.[9] The first essay in this volume, "The Recombinant DNA Debate," began as a lecture in my Science and Society class. My goal was to help the students think clearly about the moral issues posed by a new technology that might lead to enormous benefits but might also do catastrophic harm. Though the debate about the use of recombinant DNA technology has largely grown quiet, the template the article provides for thinking about similar issues is apparently still useful, since it continues to be anthologized in textbooks and assigned in courses.

In my Contemporary Moral Issues course, I often used the familiar strategy of challenging students to justify moral distinctions they were inclined to make by specifying some morally relevant difference between the sorts of cases they found acceptable and those they found unacceptable. For example, since most students were not vegetarians, I would ask whether they approved of killing and eating people. The answer, of course, was always no. But they found it exceptionally difficult to specify a difference between harvesting pigs and harvesting people that, on reflection, they were prepared to defend as marking a morally important boundary. They came up with lots of candidates, but it was usually pretty easy, and always great fun, to construct a hypothetical case—severely retarded babies, senile senior citizens with no friends or relatives, etc.—that fell on the wrong side of the boundary they had proposed. In "Moral Philosophy and Mental Representation" (chapter 5), I reconstruct a typical classroom episode of this sort. It was not at all uncommon for students to react by starting to question their previous moral convictions, and this sometimes led to a real moral crisis. However, in the late 1980s, having used this didactic strategy for well over a decade, I found myself confronting a moral crisis of my own.

The crisis was provoked by my growing interest in the fascinating empirical literature on the mental representation of concepts and categories, inspired by the groundbreaking work of Berkeley psychologist Eleanor Rosch. In "Moral Philosophy and Mental Representation," I argue that both the strategy of seeking morally relevant differences and the venerable Platonic project of seeking definitions for important moral concepts seem to presuppose that we already have something like a tacitly known set of necessary and sufficient conditions to guide our judgments about particular cases. But Rosch and the many researchers she inspired had amassed an impressive body of evidence indicating that, in most cases at least, that simply isn't how concepts or categories are represented in the mind. And if that's right, then I was gleefully provoking moral crises in my students by challenging them to do something that could not be done. A few years after I moved to Rutgers, this worry played a significant role in my decision to stop teaching Contemporary Moral Issues.

---

8. Jackson and Stich 1979.

9. Stich 1983.

Much of the early work in the Rosch tradition was devoted to exploring the idea, inspired by Wittgenstein, that moral judgments are subserved by mentally represented prototypes or exemplars, rather than by mentally represented necessary and sufficient conditions. Toward the end of "Moral Philosophy and Mental Representation," I noted that this was not the only philosophically inspired game in town. In *A Theory of Justice* (1971), Rawls had drawn attention to the analogy between the attempt to capture moral intuitions in moral philosophy and the attempt to capture grammatical intuitions in Chomskian linguistics. The linguistic analogy suggests that moral judgment might be subserved not by prototypes or exemplars but by something like a Chomskian generative grammar. Moreover—though Rawls did not make the point—if the analogy is a good one, and if Chomsky is right about grammar, then there may be important innate constraints on the sorts of moral systems humans can adopt; all human moral systems might share important innate components. If anything like this is true, it would, of course, have enormous implications for moral theory. But there was no way of knowing whether it *is* true without doing quite a lot of very sophisticated cognitive science. It was, I thought, time for philosophers and cognitive scientists to collaborate much more actively in the attempt to understand the mental mechanisms and processes underlying moral judgment.

I was certainly not the only person who had that thought. As the twentieth century drew to a close, it became increasingly clear that moral philosophers had much to gain by attending more closely to the work of colleagues in psychology and neuroscience. No one made the case more forcefully than Gilbert Harman, who, in an influential series of papers, argued that findings in social psychology pose an important challenge to virtue ethics (Harman 1999, 2000). Gil was a neighbor and an old friend—he had been co-chair of my dissertation committee three decades earlier—so we found lots of opportunities to discuss our overlapping interests. During these conversations an intriguing idea emerged. Since there was a growing body of empirical work that was relevant to issues in moral philosophy, and a growing number of philosophers trying to understand the implications of this work, we could pool our resources, organize a joint Princeton-Rutgers graduate seminar, and invite guest speakers—both philosophers and empirical researchers—whose work we wanted to learn more about. To round out the planning committee for the seminar, we recruited Princeton psychologist John Darley, who was one of the pioneers in studying the social psychology of moral judgment and decision making. The seminar met during the first semester of the new century; we called it Ethics 2000.

As it happened, John Doris, who had also done important work on the implications of social psychology for virtue ethics, was visiting Princeton that year, and he came along to the seminar.[10] Actually, "came along" doesn't begin to capture John's contribution. It quickly became clear that he was, de facto, the fourth instructor in the seminar, and also the liveliest and most provocative—no easy task in that group. By the time the seminar was

---

10. Doris 1998, 2002.

over, John and I had launched an ongoing collaboration aimed at exploring the implications of empirical findings for questions in moral philosophy. To date, that collaboration has resulted in five papers, two of which are included in this collection. "As a Matter of Fact: Empirical Perspectives on Ethics" (chapter 11) discusses character and virtue ethics, moral motivation, moral disagreement, and the role of thought experiments in ethics. Though it covers a lot of ground, the leitmotif that runs through the paper—and through all my work with Doris—is that there is a growing body of empirical evidence in psychology and neuroscience that philosophers interested in these issues cannot afford to ignore. In "Altruism" (chapter 15), Doris, Erica Roedder, and I focus on an issue that has vexed philosophers since Plato: is genuinely altruistic behavior possible, or is all human behavior ultimately selfish? Hobbes, famously, argued for the second option, and many towering figures in the history of ethics, including Bentham and John Stuart Mill, agreed. If this view, often called "psychological egoism," is true, the implications for both ethics and political philosophy are vast. Psychological egoism is an empirical claim about the nature of human motivation. But, as the centuries-long debate over its plausibility makes clear, the sorts of evidence philosophers traditionally appeal to—introspection, anecdote, and careful observation of human behavior—are not rich enough to settle the issue. In recent years, both psychologists and evolutionary biologists have joined the conversation. As Doris, Roedder, and I see it, the evolutionary considerations that have been offered both for and against the existence of altruism have done very little to advance the debate. But the evidence from experimental social psychology, more specifically the work of Daniel Batson and his collaborators, has made a major contribution. We end our paper on altruism with the modest conclusion that Batson and his collaborators have made more progress on this issue in the last three decades than philosophers have made in the previous two millennia.

The Ethics 2000 seminar was a great success. New conversations were started, collaborative projects were launched, and a great deal of enthusiasm was generated. We had all learned a great deal, and many of us wanted to keep the kettle boiling. How to do that was less clear. In April 2003, I sponsored a meeting at Rutgers to discuss the creation of an ongoing group that could foster collaborative interdisciplinary research in moral psychology. By the end of the meeting, the Moral Psychology Research Group (MPRG) had been formed. Meeting twice a year for an intense weekend of discussion and debate, the MPRG has, I think, played a significant role in promoting the now flourishing field of philosophically sophisticated and empirically informed moral psychology. From the beginning, gifted graduate students were included as full members of the MPRG and welcomed as equal partners, sometimes first authors, in the many collaborative research and writing projects that emerged from MPRG discussions.[11]

One of those collaborative research products resulted in "A Framework for the Psychology of Norms" (chapter 12). Chandra Sripada, the first author and primary architect

---

11. A baker's dozen of those projects are collected in Doris and the Moral Psychology Research Group 2010.

of the paper, was a Rutgers graduate student with an awesome ability to devour and master huge amounts of literature from a wide variety of fields, ranging from philosophy, psychology, and psychiatry to anthropology, economics, and neuroscience. A particular interest of his, and mine, was the literature on gene-culture co-evolution growing out of the seminal work of Rob Boyd and Pete Richerson (1985, 2005). Chandra believed, and quickly convinced me, that there was enough information scattered in these diverse literatures to motivate at least a first pass at a model of the psychological systems underlying the acquisition and implementation of human norms. That's the first task that we tackled in the "Framework" paper. But once we constructed the model, it became clear that there are many important questions that the available literature does not answer. The second half of the paper is devoted to a discussion of some of those questions. One of the main virtues of models like the one we sketch is that they enable us to focus more clearly on questions we do not yet know how to answer, and thus act as guides to the sort of research that needs to be done if we are to have a better understanding of the psychology of norms.

The two papers I have not yet discussed were both written with Dan Kelly, who was another graduate student member of the MPRG. Both papers focus on the literature on the moral/conventional distinction growing out of the work of Elliott Turiel (1983) and his followers. Turiel designed an experimental paradigm, often called the "moral/conventional task," in which subjects are presented with prototypical examples of moral transgressions, like one child pushing another off a swing, and prototypical examples of conventional transgressions, like a child talking in class when he has not been called on by the teacher. In just about all of the moral/conventional task studies conducted by Turiel and his followers, the prototypical moral transgressions involve a victim who is clearly harmed by the protagonist's transgression; no one is harmed in the prototypical conventional transgressions. After reading or listening to a description of the transgression, subjects are asked a series of questions aimed at determining whether they think the transgression is serious, whether they think the wrongness of the transgression is "authority dependent," and whether the wrongness of the action generalizes to other times and other places.[12] In many experiments, it was found that when the scenario recounts a transgression in which someone is harmed, subjects typically reply that the transgression is serious and authority independent, and that the wrongness of the transgression generalizes—it would be wrong at other times and in other places. When the scenario recounts a transgression in which no one is harmed, subjects typically judge that the transgression is less serious and authority dependent, and that the wrongness does not generalize. This pattern of responses is sometimes described as "passing" or "succeeding" in the moral/conventional task.

---

12. To assess authority dependence, a subject might be asked: "What if the teacher said that there is no rule in this school prohibiting that sort of behavior? Would it be wrong to do it then?" If the subject says it would not be wrong under those circumstances, it is taken to indicate that the subject regards the rule as authority dependent. But if the subject thinks it would still be wrong, this indicates that she thinks the rule is authority independent.

I first became aware of this work when I read the manuscript of Shaun Nichols' book *Sentimental Rules*, where the moral/conventional task plays a central role. Shaun thought that the capacity to pass the moral/conventional task "reflects the ability to appreciate the distinctive status of morality" (2004, 4). The task, he claimed, "plumbs a fairly deep feature of moral judgment" (6) and can be used as "a measure of moral cognition" (196). Nichols was certainly not alone in his assessment of the importance of the moral/conventional task. James Blair (1995, 1996) uses the task to draw widely cited conclusions about the moral capacities of psychopaths and people with autism. Susan Dwyer (1999, 2006) uses the alleged early emergence and pan-cultural nature of the task as evidence for claims about the innateness of moral knowledge. Many other writers take the ability to pass the moral/conventional task to be an important early milestone in moral development.

From the get-go, I was skeptical. And as I plunged into the literature, my skepticism increased. People working in cultural psychology had reported lots of cases in which subjects in other cultures judged that harmless transgressions had one or more of the features that, according to Turiel, were associated with moral transgressions. And even some of Nichols' own work, reported in *Sentimental Rules*, seemed to me to be incompatible with the most natural interpretation of Turiel's claims. Oddly, however, I could find no reports of experiments in which harmful transgressions failed to exhibit the pattern of responses that Turiel predicted. There was also another odd feature of this literature. Since Turiel was a developmental psychologist, all the harmful transgressions he used in his initial experiments were behaviors that young children would be familiar with, like one child hitting another, or throwing sand in his eyes in the sandbox, or pushing him off a swing. The tradition of using these sorts of schoolyard transgressions became entrenched in the literature, and they continued to be used even when the moral/conventional task was given to much older children, or to normal adults, or to incarcerated psychopathic murderers! It seemed far from obvious to me that the pattern of responses to harmful transgressions that Turiel found would be preserved if we asked people to consider a wider range of harmful transgressions. In a lunchtime conversation with evolutionary anthropologist Dan Fessler, at a meeting of the Innateness and the Structure of the Mind Project, I discovered that he shared my suspicion that people's responses might be quite different if grown-up harmful transgressions were used in the moral/conventional task.[13] By the end of that Innateness Project meeting, Fessler and I had agreed to collaborate on an experiment. Fessler recruited

---

13. The Innateness and the Structure of the Mind Project (www.philosophy.dept.shef.ac.uk/AHRB-Project) was a three-year interdisciplinary project based at the University of Sheffield. It brought together leading researchers in a broad range of disciplines—including animal psychology, anthropology, cognitive psychology, developmental psychology, economics, linguistics and psycholinguistics, neuroscience, and philosophy—to investigate the current status and most promising future directions of nativist research. Stephen Laurence directed the project, and I was on the organizing committee, along with Peter Carruthers. The project produced the three-volume Innate Mind series (Carruthers, Laurence, and Stich 2005, 2006, 2007). Two of the essays in this collection first appeared in that series.

two of his graduate students to help with the project, and I dragooned Dan Kelly, who quickly became the project leader. Our experiment, the first one I had conducted using the Internet, confirmed our suspicion. The Turiel pattern often disappears when the moral/conventional task uses grown-up transgressions. The results of our study were reported in "Harm, Affect, and the Moral/Conventional Distinction" (chapter 13).

Though Turiel has never offered an explicit account of the mental mechanisms underlying moral and conventional judgment, Kelly and I were curious about what sort of psychological model would be required to explain the data that Turiel and his followers assembled to support their theory. So, in "Two Theories About the Cognitive Architecture Underlying Morality" (chapter 14), we set out to construct one—we call it the "M/C model." Not surprisingly, it looks very different from the model that Sripada and I had proposed in "A Framework for the Psychology of Norms," and it makes significantly different predictions. In light of the prominence of Turiel's work in moral psychology, a good case can be made that the M/C model is the most important competitor to the Sripada and Stich model. However, Kelly and I argue that the Sripada and Stich model does a considerably better job at handling the available data.

Two paragraphs back, I mentioned that Dan Fessler and I began planning the experiment reported in "Harm, Affect, and the Moral/Conventional Distinction" at a meeting of the Innateness and the Structure of the Mind Project. When that project came to an end, Steve Laurence and I launched another project, the Culture and the Mind Project, with the goal of bringing anthropologists, psychologists, and philosophers together to design and conduct cross-cultural research on issues that are of interest to all three disciplines.[14] Though it took some doing, the core group of the Culture and the Mind Project has evolved into a remarkably cohesive and productive interdisciplinary research team. Under the auspices of the project, Dan Fessler and I have been conducting a new study looking at the moral/conventional distinction in a number of small-scale societies. And in collaboration with Joe Henrich, I have helped to design what we believe to be the first experimental study of epistemic norms in small-scale societies. This is not the place to describe these studies in detail, though I can say that preliminary findings look very exciting indeed. So stay tuned, gentle reader, the best is still to come.

On the Beatles' *Sgt. Pepper* album, Ringo Starr told us that he got by with a little help from his friends. Well, I get by, too, but I've had a *lot* of help from my friends. Though many of my co-authors started as my students, I have learned far more from them than they learned from me. It's been an honor and a privilege to work with them; it's also been great fun. Thanks, guys![15]

---

14. See www.philosophy.dept.shef.ac.uk/culture&;mind.

15. Special thanks to John Doris for his helpful comments on an earlier draft of this introduction.

REFERENCES

Blair, R. 1995. A Cognitive Developmental Approach to Morality: Investigating the Psychopath. *Cognition* 57.

———. 1996. Brief Report: Morality in the Autistic Child. *Journal of Autism and Developmental Disorders* 26.

Boyd, R., and P. Richerson. 1985. *Culture and the Evolutionary Process*. Chicago: University of Chicago Press.

———. 2005. *The Origin and Evolution of Cultures*. New York: Oxford University Press.

Carruthers, P., S. Laurence, and S. Stich, eds. 2005. *The Innate Mind: Structure and Contents*. Oxford: Oxford University Press.

———, eds. 2006. *The Innate Mind: Culture and Cognition*. New York: Oxford University Press.

———, eds. 2007. *The Innate Mind: Foundations and the Future*. New York: Oxford University Press.

Cosmides, L., and J. Tooby. 1996. Are Humans Good Intuitive Statisticians After All? Rethinking Some Conclusions from the Literature on Judgment Under Uncertainty. *Cognition* 58.

Doris, J. 1998. Persons, Situations and Virtue Ethics. *Nous* 32.

———. 2002. *Lack of Character: Personality and Moral Behavior*. New York: Cambridge University Press.

Doris, J., and the Moral Psychology Research Group, eds. 2010. *The Moral Psychology Handbook*. Oxford: Oxford University Press.

Dwyer, S. 1999. Moral Competence. In K. Murasugi and R. Stainton, eds., *Philosophy and Linguistics*. Boulder, CO: Westview Press.

———. 2006. How Good Is the Linguistic Analogy? In P. Carruthers, S. Laurence, and S. Stich, eds., *The Innate Mind: Culture and Cognition*. Oxford University Press.

Goodman, N. 1965. *Fact, Fiction and Forecast*. 2nd ed. Indianapolis: Bobbs-Merrill.

Harman, G. 1999. Moral Philosophy Meets Social Psychology: Virtue Ethics and the Fundamental Attribution Error. *Proceedings of the Aristotelian Society* 99.

———. 2000. The Nonexistence of Character Traits. *Proceedings of the Aristotelian Society* 100.

Henrich, J., S. Heine, and A. Norenzayan. 2010. The Weirdest People in the World? *Behavioral and Brain Sciences* 33.

Jackson, D., and S. Stich. 1979. *The Recombinant DNA Debate*. Englewood Cliffs, NJ: Prentice-Hall.

Nichols, S. 2004. *Sentimental Rules: On the Natural Foundations of Moral Judgment*. New York: Oxford University Press.

Nichols, S., and S. Stich. 2003. *Mindreading*. Oxford: Oxford University Press.

Nisbett, R., and E. Borgida. 1975. Attribution and the Social Psychology of Prediction. *Journal of Personality and Social Psychology* 32.

Pinker, S. 1997. *How the Mind Works*. New York: W. W. Norton.

Quine, W. 1969. Epistemology Naturalized. In *Ontological Relativity and Other Essays*. New York: Columbia University Press.

Rawls, J. 1971. *A Theory of Justice*. Cambridge, MA: Harvard University Press.

Salmon, W. 1957. Should We Attempt to Justify Induction? *Philosophical Studies* 8.

Samuels, R., S. Stich, and L. Faucher. 2004. Reasoning and Rationality. In I. Niiniluoto, M. Sintonen, and J. Wolenski, eds., *Handbook of Epistemology*. Dordrecht: Kluwer.

Slovic, P., B. Fischhoff, and S. Lichtenstein. 1976. Cognitive Processes and Societal Risk Taking. In L. Hirschfeld and S. Gelman, eds., *Cognition and Social Behavior*. Hillsdale, NJ: Erlbaum.

Stanovich, K. 1999. *Who Is Rational? Studies of Individual Differences in Reasoning*. Mahwah, NJ: Erlbaum.

Stich, S. 1982. On the Ascription of Content. In A. Woodfield, ed., *Thought and Object: Essays on Intentionality*. Oxford: Oxford University Press.

———. 1983. Testimony on Genetic Engineering. In *Human genetic engineering: Hearings before the Subcommittee on Investigations and Oversight of the Committee on Science and Technology, U.S. House of Representatives*. Ninety-Seventh Congress, Second Session. Washington, D.C.: U.S. Government Printing Office.

———. 1990. *The Fragmentation of Reason: Preface to a Pragmatic Theory of Cognitive Evaluation*. Cambridge, MA: Bradford Books/MIT Press.

Turiel, E. 1983. *The Development of Social Knowledge*. Cambridge: Cambridge University Press.

1

THE RECOMBINANT DNA DEBATE

THE DEBATE OVER recombinant DNA research is a unique event, perhaps a turning point, in the history of science. For the first time in modern history there has been widespread public discussion about whether and how a promising though potentially dangerous line of research shall be pursued. At root the debate is a moral debate and, like most such debates, requires proper assessment of the facts at crucial stages in the argument. A good deal of the controversy over recombinant DNA research arises because some of the facts simply are not yet known. There are many empirical questions we would like to have answered before coming to a decision—questions about the reliability of proposed containment facilities, about the viability of enfeebled strains of *E. coli*, about the ways in which pathogenic organisms do their unwelcome work, and much more. But all decisions cannot wait until the facts are available; some must be made now. It is to be expected that people with different hunches about what the facts will turn out to be will urge different decisions on how recombinant DNA research should be regulated. However, differing expectations about the facts have not been the only fuel for controversy. A significant part of the current debate can be traced to differences over moral principles. Also, unfortunately, there has been much unnecessary debate generated by careless moral reasoning and a failure to attend to the logical structure of some of the moral arguments that have been advanced.

In order to help sharpen our perception of the moral issues underlying the controversy over recombinant DNA research, I shall start by clearing away some frivolous arguments that have deflected attention from more serious issues. We may then examine the problems involved in deciding whether the potential benefits of recombinant DNA research justify pursuing it despite the risks that it poses.

I. Three Bad Arguments

My focus in this section will be on three untenable arguments, each of which has surfaced with considerable frequency in the public debate over recombinant DNA research.

The first argument on my list concludes that recombinant DNA research should not be controlled or restricted. The central premise of the argument is that scientists should have full and unqualified freedom to pursue whatever inquiries they may choose to pursue. This claim was stated repeatedly in petitions and letters to the editor during the height of the public debate over recombinant DNA research in the University of Michigan community.[1] The general moral principle which is the central premise of the argument plainly does entail that investigators using recombinant DNA technology should be allowed to pursue their research as they see fit. However, we need only consider a few examples to see that the principle invoked in this "freedom of inquiry" argument is utterly indefensible. No matter how sincere a researcher's interest may be in investigating the conjugal behavior of American university professors, few would be willing to grant him the right to pursue his research in my bedroom without my consent. No matter how interested a researcher may be in investigating the effects of massive doses of bomb-grade plutonium on preschool children, it is hard to imagine that anyone thinks he should be allowed to do so. Yet the "free inquiry" principle, if accepted, would allow both of these projects and countless other Dr. Strangelove projects as well. So plainly the simplistic "free inquiry" principle is indefensible. It would, however, be a mistake to conclude that freedom of inquiry ought not to be protected. A better conclusion is that the right of free inquiry is a qualified right and must sometimes yield to conflicting rights and to the demands of conflicting moral principles. Articulating an explicit and properly qualified principle of free inquiry is a task of no small difficulty. We will touch on this topic again toward the end of Section II.

The second argument I want to examine aims at establishing just the opposite conclusion from the first. The particular moral judgment being defended is that there should be a total ban on recombinant DNA research. The argument begins with the observation that even in so-called low-risk recombinant DNA experiments there is at least a possibility of catastrophic consequences. We are, after all, dealing with a relatively new and

---

1. For example, from a widely circulated petition signed by both faculty and community people: "The most important challenge may be a confrontation with one of our ancient assumptions—that there must be an absolute and unqualified freedom to pursue scientific inquiries. We will soon begin to wonder what meaning this freedom has if it leads to the destruction or demoralization of human beings, the only life forms able to exercise it." And from a letter to the editor written by a professor of engineering humanities: "Is science beyond social and human controls, so that freedom of inquiry implies the absence of usual social restrictions which we all, as citizens, obey, respecting the social contract?"

It is interesting to note that the "freedom of inquiry" argument is rarely proposed by defenders of recombinant DNA research. Rather, it is proposed, then attacked, by those who are opposed to research involving recombinant molecules. Their motivation, it would seem, is to discredit the proponents of recombinant DNA research by attributing a foolish argument to them, then demonstrating that it is indeed a foolish argument.

unexplored technology. Thus it is at least possible that a bacterial culture whose genetic makeup has been altered in the course of a recombinant DNA experiment may exhibit completely unexpected pathogenic characteristics. Indeed, it is not impossible that we could find ourselves confronted with a killer strain of, say, *E. coli* and, worse, a strain against which humans can marshal no natural defense. Now if this is possible—if we cannot say with assurance that the probability of it happening is zero—then, the argument continues, all recombinant DNA research should be halted. For the negative utility of the imagined catastrophe is so enormous, resulting as it would in the destruction of our society and perhaps even of our species, that no work which could possibly lead to this result would be worth the risk.

The argument just sketched, which might be called the "doomsday scenario" argument, begins with a premise which no informed person would be inclined to deny. It is indeed *possible* that even a low-risk recombinant DNA experiment might lead to totally catastrophic results. No ironclad guarantee can be offered that this will not happen. And while the probability of such an unanticipated catastrophe is surely not large, there is no serious argument that the probability is zero. Still, I think the argument is a sophistry. To go from the undeniable premise that recombinant DNA research might possibly result in unthinkable catastrophe to the conclusion that such research should be banned requires a moral principle stating that *all* endeavors that might possibly result in such a catastrophe should be prohibited. Once the principle has been stated, it is hard to believe that anyone would take it at all seriously. For the principle entails that, along with recombinant DNA research, almost all scientific research and many other commonplace activities having little to do with science should be prohibited. It is, after all, at least logically possible that the next new compound synthesized in an ongoing chemical research program will turn out to be an uncontainable carcinogen many orders of magnitude more dangerous than aerosol plutonium. And, to vary the example, there is a non-zero probability that experiments in artificial pollination will produce a weed that will, a decade from now, ruin the world's food grain harvest.[2]

I cannot resist noting that the principle invoked in the doomsday scenario argument is not new. Pascal used an entirely parallel argument to show that it is in our own best interests to believe in God. For though the probability of God's existence may be very low, if He nonetheless should happen to exist, the disutility that would accrue to the disbeliever would be catastrophic—an eternity in hell. But, as introductory philosophy students should all know, Pascal's argument only looks persuasive if we take our options to be just two: Christianity or atheism. A third possibility is belief in a jealous non-Christian God who will see to our damnation if and only if we *are* Christians. The probability of such a

---

2. Unfortunately, the doomsday scenario argument is *not* a straw man conjured only by those who would refute it. Consider, for example, the remarks of Anthony Mazzocchi, spokesman for the Oil, Chemical and Atomic Workers International Union, reported in *Science News*, 19 March 1977, p. 181: "When scientists argue over safe or unsafe, we ought to be very prudent.... If critics are correct and the Andromeda scenario has *even the smallest possibility* of occurring, we must assume it will occur on the basis of our experience" (emphasis added).

deity existing is again very small, but non-zero. So Pascal's argument is of no help in deciding whether or not to accept Christianity. For we may be damned if we do and damned if we don't.

I mention Pascal's difficulty because there is a direct parallel in the doomsday scenario argument against recombinant DNA research. Just as there is a non-zero probability that unforeseen consequences of recombinant DNA research will lead to disaster, so there is a non-zero probability that unforeseen consequences of *failing* to pursue the research will lead to disaster. There may, for example, come a time when, because of natural or man-induced climatic change, the capacity to alter quickly the genetic constitution of agricultural plants will be necessary to forestall catastrophic famine. And if we fail to pursue recombinant DNA research now, our lack of knowledge in the future may have consequences as dire as any foreseen in the doomsday scenario argument.

The third argument I want to consider provides a striking illustration of how important it is, in normative thinking, to make clear the moral *principles* being invoked. The argument I have in mind begins with a factual claim about recombinant DNA research and concludes that stringent restrictions, perhaps even a moratorium, should be imposed. However, advocates of the argument are generally silent on the normative principle(s) linking premise and conclusion. The gap thus created can be filled in a variety of ways, resulting in very different arguments. The empirical observation that begins the argument is that recombinant DNA methods enable scientists to move genes back and forth across natural barriers, "particularly the most fundamental such barrier, that which divides prokaryotes from eukaryotes. The results will be essentially new organisms, self-perpetuating and hence permanent."[3] Because of this, it is concluded that severe restrictions are in order. Plainly this argument is an enthymeme; a central premise has been left unstated. What sort of moral principle is being tacitly assumed?

The principle that comes first to mind is simply that natural barriers should not be breached, or perhaps that "essentially new organisms" should not be created. The principle has an almost theological ring to it, and perhaps there are some people who would be prepared to defend it on theological grounds. But short of a theological argument, it is hard to see why anyone would hold the view that breaching natural barriers or creating new organisms is *intrinsically* wrong. For if a person were to advocate such a principle, he would have to condemn the creation of new bacterial strains capable of, say, synthesizing human clotting factor or insulin, *even if* creating the new organism generated *no unwelcome side effects*.

There is quite a different way of unraveling the "natural barriers" argument which avoids appeal to the dubious principles just discussed. As an alternative, this second reading of the argument ties premise to conclusion with a second factual claim and a

---

3. The quotation is from George Wald, "The Case Against Genetic Engineering," *The Sciences*, September/October 1976, reprinted in David A. Jackson and Stephen P. Stich, eds., *The Recombinant DNA Debate* (Englewood Cliffs, NJ: Prentice-Hall, 1979).

quite different normative premise. The added factual claim is that at present our knowledge of the consequences of creating new forms of life is severely limited; thus we cannot know with any assurance that the probability of disastrous consequences is very low. The moral principle needed to mesh with the two factual premises would be something such as the following:

> If we do not know with considerable assurance that the probability of an activity leading to disastrous consequences is very low, then we should not allow the activity to continue.

Now this principle, unlike those marshaled in the first interpretation of the natural barriers argument, is not lightly dismissed. It is, to be sure, a conservative principle, and it has the odd feature of focusing entirely on the dangers an activity poses while ignoring its potential benefits.[4] Still, the principle may have a certain attraction in light of recent history, which has increasingly been marked by catastrophes attributable to technology's unanticipated side effects. I will not attempt a full-scale evaluation of this principle just now. For the principle raises, albeit in a rather extreme way, the question of how risks and benefits are to be weighed against each other. In my opinion, that is the really crucial moral question raised by recombinant DNA research. It is a question which bristles with problems. In Section II I shall take a look at some of these problems and make a few tentative steps toward some solutions. While picking our way through the problems we will have another opportunity to examine the principle just cited.

II. Risks and Benefits

At first glance it might be thought that the issue of risks and benefits is quite straightforward, at least in principle. What we want to know is whether the potential benefits of recombinant DNA research justify the risks involved. To find out we need only determine the probabilities of the various dangers and benefits. And while some of the empirical facts—the probabilities—may require considerable ingenuity and effort to uncover, the assessment poses no particularly difficult normative or conceptual problems. Unfortunately, this sanguine view does not survive much more than a first glance. A closer look at the task of balancing the risks and benefits of recombinant DNA research reveals a quagmire of sticky conceptual problems and simmering moral disputes. In the next few pages I will try to catalogue and comment on some of these moral disputes. I wish I could also promise solutions to all of them, but to do so would be false advertising.

---

4. It is important to note, however, that the principle is considerably less conservative, and correspondingly more plausible, than the principle invoked in the doomsday scenario argument. That latter principle would have us enjoin an activity if the probability of the activity leading to catastrophe is anything other than zero.

PROBLEMS ABOUT PROBABILITIES

In trying to assess costs and benefits, a familiar first step is to set down a list of possible actions and possible outcomes. Next, we assign some measure of desirability to each possible outcome, and for each action we estimate the conditional probability of each outcome given that the action is performed. In attempting to apply this decision-making strategy to the case of recombinant DNA research, the assignment of probabilities poses some perplexing problems. Some of the outcomes whose probabilities we want to know can be approached using standard empirical techniques. Thus, for example, we may want to know what the probability is of a specific enfeebled host *E. coli* strain surviving passage through the human intestinal system, should it be accidentally ingested. Or we may want to know what the probability is that a host organism will escape from a P4 laboratory. In such cases, while there may be technical difficulties to be overcome, we have a reasonably clear idea of the sort of data needed to estimate the required probabilities. But there are other possible outcomes whose probabilities cannot be determined by experiment. It is important, for example, to know what the probability is of recombinant DNA research leading to a method for developing nitrogen-fixing strains of corn and wheat. And it is important to know how likely it is that recombinant DNA research will lead to techniques for effectively treating or preventing various types of cancer. Yet there is no experiment we can perform nor any data we can gather that will enable us to *empirically* estimate these probabilities. Nor are these the most problematic probabilities we may want to know. A possibility that weighs heavily on the minds of many who are worried about recombinant DNA research is that this research may lead to negative consequences for human health or for the environment *which have not yet even been thought of.* The history of technology during the last half century surely demonstrates that this is not a quixotic concern. Yet here again there would appear to be no data we can gather that would help much in estimating the probability of such potential outcomes.

It should be stressed that the problems just sketched are not to be traced simply to a paucity of data. Rather, they are conceptual problems; it is doubtful whether there is *any clear empirical sense* to be made of objective probability assignments to contingencies like those we are considering.

Theorists in the Bayesian tradition may be unmoved by the difficulties we have noted. On their view all probability claims are reports of subjective probabilities.[5] And, a Bayesian might quite properly note, there is no special problem about assigning *subjective* probabilities to outcomes such as those that worried us. But even for the radical Bayesian, there remains the problem of *whose* subjective probabilities ought to be employed in making a *social* or *political* decision. The problem is a pressing one since the subjective probabilities assigned to potential dangers and benefits of recombinant DNA research

---

5. For an elaboration of the Bayesian position, see Leonard J. Savage, *The Foundations of Statistics* (New York: John Wiley & Sons, 1954); also cf. Leonard J. Savage, "The Shifting Foundations of Statistics," in Robert G. Colodny, ed., *Logic, Laws and Life* (Pittsburgh: University of Pittsburgh Press, 1977).

would appear to vary considerably even among reasonably well-informed members of the scientific community.

The difficulties we have been surveying are serious ones. Some might feel they are so serious that they render rational assessment of the risks and benefits of recombinant DNA research all but impossible. I am inclined to be rather more optimistic, however. Almost all of the perils posed by recombinant DNA research require the occurrence of a sequence of separate events. For a chimerical bacterial strain created in a recombinant DNA experiment to cause a serious epidemic, for example, at least the following events must occur:

1. A pathogenic bacterium must be synthesized.
2. The chimerical bacteria must escape from the laboratory.
3. The strain must be viable in nature.
4. The strain must compete successfully with other micro-organisms which are themselves the product of intense natural selection.[6]

Since *all* of these must occur, the probability of the potential epidemic is the product of the probabilities of each individual contingency. And there are at least two items on the list, namely (2) and (3), whose probabilities are amenable to reasonably straightforward empirical assessment. Thus the product of these two individual probabilities places an upper limit on the probability of the epidemic. For the remaining two probabilities, we must rely on subjective probability assessments of informed scientists. No doubt there will be considerable variability. Yet even here the variability will be limited. In the case of (4), as an example, the available knowledge about microbial natural selection provides no precise way of estimating the probability that a chimerical strain of enfeebled *E. coli* will compete successfully outside the laboratory. But no serious scientist would urge that the probability is *high*. We can then use the highest responsible subjective estimate of the probabilities of (1) and (4) in calculating the "worst-case" estimate of the risk of epidemic. If in using this highest "worst-case" estimate, our assessment yields the result that benefits outweigh risks, then lower estimates of the same probabilities will, of course, yield the same conclusion. Thus it may well be the case that the problems about probabilities we have reviewed will not pose insuperable obstacles to a rational assessment of risks and benefits.

WEIGHING HARMS AND BENEFITS

A second cluster of problems that confronts us in assessing the risks and benefits of recombinant DNA research turns on the assignment of a measure of desirability to the

---

6. For an elaboration of this point, see Bernard D. Davis, "Evolution, Epidemiology, and Recombinant DNA," in David A. Jackson and Stephen P. Stich, eds., *The Recombinant DNA Debate* (Englewood Cliffs, NJ: Prentice-Hall, 1979).

various possible outcomes. Suppose that we have a list of the various harms and benefits that might possibly result from pursuing recombinant DNA research. The list will include such "benefits" as development of an inexpensive way to synthesize human clotting factor and development of a strain of nitrogen-fixing wheat and such "harms" as release of a new antibiotic-resistant strain of pathogenic bacteria and release of a strain of *E. coli* carrying tumor viruses capable of causing cancer in man.

Plainly, it is possible that pursuing a given policy will result in more than one benefit and in more than one harm. Now if we are to assess the potential impact of various policies or courses of action, we must assign some index of desirability to the possible *total outcomes* of each policy, outcomes which may well include a mix of benefits and harms. To do this we must confront a tangle of normative problems that are as vexing and difficult as any we are likely to face. We must *compare* the moral desirabilities of various harms and benefits. The task is particularly troublesome when the harms and benefits to be compared are of different kinds. Thus, for example, some of the attractive potential benefits of recombinant DNA research are economic: we may learn to recover small amounts of valuable metals in an economically feasible way, or we may be able to synthesize insulin and other drugs inexpensively. By contrast, many of the risks of recombinant DNA research are risks to human life or health. So if we are to take the idea of cost-benefit analysis seriously, we must at some point decide how human lives are to be weighed against economic benefits.

There are those who contend that the need to make such decisions indicates the moral bankruptcy of attempting to employ risk-benefit analyses when human lives are at stake. On the critics' view, we cannot reckon the possible loss of a human life as just another negative outcome, albeit a grave and heavily weighted one. To do so, it is urged, is morally repugnant and reflects a callous lack of respect for the sacredness of human life.

On my view, this sort of critique of the very idea of using risk-benefit analyses is ultimately untenable. It is simply a fact about the human condition, lamentable as it is inescapable, that in many human activities we run the risk of inadvertently causing the death of a human being. We run such a risk each time we drive a car, allow a dam to be built, or allow a plane to take off. Moreover, in making social and individual decisions, we cannot escape weighing economic consequences against the risk to human life. A building code in the Midwest will typically mandate fewer precautions against earthquakes than a building code in certain parts of California. Yet earthquakes are not impossible in the Midwest. If we elect not to require precautions, then surely a major reason must be that it would simply be too expensive. In this judgment, as in countless others, there is no escaping the need to balance economic costs against possible loss of life. To deny that we must and do balance economic costs against risks to human life is to assume the posture of a moral ostrich.

I have been urging the point that it is not *morally objectionable* to try to balance economic concerns against risks to human life. But if such judgments are unobjectionable, indeed necessary, they also surely are among the most difficult any of us has to face. It is hard to imagine a morally sensitive person not feeling extremely uncomfortable when confronted with the need to put a dollar value on human lives. It might be thought that the moral dilemmas engendered by the need to balance such radically different costs and benefits pose insuperable practical obstacles for a rational resolution of the recombinant DNA debate. But here, as in the case of problems with probabilities, I am more sanguine. For while some of the risks and potential benefits of recombinant DNA research are all but morally incommensurable, the most salient risks and benefits are easier to compare. The major risks, as we have noted, are to human life and health. However, the major potential benefits are *also* to human life and health. The potential economic benefits of recombinant DNA research pale in significance when set against the potential for major breakthroughs in our understanding and ability to treat a broad range of conditions, from birth defects to cancer. Those of us, and I confess I am among them, who despair of deciding how lives and economic benefits are to be compared can nonetheless hope to settle our views about recombinant DNA research by comparing the potential risks to life and health with the potential benefits to life and health. Here we are comparing plainly commensurable outcomes. If the balance turns out to be favorable, then we need not worry about factoring in potential economic benefits.

There is a certain irony in the fact that we may well be able to ignore economic factors entirely in coming to a decision about recombinant DNA research. For I suspect that a good deal of the apprehension about recombinant DNA research on the part of the public at large is rooted in the fear that (once again) economic benefits will be weighed much too heavily and potential damage to health and the environment will be weighed much too lightly. The fear is hardly an irrational one. In case after well-publicized case, we have seen the squalid consequences of decisions in which private or corporate gain took precedence over clear and serious threats to health and to the environment. It is the profit motive that led a giant chemical firm to conceal the deadly consequences of the chemical which now threatens to poison the James River and perhaps all of Chesapeake Bay. For the same reason, the citizens of Duluth drank water laced with a known carcinogen. And the ozone layer that protects us all was eroded while regulatory agencies and legislators fussed over the loss of profits in the spray deodorant industry. Yet while public opinion about recombinant DNA research is colored by a growing awareness of these incidents and dozens of others, the case of recombinant DNA is fundamentally different in a crucial respect. The important projected benefits which must be set against the risks of recombinant DNA research are not economic at all; they are medical and environmental.

PROBLEMS ABOUT PRINCIPLES

The third problem I want to consider focuses on the following question. Once we have assessed the potential harms and benefits of recombinant DNA research, how should we use this information in coming to a decision? It might be thought that the answer is trivially obvious. To assess the harms and benefits is, after all, just to compute, for each of the various policies that we are considering, what might be called its *expected utility*. The expected utility of a given policy is found by first multiplying the desirability of each possible total outcome by the probability that the policy in question will lead to that total outcome, and then adding the numbers obtained. As we have seen, finding the needed probabilities and assigning the required desirabilities will not be easy. But once we know the expected utility of each policy, is it not obvious that we should choose the policy with the highest expected utility? The answer, unfortunately, is no, it is not at all obvious.

Let us call the principle that we should adopt the policy with the highest expected utility the *utilitarian principle*. The following example should make it clear that, far from being trivial or tautological, the utilitarian principle is a substantive and controversial moral principle. Suppose that the decision which confronts us is whether or not to adopt policy *A*. What is more, suppose we know there is a probability close to 1 that 100,000 lives will be saved if we adopt *A*. However, we also know that there is a probability close to 1 that 1,000 will die as a direct result of our adopting policy *A*, and these people would survive if we did not adopt *A*. Finally, suppose that the other possible consequences of adopting *A* are relatively inconsequential and can be ignored. (For concreteness, we might take *A* to be the establishment of a mass vaccination program, using a relatively risky vaccine.) Now plainly if we take the moral desirability of saving a life to be exactly offset by the moral undesirability of causing a death, then the utilitarian principle dictates that we adopt policy *A*. But many people feel uncomfortable with this result, the discomfort increasing with the number of deaths that would result from *A*. If, to change the example, the choice that confronts us is saving 100,000 lives while causing the deaths of 50,000 others, a significant number of people are inclined to think that the morally right thing to do is to refrain from doing *A* and "let nature take its course."

If we reject policy *A*, the likely reason is that we also reject the utilitarian principle. Perhaps the most plausible reason for rejecting the utilitarian principle is the view that our obligation to *avoid doing harm* is stronger than our obligation to do good. There are many examples, some considerably more compelling than the one we have been discussing, which seem to illustrate that in a broad range of cases we do feel that our obligation to avoid doing harm is greater than our obligation to do good.[7] Suppose, to take but one example, that my neighbor requests my help in paying off his gambling debts. He owes $5,000 to a certain bookmaker with underworld connections. Unless the neighbor pays the debt immediately, he will be shot. Here, I think we are all inclined to say, I have no strong obligation to give my neighbor the money he needs, and if I were to do so it would be a supererogatory gesture. By contrast, suppose a representative of my neighbor's bookmaker approaches me and requests that I shoot my neighbor. If I refuse, he will see to it

---

7. For an interesting discussion of these cases, see J. O. Urmson, "Saints and Heros," in A. I. Melden, ed., *Essays in Moral Philosophy* (Seattle: University of Washington Press, 1958). Also see the discussion of positive and negative duties in Philippa Foot, "The Problem of Abortion and the Doctrine of Double Effect," *Oxford Review* 5 (1967), reprinted in James Rachels, ed., *Moral Problems* (New York: Harper & Row, 1971).

that my new car, which cost $5,000, will be destroyed by a bomb while it sits unattended at the curb. In this case, surely, I have a strong obligation not to harm my neighbor, although not shooting him will cost me $5,000.

Suppose that this example and others convince us that we cannot adopt the utilitarian principle, at least not in its most general form, where it purports to be applicable to all moral decisions. What are the alternatives? One cluster of alternative principles would urge that in some or all cases we weigh the harm a contemplated action will cause more heavily than we weigh the good it will do. The extreme form of such a principle would dictate that we ignore the benefits entirely and opt for the action or policy that produces the *least* expected harm. (It is this principle, or a close relation, which emerged in the second reading of the "natural barriers" argument discussed in the third part of Section I above.) A more plausible variant would allow us to count both benefits and harms in our deliberations but would specify how much more heavily harms were to count.

On my view, some moderate version of a "harm-weighted" principle is preferable to the utilitarian principle in a considerable range of cases. *However, the recombinant DNA issue is not one of these cases.* Indeed, when we try to apply a harm-weighted principle to the recombinant DNA case we run head-on into a conceptual problem of considerable difficulty. The distinction between doing good and doing harm presupposes a notion of the normal or expectable course of events. Roughly, if my action causes you to be worse off than you would have been in the normal course of events, then I have harmed you; if my action causes you to be better off than in the normal course of events, then I have done you some good; and if my action leaves you just as you would be in the normal course of events, then I have done neither. In many cases, the normal course of events is intuitively quite obvious. Thus in the case of the neighbor and the bookmaker, in the expected course of events I would neither shoot my neighbor nor give him $5,000 to pay off his debts. Thus I am doing good if I give him the money and I am doing harm if I shoot him. But in other cases, including the recombinant DNA case, it is not at all obvious what constitutes the "expected course of events," and thus it is not at all obvious what to count as a harm. To see this, suppose that as a matter of fact many more deaths and illnesses will be prevented as a result of pursuing recombinant DNA research than will be caused by pursuing it. But suppose that there *will* be at least some people who become ill or die as a result of recombinant DNA research being pursued. If these are the facts, then who would be harmed by imposing a ban on recombinant DNA research? That depends on what we take to be the "normal course of events." Presumably, if we do not impose a ban, then the research will continue and the lives will be saved. If this is the normal course of events, then if we impose a ban we have *harmed* those people who would be saved. But it is equally natural to take as the normal course of events the situation in which recombinant DNA research is not pursued. And if *that* is the normal course of events, then those who would have been saved are not harmed by a ban, for they are no worse off than they would be in the normal course of events. However, on this reading of "the normal course of events," if we *fail* to impose a ban, then we have harmed those people who will ultimately become ill or die as a result of recombinant DNA research, since as a result of not imposing a ban they are worse off than they would have been in the normal course of events. I conclude that, in the absence of a theory detailing how we are to recognize the normal course of events, harm-weighted principles have no clear application to the case of recombinant DNA research.

Harm-weighted principles are not the only alternatives to the utilitarian principle. There is another cluster of alternatives that take off in quite a different direction. These principles urge that in deciding which policy to pursue there is a strong presumption in favor of policies that adhere to certain formal moral principles (that is, principles which do not deal with the *consequences* of our policies). Thus, to take the example most directly relevant to the recombinant DNA case, it might be urged that there is a strong presumption in favor of a policy which preserves freedom of scientific inquiry. In its extreme form, this principle would protect freedom of inquiry *no matter what the consequences;* and as we saw in the first part of Section I, this extreme position is exceptionally implausible. A much more plausible principle would urge that freedom of inquiry be protected until the balance of negative over positive consequences reaches a certain specified amount, at which point we would revert to the utilitarian principle. On such a view, if the expected utility of banning recombinant DNA research is a bit higher than the expected utility of allowing it to continue, then we would nonetheless allow it to continue. But if the expected utility of a ban is enormously higher than the expected utility of continuation, banning is the policy to be preferred.[8]

III. Long-Term Risks

Thus far in our discussion of risks and benefits, the risks that have occupied us have been what might be termed "short-term" risks, such as the release of a new pathogen. The negative effects of these events, though they might be long-lasting indeed, would be upon us relatively quickly. However, some of those who are concerned about recombinant DNA research think there are longer-term dangers that are at least as worrisome. The dangers they have in mind stem not from the accidental release of harmful substances in the course of recombinant DNA research, but rather from the unwise use of the *knowledge* we will likely gain in pursuing the research. The scenarios most often proposed are nightmarish variations on the theme of human genetic engineering. With the knowledge we acquire, it is conjectured, some future tyrant may have people built to order, perhaps creating a whole class of people who willingly and cheaply do the society's dirty or dangerous work, as in Huxley's *Brave New World*. Though the proposed scenarios clearly are

---

8. Carl Cohen defends this sort of limited protection of the formal free inquiry principle over a straight application of the utilitarian principle in his interesting essay "When May Research Be Stopped?" *New England Journal of Medicine* 296 (1977), reprinted in David A. Jackson and Stephen P. Stich, eds., *The Recombinant DNA Debate* (Englewood Cliffs, NJ: Prentice-Hall, 1979).

science fiction, they are not to be lightly dismissed. For if the technology they conjure is not demonstrably achievable, neither is it demonstrably impossible. And if only a bit of the science fiction turns to fact, the dangers could be beyond reckoning.

Granting that potential misuse of the knowledge gained in recombinant DNA research is a legitimate topic of concern, how ought we to guard ourselves against this misuse? One common proposal is to try to prevent the acquisition of such knowledge by banning or curtailing recombinant DNA research now. Let us cast this proposal in the form of an explicit moral argument. The conclusion is that recombinant DNA research should be curtailed, and the reason given for the conclusion is that such research could possibly produce knowledge which might be misused with disastrous consequences. To complete the argument we need a moral principle, and the one which seems to be needed is something such as this:

If a line of research can lead to the discovery of knowledge which might be disastrously misused, then that line of research should be curtailed.

Once it has been made explicit, I think relatively few people would be willing to endorse this principle. For recombinant DNA research is hardly alone in potentially leading to knowledge that might be disastrously abused. Indeed, it is hard to think of an area of scientific research that could *not* lead to the discovery of potentially dangerous knowledge. So if the principle is accepted it would entail that almost all scientific research should be curtailed or abandoned.

It might be thought that we could avoid the extreme consequences just cited by retreating to a more moderate moral principle. The moderate principle would urge only that we should curtail those areas of research where the probability of producing dangerous knowledge is comparatively high. Unfortunately, this more moderate principle is of little help in avoiding the unwelcome consequences of the stronger principle. The problem is that the history of science is simply too unpredictable to enable us to say with any assurance which lines of research will produce which sorts of knowledge or technology. There is a convenient illustration of the point in the recent history of molecular genetics. The idea of recombining DNA molecules is one which has been around for some time. However, early efforts proved unsuccessful. As it happened, the crucial step in making recombinant DNA technology possible was provided by research on restriction enzymes, research that was undertaken with no thought of recombinant DNA technology. Indeed, until it was realized that restriction enzymes provided the key to recombining DNA molecules, the research on restriction enzymes was regarded as a rather unexciting (and certainly uncontroversial) scientific backwater.[9] In an entirely analogous way, crucial pieces of information that may one day enable us to manipulate the human genome may come

9. I am indebted to Prof. Ethel Jackson for both the argument and the illustration.

from just about any branch of molecular biology. To guard against the discovery of that knowledge we should have to curtail not only recombinant DNA research but all of molecular biology.

Before concluding, we would do well to note that there is a profound pessimism reflected in the attitude of those who would stop recombinant DNA research because it might lead to knowledge that could be abused. It is, after all, granted on all sides that the knowledge resulting from recombinant DNA research will have both good and evil potential uses. So it would seem the sensible strategy would be to try to prevent the improper uses of this knowledge rather than trying to prevent the knowledge from ever being uncovered. Those who would take the more extreme step of trying to stop the knowledge from being uncovered presumably feel that its improper use is all but inevitable, that our political and social institutions are incapable of preventing morally abhorrent applications of the knowledge while encouraging beneficial applications. On my view, this pessimism is unwarranted; indeed, it is all but inconsistent. The historical record gives us no reason to believe that what is technologically possible will be done, no matter what the moral price. Indeed, in the area of human genetic manipulation, the record points in quite the *opposite* direction. We have long known that the same techniques that work so successfully in animal breeding can be applied to humans as well. Yet there is no evidence of a "technological imperative" impelling our society to breed people as we breed dairy cattle simply because we know that it can be done. Finally, it is odd that those who express no confidence in the ability of our institutions to forestall such monstrous applications of technology are not equally pessimistic about the ability of the same institutions to impose an effective ban on the uncovering of dangerous knowledge. If our institutions are incapable of restraining the application of technology when those applications would be plainly morally abhorrent, one would think they would be even more impotent in attempting to restrain a line of research which promises major gains in human welfare.

2

JUSTIFICATION AND THE PSYCHOLOGY OF HUMAN REASONING

Stephen Stich and Richard E. Nisbett

THIS ESSAY GROWS out of the conviction that recent work by psychologists studying human reasoning has important implications for a broad range of philosophical issues. To illustrate our thesis we focus on Nelson Goodman's elegant and influential attempt to "dissolve" the problem of induction. In the first section of the paper we sketch Goodman's account of what it is for a rule of inference to be justified. We then marshal empirical evidence indicating that, on Goodman's account of justification, patently invalid inferential rules turn out to be "justified." We conclude that something is seriously wrong with Goodman's story about justification. In the second section we attempt to patch Goodman's account. The notion of epistemic authority and the social aspect of justification play central roles in the alternative account of justification that we propose.

There was a time, Hume's time, when the empirical study of human reasoning went hand in hand with the philosophical study of the justification of inference. But more recently, philosophers have held the empirical study of reasoning to be beyond their province. And modern experimental psychologists, until recently, simply ignored human inference altogether. Happily, a growing number of experimental psychologists have begun to study how human subjects actually go about the business of reasoning. Philosophers, however, have as yet given this work little notice. We are convinced that philosophers ignore this work at their peril.[1]

---

1. For a parallel view, cf. Goldman (1978).

The present paper makes an extended case for the philosophical relevance of recent empirical work on reasoning. The paper will focus on the implications of this work for an analysis of justification of inductive procedures. We shall argue that Nelson Goodman's elegant and enormously influential attempt to "dissolve" the problem of induction is seriously flawed.[2] At the root of the difficulty is the fact that Goodman makes tacit assumptions about the ways in which people actually infer. These are empirical assumptions, and recent studies of inference indicate that the assumptions are false. This is the burden of the first section of our paper.

In the second section we try our hand at repairing the damage. The trouble with Goodman's story about induction centers on his analysis of what we are saying when we say that a rule of inference is justified. We will offer a new account of what is going on when people say that an inference or a rule of inference is (or is not) justified. In the course of developing our analysis we begin to explore the much neglected social component of justification and the role of expert authority in our cognitive lives.

I Facts and Fictions About Forecasts

1. GOODMAN'S SOLUTION TO THE RIDDLE OF INDUCTION

Hume's riddle about inductive reasoning is easy enough to state. We know that a certain kind of food has nourished us in the past, and on the basis of this evidence we come to believe it will continue to nourish us in the future. But what justification do we have for such an inference? Surely it is possible that food which nourished us in the past should poison us now. There is no contradiction in assuming that this will happen. More generally, what justification do we have for believing that the regularities we have observed in nature will obtain in those parts of nature we have yet to observe?

The central move in Goodman's solution to Hume's riddle is a strategic one. Before attempting a justification of inductive reasoning, Goodman notes, it would be sensible to reflect on just what it is we ask for when we ask for a justification. If, for example, what we seek is a guarantee that inductive inferences will turn out to be correct, then there can be no justification of induction. For there simply is no guarantee. Some good inductive arguments with true premises turn out to have false conclusions. That is just the nature of the beast.[3]

---

2. References to this volume (Goodman 1965) will be given in parentheses in the text.

3. Goodman makes the point with more grace though less caution:

> If the problem is to explain how we know that certain predictions will turn out to be correct, the sufficient answer is that we don't know any such thing. If the problem is to *find* some way of distinguishing antecedently between true and false predictions, we are asking for prevision rather than for philosophical explanation. (62)

> Read literally, Goodman seems to be claiming that we do not *know* some predictions will turn out to be correct while others will not. But surely this is perverse if the word "know" is being used with its ordinary meaning. Suppose that a gypsy fortune teller predicted last week that the sun would not rise yesterday. We certainly think that we knew her prediction would turn out not to be correct even before yesterday's sunrise. And as the word "know" is ordinarily used, we are surely right.

But if it is not a guarantee we seek, just what do we want when we ask for a justification of induction? Before we can productively ask for a justification of induction, we need an analysis of the notion of justification.

Goodman begins his analysis of justification by asking what a justification amounts to in the case of *deductive* reasoning. To begin, of course, a deductive inference is justified if it conforms to the general rules of deductive inference. But not just any set of rules will do here; the rules themselves must be valid ones. How, then, do we justify a deductive *rule*? On Goodman's view,

> principles of deductive inference are justified by their conformity with accepted deductive practice. Their validity depends on accordance with the particular deductive inferences we actually make and sanction. If a rule yields inacceptable inferences, we drop it as invalid. Justification of general rules thus derives from judgements rejecting or accepting particular inferences. (63–64)

Now, as Goodman notes, this account of justification "looks flagrantly circular" (64). Particular inferences are supposed to be justified by their conformity to general rules, and general rules are supposed to be justified by their conformity to valid inferences. But, Goodman urges, the

> circle is a virtuous one. The point is that rules and particular inferences alike are justified by being brought into agreement with each other. *A rule is amended if it yields an inference we are unwilling to accept; an inference is rejected if it violates a rule we are unwilling to amend.* The process of justification is the delicate one of making mutual adjustments between rules and accepted inferences; and in the agreement achieved lies the only justification needed for either. (64, emphasis Goodman's)

So, on Goodman's account, a deductive rule is justified if it accords with the deductive inferences that we would reflectively make or sanction. We shall refer to this sort of accord by saying that a rule is in *reflective equilibrium* with inferential practice.[4]

Finally, Goodman proposes that his account of justification in deduction can be extended *mutatis mutandis* to inductive reasoning as well. There too, a particular inference is justified by conformity to general rules, in this case the rules of induction. And the general principles are justified by their conformity to the inductive references we reflectively make and accept.

> Predictions are justified if they conform to valid canons of induction; and the canons are valid if they accurately codify accepted inductive practice. (64)

There is an elegant simplicity to Goodman's account. To justify a particular inductive inference we need only show that it conforms with justified rules of inductive inference.

---

4. We borrow the term *reflective equilibrium* from John Rawls (1971, p. 20). Rawls, in turn, attributes the idea to Goodman.

And to justify the rules we need only show that they accurately describe the inductive inferences we are willing to accept. Actually, the portrayed simplicity of the justificatory process is a bit deceptive. For there may be those awkward times when a rule we are loath to amend sanctions an inference we are unwilling to accept. And conversely there may be times when canons of induction which we are reluctant to fiddle with *fail* to sanction an induction we are unwilling to reject. Here Goodman's counsel is that we resort to the "delicate" process of making mutual adjustments between rules and accepted inferences, though he gives us no guidance on how to resolve the competing claims of an irresistible inference and an immovable rule. His view would seem to be that there is no right or wrong way to resolve such an impasse, or at least that any of a wide range of potential resolutions are all equally acceptable.[5] For our purposes, however, we may ignore those problematic cases where rule and inference conflict. In the remaining cases, those where a rule we are inclined to endorse sanctions inferences we are inclined to accept, Goodman takes both rule and inferences to be justified.

A conspicuous virtue of Goodman's account of justification is that, if it is correct, then the problem of induction is straightforwardly solvable. Hume asked what justification we have for believing that bread will continue to nourish us. The answer is that we have inferred this belief from true premises *via* valid inductive rules. And if Hume were to ask what justification we have for the rules, the reply would be that they are in reflective equilibrium with our inductive practice. There remains, of course, the formidable job of explicitly articulating the rules which capture our reflective practice. This is the project which occupies the remainder of Goodman's book. However, we will retrace Goodman's thinking no further, for it is our contention that his account of justification is simply wrong.

2. SOME TROUBLESOME FACTS ABOUT HUMAN INFERENCE

What we propose to show is that, *pace* Goodman, being in reflective equilibrium with inductive practice is neither necessary nor sufficient for a rule of inductive inference to be justified. Our strategy will be to take the reflective equilibrium idea seriously and ask what sorts of rules do, as a matter of empirical fact, pass the reflective equilibrium test. Pursuing this course we will find numerous examples of patently invalid rules which pass the test for many subjects. In most of these cases there will be a valid rule which fails to pass the reflective equilibrium test. Some of the cases we will cite rest heavily on anecdotal evidence, and on conjecture about what more careful study would show. However, there is also a growing body of empirical work which points to the conclusion that human subjects regularly and systematically make invalid inductive inferences. While some of these studies provide little evidence about subjects' explicit acceptance of the invalid rule tacitly guiding their inferences, there is no reason to think that they would have any qualms about accepting these invalid rules, or about rejecting valid ones that ought to govern the inference at hand.

---

5. Cf. Nelson Goodman (1966), chapter I.

i. The Gambler's Fallacy

To begin, let us consider the notorious case of the gambler's fallacy. Most readers will be able to provide their own anecdote of a person involved in a game of chance like roulette who has been losing heavily while betting on a certain number. In some circumstances it might be reasonable for the subject to infer that the game itself is crooked. In other circumstances, where the hypothesis of a dishonest game can be ruled out as extremely unlikely, the reasonable expectation is that the chance of hitting the favored number after a long losing streak is exactly the same as the chance of hitting the number at any other time. But the subject of our anecdote makes neither inference. Rather, his losing streak leads him to stick all the more doggedly to his favored number, in the belief that the chance of hitting that number increases as the number of turns in which it fails to win increases. The anecdote has two possible endings. In one, the subject does hit the jackpot, thus reinforcing his adherence to the gambler's fallacy. In the other, the subject leaves the game in a barrel, either metaphorically or literally.

The principle of inference invoked by our misguided subject would seem to be something like the following:

> In a fair game of chance, the probability of a given sort of outcome occurring after $n + 1$ consecutive instances of non-occurrence is greater than the probability of its occurrence after n consecutive instances of non-occurrence.

There can be little doubt that many people do in fact persistently infer in accord with this principle. So the principle does accurately describe the inductive practice of these subjects. Moreover, there is no reason to think that if these subjects were explicitly queried about whether the rule is intuitively reasonable or acceptable to them they would be at all reluctant to endorse it. Indeed a number of reflective people *have* endorsed the gambler's fallacy principle. Consider, for example, the following eye-catching passage from Henry Coppée's *Elements of Logic* (revised edition, 1874; Philadelphia: J. H. Butler & Company, p. 162).

> Thus, in throwing dice, we cannot be sure that any single face or combination of faces will appear; but if, in very many throws, some particular face has not appeared, the chances of its coming up are stronger and stronger, until they approach very near to certainty. It must come; and as each throw is made and it fails to appear, the certainty of its coming draws nearer and nearer.[6, 7]

---

6. We are grateful to Prof. Arnold Wilson for bringing this quote to our attention. There is a delightful irony in the fact that Coppée's book first appeared while he was Professor of Philosophy at the University of Pennsylvania. Goodman held the same position when *Fact, Fiction and Forecast* first appeared.

7. Perhaps we should note that there are circumstances in which an inferential strategy similar to the gambler's fallacy would be perfectly appropriate. Suppose you are waiting for an elevator, but you could walk up the stairs. The longer you wait, the more likely the elevator is to come in the next few seconds (assuming that the elevator is functioning properly and is going through its appointed rounds). It is tempting to conjecture that the gambler's fallacy has its psychological roots in an overgeneralization. An inferential strategy which is perfectly reasonable in a given range of cases is extended to other cases where it is inappropriate. (For the example our thanks go to an anonymous reviewer.)

Now the existence of large numbers of subjects like Coppée is something of an embarrassment to Goodman. The gambler's fallacy rule is in reflective equilibrium with actual inductive practice for these subjects. So on Goodman's account of justification, both the gambler's fallacy and the inferences made in accord with it are justified for these subjects.

ii. Regression Errors

To introduce our second example, consider the following little quiz: It is well known that people's height is correlated with the height of their parents. Tall persons generally have tall parents and short persons generally have short parents, though of course there are exceptions. Now consider those families in which both parents are in the 95th percentile for height. That is, the father is taller than 94% of all men and the mother is taller than 94% of all women. What would you expect the average height of children in these families to be?

   a. Taller than the 95th percentile height
   b. Shorter than the 95th percentile height
   c. Approximately equal to the 95th percentile height.

Most subjects who take this little quiz answer c, though, of course, the correct answer is b since regression toward the mean is to be expected in such cases. Extensive work by Tversky and Kahneman (1974) has demonstrated that most subjects have little or no grasp of the notion of statistical regression. In a wide range of cases in which a pair of dimensions are imperfectly correlated (e.g., student I.Q. and grade point average; or success in graduate school and success in career), subjects expect that values on the dimension to be predicted will on the average be as discrepant from the mean as values on the predictor dimension. Moreover, when questioned on the principle behind their inference, the rules offered by subjects take no account of regression to the mean.[8] These subjects, like those in the gambler's fallacy example, pose a problem for Goodman. Their non-regressive rule is in reflective equilibrium with their actual inductive practice. So for Goodman, both their rule and their individual inferences are justified.

iii. Erroneous Analysis of Covariation

As a final example, consider the sort of inference that sometimes leads people to believe in the efficacy of quack medical "cures," occasionally with tragic results:

> Aunt Maude has been all but crippled with painful backaches. On the advice of a friend, she seeks treatment from Dr. Snapbone. After three months in Snapbone's care, Maude's backaches are entirely gone. On hearing of Aunt Maude's "cure," Uncle Rupert comes to believe that Dr. Snapbone's treatment is helpful for backaches, i.e., that one's chances of recovery are better with Snapbone's treatment than without.

---

8. For a more detailed account of the rule which subjects endorse, cf. Nisbett and Ross 1980.

Of course, without information about the spontaneous "cure" rate among persons whose backaches are left untreated, along with information about the rate of both "cures" and "non-cures" among people who have received Snapbone's therapy, Rupert is in no position to draw the inference he does. However, Smedslund and Ward and Jenkins[9] have shown that many subjects take no account of information about spontaneous "cures" even when the information is available. Given data like the following:

	Cure	No Cure
treatment	581	83
no treatment	287	41

many subjects will conclude that the chances of a cure are better with treatment than without. Such subjects often point to the treatment/cure cell of the matrix and say, "Many people who got the treatment were cured, so the treatment is effective." Other subjects, slightly more sophisticated, point to the treatment/no cure cell in addition, and say, "Since most of the subjects who received the treatment were cured, the treatment was effective." In fact, these data provide no evidence that the treatment has any value whatever. Yet subjects in these experiments are prepared to endorse the fallacious rule they appear to be using, *viz*.:

> If the presence of A (in this case treatment) is often followed by the presence of B (in this case cure) then the chance of B occurring is greater when A has occurred than when A has not occurred.

As in our previous two examples, such subjects are an embarrassment for Goodman. The rule they endorse is in reflective equilibrium with their actual inductive practice. So on Goodman's account of justification both the rule and the particular inference are justified.

The examples we have elaborated are not the only ones that might be given. In the last two decades psychologists have become increasingly interested in the inferential patterns people actually invoke and accept in ordinary life.[10] The picture that emerges from this work is hardly a flattering one. Subjects frequently and systematically invoke inference patterns ranging from the merely invalid to the bizarre. And, though the evidence is less substantial on this point, there is every reason to think that many of these patterns are in reflective equilibrium.

---

9. Smedslund 1963; Ward and Jenkins 1965.

10. See especially Tversky and Kahneman 1974 and Nisbett and Ross 1980.

3. SOME COUNTERMOVES

On the face of it, the facts we have reviewed would seem to show that Goodman's account of justification is well off target. In the next few pages we want to anticipate and respond to possible moves a Goodmanian might make in an effort to shield his view from the damage threatened by the facts.

i. Instruction and Reflective Equilibrium

The first move we want to examine denies that the rules invoked by subjects in our examples actually are in *stable* reflective equilibrium. The Goodmanian who makes this move grants that subjects do frequently infer in accordance with these invalid rules, and do accept the rules when questioned. However, he continues, reasonable subjects can be shown the error of their ways. We can, with a bit of effort, *teach* these subjects that the inferential principle they accept is an invalid one. To do this we might show the subjects that the rule they use is in conflict with other rules they also accept, or with beliefs they already have or can be gotten to acquire. With appropriate instruction they can be weaned away from their invalid rules. Now, the Goodmanian claims, for a rule to be in stable reflective equilibrium is not merely for it to codify actual inductive practice. An inferential principle is in stable reflective equilibrium only when it codifies inferential practice and also would survive the further reflective process of carefully comparing rules with each other and with the beliefs subjects have or can be led to have. Since the principles considered in the previous section do not pass this test they are not counter-examples to Goodman's account of justification.

Before attempting to parry this move, let us note one claim made by our hypothetical Goodmanian with which we have no quarrel. It is quite true that a rational subject often can be persuaded to reject an invalid rule in favor of a valid one. It has been our experience, for example, that a subject who endorses the gambler's fallacy can often be led to reject the rule by asking him to consider whether he thinks there is any causal relation between past throws of dice and future throws of the same dice. When the subject concedes that there is no such causal relation, we ask him to consider how it could be that long runs in which a certain number does not appear are followed by higher probabilities of that number appearing, unless there is a causal relation between past and future throws. Stymied by the question, the subject is quite receptive to the suggestion that with fair dice the chance of a given number appearing is independent of the outcome of preceding tosses.

However, we do not think that the teachability of rational subjects can save Goodman from our counter-examples. The problem is that teachability is a two-edged sword. While it is quite true that subjects can often be gotten to reject invalid rules they had previously accepted, *it is also true that they can be gotten to accept invalid rules they had previously rejected.* For example, we have gotten a few subjects to wonder about their rejection of the gambler's fallacy by arguing as follows: "If the coin is a fair one, then in the long run the number of heads and tails should be about equal. But then if a fair coin produces a long run of heads, there will have to be some excess of tails in the following flips in order to achieve the rough equality expected from a fair coin." For obvious moral reasons we did not pursue this line of argument to the point where the subjects became converts to the gambler's fallacy. But there is little reason to doubt that such an effort at persuasion would often meet with success, particularly when the subject is, say, an undergraduate largely innocent of formal training in statistics, and the people offering the arguments are authority figures, perhaps university professors. Our point, then, is that with suitable argument subjects can often be convinced of an invalid rule just as they can be convinced of a valid one. What is more, we know of no reason to think that valid rules are easier to teach than plausible invalid ones. Indeed, because of the counter-intuitive nature of some inductive rules, regression principles, for example, there is good reason to suppose that some invalid rules would be substantially *easier* to teach, and more stable once learned.

Now recall that our imagined Goodmanian proposed to save Goodman's account of justification by interpreting the standards for reflective equilibrium more stringently. To be in stable reflective equilibrium a rule must not only accord with inferential practice, it must also survive careful comparison with other rules the subject accepts and with the body of beliefs he either has or may acquire during the reflective process. Our rejoinder is simply this. There is no reason to think that this more stringent reflective process would have a unique outcome for a given subject. With suitable "guidance" many subjects could be led either to accept or reject a large number of inferential principles, both valid and invalid.

ii. Digging In

There is a second strategy a Goodmanian might try in an effort to protect his account of justification from our embarrassing facts. This is the bold strategy of simply digging in his heels and insisting that whatever inferential principles pass the reflective equilibrium test are indeed justified, at least for the subjects involved. The subject, it might be argued, has no higher court of appeal than the reflective equilibrium test. So if the principles cited are in reflective equilibrium for the subjects in question, then the rules are justified *for them*. Of course, the rules are not justified for us. But no matter. They are justified for the subjects who invoke them, and that is all Goodman's theory need claim.

We are a bit hard put to reply to our imagined Goodmanian. For he is denying a premise we took to be completely obvious. In our critique of Goodman we simply assumed that the craps shooter in Las Vegas who systematically invoked and acted on the gambler's fallacy was relying on a patently invalid rule. Perhaps the best reply is to remind ourselves of just what we are up to. Goodman proposed to (dis)solve the problem of induction by first analyzing what we mean when we say an inferential principle is justified. And the test of such an account, surely, is how well the proposed analysand captures the extension of our intuitive use of the analysandum. By our lights it is no less than bizarre to suggest that the gambler's fallacy is justified for the Las Vegas craps shooter. This judgment seems to be all but universally shared by native philosophical informants.

II An Analysis of Justification

It is time for us to stick our own necks out a bit and offer our account of justification. The story we have to tell is a complicated one, best set out in pieces. To begin we will sketch an account of justification that is, we think, almost right. We will then go on to say why our account is only a near miss, and how it fits into the more complicated story of how the notion of justification is used.

I. EPISTEMIC AUTHORITY: THE SOCIAL COMPONENT OF JUSTIFICATION

Why does Goodman's account of justification fail? A suggestive way to approach this question is to reflect on the sort of defense one of our imagined Goodmanians offered for the Las Vegas craps shooter: "The subject has no higher court of appeal than the reflective equilibrium test." The suggestion left tacit is that the alternative to the reflective equilibrium test is skepticism. Once he has established that a rule is in reflective equilibrium with his own inductive practice, the subject has done everything he can do. If this is not enough to show the rule in question is justified, then the subject might invoke an unjustified rule though he could never know he was doing so. But surely all of this is quite wrong. There is a higher court of appeal than this subject's reflective equilibrium. It is the reflective equilibrium of his cognitive betters. There are people in our subject's society who are recognized as *authorities* on one or another sort of inference. And if our subject wanted to appeal to a higher court than his own reflective equilibrium, he could do so. He need only seek out the experts and ask them.

The role of experts and authorities in our cognitive lives has been all but ignored by modern epistemologists. Yet it is a hallmark of an educated and reflective person that he recognizes, consults, and defers to authority on a wide range of topics. We defer to the judgment of experts not only in assessing inference, but on factual questions as well, in medicine, science, history, and many other areas. Few educated laypersons would consider questioning the consensus of authorities on the authenticity of a painting, the cause of an airline crash, or the validity of a new theorem. Indeed, it is our suspicion that one of the principal effects of education is to socialize people to defer to cognitive authorities. (We are following up our hunch in an empirical study now under way.)

Deference to authority is not merely the habitual practice of educated people; it is, generally, the right thing to do, from a normative point of view. The man who persists in believing that his theorem is valid, despite the dissent of leading mathematicians, is a fool. The man who acts on his belief that a treatment, disparaged by medical experts, will cure his child's leukemia is worse than a fool.

Of course, it is rarely the case that even a well-educated person actually knows who the experts on a given topic are. And it is even more infrequent that he seeks them out or reads what they have written. It is more common to rely on secondhand accounts in the popular press, though the extent and influence of such secondhand appeals to authority is very much an open question. In claiming that people recognize the force of cognitive authority, we are not claiming that they often consult such authorities, but only that people believe there are experts and that they are prepared to defer to the experts' views.[11]

The last three paragraphs constitute little more than a gesture at the phenomena of epistemic authority. There are many questions about the social psychology and sociology of epistemic authority that must be explored before we have even the beginnings of an adequate understanding of the subject. Perhaps the most interesting question concerns the vesting of epistemic authority: In virtue of what do people come to count as experts on a given issue for a society or a subculture? Yet another set of questions focuses on opinion change among the community of experts: Are there general patterns to be observed? What factors influence the dynamics of opinion change among experts? In addition, it would be fascinating to know the extent to which subcultures within our society recognize disparate sets of experts on one or another issue. Equally intriguing is the question of what happens when cultures recognizing different experts come in contact with one another. Plainly, this is not the place to essay answers to these questions. Our purpose here is only to urge the importance of the questions and to lament their neglect.

The relevance of the notion of epistemic authority to Goodman's ailing analysis of justification will become clear by returning to a consideration of our Las Vegas craps shooter. Why is it that his inference is not justified? The answer we would urge is that the rule he invokes, though in reflective equilibrium for him, is not in reflective equilibrium for the experts on inductive inference in our society. This suggests a modification of Goodman's account which recognizes the special role of cognitive authorities. On the modified account, a rule of inference is justified if it captures the reflective practice not of the person using it but of the appropriate experts in our society. We think that this "expert reflective equilibrium" (hereafter: expert r.e.) account of justification does a much better job than Goodman's account at capturing what one does when attributing and denying justification. In particular, it handles with dispatch all the examples assembled in I, 2. Each of these was an example of an invalid inferential rule accepted and adhered to by many subjects. On the expert r.e. account, in contrast to Goodman's, none of these rules is justified, since none are accepted by experts on inference.

It has been suggested to us that, read with maximal charity, Goodman might actually be construed as offering the expert r.e. account himself. Goodman's account of justification refers to "inferences we actually make and sanction," inferences "we are willing to accept," rules "we are unwilling to amend," etc. Unfortunately he never pauses to say who "we" are. Now on the most charitable reading, Goodman's "we" is taken to refer only to himself and other authorities on inductive inference. This reading of Goodman strikes us as an unlikely one, in light of his total silence on the matter of cognitive authority. But if this is the intended interpretation, our disagreements with Goodman are still not at an end. We do not think the expert reflective equilibrium account of justification is the right one.

---

11. For some related remarks, see Hilary Putnam 1975, 127–29.

2. THE COGNITIVE REBEL AND THE ANALYSIS OF JUSTIFICATION

The difficulty we see with the expert r.e. account is that it ties the notion of justified inference too closely to the reflective equilibrium of socially designated authorities. To knowingly disagree with expert opinion is frequently seen as foolish. But on the expert r.e. view, it is more than foolish; it is self-contradictory. Consider the case of the subject who espouses an inferential principle while knowing full well that the experts of our society consider the principle to be unjustified. Such a subject might say, "I have thought about the principle carefully and I think it is a justified one; I realize that the recognized authorities reject the principle, but I think they are wrong." Now on the expert r.e. account, our subject is literally contradicting himself. He is saying that the principle both does capture the reflective practice of the authorities (*is justified*, on the expert r.e. account), and that it does not. We take this consequence of the expert r.e. analysis to be unacceptable. The person who refuses to defer to socially recognized cognitive authority is often regarded as unwise, but not quite *that* unwise. He is not literally contradicting himself.[12] What we need, then, is some account of justification which gives the cognitive rebel his due. The cognitive rebel is, in effect, proclaiming that the reflective equilibrium of socially designated authorities doesn't count, and that his own reflective equilibrium is, for the matter at hand, to be preferred. Since he can carry off his proclamation without contradiction, our analysis cannot make the reflective equilibrium of socially designated experts necessary or sufficient for justification.

On our amended view, an attribution of justification to a rule of inference can be unpacked as a claim that the rule accords with the reflective inductive practice *of the people the speaker takes to be appropriate*. But the attribution of justification does not, by itself, *specify* whose reflective equilibrium the speaker takes to be appropriate. That job of specification can be done in varying ways by the context of the utterance. Or it can be left quite open or ambiguous. So, on the view we are urging,

Rule r is justified.

is to be analyzed as:

Rule *r* accords with the reflective inferential practice of the (person or) group of people I (the speaker) think appropriate.

Now most people are cognitive conservatives most of the time. They take the appropriate group to be the socially, consensually designated authorities. The disagreement between the cognitive rebel and the cognitive conservative is, in effect, a dispute over whose reflective judgment ought to be heeded in the issue at hand. On our view, such

---

12. We are indebted to Allan Gibbard, who first urged this argument on us.

disputes are not exclusively cognitive disputes. They are better viewed on the model of political disputes whose resolution, like the resolution of other political disputes, is determined by such factors as social power, personal style, and historical accident. There is something a bit radical about the view we are urging. To take some of the sting out, we should note that our view leaves abundant room for rational argument about justification *among* cognitive conservatives. Also, there may be rational argument about justification among cognitive rebels who agree about the appropriate authority group. However, if our account succeeds in capturing what we mean when we say that an inference is justified, then it is to be expected that there will be some disputes over justification that admit of no rational resolution. It is our guess that the history of scientific revolutions will provide examples of such disputes. And we expect that another, richer, source of examples would come from a careful study of the social psychology of cranks and scientific "crackpots," those forlorn souls who proclaim cognitive revolutions that win no converts. But to elaborate on this theme would require another paper, and another pair of authors.

REFERENCES

Goldman, A. 1978. Epistemics: The Regulative Theory of Cognition. *Journal of Philosophy* 75, 10: 509–23.

Goodman, N. 1965. *Fact, Fiction and Forecast*. 2nd ed. Indianapolis: Bobbs-Merrill.

———. 1966. *The Structure of Appearance*. 2nd ed. Indianapolis: Bobbs-Merrill.

Nisbett, R., and L. D. Ross. 1980. *Human Inference: Strategies and Shortcomings*. Englewood Cliffs, NJ: Prentice-Hall.

Putnam, H. 1975. The Meaning of "Meaning." In *Mind, Language and Reality*. Cambridge: Cambridge University Press, 127–29.

Rawls, J. 1971. *A Theory of Justice*. Cambridge, MA: Harvard University Press.

Smedslund, J. 1963. The Concept of Correlation in Adults. *Scandinavian Journal of Psychology* 4: 165–73.

Tversky, A., and D. Kahneman. 1974. Judgment Under Certainty: Heuristics and Biases. *Science* 185: 1124–31.

Ward, W. D., and H. M. Jenkins. 1965. The Display of Information and the Judgment of Contingency. *Canadian Journal of Psychology* 19: 231–41.

3

COULD MAN BE AN IRRATIONAL ANIMAL?

Some Notes on the Epistemology of Rationality

1

Aristotle thought man was a rational animal. From his time to ours, however, there has been a steady stream of writers who have dissented from this sanguine assessment. For Bacon, Hume, Freud, or D. H. Lawrence, rationality is at best a sometimes thing. On their view, episodes of rational inference and action are scattered beacons on the irrational coastline of human history. During the last decade or so, these impressionistic chroniclers of man's cognitive foibles have been joined by a growing group of experimental psychologists who are subjecting human reasoning to careful empirical scrutiny. Much of what they have found would appall Aristotle. Human subjects, it would appear, regularly and systematically invoke inferential and judgmental strategies ranging from the merely invalid to the genuinely bizarre.

Recently, however, there have been rumblings of a reaction brewing—a resurgence of Aristotelian optimism. Those defending the sullied name of human reason have been philosophers, and their weapons have been conceptual analysis and epistemological argument. The central thrust of their defense is the claim that empirical evidence could not possibly support the conclusion that people are systematically irrational. And thus the experiments which allegedly show that they are must be either flawed or misinterpreted.

In this paper I propose to take a critical look at these philosophical defenses of rationality. My sympathies, I should note straightaway, are squarely with the psychologists. My central thesis is that the philosophical arguments aimed at showing irrationality cannot be experimentally demonstrated are mistaken. Before considering these arguments, however, we would do well to set out a few illustrations of the sort of empirical studies which allegedly show that people depart from normative standards of rationality in systematic ways. This is the chore that will occupy us in the following section.

2

One of the most extensively investigated examples of inferential failure is the so-called "selection task" studied by P. C. Wason, P. N. Johnson-Laird, and their colleagues (Johnson-Laird, Legrenzi, and Sonino Legrenzi 1972; Johnson-Laird and Wason 1977; Wason 1977; Wason and Johnson-Laird 1972, chaps. 13–15). A typical selection task experiment presents subjects with four cards like those in Figure 3.1. Half of each card is masked. Subjects are then given the following instructions:

Wason and Johnson-Laird discovered that subjects, including very intelligent subjects, find the problem remarkably difficult. In one group of 128 university students, only *five* got the right answer. Moreover, the mistakes that subjects make are not randomly distributed. The two most common wrong answers are that one must see both (a) and (c), and that one need only see (a). The phenomenon turns out to be a remarkably robust one,

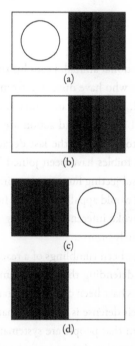

FIGURE 3.1

Which of the hidden parts of these cards do you need to see in order to answer the following question decisively?
FOR THESE CARDS IS IT TRUE THAT IF THERE IS A CIRCLE ON THE LEFT THERE IS A CIRCLE ON THE RIGHT?
You have only one opportunity to make this decision; you must not assume that you can inspect cards one at a time. Name those cards which it is absolutely essential to see.

producing essentially the same results despite significant variation in the experimental design, the wording of the question, and the details of the problem. For example, subjects presented with the four envelopes in Figure 3.2 and asked which must be turned over to determine the truth of the rule "If it has a vowel on one side it has an even number on the other side" do just as badly as subjects given the cards in Figure 3.1. However, there are variations in the experimental design which substantially improve inferential performance. One of these is making the relation between the antecedent and the consequent of the conditional rule in the instructions more "realistic." So, for example, subjects presented with the envelopes in Figure 3.3 and asked which must be turned over to determine the truth of the rule "If it is sealed, then it has a 5d stamp on it" do vastly better than subjects presented with the envelope in Figure 3.2. In one experiment using the "realistic" material, 22 out of 24 subjects got the right answer.[1]

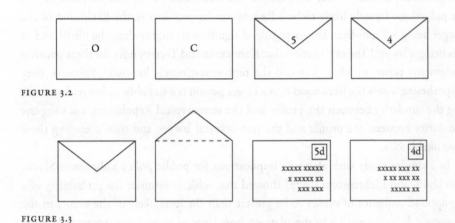

FIGURE 3.2

FIGURE 3.3

Wason and Johnson-Laird have also explored the ways in which subjects react when they are shown that their initial inferences are mistaken. In Figure 3.1, for example, a subject who said he must see only the hidden side of (a) might be asked to remove the masks on both (a) and (d), discovering a circle under each mask. Many subjects have a startling reaction. They note that the rule is false for these cards—in virtue of card (d)—and they continue to insist that it was only necessary to see card (a)! In further work Wason, Johnson-Laird, and their colleagues have looked at the ways in which subjects react when the apparent contradiction in their claims is pointed out. The intriguing details of these studies need not detain us here.

My second example of research revealing *prima facie* deviation from normative standards of inference focuses on the way people assess the probability of logically compound events or states of affairs. It is a truism of probability theory that the likelihood of a compound event or state of affairs must be less than or equal to the likelihood of the component events or states of affairs. If the components are probabilistically independent, the probability of the compound is equal to the product of the probabilities of the

---

1. Johnson-Laird, Legrenzi, and Sonino Legrenzi 1972. However, see also Griggs and Cox 1982.

components. If the components are not probabilistically independent, matters are more complicated. But in no case will the probability of the compound be *greater* than the probability of the components. There are, however, a number of experiments which demonstrate that people regularly violate this basic tenet of probabilistic reasoning. In one such experiment Kahneman and Tversky gave subjects personality profiles of various target persons. Subjects were then asked to assess the likelihood that the persons described in the profiles belonged to various groups. One group of subjects was asked to estimate the likelihood that profiled persons were members of noncompound groups like *lawyers* or *Republicans*. Another group of subjects was asked to estimate the probability that the profiled persons were members of compound groups like *Republican lawyers*. What Tversky and Kahneman (1982) found is that if a profiled person is judged rather unlikely to be, say, a lawyer, and rather likely to be a Republican, he will be judged moderately likely to be a Republican lawyer. That is, the likelihood of the target being a Republican lawyer is judged significantly higher than the likelihood of his being a lawyer! The explanation that Kahneman and Tversky offer for these peculiar judgments turns on what they call the representativeness heuristic. Subjects, they hypothesize, assess the likelihood that a target person is a Republican lawyer by assessing the similarity between the profile and the stereotypical Republican, assessing the similarity between the profile and the stereotypical lawyer, and then averaging these two likelihoods.

In a similar study with alarming implications for public policy judgments, Slovic, Fischhoff, and Lichtenstein (1977) showed that subjects estimate the probability of a compound sequence of events to be greater than the least likely of the events in the sequence. It is disquieting to speculate on how large an impact this inferential failing may have on people's assessments of the chance of such catastrophes as nuclear reactor failures which require a number of distinct events to occur in sequence (Slovic and Fischhoff, 1978).

My final example of an experimental program exploring human irrationality is the work on belief perseverance by Ross, Lepper, and their colleagues (Ross, Lepper, and Hubbard 1975). One of the experimental strategies used in this work is the so-called "debriefing" paradigm. In these experiments subjects are given evidence which is later completely discredited. But despite being "debriefed" and told exactly how they had been duped, subjects tend to retain to a substantial degree the beliefs they formed on the basis of the discredited evidence. In one such experiment subjects were presented with a task of distinguishing between authentic and unauthentic suicide notes. As they worked they were provided with false feedback indicating that overall they were performing at close to the average level, or (for other subjects) much above the average level, or (for a third group of subjects) much below the average level. Following this, each subject was debriefed, and the predetermined nature of the feedback was explained to him. They were not only told that their feedback had been false but were also shown the experimenter's instruction sheet assigning them to the success, failure, or average group, and specifying the feedback to be presented. Subsequent to this, and allegedly for quite a different reason, subjects were asked to fill out a questionnaire on which they were asked to estimate their actual performance at the suicide note task, to predict their probable success on related future tasks, and to rate their ability at suicide note discrimination and other related tasks. The results revealed that even after debriefing subjects who had initially been assigned to the success group continued to rate their performance and abilities far more favorably than did subjects in the average group. Subjects initially assigned to the failure group showed the opposite pattern of results. Once again, these results appear to reflect a robust phenomenon which manifests itself in many variations on the experimental theme, including some conducted outside the laboratory setting.

The three examples I have sketched could easily be supplemented by dozens more, all apparently demonstrating that human reasoning often deviates substantially from the standard provided by normative canons of inference. Let us now turn our attention to the arguments aimed at showing that these experiments are being misinterpreted.

3

Of the three arguments I shall consider, two are due to D. C. Dennett. Both arguments are embedded in Dennett's much more elaborate theory about the nature of intentional attributions, though neither argument is developed in much detail. In a pair of previous papers (Stich 1980, 1981a) I have tried to give a systematic critique of Dennett's views with due attention to problems of interpretation and the possibilities of alternative construals. In the present paper I will sidestep most of these niceties. What I wish to show is that a pair of arguments are mistaken. I think it is clear that Dennett has at least flirted with each of these arguments. But for the purposes at hand, pinning the tail on the donkey is of little importance.

The first of the arguments I am attributing to Dennett might be called *the argument from the inevitable rationality of believers*. On Dennett's view, when we attribute beliefs, desires, and other states of common sense psychology to a person, or for that matter to an animal or an artifact, we are assuming or presupposing that the person or object can be treated as what Dennett calls an *intentional system*. An intentional system is one which is rational through and through; its beliefs are "those it ought to have, given its perceptual capacities, its epistemic needs, and its biography. . . . Its desires are those it ought to have, given its biological needs and the most practicable means of satisfying them. . . . And its behavior will consist of those acts that it *would be rational* for an agent with those beliefs and desires to perform" (1981b). According to Dennett it is in the context of this set of assumptions about rationality that our ordinary talk about beliefs, desires, or other intentional states gains its meaning. If this is right, then we should expect that when a person's behavior is less than fully rational the intentional scheme would no longer apply. We could not rest content with a description of a person as holding an incoherent or irrational set of beliefs, for if rationality is absent, we cannot coherently ascribe beliefs at all. Dennett (1978, 20) puts the matter as follows:

> Conflict arises . . . when a person falls short of perfect rationality, and avows beliefs that either are strongly disconfirmed by the available empirical evidence or are self-contradictory or contradict other avowals he has made. If we lean on the myth that a man is perfectly rational, we must find his avowals less than authoritative: "You can't mean—understand—what you're saying!"; if we lean on his right as a speaking intentional system to have his word accepted, we grant him an irrational set of beliefs. Neither position provides a stable resting place; for, as we saw earlier, intentional explanation and prediction cannot be accommodated either to breakdown or to less than optimal design, so there is no coherent intentional description of such an impasse.

Given this much of Dennett's view, it follows straightforwardly that no experiment could demonstrate that people systematically invoke invalid or irrational inferential strategies. The point is not that people *must* be rational. No such conclusion follows from Dennett's view. What does follow from Dennett's view is that people must be rational *if they can usefully be viewed as having any beliefs at all*. We have no guarantee that people will behave in a way that makes it profitable for us to assume the intentional stance toward them. But intentional descriptions and rationality come in the same package; there is no getting one without the other. Thus if people infer at all, that is, if they generate new beliefs from old ones, from perceptual experience, or what have you, then they must do so rationally. Dennett is, in effect, offering us a *reductio* on the claim that people infer irrationally. If a system infers irrationally, it cannot be an intentional system; thus we cannot ascribe beliefs and desires to it. But since inference is a belief-generating process, the system does not infer at all.

Now as I see it, the problem with Dennett's argument comes right at the beginning. He is simply wrong about the relationship between our ordinary notions of belief and desire and his notion of an idealized fully rational intentional system. *Pace* Dennett, it is simply not the case that our ordinary belief and desire ascriptions presuppose full rationality. There is nothing in the least incoherent or unstable about a description, cast in intentional terms, of a person who has inconsistent beliefs. The subjects in Wason and Johnson-Laird's experiments provide a clear example, one among endlessly many. Some of these subjects clearly believe that cards (a) and (c) must be removed, and defend their view with considerable vigor. Yet these subjects clearly understand the conditions of the problem and have no false beliefs about what they are being asked to do.[2]

In defending his contention that ordinary intentional ascriptions gain their meaning against the background of a theory of intentional systems, Dennett offers a pair of

---

2. For Dennett's attempt to blunt this point, see Dennett 1981a.

arguments, one long and one short. The short one is the observation, attributed to Quine, that blatant or obvious inconsistency is the best evidence we can have that we are misdescribing a subject's beliefs. This fact is readily explained if belief ascription presupposes full rationality. The longer argument has much the same structure. In effect, Dennett maintains that his intentional system explication of ordinary belief and desire talk explains many of the facts about the way we use these locutions in describing and explaining the behavior of persons, animals, and artifacts. All of this I cheerfully grant. I also grant that, until recently at least, Dennett's explication of ordinary intentional locutions was the best—indeed pretty near the only—game in town. None of this, however, persuades me to accept Dennett's explication. The reason is that I think there is a better explication of the way we use our workaday belief and desire locutions, an explication that handles all the facts Dennett's can handle without the paradoxical consequence that intentional descriptions of irrational beliefs are unstable or incoherent. The basic idea of this alternative explication is that in using intentional locutions we are presupposing that the person or system to which they are applied is, in relevant ways, similar to ourselves. Thus inferential errors that we can imagine ourselves making—errors like those recounted in my previous section—can be described comfortably in intentional terms. It is only the sort of error or incoherence that we cannot imagine falling into ourselves that undermines intentional description. This is the reason that blatant inconsistency of the sort Quine has in mind is evidence that something has gone wrong in our intentional attributions. Plainly the alternative "similar-to-us" account of intentional locutions needs a much more detailed elaboration. I have made a beginning at this in Stich 1981b.[3]

4

Dennett concedes that his second argument is uncomfortably vague, so a fair bit of interpretation is needed. I will call this one *the argument from natural selection.* The closest Dennett comes to setting out the argument is in a passage where he reflects on whether

---

3. See also Stich 1983, ch. 5. Dennett's view is often described as of a piece with Davidson's. But this is clearly mistaken. Davidson makes no use of the notion of an ideally rational system. Like me, he insists that a person must be cognitively *similar* to ourselves if we are to succeed in understanding his speech and ascribing beliefs to him. In particular, he maintains that "if I am right in attributing a particular belief to you, then you must have a pattern of beliefs much like mine" (Davidson 1979, 295). Davidson goes on to argue that most of these beliefs must be *true*. This is a view that Dennett holds as well. But as we shall see in the next section, Dennett's defense of this doctrine turns on evolutionary considerations, while Davidson's does not. The least obscure argument Davidson offers for this conclusion goes like this: "There is nothing absurd in the idea of an omniscient interpreter" (ibid.). To interpret us, this omniscient interpreter must share the bulk of our beliefs. And since by hypothesis all of his beliefs are true, it follows that the bulk of ours must be true as well. End of argument. It should be pretty clear, however, that this argument simply begs the question. Granting the point about belief similarity being necessary for interpretation, it is an open question whether an omniscient interpreter could interpret our utterances as meaning something in his language. He could do so only if the bulk of our beliefs are true. And that is just what the argument was supposed to establish.

we could adopt the intentional stance toward thoroughly exotic creatures encountered on another planet. His answer is that we could, provided "we have reason to suppose that a process of natural selection has been in effect." But why would the mere existence of natural selection suffice to ensure that the creatures would be good approximations to the thoroughly rational ideal embodied in the notion of an intentional system? Dennett offers no detailed answer, but provides us with a few hints, as have other writers who have sounded similar themes. These hints may be elaborated into the following argument.

1. Natural selection will favor (i.e., select for) inferential strategies which generally yield true beliefs. This is because, in general, true beliefs are more adaptive than false ones; they enable the organism to cope better with its environment. There are exceptions, of course. But on the whole organisms will outcompete their conspecifics if their ratio of true beliefs to false ones is higher. After an extended period of natural selection we can expect that the inferential strategies an organism uses will be ones which generally yield true beliefs.
2. An inferential strategy which generally yields true beliefs is a rational inferential strategy. Therefore,
3. Natural selection will favor rational inferential strategies.

Since Dennett's Martians are, by hypothesis, the product of an extended process of natural selection we can conclude that they use rational inferential strategies. And, closer to home, since human beings are the result of millions of years of natural selection we know that they too must use rational inferential strategies. Thus any research program which claims to have evidence for widespread and systematic irrationality among humans must be misinterpreting its results. It is my suspicion that many writers who have recently been urging a naturalized or evolutionary reinterpretation of epistemology have had something very like this argument in mind. If so, then it is all the more important to focus critical scrutiny on the argument, for such scrutiny shows the argument to be seriously flawed.

Consider the first step. Is it true that natural selection favors inferential strategies which generally yield true beliefs? The answer, I think, is clearly no. Perhaps the most vivid way to make the point is with a brief description of some intriguing experiments by John Garcia and his co-workers (Garcia, McGowan, and Green 1972). In one series of experiments Garcia's group fed rats distinctively flavored water or food, and then subjected them to substantial doses of radiation, enough to induce radiation sickness. After a single episode, the rats developed a strong aversion to the distinctively flavored food or water that had been used. Workers in other laboratories have demonstrated that the same phenomenon occurs even when the rat is exposed to radiation as much as 12 hours after eating or drinking. It has also been shown that the taste of the food is the object of the rat's aversion. The rats acquire no aversion to the cage in which the distinctive food was eaten, nor do they acquire an aversion to food pellets of a distinctive size. But if two substances are eaten in sequence prior to illness, novelty is a much more potent factor than recency in determination of the aversion. In short, the rat behaves as though it believes that anything which tastes like the distinctive-tasting stuff it has eaten will cause it to become deathly ill. Moreover, it is clear that this belief, if that is what it is, is the result of an innate belief- (or aversion-) forming strategy which is surely the result of natural selection.

Consider now how often the inferential strategy which leads to the rat's belief will lead to a true belief. In the laboratory, of course, the inferential strategy is thoroughly unreliable. It is the radiation, not the food, which causes the rat's illness. But what about the rats in their natural environment? I know of no studies of rat epidemiology which indicate the most common causes of acute illness among rats. I would suspect, however, that rats, like people, fall victim to all manner of acute afflictions caused by viruses and bacteria which are not transmitted through food, still less through distinctively flavored food. If this is right, if, to be more specific, more than half of the illnesses rats endure in the wild which lead to the development of Garcia aversions are not transmitted by distinctively flavored food, it follows that *most* of the beliefs produced by the innate inferential strategy Garcia discovered are *false* beliefs. So it is just not true that natural selection favors inferential strategies which generally yield true beliefs. It is important to note that this argument does not turn essentially on my conjecture about the percentage of rat illnesses caused by distinctive-tasting food. The real point of my argument is that *if* my conjecture is correct, it would pose no puzzle for the student of natural selection.

Natural selection might perfectly well opt for an inferential strategy which produces false beliefs more often than true ones. The sole concern of natural selection is with reproductive success and those features that foster it. When it comes to food poisoning, natural selection may well prefer an extremely cautious inferential strategy which is very often wrong to a less cautious one which more often gets the right answer. It might be protested that the Garcia phenomenon does not really join the issue of irrational inference since the rats acquire an aversion, and aversions are not plausibly treated as beliefs. But this reply misses the essential point. Natural selection *could* perfectly well lead to inferential strategies which generally get the wrong answer but are right when it counts most, just as it leads to aversions to foods most of which are harmless and nourishing. Often it is more adaptive to be safe than sorry.

Thus far my critique of the argument from natural selection has been aimed at the first step, the one which claims that natural selection favors inferential strategies that generally yield true beliefs. But even if we were to grant this dubious claim, the argument from natural selection would still be defective. For its second premise is false as well. That premise, recall, is that inferential strategies which generally yield the right answer are rational inferential strategies. In many cases this simply is not so. Perhaps the clearest examples of generally truth-generating inferential strategies which are not rational are the cases in which a strategy is being invoked in a domain or setting significantly different from the one in which it presumably evolved. Once again an example from the study of animal behavior provides a striking illustration. Alcock (1979) recounts that a certain species of toad is capable of learning on a single trial to avoid eating a noxious species of millipede. However, the very same toad will continue to consume BBs that are rolled past it until it quite literally becomes a living beanbag! With only a bit of anthropomorphism, we might describe the case as follows. On seeing a millipede of a species previously found to be noxious, the toad comes to believe (i.e., infers) that it is not good to eat. But BBs, with their bland flavor, produce no such belief. Each time a new BB is rolled by, the toad infers that it is good to eat. This belief, of course, is quite false, a fact which will become obvious the first time the BB-filled toad attempts to leap out of harm's way. But, of course, the inferential strategy which led to the belief *generally* yields true beliefs. Does this show that the strategy is normatively appropriate for the toad to use on the BBs? I am inclined to think that the answer is no.

For all its vividness, the toad example may not be the best one to make my point. For some would protest that they just don't know what counts as a rational inferential strategy for a toad, a protest with which I have considerable sympathy. But the moral I want to draw from the toad example is one which can be drawn also from many cases involving human inference. A common theme in the research on human inference is that people are inclined to overextend the domain of an inferential strategy, applying it to cases where it is normatively inappropriate. Nisbett and Wilson (1977), for example, suggest that many causal inferences are influenced by a primitive version of the representativeness heuristic.

> People have strong *a priori* notions of the types of causes that ought to be linked to particular types of effects, and the simple "resemblance criterion" often figures heavily in such notions. Thus, people believe that great events ought to have great causes, complex events ought to have complex causes, and emotionally relevant events ought to have emotionally relevant causes. . . . The resemblance criterion is transparently operative in the magical thinking of prescientific cultures. For example Evans-Pritchard . . . reported such Azande beliefs as the theory that fowl excrement was a cure for ringworm and the theory that burnt skull of red bush-monkey was an effective treatment for epilepsy. Westerners unacquainted with Azande ecology might be tempted to guess that such treatments were the product of trial and error or laboriously accumulated folk wisdom. Unfortunately, the truth is probably less flattering to Azande medical science. Fowl excrement resembles ringworm infection: the jerky, frenetic movements of the bush-monkey resemble the convulsive movements that occur during an epileptic seizure. (Nisbett and Ross 1980, 115–16)

Now it may well be that in a sufficiently primitive setting the primitive representativeness heuristic generally does get the right answer; it may have served our hunter-gatherer forebears in good stead. But it seems clear that the Azande are invoking the strategy in a domain where its applicability is, to say the least, normatively dubious. Nisbett and Ross go on to argue that the primitive representativeness heuristic plays a central role in psychoanalytic inference and in contemporary lay inference about the causes of disease, crime, success, etc. The normative inappropriateness of the heuristic in these settings is, I should think, beyond dispute.

The primitive representativeness heuristic is an extreme example of the overextension of an inferential strategy. For we have to go a long way back into our hunter-gatherer ancestry before coming upon life situations in which the heuristic is generally reliable and adaptive. But many of the other inferential failings recounted in the recent literature would seem to arise in a similar way. An inference pattern which generally gets the right answer in a limited domain is applied outside that domain, often to problems without precedent during the vast stretches of human and pre-human history when our cognitive apparatus evolved. Indeed, it is disquieting to reflect on how vast a gap there likely is between the inferences that are important to modern science and society and those that were important to our prehistoric forebears. As Einstein noted, "the most incomprehensible thing about the universe is that it is comprehensible."[4]

I have been arguing that inferential strategies which generally get the right answer may nonetheless be irrational or normatively inappropriate when applied outside the problem domain for which they were shaped by natural selection. If this is right, then the second premise of the argument from natural selection must be rejected. Before leaving this topic I want to digress briefly to raise a thornier issue about normatively appropriate inference. It seems beyond dispute that an inferential strategy like the primitive representativeness heuristic is out of place in modern inquiries about the causes of cancer or of reactor failures. But what about the use of these heuristics in their natural settings? Are they normatively appropriate in those domains to which natural selection has molded them and in which (let us assume) they generally do produce the right answer? If I understand Professor Goldman's view correctly, he would answer with an unqualified affirmative. But I am less confident. At issue here is the deep and difficult question of just what we are saying of an inferential strategy when we judge that it is or is not normatively appropriate. This issue will loom large in the remaining pages of this paper.

Before leaving the argument from natural selection, we would do well to note one account of what it is for an inference strategy to be rational or normatively appropriate which had best be avoided. This is the reading which turns the conclusion of the argument from natural selection into a tautology by the simple expedient of defining *rational inferential strategy* as *inferential strategy favored by natural selection*. Quite apart from its *prima facie* implausibility, this curious account of rationality surely misses the point of psychological studies of reasoning. These studies are aimed at showing that people regularly violate the normative canons of deductive and inductive logic, probability theory,

4. Quoted in Sinsheimer 1971.

decision theory, etc. They do not aim at showing that people use inferential strategies which have not evolved by natural selection!

5

The final argument I want to consider is one proposed by L. Jonathan Cohen (1981). Cohen's argument grows out of an account of how we establish or validate normative theses about cognitive procedures—how we justify claims about rational or irrational inference. On Cohen's view normative theses about cognitive procedures are justified by what in ethics has come to be known as the method of *reflective equilibrium*. The basic input to the method, the data if you will, are intuitions, which Cohen characterizes as "immediate and untutored inclinations . . . to judge that" something is the case. In ethics the relevant intuitions are judgments about how people ought or ought not to behave. In the normative theory of reasoning they are judgments about how people ought or ought not to reason.

According to Cohen, a normative theory of reasoning is simply an idealized theory built on the data of people's individualized intuitions about reasoning. As in science, we build our theory so as to capture the bulk of the data in the simplest way possible. Our theory, in the case at hand, will be an interlocking set of normative principles of reasoning which should entail most individualized intuitions about how we should reason in the domain in question. An idealized theory need not aim at capturing all the relevant intuitions of all normal adults. Scattered exceptions—intuitions that are not entailed by the theory—can be tolerated in the same spirit that we tolerate exceptions to the predictions of the ideal gas laws.

Cohen stresses that normative theories of reasoning are not theories about the data (that is, about intuitions) any more than physics is a theory about observed meter readings, or ethics a theory about intuitions of rightness and wrongness. Just what normative theories *are* about is a question Cohen sidesteps.

> Fortunately, it is not necessary for present purposes to determine what exactly the study of moral value, probability or deducibility has as its proper subject matter. For example, an applied logician's proper aim may be to limn the formal consequences of linguistic definitions . . . the most general features of reality . . . or the structure of ideally rational beliefs systems. . . . But, whatever the ontological concerns of applied logicians, they have to draw their evidential data from intuitions in concrete, individual cases; and the same is true for investigations into the norms of everyday probabilistic reasoning. (321)

But although a normative theory of reasoning is not a theory about reasoning intuitions, it is perfectly possible, on Cohen's view, to construct an empirical theory which is concerned to describe or predict the intuitive judgments which provide the data for the corresponding normative theory. This second theory will be a psychological theory, not a logical . . . one. It will describe a competence that human beings have—an ability, uniformly operative under ideal conditions and often under others, to form intuitive judgements about particular instances of . . . right or wrong, deducibility or nondeducibility, probability or improbability. This theory will be just as idealized as the normative theory. (321)

Having said this much, Cohen can now neatly complete his argument for the inevitable rationality of normal people. The essential point is that the empirical theory of human reasoning, that is, the psychological theory that aims to describe and predict intuitive judgments, exploits the same data as the normative theory of reasoning, and exploits them in the same way. In both cases, the goal is to construct the simplest and most powerful set of principles that accounts for the bulk of the data. Thus, once a normative theory is at hand, the empirical theory of reasoning competence will be free for the asking, since it will be *identical* with the normative theory of reasoning! Though the empirical theory of reasoning competence "is a contribution to the psychology of cognition," Cohen writes,

it is a by-product of the logical or philosophical analysis of norms rather than something that experimentally oriented psychologists need to devote effort to constructing. It is not only all the theory of competence that is needed in its area. It is also all that is possible, since a different competence, if it actually existed, would just generate evidence that called for a revision of the corresponding normative theory.

In other words, where you accept that a normative theory has to be based ultimately on the data of human intuition, you are committed to the acceptance of human rationality as a matter of fact in that area, in the sense that it must be correct to ascribe to normal human beings a cognitive competence—however often faulted in performance—that corresponds point by point with the normative theory. (321)

It is important to see that Cohen's view does not entail that people never reason badly. He can and does happily acknowledge that people make inferential errors of many sorts and under many circumstances. But he insists that these errors are performance errors, reflecting nothing about the underlying, normatively unimpeachable competence. The account Cohen would give of inferential errors is analogous to the account a Chomskian would give about the errors a person might make in speaking or understanding his own language. We often utter sentences which are ungrammatical in our own dialect, but this is no reflection on our underlying linguistic competence. On the Chomskian view, our competence consists in a tacitly internalized set of rules which determines the strings of words that are grammatical in our language, and these rules generate no ungrammatical strings. Our utilization of these rules is subject to a whole host of potential misadventures which may lead us to utter ungrammatical sentences: there are slips of the tongue, failures of memory, lapses of attention, and no doubt many more. It is certainly possible to study these failures and thereby to learn something about the way the mind exploits its underlying competence. But while such studies might reveal interesting defects in performance, they could not reveal defects in competence. Analogously, we may expect all sorts of defects in inferential performance, due to inattention, memory limitations, or what have you. Study of these failings may indicate something interesting about the way we exploit our underlying cognitive competence. But such a study could no more reveal an irrational or defective cognitive competence than a study of grammatical errors could reveal that the speaker's linguistic competence was defective.

This is all I shall have to say by way of setting out Cohen's clever argument. As I see it, the argument comes to grief in the account it offers of the justification of normative theses about cognitive procedures. Perhaps the clearest way to underscore the problem with Cohen's epistemological account is to pursue the analogy between grammar and the empirical or descriptive theory of reasoning competence. Both theories are based on the data of intuition and both are idealized. But on Cohen's account there is one striking and paradoxical dis-analogy. In grammar we expect different people to have different underlying competences which manifest themselves in significantly different linguistics intuitions. The linguistic competence of a Frenchman differs radically from the linguistic competence of an Englishman, and both differ radically from the linguistic competence of a Korean. Less radical, but still significant, are the differences between the competence of an Alabama sharecropper, an Oxford don, and a Shetland Island crofter. Yet on Cohen's account of the empirical theory of reasoning there is no mention of different people having different idealized competences. Rather, he seems to assume that in the domain of reasoning all people have exactly the same competence. But why should we not expect that cognitive competence will vary just as much as linguistic competence? The only answer I can find in Cohen's writing is a brief suggestion that cognitive competence may be *innate*. Yet surely this suggestion is entirely gratuitous. Whether or not individuals, social groups, or cultures differ in their cognitive competence is an *empirical* question, on all fours with the parallel question about linguistic competence. It is a question to be settled by the facts about intuitions and practice, not by a priori philosophical argument. And while the facts are certainly far from all being in, I am inclined to think that studies like those reviewed at the beginning of this paper, along with hundreds of others that might have been mentioned, make it extremely plausible that there are substantial individual differences in cognitive competence.

Now if this is right, if different people have quite different cognitive competences, then Cohen's account of the justification of a *normative* theory of reasoning faces some embarrassment. For recall that on this account a normative theory of reasoning is identical with a descriptive theory of cognitive competence; they are built on the same data and idealized in the same way. So if there are *many* cognitive competences abroad in our society and others, then there are *many* normative theories of cognition. But if there are many normative theories of cognition, which is the right one? Note that just here the analogy between linguistic competence and cognitive competence breaks down in an illuminating way. For although there are obviously great variations in linguistic competence, there is no such thing as a normative theory in linguistics (or at least none that deserves to be taken seriously). Thus there is no problem about which of the many linguistic competences abroad in the world corresponds to the normatively correct one.

The problem I have been posing for Cohen is analogous to a familiar problem in ethics. For there too there is good reason to suspect that the method of reflective equilibrium would yield different normative theories for different people, and we are left with the problem of saying which normative theory is the right one. One response to the problem in ethics, though to my mind an unsatisfactory one, is a thoroughgoing relativism: my normative theory is the right one *for me*, yours is the right one *for you*. One way for Cohen to deal with the problem of the multiplicity of normative theories of cognition might be to adopt an analogous relativism. My inferential competence is right for me, yours is right for you. But this move is even more unpalatable for the normative theory of cognition than it is for ethics. We are not in the least inclined to say that any old inference is normatively acceptable for a subject merely because it accords with the rules which constitute his cognitive competence. If the inference is stupid or irrational, and if it accords with the subject's cognitive competence, then his competence is stupid or irrational too, in this quarter at least.

A second strategy for dealing with the multiplicity of normative theories might be to adopt a majoritarian view according to which it is the cognitive competence of the majority that is normatively correct. This is no more plausible than the relativist alternative, however. First, it is not at all clear that there is a majority cognitive competence, any more than there is a majority linguistic competence. It may well be that many significantly different competences co-exist in the world, with the most common having no more than a meager plurality. Moreover, even if there is a majority cognitive competence, there is little inclination to insist that it must be the normatively correct one. If, as seems very likely, most people disregard the impact of regression in estimating the likelihood of events, then most infer badly! (Nisbett and Ross 1980, 150ff.)

The upshot of these reflections is that Cohen has simply told the wrong story about the justification of normative theories of cognition. Given the possibility of alternative cognitive competences, he has failed to tell us which one is normatively correct. Should he supplement his story along either relativist or majoritarian lines he would be stuck with the unhappy conclusion that a patently irrational inferential strategy might turn out to be the normatively correct one.[5]

---

5. We should note in passing that Cohen was not the first to introduce the competence/performance distinction into the debate about human rationality. Fodor (1981) has an extended and illuminating discussion of the possibility that "the postulates of . . . logic are mentally represented by the organism, and this mental representation contributes (in appropriate ways) to the causation of its beliefs" (120). Since the internally represented logic would be only one among many interacting causes of belief and behavior, "the evidence for attributing a logic to an organism would not be that the organism believes whatever the logic entails. Rather, the appropriate form of argument is to show that the assumption that the organism internally represents the

By way of conclusion, let me note that there is a variation on Cohen's reflective equilibrium story which does a much better job of making sense of our normative judgments about reasoning, both in everyday life and in the psychology laboratory. It seems clear that we do criticize the reasoning of others, and we are not in the least swayed by the fact that the principles underlying a subject's faulty reasoning are a part of his—or most people's—cognitive competence. We are, however, swayed by finding that the inference at hand is sanctioned or rejected by the cognitive competences of experts in the field of reasoning in question. Many well-educated people find statistical inferences involving regression to the mean to be highly counter-intuitive, at least initially. But sensible people come to distrust their own intuition on the matter when they learn that principles requiring regressive inference are sanctioned by the reflective equilibrium of experts in statistical reasoning. In an earlier paper, Nisbett and I (Stich and Nisbett 1980) tried to parlay this observation into a general account of what it is for a normative principle of reasoning to be justified. On our view, when we judge someone's inference to be normatively inappropriate, we are comparing it to (what we take to be) the applicable principles of inference sanctioned by expert reflective equilibrium. On this account, there is no puzzle or paradox implicit in the practice of psychologists who probe human irrationality. They are evaluating the inferential practice of their subjects by the sophisticated and evolving standard of expert competence. From this perspective, it is not all that surprising that lay practice has been found to be markedly defective in many areas. We would expect the same, and for the same reason, if we examined lay competence in physics or in economics.

There is a hopeful moral embedded in this last observation. If, as Cohen suggests, cognitive competence is innate, then normatively inappropriate competence is ominous and inalterable. But if, as I have been urging, there is every reason to think that cognitive competence, like linguistic competence, is to a significant extent acquired and variable, then there is reason to hope that competence can be improved through education and practice, much as a child from Liverpool can acquire the crisp linguistic competence of an Oxford don. There is an important dis-analogy, of course. Liverpudlian cadences are harmless and charming; normatively defective inference is neither. I am inclined to think it a singular virtue of recent studies of reasoning that they point to the areas where remedial education is needed most.

---

logic, when taken together with independently motivated theories of the character of the other interacting variables, yields the best explanation of the data about the organism's mental states and processes and/or the behaviors in which such processes eventuate." But if the facts turn out right, it would seem that the same sort of evidentiary considerations might also lead to the conclusion that the organism had internally represented a peculiar or normatively inappropriate "logic." This is not a possibility Fodor pursues, however, since he has been seduced by Dennett's argument from natural selection. Darwinian selection, he claims, "guarantees that organisms either know the elements of logic or become posthumous" (121).

REFERENCES

Alcock, J. 1979. *Animal Behavior: An Evolutionary Approach*. Sunderland, MA: Sinauer Associates.

Cohen, L. J. 1981. Can Human Irrationality Be Experimentally Demonstrated? *Behavioral and Brain Sciences* 4, 3.

Davidson, D. 1979. The Method of Truth in Metaphysics. In P. A. French, T. E. Uehling Jr., and H. K. Wettstein, eds., *Contemporary Perspectives in the Philosophy of Language*. Minneapolis: University of Minnesota Press.

Dennett, D. 1978. *Brainstorms*. Montgomery, VT: Bradford Books.

———. 1981a. Making Sense of Ourselves. *Philosophical Topics* 12, 1.

———. 1981b. Three Kinds of Intentional Psychology. In R. Healey, ed., *Reduction, Time and Reality*. Cambridge: Cambridge University Press.

Fodor, J. 1981. Three Cheers for Propositional Attitudes. In *Representations: Philosophical Essays on the Foundations of Cognitive Science*. Cambridge, MA: MIT Press and Bradford Books.

Garcia, J., B. K. McGowan, and K. F. Green. 1972. Biological Constraints on Conditioning. In A. H. Black and W. F. Prokasy, eds., *Classical Conditioning II: Current Research and Theory*. New York: Appleton-Century-Crofts.

Griggs, R. A., and J. R. Cox. 1982. The Elusive Thematic-Materials Effect in Wason's Selection Task. *British Journal of Psychology* 73.

Johnson-Laird, P. N., P. Legrenzi, and M. Sonino Legrenzi. 1972. Reasoning and a Sense of Reality. *British Journal of Psychology* 63.

Johnson-Laird, P. N., and P. C. Wason. 1977. A Theoretical Analysis of Insight into a Reasoning Task [1970, with a 1977 postscript]. In P. N. Johnson-Laird and P. C. Wason, eds., *Thinking*. Cambridge: Cambridge University Press.

Nisbett, E. W., and T. D. Wilson. 1977. Telling More than We Can Know: Verbal Reports on Mental Processes. *Psychological Review* 84.

Nisbett, R. E., and L. Ross. 1980. *Human Inference: Strategies and Shortcomings of Social Judgment*. Englewood Cliffs, NJ: Prentice-Hall.

Ross, L., M. R. Lepper, and M. Hubbard. 1975. Perseverance in Self Perception and Social Perception: Biased Attributional Processes in the Debriefing Paradigm. *Journal of Personality and Social Psychology* 32.

Sinsheimer, R. L. 1971. The Brain of Pooh: An Essay on the Limits of Mind. *Science* 59.

Slovic, P., and B. Fischhoff. 1978. How Safe Is Safe Enough? In L. Gould and C. A. Walker, eds., *The Management of Nuclear Wastes*. New Haven: Yale University Press. Reprinted in J. Dowie and P. Lefrere, eds., *Risk and Chance*. Milton Keynes: Open University Press, 1980.

Slovic, P., B. Fischhoff, and S. Lichtenstein. 1977. Behavioral Decision Theory. *Annual Review of Psychology* 28.

Stich, S. P. 1980. Headaches. *Philosophical Books* 21, 2.

———. 1981a. Dennett on Intentional Systems. *Philosophical Topics* 12, 1.

———. 1981b. On the Ascription of Content. In A. Woodfield, ed., *Thought and Object*. Oxford: Oxford University Press.

———. 1983. *From Folk Psychology to Cognitive Science*. Cambridge, MA: MIT Press.

Stich, S. P., and R. E. Nisbett. 1980. Justification and the Psychology of Human Reasoning. *Philosophy of Science* 47.

Tversky, A., and D. Kahneman. 1982. Judgments of and by Representativeness. In D. Kahneman, P. Slovic, and A. Tversky, eds., *Judgment Under Uncertainty: Heuristics and Biases*. Cambridge: Cambridge University Press.

Wason, P. C. 1977. Self-Contradiction. In P. N. Johnson-Laird and P. C. Wason, eds., *Thinking*. Cambridge: Cambridge University Press.

Wason, P. C., and P. N. Johnson-Laird. 1972. *The Psychology of Reasoning: Structure and Content*. London: B. T. Batsford.

4

REFLECTIVE EQUILIBRIUM, ANALYTIC EPISTEMOLOGY,

AND THE PROBLEM OF COGNITIVE DIVERSITY

THIS IS A paper about different ways of thinking—or cognitive diversity, as I shall sometimes say—and the problem of choosing among them. In the pages to follow I will defend a pair of claims. The first is that one influential proposal for solving the problem of cognitive diversity, a proposal that invokes the notion of reflective equilibrium, will not work. The second is much more radical. What I propose to argue is that although some of the objections to the reflective equilibrium solution turn on details of that idea, the most serious objection generalizes into an argument against an entire epistemological tradition—the tradition that I shall call "analytic epistemology." Before attending to either of these claims, however, I will have to say something about how I conceive of cognition and cognitive diversity.

1. Cognition and Cognitive Diversity

Let me begin with a simplifying assumption that I hope you will not find wildly implausible. I shall assume that in humans and other higher animals there is a distinct category of mental states whose function it is to store information about the world. When the organisms in question are normal, adult humans in a culture not too remote from our own, folk psychology labels these states *beliefs*. Whether or not this folk label can be used appropriately for the belief-like states of animals, automata, young children, and exotic folk is a question of considerable controversy.[1] For present purposes, however, it is a controversy best avoided. Thus I propose to adopt the term "cognitive state" as a broad cover

---

1. See Davidson 1982; Stich 1979; Routley 1981; Stich 1983, 89–106; Stich 1984.

term whose extension includes not only beliefs properly so called, but also the belief-like information-storing mental states of animals, young children, and those adult humans, if any there be, whose cognitive lives differ substantially from our own.

Our beliefs, and the cognitive states of other creatures, are in a constant state of flux. New ones are added and old ones removed as the result of perception, and as a result of various processes in which cognitive states interact with each other. In familiar cases, folk psychology provides us with labels like "thinking" and "reasoning" for these processes, though once again the propriety of these labels becomes controversial when the cognitive states being modified are those of children, animals or exotic folk. So I will use the term "cognitive processes" as a cover term whose extension includes our own reasoning processes, the updating of our beliefs as the result of perception, and the more or less similar processes that occur in other organisms.

Cognitive processes are biological processes; they are something that brains do. And, like other biological processes, they have been shaped by natural selection. Thus it is to be expected that our genes exert an important influence on the sorts of cognitive processes we have. It is also to be expected that the cognitive processes of other species with other needs and other natural environments will be in varying degrees different from those to be found among humans. But from the fact that genes inevitably exert a major influence on cognitive processes it does *not* follow that all of our cognitive processes are innate, or, indeed, that any of them are.

To see the point, we need only reflect on the case of language. My ability to speak English is a biological ability; processing English is something my brain does. Moreover, my genes are surely heavily implicated in the explanation of how I came to have a brain that could process English. Still, English is not innate. The ability to process English is an ability I acquired, and had I been raised in a different environment I might have acquired instead the ability to speak Korean or Lapp. This is not to deny that *something* relevant to language is innate. All normal human children have the ability to acquire the language spoken around them. And that is a very special ability. There is no serious evidence indicating that members of any other species can acquire human languages or anything much like them.

Now the point I want to stress is that, as far as we know, human cognitive processes may be like human language-processing abilities. They may be acquired in ways that are deeply dependent on environmental variables, and they may differ quite radically from one individual or culture to another. Of course, it is also possible that human cognitive processes are much less plastic and much less under the influence of environmental variables. It is possible that cognition is more similar to digestion than to language. To make matters a bit messier, there is no reason a priori for all cognitive processes to be at the same point on this continuum. It may be that some of our cognitive processes are shared by all normal humans, while others are a part of our cultural heritage.[2] I am inclined to

---

2. Nor are these the only alternatives. There are lots of characteristics which are innate (not part of our cultural heritage) though they differ substantially from one group to another. Sex, hair color, and blood type are three obvious examples.

think that this last possibility is the most plausible one in the light of available evidence, and for the remainder of this paper I will take it for granted. But it must be admitted that the evidence is both fragmentary and very difficult to interpret.[3]

If we suppose that there is a fair amount of acquired diversity in human cognitive processes, and that patterns of reasoning or cognitive processing are to some substantial degree molded by cultural influences, it adds a certain urgency to one of the more venerable questions of epistemology. For if there are lots of different ways in which the human mind/brain can go about ordering and reordering its cognitive states, if different cultures could or do go about the business of reasoning in very different ways, *which of these ways should we use?* Which cognitive processes are the *good* ones? It is just here that the analogy with language breaks down in an illuminating way. Most of us are inclined to think that, at least to a first approximation, one language is as good as another. The one you should use is the one spoken and understood by the people around you.[4] By contrast, most of us are *not* inclined to accept this sort of thoroughgoing relativism about cognitive processes. If primitive tribesmen or pre-modern scientists or our own descendants think in ways that are quite different from the ways we think, few of us would be inclined to suggest that all of these ways are equally good. Some ways of going about the business of belief revision are better than others. But just what is it that makes one system of cognitive processes better than another, and how are we to tell which system of reasoning is best? In the remaining sections of this paper I want to consider one influential answer to this question. I shall argue that both the answer itself and the philosophical tradition it grows out of should be rejected.

2. Reflective Equilibrium as a Criterion for Assessing Cognitive Processes

The answer I will disparage was first suggested about three decades ago when, in one of the more influential passages of twentieth-century philosophy, Nelson Goodman described a process of bringing judgments about particular inferences and about general principles of inference into accord with one another. In the accord thus achieved, Goodman maintained, lay all the justification needed, and all the justification possible for the inferential principles that emerged. Other writers, most notably John Rawls, have adopted a modified version of Goodman's process as a procedure for justifying moral principles and moral judgments. To Rawls, too, we owe the term "reflective equilibrium," which has been widely used to characterize a system of principles and judgments that have been brought into coherence with one another in the way that Goodman describes.[5]

---

3. See Cole and Scribner 1974; Cole and Means 1981.

4. Actually, the issue is not so straightforward if we compare languages at very different stages of development, or languages involving different theoretical assumptions. It is only when the choice is between languages that are more or less inter-translatable with our own that we are inclined to judge that one is as good as another. Thanks to Paul Churchland for reminding me of this point.

5. Rawls 1971, 20 ff.

It is hard to imagine the notion of reflective equilibrium explained more eloquently than Goodman himself explains it.

> How do we justify a *deduction*? Plainly by showing that it conforms with the general rules of deductive inference. An argument that so conforms is justified or valid, even if its conclusion happens to be false. An argument that violates a rule is fallacious even if its conclusion happens to be true. . . . Analogously, the basic task in justifying an inductive inference is to show that it conforms to the general rules of *induction*. . . .
>
> Yet, of course, the rules themselves must ultimately be justified. The validity of a deduction depends not upon conformity to any purely arbitrary rules we may contrive, but upon conformity with valid rules. When we speak of *the* rules of inference we mean the valid rules—or better, *some* valid rules, since there may be alternative sets of equally valid rules. But how is the validity of rules to be determined? Here . . . we encounter philosophers who insist that these rules follow from some self-evident axiom, and others who try to show that the rules are grounded in the very nature of the human mind. I think the answer lies much nearer to the surface. Principles of deductive inference are justified by their conformity with accepted deductive practice. Their validity depends upon accordance with the particular deductive inferences we actually make and sanction. If a rule yields unacceptable inferences, we drop it as invalid. Justification of general rules thus derives from judgments rejecting or accepting particular deductive inferences.
>
> This looks flagrantly circular. I have said that deductive inferences are justified by their conformity to valid general rules, and that general rules are justified by their conformity to valid inferences. But this circle is a virtuous one. *A rule is amended if it yields an inference we are unwilling to accept; an inference is rejected if it violates a rule we are unwilling to amend.* The process of justification is the delicate one of making mutual adjustments between rules and accepted inferences; and in the agreement thus achieved lies the only justification needed for either.
>
> All this applies equally well to induction. An inductive inference, too, is justified by conformity to general rules, and a general rule by conformity to accepted inductive inferences.[6]

There are three points in this passage that demand a bit of interpretation. First, Goodman claims to be explaining what justifies deductive and inductive inferences. However, it is not clear that, as he uses the term, *inference* is a cognitive process. It is possible to read Goodman as offering an account of the justification of principles of logic and of steps in logical derivations. Read in this way, Goodman's account of justification would be of no help in dealing with the problem of cognitive diversity unless it was supplemented with a

---

6. Goodman 1965, 66–67; emphasis is Goodman's.

suitable theory about the relation between logic and good reasoning. But as several authors have lately noted, that relation is much less obvious than one might suppose.[7] It is also possible to read Goodman as speaking directly to the question of how we should go about the business of reasoning,[8] and offering a solution to the problem of cognitive diversity. This is the reading I propose to adopt.

A second point that needs some elaboration is just what status Goodman would claim for the reflective equilibrium test he describes. It is clear Goodman thinks we can conclude that a system of inferential rules is justified if it passes the reflective equilibrium test. But it is not clear *why* we can conclude this. Two different sorts of answers are possible. According to one answer, the reflective equilibrium test is *constitutive* of justification or validity. For a system of inferential rules to be justified just *is* for them to be in reflective equilibrium. Another sort of answer is that if a set of inferential principles passes the reflective equilibrium test, this counts as good *evidence* for them being valid or justified. But, on this second view, being in reflective equilibrium and being justified are quite different. One is not to be identified with the other. I am inclined to think that it is the former, constitutive, view that best captures Goodman's intentions. But since my concern is to criticize a view and not an author, I don't propose to argue the point. Rather, I will simply stipulate that the constitutive reading is the one I'm stalking.[9]

The third point of interpretation concerns the status of the claim that reflective equilibrium is constitutive of justification. On this point, there are at least three views worth mentioning. The first is that the claim is a *conceptual truth*—that it follows from the meaning of "justification" or from the analysis of the concept of justification. Like other conceptual truths, it is both necessarily true and knowable a priori. If we adopt this view, the status of the claim that reflective equilibrium is constitutive of justification would be akin to the status of the claim that being a closed, three-sided plane figure is constitutive of being a triangle, though the claim about justification is, of course, a much less obvious conceptual truth. A second view is that the claim is a non-conceptual necessary truth that is knowable only a posteriori. This would accord it much the same status that some philosophers accord to the claim water is H_2O. Finally, it might be urged that the claim is being offered as a stipulative proposal. It is not telling us what our pre-existing concept of justification amounts to, nor what is essential to the referent of that concept. Rather, in a

---

7. Cherniak 1986, chap. 4; Harman 1986, chap. 2; Goldman 1986, section 5.1.

8. L. J. Cohen (1981) seems to read Goodman this way since he exploits Goodman's notion of reflective equilibrium in giving an account of good reasoning.

9. Well, I will argue it a little. Note first that according to Goodman the only justification needed for either rules or inferences "lies in" the agreement achieved by the reflective equilibrium process. This talk of justification *lying in* the agreement strongly suggests the constitutive reading. Moreover, on the non-constitutive reading, Goodman's doctrine would be an oddly incomplete one. It would present us with a test for justification without telling us why it was a test or giving us any account of what it is that is being tested for. On the constitutive reading, by contrast, no such problem arises. We have in one tidy package both an analysis of the notion of justification and an unproblematic explanation of the relation between justification and the process Goodman describes.

revisionary spirit, it is proposing a new notion of justification. Actually, the divide between the first and the last of these alternatives is not all that sharp, for one might start with an analysis of our ordinary notion and go on to propose modifications in an effort to tidy the notion up a bit here and there. As the changes proposed get bigger and bigger, this sort of "explication" gradually shades into pure stipulation. So long as the changes an explication urges in a pre-existing concept are motivated by considerations of simplicity and don't result in any radical departures from the ordinary concept, I'll count them as a kind of conceptual analysis. I think a good case can be made that Goodman took himself to be providing just such a conservative explication. But again, since it is a view rather than an author that I hope to refute, I will simply stipulate that the conceptual analysis or conservative explication interpretation is the one to be adopted here.

3. Does the Reflective Equilibrium Account Capture Our Notion of Justification?

Goodman, as I propose to read him, offers us an account of what our concept of justified inference comes to. How can we determine whether his analysis is correct? One obvious strategy is to ask just what systems of inferential rules result from the process of mutual adjustment that Goodman advocates. If the inferential systems generated by the reflective equilibrium process strike us as systems that a rational person ought to invoke, this will count in favor of Goodman's analysis. If, on the other hand, the reflective equilibrium process generates what we take to be irrational or unjustified inferential rules or practices, this will cast doubt on Goodman's claim to have captured our concept of justification. Since we are viewing conceptual explication as a kind of analysis, we should not insist that Goodman's account coincide perfectly with our intuitive judgments. But if there are lots of cases in which Goodman's account entails that a system of inferential rules is justified and intuition decrees that it is not, this is a symptom that the analysis is in serious trouble.

In an earlier paper, Nisbett and I exploited the strategy just described to argue that the reflective equilibrium account does not capture anything much like our ordinary notion of justification.[10] On the basis of both controlled studies and anecdotal evidence, we argued that patently unacceptable rules of inference would pass the reflective equilibrium test for many people. For example, it appears likely that many people infer in accordance with some version of the gambler's fallacy when dealing with games of chance. These people infer that the likelihood of throwing a seven in a game of craps increases each time a non-seven is thrown. What is more, there is every reason to think that the principle underlying their inference is in reflective equilibrium for them. When the principle is articulated and the subjects have had a chance to reflect upon it and upon their own inferential practice, they accept both. Indeed, one can even find some nineteenth-century logic texts in which versions of the gambler's fallacy are explicitly endorsed. (In a delightful

---

10. Stich and Nisbett 1980.

irony, one of these books was written by a man who held the same chair Goodman held when he wrote *Fact, Fiction and Forecast.*)[11] It can also be shown that many people systematically ignore the importance of base rates in their probabilistic reasoning, that many find the principle of regression to the mean to be highly counter-intuitive, that many judge the probability of certain sequences of events to be higher than the probability of components in the sequence, etc.[12] In each of these cases, and in many more that might be cited, it is very likely that, for some people at least, the principles that capture their inferential practice would pass the reflective equilibrium test. If this is right, it indicates there is something very wrong with the Goodmanian analysis of justification. For on that analysis, to be justified *is* to pass the reflective equilibrium test. But few of us are prepared to say that if the gambler's fallacy is in reflective equilibrium for a person, then his inferences that accord with that principle are justified.

Of course, each example of the infelicitous inferential principle that allegedly would pass the reflective equilibrium test is open to challenge. Whether or not the dubious principles that appear to guide many people's inferential practice would stand up to the reflective scrutiny Goodman's test demands is an empirical question. And for any given rule, a Goodmanian might protest that the empirical case has just not been made adequately. I am inclined to think that the Goodmanian who builds his defenses here is bound to be routed by a growing onslaught of empirical findings. But the issue need not turn on whether this empirical hunch is correct. For even the *possibility* that the facts will turn out as I suspect they will poses a serious problem for the Goodmanian story. It is surely not an a priori fact that strange inferential principles will always fail the reflective equilibrium test for all subjects. And if it is granted, as surely it must be, that the gambler's fallacy (or any of the other inferential oddities that have attracted the attention of psychologists in recent years) could possibly pass the reflective equilibrium test for some group of subjects, this is enough to cast doubt on the view that reflective equilibrium is constitutive of justification as that notion is ordinarily used. For surely we are not at all inclined to say that a person is justified in using any inferential principle—no matter how bizarre it may be—simply because it accords with his reflective inferential practice.

Faced with this argument the friends of reflective equilibrium may offer a variety of responses. The one I have the hardest time understanding is simply to dig in one's heels and insist that if the gambler's fallacy (or some other curious principle) is in reflective equilibrium for a given person or group, then that principle is indeed justified for them. Although I have heard people advocate this line in conversation, I know of no one who

---

11. The writer was Henry Coppée (1874). Here is a brief quote:

> Thus, in throwing dice, we cannot be sure that any single face or combination of faces will appear; but if, in very many throws, some particular face has not appeared, the chances of its coming up are stronger and stronger, until they approach very near to certainty. It must come; and as each throw is made and it fails to appear, the certainty of its coming draws nearer and nearer. (162)

12. For an excellent survey of the literature in this area see Nisbett and Ross 1980; a number of important studies are collected in Kahneman, Slovic, and Tversky 1982.

has been bold enough to urge the view in print. Since no one else seems willing to take the view seriously, I won't either.

A very different sort of response is to urge that the notion of reflective equilibrium is itself in need of patching—that some bells and whistles must be added to the justificatory process Goodman describes. One idea along these lines is to shift from narrow Goodmanian reflective equilibrium to some analog of Rawls's "wide reflective equilibrium."[13] Roughly, the idea here is to broaden the scope of the judgments and convictions that are to be brought into coherence with one another. Instead of attending only to our assessments of inferential principles, wide reflective equilibrium also requires that our system of inferential rules is to cohere with our semantic, epistemological, metaphysical, or psychological views. Just how various philosophical or psychological convictions are supposed to constrain a person's inferential principles and practice has not been spelled out in much detail, though Norman Daniels, whose papers on wide reflective equilibrium are among the best around, gives us a hint when he suggests, by way of example, that Dummett's views on logic are constrained by his semantic views.[14] It would also be plausible to suppose that the classical intuitionists in logic rejected certain inferential principles on epistemological grounds.

A rather different way of attempting to preserve a reflective equilibrium account of justification is to restrict the class of people whose reflective equilibrium is to count in assessing the justification of inferential principles. For example, Nisbett and I proposed that in saying an inferential principle is justified, what we are saying is that it would pass the (narrow) reflective equilibrium test for those people whom we regard as experts in the relevant inferential domain.[15]

A dubious virtue of both the wide reflective equilibrium and the expert reflective equilibrium accounts is that they make clear-cut counter-examples harder to generate. That is, they make it harder to produce actual examples of inferential rules which the analysis counts as justified and intuition does not. In the case of wide reflective equilibrium, counter-examples are hard to come by just because it is so hard to show that anything is in wide reflective equilibrium for anyone. ("Would she continue to accept that rule if she thought through her epistemological and metaphysical views and came to some stable equilibrium view?" Well, God knows.) In the case of the expert reflective equilibrium account, the dubious but reflectively self-endorsed inferential practices of the experimental subject or the Las Vegas sucker just don't count as counter-examples, since these people don't count as experts.

But though clear-cut cases involving actual people may be harder to find, each of these elaborations of the reflective equilibrium story falls victim to the argument from possible cases offered earlier. Consider wide reflective equilibrium first. No matter how the details

---

13. Rawls 1974.

14. Daniels 1979, 1980a, 1980b.

15. Stich and Nisbett 1980.

of the wide reflective equilibrium test are spelled out, it is surely not going to turn out to be impossible for a person to reach wide reflective equilibrium on a set of principles and convictions that includes some quite daffy inferential rule. Indeed, one suspects that by allowing people's philosophical convictions to play a role in filtering their inferential principles, one is inviting such daffy principles, since many people are deeply attached to outlandish philosophical views. The expert reflective equilibrium move fares no better. For unless experts are picked out in a question-begging way (e.g., those people whose inferential practices are in fact justified) it seems entirely possible for the expert community, under the influence of ideology, recreational chemistry, or evil demons, to end up endorsing some quite nutty set of rules.[16]

4. A "Neo-Goodmanian" Project

At this point, if the friend of reflective equilibrium is as impressed by these arguments as I think he should be, he might head off to his study to work on some further variations on the reflective equilibrium theme that will do better at capturing our concept of justification. Despite a string of failures, he might be encouraged to pursue this project by a line of thought that runs something like the following. I'll call it the *neo-Goodmanian* line.

> It can hardly be denied that we do *something* to assess whether or not an inferential practice is justified. Our decisions on these matters are certainly not made at random. Moreover, if there is some established procedure that we invoke in assessing justification, then it must surely be possible to describe this procedure. When we have succeeded at this we will have an account of what it is for an inferential practice to be justified. For, as Goodman has urged, to be justified just *is* to pass the tests we invoke in assessing an inferential practice. Our procedures for assessing an inferential practice are constitutive of justification. Granted, neither Goodman's narrow reflective equilibrium story nor the more elaborate stories told by others has succeeded in capturing the procedure we actually use in assessing justification. But that just shows we must work harder. The rewards promise to repay our efforts, since once we have succeeded in describing our assessment procedure, we will have taken a giant step forward in epistemology. We will have explained what it is for a cognitive process to be justified. In so doing we will have at least begun to resolve the problem posed by cognitive diversity. For once we have a clear specification of what justification amounts to, we can go on to ask whether our own cognitive processes are justified or whether, perhaps, those of some other culture come closer to the mark.

16. As Conee and Feldman (1983) point out, the situation is actually a bit worse for the version of the expert reflective equilibrium analysis that Nisbett and I offered. On that account, different groups may recognize different people as experts. And it is surely at least possible for a group of people to accept as an expert some guru who is as bonkers as he is charismatic. But we certainly don't want to say that the followers of such a guru would be rational to invoke whatever wild inferential principle might be in reflective equilibrium for their leader.

There is no doubt that this neo-Goodmanian line can be very appealing. I was myself under its sway for some years. However, I am now persuaded that the research program it proposes for epistemology is a thoroughly wrong-headed one. In the pages that follow I will try to say why. My case against the neo-Goodmanian project divides into two parts. First I shall raise some objections that are targeted more or less specifically on the details of the neo-Goodmanian program. Central to each of these objections is the fact that the neo-Goodmanian is helping himself to a healthy serving of empirical assumptions about the conceptual structures underlying our commonsense judgments of cognitive assessment, and each of these assumptions stands in some serious risk of turning out to be false. If one or more of them is false, then the project loses much of its initial attractiveness. In the following section I will set out a brief catalog of these dubious assumptions. The second part of my critique is much more general and I'll be after much bigger game. What I propose to argue is that neither the neo-Goodmanian program nor any alternative program that proposes to analyze or explicate our pre-systematic notion of justification will be of any help at all in resolving the problem posed by cognitive diversity. But here I am getting ahead of myself. Let me get back to the neo-Goodmanian and his dubious empirical presuppositions.

5. Some Questionable Presuppositions of the Neo-Goodmanian Project

Let me begin with a fairly obvious point. The neo-Goodmanian, as I have portrayed him, retains his allegiance to the idea of reflective equilibrium. We last saw him heading back to his study to seek a more adequate elaboration of this notion. But nothing the neo-Goodmanian has said encourages us to expect that reflective equilibrium or anything much like it plays a role in our procedure for assessing the justification of a cognitive process. So even if it is granted that we have good reason to work hard at characterizing our justification-assessing procedure, we may find that the notion of reflective equilibrium is simply a nonstarter. Confronted with this objection, I think the only move open to the neo-Goodmanian is to grant the point and concede that in trying to patch the notion of reflective equilibrium he is simply playing a hunch. Perhaps it will turn out that something like reflective equilibrium plays a central role in our assessments of justification. But until we have an accurate characterization of the assessment process there can be no guarantees.

Two further assumptions of the neo-Goodmanian program are that we ordinarily invoke only *one* notion of justification for inferential processes, and that this is a *coherent* notion for which a set of necessary and sufficient conditions can be given. But once again these are not matters that can be known in advance. It might be that different people mean different things when they call a cognitive process "justified" because there are different notions of justification in circulation. These different meanings might cluster around a central core. But then again they might not. There are lots of normatively loaded terms that seem to be used in very different ways by different individuals or groups in society. I would not be at all surprised to learn that what I mean by terms like "morally right" and "freedom" is very different from what the followers of the Rev. Falwell or admirers of Col. Khadafi mean. And I wouldn't be much more surprised if terms of epistemic evaluation turned out to manifest similar interpersonal ambiguities.

Even discounting the possibility of systematic interpersonal differences, it might be that in assessing the justification of a cognitive process we use different procedures on different occasions, and that these procedures have different outcomes. Perhaps, for example, our intuitive notion of justification is tied to a number of prototypical exemplars, and that in deciding new cases we focus in some context-sensitive way on one or another of these exemplars, making our decision about justification on the basis of how similar the case at hand is to the exemplar on which we are focusing. This is hardly a fanciful idea, since recent work on the psychological mechanisms underlying categorization suggests that in *lots* of cases our judgment works in just this way.[17] If it turns out that our judgments about the justification of cognitive processes are prototype or exemplar based, then it will be a mistake to look for a property or characteristic that all justified cognitive processes have. It will not be the case that there is any single test passed by all the cognitive processes we judge to be justified. I am partial to a reading of the later Wittgenstein on which this is just what he would urge about our commonsense notion of justification, and I am inclined to suspect that this Wittgensteinian story is right. But I don't pretend to have enough evidence to make a convincing case. For present purposes it will have to suffice to note that this *might* be how our commonsense concept of justification works. If it is, then the neo-Goodmanian program is in for some rough sledding.

A final difficulty with the neo-Goodmanian program is that it assumes, without any evidence, that the test or procedure we use for assessing the justification of cognitive processes exhausts our concept of inferential justification, and thus that we will have characterized the concept when we have described the test. But this is hardly a claim that can be assumed without argument. It might be the case that our procrustean concept of justification is an amalgam composed in part of folk epistemological theory specifying certain properties or characteristics that are essential to justification, and in part of a test or cluster of tests that folk wisdom holds to be indicative of those properties. Moreover, the tests proposed might not always (or ever) be reliable indicators of the properties.[18] I don't have any compelling reason to believe that our commonsense notion of justification will turn out like this. But I wouldn't be much surprised. Though our understanding of the mechanisms underlying commonsense concepts and judgments is still *very* primitive, as I read the literature it points to two important morals. First, the mental representation of concepts is likely to turn out to be a very messy business. Second, it is no easy job to separate commonsense concepts from the folk theories in which they are enmeshed. All of this bodes ill for the neo-Goodmanian who hopes that the analysis or explication of our concept of justification will yield some relatively straightforward elaboration of the reflective equilibrium test.

---

17. For a good review of the literature, see Smith and Medin 1981.

18. For some insightful observations on the potential complexity of commonsense concepts and the ways in which intuitive tests can fail to capture the extension of concepts, see Rey 1983.

6. Against Analytic Epistemology

The problems posed in the previous section shared a pair of properties. They all turned on empirical assumptions about the nature of our ordinary concept of justification, and they were all targeted fairly specifically at the neo-Goodmanian project.[19] In the current section I want to set out a very different sort of argument, an argument which if successful will undermine not only reflective equilibrium theories but also the whole family of epistemological theories to which they belong.

To give some idea of the range of theories that are in the intended scope of my critique, it will be helpful to sketch a bit of the framework for epistemological theorizing suggested by Alvin Goldman in his recent book, *Epistemology and Cognition*.[20] Goldman notes that one of the major projects of both classical and contemporary epistemology has been to develop a theory of epistemic justification. The ultimate job of such a theory is to say which cognitive states are epistemically justified and which are not. Thus, a fundamental step in constructing a theory of justification will be to articulate a system of rules evaluating the justificatory status of beliefs and other cognitive states. These rules (Goldman calls them *justificational rules* or *J-rules*) will specify permissible ways in which a cognitive agent may go about the business of forming or updating his cognitive states. They "permit or prohibit beliefs, directly or indirectly, as a function of some states, relations, or processes of the cognizer."[21]

Of course, different theorists may have different views on which beliefs are justified or which cognitive processes yield justified beliefs, and thus they may urge different and incompatible sets of J-rules. It may be that there is more than one right system of justificational rules, but it is surely not the case that all systems are correct. So in order to decide whether a proposed system of J-rules is right, we must appeal to a higher criterion which Goldman calls a "criterion of rightness." This criterion will specify a "set of conditions that are necessary and sufficient for a set of J-rules to be right."[22]

But now the theoretical disputes emerge at a higher level, for different theorists have suggested very different criteria of rightness. Indeed, as Goldman notes, an illuminating taxonomy of epistemological theories can be generated by classifying theories or theo-

---

19. Actually, the last three of my four objections might, with a bit of reworking, be generalized so as to apply to all of analytic epistemology, as it is defined below. But I don't propose to pursue them since, as we shall see, analytic epistemology has more pressing problems.
20. Goldman 1986.
21. Ibid., 60. For the reader who wants a more hands-on feel for Goldman's notion of a J-rule, the quote continues as follows:

For example, J-rules might permit a cognizer to form a given belief because of some appropriate antecedent or current state. Thus, someone being "appeared to" in a certain way at *t* might be permitted to believe *p* at *t*. But someone else not in such a state would not be so permitted. Alternatively, the rules might focus on mental operations. Thus, if *S*'s believing *p* at *t* is the result of a certain operation, or sequence of operations, then his belief is justified if the system of J-rules permits that operation or sequence of operations.

22. Ibid., 64.

rists on the basis of the sort of criterion of rightness they endorse. Coherence theories, for example, take the rightness of a system of J-rules to turn on whether conformity with the rules would lead to a coherent set of beliefs. Truth-linked or reliability theories take the rightness of a set of J-rules to turn in one way or another on the truth of the set of beliefs that would result from conformity with the rules. Reflective equilibrium theories judge J-rules by how well they do on their favored version of the reflective equilibrium test. And so on. How are we to go about deciding among these various criteria of rightness? Or, to ask an even more basic question, just what does the correctness of a criterion of rightness come to; what makes a criterion right or wrong? On this point Goldman is not as explicit as one might wish. However, much of what he says suggests that, on his view, *conceptual analysis* or *conceptual explication* is the proper way to decide among competing criteria of rightness. The correct criterion of rightness is the one that comports with the conception of justifiedness that is "embraced by everyday thought or language."[23] To test a criterion we explore the judgments it would entail about specific cases, and we test these judgments against our "pretheoretic intuition." "A criterion is supported to the extent that implied judgments accord with such intuitions, and weakened to the extent that they do not."[24] Goldman is careful to note that there may be a certain amount of vagueness in our commonsense notion of justifiedness, and thus there may be no unique best criterion of rightness. But despite the vagueness, "there seems to be a common core idea of justifiedness" embedded in everyday thought and language, and it is this common core idea that Goldman tells us he is trying to capture in his own epistemological theorizing.[25]

The view I am attributing to Goldman on what it is for a criterion of rightness to itself be right is hardly an idiosyncratic or unfamiliar one. We saw earlier that a very natural reading of Goodman would have him offering the reflective equilibrium story as an explication or conceptual analysis of the ordinary notion of justification. And many other philosophers have explicitly or implicitly adopted much the same view. I propose to use the term *analytic epistemology* to denote any epistemological project that takes the choice between competing justificational rules or competing criteria of rightness to turn on conceptual or linguistic analysis. There can be little doubt that a very substantial fraction of the epistemological writing published in English in the last quarter of a century has been analytic epistemology.[26]

---

23. Ibid., 58.
24. Ibid., 66.
25. Ibid., 58–59.
26. For an extended review of part of this literature see Shope 1983. As Shope notes, relatively few of the philosophers who have tried their hands at constructing an "analysis" of knowledge (or of some other epistemic notion) have been explicit about their objectives (see 34–44). However, absent indications to the contrary, I am inclined to think that if a philosophical project proceeds by offering definitions or "truth conditions," and testing them against our intuitions about real or imaginary cases, then the project should be viewed as an attempt at conceptual analysis or explication. Unless one has some pretty strange views about intuitions, it is hard to see what we could hope to gain from capturing them apart from some insight into the concepts that underlie them.

However, it is my contention that if an analytic epistemological theory is taken to be part of the serious normative inquiry whose goal is to tell people which cognitive processes are good ones, or which ones they should use, then for most people it will prove to be an irrelevant failure.

I think the most intuitive way to see this point is to begin by recalling how the specter of culturally based cognitive diversity lends a certain urgency to the question of which cognitive processes we should use. If patterns of inference are acquired from the surrounding culture, much as language or fashions or manners are, and if we can learn to use cognitive processes quite different from the ones we have inherited from our culture, then the question of whether our culturally inherited cognitive processes are good ones is of more than theoretical interest. If we *can* go about the business of cognition differently, and if others actually *do*, it is natural to ask whether there is any reason why we should continue to do it our way. Even if we cannot change our cognitive processes once we've acquired them, it is natural to wonder whether those processes are good ones. Moreover, for many people the absence of a convincing affirmative answer can be seriously disquieting. For if we cannot say why our cognitive processes are any better than those prevailing elsewhere, it suggests that it is ultimately no more than an historical accident that we use the cognitive processes we do, or that we hold the beliefs that those processes generate, just as it is an historical accident that we speak English rather than Spanish and wear trousers rather than togas.

Consider now how the analytic epistemologist would address the problem that cognitive diversity presents. To determine whether our cognitive processes are good ones, he would urge, we must first *analyze* our concept of justification (or perhaps some other commonsense epistemic notion like rationality). If our commonsense epistemic notion is not too vague or ambiguous, the analysis will give us a criterion of rightness for J-rules (or perhaps a cluster of closely related criteria). Our next step is to investigate which sets of J-rules fit the criterion. Having made some progress there, we can take a look at our own cognitive processes and ask whether they do in fact accord with some right set of J-rules. If they do, we have found a reason to continue using those processes; we have shown that they are good ones because the beliefs they lead to are justified. If it turns out that our cognitive processes don't accord with a right set of J-rules, we can try to discover some alternative processes that do a better job, and set about training ourselves to use them.

It is my contention that something has gone very wrong here. For the analytic epistemologist's effort is designed to determine whether our cognitive states and processes accord with our commonsense notion of justification (or some other commonsense concept of epistemic evaluation). Yet surely the evaluative epistemic concepts embedded in everyday thought and language are every bit as likely as the cognitive processes they evaluate to be culturally acquired and to vary from culture to culture.[27] Moreover, the analytic epistemologist offers us no reason whatever to think that the notions of evaluation prevailing in our own language and culture are any better than the alternative evaluative notions that might or do prevail in other cultures. But in the absence of any reason to think that the locally prevailing notions of epistemic evaluation are superior to the alternatives, why should we care one whit whether the cognitive processes we use are sanctioned by those evaluative concepts? How can the fact that our cognitive processes are approved by the evaluative notions embraced in our culture alleviate the worry that our cognitive processes are no better than those of exotic folk, if we have no reason to believe that our evaluative notions are any better than alternative evaluative notions?

To put the point a bit more vividly, imagine that we have located some exotic culture that does in fact exploit cognitive processes very different from our own, and that the notions of epistemic evaluation embedded in their language also differ from ours. Suppose further that the cognitive processes prevailing in that culture accord quite well with *their* evaluative notions, while the cognitive processes prevailing in our culture accord quite well with *ours*. Would any of this be of any help at all in deciding which cognitive processes we should use? Without some reason to think that one set of evaluative notions was preferable to the other, it seems clear that it would be of no help at all.

In the philosophical literature there is a tradition, perhaps traceable to Wittgenstein, that would reject the suggestion that our evaluative notions should themselves be evaluated. Justifications, this tradition insists, must come to an end. And once we have shown that our practice accords with our evaluative concepts, there is nothing more to show. Our language game (or form of life) does not provide us with any way to go about evaluating our evaluative notions. There is no logical space in which questions like "Should we hold justified beliefs?" or "Should we invoke rational cognitive processes?" can be asked seriously. If a person did not recognize that the answers to these questions had to be affirmative, it

---

27. Evidence on this point, like evidence about cross-cultural differences in cognitive processes, is hard to come by and hard to interpret. But there are some intriguing hints in the literature. Hallen and Sodipo (1986) studied the terms of epistemic evaluation exploited by the Yoruba, a West African people. It is their contention that the Yoruba do not have a distinction corresponding to our distinction between knowledge and (mere) true belief. They do, however, divide beliefs into two other categories: those for which a person has immediate, eyewitness evidence, and those for which he does not. In the standard Yoruba-English dictionaries, the Yoruba term for the former sort of belief, "mo," is translated as "knowledge," while the term for the latter sort, "gbagbo," is translated as "belief." However, Hallen and Sodipo argue that these translations are mistaken, since "mo" has a much narrower extension than "knowledge." Most of what we would classify as scientific knowledge, for example, would not count as "mo" for the Yoruba, because it is based on inference and secondhand report. Since the Yoruba do not draw the distinction between knowledge and (mere) true belief, they have no use for our notion of epistemic justification, which earns its keep in helping to draw that distinction. Instead, the Yoruba presumably have another notion which they exploit in distinguishing "mo" from "gbagbo." Hallen and Sodipo do not indicate whether the Yoruba have a single word for this notion, but if they do, it would be a mistake to translate the word as "(epistemic) justification." Clearly, if Hallen and Sodipo are right, the Yoruba categories of epistemic evaluation are significantly different from our own.

would simply indicate that he did not understand the logical grammar of words like "should" and "justified" and "rational."

I am inclined to think that there is at least a kernel of truth in this "Wittgensteinian" stand. Justifications do ultimately come to an end. However, it is, I think, a disastrous mistake to think that they come to an end *here*. For there are *lots* of values that are both widely shared and directly relevant to our cognitive lives, though they are quite distinct from the "epistemic values" that lie behind our ordinary use of terms like "justified" and "rational." It is against the background of these non-epistemic values that our socially shared system of epistemic evaluation can itself be evaluated. Thus, for example, many people attach high value to cognitive states that foster happiness (their own or everyone's), and many people value cognitive states that afford them the power to predict and control nature. Some people share Mother Nature's concern that our cognitive lives should foster reproductive success. And, on a rather different dimension, many people care deeply that their beliefs be true.[28] Each of these values, along with many others that might be mentioned, affords a perspective from which epistemic values like justification and rationality can be evaluated. We can ask whether the cognitive states and processes endorsed by our notions of epistemic value foster happiness, or power, or accurate prediction, or reproductive success, or truth. More interestingly, we can ask whether the cognitive states and processes we actually have or use foster happiness, power, or the rest. And if they do not, we can explore alternatives that may do a better job, though there is of course no guarantee that all of these values can be maximized together.[29]

At this point, it might be protested that the values I am proposing to use in evaluating our socially shared notions of epistemic evaluation are themselves lacking any deeper justification. If someone can accept *these* as ultimate values, why couldn't someone do the same for justification or rationality? My reply is that of course someone could, but this is no objection to the view I am urging. There are many things that people might and do find ultimately or intrinsically valuable. Some of these values may be rooted more or less directly in our biological nature, and these we can expect to be widely shared. Other

---

28. I should note, in passing, that I think it is a mistake to include truth on the list of intrinsically valuable features of one's cognitive life. But that is a topic for another paper, (see Stich 1990, chap. 5) and I will ignore the point here.

29. The point I am making here is really just a generalization of a point made long ago by Salmon 1957, Skyrms 1975, and a number of other authors. Strawson (1952) argued that the rationality or reasonableness of inductive reasoning was easy to demonstrate, since being supported by inductive inference is part of what we *mean* when we say that an empirical belief is reasonable. To which Salmon replied that if Strawson is right about the meaning of "*reasonable*" it is not at all clear why anyone should *want* to be reasonable. What most of us do care about, Salmon notes, is that our inferential methods be those that are "best suited to the attainment of our ends" (41). "If we regard beliefs as reasonable simply because they are arrived at inductively and we hold that reasonable beliefs are valuable for their own sake, it appears that we have elevated inductive method to the place of an intrinsic good" (42). The analytic epistemologist elevates being within the extension of our ordinary terms of epistemic evaluation to the place of an intrinsic good. In so doing, the analytic epistemologist embraces a system of value that few of us are willing to share.

values, including intrinsic, life-shaping values, may be socially transmitted, and vary from society to society. Still others may be quite idiosyncratic. It is entirely possible for someone in our society to attach enormous value to having justified beliefs or to using rational inferential strategies—that is, to having beliefs or inferential processes that fall within the extension of "justified" or "rational" as they are used in our language. Similarly, it is entirely possible for someone in another society to attach enormous value to having cognitive states that fall within the extension of the terms of cognitive evaluation current in that society. In each case the evaluation may be either instrumental or intrinsic. A person in our culture may value the states and processes that fall within the extension of "rational" or "justified" because he thinks they are likely to be true, to lead to happiness, etc., or he may value them for no further reason at all. And a person in another culture may have either sort of attitude in valuing what falls within the extension of his language's terms of cognitive evaluation. Where the value attached is instrumental, there is plenty of room for productive inquiry and dialogue. We can try to find out whether rational or justified cognitive processes do lead to happiness or power or truth, and if they do we can try to understand why. But where the value accorded to one or another epistemic virtue is intrinsic, there is little room for debate. If you value rationality for its own sake, and the native of another culture values some rather different cognitive characteristic ("shmashinality," as Hilary Putnam might put it) for *its* own sake, there is not much you can say to each other. Moreover, there is not much I can say to either of you, since on my view the fact that a cognitive process is sanctioned by the venerable standards embedded in our language of epistemic evaluation, or theirs, is of no more interest than the fact that it is sanctioned by the venerable standards of a religious tradition or an ancient text—unless, of course, it can be shown that those standards correlate with something more generally valued.[30] But I do not pretend to have any arguments that will move the true epistemic xenophobe. If a person really does attach deep intrinsic value to the epistemic virtues favored by folk epistemology, then dialogue has come to an end.

Finally, let me say how all of this relates to analytic epistemology. The analytic epistemologist proposes to arbitrate between competing criteria of rightness by seeing which one accords best with the evaluative notions "embraced by everyday thought and language." However, it is my contention that this project is of no help whatever

---

30. Let me try to head off a possible misunderstanding. Some analytic epistemologists claim that our ordinary notions of epistemic evaluation are conceptually linked to truth. On Goldman's account, for example, the rightness of a set of J-rules is a function of how well the processes sanctioned by those rules do at producing truths. If this is right, then a person who attached intrinsic value to having true beliefs would, of course, have reason to be interested in whether his cognitive states and processes were sanctioned by the standards embedded in our language. But here it is the appeal to truth that is doing the work, not the appeal to traditional standards. For if Goldman is wrong in his conceptual analysis and "(epistemic) justification" is not conceptually tied to truth, the person who values truth will stay just as interested in whether his cognitive processes reliably lead to truth, though he may have no interest whatever in how traditional notions of epistemic evaluation judge his cognitive processes. Thanks to Steven Luper-Foy for the query that prompted this note.

in confronting the problem of cognitive diversity unless one is an epistemic xenophobe. The program of analytic epistemology views conceptual analysis or explication as a stopping place in disputes about how we should go about the business of cognition. When we know that a certain cognitive process falls within the extension of our ordinary terms of epistemic evaluation—whatever the analysis of those terms may turn out to be—we know all that can be known that is relevant to the question of how we should go about the business of reasoning. But as I see it, the only people who should take this information to be at all relevant to the question are the profoundly conservative people who find intrinsic value in having their cognitive processes sanctioned by culturally inherited standards, whatever those standards may be. Many of us care very much whether our cognitive processes lead to beliefs that are true, or give us power over nature, or lead to happiness. But only those with a deep and free-floating conservatism in matters epistemic will care whether their cognitive processes are sanctioned by the evaluative standards that happen to be woven into our language.[31]

REFERENCES

Cherniak, C. 1986. *Minimal Rationality*. Cambridge, MA: MIT Press.

Cohen, L. J. 1981. Can Human Irrationality Be Experimentally Demonstrated? *Behavioral and Brain Sciences* 4: 317–30.

Cole, M., and B. Means. 1981. *Comparative Studies of How People Think*. Cambridge, MA: Harvard University Press.

Cole, M., and S. Scribner. 1974. *Culture and Thought*. New York: John Wiley.

Conee, E., and R. Feldman. 1983. Stich and Nisbett on Justifying Inference Rules. *Philosophy of Sciences* 50: 326–31.

Daniels, N. 1979. Wide Reflective Equilibrium and Theory Acceptance in Ethics. *Journal of Philosophy* 76: 256–82.

———. 1980a. Reflective Equilibrium and Archimedean Points. *Canadian Journal of Philosophy* 10: 83–103.

———. 1980b. On Some Methods of Ethics and Linguistics. *Philosophical Studies* 37: 21–36.

Davidson, D. 1982. Rational Animals. *Dialectica* 36: 317–27.

Goldman, A. 1986. *Epistemology and Cognition*. Cambridge, MA: Harvard University Press.

Goodman, N. 1965. *Fact, Fiction and Forecast*. Indianapolis, IN: Bobbs-Merrill.

Hallen, B., and J. O. Sodipo. 1986. *Knowledge, Belief and Witchcraft*. London: Ethnographica.

---

31. This paper has been evolving for a long time. Earlier versions were presented in my seminars at the University of Sydney, the University of Maryland, and the University of California, San Diego, and in colloquia at the University of Adelaide, La Trobe University, the Australian National University, the University of Illinois at Chicago, the University of Vermont, Tulane University, the University of Southern California, and the University of Colorado. Suggestions and criticism from these varied audiences have led to more changes than I can remember or acknowledge. My thanks to all who helped, or tried. Special thanks are due to Philip Kitcher, David Stove, and Joseph Tolliver.

Harman, G. 1986. *Change in View*. Cambridge, MA: MIT Press.

Kahneman, D., P. Slovic, and A. Tversky. 1982. *Judgment Under Uncertainty: Heuristics and Biases*. New York: Cambridge University Press.

Nisbett, R., and L. Ross. 1980. *Human Inference: Strategies and Shortcoming of Social Judgment*. Englewood Cliffs, NJ: Prentice-Hall.

Rawls, J. 1971. *A Theory of Justice*. Cambridge, MA: Harvard University Press.

———. 1974. The Independence of Moral Theory. *Proceeding and Addresses of the American Philosophical Association* 48: 4–22.

Rey, G. 1983. Concepts and Stereotypes. *Cognitions* 15: 237–62.

Routley, R. 1981. Alleged Problems in Attributing Beliefs, and Intentionality, to Animals. *Inquiry* 24: 385–417.

Salmon, W. 1957. Should We Attempt to Justify Induction? *Philosophical Studies* 8: 33–48.

Shope, R. 1983. *The Analysis of Knowing: A Decade of Research*. Princeton, NJ: Princeton University Press.

Skyrms, B. 1975. *Choice and Chance*. Belmont, CA: Wadsworth.

Smith, E., and D. Media. 1981. *Concepts and Categories*. Cambridge, MA: Harvard University Press.

Stich, S. 1979. Do Animals Have Beliefs? *Australasian Journal of Philosophy* 57: 15–28.

———. 1983. *From Folk Psychology to Cognitive Science*. Cambridge, MA: MIT Press.

———. 1984. Relativism, Rationality and the Limits of International Description. *Pacific Philosophical Quarterly* 65: 211–35.

———. 1990. *The Fragmentation of Reason: Preface to a Pragmatic Theory of Cognitive Evaluation*. Cambridge, MA: Bradford Books/MIT Press.

Stich, S., and R. Nisbett. 1980. Justification and the Psychology of Human Reasoning. *Philosophy of Science* 47: 188–202.

Strawson, P. 1952. *Introduction to Logical Theory*. New York: John Wiley.

5

MORAL PHILOSOPHY AND MENTAL REPRESENTATION

LET ME BEGIN with a bit of autobiography. I am, by profession, a teacher of philosophy. Year in and year out, for the last 15 or 20 years, I have taught a large undergraduate course on contemporary moral issues—issues such as abortion, euthanasia, reverse discrimination, genetic engineering, and animal rights. Over the years, I have written a handful of papers on some of these topics. However, most of my research and writing has been in a very different domain. It has been concerned with problems in the philosophy of language, the philosophy of mind, and the philosophy of psychology. During the last decade, much of my work has been on the philosophical foundations of cognitive science, and I have spent a great deal of time thinking and writing about the nature of mental representation.

For a long time I assumed that the two branches of my professional life were quite distinct. However, a few years ago I began to suspect that there might actually be important connections between them. The invitation to participate in the Tucson conference on the Scientific Analysis of Values has provided the motivation to set out my suspicions a bit more systematically. In reading what follows, do keep in mind that it is very much a first stab at these matters. I suspect that much of what I have to say is seriously oversimplified, and no doubt some of it is muddled or mistaken.

Here is an overview of what is to come. In Sections I and II, I will sketch two of the projects frequently pursued by moral philosophers, and the methods typically invoked in those projects. I will argue that these projects presuppose (or at least suggest) a particular sort of account of the mental representation of human value systems, since the methods make sense only if we assume a certain kind of story about how the human mind stores information about values. The burden of my argument in Section III will be that while the jury is still out, there is some evidence suggesting that this account of mental representation is mistaken. If it is mistaken, it follows that two of the central methods of moral philosophy may have to be substantially modified, or perhaps abandoned, and that the goals philosophers have sought to achieve with these methods may themselves be misguided. I fear that many of my philosophical colleagues will find this a quite radical suggestion. But if anything is clear in this area, it is that the methods we will be considering have not been conspicuously successful, though it certainly has not been for want of trying. So perhaps it is time for some radical, empirically informed rethinking of goals and methods in these parts of moral philosophy.

In Section IV, I will take a brief look at a rather different project in moral philosophy. This project, I will argue, is compatible with a wide range of theories about the structures subserving mental representation. But to pursue the project seriously, it will be necessary to determine which of these theories is correct. And that is a job requiring input from anthropologists, linguists, artificial intelligence (AI) researchers, and cognitive psychologists as well as philosophers. If this is right, a surprising redrawing of traditional disciplinary boundaries is in order. For a central project in ethics will turn out to be located squarely within the domain of cognitive science.

I. Plato's Quest: The Analysis of Moral Concepts

> Well said, Cephalus, I replied; but as concerning justice, what is it?—to speak the truth and to pay your debts—no more than this? And even to this are there not exceptions?

With this passage in the *Republic*,[1] Plato launches a long inquiry whose goal is to find the definition of justice. Let me pick up the quote where I left off, since the next few sentences provide a paradigm for the process of inquiry Plato will pursue.

> Suppose that a friend when in his right mind has deposited arms with me and he asks for them when he is not in his right mind, ought I to give them back to him? No one would say that I ought or that I should be right in doing so, any more than they would say that I ought always to speak the truth to one who is in his condition.
> You are quite right, he replied.
> But then, I said, speaking the truth and paying your debts is not a correct definition of justice.

---

1. Plato 1892, *The Republic* I, 331, p. 595.

Quite correct, Socrates.[2]

Much the same pattern recurs frequently in Plato's dialogues. Here's another example.

> *SOCRATES*: I abjure you to tell me the nature of piety and impiety, which you say that you know so well, and of murder, and of other offenses against the gods. What are they? Is not piety in every action always the same?
> *EUTHYPHRO*: To be sure, Socrates.
> *SOCRATES*: And what is piety, and what is impiety? . . . Tell me what is the nature of this idea, and then I shall have a standard to which I may look, and by which I may measure actions, whether yours or those of any one else, and then I shall be able to say that such and such an action is pious, such another impious.
> *EUTHYPHRO*: I will tell you, if you like. . . . Piety . . . is that which is dear to the gods, and impiety is that which is not dear to them.
> *SOCRATES*: Very good, Euthyphro; you have now given me the sort of answer which I wanted. But whether what you say is true or not I cannot as yet tell. . . .
> The quarrels of the gods, noble Euthyphro, when they occur, are of a like nature [to the quarrels of men]. . . . They have differences of opinion . . . about good and evil, just and unjust, honorable and dishonorable. . . .
> *EUTHYPHRO*: You are quite right.
> *SOCRATES*: Then, my friend, I remark with surprise that you have not answered the question which I asked. For I certainly did not ask you to tell me what action is both pious and impious: but now it would seem that what is loved by the gods is also hated by them.[3]

Throughout the history of philosophy, there has been no shortage of authors who have followed in Plato's footsteps, seeking definitions of such central moral notions as justice, goodness, obligation, responsibility, equality, fairness, and a host of others. Typically, those pursuing these projects share with Plato a cluster of assumptions about how the game is to be played. The first is that a correct definition must provide *individually necessary and jointly sufficient conditions* for the application of the concept being defined. It must specify what every instance falling under the concept, and only these, have in common. If there are exceptions to the definition—either cases that fit the definition but to which the concept does not apply, or cases that do not fit the definition but to which the concept does apply—then the definition is mistaken.

A second widely shared Platonic assumption is that we already have a great deal of knowledge relevant to the definition we seek. The central strategy in testing a proposed definition is to compare what the definition says to what *we* would say about a variety of actual and hypothetical cases. On the definition offered by Cephalus, justice requires

2. Ibid.
3. Plato 1892, *Euthyphro*, 5–7, pp. 386–89.

paying your debts. But we would not say that a man is unjust if he refuses to return the weapons of a friend who is no longer in his right mind. So Cephalus's definition must be mistaken. To make this sort of test work we must suppose that we already know whether or not refusing to return the arms would be unjust—we must have this sort of knowledge prior to articulating the sought after definition. Indeed, the Platonic inquiry seems to make the most sense if we assume that we already know necessary and sufficient conditions for the application of the concept, and that this knowledge is being put to work in guiding our judgments about the various cases, both real and hypothetical, that are offered as potential counterexamples to proposed definitions. Though of course at the beginning of the inquiry our knowledge of necessary and sufficient conditions is largely tacit; it is not available in a form that enables us to specify those conditions. If it were, the Platonic quest for definitions would be much easier than it is.

A third assumption underlying the Platonic project is that it will do some good to articulate and make explicit the necessary and sufficient conditions that, presumably, we already tacitly know. Socrates motivates his request for a definition by saying that when he has it "then I shall have a standard to which I may look, and by which I may measure actions, . . . and then I shall be able to say that such and such an action is pious, such another impious." There is something of a paradox lurking here, however. For, as we have just seen, the method that Plato and the many who follow him invoke seems to require that we already know how to "measure actions . . . and say that such and such an action" is just or pious or what have you. Judgments about the applicability of the term we are seeking to define are the *input* into the process of testing proposed definitions. Having noted this paradox, I do not propose to pursue it any further, since doing so would take us too far afield.

II. Morally Relevant Difference Arguments

My second example of a project in moral philosophy that seems to make some strong assumptions about the mental representation of values is one that I find myself pursuing over and over again in my courses in contemporary moral issues. To motivate the project for my students, I begin with the observation that if two cases are to be judged differently from a moral point of view—if, for example, one action is judged morally right while another is morally wrong—then it must be the case that there is some nonmoral feature with respect to which they differ. Two cases that are *exactly* the same in every descriptive or nonmoral respect must be morally the same as well. Philosophers like to make this point by saying that the moral properties of a situation *supervene* on the nonmoral properties. Once the latter have been determined, the former are fixed as well.

Now, by itself, this principle of the supervenience of the moral on the nonmoral cannot do much work for us, since in the real world there are no two cases that are exactly alike. There will always be *some* differences between any two situations. However, if we are going to draw a moral distinction between a pair of cases, the descriptive differences between them must be differences that we take to be *morally relevant*—they must be aspects of the situation that we are seriously prepared to accept as justifying the drawing of a moral distinction. And if they justify the drawing of a moral distinction in the case at hand, then presumably they justify the drawing of a parallel moral distinction in other cases that differ in the same way.

All of this will be a bit clearer if we consider an example. The illustration I will use is one of my favorites in the classroom—the issue of animal rights. I begin the discussion by noting that most people have reasonably stable and reasonably clear views about what is right and wrong in this domain. The goal I propose to the students is the apparently modest one of making their own views explicit.

Most students are not vegetarians. They are prepared to say that there is nothing morally wrong with the practice of raising and slaughtering a variety of agricultural animals for no better reason than that some people like to eat the meat of those animals. There is, in particular, nothing at all morally wrong with raising pigs destined for slaughter and ultimately for pork chops and ham sandwiches. Nonvegetarian students typically do not condone the *cruel* treatment of farm animals. And, of course, some of the most powerful arguments of animal rights advocates turn on what is alleged to be the intrinsically cruel nature of modern farming methods. But for the purposes of the current illustration, let us leave the issue of cruelty to one side. Let us assume that the animals we are considering are treated well and slaughtered as painlessly as possible. Under these circumstances most of my students are prepared to agree, indeed insist, that there is nothing wrong with raising cows, pigs, and other common farm animals for food.

Now consider a parallel case. Suppose a group of very wealthy gourmets decide that it would be pleasant to dine occasionally on human flesh. To achieve their goal they hire a number of couples who are prepared to bear infants to be harvested for the table. Typically, my students' first reaction to this proposal is horror and disgust, accompanied with considerable moral indignation. They are quite certain that such a practice would be morally intolerable. Very well, then, I ask, what is the morally relevant difference between farming children and farming animals? Why do you draw a moral distinction between babies and pigs? To start the ball rolling, I note that there are all sorts of features that distinguish adult humans from pigs that they cannot appeal to here. It is not the case that a human baby is more intelligent than an adult pig, or more self-conscious, or more rational, or more aware of its environment. With respect to all of these features, adult pigs are *superior* to babies.

Well, the answer usually comes back, perhaps it is true that an adult pig is more intelligent and self-aware than a human infant. But the difference is one of *potential*. Human babies have the potential to become significantly more intelligent, rational, self-aware, etc. than any pig can ever be. Human babies grow up to be moral agents. Pigs do not. And it is the potential for developing in these ways that marks the moral boundary between pigs and babies.

Ah, I reply, not so fast. Let me change the case a bit. Suppose that our gourmets, sensitive to concerns about potential, have arranged to treat the sperm with which the women are impregnated. The treatment makes some small changes in the genetic makeup of the sperm, with the result that the children produced are all very severely retarded. None of *these* children has the potential for developing into rational, reflective adults. On any reasonable measure, none of them will ever be as rational as a normal adult pig. Or, if you prefer, we can imagine yet another variation on the theme. Suppose our gourmets have entered into an arrangement with the administration of several large hospitals. Whenever there is an extremely senile patient in one of the hospitals who has no close relatives or friends, the patient is turned over to the gourmets, and ends up in the stew at their next banquet. Here again, there is no potential for rationality, or for becoming a moral agent. The people who end up on the dinner table have less potential, along these lines, than a normal adult pig.

At this point the students are generally getting a bit uncomfortable, and it is common for someone to propose that the crucial difference between the pig and the senile person or the severely retarded child is simply that the latter two are *humans*—they are members of *our* species. It is the difference between humans and nonhumans that marks a major moral boundary. A first response to this suggestion, one that often comes from another student, is the observation that this is *speciesism*—a doctrine that bears a distressing similarity to racism. But if a student is unmoved by the analogy, the following tale will typically be very unsettling. Suppose it were to be found that some small group of people living among us—people of Icelandic descent, for example—turn out not to be able to have children when married to partners outside their group. On further investigation it turns out that the Icelanders are incapable of interbreeding with the rest of us because they are actually genetically different from us. They have a different number of chromosomes, and a significantly different genetic structure. They are, in short, members of a different species. The difference went unnoticed for so long because Icelanders generally marry other Icelanders. Despite the differences, however, Icelanders typically make exemplary citizens, and they are often the best of friends with non-Icelanders. Some of them do superb science, others write first-rate poetry, and a fair number of them are skilled at sports. Nonetheless, they are members of another species. And because of the difference in species, our gourmets conclude they are morally justified in having the occasional Icelander for dinner—as the main course.

Not at all surprisingly, the students find this morally repugnant, and they concede that mere difference in species is not enough to mark the moral boundary they seek. Indeed, what often happens at this point in the discussion is that students start to question their initial moral judgments. If it is so *hard* to specify the morally relevant difference between pigs and babies, perhaps that is because there are no differences that they are prepared to take seriously. Perhaps when the issue at hand is killing for food, pigs and babies should not be treated differently. Perhaps what we do to pigs is horribly *wrong*. It is not at all uncommon for students to suffer a small moral crisis when confronted with these considerations. And in at least a few cases students who came back to visit a number of years later have told me that they had been strict vegetarians ever since taking my course.

The search for morally relevant differences between harvesting pigs and harvesting people is in some ways quite different from the Platonic search for definitions. In Plato's project, we are seeking to characterize conditions for the application of a particular moral notion such as justice or responsibility or piety. In debating the morality of using animals for food, we are seeking to characterize an important moral boundary—the boundary between those creatures that it is morally acceptable to kill simply to satisfy our own tastes, and those that it would be morally repugnant to kill for this reason. However, there are also some important similarities between the two endeavors. In both investigations, we are trying to specify the extension of categories by seeking necessary and sufficient conditions. We want an account that will cleanly divide cases into two distinct classes—the just and the unjust, or the things it is permissible to kill for food and the things it is not permissible to kill for food. Also, it seems that in both cases we must assume that we already know a great deal about the categories we are seeking to characterize. The methods proceed by testing proposed conditions against our "intuitive" judgments about actual and hypothetical cases. And, as we noted earlier, it is plausible to suppose that if this process is to succeed we must already have something like a set of tacitly known necessary and sufficient conditions to guide our judgments about particular cases. Thus, both the Platonic quest for definitions and the search for morally relevant differences appear to presuppose a view about the process underlying our ability to classify items into categories: *Categorization exploits tacitly known necessary and sufficient conditions.* In the section that follows, I will sketch some of the reasons to suspect that this account of categorization may be mistaken.

III. Categorization and Concepts

In the psychological literature, the cognitive structures underlying categorical judgments are generally referred to as *concepts*.[4] And in psychology, as in philosophy, there is a long-standing tradition that insists that concepts must specify necessary and sufficient conditions. However, since the early 1970s there has been a growing body of experimental literature challenging this "classical view" of concepts. Perhaps the most well known work in this area has been done by Eleanor Rosch and her associates.

In one series of experiments it was shown that people can reliably order instances falling under a concept when asked how "typical" or "representative" the instances are. Thus, for example, an apple will be rated as a more typical fruit than a lemon; a lemon will be rated as more typical than a coconut; and a coconut will be rated as more typical than

---

4. Philosophers too sometimes use the term "concept" in this way, though they also use the term in some very different ways. For a useful discussion of the contrast, see Rey 1983, 1985; Smith, Medin, and Rips 1984; and Smith 1989.

an olive (Mervis, Catlin, and Rosch 1976; Rosch 1978; Malt and Smith 1984). What is important about these ratings is that they predict performance on a wide variety of tasks including categorization.

If subjects are asked whether a particular item is or is not a fruit, and are told to respond as quickly as possible, their responses are faster for more typical instances and slower for less typical instances (Smith, Shoben, and Rips 1974). Also, when subjects are asked to generate examples of subcategories of a given concept they mention typical ones before atypical ones. Thus, for example, subjects asked to name kinds of fruit will mention apples, peaches, and pears before blueberries, and blueberries will be mentioned before avocados or pumpkins (Rosch 1978).

Now if a concept is the cognitive structure that subjects are using when they make categorical judgments, then these results begin to make the classical view of concepts look a bit problematic. For if concepts specify necessary and sufficient conditions, they apply equally to every instance of the concept, and it is not obvious why some instances should be more typical, easier to categorize and easier to recall.

Another line of research that has been taken to undermine the classical view of concepts suggests that typicality effects can be explained by appeal to properties that are common in members of the category, though they are not necessary conditions for membership in the category. In a number of studies, subjects were provided with a list of instances or subcategories falling under a given concept, and they were asked to specify properties of the items on the list. Thus, for example, if the category in question is *birds*, subjects will be given a list that includes *robin, canary, vulture, chicken,* and *penguin.* The properties that subjects offer for canary might include *has feathers, flies, small size, sings,* etc. Only the first two of these would be offered for *vulture,* and only the first for *penguin.* Given these data, we can compute what Rosch and her associates call the *family resemblance score* for various kinds of birds. This is done by assigning to each property (*has feathers, flies,* etc.) a number proportional to the number of bird kinds for which the property was mentioned. (Thus the number assigned to *has feathers* would be higher than the number assigned to *sings.*) Having weighted the properties, the family resemblance score for a particular kind of bird is simply the sum of the weights of the properties mentioned for that bird. The high family resemblance score for *robin* indicates that robins have many properties that occur frequently in other kinds of birds, while the low family resemblance score for *chicken* and *penguin* indicates that these birds do not have many of the properties that occur frequently in other sorts of birds. Not surprisingly, the family resemblance score turns out to be an excellent predictor of typicality, and thus an excellent predictor of categorization speed, recall, etc.

In light of these results, a number of investigators have proposed accounts of concepts that are at odds with the classical (necessary and sufficient conditions) view. One widely discussed idea is that a concept consists of a set of salient features or properties that characterizes only the best or "prototypical" members of category. This prototype representation will, of course, contain a variety of properties that are lacking in some members of the category. The prototypical bird flies, but emus do not. On the prototype view of concepts, objects are classified as members of a category if they are sufficiently similar to the prototype—that is, if they have a sufficient number of properties specified in the prototype representation. The more similar an item is to the target prototype, the faster one can determine that it exceeds the similarity threshold. Thus a more typical member of a category will be recognized and classified more rapidly than a less typical one.

Another proposal for dealing with the experimental results posits the mental representation of one or more specific exemplars. An exemplar is a specific instance of an item falling under a concept—the spaniel that was my boyhood companion (for *dog*) or the couch in our living room (for *couch*). On this view, categorization proceeds by activating the mental representations of one or more exemplars for the concept at hand, and then assessing the similarity between the exemplars and the item to be categorized. When developed in detail, exemplar models and prototype models yield different predictions, and there are some sophisticated empirical studies aimed at determining which model is superior in various conceptual domains (see, for example, Estes 1986).

Recent research strongly suggests that neither the prototype approach nor the exemplar approach can tell the whole story about conceptual representation, even for simple object concepts such as *fruit* and *bird* (Medin and Smith 1984; Smith 1990). The consensus seems to be that conceptual representation is a complex affair combining prototypes or exemplars with less observationally salient, more theoretical features. Also, it may well turn out that conceptual representation works differently in different domains. If this is right, then the mental representation of "goal-derived" categories such as *things not to eat on a diet* and social concepts such as *extrovert* or *communist* may have a format that is quite different from the mental representation of *apple, fruit,* or *dog* (Barsalou 1987).

While the empirical story about the mental structures underlying categorization is far from complete, it should be clear that much of the work I have been reviewing poses a major challenge to the two methods in moral philosophy sketched in Sections I and II. For both of those methods assume that categorization exploits tacitly known necessary and sufficient conditions, and much of the empirical work on categorization suggests that classical necessary and sufficient conditions play little or no role in the process. To the best of my knowledge, there have been no empirical studies aimed at exploring the mental representation of moral concepts like *justice* or *responsibility*. Nor has anyone looked carefully at the cognitive structures underlying our ability to use categories such as *things it is morally acceptable to kill for food*. However, if the story for those concepts is at all like the story elsewhere, it will explain why it is that moral philosophers working with the methods I sketched have been so unsuccessful for so long. For if the mental representation of moral concepts is similar to the mental representation of other concepts that have been studied, then the tacitly known necessary and sufficient conditions that moral philosophers are seeking *do not exist*.

Exemplar models of conceptual representation, and more sophisticated variations on the theme that invoke "scripts" or stories, also suggest an explanation for the fact that those engaged in moral pedagogy generally prefer examples to explicit principles or definitions. Myths, parables, fables, snippets of biography (real or fanciful)—these seem to be the principal tools of a successful moral teacher. Perhaps this is because moral knowledge is *stored* in the form of examples and stories. It may well be that moral doctrines cast in the form of necessary and sufficient conditions are didactically ineffective because they are presented in a form that the mind cannot readily use.

IV. Some Alternative Models for the Mental Representation of Moral Systems

The two projects in moral philosophy that we have looked at so far seem to presuppose that the mental structures underlying moral judgments are rather like definitions—they specify individually necessary and jointly sufficient conditions for the application of moral concepts. The psychological models that challenge this presupposition offer alternative accounts of conceptual representation, accounts that do not involve necessary and sufficient conditions. But these alternatives are still very much *like* definitions. Indeed, as Quine pointed out long ago, a typical dictionary definition of a word such as *tiger* or *lemon* will not offer necessary and sufficient conditions. Often it will present a list of features of a typical tiger or a typical lemon—very much in the spirit of the prototype account of mental representation (Quine 1953).

However, in the philosophical literature there is a venerable tradition that suggests a rather different account of how moral judgments are made. Instead of relying on something akin to definitions, this tradition assumes that our moral judgments are derived from an interconnected set of *rules* or *principles* specifying what sort of actions are just or unjust, permissible or not permissible, and so on. There are some clever ways in which certain systems of rules can be recast as a set of necessary and sufficient conditions. Thus the distinction between these two approaches is not a hard and fast one. Still, in many cases the style and complexity of rule-based theories give them a very different appearance and a very different feel.

In his seminal book, A *Theory of Justice*, John Rawls (1971, 46) urges that a first goal of moral philosophy should be the discovery of the set of rules or principles underlying our reflective moral judgment. These principles along with our beliefs about the circumstances of specific cases should entail the intuitive judgments we would be inclined to make about the cases, at least in those instances where our judgments are clear, and there are no extraneous factors likely to be influencing them. There is, of course, no reason to suppose that the principles guiding our moral judgments are fully (or even partially) available to conscious introspection. To uncover them we must collect a wide range of intuitions about specific cases (real or hypothetical) and attempt to construct a system of principles that will entail them.

As Rawls notes, this method for uncovering the system of principles presumed to underlie our intuitive moral judgments is analogous to the method used in modern linguistics. Following Chomsky, linguists typically assume that speakers of a natural language have internalized a system of generative grammatical rules, and that these rules play a central role in language production and comprehension. The rules are also assumed to play a central role in the production of linguistic intuitions—the more or less spontaneous judgments speakers offer about the grammaticality and other linguistic properties of sentences presented to them. In attempting to discover what a speaker has internalized, linguists construct systems of generative rules, and check them against the speaker's intuitions. However, the internalized rules are not the only psychological system that plays a part in producing reported intuitions. Memory, motivation, attention, and other factors all interact in the production of the judgments speakers offer. Thus the rules the linguist produces should not be expected to capture the exact details of the speakers' judgments. As in the case of moral principles, we expect the rules to capture only the clearest intuitions, and even these may be ignored when there is some reason to suspect that other factors are distorting the subject's judgment.

Now, as Rawls (1971, 47) observes, it is very likely that the grammatical rules for a natural language such as English will "require theoretical constructions that far outrun the ad hoc precepts of our explicit grammatical knowledge." So if the analogy between grammar and ethics is a good one, "there is no reason to assume that our sense of justice can be adequately characterized by familiar common sense precepts" (Rawls 1971, 47). It may also be the case that the principles underlying our moral intuitions, like those underlying our grammatical intuitions, are both numerous and enormously complex. Indeed, in the case of language, Chomsky has long maintained that the rules are so complex that they could not possibly be learned from the relatively limited data available to the child. Rather, he contends, the range of grammars that it is possible for a child to learn is a small and highly structured subset of the set of logically possible grammars. Thus much of the fundamental structure of the grammars that children ultimately internalize must be innate. One of the more intriguing possibilities suggested by the analogy between grammatical theory and moral theory is that, as we learn more about the mental representations underlying moral judgment, we may find that they sustain a similar sort of "argument from the poverty of the stimulus." Thus it may be that "humanly possible" moral systems are a very small subset of the logically possible systems, and that much of the structure of moral systems is innate, not acquired.

Though grammatical knowledge was one of the first domains to be systematically investigated by cognitive scientists, there has been a great deal of work on the mental structures underlying other sorts of knowledge, belief, and skill during the last two decades. Mathematical knowledge, knowledge of various sciences, and commonsense knowledge in various domains have all been explored. The cognitive systems underlying various skills, from chess and computer programming to musical composition and medical diagnosis, have also been investigated. Theories attempting to account for people's abilities in these areas have invoked a wide range of knowledge-representing systems, some of them rather like the generative systems that loom large in linguistics, and others quite different. What makes this work relevant to our current concerns is that many of the knowledge or belief systems that have been explored are at least roughly analogous to moral systems. In many cases people can offer a complex, subtle, and apparently systematic array of judgments about particular cases, with little or no conscious access to the mechanisms or principles underlying these judgments. Thus, while Rawls was certainly right in noting parallels between ethics and grammar, there are other analogies that are at least as plausible. Perhaps the mental structures underlying moral judgment are similar to those underlying expert medical diagnosis, or commonsense physical intuition. Perhaps the best analogy is with the knowledge structures that guide our expectations in reading stories about restaurants and other common social situations.

Which account of the mental representation of moral systems is best is certainly not a matter to be settled a priori. The question is an empirical one. But it is, I think, the sort of empirical question that is best approached in a resolutely interdisciplinary way. Philosophers have lavished a great deal of attention on the exploration of moral intuitions, and have amassed a very substantial body of cases illustrating the richness, subtlety, and complexity of our moral judgments. Linguists and deontic logicians have studied the semantic and logical structure of moral language. Anthropologists have much to say about the moral systems in cultures very different from our own. AI researchers, particularly those concerned with knowledge representation, have explored the strengths and weaknesses of many strategies for storing and using complex bodies of information. And, of course, cognitive psychologists have a sophisticated bag of tricks for testing hypotheses about the form and content of mentally represented information.

It is my strong suspicion that progress in understanding how people represent and use moral systems will not be made until scientists and scholars from these various disciplines begin to address the problem collaboratively. Indeed, one of my goals in writing this chapter is to convince at least some of my readers that it is time to launch such a collaborative effort.

A final note: If I am right about the way to make headway in understanding how moral systems are mentally represented, and if Rawls is right in suggesting that such an understanding is a first essential step in moral philosophy, then the beginnings of moral philosophy fall squarely within the domain of cognitive science.

REFERENCES

Barsalou, L. 1987. The Instability of Graded Structure: Implications for the Nature of Concepts. In U. Neisser, ed., *Concepts and Conceptual Development: Ecological and Intellectual Factors in Categorization*, 101–40. Cambridge: Cambridge University Press.
Estes, W. 1986. Array Models for Category Learning. *Cognitive Psychology* 18: 500–49.
Malt, B., and E. Smith. 1984. Correlated Properties in Natural Categories. *Journal of Verbal Learning and Verbal Behavior* 23: 250–69.
Medin, D., and E. Smith. 1984. Concepts and Concept Formation. *Annual Review of Psychology* 35: 113–38.

Mervis, C., J. Catlin, and E. Rosch. 1976. Category Structure and the Development of Categorization. In R. Spiro, B. Bruce, and W. Brewer, eds., *Theoretical Issues in Reading Comprehension*,
279–307. Hillsdale, NJ: Lawrence Erlbaum.

Plato. 1892. *The Dialogues of Plato*, vol. 1. Trans. B. Jowett. New York: Random House.

Quine, W. 1953. Two Dogmas of Empiricism. In *From a Logical Point of View*, 20–46. Cambridge,
MA: Harvard University Press.

Rawls, J. 1971. *A Theory of Justice*. Cambridge, MA: Harvard University Press.

Rey, G. 1983. Concepts and Stereotypes. *Cognition* 15: 237–62.

———. 1985. Concepts and Conceptions: A Reply to Smith, Medin and Rips. *Cognition* 19:
297–303.

Rosch, E. 1978. Principles of Categorization. In E. Rosch and B. Lloyd, eds., *Cognition and Categorization*, 27–48. Hillsdale, NJ: Lawrence Erlbaum.

Smith, E. 1989. Three Distinctions About Concepts and Categorization. *Language and Mind* 4,
1–2: 57–61.

———. 1990. Categorization. In D. Osherson and E. Smith, eds., *Thinking: An Invitation to Cognitive Science*, vol. 3. Cambridge, MA: MIT Press.

Smith, E., D. Medin, and L. Rips. 1984. A Psychological Approach to Concepts: Comments on
Rey's "Concepts and Stereotypes." *Cognition* 17: 265–74.

Smith, E., E. Shoben, and L. Rips. 1974. Structure and Process in Semantic Memory: A Featural
Model for Semantic Decisions. *Psychological Review* 81: 214–41.

6

NATURALIZING EPISTEMOLOGY

Quine, Simon, and the Prospects for Pragmatism

1. Introduction

In recent years there has been a great deal of discussion about the prospects of developing a "naturalized epistemology," though different authors tend to interpret this label in quite different ways.[1] One goal of this paper is to sketch three projects that might lay claim to the "naturalized epistemology" label, and to argue that they are not all equally attractive. Indeed, I'll maintain that the first of the three—the one I'll attribute to Quine—is simply incoherent. There is no way we could get what we want from an epistemological theory by pursuing the project Quine proposes. The second project on my list is a naturalized version of reliabilism. This project is not fatally flawed in the way that Quine's is. However, it's my contention that the sort of theory this project would yield is much less interesting than might at first be thought.

The third project I'll consider is located squarely in the pragmatist tradition. One of the claims I'll make for this project is that if it can be pursued successfully the results will be both more interesting and more useful than the results that might emerge from the reliabilist project. A second claim I'll make for it is that there is some reason to suppose that it *can* be pursued successfully. Indeed, I will argue that for over a decade one version of the project *has* been pursued with considerable success by Herbert Simon and his

---

1. For useful discussions of these various interpretations see Kornblith 1985b and Kitcher 1992.

co-workers in their ongoing attempt to simulate scientific reasoning. In the final section of the paper, I will offer a few thoughts on the various paths Simon's project, and pragmatist naturalized epistemology, might follow in the future.

Before I get on to any of this, however, I had best begin by locating the sort of naturalistic epistemology that I'll be considering in philosophical space. To do this I'll need to say something about how I conceive of epistemology, and to distinguish two rather different ideas on what "naturalizing" might come to. Much of traditional epistemology, and much of contemporary epistemology as well, can be viewed as pursuing one of three distinct though interrelated projects. One of these projects is the assessment of strategies of belief formation and belief revision. Those pursuing this project try to say which ways of building and rebuilding our doxastic house are good ways, which are poor ways, and why. A fair amount of Descartes' epistemological writing falls under this heading, as does much of Bacon's best-known work. It is also a central concern in the work of more recent writers like Mill, Carnap, and Goodman. A second traditional project aims to provide a definition or characterization of knowledge, explaining how knowledge differs from mere true opinion, as well as from ignorance and error. A third project has as its goal the refutation of the skeptic—the real or imagined opponent who claims that we can't have knowledge or certainty or some other putatively valuable epistemological commodity.[2] Although these three projects are obviously intertwined in various ways, my focus in this paper will be exclusively on the first of the three. The branch of epistemology whose "naturalization" I'm concerned with here is the branch that attempts to evaluate strategies of belief formation.

Let me turn now to "naturalizing." What would it be to "naturalize" epistemology? There are, I think, two rather different answers that might be given here. I'll call one of them Strong Naturalism and the other Weak Naturalism. What the answers share is the central idea that empirical science has an important role to play in epistemology—that epistemological questions can be investigated and resolved using the methods of the natural or social sciences. The issue over which Strong Naturalism and Weak Naturalism divide is the *extent* to which science can resolve epistemological questions. Strong Naturalism maintains that *all* legitimate epistemological questions are scientific questions, and thus that epistemology can be reduced to or replaced by science. Weak Naturalism, by contrast, claims only that *some* epistemological questions can be resolved by science. According to Weak Naturalism there are some legitimate epistemological questions that are *not* scientific questions and cannot be resolved by scientific research. The sort of epistemological pragmatism that I'll be advocating in this paper is a version of Weak Naturalism. It claims that while some epistemological questions can be resolved by doing science, there is at least one quite fundamental epistemological issue that science cannot settle.

2. For more on these three projects, see Stich 1990, 1–4.

2. Quine(?)'s Version of Strong Naturalism

The most widely discussed proposal for naturalizing epistemology is the one sketched by Quine in "Epistemology Naturalized" (1969b) and a number of other essays (1969c, 1975). According to Quine,

> [Naturalized epistemology] studies a natural phenomenon, viz., a physical human subject. This human subject is accorded a certain experimentally controlled input—certain patterns of irradiation in assorted frequencies, for instance—and in the fullness of time the subject delivers as output a description of the three-dimensional external world and its history. The relation between the meager input and the torrential output is a relation that we are prompted to study for somewhat the same reasons that always prompted epistemology; namely, in order to see how evidence relates to theory, and in what ways one's theory of nature transcends any available evidence. (1969b, 82–83).
>
> The stimulation of his sensory receptors is all the evidence anybody has had to go on, ultimately, in arriving at his picture of the world. Why not just see how this construction really proceeds? Why not settle for psychology? (1969b, 75–76)

There are various ways in which this Quinean proposal might be interpreted. On one reading, Quine is proposing that psychological questions can replace traditional epistemological questions—that instead of asking: How *ought* we to go about forming beliefs and building theories on the basis of evidence? we should ask: How do people actually go about it? And that the answer to this latter, purely psychological question will tell us what we've really wanted to know all along in epistemology. It will tell us "how evidence relates to theory." I'm not at all sure that this is the best interpretation of Quine.[3] What I am sure of is that many people do interpret Quine in this way. I am also sure that on this interpretation, Quine's project is a non-starter.

To see why, let us begin by asking *which* "physical human subject" or subjects Quine is proposing that we study. Quine doesn't say. Perhaps this is because he supposes that it doesn't much matter, since we're all very much alike. But that is simply not the case.

Consider, for example, those "physical human subjects" who suffer from Capgras syndrome. These people typically believe that some person close to them has been kidnapped and replaced by a duplicate who looks and behaves almost exactly the same as the original. Some people afflicted with Capgras come to believe that the replacement is not human at all; rather it is a robot with electrical and mechanical components inside. There have even been a few cases reported in which the Capgras sufferer attempted to prove

---

3. Indeed, in earlier drafts of this paper I attributed the view to someone called "Quine(?)" as a way of emphasizing my uncertainty about the interpretation. But that device survives only in the title of this section; it gets old very quickly.

that the "duplicate" was a robot by attacking it with an axe or a knife in order to expose the wires and transistors concealed beneath the "skin." Unfortunately, not even the sight of the quite real wounds and severed limbs that result from these attacks suffice to persuade Capgras patients that the "duplicate" is real.[4] Now for a Capgras patient, as much as for the rest of us, "the stimulation of his sensory receptors is all the evidence [he] has had to go on, ultimately, in arriving at his picture of the world." And psychology might well explore "how this construction really proceeds." But surely this process is *not* one that "we are prompted to study for the same reasons that always prompted epistemology." For what epistemologists want to know is not how "evidence relates to theory" in any arbitrary human subject. Rather they want to know how evidence relates to theory in subjects who do a good job of relating them. Among the many actual and possible ways in which evidence might relate to theories, which are the *good* ways and which are the bad ones? That is the question that "has always prompted epistemology." And the sort of study that Quine seems to be proposing cannot possibly answer it.

People suffering from Capgras syndrome are, of course, pathological cases. But much the same point can be made about perfectly normal subjects. During the last two decades cognitive psychologists have lavished considerable attention on the study of how normal subjects go about the business of inference and belief revision. Some of the best-known findings in this area indicate that in lots of cases people relate evidence to theory in ways that seem normatively dubious to put it mildly (Nisbett and Ross 1980; Kahneman, Slovic, and Tversky 1982). More recent work has shown that there are significant interpersonal differences in reasoning strategies, some of which can be related to prior education and training (Fong, Krantz, and Nisbett, 1986; Nisbett, Fong, Lehman, and Cheng 1987). The Quinean naturalized epistemologist can explore in detail the various ways in which different people construct their "picture of the world" on the basis of the evidence available to them. But he has no way of ranking these quite different strategies for building world descriptions; he has no way of determining which are better and which are worse. And since the Quinean naturalized epistemologist can provide no normative advice whatever, it is more than a little implausible to claim that his questions and projects can replace those of traditional epistemology. We can't "settle for psychology" because psychology tells us how people *do* reason; it does not (indeed cannot) tell us how they *should*.[5]

3. Reliabilism: Evaluating Reasoning by Studying Reasoners Who Are Good at Forming True Beliefs

The problem with Quine's proposal is that it doesn't tell us *whose* psychology to "settle for." But once this has been noted, there is an obvious proposal for avoiding the problem.

4. Foerstl 1990. I am grateful to Lynn Stephens for guiding me to the literature on Capgras syndrome.

5. For a similar critique of Quine, see Kim 1988.

If someone wants to improve her chess game, she would be well advised to use the chess strategies that good chess players use. Similarly, if someone wants to improve her reasoning, she would be well advised to use the reasoning strategies that good reasoners use. So rather than studying just anyone, the naturalized epistemologist can focus on those people who do a good job of reasoning. If we can characterize the reasoning strategies that good reasoners employ, then we will have a descriptive theory that has some normative clout.[6]

This, of course, leads directly to another problem. How do we select the people whose reasoning strategies we are going to study? How do we tell the good reasoners from the bad ones? Here there is at least one answer that clearly will *not* do. We can't select people to study by first determining the reasoning strategies that various people use, and then confining our attention to those who use good ones. For that would require that we already know which strategies are good ones; we would be trying to pull ourselves up by our own bootstraps. However, as the analogy with chess suggests, there is a very different way to proceed. We identify good chess players by looking at the consequences of their strategies—the good players are the ones who win, and the good strategies are the ones that good players use. So we might try to identify good reasoners by looking at the outcome of the reasoning. But this proposal raises further questions: Which "outcomes" should we look at, and how should we assess them? What counts as "winning" in epistemology?

One seemingly natural way to proceed here is to focus on *truth*. Reasoning, as Quine stresses, produces "descriptions of the . . . world and its history." A bit less behavioristically, we might say that reasoning produces *theories* that the reasoner comes to *believe*. Some of those theories are true, others are not. And, as the example of the Capgras sufferer's belief makes abundantly clear, false theories can lead to disastrous consequences. So perhaps what we should do is locate reasoners who do a good job at forming *true* beliefs, and try to discover what strategies of reasoning they employ. This project has an obvious affinity with the reliabilist tradition in epistemology. According to reliabilists, *truth* is a quite basic cognitive virtue, and beliefs are justified if they are produced by a belief-forming strategy that generally yields true beliefs. So it would be entirely in order for a naturalistically inclined reliabilist to propose that reasoning strategies should be evaluated by their success in producing true beliefs.[7]

It might be thought that this proposal suffers from something like the same sort of circularity that scuttled the proposal scouted two paragraphs back since we can't identify

---

6. A number of people have suggested to me that this strategy of studying the reasoning of people who are good at it is what Quine actually had in mind. I find relatively little in Quine's writing to support this interpretation. But I do not pretend to be a serious scholar on such matters. If those who know Quine's work better than I decide that this is what he really intended, I'll be delighted. I can use all the support I can get.

7. The sort of naturalized reliabilism that I am sketching bears an obvious similarity to the psychologically sophisticated reliabilism championed by Alvin Goldman. See, for example, Goldman 1986.

reasoners who do a good job at producing true theories unless we already know how to distinguish true theories from false ones. On my view, this charge of circularity can't be sustained. There is no overt circularity in the strategy that's been sketched, and the only "covert" circularity lurking is completely benign, and is to be found in all other accounts of how to tell good reasoning strategies from bad ones. However, I won't pause to set out the arguments rebutting the charge of circularity, since Goldman has already done a fine job of it.[8]

But while this reliabilist project is not viciously circular, it is, I think, much less appealing than might at first be thought. In support of this claim, I'll offer two considerations, one of which I've defended at length elsewhere. The project at hand proposes to distinguish good reasoning strategies from bad ones on the basis of how well they do at producing true beliefs. But, one might well ask, what's so good about having true beliefs? Why should having true beliefs be taken to be a fundamental goal of cognition? One's answer here must, of course, depend on what one takes true beliefs to be. If, along with Richard Rorty, one thinks that true beliefs are just those that one's community will not challenge when one expresses them, then it is not at all clear why one should want to have true beliefs, unless one values saying what one thinks while avoiding confrontation.[9]

I am not an advocate of Rorty's account of truth, however. On the account I favor, beliefs are mental states of a certain sort that are mapped to propositions (or content sentences) by an intuitively sanctioned "interpretation function." Roughly speaking, the proposition to which a belief-like mental state is mapped may be thought of as its truth condition. The true beliefs are those that are mapped by this function to true propositions; the false beliefs are those that are mapped to false propositions. However, it is my contention that the intuitively sanctioned function that determines truth conditions— the one that maps beliefs to propositions—is both arbitrary and idiosyncratic. There are lots of other functions mapping the same class of mental states to propositions in quite different ways. And these alternative functions assign different (albeit counter-intuitive) truth conditions. The class of beliefs mapped to true propositions by these counter-intuitive functions may be slightly different, or very different from the class of beliefs mapped to true propositions by the intuitive function. So, using the counter-intuitive functions we can define classes of beliefs that might be labeled TRUE* beliefs, TRUE** beliefs, and so on. A TRUE* belief is just one that is mapped to a true proposition by a counter-intuitive mapping function. Yet many of the alternative functions are no more arbitrary or idiosyncratic than the intuitively sanctioned function. Indeed, the only special feature that the intuitively sanctioned function has is that it is the one we happened to have been bequeathed by our language and culture. If all of this is right, then it is hard

---

8. See Goldman 1986, 116–21. In Stich 1990, Section 6.3, I have added a few of my own bells and whistles to Goldman's arguments.

9. This is, of course, no more than a caricature of Rorty's view. The full view defies easy summary. See Rorty 1979, Ch. 8; 1982, xiii–xlvii; 1988.

to see why we should prefer a system of reasoning that typically yields true beliefs over a system that typically yields TRUE* beliefs. The details on all of this, and the supporting arguments, have been set out elsewhere (Stich 1990, ch. 5; 1991a; 1991b). Since there is not space enough to reconstruct them here, let me offer a rather different sort of argument to challenge the idea that good reasoning strategies are those that typically yield true beliefs.

If one wants to play excellent chess, one would be well advised to use the strategies used by the best players in their best games. Of course, it *may* be possible to do even better than the best players of the past. One can always hope. But surely a good first step would be to figure out the strategies that the best players were using at the height of their power. For, barring cosmic accident, those are likely to be very good strategies indeed. Now suppose we were to try to apply this approach not to chess strategies but to reasoning strategies. Whose reasoning would we study?

Here opinions might differ, of course. But I suspect that most of us would have the great figures of the history of science high on our list. Aristotle, Newton, Dalton, Mendel— these are some of the names that would be on my list of Grand Masters at the "game" of reasoning. If one is a reliabilist, however, there is something quite odd about this list. For in each case the theories for which the thinker is best known, the theories they produced at the height of their cognitive powers, have turned out not to be true. Nor is this an idiosyncratic feature of this particular collection of thinkers. It is a commonplace observation in the history of science that much of the best work of many of the best scientific thinkers of the past has turned out to be mistaken. In some cases historical figures seem to be getting "closer" to the truth than their predecessors. But in other cases they seem to be getting further away. And in many cases this notoriously obscure notion of "closer to the truth" seems to make little sense.

The conclusion that I would draw here is that if we adopt the strategy of locating good reasoners by assessing the *truth* of their best products, we will end up studying the wrong class of thinkers. For some of the best examples of human reasoning that we know of do not typically end up producing true theories. If we want to know how to do a good job of reasoning—if we want to be able to do it the way Newton did it—then we had better not focus our attention exclusively on thinkers who got the right answer.

4. Pragmatism: There Are No Special Cognitive Goals or Virtues

The project sketched in the previous section might be thought of as having two parts. The first part was entirely normative. It was claimed that truth was a quite special cognitive virtue, and that achieving true beliefs was the goal in terms of which strategies of reasoning should be evaluated. The second part was empirical. Having decided that good cognition was cognition that produced true belief, we try to identify people who excel by that measure, and then study the way they go about the business of reasoning. Using the terminology suggested in Section 1, the project is a version of Weak Naturalism. Science, broadly construed, can tell us which reasoners do a good job at producing true beliefs, and what strategies of reasoning they exploit. But science can't either confirm or discon-firm the initial normative step. Science can't tell us by what standard strategies of rea-soning *should* be evaluated. The critique of the project that I offered in the previous section was aimed entirely at the normative component. It is, I argued, far from obvious that producing true beliefs is the standard against which strategies of reasoning should be measured.

But if truth is not to be the standard in epistemology, what is? The answer that I favor is one that plays a central role in the pragmatist tradition. For pragmatists, there are *no* special cognitive or epistemological values. There are just *values*. Reasoning, inquiry, and cognition are viewed as tools that we use in an effort to achieve what we value. And like any other tools, they are to be assessed by determining how good a job they do at achieving what we value. So on the pragmatist view, the good cognitive strategies for a person to use are those that are likely to lead to the states of affairs that he or she finds intrinsically valuable. This is, of course, a thoroughly relativistic account of good reasoning. For if two people have significantly different intrinsic values, then it may well turn out that a strategy of reasoning that is good for one may be quite poor for the other. There is, in the pragma-tist tradition, a certain tendency to down play or even deny the epistemic relativism to which pragmatism leads. But on my view this failure of nerve is a great mistake. Rela-tivism in the evaluation of reasoning strategies is no more worrisome than relativism in the evaluation of diets or investment strategies or exercise programs. The fact that dif-ferent strategies of reasoning may be good for different people is a fact of life that prag-matists should accept with equanimity.[10]

As I envision it, the pragmatist project for assessing reasoning strategies proceeds as follows. First, we must determine which goal or goals are of interest for the assessment at hand. We must decide what it is that we want our reasoning to achieve. This step, of course, is fundamentally normative. Empirical inquiry may be of help in making the decision, but science alone will not tell you what your goals are. Thus the pragmatist's project, like the reliabilist's, is a version of Weak Naturalism. The second step is to locate people who have done a good job at achieving the goal or goals selected. The third step—and typically it is here that most of the hard work comes in—is to discover the strategies of reasoning and inquiry that these successful subjects have used in achieving the speci-fied goal. Just as in the case of chess, the expectation is that if we can discover the strat-egies used by those who have done a good job at achieving the goals we value, these will be good strategies for us to use as well. But we need not assume that they are the best possible strategies. It may well be that once we gain some understanding of the strategies used by people who have excelled in achieving the specified goals, we may find ways of improving on their strategies. Exploring the possibility of improving on the actual strat-egies of successful cognitive agents is the fourth step in the pragmatist project.

---

10. For more on pragmatism and relativism, see Stich 1990, Section 6.2.

5. Herbert Simon's Computational Pragmatism

The pragmatist project sketched in the previous section is of a piece with the epistemological theory I defended in *The Fragmentation of Reason*. Shortly after that book was completed I was delighted to discover that for more than two decades Herbert Simon and his colleagues had been hard at work on a project that had all the essential features of the one I have proposed. They had long been practicing what I had only recently started to preach.[11]

Simon's project is an ambitious research program in artificial intelligence. He characterizes the project, rather provocatively, as an attempt to construct a "logic of scientific discovery." The "logic" that Simon seeks would be an explicit set of principles for reasoning and the conduct of inquiry which, when followed systematically, will result in the production of good scientific hypotheses and theories. As is generally the case in artificial intelligence, the principles must be explicit enough to be programmed on a computer. Simon and his co-workers don't propose to construct their logic of discovery by relying on *a priori* principles or philosophical arguments about how science should proceed; their approach is much more empirical. To figure out how to produce good scientific theories, they study and try to simulate what good scientists do. In some ways their project is quite similar to "expert systems" studies in AI. The initial goal is to produce a computational simulation of the reasoning of people who are "experts" at doing science.

Though Simon does not stress the point, he acknowledges that a largely parallel project might be undertaken with the goal of simulating the reasoning of some other class of "experts." We might, for example, focus on the reasoning of people who have done outstanding work in history, or in literary criticism, or in theology. In some of these cases (or all of them) we might end up with pretty much the same principles of reasoning. But then again, we might not. It might well turn out that different strategies of reasoning work best in different domains. The choice of which group of reasoners to study—and ultimately, the choice of which strategy to use in one's own reasoning—is the initial normative step in Simon's pragmatic project.

Having decided that the reasoning he wants to study is the sort that leads to success in science, the second step in Simon's project is to identify people who have achieved scientific success. As a practical matter, of course, this is easy enough. There is a fair amount of agreement on who the great scientists of the past have been. But when pressed to provide some justification for the scientists he selects, Simon (only half jokingly) suggests the

---

11. The literature in this area is extensive and growing quickly. While Simon is clearly a seminal figure, many others have done important work. In much of what follows, "Simon" should be read as shorthand for "Simon and his co-workers." Perhaps the best place to get an overview of Simon's work in this area is in Langley, Simon, Bradshaw, and Zytkow 1987. For a review of more recent work see Shrager and Langley 1990b and the other essays in Shrager and Langley 1990a. Other useful sources include Simon 1966, 1973; Buchanan 1983; Kulkarni and Simon 1988, 1990; Zytkow and Simon 1988; Thagard 1988.

following way to "operationalize" the choice: Go to the library and get a collection of the most widely used basic textbooks in various fields. Then sit down and make a list of the people whose pictures appear in the textbooks. Those are the people whose reasoning we should study. Though I rather doubt that Simon has ever actually done this, the joke makes a serious point. The criterion of success that Simon is using is not the *truth* of the theories that various scientists produce. To be a successful scientist, as Simon construes the notion, is to be famous enough to get one's picture in the textbooks.

With a list of successful scientists at hand, the really challenging part of Simon's project can begin. The goal is to build a computational simulation of the cognitive processes that led successful scientists to their most celebrated discoveries. To do this, a fair amount of historical information is required, since optimally the input to the simulation should include as much as can be discovered about the data available to the scientist who is the target of the simulation, along with information about the received theories and background assumptions that the scientist was likely to bring to the project. As with other efforts at cognitive simulation, there is a variety of evidence that can be used to confirm or disconfirm the simulation as it develops. First, of course, the simulation must end up producing the same law or theory that the target scientist produced. Second, the simulation should go through intermediate steps parallel to those that the scientist went through in the course of making his or her discovery. In some cases, laboratory notebooks and other historical evidence provide a quite rich portrait of the inferential steps (and missteps) that the target scientist made along the way. But in most cases the details of the scientist's reasoning are at best very sketchy. In an effort to generate more data against which the simulation can be tested, Simon and his co-workers have used laboratory studies of problem solving and "rediscovery" in which talented students are asked to come up with a law or theory that will capture a set of data, where the data provided are at least roughly similar to the data available to the target scientist. While they are working, the students are asked to "think out loud" and explain the various steps they make. The problems are often very hard ones, and relatively few students succeed. But the protocols generated by the successful students can be used as another source of data against which simulation programs can be tested (Kulkarni and Simon 1988; Dunbar 1989; Qin and Simon 1990).

It should be stressed that there is no *a priori* guarantee that Simon's research program will be successful. There is a long tradition which insists that scientific creativity, indeed all creativity, is a deeply mysterious process, far beyond the reach of computational theories. And even if we don't accept the mystery theory of creativity, it is entirely possible that efforts to simulate the reasoning which led one or another important scientist to a great discovery will fail. The only way to silence these concerns is to deliver the goods. It is also possible that while each individual scientist's reasoning can be simulated successfully, each case is different. There might be no interesting regularities that all cases of successful scientific reasoning share. Perhaps successful scientific reasoning is discipline specific, and different strategies of reasoning are successful in different disciplines. Worse still, it might turn out that no two successful scientists exploit the same strategies. Styles of successful reasoning might be entirely idiosyncratic. Having noted these concerns, however, I should also note that it doesn't look like things *are* turning out this way. While there is still lots of work to be done, Simon and his group have produced impressive simulations of Kepler's discovery of his third law, Krebs' discovery of the urea cycle, and a variety of other important scientific discoveries. While some of the heuristics used in these simulations are specific to a particular scientific domain, none are specific to a particular problem, and many appear to be domain independent (Kulkarni and Simon 1990, Section 5). So, though the jury is still out, I think it is entirely reasonable to view Simon's successes to date as an excellent beginning on the sort of pragmatist naturalization of epistemology that I advocated in the previous section. In the final section of this paper, I want to consider some of the ways in which Simon-style pragmatist projects may develop in the future.

6. Beyond History's Best: Future Projects for Naturalistic Pragmatism

The project of simulating successful scientific reasoning is the one that has preoccupied Simon and his co-workers up until now. However, once some substantial success has been achieved along these lines—and it is my reading of the situation that we are now at just about that stage—it becomes possible to explore some new and very exciting territory. As the historical record indicates, important discoveries are often slow in coming and they frequently involve steps that later come to be seen as unnecessary or unfruitful. To the extent that simulations like Simon's have as their goal understanding the details of the psychological process that lead to discoveries, it is, of course, a virtue if they explore blind alleys just where the scientists they were modeling did. However, if we want a normative rather than a descriptive theory of discovery, it is no particular virtue to mimic the mistaken steps and wasted efforts of gifted scientists. Thus rather than aiming to describe the cognitive strategies of gifted scientists, we might aspire to *improve* on those strategies. By tinkering with the program—or, more interestingly, by developing a substantive theory of how and why they work—we may well be able to design programs that do *better* than real people, including very gifted and highly trained people, be they important historical figures or clever students in laboratory studies of reasoning. I think that to a certain extent this sort of tinkering and theory-driven improvement is already a part of Simon's project, though it is often not clearly separated from the process of modeling actual discovery. The process of improvement can be pursued along several rather different lines. What distinguishes them is the sort of constraints that the computational model takes to be important. In the remaining pages of this paper I want to sketch some of the *constraints* that might be imposed or ignored, and consider the sorts of projects that might ensue.

A first division turns on how much importance we attach to the idea that normative rules and strategies of reasoning have to be usable by human beings. To the extent that we take that constraint seriously, we will not propose strategies of reasoning that are difficult or impossible for a human cognitive system. Our normative theory will respect the limitations imposed by human psychology and human hardware. A natural label for this project might be *Human Epistemology*. Of course, the more our normative theory of Human Epistemology respects the limits and idiosyncrasies of human cognition, the closer it will resemble the descriptive theory of good reasoning. But there is no reason to think that the two will collapse. For it may well be the case that there are readily learnable and readily usable strategies of reasoning that would improve on those that were in fact used in the "exemplary" cases of scientific discovery. In order to pursue Human Epistemology in a serious way we will need detailed information about the nature and the rigidity of constraints on human cognition. And the only way to get this information is to do the relevant empirical work. This is yet another way in which the sort of naturalized epistemology that I am advocating requires input from empirical science.[12]

What happens if we are not much concerned with constraining our epistemological system by taking account of the facts of human cognition? We aren't free of all constraints, since the commitment to construct theories of scientific discovery that are explicit enough to be *programmable* imposes its own constraints. The theories we build must be implementable with available hardware and available software. But, of course, there are lots of things that available systems can do quite easily that human brains cannot do at all. So if we are prepared to ignore the facts about human cognition, we are likely to get a very different family of normative theories of scientific discovery. In recent work, Clark Glymour has introduced the term *Android Epistemology*, and I think that would be an ideal label to borrow for normative theories like these.

If there were more space available, I would spend it exploring the prospects for Android Epistemology. For it seems to me that they are very exciting prospects indeed. What is slowly emerging from the work of Simon's group, and from the work of other groups focusing on related problems, is, in effect, a *technology of discovery*. We are beginning to see the development of artifacts that can discover useful laws, useful concepts, and useful theories. It is, of course, impossible to know how successful these efforts will ultimately be. But I, for one, would not be at all surprised if future historians viewed this work as a major juncture in human intellectual history.

Let me return to the domain of Human Epistemology. For there is one more distinction that needs to be drawn here. Once again the notion of constraints provides a convenient way to draw the distinction. One of the facts about real human cognizers is that they are embedded in a social context. They get information and support from other people, they compete with others in various ways, and their work is judged by others. Many of the rewards for their efforts come from the surrounding society as the result of

---

12. For some interesting studies aimed at discovering how much plasticity there is in human reasoning, see the papers in Nisbett 1993, Part VI.

these judgments. In building our *Normative Human Epistemology* we may choose to take account of these factors or to ignore them.

In their work to date, Simon and his colleagues have largely chosen to ignore these social constraints. And for good reason. Things are complicated enough already, without trying to see how well our simulations do when competing with other simulations in a complex social environment. Nonetheless, I think there may ultimately be a great deal to learn by taking the social constraints seriously, and exploring what we might label *Social Epistemology*. For example, Philip Kitcher (1990) has recently tried to show that the likely payoff of pursuing long shots in science—the expected utility of working hard to defend implausible theories—depends in important ways on the distribution of intellectual labor in the rest of the community. I think there is reason to hope that if we take seriously the idea of building epistemological theories for socially embedded cognitive agents we may begin to find ways in which the organization of the inquiring community itself may be improved. We may find better ways to fund research, channel intellectual effort, deal with dishonesty, and distribute rewards. As a pragmatist, I can think of no finer future for epistemology.[13]

REFERENCES

Buchanan, B. 1983. Mechanizing the Search for Explanatory Hypotheses. In P. Asquith and T. Nichols, eds., *PSA 1982*, vol. 2. East Lansing, MI: Philosophy of Science Association.
Dunbar, K. 1989. Scientific Reasoning Strategies in a Simulated Molecular Genetics Environment. In *Proceedings of the Eleventh Annual Meeting of the Cognitive Science Society*. Ann Arbor, MI: Erlbaum.
Foerstl, H. 1990. Capgras' delusion. *Comprehensive Psychiatry* 31: 447–49.
Fong, G., D. Krantz, and R. Nisbett. 1986. The Effects of Statistical Training on Thinking About Everyday Problems. *Cognitive Psychology* 18: 253–92.
Goldman, A. 1986. *Epistemology and Cognition*. Cambridge, MA: Harvard University Press.
Kahneman, D., P. Slovic, and A. Tversky, eds. 1982. *Judgment Under Uncertainty*. Cambridge: Cambridge University Press.
Kim, J. 1988. What Is "Naturalized Epistemology"? *Philosophical Perspectives* 2: 381–405.
Kitcher, P. 1990. The Division of Cognitive Labor. *Journal of Philosophy* 87: 5–22.
———. 1992. The Naturalists Return. *Philosophical Review* 101: 53–114.
Kornblith, H., ed. 1985a. *Naturalizing Epistemology*. Cambridge, MA: MIT Press.
———. 1985b. What Is Naturalistic Epistemology? In Kornblith 1985a, 1–13.

13. Earlier versions of this paper were presented at the Conference on Methods at the New School for Social Research, the Southern Society for Philosophy and Psychology, the Australasian Association for Philosophy and the conference on Philosophy and Cognitive Science at the University of Birmingham. I am grateful to the audiences at all these meetings for many helpful suggestions. Thanks are also due to Peter Klein for extended comments on the penultimate version of the paper, and to Paul Lodge for help in preparing the final version of the manuscript.

Kulkarni, D., and H. Simon. 1988. The Processes of Scientific Discovery: The Strategy of Experimentation. *Cognitive Science* 12: 139–75.

———. 1990. Experimentation in Machine Discovery. In Shrager and Langley 1990a.

Langley, P., H. Simon, G. Bradshaw, and J. Zytkow. 1987. *Scientific Discovery: Computational Explorations of the Creative Processes*. Cambridge, MA: MIT Press.

Nisbett, R., ed. 1993. *Rules for Reasoning*. Hillsdale, NJ: Erlbaum.

Nisbett, R., G. Fong, D. Lehman, and P. Cheng. 1987. Teaching Reasoning. *Science* 238: 625–31.

Nisbett, R., and L. Ross. 1980. *Human Inference*. Englewood Cliffs, NJ: Prentice-Hall.

Qin, Y., and H. Simon. 1990. Laboratory Replication of Scientific Discovery Processes. *Cognitive Science* 14: 281–312.

Quine, W. 1969a. *Ontological Relativity and Other Essays*. New York: Columbia University Press.

———. 1969b. Epistemology Naturalized. In Quine 1969a, 69–90. Reprinted in Kornblith 1985a.

———. 1969c. Natural Kinds. In Quine 1969a, 114–38. Reprinted in Kornblith 1985a.

———. 1975. The Nature of Natural Knowledge. In S. Guttenplan, ed., *Mind and Language*. Oxford: Clarendon Press.

Rorty, R. 1979. *Philosophy and the Mirror of Nature*. Princeton: Princeton University Press.

———. 1982. *Consequences of Pragmatism*. Minneapolis: University of Minnesota Press.

———. 1988. Representation, Social Practice, and Truth. *Philosophical Studies* 54: 215–28.

Shrager, J., and P. Langley, eds. 1990a. *Computational Models of Scientific Discovery and Theory Formation*. San Mateo, CA: Morgan Kaufmann Publishers.

———. 1990b. Computational Approaches to Scientific Discovery. In Shrager and Langley 1990a.

Simon, H. 1966. Scientific Discovery and the Psychology of Problem Solving. In R. Colodny, ed., *Mind and Cosmos: Essays in Contemporary Science and Philosophy*. Pittsburgh: University of Pittsburgh Press.

———. 1973. Does Scientific Discovery Have a Logic? *Philosophy of Science* 40: 471–80.

Stich, S. 1990. *The Fragmentation of Reason*. Cambridge, MA: MIT Press.

———. 1991a. *The Fragmentation of Reason*—Precis of Two Chapters. *Philosophy and Phenomenological Research* 51: 179–83.

———. 1991b. Evaluating Cognitive Strategies: A Reply to Cohen, Goldman, Harman and Lycan. *Philosophy and Phenomenological Research* 51: 207–213.

Thagard, P. 1988. *Computational Philosophy of Science*. Cambridge, MA: MIT Press.

Zytkow, J., and H. Simon. 1988. Normative Systems of Discovery and Logic of Search. *Synthese* 74: 65–90.

7

RETHINKING RATIONALITY

From Bleak Implications to Darwinian Modules

Richard Samuels, Stephen Stich, and Patrice D. Tremoulet

1 Introduction

THERE IS A venerable philosophical tradition that views human beings as intrinsically rational, though even the most ardent defender of this view would admit that under certain circumstances people's decisions and thought processes can be very irrational indeed. When people are extremely tired, or drunk, or in the grip of rage, they sometimes reason and act in ways that no account of rationality would condone. About 30 years ago, Amos Tversky, Daniel Kahneman, and a number of other psychologists began reporting findings suggesting much deeper problems with the traditional idea that human beings are intrinsically rational animals. What these studies demonstrated is that even under quite ordinary circumstances where fatigue, drugs, and strong emotions are not factors, people reason and make judgments in ways that systematically violate familiar canons of rationality on a wide array of problems. Those first surprising studies sparked the growth of a major research tradition whose impact has been felt in economics, political theory, medicine, and other areas far removed from cognitive science. In section 2, we will sketch a few of the better-known experimental findings in this area. We've chosen these particular findings because they will play a role at a later stage of the paper. For readers who would like a deeper, more systematic account of the fascinating and disquieting research on reasoning and judgment, there are now several excellent texts and anthologies available (Nisbett and Ross 1980; Kahneman, Slovic, and Tversky 1982; Baron 1988; Piattelli-Palmarini 1994; Dawes 1988; Sutherland 1994).

Though there is little doubt that most of the experimental results reported in the literature are robust and can be readily replicated, there is considerable debate over what these experiments indicate about the intrinsic rationality of ordinary people. One widely discussed interpretation of the results claims that they have "bleak implications" for the rationality of the man and woman in the street. What the studies show, according to this interpretation, is that ordinary people lack the underlying *competence* to handle a wide array of reasoning tasks, and thus that they must exploit a collection of simple *heuristics* which often lead to seriously counter-normative conclusions. Advocates of this interpretation would, of course, acknowledge that there are some people who have mastered the correct rules or procedures for handling some of these problems. But, they maintain, this knowledge is hard to acquire and hard to use. It is not the sort of knowledge that the human mind acquires readily or spontaneously in normal environments, and even those who have it often do not use it unless they make a special effort. In section 3, we will elaborate on this interpretation and explain the technical notion of competence that it invokes.

The pessimistic interpretation of the experimental findings has been challenged in a number of ways. One of the most recent and intriguing of these challenges comes from the emerging interdisciplinary field of evolutionary psychology. Evolutionary psychologists defend a highly *modular* conception of mental architecture, which views the mind as composed of a large number of special-purpose information-processing organs, or "modules," that have been shaped by natural selection to handle the sorts of recurrent information-processing problems that confronted our hunter-gatherer forebears. Since good performance on a variety of reasoning tasks would likely have served our Pleistocene ancestors in good stead, evolutionary psychologists hypothesize that we should have evolved mental modules for handling these tasks well. However, they also maintain that the modules should be well adapted to the sorts of information that was available in the pre-human and early human environment. Thus, they hypothesize, when information is presented in the right way, performance on reasoning tasks should improve dramatically. In section 4 we will offer a more detailed sketch of the richly modular picture of the mind advanced by evolutionary psychologists and of the notion of a mental module that plays a fundamental role in that picture. We will also take a brief look at the sorts of arguments offered by evolutionary psychologists for their contention that the mind is massively modular. Then, in section 5, we will consider several recent studies that appear to confirm the evolutionary psychologists' prediction: When information is presented in ways that would have been important in our evolutionary history, performance on reasoning tasks soars. While the arguments and the experimental evidence offered by evolutionary psychologists are tantalizing, they hardly constitute a conclusive case for the evolutionary psychologists' theory about the mind and its origins. But a detailed critique of that theory would be beyond the scope of this essay. Rather, what we propose to do in our final section is to ask a hypothetical question: If the evolutionary psychologists' account turns out to be on the right track, what implications would this have for questions about the nature and the extent of human rationality or irrationality?

2 Exploring Human Reasoning and Judgment: Four Examples

2.1 THE SELECTION TASK

In 1966, Peter Wason reported the first experiments using a cluster of reasoning problems that came to be called the *selection task*. A recent textbook on reasoning has described that task as "the most intensively researched single problem in the history of the psychology of reasoning" (Evans, Newstead, and Byrne 1993, 99). A typical example of a selection task problem is shown in figure 7.1.

Here are four cards. Each of them has a letter on one side and a number on the other side. Two of these cards are shown with the letter side up, and two with the number side up.

Indicate which of these cards you have to turn over in order to determine whether the following claim is true: **If a card has a vowel on one side, then it has an odd number on the other side.**

FIGURE 7.1

What Wason and numerous other investigators have found is that subjects typically do very poorly on questions like this. Most subjects respond, correctly, that the E card must be turned over, but many also judge that the 5 card must be turned over, despite the fact that the 5 card could not falsify the claim no matter what is on the other side. Also, a large majority of subjects judge that the 4 card need *not* be turned over, though without turning it over there is no way of knowing whether it has a vowel on the other side. And, of course, if it does have a vowel on the other side then the claim is not true. It is not the case that subjects do poorly on all selection task problems, however. A wide range of variations on the basic pattern have been tried, and on some versions of the problem a much larger percentage of subjects answer correctly. These results form a bewildering pattern, since there is no obvious feature or cluster of features that separates versions on which subjects do well from those on which they do poorly. As we will see in section 5, some evolutionary psychologists have argued that these results can be explained if we focus on the sorts of mental mechanisms that would have been crucial for reasoning about social exchange (or "reciprocal altruism") in the environment of our hominid forebears. The versions of the selection task we're good at, these theorists maintain, are just the ones that those mechanisms would have been designed to handle. But, as we will also see in section 5, this explanation is hardly uncontroversial.

2.2 THE CONJUNCTION FALLACY

Ronald Reagan was elected President of the United States in November 1980. The following month, Amos Tversky and Daniel Kahneman administered a questionnaire to 93 subjects who had had no formal training in statistics. The instructions on the questionnaire were as follows:

> In this questionnaire you are asked to evaluate the probability of various events that may occur during 1981. Each problem includes four possible events. Your task is to rank order these events by probability, using 1 for the most probable event, 2 for the second, 3 for the third and 4 for the least probable event.

Here is one of the questions presented to the subjects:

> Please rank order the following events by their probability of occurrence in 1981:
> (a) Reagan will cut federal support to local government.
> (b) Reagan will provide federal support for unwed mothers.
> (c) Reagan will increase the defense budget by less than 5%.
> (d) Reagan will provide federal support for unwed mothers and cut federal support to local governments.

The unsettling outcome was that 68 percent of the subjects rated (d) as more probable than (b), despite the fact that (d) could not happen unless (b) did (Tversky and Kahneman 1982). In another experiment, which has since become quite famous, Tversky and Kahneman (1982) presented subjects with the following task:

> Linda is 31 years old, single, outspoken, and very bright. She majored in philosophy. As a student, she was deeply concerned with issues of discrimination and social justice, and also participated in anti-nuclear demonstrations.
> Please rank the following statements by their probability, using 1 for the most probable and 8 for the least probable.
> (a) Linda is a teacher in elementary school.
> (b) Linda works in a bookstore and takes Yoga classes.
> (c) Linda is active in the feminist movement.
> (d) Linda is a psychiatric social worker.
> (e) Linda is a member of the League of Women Voters.
> (f) Linda is a bank teller.
> (g) Linda is an insurance salesperson.
> (h) Linda is a bank teller and is active in the feminist movement.

In a group of naive subjects with no background in probability and statistics, 89 percent judged that statement (h) was more probable than statement (f). When the same question was presented to statistically sophisticated subjects—graduate students in the decision science program of the Stanford Business School—85 percent made the same judgment! Results of this sort, in which subjects judge that a compound event or state of affairs is more probable than one of the components of the compound, have been found repeatedly since Kahneman and Tversky's pioneering studies.

2.3 BASE-RATE NEGLECT

On the familiar Bayesian account, the probability of a hypothesis on a given body of evidence depends, in part, on the prior probability of the hypothesis. However, in a series of elegant experiments, Kahneman and Tversky (1973) showed that subjects often seriously undervalue the importance of prior probabilities. One of these experiments presented half of the subjects with the following "cover story."

> A panel of psychologists have interviewed and administered personality tests to 30 engineers and 70 lawyers, all successful in their respective fields. On the basis of this information, thumbnail descriptions of the 30 engineers and 70 lawyers have been written. You will find on your forms five descriptions, chosen at random from the 100 available descriptions. For each description, please indicate your probability that the person described is an engineer, on a scale from 0 to 100.

The other half of the subjects were presented with the same text, except the "base rates" were reversed. They were told that the personality tests had been administered to 70 engineers and 30 lawyers. Some of the descriptions that were provided were designed to be compatible with the subjects' stereotypes of engineers, though not with their stereotypes of lawyers. Others were designed to fit the lawyer stereotype, but not the engineer stereotype. And one was intended to be quite neutral, giving subjects no information at all that would be of use in making their decision. Here are two examples, the first intended to sound like an engineer, the second intended to sound neutral:

> Jack is a 45-year-old man. He is married and has four children. He is generally conservative, careful and ambitious. He shows no interest in political and social issues and spends most of his free time on his many hobbies which include home carpentry, sailing, and mathematical puzzles.
>   Dick is a 30-year-old man. He is married with no children. A man of high ability and high motivation, he promises to be quite successful in his field. He is well liked by his colleagues.

As expected, subjects in both groups thought that the probability that Jack is an engineer is quite high. Moreover, in what seems to be a clear violation of Bayesian principles, the difference in cover stories between the two groups of subjects had almost no effect at all.

The neglect of base-rate information was even more striking in the case of Dick. That description was constructed to be totally uninformative with regard to Dick's profession. Thus the only useful information that subjects had was the base-rate information provided in the cover story. But that information was entirely ignored. The median probability estimate in both groups of subjects was 50 percent. Kahneman and Tversky's subjects were not, however, completely insensitive to base-rate information. Following the five descriptions on their form, subjects found the following "null" description:

> Suppose now that you are given no information whatsoever about an individual chosen at random from the sample.
> The probability that this man is one of the 30 engineers [or, for the other group of subjects: one of the 70 engineers] in the sample of 100 is ___%.

In this case subjects relied entirely on the base rate; the median estimate was 30 percent for the first group of subjects and 70 percent for the second. In their discussion of these experiments, Nisbett and Ross offer this interpretation.

> The implication of this contrast between the "no information" and "totally nondiagnostic information" conditions seems clear. When *no* specific evidence about the target case is provided, prior probabilities are utilized appropriately; when *worthless* specific evidence is given, prior probabilities may be largely ignored, and people respond as if there were no basis for assuming differences in relative likelihoods. People's grasp of the relevance of base-rate information must be very weak if they could be distracted from using it by exposure to useless target case information. (Nisbett and Ross 1980, 145–46)

Before leaving the topic of base-rate neglect, we want to offer one further example illustrating the way in which the phenomenon might well have serious practical consequences. Here is a problem that Casscells et al. (Casscells, Schoenberger, and Grayboys 1978) presented to a group of faculty, staff, and fourth-year students at Harvard Medical School.

> If a test to detect a disease whose prevalence is 1/1000 has a false positive rate of 5%, what is the chance that a person found to have a positive result actually has the disease, assuming that you know nothing about the person's symptoms or signs? ___%

Under the most plausible interpretation of the problem, the correct Bayesian answer is 2 percent. But only 18 percent of the Harvard audience gave an answer close to 2 percent. Forty-five percent of this distinguished group completely ignored the base-rate information and said that the answer was 95 percent.

2.4 OVERCONFIDENCE

One of the most extensively investigated and most worrisome clusters of phenomena explored by psychologists interested in reasoning and judgment involves the degree of confidence that people have in their responses to factual questions—questions like:

In each of the following pairs, which city has more inhabitants?
(a) Las Vegas   (b) Miami
(a) Sydney   (b) Melbourne
(a) Hyderabad   (b) Islamabad
(a) Bonn   (b) Heidelberg

In each of the following pairs, which historical event happened first?
(a) Signing of the Magna Carta   (b) Birth of Mohammed
(a) Death of Napoleon   (b) Louisiana Purchase
(a) Lincoln's assassination   (b) Birth of Queen Victoria

After each answer subjects are also asked:

How confident are you that your answer is correct?
50% 60% 70% 80% 90% 100%

In an experiment using relatively hard questions it is typical to find that for the cases in which subjects say they are 100 percent confident, only about 80 percent of their answers are correct; for cases in which they say that they are 90 percent confident, only about 70 percent of their answers are correct; and for cases in which they say that they are 80 percent confident, only about 60 percent of their answers are correct. This tendency to overconfidence seems to be very robust. Warning subjects that people are often overconfident has no significant effect, nor does offering them money (or bottles of French champagne) as a reward for accuracy. Moreover, the phenomenon has been demonstrated in a wide variety of subject populations, including undergraduates, graduate students, physicians, and even CIA analysts. (For a survey of the literature see Lichtenstein, Fischhoff, and Phillips 1982.)

3 Bleak Implications: Shortcomings in Reasoning Competence

The experimental results we've been recounting and the many related results reported in the extensive literature in this area are, we think, intrinsically disquieting. They are even more alarming if, as has occasionally been demonstrated, the same patterns of reasoning and judgment are to be found outside the laboratory. None of us want our illnesses to be diagnosed by physicians who ignore well-confirmed information about base rates. Nor do we want our public officials to be advised by CIA analysts who are systematically overconfident. The experimental results themselves do not entail any conclusions about the nature or the normative status of the cognitive mechanisms that underlie people's reasoning and judgment. But a number of writers have urged that these results lend considerable support to a pessimistic hypothesis about those mechanisms, a hypothesis which may be even more disquieting than the results themselves. On this view, the examples of faulty reasoning and judgment that we've sketched are not mere *performance errors*. Rather, they indicate that most people's underlying *reasoning competence* is irrational or at least normatively problematic. In order to explain this view more clearly, we'll have to back up a bit and explain the rather technical distinction between competence and performance on which it is based.

The competence/performance distinction, as we will characterize it, was first introduced into cognitive science by Chomsky, who used it in his account of the explanatory strategy of theories in linguistics (Chomsky 1965, ch. 1; 1975; 1980). In testing linguistic theories, an important source of data are the "intuitions" or unreflective judgments that speakers of a language make about the grammaticality of sentences and about various linguistic properties (e.g., Is the sentence ambiguous?) and relations (e.g., Is this phrase the subject of that verb?). To explain these intuitions, and also to explain how speakers go about producing and understanding sentences of their language in ordinary speech, Chomsky and his followers proposed what has become one of the most important hypotheses about the mind in the history of cognitive science. What this hypothesis claims is that a speaker of a language has an internally represented grammar of that language—an integrated set of generative rules and principles that entail an infinite number of claims about the language. For each of the infinite number of sentences in the speaker's language, the internally represented grammar entails that it is grammatical; for each ambiguous sentence in the speaker's language, the grammar entails that it is ambiguous, etc. When speakers make the judgments that we call "linguistic intuitions," the information in the internally represented grammar is typically accessed and relied upon, though neither the process nor the internally represented grammar is accessible to consciousness. Since the internally represented grammar plays a central role in the production of linguistic intuitions, those intuitions can serve as an important source of data for linguists trying to specify what the rules and principles of the internally represented grammar are.

A speaker's intuitions are not, however, an infallible source of information about the grammar of the speaker's language, because the grammar cannot produce linguistic intuitions by itself. The production of intuitions is a complex process in which the internally represented grammar must interact with a variety of other cognitive mechanisms, including those subserving perception, motivation, attention, short-term memory, and perhaps a host of others. In certain circumstances, the activity of any one of these mechanisms may result in a person offering a judgment about a sentence which does not accord with what the grammar actually entails about that sentence. The attention mechanism offers a clear example of this phenomenon. It is very likely the case that the grammar internally represented in typical English-speakers entails that an infinite number of sentences of the form

A told B that p, and B told C that q, and C told D that r, and . . .

are grammatical in the speaker's language. However, if the present authors were asked to judge the grammaticality of a sentence containing a few hundred of these conjuncts, or perhaps even a few dozen, there is a good chance that our judgments would not reflect what our grammars entail, since in cases like this our attention easily wanders. Short-term memory provides a more interesting example of the way in which a grammatical judgment may fail to reflect the information actually contained in the grammar. There is considerable evidence indicating that the short-term memory mechanism has difficulty handling center-embedded structures. Thus it may well be the case that our internally represented grammars entail that the following sentence is grammatical:

What what what he wanted cost would buy in Germany was amazing.

though our intuitions suggest, indeed shout, that it is not.

Now in the jargon that Chomsky introduced, the rules and principles of a speaker's internalized grammar constitute the speaker's *linguistic competence*; the judgments a speaker makes about sentences, along with the sentences the speaker actually produces, are part of the speaker's *linguistic performance*. Moreover, as we have just seen, some of the sentences a speaker produces and some of the judgments the speaker makes about sentences will not accurately reflect the speaker's linguistic competence. In these cases, the speaker is making a *performance error*.

There are some obvious analogies between the phenomena studied in linguistics and those studied by cognitive scientists interested in reasoning. In both cases there is spontaneous and largely unconscious processing of an open-ended class of inputs; people are able to understand endlessly many sentences and to draw inferences from endlessly many premises. Also, in both cases, people are able to make spontaneous intuitive judgments about an effectively infinite class of cases—judgments about grammaticality, ambiguity, etc. in the case of linguistics, and judgments about validity, probability, etc. in the case of reasoning. Given these analogies, it is plausible to explore the idea that the mechanism underlying our ability to reason is similar to the mechanism underlying our capacity to process language. And if Chomsky is right about language, then the analogous hypothesis about reasoning would claim that people have an internally represented integrated set of rules and principles of reasoning—a "psycho-logic" as it has been called—which is usually accessed and relied upon when people draw inferences or make judgments about them. As in the case of language, we would expect that neither the processes involved nor the principles of the internally represented psycho-logic are readily accessible to consciousness. We should also expect that people's inferences and judgments would not be an infallible guide to what the underlying psycho-logic actually entails about the validity or plausibility of a given inference. For here, as in the case of language, the internally represented rules and principles must interact with lots of other cognitive mechanisms—including attention, motivation, short-term memory, and many others. The activity of these mechanisms can give rise to *performance errors*—inferences or judgments that do not reflect the psycho-logic which constitutes a person's *reasoning competence*.

There is, however, an important difference between reasoning and language, even if we assume that a Chomsky-style account of the underlying mechanism is correct in both cases. For in the case of language, it makes no clear sense to offer a normative assessment of a normal person's competence. The rules and principles that constitute a French-speaker's linguistic competence are significantly different from the rules and principles that underlie language processing in a Chinese-speaker. But if we were asked which system was better or which one was correct, we would have no idea what was being asked. Thus, on the language side of the analogy, there are performance errors, but there is no such thing as a competence error or a normatively problematic competence. If two otherwise normal people have different linguistic competences, then they simply speak different languages or different dialects. On the reasoning side of the analogy, things look very different. It is not clear whether there are significant individual and group differences in the rules and principles underlying people's performance on reasoning tasks, as there so clearly are in the rules and principles underlying people's linguistic performance. But if there are significant interpersonal differences in reasoning competence, it surely *appears* to make sense to ask whether one system of rules and principles is better than another.[1] If Adam's psycho-logic ignores base rates, endorses the conjunction fallacy, and approves of affirming the consequent, while Bertha's does not, then, in these respects at least, it seems natural to say that Bertha's reasoning competence is better than Adam's. And even if all normal humans share the same psycho-logic, it still makes sense to ask how rational it is. If everyone's psycho-logic contains rules that get the wrong answer on certain versions of the selection task, then we might well conclude that there is a normative shortcoming that we all share.

We are now, finally, in a position to explain the pessimistic hypothesis that some authors have urged to account for the sort of experimental results sketched in section 2. According to this hypothesis, the errors that subjects make in these experiments are very different from the sorts of reasoning errors that people make when their memory is over-extended or when their attention wanders. They are also different from the errors people make when they are tired or drunk or blind with rage. These are all examples of *performance errors*—errors that people make when they infer in ways that are *not* sanctioned by

---

1. Though at least one philosopher has argued that this appearance is deceptive. In an important and widely debated article, Cohen (1981) offers an account of what it is for reasoning rules to be normatively correct, and his account entails that a normal person's reasoning competence *must* be normatively correct. So on Cohen's view normal people can and do make lots of performance errors in both reasoning and language, but there is no such thing as a competence error in either domain. However, a number of critics, including one of the current authors, have argued that Cohen's account of what it is for reasoning rules to be correct is mistaken (Stich 1990, ch. 4). For Cohen's reply see Cohen 1986, and for a well-informed assessment of the debate, see Stein 1996.

their own psycho-logic. But the sorts of errors described in section 2 are *competence errors*. In these cases people *are* reasoning and judging in ways that accord with their psycho-logic. The subjects in these experiments do not use the right rules because they do not have access to them; they are not part of the subjects' internally represented reasoning competence. What they have instead is a collection of simpler rules, or "heuristics," that may often get the right answer, though it is also the case that often they do not. So, according to this bleak hypothesis, the subjects make mistakes because their psycho-logic is normatively defective; their internalized rules of reasoning are less than fully rational. It is not at all clear that Kahneman and Tversky would endorse this interpretation of the experimental results, though a number of other leading researchers clearly do.[2] According to Slovic, Fischhoff, and Lichtenstein, for example, "It appears that people lack the correct programs for many important judgmental tasks. ... We have not had the opportunity to evolve an intellect capable of dealing conceptually with uncertainty" (1976, 174).

Suppose it is in fact the case that many of the errors made in reasoning experiments are competence errors. This is not a flattering explanation, certainly, and it goes a long way toward undermining the traditional claim that man is a rational animal. But just how pessimistic a conclusion would it be? In part, the answer depends on how hard it would be to improve people's performance, and that in turn depends on how hard it is to improve reasoning competence. Very little is known about this at present.[3] By invoking evolution as an explanation of our defective competence, however, Slovic, Fischhoff, and Lichtenstein certainly do not encourage much optimism, since characteristics and limitations attributable to evolution are often innate, and innate limitations are not easy to overcome. The analogy with language points in much the same direction. For if Chomsky is right about language, then though it is obviously the case that people who speak different languages have internalized different grammars, the class of grammars that humans can internalize and incorporate into their language-processing mechanism is severely restricted, and a significant part of an adult's linguistic competence is innate. If reasoning competence is similar to language competence, then it may well be the case that many improvements are simply not psychologically possible, because our minds are not designed to reason well on these sorts of problems. This deeply pessimistic interpretation

---

2. In a frequently cited passage, Kahneman and Tversky write: "In making predictions and judgments under uncertainty, people do not appear to follow the calculus of chance or the statistical theory of prediction. Instead, they rely on a limited number of heuristics which sometimes yield reasonable judgments and sometimes lead to severe and systematic errors" (1973, 237). But this does not commit them to the claim that people do not follow the calculus of chance or the statistical theory of prediction because these are not part of their cognitive competence, and in a more recent paper they acknowledge that in *some* cases people *are* guided by the normatively appropriate rules (Kahneman and Tversky 1996, 587). So presumably they do not think that people are simply ignorant of the appropriate rules, only that they often do not exploit them when they should.

3. For some pioneering empirical explorations of this issue, see Nisbett et al. 1987; Lehman, Lempert, and Nisbett 1988; Lehman and Nisbett 1990.

of the experimental results has been endorsed by a number of well-known authors, including Stephen J. Gould, who makes the point with his characteristic panache.

> I am particularly fond of [the Linda] example, because I know that the [conjunc-
> tion] is least probable, yet a little homunculus in my head continues to jump up and
> down, shouting at me—"but she can't just be a bank teller; read the description." ...
> Why do we consistently make this simple logical error? Tversky and Kahneman
> argue, correctly I think, that our minds are not built (for whatever reason) to work
> by the rules of probability. (1992, 469)

It is important to be clear about what it means to claim that improving our reasoning
competence may be "psychologically impossible." In the case of language, people clearly
do learn to use artificial languages like BASIC and LISP, which violate many of the constraints that a Chomskian would claim that all natural (or "psychologically possible")
languages must satisfy. However, people do not acquire and use BASIC in the way they
acquire English or Arabic. Special effort and training are needed to learn it, and those
who have mastered it only use it in special circumstances. No one "speaks" BASIC or uses
it in the way that natural languages are used. Similarly, with special effort, it may be
possible to learn rules of reasoning that violate some of the constraints on "natural" or
"psychologically possible" rules and to use those rules in special circumstances. But in
confronting the myriad inferential challenges of everyday life, a person who had mastered
a non-natural (but normatively superior) rule would typically use a less demanding and
more natural "heuristic" rule. This is the point that Gould makes so vividly by conjuring
up a little homunculus jumping up and down in his head, and it might explain the otherwise surprising fact that graduate students in a prestigious decision science program are
no better than the rest of us at avoiding the conjunction fallacy.

As we noted in the introduction, there have been many attempts to challenge the pessimistic interpretation of the experimental findings on reasoning. In the two sections to
follow we will focus on one of the boldest and most intriguing of these, the challenge
from evolutionary psychology. If evolutionary psychologists are right, the rules and principles of reasoning available to ordinary people are much better than the "bleak implications" hypothesis would lead us to expect.

4 The Challenge from Evolutionary Psychology

In explaining the challenge from evolutionary psychology, the first order of business is to
say what evolutionary psychology is, and that is not an easy task since this interdisciplinary
field is too new to have developed any precise and widely agreed upon body of doctrines.
There are, however, two basic ideas that are clearly central to evolutionary psychology. The
first is that the mind consists of a large number of special-purpose systems—often called

"modules," or "mental organs." The second is that these systems, like other systems in the body, have been shaped by natural selection to perform specific functions or to solve information-processing problems that were important in the environment in which our hominid ancestors evolved. In this section, we propose to proceed as follows. First, in section 4.1, we'll take a brief look at some of the ways in which the notion of a "module" has been used in cognitive science and focus on the sorts of modules that evolutionary psychologists typically have in mind. In section 4.2, we will contrast the massively modular account of the mind favored by evolutionary psychologists with another widely discussed conception of the mind according to which modules play only a peripheral role. In section 4.3, we will consider an example of the sort of theoretical considerations that evolutionary psychologists have offered in support of their contention that the mind consists of large numbers of modules—and perhaps nothing else. Finally, in section 4.4, we will give a very brief sketch of the evolutionary psychology research strategy.

4.1 WHAT IS A MENTAL MODULE?

Though the term "module" has gained considerable currency in contemporary cognitive science, different theorists appear to use it in importantly different ways. In this section we will outline some of these uses, with the intention of getting a clearer picture of what evolutionary psychologists mean—and what they don't mean—by "module." The notions of modularity discussed in this section by no means exhaust the ways in which the term is used in contemporary cognitive science. For a more comprehensive review see Segal 1996.

When speaking of modules, cognitive scientists are typically referring to mental structures or components of the mind that can be invoked in order to explain various cognitive capacities. Moreover, it is ordinarily assumed that modules are domain-specific (or functionally specific), as opposed to domain-general. Very roughly, this means that modules are dedicated to solving restricted classes of problems in unique domains. For instance, the claim that there is a vision module implies that there are mental structures which are brought into play in the domain of visual processing and are not recruited in dealing with other cognitive tasks. Later in this section we will discuss the notion of domain specificity in greater detail. For the moment, however, we want to focus on the fact that the term "module" is used to refer to two fundamentally different sorts of mental structures. (i) Sometimes it is used to refer to systems of mental representations. (ii) On other occasions the term "module" is used in order to talk about computational mechanisms. We will call modules of the first sort *Chomskian modules* and modules of the second sort *computational modules*.

4.1.1 Chomskian Modules

A Chomskian module is a domain-specific body of mentally represented knowledge or information that accounts for a cognitive capacity. As the name suggests, the notion of a Chomskian module can be traced to Chomsky's work in linguistics. As we saw in section

3, Chomsky claims that our linguistic competence consists in the possession of an internally represented grammar of our natural language. This grammar is a paradigm example of what we mean when speaking of Chomskian modules. But, of course, Chomsky is not the only theorist who posits the existence of what we are calling Chomskian modules. For instance, developmental psychologists such as Susan Carey and Elizabeth Spelke have argued that young children have domain-specific, mentally represented theories—systems of principles—for physics, psychology, and mathematics (Carey and Spelke 1994). Theory-like structures of the sort posited by Carey and Spelke are an important kind of Chomskian module. However, if we assume that a theory is a *truth-evaluable* system of representations—that is, one in which it makes sense to ask whether the representations are true or false—then not all Chomskian modules must be theories. There can also be Chomskian modules that consist entirely of non-truth-evaluable systems of representations. There may, for example, be Chomskian modules that encode domain-specific knowledge of how to perform certain tasks—for example, how to play chess, how to do deductive reasoning, or how to detect cheaters in social exchange settings.

As we have already noted, a domain-specific mental structure is one that is dedicated to solving problems in a restricted domain. In the case of Chomskian modules, it is ordinarily assumed that they are dedicated in this way for a specific reason: the content of the representations that constitute a given Chomskian module represent only properties and objects that belong to a specific domain. So, for example, if physics is a domain, then a Chomskian module for physics will contain only information about physical properties and physical objects. Similarly, if geometry constitutes a domain, then a Chomskian module for geometry will contain only information about geometrical properties and objects.

There are many problems with trying to characterize the notion of a Chomskian module in more precise terms. Clearly we do not want to treat just any domain-specific collection of mental representations as a Chomskian module, since this would render the notion theoretically uninteresting. We do not, for example, want to treat a child's beliefs about toy dinosaurs as a module. Consequently, it is necessary to impose additional constraints, in order to develop a useful notion of a Chomskian module. Two commonly invoked constraints are (i) innateness and (ii) restrictions on information flow. So, for example, according to Chomsky, Universal Grammar is an innate system of mental representations, and most of the information that is contained in the Universal Grammar is not accessible to consciousness. (See Segal 1996 for an elaboration of these points.) We don't propose to pursue the issue of constraints any further, however, since, as will soon become clear, when evolutionary psychologists speak of modules, they are usually concerned with a rather different kind of module—a computational module.

4.1.2 Computational Modules

Computational modules are a species of computational device. As a first pass, we can characterize them as domain-specific, computational devices. A number of points of elaboration and clarification are in order, however. First, computational modules are ordinarily assumed to be classical computers—that is, symbol- (or representation-) manipulating devices which receive representations as inputs and manipulate them according to formally specifiable rules in order to generate representations (or actions) as outputs. (For detailed discussions of the notion of classical computation see Haugeland 1985 and Pylyshyn 1984.) Classical computers of this sort contrast sharply with certain sorts of connectionist computational systems, which cannot plausibly be viewed as symbol-manipulating devices.[4]

Second, it is ordinarily assumed that computational modules are dedicated to solving problems in a specific domain because they are only capable of carrying out computations on a restricted range of inputs—namely, representations of the properties and objects found in a particular domain (Fodor 1983, 103). So, for instance, if phonology constitutes a domain, then a phonology computational module will only provide analyses of inputs which are about phonological objects and properties. Similarly, if arithmetic is a domain, then an arithmetic computational module will only provide solutions to arithmetical problems.

Third, computational modules are usually assumed to be relatively autonomous components of the mind. Though they receive input from, and send output to, other cognitive processes or structures, they perform their own internal information processing unperturbed by external systems. For example, David Marr claims that the various computational modules on which parts of the visual process are implemented "are as nearly independent of each other as the overall task allows" (Marr 1982, 102).

Fourth, we want to emphasize the fact that computational modules are a very different kind of mental structure from Chomskian modules. Chomskian modules are *systems of representations.* By contrast, computational modules are processing devices—they *manipulate* representations. However, computational modules can coexist with Chomskian modules. Indeed, it may be that Chomskian modules, being bodies of information, are often manipulated by computational modules. Thus, for example, a parser might be conceived of as a computational module that deploys the contents of a Chomskian module devoted to linguistic information in order to generate syntactic and semantic representations of physical sentence-forms (Segal 1996, 144). Moreover, some Chomskian modules may be accessible only to a single computational module. When a Chomskian module and a computational module are linked in this way, it is natural to think of the two as a unit, which we might call a *Chomskian/computational module.* But it is also important to note that the existence of Chomskian modules does not entail the existence of computational modules, since it is possible for a mind to contain Chomskian modules while not

---

4. Though we can't pursue the issue here, we see no reason why the notion of a connectionist computational module—i.e., a domain-specific, connectionist computational system—might not turn out to be a theoretically interesting notion. See Tanenhaus, Dell, and Carson 1987 for an early attempt to develop connectionist modules of this sort.

containing any computational modules. For example, while humans may possess domain-specific systems of knowledge for physics or geometry, it does not follow that we possess domain-specific computational mechanisms for processing information about physical objects or geometrical properties. Rather, it may be that such domain-specific knowledge is utilized by domain-general reasoning systems.

A final point worth making is that the notion of a computational module has been elaborated in a variety of different ways in the cognitive science literature. Most notably, Fodor (1983) developed a conception of modules as domain-specific, computational mechanisms that are also (1) informationally encapsulated, (2) mandatory, (3) fast, (4) shallow, (5) neurally localized, (6) susceptible to characteristic breakdown, and (7) largely inaccessible to other processes.[5] Although the full-fledged Fodorian notion of a module has been highly influential in cognitive science (Garfield 1987), evolutionary psychologists have not typically adopted his conception of modules. In his recent book *Mindblindness*, for example, Simon Baron-Cohen explicitly denies that the modules involved in his theory of "mind reading"[6] need to be informationally encapsulated or have shallow outputs (1994, 515).

4.1.3 Darwinian Modules

What, then, do evolutionary psychologists typically mean by the term "module"? The answer, unfortunately, is far from clear, since evolutionary psychologists don't attempt to provide any precise characterization of modularity and rarely bother to distinguish between the various notions of module that we have set out in this section. Nevertheless, from what they do say about modularity, we think it is possible to piece together an account of what we propose to call a *Darwinian module*, which can be viewed as a sort of prototype of the evolutionary psychologists' notion of modularity. Darwinian modules

---

5. Here are brief explanations of the characteristics that Fodor ascribes to modules:

1. Informational encapsulation: A module has little or no access to information that is not contained in its own proprietary data base. This should not be confused with the sort of limited access characteristic of a Chomskian/computational module, where the proprietary information to which a computational module has access is not available to *other* components in the system.
2. Mandatoriness: One cannot control whether or not a module applies to a given input.
3. Speed: By comparison to nonmodular systems, modules process information very swiftly.
4. Shallow output: Modules provide only a preliminary characterization of input.
5. Neural localization: Modular mechanisms are associated with fixed neural architecture.
6. Susceptibility to characteristic breakdown: Since modules are associated with fixed neural architecture, they exhibit characteristic breakdown patterns (Fodor 1986, 15).
7. Lack of access of other processes to its intermediate representations: Other systems have limited access to what is going on inside a module.

6. This is his theory of how people attribute mental states to each other and use them to predict behavior.

have a cluster of features, and when evolutionary psychologists talk about modules, they generally have in mind something that has most or all of the features in the cluster.

The first feature of Darwinian modules is that they are domain-specific. According to Cosmides and Tooby, who are perhaps the best-known proponents of evolutionary psychology, our minds consist primarily of "a constellation of specialized mechanisms that have domain-specific procedures, operate over domain-specific representations, or both" (Cosmides and Tooby 1994, 94).

Second, Darwinian modules are computational mechanisms. On the colorful account offered by Tooby and Cosmides, "our cognitive architecture resembles a confederation of hundreds or thousands of functionally dedicated computers (often called modules)" (Tooby and Cosmides 1995, xiii). Thus Darwinian modules are not Chomskian modules but, rather, a species of computational module. However, evolutionary psychologists also assume that many Darwinian modules utilize domain-specific systems of knowledge (i.e., Chomskian modules) when doing computations or solving problems, and that in some cases this domain-specific knowledge is accessible only to a single Darwinian module. Thus some Darwinian modules are a kind of Chomskian/computational module. The "theory of mind" module posited by a number of recent theorists may provide an example. This module is typically assumed to employ innate, domain-specific knowledge about psychological states when predicting the behavior of agents, and much of that information may not be available to other systems in the mind.

A third feature of Darwinian modules is that they are innate cognitive structures whose characteristic properties are largely or wholly determined by genetic factors. In addition, evolutionary psychologists make the stronger claim that the many Darwinian modules which predominate in our cognitive architecture are the products of natural selection. They are, according to Tooby and Cosmides, "kinds invented by natural selection during the species' evolutionary history to produce adaptive ends in the species' natural environment" (Tooby and Cosmides 1995, xiii; see also Cosmides and Tooby 1992). Thus, not only do evolutionary psychologists commit themselves to the claim that modules are innate, they also commit themselves to a theory about how modules came to be innate—namely, via natural selection. Though Darwinian modules need not enhance reproductive fitness in modern environments, they exist because they did enhance fitness in the environment of our Pleistocene ancestors. Or, to make much the same point in the jargon favored by evolutionary psychologists, though Darwinian modules need not now be adaptive, they are *adaptations*. This account of the origins of these modules is, of course, the reason that we have chosen to call them "Darwinian," and as we shall see in section 4.4 the fact that Darwinian modules are adaptations plays an important role in structuring the research program that evolutionary psychologists pursue.

Finally, evolutionary psychologists often insist that Darwinian modules are universal features of the human mind, and thus that we should expect to find that all (normally functioning) human beings possess the same specific set of modules. According to evolutionary psychologists, then, not only has natural selection designed the human mind so that it is rich in innate, domain-specific, computational mechanisms; it has also given us all more or less the same design. (For an interesting critique of this claim, see Griffiths 1997, ch. 5.)

To sum up, a (prototypical) Darwinian module is an innate, naturally selected, functionally specific, and universal computational mechanism which may have access (perhaps even unique access) to a domain-specific system of knowledge of the sort we've been calling a Chomskian module.

4.2 PERIPHERAL VERSUS MASSIVE MODULARITY

Until recently, even staunch proponents of modularity typically restricted themselves to the claim that the mind is modular at its periphery.[7] So, for example, although the discussion of modularity as it is currently framed in cognitive science derives largely from Jerry Fodor's arguments in *The Modularity of Mind* (1983), Fodor insists that much of our cognition is subserved by nonmodular systems. According to Fodor, only input systems (those responsible for perception and language processing) and output systems (those responsible for action) are plausible candidates for modularity. By contrast, "central systems" (those systems responsible for reasoning and belief fixation) are likely to be nonmodular. As Dan Sperber has observed:

> Although this was probably not intended and has not been much noticed, "modularity of mind" was a paradoxical title, for, according to Fodor, modularity is to be found only at the periphery of the mind. . . . In its center and bulk, Fodor's mind is decidedly nonmodular. Conceptual processes—that is, thought proper—are presented as a holistic lump lacking joints at which to carve. (Sperber 1994, 39)

Evolutionary psychologists reject the claim that the mind is only peripherally modular in favor of the view that the mind is largely or even entirely composed of Darwinian modules. We will call this thesis the Massive Modularity Hypothesis (MMH). Tooby and Cosmides elaborate on the Massive Modularity Hypothesis as follows:

> [O]ur cognitive architecture resembles a confederation of hundreds or thousands of functionally dedicated computers (often called modules) designed to solve adaptive problems endemic to our hunter-gatherer ancestors. Each of these devices has its own agenda and imposes its own exotic organization on different fragments of the world. There are specialized systems for grammar induction, for face recognition, for dead reckoning, for construing objects and for recognizing emotions from the face. There are mechanisms to detect animacy, eye direction, and cheating.

---

7. See Gardner 1983 for an early attempt to develop a more fully modular account of the mind.

There is a "theory of mind" module . . . a variety of social inference modules . . . and a multitude of other elegant machines. (Tooby and Cosmides 1995, xiv)

According to the MMH, "central capacities too can be divided into domain-specific modules" (Jackendoff 1992, 70). So, for example, the linguist and cognitive neuroscientist Steven Pinker has suggested that not only are there modules for perception, language, and action, but there may also be modules for many tasks traditionally classified as central processes, including:

> Intuitive mechanics: knowledge of the motions, forces, and deformations that objects undergo . . . Intuitive biology: understanding how plants and animals work. . . . Intuitive psychology: predicting other people's behavior from their beliefs and desires. . . . Self-concept: gathering and organizing information about one's value to other people, and packaging it for others. (Pinker 1994, 420)

According to this view, then, "the human mind . . . [is] . . . not a general-purpose computer but a collection of instincts adapted for solving evolutionary significant problems—the mind as a Swiss Army knife" (Pinker 1994).[8]

4.3 ARGUMENTS FOR MASSIVE MODULARITY

Is the Massive Modularity Hypothesis correct? Does the human mind consist largely or even entirely of Darwinian modules? This question is fast becoming one of the central issues in contemporary cognitive science. Broadly speaking, the arguments in favor of MMH can be divided into two kinds, which we'll call "theoretical" and "empirical." Arguments of the first sort rely heavily on quite general theoretical claims about the nature of evolution, cognition, and computation, while those of the second sort focus on experimental results which, it is argued, support the MMH view of the mind. While a systematic review of the arguments that have been offered in support of the MMH would be beyond the scope of this essay, we think it is important for the reader to have some feel for what these arguments look like. Thus, in this section we'll present a brief sketch of one of the theoretical arguments offered by Cosmides and Tooby and suggest one way in which the argument might be criticized.[9] In section 5, we'll consider some of the empirical results about reasoning that have been interpreted as supporting the MMH.

8. For some additional discussion of the Massive Modularity Hypothesis, see Pinker 1997, 27–28.

9. For other theoretical arguments in support of the claim that the mind is massively modular, see Marr 1982, 102; Cosmides and Tooby 1987, 1992, 1994; Pinker 1994, 1997; and Sperber 1994. For some arguments *against* the MMH, see Fodor 1983, part 4; Karmiloff-Smith 1992, ch. 1; Quartz and Sejnowski 1994. For a more systematic review of the debate, see Samuels 1998.

Cosmides and Tooby's argument focuses on the notion of an *adaptive problem*, which can be defined as an evolutionary recurrent problem whose solution promoted reproduction, however long or indirect the chain by which it did so (Cosmides and Tooby 1994, 87). For example, in order to reproduce, an organism must be able to find a mate. Thus finding a mate is an adaptive problem. Similarly, in order to reproduce, one must avoid being eaten by predators before one mates. Thus predator avoidance is also an adaptive problem. According to Cosmides and Tooby, once we appreciate both the way in which natural selection operates and the specific adaptive problems that human beings faced in the Pleistocene era, we will see that there are good reasons for thinking that the mind contains a number of distinct, modular mechanisms. In developing the argument, Cosmides and Tooby first attempt to justify the claim that when it comes to solving adaptive problems, selection pressures can be expected to produce highly *specialized* cognitive mechanisms—that is, modules.

> [D]ifferent adaptive problems often require different solutions and different solutions can, in most cases, be implemented only by different, functionally distinct mechanisms. Speed, reliability and efficiency can be engineered into specialized mechanisms because there is no need to engineer a compromise between different task demands. (Cosmides and Tooby 1994, 89)

By contrast, "a jack of all trades is necessarily a master of none, because generality can be achieved only by sacrificing effectiveness" (ibid.). In other words, while a specialized mechanism can be fast, reliable, and efficient, because it is dedicated to solving a specific adaptive problem, a general mechanism that solves many adaptive problems with competing task demands will attain generality only at the expense of sacrificing these virtues. Consequently:

(1) "As a rule, when two adaptive problems have solutions that are incompatible or simply different, a single general solution will be inferior to two specialized solutions" (ibid.).

Notice that the above quotation is not specifically about *cognitive* mechanisms. Rather, it is supposed to apply generally to all solutions to adaptive problems. Nevertheless, according to Cosmides and Tooby, what applies generally to solutions to adaptive problems also applies to the specific case of cognitive mechanisms for solving adaptive problems. Thus, they claim, we have good reason to expect task-specific or domain-specific cognitive mechanisms to be superior solutions to adaptive problems than domain-general systems. Moreover, since natural selection can be expected to favor superior solutions to adaptive problems over inferior ones, Cosmides and Tooby conclude that when it comes to solving adaptive problems:

(2) "domain specific cognitive mechanisms . . . can be expected to systematically out-perform (and hence preclude or replace) more general mechanisms" (ibid.).

So far, then, we have seen that Cosmides and Tooby argue for the claim that selection pressures can be expected to produce domain-specific cognitive mechanisms—modules—for solving adaptive problems. But this alone is not sufficient to support the claim that the mind contains a *large number* of modules. It must also be the case that our ancestors were confronted by a large number of adaptive problems that could be solved only by cognitive mechanisms. Accordingly, Cosmides and Tooby insist that:

(3) "Simply to survive and reproduce, our Pleistocene ancestors had to be good at solving an enormously broad array of adaptive problems—problems that would defeat any modern artificial intelligence system. A small sampling includes foraging for food, navigating, selecting a mate, parenting, engaging in social exchange, dealing with aggressive threat, avoiding predators, avoiding pathogenic contamination, avoiding naturally occurring plant toxins, avoiding incest, and so on." (ibid., 90)

Yet, if this is true, and if it is also true that when it comes to solving adaptive problems, domain-specific cognitive mechanisms can be expected to preclude or replace more general cognitive mechanisms, then it would seem to follow that:

(4) The human mind can be expected to include a large number of distinct, domain specific mechanisms.

And this, of course, is just what the Massive Modularity Hypothesis requires.

This argument is not supposed to be a deductive proof that the mind is massively modular. Rather, it is offered as a plausibility argument. It is supposed to provide us with plausible grounds to expect the mind to contain many modules (ibid., 89). Nonetheless, if the conclusion of the argument is interpreted as claiming that the mind contains lots of *prototypical Darwinian* modules, then we suspect that the argument claims more than it is entitled to. For even if we grant that natural selection has contrived to provide the human mind with many specialized solutions to adaptive problems, it does not follow that these specialized solutions will be prototypical Darwinian modules. Rather than containing a large number of specialized computational devices, it might instead be the case that the mind contains lots of innate, domain-specific items of knowledge, and that these are employed in order to solve various adaptive problems. Thus, rather than exploiting Darwinian modules, our minds might contain lots of innate, *Chomskian* modules.

And it is perfectly consistent with the claim that we possess Chomskian modules for solving adaptive problems that the information contained within such modules is utilized only by *domain-general* and hence nonmodular computational devices. Moreover, the claim that natural selection prefers certain kinds of adaptive specializations to others—namely, Darwinian computational modules to Chomskian modules—surely does not follow from the general claim that specialized solutions (of some kind) typically outperform more general ones. So instead of producing Darwinian modules as solutions to adaptive problems, natural selection might instead have provided specialized solutions in the form of innate, domain-specific knowledge that is utilized by a domain-general computational mechanism. In order to make it plausible that the mind contains large numbers of Darwinian modules, one must argue for the claim that natural selection can be expected to prefer domain-specific *computational* devices over domain-specific *bodies of information* as solutions to adaptive problems. And, at present, it is far from clear that anyone knows how such an argument would go.

4.4 THE RESEARCH PROGRAM OF EVOLUTIONARY PSYCHOLOGY

A central goal of evolutionary psychology is to construct and test hypotheses about the Darwinian modules which, the theory maintains, make up much of the human mind. In pursuit of this goal, research may proceed in two quite different stages. The first, which we'll call *evolutionary analysis*, has as its goal the generation of plausible hypotheses about Darwinian modules. An evolutionary analysis tries to determine as much as possible about recurrent information-processing problems that our forebears would have confronted in what is often called *the environment of evolutionary adaptation* or EEA—the environment in which *Homo sapiens* evolved. The focus, of course, is on *adaptive* problems whose successful solution would have directly or indirectly contributed to reproductive success. In some cases these adaptive problems were posed by physical features of the EEA; in other cases they were posed by biological features; and in still other cases they were posed by the social environment in which our forebears were embedded. Since so many factors are involved in determining the sorts of recurrent information-processing problems that our ancestors confronted in the EEA, this sort of evolutionary analysis is a highly interdisciplinary exercise. Clues can be found in many different sort of investigations, from the study of the Pleistocene climate to the study of the social organization in the few remaining hunter-gatherer cultures. Once a recurrent adaptive problem has been characterized, the theorist may hypothesize that there is a module which would have done a good job at solving that problem in the EEA.

An important part of the effort to characterize these recurrent information-processing problems is the specifications of the sorts of constraints that a mechanism solving the problem could take for granted. If, for example, the important data needed to solve the problem was almost always presented in a specific format, then the mechanism need not be able to handle data presented in other ways. It could "assume" that the data would be presented in the typical format. Similarly, if it was important to be able to detect people or objects with a certain property that is not readily observable, and if in the EEA that property was highly correlated with some other property that is easier to detect, the system could simply assume that people or objects with the detectable property also had the one that was hard to observe.

It is important to keep in mind that evolutionary analyses can be used only as a way of *suggesting plausible hypotheses* about mental modules. By themselves, evolutionary analyses provide no assurance that these hypotheses are true. The fact that it would have enhanced our ancestors' fitness if they had developed a module that solved a certain problem is no guarantee that they *did* develop such a module, since there are many reasons why natural selection and the other processes that drive evolution may fail to produce a mechanism that would enhance fitness (Stich 1990, ch. 3).

Once an evolutionary analysis has succeeded in suggesting a plausible hypothesis, the next stage in the evolutionary psychology research strategy is to *test* the hypothesis by looking for evidence that contemporary humans actually have a module with the properties in question. Here, as earlier, the project is highly interdisciplinary. Evidence can come from experimental studies of reasoning in normal humans (Cosmides 1989; Cosmides and Tooby 1992, 1996; Gigerenzer 1991; Gigerenzer and Hug 1992), from developmental studies focused on the emergence of cognitive skills (Carey and Spelke 1994; Leslie 1994; Gelman and Brenneman 1994), or from the study of cognitive deficits in various abnormal populations (Baron-Cohen 1995). Important evidence can also be gleaned from studies in cognitive anthropology (Barkow 1992; Hutchins 1980), history, and even from such surprising areas as the comparative study of legal traditions (Wilson and Daly 1992). When evidence from a number of these areas points in the same direction, an increasingly strong case can be made for the existence of a module suggested by evolutionary analysis.

5 Evolutionary Psychology Applied to Reasoning: Theory and Results

In this section we will consider two lines of research on human reasoning in which the two-stage strategy described in the previous section has been pursued. Though the interpretation of the studies we will sketch is the subject of considerable controversy, a number of authors have suggested that they show there is something deeply mistaken about the "bleak" hypothesis set out in section 3. That hypothesis claims that people lack normatively appropriate rules or principles for reasoning about problems like those set out in section 2. But when we look at variations on these problems that may make them closer to the sort of recurrent problems our forebears would have confronted in the EEA, performance improves dramatically. And this, it is argued, is evidence for the existence of at least two normatively sophisticated Darwinian modules, one designed to deal with probabilistic reasoning when information is presented in a relative frequency format, the other designed to deal with reasoning about cheating in social exchange settings.

5.1 THE FREQUENTIST HYPOTHESIS

The experiments reviewed in sections 2.2–2.4 indicate that in many cases people are quite bad at reasoning about probabilities, and the pessimistic interpretation of these results claims that people use simple ("fast and dirty") heuristics in dealing with these problems because their cognitive systems have no access to more appropriate principles for reasoning about probabilities. But, in a series of recent, very provocative papers, Gigerenzer (1994; Gigerenzer and Hoffrage 1995) and Cosmides and Tooby (1996) argue that from an evolutionary point of view this would be a surprising and paradoxical result. "As long as chance has been loose in the world," Cosmides and Tooby note, "animals have had to make judgments under uncertainty" (1996, 14). Thus making judgments when confronted with probabilistic information posed adaptive problems for all sorts of organisms, including our hominid ancestors, and "if an adaptive problem has endured for a long enough period and is important enough, then mechanisms of considerable complexity can evolve to solve it" (ibid.). But, as we saw in the previous section, "one should expect a mesh between the design of our cognitive mechanisms, the structure of the adaptive problems they evolved to solve, and the typical environments that they were designed to operate in—that is, the one that they evolved in" (ibid.). So, in launching their evolutionary analysis, Cosmides and Tooby's first step is to ask: "what kinds of probabilistic information would have been available to any inductive reasoning mechanisms that we might have evolved?" (ibid., 15).

In the modern world we are confronted with statistical information presented in many ways: weather forecasts tell us the probability of rain tomorrow, sports pages list batting averages, and widely publicized studies tell us how much the risk of cancer of the colon is reduced in people over 50 if they have a diet high in fiber. But information about the probability of single events (like rain tomorrow) and information expressed in percentage terms would have been rare or unavailable in the EEA.

> What *was* available in the environment in which we evolved was the encountered frequencies of actual events—for example, that we were successful 5 times out of the last 20 times we hunted in the north canyon. Our hominid ancestors were immersed in a rich flow of observable frequencies that could be used to improve decision-making, given procedures that could take advantage of them. So if we have adaptations for inductive reasoning, they should take frequency information as input. (ibid., 15–16)

After a cognitive system has registered information about relative frequencies, it might convert this information to some other format. If, for example, the system has noted that 5 out of the last 20 north canyon hunts were successful, it might infer and store the conclusion that there is a 0.25 chance that a north canyon hunt will be successful. However, Cosmides and Tooby argue, "there are advantages to storing and operating on frequentist representations because they preserve important information that would be lost by conversion to single-event probability. For example, . . . the number of events that the judgment was based on would be lost in conversion. When the *n* disappears, the index of reliability of the information disappears as well" (ibid., 16).

These and other considerations regarding the environment in which our cognitive systems evolved lead Cosmides and Tooby to hypothesize that our ancestors "evolved mechanism that took frequencies as input, maintained such information as frequentist representations, and used these frequentist representations as a database for effective inductive reasoning."[10] Since evolutionary psychologists expect the mind to contain many specialized modules, Cosmides and Tooby are prepared to find other modules involved in inductive reasoning that work in other ways.

> We are not hypothesizing that every cognitive mechanism involving statistical induction necessarily operates on frequentist principles, only that at least one of them does, and that this makes frequentist principles an important feature of how humans intuitively engage the statistical dimension of the world. (ibid., 17)

But, while their evolutionary analysis does not preclude the existence of inductive mechanisms that are not focused on frequencies, it does suggest that when a mechanism that operates on frequentist principles is engaged, it will do a good job, and thus the probabilistic inferences it makes will generally be normatively appropriate ones. This, of course, is in stark contrast to the bleak implications hypothesis, which claims that people simply do not have access to normatively appropriate strategies in this area.

From their hypothesis, Cosmides and Tooby derive a number of predictions:

1. Inductive reasoning performance will differ depending on whether subjects are asked to judge a frequency or the probability of a single event.
2. Performance on frequentist versions of problems will be superior to nonfrequentist versions.
3. The more subjects can be mobilized to form a frequentist representation, the better performance will be.
4. . . . Performance on frequentist problems will satisfy some of the constraints that a calculus of probability specifies, such as Bayes's rule. This would occur because some inductive reasoning mechanisms in our cognitive architecture embody aspects of a calculus of probability. (ibid., 17)

---

10. Cosmides and Tooby call "the hypothesis that our inductive reasoning mechanisms were designed to operate on and to output frequency representations" *the frequentist hypothesis* (1996, 21), and they give credit to Gerd Gigerenzer for first formulating the hypothesis. See, e.g., Gigerenzer 1994, 142.

To test these predictions, Cosmides and Tooby ran an array of experiments designed around the medical diagnosis problem which Casscells et al. used to demonstrate that even very sophisticated subjects ignore information about base rates. In their first experiment Cosmides and Tooby replicated the results of Casscells et al. using exactly the same wording that we reported in section 2.4. Of the 25 Stanford University undergraduates who were subjects in this experiment, only 3 (= 12 percent) gave the normatively appropriate bayesian answer of "2 percent," while 14 subjects (= 56 percent) answered "95 percent."[11] As we noted in 2.3, the Harvard Medical School subjects in the original Casscells et al. study did slightly better; 18 percent of those subjects gave answers close to "2 percent" and 45 percent answered "95 percent."

In another experiment, Cosmides and Tooby gave 50 Stanford students a similar problem in which relative frequencies rather than percentages and single-event probabilities were emphasized. The "frequentist" version of the problem read as follows:

> 1 out of every 1000 Americans has disease X. A test has been developed to detect when a person has disease X. Every time the test is given to a person who has the disease, the test comes out positive. But sometimes the test also comes out positive when it is given to a person who is completely healthy. Specifically, out of every 1000 people who are perfectly healthy, 50 of them test positive for the disease.
>
> Imagine that we have assembled a random sample of 1000 Americans. They were selected by lottery. Those who conducted the lottery had no information about the health status of any of these people.
> Given the information above:
>
> on average,
>
> How many people who test positive for the disease will *actually* have the disease?
> ___ out of ___.[12]

On this problem the results were dramatically different: 38 of the 50 subjects (= 76 percent) gave the correct Bayesian answer.[13]

A series of further experiments systematically explored the differences between the problem used by Casscells et al. and the problems on which subjects perform well, in an

---

11. Cosmides and Tooby use "bayesian" with a small "b" to characterize any cognitive procedure that reliably produces answers that satisfy Bayes's rule.

12. This is the text used in Cosmides and Tooby's (1996) experiments E2-C1 and E3-C2.

13. In yet another version of the problem, Cosmides and Tooby explored whether an even greater percentage would give the correct bayesian answer if subjects were forced "to actively construct a concrete, visual frequentist representation of the information in the problem" (ibid., 34). On that version of the problem, 92 percent of subjects gave the correct bayesian response.

effort to determine which factors had the largest effect. Although a number of different factors affect performance, two predominate. "Asking for the answer as a frequency produces the largest effect, following closely by presenting the problem information as frequencies" (ibid., 58). The most important conclusion that Cosmides and Tooby want to draw from these experiments is that "frequentist representations activate mechanisms that produce bayesian reasoning, and that this is what accounts for the very high level of Bayesian performance elicited by the pure frequentist problems that we tested" (ibid., 59).

As further support for this conclusion, Cosmides and Tooby cite several striking results reported by other investigators. In one study, Fiedler (1988), following up on some intriguing findings of Tversky and Kahneman (1983), showed that the percentage of subjects who commit the conjunction fallacy can be radically reduced if the problem is cast in frequentist terms. In the "feminist bank teller" example, Fiedler contrasted the wording reported in section 2.2 with a problem that read as follows:

> Linda is 31 years old, single, outspoken, and very bright. She majored in philosophy. As a student, she was deeply concerned with issues of discrimination and social justice, and also participated in anti-nuclear demonstrations.
>
> There are 200 people who fit the description above. How many of them are:
> bank tellers?
> bank tellers and active in the feminist movement?
> ...

In Fiedler's replication using the original formulation of the problem, 91 percent of subjects judged the feminist bank teller option to be more probable than the bank teller option. However, in the frequentist version only 22 percent of subjects judged that there would be more feminist bank tellers than bank tellers. In yet another experiment, Hertwig and Gigerenzer (1994; reported in Gigerenzer 1994) told subjects that there were 200 women fitting the "Linda" description, and asked them to estimate the number who were bank tellers, feminist bank tellers, and feminists. Only 13 percent committed the conjunction fallacy.

Studies on overconfidence have also been marshaled in support of the frequentist hypothesis. In one of these Gigerenzer, Hoffrage, and Kleinbölting (1991) reported that the sort of overconfidence described in section 2.4 can be made to "disappear" by having subjects answer questions formulated in terms of frequencies. Gigerenzer and his colleagues gave subjects lists of 50 questions similar to those described in section 2.4, except that in addition to being asked to rate their confidence after each response (which, in effect, asks them to judge the probability of that single event), subjects were, at the end, also asked a question about the frequency of correct responses: "How many of these 50 questions do you think you got right?" In two experiments, the average overconfidence was about 15 percent, when single-event confidences were compared with actual relative frequencies of correct answers, replicating the sorts of findings we sketched in section 2.4. However, comparing the subjects' "estimated frequencies with actual frequencies of correct answers made 'overconfidence' *disappear* . . . Estimated frequencies were practically identical with actual frequencies, with even a small tendency towards underestimation. The 'cognitive illusion' was gone" (Gigerenzer 1991, 89).

Both the experimental studies we have been reviewing and the conclusions that Gigerenzer, Cosmides, and Tooby want to draw from them have provoked a fair measure of criticism. For our purposes, perhaps the most troublesome criticisms are those demonstrating that various normatively problematic patterns of reasoning arise even when a problem is stated in terms of frequencies. In their detailed study of the conjunction fallacy, for example, Tversky and Kahneman (1983) reported an experiment in which subjects were asked to estimate both the number of "seven-letter words of the form '—n-' in four pages of text" and the number of "seven-letter words of the form '—ing' in four pages of text." The median estimate for words ending in "ing" was about three times *higher* than for words with "n" in the next-to-last position. As Kahneman and Tversky (1996) note, this appears to be a clear counter-example to Gigerenzer's claim that the conjunction fallacy disappears in judgments of frequency.

As another challenge to the claim that frequency representations eliminate base-rate neglect, Kahneman and Tversky cite a study by Gluck and Bower (1988). In that study subjects were required to learn to diagnose whether a patient had a rare disease (25 percent) or a common disease (75 percent) on the basis of 250 trials in which they were presented with patterns of four symptoms. After each presentation subjects guessed which disease the patient had, and were given immediate feedback indicating whether their guess was right or wrong. Though subjects encountered the common disease three times more often than the rare disease, they largely ignored this base-rate information and acted as if the two diseases were equally likely.

There is also a substantial body of work demonstrating that antecedent expectations can lead people to report illusory correlations when they are shown data about a sequence of cases. In one well-known and very disquieting study, Chapman and Chapman (1967, 1969) showed subjects a series of cards each of which was said to reproduce a drawing of a person made by a psychiatric patient. Each card also gave the diagnosis for that patient. Subjects reported seeing "intuitively expected" correlations (e.g., drawings with peculiar eyes and diagnoses of paranoia) even when there was no such correlation in the data they were shown. In another widely discussed study, Gilovich, Vallone, and Tversky (1985) showed that people "see" a positive correlation between the outcome of successive shots in basketball (thus giving rise to the illusion of a "hot hand") even when there is no such correlation in the data.

In our view, what these criticisms show is that the version of the frequentist hypothesis suggested by Gigerenzer, Cosmides, and Tooby is too simplistic. It is not the case that all frequentist representations activate mechanisms that produce good bayesian reasoning; nor is it the case that presenting data in a sequential format from which frequency distribution can readily be extracted always activates mechanisms that do a good job at detecting correlations. More experimental work is needed to determine what additional factors are required to trigger good bayesian reasoning and good correlation detection.

And more subtle evolutionary analyses are needed to throw light on why these more complex triggers evolved. But despite the polemical fireworks there is actually a fair amount of agreement between the evolutionary psychologists and their critics. Both sides agree that people *do* have mental mechanisms which can do a good job at bayesian reasoning, and that presenting problems in a way that makes frequency information salient can play an important role in activating these mechanisms. Both sides also agree that people have other mental mechanisms that exploit quite different reasoning strategies, though there is little agreement on how to characterize these non-bayesian strategies, what factors trigger them, or why they evolved. The bottom line, we think, is that the experiments demonstrating that people sometimes do an excellent job of bayesian reasoning go a long way toward refuting the gloomy hypothesis sketched in section 3. Gould's claim that "our minds are not built ... to work by the rules of probability" is much too pessimistic. Our cognitive systems clearly do have access to reasoning strategies that accord with the rules of probability, though it is also clear that we don't always use them. We also think that the evidence reviewed in this section is compatible with the hypothesis that good probabilistic reasoning, when it occurs, is subserved by one or more Darwinian modules, though of course the evidence is compatible with lots of alternative hypotheses as well.

5.2 THE CHEATER DETECTION HYPOTHESIS

In section 2 we reproduced one version of Wason's four-card selection task on which most subjects perform very poorly, and we noted that, while subjects do equally poorly on

In its crackdown against drunk driver, Massachusetts law enforcement officials are revoking liquor licenses left and right. You are a bouncer in a Boston bar, and you'll lose your job unless you enforce the following law:

"If a person is drinking beer, then he must be over 20 years old."

The cards below have information about four people sitting at a table in your bar. Each card represents one person. One side of the card tells what a person is drinking and the other side of the card tells that person's age. Indicate only those card(s) you definitely need to turn over to see if any of these people are breaking the law.

| drinking beer | drinking coke | 25 years old | 16 years old |

FIGURE 7.2

many other versions of the selection task, there are some versions on which performance improves dramatically. An example from Griggs and Cox (1982) is shown in figure 7.2. From a logical point of view, this problem is structurally identical to the problem in section 2.1, but the *content* of the problems clearly has a major effect on how well people perform. About 75 percent of college student subjects get the right answer on this version of the selection task, while only 25 percent get the right answer on the other version. Though there have been dozens of studies exploring this "content effect" in the selection task, the results have been, and continue to be, rather puzzling, since there is no obvious property or set of properties shared by those versions of the task on which people perform well. However, in several recent and widely discussed papers, Cosmides and Tooby have argued that an evolutionary analysis enables us to see a surprising pattern in these otherwise bewildering results (Cosmides 1989; Cosmides and Tooby 1992).

The starting point of their evolutionary analysis is the observation that in the environment in which our ancestors evolved (and in the modern world as well) it is often the case that unrelated individuals can engage in "non-zero-sum" exchanges, in which the benefits to the recipient (measured in terms of reproductive fitness) are significantly greater than the costs to the donor. In a hunter-gatherer society, for example, it will sometimes happen that one hunter has been lucky on a particular day and has an abundance of food, while another hunter has been unlucky and is near starvation. If the successful hunter gives some of his meat to the unsuccessful hunter rather than gorging on it himself, this may have a small negative effect on the donor's fitness, since the extra bit of body fat that he might add could prove useful in the future, but the benefit to the recipient will be much greater. Still, there is *some* cost to the donor; he would be slightly better off if he didn't help unrelated individuals. Despite this, it is clear that people sometimes do help non-kin, and there is evidence to suggest that non-human primates (and even vampire bats) do so as well. On first blush, this sort of "altruism" seems to pose an evolutionary puzzle, since if a gene which made an organism *less* likely to help unrelated individuals appeared in a population, those with the gene would be slightly *more* fit, and thus the gene would gradually spread through the population.

A solution to this puzzle was proposed by Robert Trivers (1971), who noted that, while one-way altruism might be a bad idea from an evolutionary point of view, *reciprocal altruism* is quite a different matter. If a pair of hunters (be they humans or bats) can each count on the other to help when one has an abundance of food and the other has none, then they may both be better off in the long run. Thus organisms with a gene or a suite of genes that inclines them to engage in reciprocal exchanges with non-kin (or "social exchanges" as they are sometimes called) would be more fit than members of the same species without those genes. But, of course, reciprocal exchange arrangements are vulnerable to cheating. In the business of maximizing fitness, individuals will do best if they are regularly offered and accept help when they need it, but never reciprocate when others need help. This suggests that if stable social exchange arrangements are to exist, the organisms involved must have cognitive mechanisms that enable them to detect cheaters and to avoid helping them in the future. And since humans apparently are capable of entering into stable social exchange relations, this evolutionary analysis leads Cosmides and Tooby to hypothesize that we have one or more Darwinian modules whose job it is to recognize reciprocal exchange arrangements and to detect cheaters who accept the benefits in such arrangements but do not pay the costs. In short, the evolutionary analysis leads Cosmides and Tooby to hypothesize the existence of one or more cheater detection modules. We call this *the cheater detection hypothesis.*

If this is right, then we should be able to find some evidence for the existence of these modules in the thinking of contemporary humans. It is here that the selection task enters the picture. For, according to Cosmides and Tooby, some versions of the selection task engage the mental module(s) which were designed to detect cheaters in social exchange situations. And since these mental modules can be expected to do their job efficiently and accurately, people do well on those versions of the selection task. Other versions of the task do not trigger the social exchange and cheater detection modules. Since we have no mental modules that were designed to deal with these problems, people find them much harder, and their performance is much worse. The bouncer-in-the-Boston-bar problem presented earlier is an example of a selection task that triggers the cheater detection mechanism. The problem involving vowels and odd numbers presented in section 2 is an example of a selection task that does not trigger the cheater detection module.

In support of their theory, Cosmides and Tooby assemble an impressive body of evidence. To begin, they note that the cheater detection hypothesis claims that social exchanges, or "social contracts," will trigger good performance on selection tasks, and this enables us to see a clear pattern in the otherwise confusing experimental literature that had grown up before their hypothesis was formulated.

> When we began this research in 1983, the literature on the Wason selection task was full of reports of a wide variety of content effects, and there was no satisfying theory or empirical generalization that could account for these effects. When we categorized these content effects according to whether they conformed to social contracts, a striking pattern emerged. Robust and replicable content effects were found only for rules that related terms that are recognizable as benefits and cost/requirements in the format of a standard social contract. . . . No thematic rule that was not a social contract had ever produced a content effect that was both robust and replicable. . . . All told, for non-social contract thematic problems, 3 experiments had produced a substantial content effect, 2 had produced a weak content effect, and 14 had produced no content effect at all. The few effects that were found did not replicate. In contrast, 16 out of 16 experiments that fit the criteria for standard social contracts . . . elicited substantial content effects. (Cosmides and Tooby 1992, 183)

Since the formulation of the cheater detection hypothesis, a number of additional experiments have been designed to test the hypothesis and rule out alternatives. Among the most persuasive of these are a series of experiments by Gigerenzer and Hug (1992). In one set of experiments, these authors set out to show that, contrary to an earlier proposal by Cosmides and Tooby, *merely* perceiving a rule as a social contract was not enough to engage the cognitive mechanism that leads to good performance in the selection task, and that cueing for the possibility of *cheating* was required. To do this, they created two quite different context stories for social contract rules. One of the stories required subjects to attend to the possibility of cheating, while in the other story cheating was not relevant. Among the social contract rules they used was the following, which, they note, is widely known among hikers in the Alps:

(i)   If someone stays overnight in the cabin, then that person must bring along a bundle of wood from the valley.

The first context story, which the investigators call the "cheating version," explained:

There is a cabin at high altitude in the Swiss Alps, which serves hikers as an overnight shelter. Since it is cold and firewood is not otherwise available at that altitude, the rule is that each hiker who stays overnight has to carry along his/her own share of wood. There are rumors that the rule is not always followed. The subjects were cued into the perspective of a guard who checks whether any one of four hikers has violated the rule. The four hikers were represented by four cards that read "stays overnight in the cabin," "carried no wood," "carried wood," and "does not stay overnight in the cabin."

The other context story, the "no-cheating version,"

the subjects were cued into the perspective of a member of the German Alpine Association who visits the Swiss cabin and tries to discover how the local Swiss Alpine Club runs this cabin. He observes people bringing wood to the cabin, and a friend suggests the familiar overnight rule as an explanation. The context story also mentions an alternative explanation: rather than the hikers, the members of the Swiss Alpine Club, who do not stay overnight, might carry the wood. The task of the subject was to check four persons (the same four cards) in order to find out whether anyone had violated the overnight rule suggested by the friend. (Gigerenzer and Hug 1992, 142–43)

The cheater detection hypothesis predicts that subjects will do better on the cheating version than on the no-cheating version, and that prediction was confirmed. In the cheating version, 89 percent of the subjects got the right answer, while in the no-cheating version, only 53 percent responded correctly.

In another set of experiments, Gigerenzer and Hug showed that when social contract rules make cheating on both sides possible, cueing subjects into the perspective of one party or the other can have a dramatic effect on performance in selection task problems. One of the rules they used that allows the possibility of bilateral cheating was:

(ii) If an employee works on the weekend, then that person gets a day off during the week.

Here again, two different context stories were constructed, one of which was designed to get subjects to take the perspective of the employee, while the other was designed to get subjects to take the perspective of the employer.

The employee version stated that working on the weekend is a benefit for the employer, because the firm can make use of its machines and be more flexible. Working on the weekend, on the other hand, is a cost for the employee. The context story was about an employee who had never worked on the weekend before, but who is considering working on Saturdays from time to time, since having a day off during the week is a benefit that outweighs the costs of working on Saturday. There are rumours that the rule has been violated before. The subject's task was to check information about four colleagues to see whether the rule has been violated. The four cards read: "worked on the weekend," "did not get a day off," "did not work on the weekend," "did get a day off."

In the employer version, the same rationale was given. The subject was cued into the perspective of the employer, who suspects that the rule has been violated before. The subjects' task was the same as in the other perspective [viz., to check information about four employees to see whether the rule has been violated]. (Gigerenzer & Hug 1992, 154)

In these experiments about 75 percent of the subjects cued to the employee's perspective chose the first two cards ("worked on the weekend" and "did not get a day off"), while less than 5 percent chose the other two cards. The results for subjects cued to the employer's perspective were radically different. Over 60 percent of subjects selected the last two cards ("did not work on the weekend" and "did get a day off"), while less than 10 percent selected the first two.

The evolutionary analysis that motivates the cheater detection hypothesis maintains that the capacity to engage in social exchange could not have evolved unless the individuals involved had some mechanism for detecting cheaters. There would, however, be no need for our hominid forebears to have developed a mechanism for detecting "pure altruists" who help others but do not expect help in return. If there were individuals like that, it might of course be useful to recognize them, so that they could be more readily exploited. However, altruists of this sort would incur fitness costs with no compensating benefits, and thus an evolutionary analysis suggests that they would have been selected against. Since altruists would be rare or non-existent, there would be no selection pressure for an altruist detection mechanism. These considerations led Cosmides and Tooby to predict that people will be much better at detecting cheaters in a selection task than at detecting altruists. To test the prediction, they designed three pairs of problems. In each pair the two stories are quite similar, though in one version subjects must look for cheaters, while in the other they must look for altruists. In one pair, both problems begin with the following text:

> You are an anthropologist studying the Kaluame, a Polynesian people who live in small, warring bands on Maku Island in the Pacific. You are interested in how Kaluame "big men"—chieftains—wield power.
>
> "Big Kiku" is a Kaluame big man who is known for his ruthlessness. As a sign of loyalty, he makes his own "subjects" put a tattoo on their face. Members of other Kaluame bands never have facial tattoos. Big Kiku has made so many enemies in other Kaluame bands, that being caught in another village with a facial tattoo is, quite literally, the kiss of death.
>
> Four men from different bands stumble into Big Kiku's village starving and desperate. They have been kicked out of their respective villages for various misdeeds, and have come to Big Kiku because they need food badly. Big Kiku offers each of them the following deal:
>
> "If you get a tattoo on your face, then I'll give you cassava root."

Cassava root is a very sustaining food which Big Kiku's people cultivate. The four men are very hungry, so they agree to Big Kiku's deal. Big Kiku says that the tattoos must be in place tonight, but that the cassava root will not be available until the following morning.

At this point the two problems diverge. The *cheater version* continues:

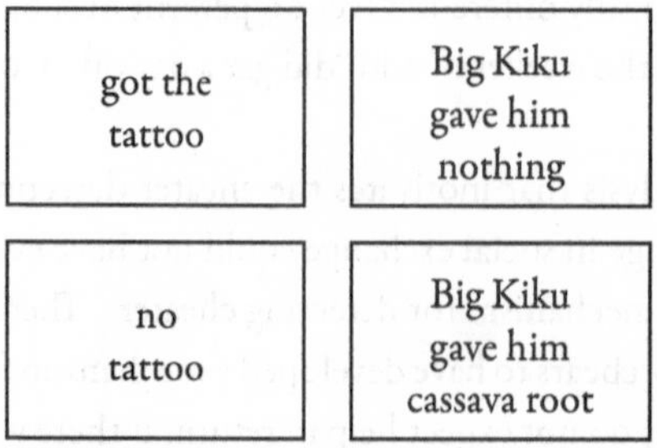

got the tattoo	Big Kiku gave him nothing
no tattoo	Big Kiku gave him cassava root

FIGURE 7.3

You learn that Big Kiku hates some of these men for betraying him to his enemies. You suspect he will cheat and betray some of them. Thus, this is a perfect opportunity for you to see first hand how Big Kiku wields his power.

The cards below have information about the fates of the four men. Each card represents one man. One side of a card tells whether or not the man went through with the facial tattoo that evening and the other side of the card tells whether or not Big Kiku gave that man cassava root the next day.

Did Big Kiku get away with cheating any of these four men? Indicate only those card(s) you definitely need to turn over to see if Big Kiku has broken his word to any of these four men.

The *altruist version* continues:

You learn that Big Kiku hates some of these men for betraying him to his enemies. You suspect he will cheat and betray some of them. However, you have also heard that Big Kiku sometimes, quite unexpectedly, shows great generosity towards others—that he is sometimes quite altruistic. Thus, this is a perfect opportunity for you to see first hand how Big Kiku wields his power.

The cards below have information about the fates of the four men. Each card represents one man. One side of a card tells whether or not the man went through with the facial tattoo that evening and the other side of the card tells whether or not Big Kiku gave that man cassava root the next day.

Did Big Kiku behave altruistically towards any of these four men? Indicate only those card(s) you definitely need to turn over to see if Big Kiku has behaved altruistically towards any of these four men.

The four cards, which were identical in both versions, are shown in figure 7.3. In the version of the problem that requires subjects to detect cheaters, Cosmides (1989) had found that 74 percent of subjects get the correct answer. In the version that requires subjects to detect altruists, however, only 28 percent answered correctly (Cosmides and Tooby 1992, 193–97).

These experiments, along with a number of others reviewed by Cosmides and Tooby (1992), are all compatible with the hypothesis that we have one or more Darwinian modules designed to deal with social exchanges and detect cheaters. However, this hypothesis is, to put it mildly, very controversial. Many authors have proposed alternative hypotheses to explain the data, and in some cases they have supported these hypotheses with additional experimental evidence. One of the most widely discussed of these alternatives is the *pragmatic reasoning schemas* approach defended by Cheng, Holyoak, and their colleagues (Cheng and Holyoak 1985, 1989; Cheng et al. 1986). On this account, reasoning is explained by the activation of domain-specific sets of rules (called "schemas") which are acquired during the lifetime of the individual through general inductive mechanisms. These rules subserve people's reasonings about permission, obligation, and other deontic concepts that may be used in their culture. Rules for reasoning about social exchanges are just one kind of reasoning schema. One virtue of this theory is that it provides an explanation for the fact that people perform well on problems like the "bar bouncer" task which are not assimilated comfortably to the model of reciprocal social exchange. However, as Cummins (1996) argues, there is little evidence for the claim that schemas involved in reasoning about permission and obligation are learned, and a fair amount of evidence suggesting that capacity to engage in deontic reasoning emerges relatively early in childhood. This, along with a number of other lines of evidence, leads Cummins to propose an intriguing hypothesis that integrates ideas from both the social exchange theory and the pragmatic reasoning schemas theory. On Cummins's hypothesis, reasoning about "permissions, obligations, prohibitions, promises, threats and warnings" (1996, 166) is subserved by an innate, domain-specific module devoted exclusively to deontic contents. This reasoning module "evolved for the very important purpose of solving problems that frequently arise within a dominance hierarchy—the social structure that characterizes most mammalian and avian species" (ibid.). A core component of the deontic reasoning module, Cummins maintains, is a mechanism whose job is violation detection. "[T]o reason effectively about deontic concepts, it is necessary to recognize what constitutes a violation, respond to it appropriately (which often depends on the respective status of the parties involved), and appreciate the necessity of adopting a violation-detection strategy whenever a deontic situation is encountered" (ibid.). Still other hypotheses to account for the content effects in selection tasks have been proposed by Oaksford and Chater (1994), Manktelow and Over (1995), and Sperber, Cara, and Girotto (1995).

This is not the place to review all these theories; nor would we venture a judgment—even a tentative one—on which theory is most promising. These are busy and exciting times for those studying human reasoning, and there is obviously much that remains to be discovered. What we believe we can safely conclude from the studies recounted in this section is that the hypothesis that much of human reasoning is subserved by a cluster of domain-specific Darwinian modules deserves to be taken very seriously. Whether or not it ultimately proves to be correct, the highly modular picture of the mechanisms underlying reasoning has generated a great deal of impressive research and will continue to do so for the foreseeable future. Thus we would do well to begin exploring what the implications would be for various claims about human rationality *if* the Massive Modularity Hypothesis turns out to be correct. In the final section of this paper we will begin this exploration by asking what implication the Massive Modularity Hypothesis might have for the "bleak implications" interpretations of some of the experimental studies of reasoning.

6 Massive Modularity, Bleak Implications, and the Panglossian Interpretation

One possible response to the Massive Modularity Hypothesis—we'll call it the *Panglossian interpretation*—maintains that if the MMH turns out to be correct, it would make

the bleak implications interpretation of the experimental studies of rationality completely untenable. According to the bleak implications interpretation, the sorts of experimental results surveyed in section 2 reflect shortcomings in human reasoning *competence*.
People deal with the problems in those experiments by exploiting various normatively
problematic heuristics, and they do this because they have nothing better available. They
"lack the correct programs for many important judgmental tasks,"[14] because, as Gould
maintained, "our minds are not built . . . to work by the rules of probability" (Gould
1992, 469). But, according to the Panglossian this is simply the wrong interpretation. If
the Massive Modularity Hypothesis is correct, then the mind contains "a multitude
of . . . elegant machines" (Tooby and Cosmides 1995, xiv). There are Darwinian modules
that reason in *normatively appropriate* ways about probability, cheating, and threats and
also about dead reckoning, intuitive mechanics, intuitive biology, and intuitive psychology, and no doubt a host of others as well. So humans *do* have access to the correct
programs for important judgmental tasks; our minds include Darwinian modules that
are built to "work by the rules of probability"; and humans are "good intuitive statisticians after all." The errors reported in the experimental literature, if indeed they really
are errors,[15] are merely *performance* errors, and the bleak implications interpretation
must be rejected.

We are not at all sure that anyone actually advocates this very strong version of the
Panglossian interpretation, though we suspect that a fair number of people would
endorse a more hedged and cautious version.[16] We don't believe that anything very close
to the strong version of the Panglossian interpretation can be defended, though we think
there is a great deal to be learned by exploring why the Panglossian interpretation fails.

One fairly straightforward objection to the Panglossian interpretation begins with the
observations that the experimental literature on human reasoning has documented many
quite different sorts of problems on which subjects perform poorly. Those reviewed in
section 2 are a small and highly selective sample. If the Panglossian interpretation is
correct, then people must have Darwinian modules capable of handling in normatively
appropriate ways *all* of the problems on which subjects perform poorly, though for one
reason or another the performance of experimental subjects does not reflect their underlying competence. That is, of course, a very strong claim, much stronger than currently
available evidence will support. Nor is there any plausible evolutionary argument for
the claim that natural selection would have provided us with Darwinian modules for

---

14. Slovic, Fischhoff, and Lichtenstein 1976, 174.
15. Gigerenzer (1991, 1994; Gigerenzer and Murray 1987) argues that in many cases the putative errors are not
really errors at all, and that those who think they are errors are relying on mistaken or overly simplistic normative theories of reasoning. Gigerenzer's challenge raises many interesting and important issues about the
nature of rationality and the assessment of reasoning. A detailed discussion of these issues would take us far
beyond the bounds of the current chapter.
16. Sec, e.g., Pinker 1997, 345.

handling *all* these cases. So the Panglossian interpretation rests on a bold speculation with relatively little empirical or theoretical support. But even if we put this concern off to the side and concentrate on those cases where there is some evidence for the existence of a Darwinian module, there are serious problems with the Panglossian idea that all errors are performance errors.

To bring these problems into focus, let us start by considering Kahneman and Tverky's seven-letter-word problem, discussed in section 5.1. In that problem subjects were not asked about the probability of a particular event. Rather, they were asked to estimate the *frequency* of words of the form "—ing" and words of the form "—n-" in four pages of text. Yet, despite being asked to estimate frequencies, most subjects said that the number of "—ing" words would be greater than the number of "—n-" words. If, as advocates of the MMH have argued, we have one or more Darwinian modules that do a good job of probabilistic reasoning when problems are couched in terms of frequencies, what sort of explanation can be offered for the error that these subjects make? One plausible hypothesis is that, rather than using their probabilistic reasoning module(s), subjects are relying on what Kahneman and Tversky call an "availability heuristic." They are searching memory for examples of words of the form "—ing" and also for words of the form "—n-," and because of the way in which our memory for such facts is organized, they are coming up with far more of the former than of the latter. But now let us ask *why* subjects (or their cognitive systems) are dealing with the problem in this way. Why *aren't* they using a probabilistic reasoning module which, presumably, would not produce responses that violate the conjunction rule? For an advocate of the MMH, perhaps the most natural hypothesis is that there is a mechanism in the mind (or maybe more than one) whose job it is to determine which of the many reasoning modules and heuristics that are available in a massive modular mind get called on to deal with a given problem, and that this mechanism, which we'll call *the allocation mechanism*, is routing the problem to the wrong component of the reasoning system. If that's right, and if we further suppose that this misallocation is the result of persisting and systematic features of the allocation mechanism, then it seems natural to conclude that the allocation mechanism itself is normatively problematic. It produces errors in reasoning by sending problems to the wrong place.

If this speculation is correct—if certain errors in reasoning are generated by a normatively problematic allocation mechanism—then it seems odd to say that the resulting errors are "performance errors." For, unlike performance errors that result from fatigue or alcohol or emotional stress, this is not a case in which factors arising outside the reasoning system interfere with the normal functioning of the system and cause it to operate in a way that it does not usually operate. In dealing with cases like the seven-letter-word problem, the allocation mechanism works just the way it normally does. The reasoning error is produced because what it normally does is send problems like these to the wrong place. Nor does this look much like the sort of performance errors that are produced in language processing as the result of limited short-term memory. There is no resource that runs out in these cases of misallocation, no parameter that is exceeded. The subject gets the wrong answer because the principles governing the operation of the allocation system are themselves normatively defective. There is (we have been assuming) a Darwinian module capable of doing a good job on the problem, and the allocation mechanism fails to send it there. At this point, a defender of the Panglossian interpretation might insist that since the correct rules for handling these cases of faulty reasoning are available in the subject's mind, the errors are not the product of a defective competence, and thus allocation errors must be just *another kind* of performance error. This argument assumes that there are only two kinds of cognitive errors—performance errors and competence errors—and that anything which doesn't count as one sort of error must be an instance of the other sort. But that is not an assumption we see any reason to accept. Since misallocation errors are not comfortably viewed either as competence errors or as performance errors, we are inclined to think that one lesson to be learned from examples like this is that in a massively modular mind the performance error/competence error distinction does not exhaust the possibilities.

Let us turn now to the original version of the feminist bank teller problem (section 2.2) and the original version of the Casscells et al. "Harvard Medical School" problem (section 2.3). In both cases subjects perform poorly. How might an advocate of the MMH explain this poor performance? One possibility is that these are further examples of allocation errors, and that there is a reasoning module that would have solved them correctly had they been routed there. But there is also a very different possibility that needs to be explored. Darwinian modules are designed by natural selection to handle recurrent information-processing problems. To enable a module to handle problems efficiently, one strategy that natural selection might exploit is to design the module in such a way that it can deal successfully with a problem only if the problem is presented in an appropriate format or in an appropriate system of representation. Thus, for example, Gigerenzer argues that since frequentist formats were the only ones to play a major role in the EEA, we would expect the mental module(s) that handle probabilistic reasoning to be designed to "expect" that format and to be unable to solve the problems successfully if they are presented in some other format. If Gigerenzer is right, then the module(s) subserving good bayesian reasoning simply cannot solve problems posed in terms of single-event probabilities. But in that case, subjects' errors in the original version of the Harvard Medical School problem and the feminist bank teller problem cannot be treated as allocation errors, since the allocation system hasn't sent them to the wrong place. It has no good place to send them. In ordinary subjects there is no module or component of the reasoning system that has the right algorithms for dealing with the problem as posed.

If these speculations are right, then it might be tempting to conclude that the errors are competence errors, and thus that the bleak implications interpretation has gained a foothold even within a massively modular picture of the mind. But, while the matter may be largely terminological, we are not entirely comfortable with the conclusion that these errors are competence errors. For while it is true that the hypothesized Darwinian module(s) don't contain algorithms that can deal with the problem as *posed*, it is also the case that the modules do contain algorithms for dealing with *reformulated* versions of the problems. Thus it may be possible to improve people's performance on these problems without modifying their competence or enriching the reasoning algorithms that the mind makes available. For we may be able to teach them to restate the problems, to put them into a format that their Darwinian modules are designed to process. Since the distinction between those errors that can be avoided by reformulation and those that cannot is potentially a very important one, we think the avoidable errors merit a category of their own. We'll call them *formulation errors*.

One central claim made by the Panglossian interpretation is that all the errors reported in the experimental literature are merely performance errors. But we've now seen two quite different reasons to be suspicious of that claim. If the MMH is correct, then some reasoning errors are likely to be misallocation errors, while others may be formulation errors. On our view, the right conclusion to draw from the MMH is not that all errors are performance errors, but rather that there are a number of importantly different kinds of errors that can't be comfortably characterized as either performance errors or competence errors. If the MMH is right, then the assumption that all reasoning errors are either performance errors or competence errors will have to be abandoned.

The other central claim made by the Panglossian interpretation is that the mind is well stocked with Darwinian modules that reason in normatively appropriate ways. In the remaining pages of this chapter we want to consider some of the problems that confront this aspect of the Panglossian interpretation. A first problem is settling on what might be called a *general normative theory of reasoning*—a theory which specifies the standards by which any inference mechanism or reasoning strategy should be evaluated. In the philosophical literature there is a great deal of debate about the attractions of competing general normative theories.[17] Some theorists defend "reliabilist" accounts in which attaining true beliefs plays a central role. Others advocate accounts on which attaining more pragmatic goals like health and happiness are central. Still others urge that reasoning strategies should be evaluated by appeal to our reflective intuitions about what is and is not rational. This is not the place to review the arguments for and against these general normative theories. Rather, we will assume, as we have throughout this chapter, that some version of reliabilism is correct, and that truth is central to the evaluation of inferential mechanisms. Other things being equal, one inferential mechanism is better than another if it does a better job at getting the right answer. But even if we assume that reliabilism is the correct general normative theory of reasoning, the domain specificity of Darwinian

---

17. See, e.g., Goldman 1986 and Stich 1990.

modules poses a cluster of new and quite unique problems that traditional epistemology has not yet explored.

Consider, for example, the module that subserves reasoning about social contracts. We can assume that this module does a relatively good job at answering questions about cheating and contract violation. But there are also indefinitely many problems— elementary arithmetic problems, for example, or "theory of mind" problems about what people would believe or decide to do in various circumstances—for which the social contract module does not produce the right answer; indeed, it produces no answer at all. But surely it would be perverse to criticize the social contract module on the grounds that it can't solve mathematical problems. This would be a bit like criticizing a toaster on the grounds that it cannot be used as a typewriter. To evaluate a toaster, we must attend to its performance on an appropriate range of tasks, and clearly typing is not one of them. Similarly, to evaluate the social contract module, we must attend to its performance on an appropriate range of tasks, and solving mathematical problems is not one of them. The moral to be drawn here seems fairly obvious: Normative evaluations of domain-specific modules must be relativized to a specific domain or a specific range of problems. But this immediately raises a new puzzle: If normative evaluations of domain-specific modules must be relativized to a domain, which domain should it be?

One suggestion is that the right domain is what Sperber (1994) calls the *actual domain*. The actual domain for a given reasoning module is "all the information in the organism's environment that (once processed by perceptual modules, and possibly by other conceptual modules) satisfies the module's input conditions" (52). By "input conditions" Sperber means those conditions that must be satisfied in order that the module be able to process a given item of information. So, for example, if a module requires that a problem be stated in a particular format, then any information not stated in that format fails to satisfy the module's input conditions.

A quite different suggestion is that the domain relevant to the evaluation of domain-specific modules is what Sperber calls the *proper domain*, which he characterizes as "all the information that it is the module's biological function to process" (ibid.). The proper domain is the information that the module was designed to process by natural selection. In recent years, many philosophers of biology have come to regard the notion of a biological function as a particularly slippery one.[18] For current purposes we can rely on the following very rough characterization. The biological functions of a system are the activities or effects of the system in virtue of which it has remained a stable feature of an enduring species.

In some cases the actual domain of a Darwinian module may coincide with its proper domain. But it is also likely that in many cases the two domains will not be identical. For example, it is plausible to suppose that the proper domain of the folk-psychology module

---

18. See, e.g., Godfrey-Smith 1994; Neander 1991; Plantinga 1993.

includes only the kind of information about the mental states of human beings and the behavior caused by those states that would have been useful to our Pleistocene forebears. But it is very likely that the module also processes information about lots of other things, including the activities of non-human animals, cartoon characters, and even mindless physical objects like trees and heavenly bodies. If this is right, then a normative evaluation of the module relativized to its proper domain is likely to be much more favorable than a normative evaluation relativized to its actual domain. We suspect that those Panglossian-inclined theorists who describe Darwinian modules as "elegant machines" are tacitly assuming that normative evaluation should be relativized to the proper domain, while those who offer a bleaker assessment of human rationality are tacitly relativizing their evaluations to the actual domain, which, in the modern world, contains a vast array of information-processing challenges that are quite different from anything that our Pleistocene ancestors had to confront.

So which domain should we use to evaluate the module, the proper domain or the actual one? Which domain is the *right* one? We don't think there is any principled way of answering this question. Rather, we maintain, normative claims about Darwinian modules or the algorithms they embody make no clear sense until they are explicitly or implicitly relativized to a domain. Moreover, the choice confronting us is actually much more complex than we have suggested so far. For both actual domains and proper domains are best viewed not as single options but as families of options. There are different ways of explicating both the notion of a proper domain and the notion of an actual domain, and these differences will make a difference, in some cases a major difference, to the outcome of relativized normative assessments. Nor should it be assumed that actual domains and proper domains are the only two families of options that might be considered. Normative assessments can serve many different purposes, and for some of these it may be appropriate to relativize to a domain which is neither actual nor proper.

Our conclusion is that neither the Panglossian interpretation nor the bleak implications interpretation offers a satisfactory response to the Massive Modularity Hypothesis. If it is indeed the case that our minds contain a large number of Darwinian modules, and that the modules subserve most of our everyday reasoning, then many of the categories and distinctions that philosophers and cognitive scientists have used to describe and assess cognition will have to be reworked or abandoned. If the Massive Modularity Hypothesis is correct, we will have to rethink what we mean by "rationality."

ACKNOWLEDGMENTS

Earlier versions of some of this material served as the basis of lectures at the City University of New York Graduate Center, Canterbury University in Christchurch, New Zealand, Rutgers University, and at the Fifth International Colloquium on Cognitive Science in San Sebastian, Spain. We are grateful for the many helpful comments and criticisms that were offered on these occasions. Special thanks are due to Kent Bach, Michael Bishop, Margaret Boden, Derek Browne, L. Jonathan Cohen, Jack Copeland, Stephen Downes, Mary Frances Egan, Richard Foley, Gerd Gigerenzer, Daniel Kahneman, Ernie Lepore, Brian McLaughlin, Brian Scholl, and Ernest Sosa.

REFERENCES

Barkow, J. 1992. Beneath New Culture Is Old Psychology: Gossip and Social Stratification. In Barkow, Cosmides, and Tooby 1992, 627–37.

Barkow, J., L. Cosmides, and J. Tooby, eds. 1992. *The Adapted Mind: Evolutionary Psychology and the Generation of Culture*. Oxford: Oxford University Press.

Baron, J. 1988. *Thinking and Deciding*. Cambridge: Cambridge University Press.

Baron-Cohen, S. 1994. How to Build a Baby That Can Read Minds: Cognitive Mechanisms in Mindreading. *Cahiers de psychologie* 13, 5: 513–52.

———. 1995. *Mindblindness: An Essay on Autism and Theory of Mind*. Cambridge, MA: MIT Press.

Carey, S., and E. Spelke. 1994. Domain-Specific Knowledge and Conceptual Change. In Hirschfeld and Gelman 1994, 169–200.

Carruthers, P., and P. Smith, eds. 1996. *Theories of Theories of Mind*. Cambridge: Cambridge University Press.

Casscells, W., A. Schoenberger, and T. Grayboys. 1978. Interpretation by Physicians of Clinical Laboratory Results. *New England Journal of Medicine* 299: 999–1000.

Chapman, L., and J. Chapman. 1967. Genesis of Popular but Erroneous Diagnostic Observations. *Journal of Abnormal Psychology* 72: 193–204.

———. 1969. Illusory Correlation as an Obstacle to the Use of Valid Psychodiagnostic Signs. *Journal of Abnormal Psychology* 74: 271–80.

Cheng, P., and K. Holyoak. 1985. Pragmatic Reasoning Schémas. *Cognitive Psychology* 17: 391–416.

———. 1989. On the Natural Selection of Reasoning Theories. *Cognition* 33: 285–313.

Cheng, P., K. Holyoak, R. Nisbett, and L. Oliver. 1986. Pragmatic Versus Syntactic Approaches to Training Deductive Reasoning. *Cognitive Psychology* 18: 293–328.

Chomsky, N. 1965. *Aspects of the Theory of Syntax*. Cambridge, MA: MIT Press.

———. 1975. *Reflections of Language*. New York: Pantheon Books.

———. 1980. *Rules and Representations*. New York: Columbia University Press.

Cohen, L. 1981. Can Human Irrationality Be Experimentally Demonstrated? *Behavioral and Brain Sciences* 4: 317–70.

———. 1986. *The Dialogue of Reason*. Oxford: Clarendon Press.

Cosmides, L. 1989. The Logic of Social Exchange: Has Natural Selection Shaped How Humans Reason? Studies with Wason Selection Task. *Cognition* 31: 187–276.

Cosmides, L., and J. Tooby. 1987. From Evolution to Behavior: Evolutionary Psychology as the Missing Link. In J. Dupré, ed., *The Latest on the Best: Essays on Evolution and Optimality*. Cambridge, MA: MIT Press.

———. 1992. Cognitive Adaptations for Social Exchange. In Barkow, Cosmides, and Tooby 1992, 163–228.

————. 1994. Origins of Domain Specificity: The Evolution of Functional Organization. In Hirschfeld and Gelman 1994, 85–116.

————. 1996. Are Humans Good Intuitive Statisticians After All? Rethinking Some Conclusions from the Literature on Judgment Under Uncertainty. *Cognition* 58, 1: 1–73.

Cummins, D. 1996. Evidence for the Innateness of Deontic Reasoning. *Mind and Language* 11: 160–90.

Dawes, R. 1988. *Rational Choice in an Uncertain World*. Orlando, FL: Harcourt Brace Jovanovich.

Evans, J. St. B. T., S. E. Newstead, and R. M. J. Byrne. 1993. *Human Reasoning: The Psychology of Deduction*. Hove, U.K.: Lawrence Erlbaum Associates Ltd.

Fiedler, K. 1988. The Dependence of the Conjunction Fallacy on Subtle Linguistic Factors. *Psychological Research* 50: 123–29.

Fodor, J. 1983. *The Modularity of Mind*. Cambridge, MA: MIT Press.

————. 1986. The Modularity of Mind. In Pylyshyn and Demopoulos 1986, 3–18.

Gallistel, C. 1990. *The Organization of Learning*. Cambridge, MA: MIT Press.

Gardner, H. 1983. *Frames of Mind: The Theory of Multiple Intelligences*. New York: Basic Books.

Garfield, J., ed. 1987. *Modularity in Knowledge Representation and Natural-language Understanding*. Cambridge, MA: MIT Press.

Gelman, S., and K. Brenneman. 1994. First Principles Can Support Both Universal and Culture-Specific Learning About Number and Music. In Hirschfeld and Gelman 1994, 369–87.

Gigerenzer, G. 1991. How to Make Cognitive Illusions Disappear: Beyond "Heuristics and Biases." *European Review of Social Psychology* 2: 83–115.

————. 1994. Why the Distinction Between Single-Event Probabilities and Frequencies Is Important for Psychology (and Vice Versa). In G. Wright and P. Ayton, eds., *Subjective Probability*, 129–61. New York: John Wiley.

Gigerenzer, G., and U. Hoffrage. 1995. How to Improve Bayesian Reasoning Without Instruction: Frequency Formats. *Psychological Review* 102: 684–704.

Gigerenzer, G., U. Hoffrage, and H. Kleinbölting. 1991. Probabilistic Mental Models: A Brunswikean Theory of Confidence. *Psychological Review* 98: 506–28.

Gigerenzer, G., and K. Hug. 1992. Domain-Specific Reasoning: Social Contracts, Cheating and Perspective Change. *Cognition* 43: 127–71.

Gigerenzer, G., and D. Murray. 1987. *Cognition as Intuitive Statistics*. Hillsdale, NJ: Erlbaum.

Gilovich, T., B. Vallone, and A. Tversky. 1985. The Hot Hand in Basketball: On the Misconception of Random Sequences. *Cognitive Psychology* 17: 295–314.

Gluck, M., and G. Bower. 1988. From Conditioning to Category Learning: An Adaptive Network Model. *Journal of Experimental Psychology: General* 117: 227–47.

Godfrey-Smith, P. 1994. A Modern History Theory of Functions. *Nous* 28: 344–62.

Goldman, A. 1986. *Epistemology and Cognition*. Cambridge, MA: Harvard University Press.

Gould, S. 1992. *Bully for Brontosaurus: Further Reflections in Natural History*. London: Penguin Books.

Griffiths, P. 1997. *What Emotions Really Are*. Chicago: University of Chicago Press.

Griggs, R., and J. Cox. 1982. The Elusive Thematic-Materials Effect in Wason's Selection Task. *British Journal of Psychology* 73: 407–20.

Haugeland, J. 1985. *Artificial Intelligence: The Very Idea*. Cambridge, MA: MIT Press.

Hertwig, R., and G. Gigerenzer. 1994. The Chain of Reasoning in the Conjunction Task. Unpublished manuscript.

Hirschfeld, L., and S. Gelman, eds. 1994. *Mapping the Mind*. Cambridge: Cambridge University Press.

Hutchins, E. 1980. *Culture and Inference: A Trobriand Case Study*. Cambridge, MA: Harvard University Press.

Jackendoff, R. 1992. Is There a Faculty of Social Cognition? In *Languages of the Mind*, 69–81. Cambridge, MA: MIT Press.

Kahneman, D., P. Slovic, and A. Tversky, eds. 1982. *Judgment Under Uncertainty: Heuristics and Biases*. Cambridge: Cambridge University Press.

Kahneman, D., and A. Tversky. 1973. On the Psychology of Prediction. *Psychological Review* 80: 237–51. Reprinted in Kahneman, Slovic, and Tversky 1982, 48–68.

———. 1996. On the Reality of Cognitive Illusions. *Psychological Review* 103: 582–91.

Karmiloff-Smith, A. 1992. *Beyond Modularity: A Developmental Perspective on Cognitive Science*. Cambridge, MA: MIT Press.

Lehman, D., and R. Nisbett. 1990. A Longitudinal Study of the Effects of Undergraduate Education on Reasoning. *Developmental Psychology* 26: 952–60.

Lehman, D., R. Lempert, and R. Nisbett. 1988. The Effects of Graduate Education on Reasoning: Formal Discipline and Thinking About Everyday Life Events. *American Psychologist* 43: 431–43.

Leslie, A. 1994. ToMM, ToBY, and Agency: Core Architecture and Domain Specificity. In Hirschfeld and Gelman 1994, 119–48.

Lichenstein, S., B. Fischhoff, and L. Phillips. 1992. Calibration of Probabilities: The State of the Art to 1980. In Kahneman, Slovic, and Tversky 1982, 306–34.

Manktelow, K., and D. Over. 1995. Deontic Reasoning. In S. Newstead and J. St. B. Evans, eds., *Perspectives on Thinking and Reasoning*, 91–114. Hillsdale, NJ: Erlbaum.

Marr, D. 1982. *Vision*. San Francisco: W. H. Freeman.

Neander, K. 1991. The Teleological Notion of "Function." *Australasian Journal of Philosophy* 59: 454–68.

Nisbett, R., G. Fong, D. Lehman, and P. Cheng. 1987. Teaching Reasoning. *Science* 238: 625–31.

Nisbett, R., and L. Ross. 1980. *Human Inference: Strategies and Shortcomings of Social Judgment*. Englewood Cliffs, NJ: Prentice-Hall.

Oaksford, M., and N. Chater. 1994. A Rational Analysis of the Selection Task as Optimal Data Selection. *Psychological Review* 101: 608–31.

Piattelli-Palmarini, M. 1994. *Inevitable Illusions: How Mistakes of Reason Rule Our Minds*. New York: John Wiley and Sons.

Pinker, S. 1994. *The Language Instinct*. New York: William Morrow and Co.

———. 1997. *How the Mind Works*. New York: W. W. Norton.

Plantinga, A. 1993. *Warrant and Proper Function*. Oxford: Oxford University Press.

Pylyshyn, Z. 1984. *Computation and Cognition*. Cambridge, MA: MIT Press.

Pylyshyn, Z., and W. Demopoulos, eds. 1986. *Meaning and Cognitive Structure: Issues in the Computational Theory of Mind*. Norwood, MA: Ablex.

Quartz, S., and T. Sejnowski. 1994. Beyond Modularity: Neural Constructivist Principles in Development. *Behavioral and Brain Sciences* 17: 725–26.

Samuels, R. 1998. Evolutionary Psychology and the Massive Modularity Hypothesis. *British Journal for the Philosophy of Science* 49: 575–602.

Segal, G. 1996. The Modularity of Theory of Mind. In Carruthers and Smith 1995, 141–57.

Slovic, P., B. Fischhoff, and S. Lichtenstein. 1976. Cognitive Processes and Societal Risk Taking. In J. S. Carol and J. W. Payne, eds., *Cognition and Social Behavior*, 165–84. Hillsdale, NJ: Erlbaum.

Sperber, D. 1994. The Modularity of Thought and Epidemiology of Representations. In Hirschfeld and Gelman 1994, 39–67.

Sperber, D., F. Cara, and W. Girotto. 1995. Relevance Theory Explains the Selection Task. *Cognition* 57, 1: 31–95.

Stein, E. 1996. *Without Good Reason*. Oxford: Clarendon Press.

Stich, S. 1990. *The Fragmentation of Reason*. Cambridge, MA: MIT Press.

Sutherland, S. 1994. *Irrationality: Why We Don't Think Straight*. New Brunswick, NJ: Rutgers University Press.

Tanenhaus, M., G. Dell, and G. Carlson. 1987. Context Effects and Lexical Processing: A Connectionist Approach to Modularity. In Garfield 1987, 83–108.

Tooby, J., and L. Cosmides. 1995. Foreword to Baron-Cohen 1995, xi–xviii.

Trivers, R. 1971. The Evolution of Reciprocal Altruism. *Quarterly Review of Biology* 46: 35–56.

Tversky, A., and D. Kahneman. 1982. Judgments of and by Representativeness. In Kahneman, Slovic, and Tversky 1982, 84–98.

———. 1983. Extensional Versus Intuitive Reasoning: The Conjunction Fallacy in Probability Judgment. *Psychological Review* 90: 293–315.

Wason, P. 1966. Reasoning. In B. Foss, ed., *New Horizons in Psychology*, 135–51. Harmondsworth: Penguin.

Wilson, M., and M. Daly. 1992. The Man Who Mistook His Wife for a Chattel. In Barkow, Cosmides, and Tooby 1992, 289–322.

8

NORMATIVITY AND EPISTEMIC INTUITIONS

Jonathan M. Weinberg, Shaun Nichols, and Stephen Stich

1. Introduction

IN THIS PAPER we propose to argue for two claims. The first is that a sizeable group of epistemological projects—a group which includes much of what has been done in epistemology in the analytic tradition—would be seriously undermined if one or more of a cluster of empirical hypotheses about epistemic intuitions turns out to be true. The basis for this claim will be set out in Section 2. The second claim is that, while the jury is still out, there is now a substantial body of evidence suggesting that some of those empirical hypotheses *are* true. Much of this evidence derives from an ongoing series of experimental studies of epistemic intuitions that we have been conducting. A preliminary report on these studies will be presented in Section 3. In light of these studies, we think it is incumbent on those who pursue the epistemological projects in question to either explain why the truth of the hypotheses does not undermine their projects, or to say why, in light of the evidence we will present, they nonetheless assume that the hypotheses are false. In Section 4, which is devoted to Objections and Replies, we'll consider some of the ways in which defenders of the projects we are criticizing might reply to our challenge. Our goal, in all of this, is not to offer a conclusive argument demonstrating that the epistemological projects we will be criticizing are untenable. Rather, our aim is to shift the burden of argument. For far too long, epistemologists who rely heavily on epistemic intuitions have proceeded as though they could simply ignore the empirical hypotheses we will set out.

We will be well satisfied if we succeed in making a plausible case for the claim that this approach is no longer acceptable.

To start, it will be useful to sketch a brief—and perhaps somewhat idiosyncratic—taxonomy of epistemological projects. With the aid of this taxonomy we will try to "locate in philosophical space" (as Wilfrid Sellars used to say) those epistemological projects which, we maintain, are threatened by the evidence we will present. There are at least four distinct, though related, projects that have occupied the attention of epistemologists. Following Richard Samuels,[1] we'll call them the Normative Project, the Descriptive Project, the Evaluative Project and the Ameliorative Project.

The Normative Project, which we're inclined to think is the most philosophically central of the four, attempts to establish norms to guide our epistemic efforts. Some of these norms may be explicitly regulative, specifying which ways of going about the quest for knowledge should be pursued and which should not. This articulation of regulative norms is one of the more venerable of philosophical undertakings, going back at least to Descartes's *Regulae* and evident in the work of Mill, Popper and many other important figures in the history of philosophy; and it continues in philosophy today. For example, when Alvin Goldman chastises internalism for being unable to provide us with "Doxastic Decision Principles," he is challenging the ability of internalism to pull its weight in this aspect of the Normative Project.[2] The Normative Project also aims to articulate what might be called *valuational* norms, which attempt to answer questions like: What is our epistemic good? and How should we prefer to structure our doxastic lives? One may not be able to generate regulative principles from the answers provided; rather, the answers tell us at what target the regulative principles should aim.

The Descriptive Project can have a variety of targets, the two most common being epistemic concepts and epistemic language. When concepts are the target, the goal is to describe (or "analyze") the epistemic concepts that some group of people actually invoke. When pursued by epistemologists (rather than linguists or anthropologists), the group in question is typically characterized rather vaguely by using the first person plural. They are "our" concepts, the ones that "we" use. Work in this tradition has led to a large literature attempting to analyze concepts like knowledge, justification, warrant, and rationality.[3] When language is the focus of the Descriptive Project, the goal is to describe the way some group of people use epistemic language or to analyze the meaning of their epistemic terms. Here again, the group is almost invariably "us."

Many epistemologists think that there are important links between the Normative and Descriptive Projects. Indeed, we suspect that these (putative) links go a long way toward explaining why philosophers think the Descriptive Project is so important. In epistemology,

1. Samuels, unpublished manuscript.
2. Goldman 1980.
3. The literature on conceptual analysis in epistemology is vast. For an elite selection, see the essays assembled in Sosa 1994.

knowledge is "the good stuff" and to call a belief an instance of knowledge is to pay it one of the highest compliments an epistemologist can bestow.[4] Thus terms like "knowledge," "justification," "warrant," etc., and the concepts they express are themselves plausibly regarded as implicitly normative. Moreover, many philosophers hold that sentences invoking epistemic terms have explicitly normative consequences. So, for example, "S's belief that p is an instance of knowledge" might plausibly be taken to entail "*Ceteris paribus*, S ought to believe that p" or perhaps "*Ceteris paribus*, it is a good thing for S to believe that p."[5] For reasons that will emerge, we are more than a bit skeptical about the alleged links between the Descriptive and Normative Projects. For the time being, however, we will leave the claim that the two projects are connected unchallenged.

The Evaluative Project tries to assess how well or poorly people's actual belief forming practices accord with the norms specified in the Normative Project. To do this, of course, another sort of descriptive effort is required. Before we can say how well or poorly people are doing at the business of belief formation and revision, we have to say in some detail how they actually go about the process of belief formation and revision.[6] The Ameliorative Project presupposes that we don't all come out with the highest possible score in the assessment produced by the Evaluative Project, and asks how we can improve the way we go about the business of belief formation. In this paper our primary focus will be on the Normative Project and on versions of the Descriptive Project which assume that the Descriptive and Normative Projects are linked in something like the way sketched above.

2. Intuition Driven Romanticism and the Normativity Problem

2.1 EPISTEMIC ROMANTICISM AND INTUITION DRIVEN ROMANTICISM

A central question that the Normative Project tries to answer is: *How ought we to go about the business of belief formation and revision?* How are we to go about finding an answer to this question? And once an answer has been proposed, how are we to assess it? If two theorists offer different answers, how can we determine which one is better? Philosophers who have pursued the Normative Project have used a variety of methods or strategies. In this section we want to begin by describing one very influential family of strategies.

---

4. This is a view with a venerable history. In Plato's *Protagoras*, Socrates says that "knowledge is a noble and commanding thing," and Protagoras, not to be outdone, replies that "wisdom and knowledge are the highest of human things" (1892/1937, 352).

5. Perhaps the most important advocate of extracting normative principles from analyses of our epistemic terms is Roderick Chisholm (1977). This approach is shared in projects as otherwise dissimilar as BonJour 1985 and Pollock and Cruz 1999.

6. For further discussion of the Evaluative Project, see Samuels, Stich and Tremoulet 1999; Samuels, Stich and Bishop 2002; Samuels, Stich and Faucher 2004.

The family we have in mind belongs to a larger group of strategies which (just to be provocative) we propose to call *Epistemic Romanticism*. One central idea of 19th century Romanticism was that our real selves, the essence of our identity, is implanted within us, and that to discover who we really are we need but let that real identity emerge. Epistemic Romanticism assumes something rather similar about epistemic norms. According to Epistemic Romanticism, knowledge of the correct epistemic norms (or information that can lead to knowledge of the correct norms) is implanted within us in some way, and with the proper process of self-exploration we can discover them. As we read him, Plato was an early exponent of this kind of Romanticism about matters normative (and about much else besides). So *Epistemic Platonism* might be another (perhaps equally provocative) label for this group of strategies for discovering or testing epistemic norms.

There are various ways in which the basic idea of Epistemic Romanticism can be elaborated. The family of strategies that we want to focus on all accord a central role to what we will call *epistemic intuitions*. Thus we will call this family of strategies *Intuition Driven Romanticism* (or IDR). As we use the notion, an epistemic intuition is simply a spontaneous judgment about the epistemic properties of some specific case—a judgment for which the person making the judgment may be able to offer no plausible justification. To count as an Intuition Driven Romantic strategy for discovering or testing epistemic norms, the following three conditions must be satisfied:

(i) The strategy must take epistemic intuitions as data or input. (It can also exploit various other sorts of data.)

(ii) It must produce, as output, explicitly or implicitly normative claims or principles about matters epistemic. Explicitly normative claims include regulative claims about how we ought to go about the business of belief formation, claims about the relative merits of various strategies for belief formation, and evaluative claims about the merits of various epistemic situations. Implicitly normative claims include claims to the effect that one or another process of belief formation leads to justified beliefs or to real knowledge or that a doxastic structure of a certain kind amounts to real knowledge.

(iii) The output of the strategy must depend, in part, on the epistemic intuitions it takes as input. If provided with significantly different intuitions, the strategy must yield significantly different output.[7]

Perhaps the most familiar examples of Intuition Driven Romanticism are various versions of the reflective equilibrium strategy in which (to paraphrase Goodman slightly) "a

---

7. Note that as we've characterized them, epistemic intuitions are spontaneous judgments about *specific cases*. Some strategies for discovering or testing epistemic norms also take intuitions about general epistemic or inferential principles as input. These will count as Intuition Driven Romantic strategies provided that the output is suitably sensitive to the intuitions about specific cases that are included in the input.

[normative] rule is amended if it yields an inference we are [intuitively] unwilling to accept [and] an inference is rejected if it violates a [normative] rule we are [intuitively] unwilling to amend."[8] In a much discussed paper called "Can Human Irrationality Be Experimentally Demonstrated?" L. J. Cohen proposes a variation on Goodman's strategy as a way of determining what counts as rational or normatively appropriate reasoning.[9] It is of some importance to note that there are many ways in which the general idea of a reflective equilibrium process can be spelled out. Some philosophers, including Cohen, advocate a "narrow" reflective equilibrium strategy. Others advocate a "wide" reflective equilibrium strategy. And both of these alternatives can be elaborated in various ways.[10] Moreover, the details are often quite important since different versions of the reflective equilibrium strategy may yield different outputs, even when provided with exactly the same input.

Another example of the IDR strategy can be found in Alvin Goldman's important and influential book, *Epistemology and Cognition* (1986). A central goal of epistemology, Goldman argues, is to develop a theory that will specify which of our beliefs are epistemically justified and which are not, and a fundamental step in constructing such a theory will be to articulate a system of rules or principles evaluating the justificatory status of beliefs. These rules, which Goldman calls *J-rules*, will specify permissible ways in which cognitive agents may go about the business of forming or updating their beliefs. They "permit or prohibit beliefs, directly or indirectly, as a function of some states, relations, or processes of the cognizer."[11] But, of course, different theorists may urge different and incompatible sets of J-rules. So in order to decide whether a proposed system of J-rules is correct, we must appeal to a higher criterion—Goldman calls it "a criterion of rightness"—which will specify a "set of conditions that are necessary and sufficient for a set of J-rules to be right."[12] But now the theoretical disputes emerge at a higher level, for different theorists have suggested very different criteria of rightness. Indeed, as Goldman notes, an illuminating taxonomy of epistemological theories can be generated by classifying them on the basis of the sort of criterion of rightness they endorse. So how are we to go about deciding among these various criteria of rightness? The answer, Goldman maintains, is that the correct criterion of rightness is the one that comports with the conception of justification that is "embraced by everyday thought and language."[13] To test a criterion, we consider the judgments it would entail about specific cases, and we test these judgments against our "pretheoretic intuition." "A criterion is supported to

8. Goodman 1965, 66.

9. Cohen 1981. For a useful discussion of the debate that Cohen's paper provoked, see Stein 1996, Ch. 5.

10. See, for example, Elgin 1996, Ch. IV, and Stein 1996, Chs. 5 and 7.

11. Goldman 1986, 60.

12. Ibid., 64.

13. Ibid., 58.

the extent that implied judgments accord with such intuitions and weakened to the extent that they do not."[14, 15]

The examples we have mentioned so far are hardly the only examples of Intuition Driven Romanticism. Indeed, we think a plausible case can be made that a fair amount of what goes on in normative epistemology can be classified as Intuition Driven Romanticism. Moreover, to the extent that it is assumed to have normative implications, much of what has been written in descriptive epistemology in recent decades also counts as Intuition Driven Romanticism. For example, just about all of the vast literature that arose in response to Gettier's classic paper uses intuitions about specific cases to test proposed analyses of the concept of knowledge.[16]

For many purposes, the details of an IDR strategy—the specific ways in which it draws inferences from intuitions and other data—will be of enormous importance. But since our goal is to raise a problem for all IDR strategies, the exact details of how they work will play no role in our argument. Thus, for our purposes, an IDR strategy can be viewed as a "black box" which takes intuitions (and perhaps other data) as input and produces implicitly or explicitly normative claims as output. The challenge we are about to raise is, we claim, a problem for IDR accounts no matter what goes on within the black box.

---

14. Ibid., 66.

15. In an insightful commentary on this paper, presented at the Conference in Honor of Alvin Goldman, Joel Pust notes that in his recent work Goldman (1992, 1999; Goldman and Pust 1998) has offered a rather different account of how epistemic intuitions are to be used:

Very roughly, Goldman's more recent view treats the targets of philosophical analysis as concepts in the psychological sense of "concept," concrete mental representations causally implicated in the production of philosophical intuitions. On this new view, intuitions serve primarily as reliable evidence concerning the intuitor's internal psychological mechanisms. . . . Especially interesting in the context of [the Weinberg, Nichols and Stich paper] is the fact that Goldman explicitly disavows the common assumption of "great uniformity in epistemic subjects" judgments about cases, noting that this assumption may result from the fact that philosophers come from a "fairly homogeneous subculture" (Goldman 1992, 160).

This new psychologistic account makes it easier to explain why intuitions are reliable evidence of some sort. However, this reliability is gained by deflating the evidential pretensions of intuitions so that they are no longer treated as relevant to the non-linguistic or non-psychological question which is the central concern of the Normative Project: "What makes a belief epistemically justified?" While Goldman's approach solves a problem about the reliability of intuitions by telling us that the fact that people have certain intuitions is a reliable indicator of their psychological constitution, it does not resolve the problem which motivated Stich's argument since that problem was whether we are justified in treating the content of our epistemic intuitions as a reliable guide to the nature of justified belief. So, while Goldman's use of intuitions in his new project seems to me largely immune to [the criticisms in the paper by Weinberg, Nichols and Stich], this is because that project has aspirations quite different from those of traditional analytic epistemology.

16. Gettier 1963. For a review of literature during the first two decades after Gettier's paper appeared, see Shope 1983. For more recent work in this tradition, see Plantinga 1993a and 1993b as well as the follow-up collection of papers in Kvanvig 1996.

2.2 THE NORMATIVITY PROBLEM

Reflective equilibrium strategies and other Intuition Driven Romantic strategies all yield as outputs claims that putatively have normative force. These outputs tell us how people ought to go about forming and revising their beliefs, which belief-forming strategies yield genuinely justified beliefs, which beliefs are warranted, which count as real knowledge rather than mere opinion, etc. But there is a problem lurking here—we'll call it the *Normativity Problem*: What reason is there to think that the output of one or another of these Intuition Driven Romantic strategies has real (as opposed to putative) normative force? Why should we care about the normative pronouncements produced by these strategies? Why should we try to do what these outputs claim we ought to do in matters epistemic? Why, in short, should we take any of this stuff seriously?

We don't think that there is any good solution to the Normativity Problem for Intuition Driven Romanticism or indeed for any other version of Romanticism in epistemology. And because there is no solution to the Normativity Problem, we think that the entire tradition of Epistemic Romanticism has been a very bad idea. These, obviously, are very big claims and this is not the place to mount a detailed argument for all of them. We do, however, want to rehearse one consideration, first raised in Stich's book, *The Fragmentation of Reason*.[17] We think it lends some plausibility to the claim that satisfying solutions to the Normativity Problem for Intuition Driven Romanticism are going to be hard to find. It will also help to motivate the empirical studies we will recount in the section to follow.

What Stich noted is that the following situation seems perfectly possible. There might be a group of people who reason and form beliefs in ways that are significantly different from the way we do. Moreover, these people might also have epistemic intuitions that are significantly different from ours. More specifically, they might have epistemic intuitions which, when plugged into your favorite Intuition Driven Romantic black box yield the conclusion that *their* strategies of reasoning and belief formation lead to epistemic states that are rational (or justified, or of the sort that yield genuine knowledge—pick your favorite normative epistemic notion here). If this is right, then it looks like the IDR strategy for answering normative epistemic questions might sanction any of a wide variety of regulative and valuational norms. And that sounds like bad news for an advocate of the IDR strategy, since the strategy doesn't tell us what we really want to know. It doesn't tell us how we should go about the business of forming and revising our beliefs. One might, of course, insist that the normative principles that should be followed are the ones that are generated when we put *our* intuitions into the IDR black box. But it is less than obvious (to put it mildly) how this move could be defended. Why should we privilege our intuitions rather than the intuitions of some other group?

---

17. Stich 1990, Sec. 4.6.

One objection that was occasionally raised in response to this challenge focused on the fact that the groups conjured in Stich's argument are just philosophical fictions.[18] While it may well be logically possible that there are groups of people whose reasoning patterns and epistemic intuitions differ systematically from our own, there is no reason to suppose that it is nomologically or psychologically possible. And without some reason to think that such people are psychologically possible, the objection continued, the thought experiment does not pose a problem that the defender of the IDR strategy needs to take seriously. We are far from convinced by this objection, though we are prepared to concede that the use of nomologically or psychologically impossible cases in normative epistemology raises some deep and difficult issues. Thus, for argument's sake, we are prepared to concede that a plausible case might be made for privileging normative claims based on actual intuitions over normative claims based on intuitions that are merely logically possible. But what if the people imagined in the thought experiment are not just logically possible, but psychologically possible? Indeed, what if they are not merely psychologically possible but real—and to all appearances normal and flourishing? Under those circumstances, we maintain, it is hard to see how advocates of an IDR strategy can maintain that their intuitions have any special standing or that the normative principles these intuitions generate when plugged into their favorite IDR black box should be privileged over the normative principles that would be generated if we plugged the other people's intuitions into the same IDR black box. In the section to follow we will argue that these "what ifs" are not *just* "what ifs." There really are people—normal, flourishing people—whose epistemic intuition are systematically different from "ours."

3. Cultural Variation in Epistemic Intuitions

3.1 NISBETT AND HAIDT: SOME SUGGESTIVE EVIDENCE

Our suspicion that people like those imagined in Stich's thought experiment might actually exist was first provoked by the results of two recent research programs in psychology. In one of these, Richard Nisbett and his collaborators have shown that there are large and systematic differences between East Asians and Westerners[19] on a long list of basic cognitive processes including perception, attention and memory. These groups also differ in the way they go about describing, predicting and explaining events, in the way they categorize objects and in the way they revise beliefs in the face of new arguments and evidence. This work makes it very plausible that the first part of Stich's

---

18. Cf. Pollock and Cruz 1999, 150.

19. The East Asian subjects were Chinese, Japanese and Korean. Some of the experiments were conducted in Asia; others used East Asian students studying in the United States or first and second generation East Asian immigrants to the United States. The Western subjects were Americans of European ancestry.

thought experiment is more than just a logical possibility. There really are people whose reasoning and belief forming strategies are very different from ours. Indeed, there are over a billion of them!

Though space does not permit us to offer a detailed account of the differences that Nisbett and his colleagues found, a few brief notes will be useful in motivating the studies we will describe later is this section. According to Nisbett and his colleagues, the differences "can be loosely grouped together under the heading of holistic vs. analytic thought." Holistic thought, which predominates among East Asians, is characterized as "involving an orientation to the context or field as a whole, including attention to relationships between a focal object and the field, and a preference for explaining and predicting events on the basis of such relationships." Analytic thought, the prevailing pattern among Westerners, is characterized as "involving detachment of the object from its context, a tendency to focus on attributes of the object in order to assign it to categories, and a preference for using rules about the categories to explain and predict the object's behavior."[20] One concomitant of East Asian holistic thought is the tendency to focus on chronological rather than causal patterns in describing and recalling events. Westerners, by contrast, focus on causal patterns in these tasks.[21] Westerners also have a stronger sense of agency and independence, while East Asians have a much stronger commitment to social harmony. In East Asian society, the individual feels "very much a part of a large and complex social organism . . . where behavioral prescriptions must be followed and role obligations adhered to scrupulously."[22]

The second research program that led us to suspect there might actually be people like those in Stich's thought experiment was the work of Jonathan Haidt and his collaborators.[23] These investigators were interested in exploring the extent to which moral intuitions about events in which no one is harmed track judgments about disgust in people from different cultural and socioeconomic groups. For their study they constructed a set of brief stories about victimless activities that were intended to trigger the emotion of disgust. They presented these stories to subjects using a structured interview technique designed to determine whether the subjects found the activities described to be disgusting and also to elicit the subjects' moral intuitions about the activities. As an illustration, here is a story describing actions which people in all the groups studied found (not surprisingly) to be quite disgusting:

A man goes to the supermarket once a week and buys a dead chicken. But before cooking the chicken, he has sexual intercourse with it. Then he cooks it and eats it.

---

20. Nisbett et al. 2001, 293.

21. Nisbett, personal communication; Watanabe 1999, abstract. See also Watanabe 1998.

22. Nisbett et al. 2001, 292–93.

23. Haidt, Koller, and Dias 1993. We are grateful to Christopher Knapp for bringing Haidt's work to our attention.

The interviews were administered to both high and low socioeconomic status (SES) subjects in Philadelphia (USA) and in two cities in Brazil. Perhaps the most surprising finding in this study was that there are large differences in moral intuitions between social classes. Indeed, in most cases the difference between social classes was significantly greater than the difference between Brazilian and American subjects of the same SES. Of course we haven't yet told you what the differences in moral intuitions were, though you should be able to predict them by noting your own moral intuitions. (Hint: If you are reading this article, you count as high SES.) Not to keep you in suspense, low SES subjects tend to think that the man who has sex with the chicken is doing something that is seriously morally wrong; high SES subjects don't. Much the same pattern was found with the other scenarios used in the study.

3.2 FOUR HYPOTHESES

For our purposes, Haidt's work, like Nisbett's, is only suggestive. Nisbett gives us reason to think that people in different cultural groups exploit very different belief-forming strategies. Haidt's work demonstrates that people in different SES groups have systematically different moral intuitions. Neither investigator explored the possibility that there might be differences in *epistemic* intuitions in different groups. However, the results they reported were enough to convince us that the following pair of hypotheses *might* be true, and that it was worth the effort to find out:

> *Hypothesis 1:* Epistemic intuitions vary from culture to culture.
> *Hypothesis 2:* Epistemic intuitions vary from one socioeconomic group to another.

To these two experimentally inspired hypotheses we added two more that were suggested by anecdotal rather than experimental evidence. It has often seemed to us that students' epistemic intuitions change as they take more philosophy courses, and we have often suspected that we and our colleagues were, in effect, teaching neophyte philosophers to have intuitions that are in line with those of more senior members of the profession. Or perhaps we are not modifying intuitions at all but simply weeding out students whose intuitions are not mainstream. If either of these is the case, then the intuitions that "we" use in our philosophical work are not those of the man and woman in the street, but those of a highly trained and self-selecting community. These speculations led to:

> *Hypothesis 3:* Epistemic intuitions vary as a function of how many philosophy courses a person has had.

It also sometimes seems that the order in which cases are presented to people can have substantial effects on people's epistemic intuitions. This hunch is reinforced by some intriguing work on neural networks suggesting that a variety of learning strategies may be "path dependent."[24] If this hunch is correct, the pattern of intuitions that people offer on a series of cases might well differ systematically as a function of the order in which the cases are presented. This suggested our fourth hypothesis:

Hypothesis 4: Epistemic intuitions depend, in part, on the order in which cases are presented.

Moreover, it might well be the case that some of the results of order effects are very hard to modify.[25]

If any one of these four hypotheses turns out to be true then, we maintain, it will pose a serious problem for the advocate of Intuition Driven Romanticism. If all of them are true, then it is hard to believe that any plausible case can be made for the claim that the normative pronouncements of Intuition Driven Romanticism have real normative force—that they are norms that we (or anyone else) should take seriously.

3.3 SOME EXPERIMENTS EXPLORING CULTURAL VARIATION IN EPISTEMIC INTUITIONS

Are any of these hypotheses true? To try to find out we have been conducting a series of experiments designed to test Hypotheses 1 and 2. While the results we have so far are preliminary, they are sufficient, we think, to at least shift the burden of argument well over in the direction of the defender of IDR strategies. What our results show, we believe, is that the advocates of IDR can no longer simply ignore these hypotheses or dismiss them as implausible, for there is a growing body of evidence which suggests that they might well be true.

In designing our experiments, we were guided by three rather different considerations. First, we wanted our intuition probes—the cases that we would ask subjects to judge—to be similar to cases that have actually been used in the recent literature in epistemology. Second, since the findings reported by Nisbett and his colleagues all focused on differences between East Asians (henceforth EAs) and European Americans (henceforth Ws, for "Westerners"), we decided that would be the obvious place to look first for differences in epistemic intuitions. Third, since Nisbett and his colleagues argue that Ws are significantly more individualistic than EAs, who tend to be much more interdependent and "collectivist" and thus much more concerned about community harmony and consensus, we tried to construct some intuition probes that would tap into this difference. Would individualistic Ws, perhaps, be more inclined to attribute knowledge to people whose

---

24. See Clark 1997, 204–7.

25. Nisbett and Ross's work on "belief perseverance" shows that, sometimes at least, once a belief is formed, it can be surprisingly impervious to change. See, for example, Nisbett and Ross 1980, Ch. 8.

beliefs are reliably formed by processes that no one else in their community shares? The answer, it seems, is yes.

3.3.1 Truetemp Cases

An issue of great moment in recent analytic epistemology is the internalism/externalism debate. Internalism, with respect to some epistemically evaluative property, is the view that *only* factors within an agent's introspective grasp can be relevant to whether the agent's beliefs have that property. Components of an agent's doxastic situation available to introspection are internalistically kosher; other factors beyond the scope of introspection, such as the reliability of the psychological mechanisms that actually produced the belief, are epistemically external to the agent. Inspired by Lehrer (1990), we included in our surveys a number of cases designed to explore externalist/internalist dimensions of our subjects' intuitions. Here is one of the questions we presented to our subjects, all of whom were undergraduates at Rutgers University.[26]

> One day Charles is suddenly knocked out by a falling rock, and his brain becomes re-wired so that he is always absolutely right whenever he estimates the temperature where he is. Charles is completely unaware that his brain has been altered in this way. A few weeks later, this brain re-wiring leads him to believe that it is 71 degrees in his room. Apart from his estimation, he has no other reasons to think that it is 71 degrees. In fact, it is at that time 71 degrees in his room. Does Charles really know that it was 71 degrees in the room, or does he only believe it?
>
> REALLY KNOWS   ONLY BELIEVES

Although Charles' belief is produced by a reliable mechanism, it is stipulated that he is completely unaware of this reliability. So his reliability is epistemically external. Therefore, to the extent that a subject population is unwilling to attribute knowledge in this case, we have evidence that the group's "folk epistemology" may be internalist. We found that while both groups were more likely to deny knowledge, EA subjects were much more likely to deny knowledge than were their W classmates. The results are shown in Figure 8.1.[27]

After finding this highly significant difference, we began tinkering with the text to see if we could construct other "Truetemp" cases in which the difference between the two groups would disappear. Our first thought was to replace the rock with some socially sanctioned intervention. The text we used was as follows:

---

26. In classifying subjects as East Asian or Western, we relied on the same ethnic identification questionnaire that Nisbett and his colleagues had used. We are grateful to Professor Nisbett for providing us with a copy of the questionnaire and for much helpful advice on its use.

27. The numerical data for all the experiments reported in this paper are assembled in the Appendix.

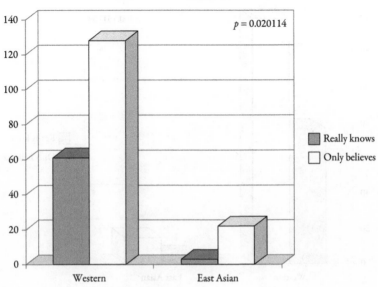

FIGURE 8.1

One day John is suddenly knocked out by a team of well-meaning scientists sent by the elders of his community, and his brain is re-wired so that he is always absolutely right whenever he estimates the temperature where he is. John is completely unaware that his brain has been altered in this way. A few weeks later, this brain re-wiring leads him to believe that it is 71 degrees in his room. Apart from his estimation, he has no other reasons to think that it is 71 degrees. In fact, it is at that time 71 degrees in his room. Does John really know that it was 71 degrees in the room, or does he only believe it?

REALLY KNOWS   ONLY BELIEVES

As we had predicted, the highly significant difference between the two groups disappeared. The results are shown in Figure 8.2.

Encouraged by this finding we constructed yet another version of the "Truetemp" case in which the mechanism that reliably leads to a true belief is not unique to a single individual, but rather is shared by everyone else in the community. The intuition probe read as follows:

The Faluki are a large but tight knit community living on a remote island. One day, a radioactive meteor strikes the island and has one significant effect on the Faluki— it changes the chemical make-up of their brains so that they are always absolutely right whenever they estimate the temperature. The Faluki are completely unaware that their brains have been altered in this way. Kal is a member of the Faluki community. A few weeks after the meteor strike, while Kal is walking along the

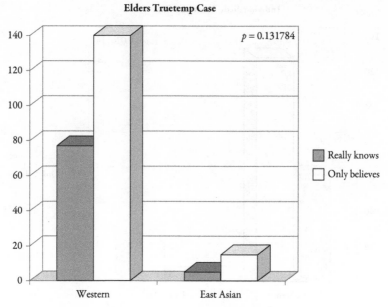

FIGURE 8.2

beach, the changes in his brain lead him to believe that it is 71 degrees where he is. Apart from his estimation, he has no other reasons to think that it is 71 degrees. In fact, it is at that time exactly 71 degrees where Kal is. Does Kal really know that it is 71 degrees, or does he only believe it?

    REALLY KNOWS   ONLY BELIEVES

As predicted, on this case too there was no significant difference between Ws and EAs. (See Figure 8.3.)

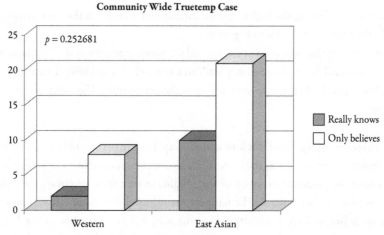

FIGURE 8.3

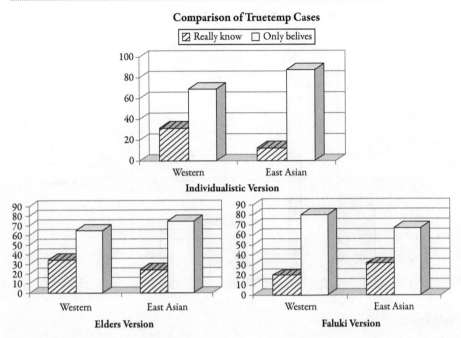

FIGURE 8.4

Intriguingly, though the difference is not statistically significant, the percentage of EAs who answered "Really Knows" in this case was *greater* than the percentage of Ws who gave that answer, reversing the pattern in the individualistic "hit by a rock" case. Figure 8.4, which is a comparison of the three Truetemp cases, illustrates the way in which the large difference between Ws and EAs in the Individualistic version disappears in the Elders version and looks to be reversing direction in the Faluki version.

3.3.2 Gettier Cases

A category of examples that has loomed large in the recent epistemology literature are "Gettier cases," in which a person has good (though, as it happens, false, or only accidentally true, or in some other way warrant-deprived) evidence for a belief which is true. These cases are, of course, by their very construction in many ways quite similar to unproblematic cases in which a person has good and true evidence for a true belief. As Norenzayan and Nisbett have shown, EAs are more inclined than Ws to make categorical judgments on the basis of similarity. Ws, on the other hand, are more disposed to focus on causation in describing the world and classifying things.[28] In a large class of Gettier cases, the evidence that *causes* the target to form a belief turns out to be false. This suggest that EAs might be much less inclined than Ws to withhold the attribution of knowledge in Gettier cases. And, indeed, they are.

---

28. Norenzayan et al. 1999.

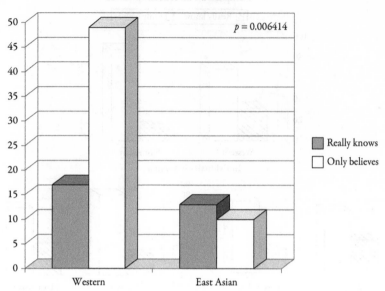

FIGURE 8.5

The intuition probe we used to explore cultural differences on Gettier cases was the following:

> Bob has a friend, Jill, who has driven a Buick for many years. Bob therefore thinks that Jill drives an American car. He is not aware, however, that her Buick has recently been stolen, and he is also not aware that Jill has replaced it with a Pontiac, which is a different kind of American car. Does Bob really know that Jill drives an American car, or does he only believe it?
> REALLY KNOWS   ONLY BELIEVES

The striking finding in this case is that a large majority of Ws give the standard answer in the philosophical literature, viz., "Only Believes." But amongst EAs this pattern is actually *reversed*! A majority of EAs say that Bob really knows. The results are shown in Figure 8.5.

3.3.3 Evidence from Another Ethnic Group

The experiments we have reported thus far were done in lower division classes and large lectures at Rutgers. Since Rutgers is the State University of New Jersey and New Jersey is home to many people of Indian, Pakistani and Bangladeshi descent, in the course of the experiments we collected lots of data about these people's intuitions. Initially we simply set these data aside since we had no theoretical basis for expecting that the epistemic intuitions of people from the Indian sub-continent (hereafter SCs) would be systematically different from the epistemic intuitions of Westerners. But, after finding the extraordinary differences between Ws and EAs on the Gettier case, we thought it might be interesting

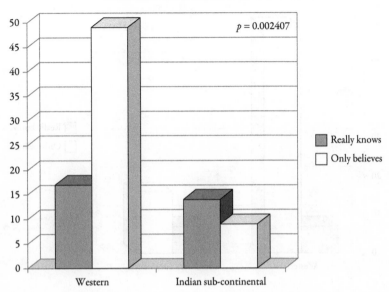

FIGURE 8.6

to analyze the SC data as well. We were right. It turns out that the epistemic intuitions of SCs are even more different from the intuitions of Ws than the intuitions of EAs are. The SC results on the Gettier case are shown in Figure 8.6. If these results are robust, then it seems that what counts as knowledge on the banks of the Ganges does not count as knowledge on the banks of the Mississippi!

There were two additional intuition probes that we used in our initial experiments which did not yield statistically significant differences between Ws and EAs. But when we analyzed the SC data, it turned out that there were significant differences between Ws and SCs. The text for one of these probes, the *Cancer Conspiracy* case, was as follows:

It's clear that smoking cigarettes increases the likelihood of getting cancer. However, there is now a great deal of evidence that just using nicotine by itself without smoking (for instance, by taking a nicotine pill) does not increase the likelihood of getting cancer. Jim knows about this evidence and as a result, he believes that using nicotine does not increase the likelihood of getting cancer. It is possible that the tobacco companies dishonestly made up and publicized this evidence that using nicotine does not increase the likelihood of cancer, and that the evidence is really false and misleading. Now, the tobacco companies did not actually make up this evidence, but Jim is not aware of this fact. Does Jim really know that using nicotine doesn't increase the likelihood of getting cancer, or does he only believe it?

REALLY KNOWS   ONLY BELIEVES

The results are shown in Figure 8.7.

Cancer Conspiracy Case: Western & Indian

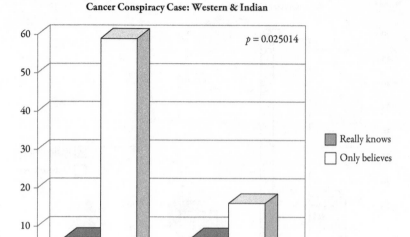

FIGURE 8.7

The other probe that produced significant differences is a version of Dretske's *Zebra-in-Zoo* case (Dretske 1970):

> Mike is a young man visiting the zoo with his son, and when they come to the zebra cage, Mike points to the animal and says, "That's a zebra." Mike is right—it is a zebra. However, as the older people in his community know, there are lots of ways that people can be tricked into believing things that aren't true. Indeed, the older people in the community know that it's possible that zoo authorities could cleverly disguise mules to look just like zebras, and people viewing the animals would not be able to tell the difference. If the animal that Mike called a zebra had really been such a cleverly painted mule, Mike still would have thought that it was a zebra. Does Mike really know that the animal is a zebra, or does he only believe that it is?
>
> REALLY KNOWS   ONLY BELIEVES

The results are shown in Figure 8.8.

What's going on in these last two cases? Why do SCs and Ws have different epistemic intuitions about them? The answer, to be quite frank, is that we are not sure how to explain these results. But, of course, for our polemical purposes, an explanatory hypothesis is not really essential. The mere fact that Ws, EAs and SCs have different epistemic intuitions is enough to make it plausible that IDR strategies which take these intuitions as inputs would yield significantly different normative pronouncements as output. And this, we think, puts the ball squarely in the court of the defenders of IDR strategies. They

Zebra-in-Zoo Case: Western & Indian

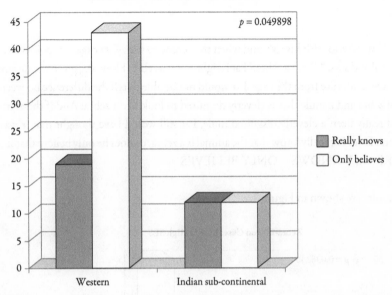

$p = 0.049898$

Really knows
Only believes

Western   Indian sub-continental

FIGURE 8.8

must either argue that intuitive differences of the sort we've found would not lead to diverging normative claims, or they must argue that the outputs of an IDR strategy are genuinely normative despite the fact that they are different for different cultures. Nor is this the end of the bad news for those who advocate IDR strategies.

3.3.4 Epistemic Intuitions and Socioeconomic Status

Encouraged by our findings in these cross-cultural studies, we have begun to explore the possibility that epistemic intuitions might also be sensitive to the socioeconomic status of the people offering the intuitions. And while our findings here are also quite prelim- inary, the apparent answer is that SES does indeed have a major impact on subjects' epistemic intuitions.

Following Haidt (and much other research in social psychology) we used years of ed- ucation to distinguish low and high SES groups. In the studies we will recount in this section, subjects were classified as low SES if they reported that they had never attended college. Subjects who reported that they had one or more years of college were coded as high SES. All the subjects were adults; they were approached near various commercial venues in downtown New Brunswick, New Jersey, and (since folks approached on the street tend to be rather less compliant than university undergraduates in classrooms) they were offered McDonald's gift certificates worth a few dollars if they agreed to participate in our study.

Interestingly, the two intuition probes for which we found significant SES differences both required the subjects to assess the importance of possible states of affairs that do not actually obtain. Here is the first probe, which is similar to the Dretske-type case discussed above:

> Pat is at the zoo with his son, and when they come to the zebra cage, Pat points to the animal and says, "That's a zebra." Pat is right—it is a zebra. However, given the distance the spectators are from the cage, Pat would not be able to tell the difference between a real zebra and a mule that is cleverly disguised to look like a zebra. And if the animal had really been a cleverly disguised mule, Pat still would have thought that it was a zebra. Does Pat really know that the animal is a zebra, or does he only believe that it is?
>
> REALLY KNOWS   ONLY BELIEVES

The results are shown in Figure 8.9.

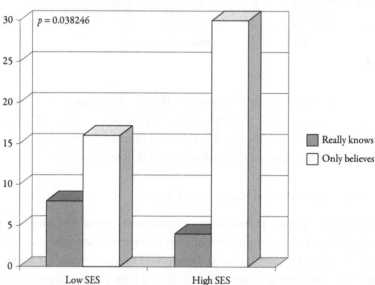

FIGURE 8.9

The second probe that produced significant (indeed enormous) differences between our two SES groups was the Cancer Conspiracy case that also generated differences between Western subjects and subjects from the Indian sub-continent. The results are shown in Figure 8.10. (For the text see 3.3.3.)

Why are the intuitions in these two SES groups so different? Here again we do not have a well worked-out theoretical framework of the sort that Nisbett and his colleagues have provided for the W vs. EA differences. So any answer we offer is only a speculation. One hypothesis is that one of the many factors that subjects are sensitive to in forming epistemic intuitions of this sort is the extent to which possible but non-actual states of affairs are relevant. Another possibility is that high SES subjects accept much weaker

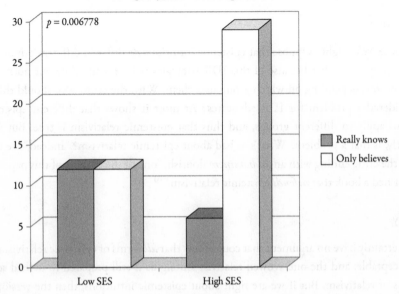

Cancer Conspiracy Case: Low & High SES

FIGURE 8.10

knowledge-defeaters than low SES subjects because low SES subjects have lower minimum standards for knowledge. More research is needed to determine whether either of these conjectures is correct. But whatever the explanation turns out to be, the data we've reported look to be yet another serious embarrassment for the advocates of IDR. As in the case of cultural difference, they must either argue that these intuitive differences, when plugged into an IDR black box, would not lead to different normative conclusions, or they must bite the bullet and argue that diverging normative claims are genuinely normative, and thus that the sorts of doxastic states that ought to be pursued by relatively rich and well-educated people are significantly different from the sorts of doxastic states that poor and less well-educated folks should seek. We don't pretend to have an argument showing that neither of these options is defensible. But we certainly don't envy the predicament of the IDR advocate who has to opt for one or the other.[29]

4. Objections and Replies

In this section we propose to assemble some objections to the case against IDR that we've set out in the preceding sections along with our replies.

---

29. We also checked for gender effects, and, while the data suggested some trends, we found significant differences on only one probe, the zebra case. On that probe, women were significantly more likely to attribute knowledge than men (p = .0487). Without a larger set of data, we are not sure how to interpret this result, but we are confident that gender differences in philosophical intuitions will be an important area for further exploration.

4.1 WHAT'S SO BAD ABOUT EPISTEMIC RELATIVISM?

Objection

Suppose we're right. Suppose that epistemic intuitions *do* differ in different ethnic and SES groups, and that because of this IDR strategies will generate different normative conclusions depending on which group uses them. Why, the critic asks, should this be considered a problem for IDR advocates? At most it shows that different epistemic norms apply to different groups, and thus that epistemic relativism is true. But why, exactly, is that a problem? What's so bad about epistemic relativism? "Indeed," we imagine the critic ending with an *ad hominem* flourish, "one of the authors of this paper has published a book that *defends* epistemic relativism."[30]

Reply

We certainly have no argument that could show that *all* forms of epistemic relativism are unacceptable, and the one avowed relativist among us is still prepared to defend some forms of relativism. But if we are right about epistemic intuitions, then the version of relativism to which IDR strategies lead would entail that the epistemic norms appropriate for the rich are quite different from the epistemic norms appropriate for the poor, and that the epistemic norms appropriate for white people are different from the norms appropriate for people of color.[31] And that we take to be quite a preposterous result. The fact that IDR strategies lead to this result is, we think, a very strong reason to think that there is something very wrong with those strategies. Of course, a defender of an IDR strategy might simply bite the bullet, and insist that the strategy he or she advocates is the right one for uncovering genuine epistemic norms, despite the fact that it leads to a relativistic consequence that many find implausible. But the IDR advocate who responds to our data in this way surely must offer some *argument* for the claim that the preferred IDR strategy produces genuine epistemic norms. And we know of no arguments along these lines that are even remotely plausible.

4.2 THERE ARE SEVERAL SENSES OF "KNOWLEDGE"

Objection

The next objection begins with the observation that epistemologists have long been aware that the word "knows" has more than one meaning in ordinary discourse. Sometimes when people say that they "know" that something is the case, what they mean is that they have a strong sense of subjective certainty. So, for example, someone at a horse

---

30. Stich 1990. See especially Ch. 6.

31. Though there is very little evidence on the point, we don't think the differences we've found are innate. Rather, we suspect, they are the product of deep differences in culture.

race might give voice to a strong hunch by saying: "I just know that Ivory Armchair is going to win." And even after Lab Bench comes in first, this colloquial sense of "know" still permits them to say, "Drat! I just knew that Ivory Armchair was going to win." At other times, though, when people use "know" and "knowledge" the sense they have in mind is the one that is of interest to epistemologists. The problem with our results, this objection maintains, is that we did nothing to ensure that when subjects answered "Really Knows" rather than "Only Believes" the sense of "know" that they had in mind was the one of philosophical interest rather than the subjective certainty sense. "So," the critic concludes, "for all you know, your subjects might have been offering you philosophically uninteresting judgments about people's sense of subjective certainty."

Reply

It is certainly possible that some of our subjects were interpreting the "Really Knows" option as a question about subjective certainty. But there is reason to think that this did not have a major impact on our findings. For all of our subject groups (W, EA and SC in the ethnic studies and high and low SES in the SES study) we included a question designed to uncover any systematic differences in our subjects' inclination to treat mere subjective certainty as knowledge. The question we used was the following:

> Dave likes to play a game with flipping a coin. He sometimes gets a "special feeling" that the next flip will come out heads. When he gets this "special feeling," he is right about half the time, and wrong about half the time. Just before the next flip, Dave gets that "special feeling," and the feeling leads him to believe that the coin will land heads. He flips the coin, and it does land heads. Did Dave really know that the coin was going to land heads, or did he only believe it?
> REALLY KNOWS   ONLY BELIEVES

As shown in Figure 8.11, there was no difference at all between the high and low SES groups on this question; in both groups almost none of our subjects judged that this was a case of knowledge. The results in the ethnic studies were basically the same.[32]

This might be a good place to elaborate a bit on what we are and are not claiming about epistemic intuitions and the psychological mechanisms or "knowledge structures"

---

32. Another possible interpretation of "Really Knows" in our intuition probes would invoke what Ernest Sosa has termed merely "animal" or "servo-mechanical" knowledge (Sosa 1991, 95). We sometimes say that a dog knows that it's about to be fed, or that the thermostat knows the temperature in the room. But we philosophers are hunting different game—fully normative game which, the critic maintains, these surveys might not capture. However, if our subjects had this notion in mind, one would predict that they would overwhelmingly attribute such knowledge in the Truetemp cases, since the protagonists in each of the stories clearly has a reliable, thermostat-like information-registering capacity. Yet they did not do so—in none of the Truetemp cases did a majority of subjects opt for "Really Knows." So this rival gloss on "knows" will not help the IDR theorist to explain our data away.

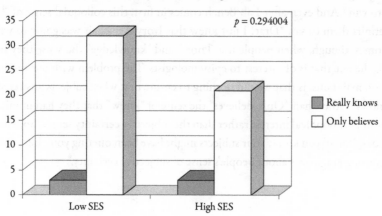

FIGURE 8.11

that may subserve them. For polemical purposes we have been emphasizing the diversity of epistemic intuitions in different ethnic and SES groups, since these quite different intuitions, when plugged into an IDR black box, will generate different normative claims. But we certainly do not mean to suggest that epistemic intuitions are completely malleable or that there are no constraints on the sorts of epistemic intuitions that might be found in different social groups. Indeed, the fact that subjects from all the groups we studied agreed in not classifying beliefs based on "special feelings" as knowledge suggests that there may well be a universal core to "folk epistemology." Whether this conjecture is true and, if it is, how this common core is best characterized, are questions that will require a great deal more research. Obviously, these are not issues that can be settled from the philosopher's armchair.

4.3 THE EFFECT SIZE WE'VE FOUND IS SMALL AND PHILOSOPHICALLY UNINTERESTING

Objection

If it were the case that virtually all Ws judged various cases in one way and virtually all EAs or SCs judged the same cases in a different way, that might be genuine cause for concern among epistemologists. But that's not at all what you have found. Rather, what you've shown is merely that in various cases there is a 20 or 30% difference in the judgments offered by subjects in various groups. So, for example, a majority in all of your groups withhold knowledge attributions in all the Truetemp cases that were designed to test the degree to which subjects' intuitions reflected epistemic internalism. Since the majority in all groups agree, we can conclude that the correct account of epistemic norms is internalist. So it is far from clear why epistemologists should find the sort of cultural diversity you've found to be at all troubling, or even interesting.

Reply

Here we have two replies. First, the sizes of the statistically significant group differences that we've reported are quite comparable with the size of the differences that Nisbett, Haidt and other social psychologists take to show important differences between groups. The second reply is more important. While in some cases what we've been reporting are just the brute facts that intuitions in different groups differ, in other cases what we've found is considerably more interesting. The differences between Ws and EAs look to be both systematic and explainable. EAs and Ws appear to be sensitive to different features of the situation, different *epistemic vectors*, as we will call them. EAs are much more sensitive to communitarian factors, while Ws respond to more individualistic ones. Moreover, Nisbett and his colleagues have given us good reason to think that these kinds of differences can be traced to deep and important differences in EA and W cognition. And we have no reason to think that equally important differences could not be found for SCs. Our data also suggest that both high and low SES Westerners stress the individualistic and non-communitarian vector, since there was no difference between high and low SES groups on questions designed to emphasize this vector. What separates high and low SES subjects is some quite different vector—sensitivity to mere possibilities, perhaps. What our studies point to, then, is more than just divergent epistemic intuitions across groups; the studies point to divergent epistemic *concerns*—concerns which appear to differ along a variety of dimensions. It is plausible to suppose that these differences would significantly affect the output of just about any IDR process.

4.4 WE ARE LOOKING AT THE WRONG SORT OF INTUITIONS; THE RIGHT SORT ARE ACCOMPANIED BY A CLEAR SENSE OF NECESSITY

Objection

The central idea of this objection is that our experiments are simply not designed to evoke the right sort of intuitions—the sort that the IDR process really requires. What we are collecting in our experiments are unfiltered spontaneous judgments about a variety of cases. But what is really needed, this objection maintains, are data about quite a different kind of intuitions. The right sort of intuitions are those that have modal import and are accompanied by a clear sense of necessity. They are the kind of intuitions that we have when confronted with principles like: If p, then not-not-p. Unless you show cultural or SES diversity in these sorts of intuitions, this objection continues, you have not shown anything that an IDR advocate needs to be concerned about, since you have not shown that the right sort of intuitions are not universal.[33]

---

33. See, for example, Bealer 1999, who insists that "the work of cognitive psychologists such as Wason, Johnson-Laird, Nisbett, Kahneman and Tversky tells us little about intuitions in our [philosophical] sense" (31).

Reply

It is true that the sorts of intuitions that our experiments collect are not the sorts that some IDR theorists would exploit. However, our findings do raise serious questions about the suggestion that intuitions which come with a clear sense of necessity and modal import—*strong intuitions*, as we propose to call them—are anything close to universal. Many epistemologists would no doubt insist that their own intuitions about many cases are strong intuitions. Simple Gettier case intuitions are a good example. Indeed, if these intuitions, which led a generation of epistemologists to seek something better than the traditional justified true belief analysis of knowledge, are not strong intuitions, then it is hard to believe that there are enough strong intuitions around to generate epistemic norms of any interest. But if philosophers' intuitions on simple Gettier cases *are* strong intuitions, then our data indicate that strong intuitions are far from universal. For, while our experiments cannot distinguish strong from weak intuitions, they do indicate that almost 30% of W subjects do not have either strong or weak intuitions that agree with those of most philosophers, since almost 30% of these subjects claim that, in our standard Gettier scenario, Bob really knows that Jill drives an American car. Among EA subjects, over 50% of subjects have the intuition (weak or strong) that Bob really knows, and among SC subjects the number is over 60! It may well be that upper middle class Westerners who have had a few years of graduate training in analytic philosophy do indeed all have strong, modality-linked intuitions about Gettier cases. But since most of the world's population apparently does not share these intuitions, it is hard to see why we should think that these intuitions tell us anything at all about the modal structure of reality, or about epistemic norms or indeed about anything else of philosophical interest.

4.5 WE ARE LOOKING AT THE WRONG SORT OF INTUITIONS; THE RIGHT SORT REQUIRE AT LEAST A MODICUM OF REFLECTION

Objection

We have also heard a rather different objection about the type of intuitions examined in our study. [34] The proper input intuitions for the IDR strategy, the critics maintain, are not "first-off" intuitions—which may be really little better than mere guesses. Rather, IDR requires what might be called *minimally reflective intuitions*—intuitions resulting from some modicum of attention, consideration, and above all reflection on the particulars of the case at hand as well as one's other theoretical commitments. We have, this objection continues, done nothing to show that such minimally reflective intuitions would exhibit the sort of diversity we have been reporting, and until we show something along those lines, the IDR theorist need not worry.

---

34. This objection was offered by Henry Jackman, Ram Neta and Jonathan Schaffer.

Reply

This objection is right as far as it goes, since we have not (yet) examined intuitions produced under conditions of explicit reflection. But the objection really does not go very
far, and certainly not far enough to allow IDR theorists to rest easy. First of all, many of
our subjects clearly did reflect at least minimally before answering, as evidenced in the
many survey forms on which the subjects wrote brief explanatory comments after their
answers. Moreover, as we stressed in Reply 4.2, it is not just that we found group differences in epistemic intuition; much more interestingly, Western and East Asian subjects'
intuitions seem to respond to quite different epistemic vectors. It is extremely likely that
such differences in sensitivities would be recapitulated—or even strengthened—in any
reflective process. If EA subjects have an inclination to take into account factors involving
community beliefs, practices and traditions, and W subjects do not have such an inclination, then we see no reason to expect that such vectors will not be differentially present
under conditions of explicit reflection. IDR theorists who want to make use of any purported difference between first-off and minimally reflective intuitions had better go get
some *data* showing that such differences would point in the direction they would want.

4.6 WE ARE LOOKING AT THE WRONG SORT OF INTUITIONS; THE RIGHT SORT ARE THOSE THAT EMERGE AFTER AN EXTENDED PERIOD OF DISCUSSION AND REFLECTION

Objection

The last objection we'll consider was proposed (though not, we suspect, endorsed) by
Philip Kitcher. What IDR strategies need, this objection maintains, is neither first-off
intuitions nor even minimally reflective intuitions, but rather the sorts of intuitions that
people develop after a lengthy period of reflection and discussion—the sort of reflection
and discussion that philosophy traditionally encourages. Kitcher suggested that they be
called *Austinian intuitions*.

Your experiments, the objection insists, do nothing to show that Austinian intuitions
would exhibit the sort of cultural diversity you've found in first-off intuitions, or, indeed,
that they would show any significant diversity at all. When sensible people reflect and
reason together, there is every reason to suppose that they will ultimately reach a meeting
of the minds.

Reply

We certainly concede that we have not shown that Austinian intuitions would not ultimately converge. However, to echo the theme of our previous reply, in the absence of any
evidence we don't think there is any reason to suppose that the sorts of marked cultural
differences in sensitivity to epistemic vectors that our experiments have demonstrated

would simply disappear after reflection and discussion. Moreover, even if these cultural differences do dissipate after extended reflection, it might well be the case that they would be replaced by the sorts of order effects suggested in our Hypothesis 4. If that hypothesis is correct, then the Austinian intuitions on which a group of reflective people would converge would depend, in part, on the order in which examples and arguments happened to be introduced. And different groups might well converge on quite different sets of Austinian intuitions which then proved quite impervious to change. Experiments demonstrating the sort of path dependence that we suggest in Hypothesis 4 are much harder to design than experiments demonstrating cultural differences in initial intuitions. In the next stage of our ongoing empirical research on intuitions, we hope to run a series of experiments that will indicate the extent to which the evolution of people's intuitions is indeed a function of the order in which examples and counter-examples are encountered. Neither those experiments nor any of the evidence we've cited in this paper will suffice to demonstrate that Austinian intuitions or IDR processes that propose to use them will fail to converge. But, to end with the theme with which we began, our goal has not been to establish that IDR strategies *will* lead to very different (putatively) normative conclusions, but simply to make it plausible that they *might*. The assumption that they won't is an empirical assumption; it is not an assumption that can be made without argument.

Our data indicate that when epistemologists advert to "our" intuitions when attempting to characterize epistemic concepts or draw normative conclusions, they are engaged in a culturally local endeavor—what we might think of as *ethno-epistemology*. Indeed, in our studies, some of the most influential thought experiments of 20th century epistemology elicited different intuitions in different cultures. In light of this, Intuition Driven Romanticism seems a rather bizarre way to determine the correct epistemic norms. For it is difficult to see why a process that relies heavily on epistemic intuitions that are local to one's own cultural and socioeconomic group would lead to genuinely normative conclusions. Pending a detailed response to this problem, we think that the best reaction to the high SES, Western philosophy professor who tries to draw normative conclusions from the facts about "our" intuitions is to ask: What do you mean "we"?

ACKNOWLEDGMENTS

We are grateful to Joe Cruz, Gilbert Harman, Philip Kitcher and Joel Pust for helpful feedback on earlier versions of this paper. Our deepest debt is to Richard Nisbett, who provided us with invaluable advice and assistance in designing and interpreting the studies reported in Section 3.

REFERENCES

Austin, J. L. 1964. *Sense and Sensibilia*. London: Oxford University Press.

Bealer, G. 1999. A Theory of the *A Priori*. In J. Tomberlin, ed., *Philosophical Perspectives*, vol. 13: *Epistemology*, 29–55. Cambridge, MA: Blackwell.

BonJour, L. 1985. *The Structure of Empirical Knowledge*. Cambridge, MA: Harvard University Press.

Cha, J.-H., and K. Nam. 1985. A Test of Kelley's Cube Theory of Attribution: A Cross-Cultural Replication of McArthur's Study. *Korean Social Science Journal* 12: 151–80.

Chisholm, R. 1977. *Theory of Knowledge*. Englewood Cliffs, NJ: Prentice-Hall.

Clark, A. 1997. *Being There: Putting Brain, Body and World Together Again*. Cambridge, MA: MIT Press.

Cohen, L. 1981. Can Human Irrationality Be Experimentally Demonstrated? *Behavioral and Brain Sciences* 4: 317–70.

Dretske, F. 1970. Epistemic Operators. *Journal of Philosophy* 67, 24: 1007–23. Reprinted in F. Dretske, *Perception, Knowledge, and Belief*. Cambridge: Cambridge University Press, 2000.

Elgin, C. 1996. *Considered Judgment*. Princeton, NJ: Princeton University Press.

Feldman, R., and E. Conee. 1985. Evidentialism. *Philosophical Studies* 48: 15–34.

Gettier, E. 1963. Is Justified True Belief Knowledge? *Analysis* 23: 121–23.

Goldman, A. 1980. The Internalist Conception of Justification. In P. A. French, T. E. Uehling, and H. K. Wettstein, eds., *Studies in Epistemology*, Midwest Studies in Philosophy vol. 5. Minneapolis: University of Minnesota Press.

———. 1986. *Epistemology and Cognition*. Cambridge, MA: Harvard University Press.

———. 1992. Epistemic Folkways and Scientific Epistemology. In *Liaisons*. Cambridge, MA: MIT Press.

———. 1999. A Priori Warrant and Naturalistic Epistemology. In J. Tomberlin, ed., *Philosophical Perspectives*, vol. 13: *Epistemology*. Cambridge, MA: Blackwell.

Goldman, A., and J. Pust. 1998. Philosophical Theory and Intuitional Evidence. In M. DePaul and W. Ramsey, eds., *Rethinking Intuition*. Lanham, MD: Rowman and Littlefield.

Goodman, N. 1965. *Fact, Fiction and Forecast*. Indianapolis: Bobbs-Merrill.

Haidt, J., S. Koller, and M. Dias. 1993. Affect, Culture and Morality. *Journal of Personality and Social Psychology* 65, 4: 613–28.

Jackson, F. 1998. *From Metaphysics to Ethics: A Defence of Conceptual Analysis*. Oxford: Oxford University Press.

Klein, P. 1999. Human Knowledge and the Infinite Regress of Reasons. In J. Tomberlin, ed., *Philosophical Perspectives*, vol. 13: *Epistemology*, 297–325. Cambridge, MA: Blackwell.

Kvanvig, J., ed. 1996. *Warrant in Contemporary Epistemology: Essays in Honor of Plantinga's Theory of Knowledge*. Lanham, MD: Rowman and Littlefield.

Lehrer, K. 1990. *Theory of Knowledge*. Boulder and London: Westview Press and Routledge.

———. 1997. *Self-Trust: A Study of Reason, Knowledge, and Autonomy*. Oxford: Oxford University Press.

Morris, M., R. Nisbett, and K. Peng. 1995. Causal Understanding Across Domains and Cultures. In D. Sperber, D. Premack, and A. J. Premack, eds., *Causal Cognition: A Multidisciplinary Debate*. Oxford: Oxford University Press.

Nisbett, R., K. Peng, I. Choi, and A. Norenzayan. 2001. Culture and Systems of Thought: Holistic vs. Analytic Cognition. *Psychological Review* 108: 291–310.

Nisbett, R., and L. Ross. 1980. *Human Inference: Strategies and Shortcomings of Social Judgment*. Englewood Cliffs, NJ: Prentice-Hall.

Norenzayan, A., R. E. Nisbett, E. E. Smith, and B. J. Kim. 1999. Rules vs. Similarity as a Basis for Reasoning and Judgment in East and West. University of Michigan, Ann Arbor.

Plantinga, A. 1993a. *Warrant: The Current Debate*. Oxford: Oxford University Press.

———. 1993b. *Warrant and Proper Function*. Oxford: Oxford University Press.

Plato. 1892/1937. *The Dialogues of Plato*. Trans. B. Jowett. New York: Random House.

Pollock, J., and J. Cruz. 1999. *Contemporary Theories of Knowledge*. Lanham, MD: Rowman and Littlefield.

Samuels, R. Unpublished manuscript. Naturalism and Normativity.

Samuels, R., S. Stich, and M. Bishop. 2002. Ending the Rationality Wars: How to Make Disputes About Human Rationality Disappear. In Renee Elio, ed., *Common Sense, Reasoning and Rationality*, Vancouver Studies in Cognitive Science, vol. 11. Oxford: Oxford University Press.

Samuels, R., S. Stich, and L. Faucher. 2004. Reasoning and Rationality. In I. Niiniluoto, M. Sintonen, and J. Wolenski, eds., *Handbook of Epistemology*. Dordrecht: Kluwer.

Samuels, R., S. Stich, and P. Tremoulet. 1999. Rethinking Rationality: From Bleak Implications to Darwinian Modules. In E. LePore and Z. Pylyshyn, eds., *What Is Cognitive Science?* Oxford: Blackwell.

Shope, R. 1983. *The Analysis of Knowing*. Princeton, NJ: Princeton University Press.

Sosa, E. 1991. *Knowledge in Perspective*. Cambridge: Cambridge University Press.

———, ed. 1994. *Knowledge and Justification*. International Research Library of Philosophy. Brookfield, VT: Dartmouth Publishing Company.

Stein, E. 1996. *Without Good Reason: The Rationality Debate in Philosophy and Cognitive Science*. Oxford: Clarendon Press.

Stich, S. 1990. *The Fragmentation of Reason*. Cambridge, MA: MIT Press.

Watanabe, M. 1998. Styles of Reasoning in Japan and the United States: Logic of Education in Two Cultures. Paper presented at the American Sociological Association Annual Meeting, San Francisco, August 1998.

———. 1999. Styles of Reasoning in Japan and the United States: Logic of Education in Two Cultures. Ph.D. thesis, Columbia University.

APPENDIX

The Fisher's Exact test was used to calculate statistical significance between groups.
Individualistic Truetemp Case (Figure 8.1)

	Really knows	Only believes
Western	61	128
East Asian	3	22

$p = 0.020114$

Elders Truetemp Case (Figure 8.2)

	Really knows	Only believes
Western	77	140
East Asian	5	15

$p = 0.131784$

Community Wide Truetemp Case (Figure 8.3)

	Really knows	Only believes
Western	2	8
East Asian	10	21

$p = 0.252681$

Gettier Case: Western and East Asian (Figure 8.5)

	Really knows	Only believes
Western	17	49
East Asian	13	10

$p = 0.006414$

Gettier Case: Western and Indian (Figure 8.6)

	Really knows	Only believes
Western	17	49
Indian sub-continental	14	9

$p = 0.002407$

Cancer Conspiracy Case: Western and Indian (Figure 8.7)

	Really knows	Only believes
Western	7	59
Indian sub-continental	7	16

$p = 0.025014$

Zebra-in-Zoo Case: Western and Indian (Figure 8.8)

	Really knows	Only believes
Western	19	43
Indian sub-continental	12	12

$p = 0.049898$

Zebra-in-Zoo Case: Low and High SES (Figure 8.9)

	Really knows	Only believes
Low SES	8	16
High SES	4	30

$p = 0.038246$

Cancer Conspiracy Case: Low and High SES (Figure 8.10)

	Really knows	Only believes
Low SES	12	12
High SES	6	29

$p = 0.006778$

Special Feeling Case: Low and High SES (Figure 8.11)

	Really knows	Only believes
Low SES	3	32
High SES	3	21

$p = 0.294004$

Special Feeling Case: Western and East Asian (no figure)

	Really knows	Only believes
Western	2	59
East Asian	0	8

$p = 0.780051$

> Blessed are the peacemakers; for they shall be
> called the children of God.
> —MATTHEW 5:9

9

ENDING THE RATIONALITY WARS

How to Make Disputes About Human Rationality Disappear

Richard Samuels, Stephen Stich, and Michael Bishop

1. Introduction

DURING THE LAST twenty-five years, researchers who studied human reasoning and judgment in what has become known as the heuristics and biases tradition have produced an impressive body of experimental work that many have seen as having "bleak implications" for the rationality of ordinary people (Nisbett and Borgida 1975). According to one proponent of this view, when we reason about probability we fall victim to "inevitable illusions" (Piattelli-Palmarini 1994). Other proponents maintain that the human mind is prone to "systematic deviations from rationality" (Bazerman and Neale 1986) and is "not built to work by the rules of probability" (Gould 1992). It has even been suggested that human beings are "a species that is uniformly probability-blind" (Piattelli-Palmarini 1994). This provocative and pessimistic interpretation of the experimental findings has been challenged from many different directions over the years. One of the most recent and energetic of these challenges has come from the newly emerging field of evolutionary psychology, where it has been argued that it's singularly implausible to claim that our species would have evolved with no "instinct for probability" and, hence, be "blind to chance" (Pinker 1997, 351). Though evolutionary psychologists concede that it is possible to design experiments that "trick our probability calculators," they go on to claim that "when people are given information in a format that meshes with the way they naturally think about probability" (Pinker 1997, 347, 351) the inevitable illusions turn out to be, to use Gerd Gigerenzer's memorable term, "evitable" (Gigerenzer 1998). Indeed, in many cases evolutionary psychologists claim that the illusions simply "disappear" (Gigerenzer 1991a).

On the face of it, the dispute between evolutionary psychology and the heuristics and biases tradition would appear to be a deep disagreement over the extent of human rationality—a conflict between two sharply divergent assessments of human reasoning. This impression is strengthened by the heated exchanges that pepper the academic literature and reinforced by steamy reports of the debate that have appeared in the popular press (Bower 1996). It is our contention, however, that the alleged conflict between evolutionary psychologists and advocates of the heuristics and biases program has been greatly exaggerated. The claims made on either side of the dispute can, we maintain, be plausibly divided into *core claims* and mere *rhetorical flourishes*.[1] And once one puts the rhetoric to one side almost all of the apparent disagreement dissolves. When one focuses on the core claims that are central to the heuristics and biases tradition and best supported by the experimental results, it turns out that these claims are not *challenged* by the evolutionary psychologists. On the contrary, some of the most intriguing avenues of research pursued by evolutionary psychologists in recent years simply make no sense unless they are interpreted as *endorsing* these central theses of the heuristics and biases tradition. Moreover, the agreement runs in the opposite direction as well. When we put aside the rhetoric of evolutionary psychologists and attend instead to their central claims about reasoning and cognitive architecture, it becomes clear that advocates of the heuristics and biases tradition have no reason at all to object to any of these claims and, in some cases, clearly should and do endorse them. Thus, we maintain that much of the dispute between evolutionary psychologists and those in the heuristics and biases tradition is itself an illusion. The fireworks generated by each side focusing on the rhetorical excesses of the other have distracted attention from what we claim is, in fact, an emerging *consensus* about the scope and limits of human rationality and about the cognitive architecture that supports it.

Our central goal in this chapter is to refocus the discussion away from the rhetoric of the debate between evolutionary psychology and the heuristics and biases tradition and toward this emerging consensus on fundamental points. To work toward this goal we will proceed as follows: In section 2, we will briefly outline the two research programs and explain what we take to be the core claims and the rhetorical excesses on both sides. Then, in section 3, we will argue that it is implausible to maintain that either research program rejects the core claims of the other. Once this is accomplished we think the illusion that

---

An earlier version of this chapter was discussed at a workshop on the evolution of mind at the Hang Seng Centre for Cognitive Studies at the University of Sheffield. We are grateful for the many helpful comments and criticisms that were offered on that occasion. Special thanks are due to George Botterill, Richard Byrne, Peter Carruthers, Gerd Gigerenzer, Brian Loar, Adam Morton, and Michael Segal.

　　1. We classify a claim as a *core claim* in one of the two research traditions if (1) it is central to the research program, (2) it is not completely implausible to suppose that the claim is supported by the empirical evidence offered by advocates of the program, and (3) advocates of the program are prepared to endorse it in their more careful moments. *Rhetorical flourishes*, by contrast, are claims that (1) are not central to the research program, (2) are not supported by the evidence offered, and (3) are typically not endorsed by advocates of the program in question when they are being careful and reflective.

evolutionary psychology and the heuristics and biases tradition have a deep disagreement about how rational human beings are should disappear. This is not to say, however, that there are *no* genuine disagreements between these two research programs. In the fourth section of this chapter, we briefly outline and discuss what we take to be some genuine disagreements between evolutionary psychology and the heuristics and biases tradition.

2. The Apparent Conflict

This section has two major parts. In the first half, we will begin by offering a few illustrations of the sorts of striking experimental findings that have been produced in the heuristics and biases tradition. Next, we will illustrate the sorts of explanations that those in the heuristics and biases tradition have offered for those findings. Finally, we will outline what we take to be the core claims of the heuristics and biases program and contrast them with some of the more rhetorically flamboyant claims that have been made. In the second half of this section, we start with an overview of the basic claims of evolutionary psychology and proceed on to a quick sketch of some of the experimental findings about probabilistic reasoning that evolutionary psychologists have presented. We'll then explain what we take to be the core claims of the evolutionary psychological approach to reasoning and assemble another short catalog of rhetorically flamboyant claims—this time claims about the implications of the evolutionary psychologists' results. Against this backdrop we'll go on, in the following section, to argue that despite all the colorful rhetoric, evolutionary psychologists and proponents of the heuristics and biases program don't really disagree at all about the extent to which human beings are rational or about any other claim that is central to either program.

THE HEURISTICS AND BIASES TRADITION: EXPERIMENTS, EXPLANATIONS, CORE CLAIMS, AND RHETORIC

On the familiar Bayesian account, the probability of a hypothesis on a given body of evidence depends, in part, on the prior probability of the hypothesis. However, in a series of elegant experiments, D. Kahneman and A. Tversky (1973) showed that subjects often seriously undervalue the importance of prior probabilities. One of these experiments presented half of the subjects with the following "cover story":

> A panel of psychologists has interviewed and administered personality tests to 30 engineers and 70 lawyers, all successful in their respective fields. On the basis of this information, thumbnail descriptions of the 30 engineers and 70 lawyers have been written. You will find on your forms five descriptions, chosen at random from the 100 available descriptions. For each description, please indicate your probability that the person described is an engineer, on a scale from 0 to 100.

The other half of the subjects were presented with the same text, except the "base rates" were reversed. They were told that the personality tests had been administered to seventy engineers and thirty lawyers. Some of the descriptions that were provided were designed to be compatible with the subjects' stereotypes of engineers, though not with their stereotypes of lawyers. Others were designed to fit the lawyer stereotype but not the engineer stereotype. And one was intended to be quite neutral, giving subjects no information at all that would be of use in making their decision. Here are two examples, the first intended to sound like an engineer, the second intended to sound neutral:

> Jack is a forty-five-year-old man. He is married and has four children. He is generally conservative, careful, and ambitious. He shows no interest in political and social issues and spends most of his free time on his many hobbies, which include home carpentry, sailing, and mathematical puzzles.
>
> Dick is a thirty-year-old man. He is married with no children. A man of high ability and high motivation, he promises to be quite successful in his field. He is well liked by his colleagues.

As expected, subjects in both groups thought that the probability that Jack was an engineer was quite high. Moreover, in what seems to be a clear violation of Bayesian principles, the difference in cover stories between the two groups of subjects had almost no effect at all. The neglect of base-rate information was even more striking in the case of Dick. That description was constructed to be totally uninformative with regard to Dick's profession. Thus, the only useful information that subjects had was the base-rate information provided in the cover story. But that information was entirely ignored. The median probability estimate in both groups of subjects was 50 percent.

How might we explain these results and the results of many similar experiments that have been reported in the psychological literature? The basic explanatory strategy that proponents of the heuristics and biases program have pursued is to posit the existence of reasoning heuristics: rules of thumb that we employ when reasoning. In the specific case of the preceding experiments, the hypothesis that Kahneman and Tversky offer is that in making probabilistic judgments people often rely on what they call *the representativeness heuristic*:

> Given specific evidence (e.g., a personality sketch), the outcomes under consideration (e.g., occupations or levels of achievement) can be ordered by the degree to which they are representative of that evidence. The thesis of this paper is that people predict by representativeness, that is, they select or order outcomes by the degree to which the outcomes represent the essential features of the evidence. In many situations, representative outcomes are indeed more likely than others. However, this is not always the case, because there are factors (e.g., prior probabilities of outcomes and the reliability of evidence) which affect the likelihood of outcomes but not their representativeness. Because these factors are ignored, intuitive predictions violate statistical rules of prediction in systematic and fundamental ways. (1973, 48)

Though many of the reasoning problems explored in the heuristics and biases literature have no great practical importance, there are some notable exceptions. In a well-known and very disquieting study, W. Casscells, A. Schoenberger, and T. Grayboys (1978) presented the following problem to a group of faculty, staff, and fourth-year students at Harvard Medical School:

> If a test to detect a disease whose prevalence is 1/1,000 has a false positive rate of 5%, what is the chance that a person found to have a positive result actually has the disease, assuming that you know nothing about the person's symptoms or signs? ____ %

Under the most plausible interpretation of the problem, the correct Bayesian answer is 2 percent. But only 18 percent of the Harvard audience gave an answer close to 2 percent. Forty-five percent of this distinguished group completely ignored the base-rate information and said that the answer was 95 percent.

What do these results and the many similar results in the heuristics and biases literature tell us about the quality of ordinary people's probabilistic reasoning and about the mental mechanisms that underlie that reasoning? Though we will return to the issue in section 3, let us grant for the time being that some of the answers that subjects provide are mistaken—that they deviate from appropriate norms of rationality. Then, since studies like those we've mentioned are both numerous and readily replicable, the following holds:

(1) People's intuitive judgments on a large number of problems that involve probability or uncertainty regularly deviate from appropriate norms of rationality.

This is clearly a core claim of the heuristics and biases program. As Kahneman and Tversky have said, "Although errors of judgment are but a method by which some cognitive processes are studied, the method has become a significant part of the message" (1982, 124). In addition, however, it is clear that proponents of the heuristics and biases program also endorse as a core claim a thesis about how to explain these deviations from appropriate norms of rationality, namely:

(2) Many of the instances in which our probabilistic judgments deviate from appropriate norms of rationality are to be explained by the fact that, in making these judgments, people rely on heuristics like representativeness "which sometimes yield reasonable judgments and sometimes lead to severe and systematic errors." (Kahneman and Tversky 1973, 48)

Moreover, if we adopt the (standard) assumption that a cognitive mechanism or program is normatively appropriate or "correct" only to the extent that it yields normatively appropriate judgments, then, given (1) and (2), it is eminently plausible to conclude, along with

P. Slovic, B. Fischhoff, and S. Lichtenstein, that "people lack the correct programs for many important judgmental tasks" (1976, 174).

Slovic, Fischhoff, and Lichtenstein are not content, however, to stop with this relatively modest conclusion. Instead, they go on to make the much more sweeping claim that "[we] have not had the opportunity to evolve an intellect capable of dealing conceptually with uncertainty" (174), thus suggesting not merely that we lack the correct programs for many tasks but also that, in dealing with uncertainty, we lack the correct programs for *all* judgmental tasks. In other words, they appear to be suggesting the following:

(3) The *only* cognitive tools that are available to untutored people when dealing with problems that involve probability or uncertainty are normatively problematic heuristics such as representativeness.

This expansive theme echoes passages like the following, in which Kahneman and Tversky, the founders of the heuristics and biases program, seem to endorse the view that people use representativeness and other normatively defective heuristics not just in some or many cases but in *all* cases—including those cases in which they get the right answer:

In making predictions and judgments under uncertainty, people do not appear to follow the calculus of chance or the statistical theory of prediction. Instead, they rely on a limited number of heuristics which sometimes yield reasonable judgments and sometimes lead to severe and systematic errors. (1973, 48)

In light of passages like this, it is perhaps unsurprising that both friends and foes of the heuristics and biases tradition suppose that it is committed to the claim that, as Gerd Gigerenzer has put it, "the untutored mind is running on shoddy software, that is, on programs that work *only* with a handful of heuristics" (1991b, 235). In another paper Gigerenzer suggests that the heuristics and biases tradition views people "as 'cognitive misers' relying on a few general heuristics due to their limited information-processing abilities" (1991a, 109). After describing one of Kahneman and Tversky's best-known experiments, S. Gould asks: "Why do we consistently make this simple logical error?" His answer is: "Tversky and Kahneman argue, correctly I think, that our minds are not built (for whatever reason) to work by the rules of probability" (1992, 469).[2]

---

2. While Kahneman and Tversky's rhetoric, and Gould's, suggests that untutored people have nothing but normatively defective heuristics or "shoddy software" with which to tackle problems dealing with probability, Piattelli-Palmarini goes on to make the even more flamboyant claim that the shoddy software is more likely to get the wrong answer than the right one.

We are . . . blind not only to the extremes of probability but also to intermediate probabilities—from which one might well adduce that we are blind about probabilities.

I would like to suggest a simple, general, probabilistic law: Any probabilistic intuition by anyone not specifically tutored in probability calculus has a greater than 50 percent chance of being wrong. (1994, 131–32)

If proponents of the heuristics and biases program would really have us believe (3), then the picture of human reasoning that they paint is bleak indeed! But should we accept this claim as anything more than mere rhetorical flourish? For several rather different reasons, we maintain that the answer is no. First, although we shall not defend this claim in detail here, it is simply not plausible to maintain that (3) is supported by the currently available experimental evidence. At *most*, what could be plausibly claimed is that we have reason to think that, in *many* instances, human beings use normatively defective heuristics. The further claim that these normatively problematic heuristics are the *only* cognitive tools that untutored folk have available is vastly stronger than anything the available evidence will support. Second, when they are being careful about what they say, leading advocates of the heuristics and biases program make it clear that they do not endorse (3). Thus, for example, Kahneman and Tversky state very clearly that the use of normatively problematic heuristics "does not preclude the use of other procedures" and insist that the currently available data do not support (3) but only the "more moderate hypothesis that intuitive predictions and probability judgments are highly sensitive to representativeness" (Tversky and Kahneman 1983, 88). This, of course, is entirely compatible with the suggestion that in many circumstances we use methods other than normatively problematic heuristics. Finally, as will become apparent in the remainder of this chapter, the heuristics and biases account of human reasoning does not presuppose a commitment to (3). It is not a central element in the heuristics and biases research program.

EVOLUTIONARY PSYCHOLOGY: THEORY, DATA, CORE CLAIMS, AND RHETORIC

Though the interdisciplinary field of evolutionary psychology is too new to have developed any precise and widely agreed upon body of doctrine, there are three basic theses that are clearly central. The first is that the mind contains a large number of special-purpose systems—often called modules or mental organs. These modules are invariably conceived of as a type of computational mechanism: namely, computational devices that are specialized or domain-specific. Many evolutionary psychologists also urge that modules are both innate and present in all normal members of the species. While this characterization of modules raises lots of interesting issues—issues about which we have had a fair amount to say elsewhere (Samuels 1998; Samuels, Stich, and Tremoulet 1999)—in this chapter we propose to put them to one side. The second central thesis of evolutionary psychology is that, contrary to what has been argued by Fodor (1983) and others, the

---

This is not, however, a claim that any other proponents of heuristics and biases have been prepared to endorse even in their least careful statements. Nor is there any reason to think that they should, since it is utterly implausible to maintain that this thesis is supported by the available data. We will, therefore, treat Piattelli-Palmarini's "probabilistic law" as a particularly extreme instance of rhetorical excess and ignore it in the remainder of this chapter.

modular structure of the mind is not restricted to input systems (those responsible for perception and language processing) and output systems (those responsible for producing actions). According to evolutionary psychologists, modules also subserve many so-called central capacities, such as reasoning and belief fixation.[3] The third thesis is that mental modules are *adaptations*—they were, as J. Tooby and L. Cosmides have put it, "invented by natural selection during the species' evolutionary history to produce adaptive ends in the species' natural environment" (1995, xiii). Here is a passage in which Tooby and Cosmides offer a particularly colorful statement of these central tenets of evolutionary psychology:

> Our cognitive architecture resembles a confederation of hundreds or thousands of functionally dedicated computers (often called modules) designed to solve adaptive problems endemic to our hunter-gatherer ancestors. Each of these devices has its own agenda and imposes its own exotic organization on different fragments of the world. There are specialized systems for grammar induction, for face recognition, for dead reckoning, for construing objects and for recognizing emotions from the face. There are mechanisms to detect animacy, eye direction, and cheating. There is a "theory of mind" module . . . a variety of social inference modules . . . and a multitude of other elegant machines. (1995, xiv)

If much of central cognition is indeed subserved by cognitive modules that were designed to deal with the adaptive problems posed by the environment in which our primate forebears lived, then we should expect that the modules responsible for reasoning would do their best job when information is provided in a format similar to the format in which information was available in the ancestral environment. And, as Gigerenzer has argued, though there was a great deal of useful probabilistic information available in that environment, this information would have been represented "as frequencies of events, sequentially encoded as experienced—for example, 3 *out of* 20 as opposed to 15 percent or p = 0.15" (1994, 142). Cosmides and Tooby make much the same point as follows:

> Our hominid ancestors were immersed in a rich flow of observable frequencies that could be used to improve decision-making, given procedures that could take advantage of them. So if we have adaptations for inductive reasoning, they should take frequency information as input. (1996, 15–16)

On the basis of such evolutionary considerations, Gigerenzer, Cosmides, and Tooby have proposed and defended a psychological hypothesis that they refer to as the *Frequentist*

---

3. The conjunction of the first two central theses of evolutionary psychology constitutes what might be called the *Massive Modularity Hypothesis*. For more on this hypothesis, see Samuels (1998) and Samuels, Stich, and Tremoulet (1999).

Hypothesis: ". . . some of our inductive reasoning mechanisms do embody aspects of a calculus of probability, but they are designed to take frequency information as input and produce frequencies as output" (Cosmides and Tooby 1996, 3).

This speculation led Cosmides and Tooby to pursue an intriguing series of experiments in which the Harvard Medical School problem used by Casscells, Schoenberger, and Grayboys was systematically transformed into a problem in which both the input and the response required were formulated in terms of frequencies. Here is one example from their study in which frequency information is made particularly salient:

> 1 out of every 1,000 Americans has disease X. A test has been developed to detect when a person has disease X. Every time the test is given to a person who has the disease, the test comes out positive. But sometimes the test also comes out positive when it is given to a person who is completely healthy. Specifically, out of every 1,000 people who are perfectly healthy, 50 of them test positive for the disease.
>
> Imagine that we have assembled a random sample of 1,000 Americans. They were selected by lottery. Those who conducted the lottery had no information about the health status of any of these people.
>
> Given the information above: on average, how many people who test positive for the disease will *actually* have the disease? ___ out of ___.

In sharp contrast to the original Casscells experiment, in which only 18 percent of subjects gave the correct Bayesian response, this problem elicited the correct Bayesian answer from 76 percent of Cosmides and Tooby's subjects. Nor is this an isolated case in which "frequentist versions" of probabilistic reasoning problems elicit high levels of performance. On the contrary, it seems that in many instances, when problems are framed in terms of frequencies rather than probabilities, subjects tend to reason in a normatively appropriate manner (Gigerenzer 1991a, 1996; Kahneman and Tversky 1996; Tversky and Kahneman 1983). Though it remains contentious how precisely to explain this fact, the phenomenon itself is now generally accepted by evolutionary psychologists and proponents of heuristics and biases alike.

It is still a matter of some controversy what precisely results of this sort show about the nature and extent of human rationality. What is clear, however, is that evolutionary psychologists take them to suggest the truth of two claims. First, they clearly think the data suggest the following:

(4) There are many reasoning problems that involve probability or uncertainty on which people's intuitive judgments *do not* deviate from appropriate norms of rationality.

Specifically, for many problems involving frequencies we reason in a normatively appropriate fashion (Cosmides and Tooby 1996; Gigerenzer 1991a, 1996). Moreover, evolutionary psychologists clearly think that the results cited earlier also provide some support for the following thesis:

(5) Many of the instances in which our probabilistic judgments accord with appropriate norms of rationality are to be explained by the fact that, in making these judgments, we rely on mental modules that were designed by natural selection to do a good job at nondemonstrative reasoning when provided with the sort of input that was common in the environment of evolutionary adaptation (EEA).

So, for example, as we have already seen, evolutionary psychologists maintain that the mind contains one or more frequentist modules that have been designed by natural selection and tend to produce normatively appropriate judgments when provided with the appropriate input. We take it that (4) and (5) are core claims of the evolutionary psychological research on probabilistic reasoning.

Like their heuristics and biases counterparts, however, evolutionary psychologists have also on occasion issued exuberant proclamations that go well beyond the core claims of the research program and cannot plausibly be viewed as anything other than rhetorical excess. In particular, evolutionary psychologists sometimes appear to maintain the following:

(6) Our probabilistic reasoning is subserved by "elegant machines" designed by natural selection and any concerns about systematic irrationality are unfounded.

This view is suggested in numerous passages in the evolutionary psychology literature. Moreover, these rhetorical flourishes tend to suggest, in our view incorrectly, that evolutionary psychology poses a direct challenge to the heuristics and biases tradition. Thus, for example, the paper in which Cosmides and Tooby reported their data on the Harvard Medical School problem appeared with the title "Are Humans Good Intuitive Statisticians After All? Rethinking Some Conclusions from the Literature on Judgment Under Uncertainty." Five years earlier, while Cosmides and Tooby's research was still in progress, Gigerenzer reported some of their early findings in a paper with the provocative title "How to Make Cognitive Illusions Disappear: Beyond 'Heuristics and Biases.'" The clear suggestion, in both of these titles, is that the findings they report pose a head-on challenge to the pessimism of the heuristics and biases tradition and to its core claim that human beings are prone to systematic deviations from appropriate norms of rationality. Nor were these suggestions restricted to titles. In paper after paper, Gigerenzer has said things like "we need not necessarily worry about human rationality" (1998b, 280); "more optimism is in order" (1991b, 245); and "Keep distinct meanings of probability straight, and much can be done— cognitive illusions disappear" (1991b, 245), and he has maintained that his view "supports intuition as basically rational" (1991b, 242). Since comments like these are widespread in the literature, it is hardly surprising that many observers have concluded that the view of the mind and of human rationality proposed by evolutionary psychologists is fundamentally at odds with the view offered by proponents of the heuristics and biases program.

3. Making the Dispute Disappear

So far we've outlined in broad strokes the dispute between evolutionary psychology and the heuristics and biases tradition. If we are to believe the rhetoric, then it would appear that these two research programs are locked in a deep disagreement over the nature and extent of human rationality. However, in this section we propose to argue that the air of apparent conflict between evolutionary psychology and the heuristics and biases program is, in large part, an illusion engendered by a failure to distinguish the core claims of the two research programs from the rhetorical embellishments to which advocates on both sides occasionally succumb. We'll argue that once one puts the rhetoric aside and tries to formulate the dispute in more precise terms, it becomes clear that there is much less disagreement here than meets the eye. To defend this surprising contention, we need to start by drawing some distinctions. In particular, we need to distinguish between (1) a variety of proposals about *what* precisely is being assessed (what the *objects of epistemic evaluation* are) in the psychological literature on rationality and (2) a range of proposals about the *standards* (the normative yardsticks) against which epistemic evaluations should be made. With these distinctions in hand, we will then argue that on any plausible understanding of the dispute over the extent of human rationality between evolutionary psychology and the heuristics and biases tradition there is, in fact, no genuine disagreement. Though the rhetoric would suggest otherwise, evolutionary psychologists and their heuristics and biases counterparts are in substantial *agreement* over the extent to which human beings are rational.

THE OBJECTS AND STANDARDS OF EPISTEMIC EVALUATION

In order to make an epistemic evaluation, one must adopt—perhaps explicitly but more often than not implicitly—positions on the following two issues. First of all, one needs to make assumptions about *what* exactly is being assessed—what the *objects* of epistemic evaluation are. In the dispute between evolutionary psychologists and advocates of the heuristics and biases tradition, there are at least two kinds of entity that might plausibly be construed as the objects of evaluation. One option is that the researchers are aiming to assess the *judgments* that subjects make—for example, the answer "95 percent" in response to the Harvard Medical School problem. If this is what is being evaluated, then it might be that the disagreement between evolutionary psychology and the heuristics and biases tradition concerns the extent to which human *judgments* about probability are normatively problematic. A second option is that psychologists who study human reason are aiming to assess the *cognitive mechanisms* that produce these judgments. In that case, the disagreement might concern the extent to which these *mechanisms* are normatively problematic.

Second, in addition to making assumptions about *what* is being assessed, the task of epistemic evaluation also requires that one adopt, if only implicitly, some *normative standard*—some yardstick—against which the evaluation is to be made. As we see it, there have been four main kinds of normative standard that have been invoked in the debate between evolutionary psychology and the heuristics and biases tradition:

1. What E. Stein (1996) calls the "standard picture"
2. Two accuracy-based normative standards:
   (a) Accuracy in the actual domain of a cognitive mechanism
   (b) Accuracy in the proper domain of a cognitive mechanism
3. An optimality-based normative standard

We will soon elaborate on these epistemic standards in some detail. For the moment, however, we wish merely to point out that when we combine them with the two objects of epistemic evaluation mentioned earlier, we can generate a 2 × 4 array of options (see Table 9.1); there are eight different kinds of epistemic evaluation that need to be kept distinct. In the remainder of this section we will argue that for each of these options there is no genuine disagreement between evolutionary psychologists and psychologists in the heuristics and biases tradition.

THE STANDARD PICTURE

When evaluating human reasoning, both evolutionary psychologists and proponents of the heuristics and biases program typically presuppose what Stein has called the standard picture of rationality:

> According to this picture, to be rational is to reason in accordance with principles of reasoning that are based on rules of logic, probability theory and so forth. If the standard picture of reasoning is right, principles of reasoning that are based on such rules are normative principles of reasoning, namely they are the principles we ought to reason in accordance with. (1996, 4)

Thus, the standard picture maintains that the appropriate criteria against which to evaluate human reasoning are the rules derived from formal theories such as classical logic, probability theory, and decision theory.[4] So, for example, one might derive something like the following principle of reasoning from the conjunction rule of probability theory:

---

4. Precisely what it is for a principle of reasoning to be *derived from* the rules of logic, probability theory, and decision theory is far from clear. For as Goldman and Harman have both pointed out, rules of rational inference cannot literally be derived from logic and probability theory (Goldman 1986, 82; Harman 1986, chapter 2). Nor is it clear which of the rules of logic, probability theory, and decision theory our judgments and reasoning mechanisms must accord with in order to count as rational. Moreover, there are serious disagreements about which *versions* of logic, decision theory, and probability theory the correct principles of rationality ought to be derived from (see, for example, Gigerenzer 1991a). Nonetheless, the essential idea is that we use the rules from these formal theories as a guide in constructing normative principles that can then be employed in order to measure the extent to which human reasoning and judgment is rational.

TABLE 9.1

Eight different kinds of epistemic evaluation

	Judgments	Mechanisms
"Standard picture"		
Accuracy in the actual domain		
Accuracy in the proper domain		
Optimal given relevant constraints		

Conjunction Principle

One ought not assign a lower degree of probability to the occurrence of event A than one does to the occurrence of A and some (distinct) event B. (Stein 1996, 6)

Given principles of this kind, one can evaluate the specific judgments issued by human subjects and the mechanisms that produce them. To the extent that a person's judgments accord with the principles of the standard picture these judgments are rational, and to the extent that they violate such principles the judgments fail to be rational. Similarly, to the extent that a reasoning mechanism produces judgments that accord with the principles of the standard picture the mechanism is rational, and to the extent that it fails to do so it is not rational. As M. Piattelli-Palmarini puts the point:

The universal principles of logic, arithmetic, and probability calculus ... tell us what we *should* ... think, not what we in fact think. ... If our intuition does in fact lead us to results incompatible with logic, we conclude that our intuition is at fault. (1994, 158)

THE STANDARD PICTURE AND THE EVALUATION OF JUDGMENTS. Proponents of the heuristics and biases program often appear to be in the business of evaluating the intuitive *judgments* that subjects make against the yardstick of the standard picture. As we noted earlier, Kahneman and Tversky say that "although errors of judgment are but a method by which some cognitive processes are studied, the method has become a significant part of the message" (1982, 124). And the method-turned-message appears to be that many of our probabilistic judgments *systematically* deviate from the norms of rationality prescribed by the standard picture, specifically from those norms derived from probability theory (Kahneman and Tversky 1972, 431; Piattelli-Palmarini 1994, 140). A recurrent theme in the heuristics and biases literature is that many of our intuitive judgments about probabilities deviate from the canons of probability theory in such a way that the deviations can be reliably reproduced under a wide range of circumstances that are related in their possession of certain key characteristics—for example, the manner in which information is presented to people or the content of the information about which people are asked to reason.

At first sight, this would appear to be a claim that evolutionary psychologists reject. Thus, Gigerenzer asserts that "most so-called errors or cognitive illusions are, contrary to the assertions of the literature, in fact *not* violations of probability theory" (1991a, 86). But on closer scrutiny, it is hard to see how evolutionary psychologists *could* reject the claim that many of our intuitive judgments systematically deviate from norms derived from probability theory. This is because some of the central features of their research program commit them to saying that human judgments *do* systematically deviate from these norms. In order to make this point we will focus on two features of the evolutionary psychological research program: (1) the empirical thesis that formulating probabilistic problems in terms of frequencies improves performance and (2) the ameliorative project of improving statistical reasoning by teaching subjects to reformulate probabilistic problems in terms of frequencies.

As we saw in section 2, evolutionary psychologists maintain that when problems are explicitly formulated in terms of frequencies performance improves dramatically. Consider, for example, the experiments on base-rate neglect. We have already discussed the Casscells study's Harvard Medical School problem and noted that it appears to show that, under certain circumstances, human beings systematically ignore information about base rates when performing diagnostic tasks (Casscells, Schoenberger, and Grayboys 1978). For our current purposes, the crucial point to notice about the Casscells et al. experiment is that the problem was formulated in a *nonfrequentist* format. Subjects were asked about the probability of single events—the probability that a *specific* person has a disease—and were provided with probabilistic information in percentile and decimal formats. The results were disconcerting: 82 percent of subjects failed to provide the appropriate Bayesian answer to the problem. By contrast, we have already seen that, when presented with variants of the Harvard Medical School problem in which frequencies rather than percentages and single event probabilities were emphasized, subjects performed far better than they did in the original Casscells experiment. Although a number of different factors affect performance, according to Cosmides and Tooby, two predominate: "Asking for the answer as a frequency produces the largest effect, followed closely by presenting the problem information as frequencies" (1996, 58).

One central conclusion that evolutionary psychologists have wanted to draw from these experiments is that human probabilistic judgment *improves* when problems are reformulated in terms of frequencies.[5] So, for example, Cosmides and Tooby claim that "good statistical reasoning reappears, when problems are posed in frequentist terms" (1996, 62). This, however, poses a serious problem for the view that evolutionary psychologists reject the heuristics and biases thesis that human beings perform poorly in many judgmental tasks that involve probabilities. After all, it's hard to make sense of the claim that probabilistic judgment *improves* or that good statistical reasoning *reappears* in frequentist tasks unless performance on nonfrequency problems was *poor*, or at any rate

---

5. Indeed, evolutionary psychologists take the fact that performance improves in frequentist tasks to *support* the frequentist hypothesis.

less good, in the first place. Moreover, it is clear that the metric that evolutionary psychologists are employing in order to evaluate whether or not probabilistic judgment improves is precisely the same as the one adopted by proponents of the heuristics and biases program: namely, the standard axioms and theorems of probability theory. It is precisely *because* judgments on many frequentist tasks accord with Bayes's theorem (and judgments on nonfrequentist tasks do not) that Cosmides and Tooby claim that good statistical reasoning reappears when problems are posed in terms of frequencies. The interpretation that evolutionary psychologists impose on their own experimental data—namely, that performance improves in frequentist tasks—*commits* them to accepting the heuristics and biases thesis that many of our probabilistic judgments deviate from appropriate norms of probabilistic reasoning.

A similar point applies to another central feature of evolutionary psychological research on human reasoning—the ameliorative project of trying to improve human probabilistic inference. In addition to providing empirical hypotheses about the cognitive mechanisms responsible for inductive reasoning, evolutionary psychologists have also been concerned with trying to improve the quality of probabilistic inference. This practical project has been vigorously pursued by Gigerenzer and his colleagues. And in a series of papers with titles such as "How to Improve Bayesian Reasoning Without Instruction: Frequency Formats" and "How to Improve Diagnostic Inferences in Physicians" they have shown how probabilistic judgment can be improved by teaching subjects to convert problems into a frequentist format (Gigerenzer and Hoffrage 1995; Hoffrage and Gigerenzer 2004). So, for example, Gigerenzer and his colleagues suggest that if physicians convert diagnostic problems into a frequentist format, then they are more likely to be accurate in their diagnoses.

This sort of ameliorative project, once again, poses a serious problem for the contention that evolutionary psychologists reject the heuristics and biases thesis that human beings perform poorly in many judgmental tasks that involve probabilities. For it is extremely hard to see how we can make sense of the idea that performance can be *improved* by converting problems into a frequency format *unless subjects were previously doing something wrong*. If there was nothing wrong, for example, with the answers that physicians provided to diagnostic problems that were formulated in nonfrequentist terms, then diagnosis *couldn't* be improved by formulating the problem in a frequentist format.[6] This is, we think,

---

6. This also poses a serious problem for Gigerenzer's claim that problems about single-event probabilities are meaningless and that, as a result, subjects' responses to such problems are not violations of the probability calculus. If problems about single events are really meaningless, then subjects' answers to such problems *couldn't* be wrong by the lights of the probability calculus. In which case, it is extremely hard to see how performance on reasoning tasks could *improve* when problems are reformulated in terms of frequencies as opposed to single events. Indeed, if, as evolutionary psychologists often appear to suggest, the frequentist problems given to experimental subjects are supposed to be *reformulations* of single-event problems, then it is hard to see how (accurate) reformulations of the original (meaningless) problems could be anything other than meaningless. In short: it is exceedingly hard to see how it could be the case that both (1) human reasoning improves when problems are reformulated in terms of frequencies and (2) nonfrequentist problems are meaningless.

an entirely uncontroversial conceptual point. According to conventional wisdom, "If it ain't broken, don't fix it." Our point is rather more basic: if it ain't broken, you *can't* fix it.

It is hard, then, to sustain the view that evolutionary psychologists reject the claim that many of our probabilistic judgments deviate from the norms of probability theory. What about a disagreement in the other direction? Do proponents of the heuristics and biases tradition deny the evolutionary psychologists' claim that many of our intuitive judgments about probability *accord* with the principles of probability theory? This is a suggestion that is hard to take seriously in the light of overwhelming textual evidence to the contrary. Kahneman, Tversky, and other advocates of the heuristics and biases program note repeatedly that normatively problematic heuristics like "representativeness" often get the *right* answer. Moreover, Kahneman and Tversky maintain (correctly) that they were responsible for discovering that formulating many judgmental problems in terms of frequencies leads to a dramatic improvement in performance (1996). And, as we'll see later on, they have also attempted to explain this phenomenon by providing an analysis of how the "extensional cues" provided by frequentist formulations of probabilistic problems facilitate reasoning. It is, therefore, singularly implausible to maintain that proponents of heuristics and biases deny that there are many probabilistic problems in which subjects' judgments accord with the probability calculus. We conclude that if there is a dispute between evolutionary psychologists and proponents of heuristics and biases, it is not located in the first box in Table 9.1. So it is time to replace Table 9.1 with Table 9.2.

TABLE 9.2

Kinds of epistemic dispute narrowed to seven options

	Judgments	Mechanisms
"Standard picture"	*no dispute*	
Accuracy in the actual domain		
Accuracy in the proper domain		
Optimal given relevant constraints		

THE STANDARD PICTURE AND THE EVALUATION OF MECHANISMS. If there is no substantive disagreement between evolutionary psychologists and proponents of the heuristics and biases tradition over whether or not our probabilistic *judgments* accord with the principles of the standard picture, then perhaps a disagreement exists over whether or not the cognitive *mechanisms* that subserve probabilistic reasoning accord with these principles? Certainly much of what has been said by participants in the debate suggests such a disagreement. Thus, for example, Cosmides and Tooby explicitly represent their project as a challenge to what they see as "the conclusion most common in the literature on judgment under uncertainty—that our inductive reasoning mechanisms do not embody a calculus of probability" (1996, 1). But when one considers the issue more carefully it becomes difficult to sustain the view that there is any genuine disagreement here—or so we shall argue.

In order to defend this claim, we'll start by arguing that the positive accounts of probabilistic reasoning that evolutionary psychologists and proponents of heuristics and biases have developed are not incompatible. Indeed, rather than being incompatible, the views that have emerged from these two research programs about the nature of probabilistic reasoning mechanisms are to a surprising degree complementary. For while the heuristics and biases program has been primarily concerned with finding cases where subjects do a bad job in their probabilistic reasoning and proposing mechanisms to explain these shortcomings, evolutionary psychologists have been more concerned with positing mechanisms in order to explain those instances in which our probabilistic reasoning is normatively unproblematic. In short, the two research programs have simply focused on different phenomena.

Evolutionary psychologists have endorsed a range of claims about the mechanisms that subserve probabilistic inference in human beings. One often-repeated claim is that the human mind contains a "multitude of elegant machines" for inductive reasoning: "many different ones, each appropriate to a different kind of decision-making problem" (Cosmides and Tooby 1996, 63). Moreover, evolutionary psychologists contend that at least some of these mechanisms—specifically, frequentist mechanisms—are normatively appropriate relative to precisely the same standard that the heuristics and biases program endorses, namely, their input-output patterns match what would be required by the Bayesian theory of probability. Thus, Cosmides and Tooby suggest that "people do have reliably developing mechanisms that allow them to apply the calculus of probability" (1996, 18).

It is important to stress, however, that these frequentist mechanisms are supposed to be *format-restricted*; they are only able to process information that is presented in the appropriate format. More specifically, frequentist mechanisms "are designed to accept probabilistic information when it is in the form of a frequency, and to produce a frequency as their output" (Cosmides and Tooby 1996, 18). When probabilistic problems are presented in a nonfrequentist format, however, evolutionary psychologists contend that our judgments will deviate from those prescribed by the calculus of probability because the frequentist mechanisms will be unable to process the information.[7] In short: according to evolutionary psychology, whether or not our probabilistic reasoning mechanisms produce judgments that accord with the probability calculus depends crucially on the format in which the information is presented.

---

7. An analogy might help to illuminate the proposal. Consider a standard electronic calculator that is designed to take as inputs mathematical problems that are presented in a standard base-10 notation. We might suppose that such a machine is a well-designed, specialized computational device that reliably solves problems that are presented in the appropriate format—i.e., base-10 Arabic notation. But suppose that we were to use the calculator to solve a problem stated in terms of Roman numerals. Since there simply are no buttons for "X" and "L" and "I" there would be no way for the calculator to deal with the problem (unless, of course, we first translate it into Arabic notation).

The previous two paragraphs provide a brief description of the main *positive* theses that evolutionary psychologists endorse about probabilistic inference in humans. But it is important to stress that this cannot be the entire story. Nor, for that matter, do evolutionary psychologists suggest that it is. Indeed, they *insist* that we may well need to posit a wide range of other inductive mechanisms, each of which operates according to different principles, in order to explain human reasoning (Cosmides and Tooby 1996, 63). One class of phenomena that is clearly in need of explanation is that of those instances in which subjects respond to probabilistic problems in ways that deviate from the norms of the probability calculus. These responses are not random but systematic in character. And presumably a complete account of human probabilistic reasoning needs to explain the inferential patterns that occur when we deviate from the probability calculus as well as those that occur when we get things right. Though evolutionary psychologists clearly accept this point and are prepared to posit additional mechanisms in order to explain the results, they have, as yet, provided no detailed theory that accounts for these results.[8] Nevertheless, they require an explanation. And presumably the explanation will need to invoke mechanisms in addition to the frequentist mechanisms discussed earlier. Moreover, these additional mechanisms will not map inputs onto the same outputs that the probability calculus would and, hence, *they will be normatively problematic by the lights of the standard picture.*

Is there any reason to think that proponents of the heuristics and biases program would or should disagree with any of this? As far as we can see, the answer is no. First of all, it is important to see that, according to the preceding picture of our reasoning architecture, the total system will yield lots of mistakes, though it will also yield lots of correct answers. And this is entirely consistent with the heuristics and biases account. Moreover, proponents of the heuristics and biases program will clearly not want to reject the claim that we possess cognitive mechanisms that *fail* to produce the input-output mappings that are sanctioned by the probability calculus. That there are such mechanisms is a central claim of the heuristics and biases approach to human probabilistic reasoning. Indeed,

---

8. One might think that the notion of format restriction provides us with at least the outline for an explanation of why we perform poorly on probabilistic problems that are presented in nonfrequentist formats: viz., frequentist mechanisms will be unable to "handle" these problems because they are encoded in the wrong format. But the fact that the normatively unproblematic mechanisms are format-restricted only tells us that problems with the wrong format *won't* be assigned to (or be handled by) them. So they must be handled by some other component of the mind. But that's *all* the notion of format restriction tells us, and that hardly counts as an explanation of why we give the wrong answer. Nor, of course, does it explain why we make the specific sorts of systematic errors that have been documented in the psychological literature. So, for example, it clearly does not explain why, for nonfrequentist problems, base rates tend to be neglected rather than over-stressed or why human beings tend to exhibit overconfidence rather than, say, underconfidence. The point that needs to be stressed here is that it is implausible to think that these normatively problematic responses are the product of normatively unproblematic, format-restricted mechanisms (both because the responses are normatively problematic and because they are in the wrong format). So there must be further mechanisms that are normatively problematic. And that is just what the heuristics and biases tradition says.

it would appear that the positive views that evolutionary psychologists endorse about the nature of our reasoning architecture are consistent with the claim that the systems responsible for producing non-Bayesian judgments employ the sorts of heuristics that Kahneman, Tversky, and their followers have invoked in order to explain deviations from the probability calculus. So, for example, it may be the case that some of the normatively problematic mechanisms that evolutionary psychologists must posit to explain normatively problematic judgments implement the representativeness and availability heuristics.

At this point it might be suggested that proponents of the heuristics and biases program reject the existence of mechanisms that operate according to principles of the probability calculus. This could be because either (1) they reject the existence of more than one reasoning mechanism or (2) while they accept the existence of more than one reasoning mechanism, they deny that any of them operate according to the principles of probability. Let's consider these options in turn.

Evolutionary psychologists sometimes appear to suggest that proponents of the heuristics and biases program are wedded to the assumptions that there are no domain-specific or modular mechanisms for reasoning and that all reasoning is subserved by general-purpose processes and mechanisms. So, for example, Cosmides and Tooby appear to attribute to the heuristics and biases program "a certain old-fashioned image of the mind: that it has the architecture of an early model, limited-resource general-purpose computer" (1996, 13). There is plenty of textual evidence, however, that proponents of the heuristics and biases program do not endorse such a picture of the mind. So, for example, in a passage that anticipates a central theme in the work of evolutionary psychologists, Kahneman and Tversky compare the processes involved in the solving of probabilistic problems "with the operation of a flexible computer program that incorporates a variety of potentially useful subroutines" (1983, 88).[9] Elsewhere, they are even more explicit on the matter and claim that "the actual reasoning process is schema-bound or content-bound so that different operations or inferential rules are available in different contexts" and that "consequently, human reasoning cannot be adequately described in terms of content-independent formal rules" (Tversky and Kahneman 1983, 499). Piattelli-Palmarini is still more explicit in his endorsement of a domain-specific conception of human reasoning and goes so far as to suggest (rightly or wrongly) that judgmental errors are "a demonstration of what modern cognitive science calls the 'modularity' of the mind" (1994, 32). In other words, Piattelli-Palmarini appears to be endorsing the claim that we possess modules for reasoning.

So proponents of the heuristics and biases program do not appear to be averse to the idea that human reasoning is subserved by a variety of domain-specific cognitive mechanisms.

---

9. Compare to Tooby and Cosmides' own suggestion that the human mind "can be likened to a computer program with millions of lines of code and hundreds or thousands of functionally specialized subroutines" (1992, 39).

Do they, perhaps, deny that any of these mechanisms operate according to the principles of the probability calculus? If they did maintain this position, then there would be a genuine disagreement between evolutionary psychologists and proponents of the heuristics and biases program. But there is, in fact, no reason to suppose that they do hold such a view. First of all, nowhere in the heuristics and biases literature have we been able to find a single passage in which it is *explicitly* denied that we possess some cognitive mechanisms that operate according to the principles of the probability calculus. What we do find, however, are passages that may be interpreted as *suggesting* that there are no such mechanisms. So, for example, as we noted earlier, Kahneman and Tversky (1973) claim that

> in making predictions and judgments under uncertainty, people do not appear to follow the calculus of chance or the statistical theory of prediction. Instead, they rely on a limited number of heuristics which sometimes yield reasonable judgments and sometimes lead to severe and systematic errors. (48)

This and other similar passages in the heuristics and biases literature might be thought to have the conversational implicature that we *only* use normatively problematic heuristics in our probabilistic reasoning and hence possess no reasoning mechanisms that operate according to the principles of the probability calculus.

We maintain, however, that there are extremely good reasons to treat such claims as instances of rhetorical excess. First, as we pointed out in section 2, the claim that we possess *no* normatively unproblematic mechanisms for probabilistic reasoning is clearly not supported by the available empirical evidence. Such a claim is vastly stronger than anything the available evidence will support. And this provides us with some reason to treat it as a rhetorical flourish rather than a core claim of the heuristics and biases research program.

Second, all the quotations from the heuristics and biases literature we have found that suggest humans possess no normatively appropriate reasoning mechanisms manifest a tendency that Kahneman and Tversky have themselves lamented—the tendency to overstate one's position by "omitting relevant quantifiers" (1996, 589). Kahneman and Tversky raise this point in response to Gigerenzer's claim that cognitive illusions disappear when problems are formulated in terms of frequencies. They suggest that "because Gigerenzer must be aware of the evidence that judgments of frequency. . . . are subject to systematic error, a charitable interpretation of his position is that he has overstated his case by omitting relevant quantifiers" (1996, 589). We maintain that much the same may be said of the position that Kahneman, Tversky, and their followers sometimes appear to endorse regarding the normative status of our reasoning mechanisms. Consider, for example, the preceding quotation from Kahneman and Tversky 1973. The natural reading of this passage is that Kahneman and Tversky are claiming that humans *always* "rely on a limited number of heuristics" (1973, 48). But notice that the relevant quantifier is omitted. It is left unspecified whether they are claiming that we *always* use normatively problematic heuristics rather than (for example) claiming that we *typically* or *often* use such heuristics. And because they must know that the truth of the natural reading is vastly underdetermined by the data, it is surely charitable to interpret this as an instance of rhetorical excess—an overstatement of their position that results from omitting relevant quantifiers. Moreover, this point generalizes: in *all* the passages from the heuristics and biases literature that we have found which suggest that humans possess no normatively appropriate reasoning mechanisms, *relevant quantifiers are systematically omitted*. We suggest, therefore, that because proponents of the heuristics and biases program are presumably aware that the available evidence fails to support the claim that humans possess *no* normatively unproblematic reasoning mechanisms, the charitable interpretation of these quotations is that they overstate the position by omitting relevant quantifiers.

A final point that further supports the conclusion of the previous paragraph is that in their more reflective moments—when quantifiers are not omitted—advocates of the heuristics and biases tradition make it clear that they are not maintaining that we *always* use normatively problematic heuristics and mechanisms in our intuitive reasoning. Instead, they explicitly claim only that we *sometimes* or *often* use such heuristics and mechanisms. So, for example, when they are being careful, Kahneman and Tversky claim only that "intuitive predictions and judgments are *often* mediated by a small number of distinct mental operations . . . [or] . . . judgmental heuristics" (1996, 582). But this position is entirely compatible with the evolutionary psychological view that we also possess some normatively unproblematic reasoning mechanisms. In short: when proponents of the heuristics and biases tradition express their views carefully and fill in the appropriate quantifiers, they end up maintaining a position about the normative status of our reasoning mechanisms that does not conflict with the claims of evolutionary psychologists. It is time, then, to replace Table 9.2 with Table 9.3.

TABLE 9.3

Kinds of epistemic dispute narrowed to six options

	Judgments	Mechanisms
"Standard picture"	*no dispute*	*no dispute*
Accuracy in the actual domain		
Accuracy in the proper domain		
Optimal given relevant constraints		

ACCURACY-BASED ASSESSMENTS

Though the standard picture is the normative yardstick most commonly invoked in the dispute between evolutionary psychology and the heuristics and biases program, it is not the only one. Another kind of normative standard is suggested by Gigerenzer's discussion of Take The Best and other members of a class of satisficing algorithms that he calls fast and frugal procedures (Gigerenzer and Goldstein 1996; Gigerenzer, Hoffrage, and Klein-bölting 1991). According to Gigerenzer, a central consideration when evaluating reasoning is its *accuracy* (Gigerenzer and Goldstein 1996, 665). And because fast and frugal algorithms get the correct answer at least as often as other computationally more expensive, "rational"[10] methods (such as standard statistical linear models) Gigerenzer clearly thinks that they are normatively unproblematic. Indeed, he thinks that the fact that these simple algorithms are accurate constitutes a refutation of the claim that only "rational" algorithms can be accurate and goes some way toward overcoming the "opposition between the rational and the psychological and. . . . reunit[ing] the two" (Gigerenzer and Goldstein 1996, 666).

Although the notion of accuracy applies to both judgments and cognitive mechanisms, Gigerenzer and other evolutionary psychologists are concerned primarily with the accuracy of mechanisms (Cosmides and Tooby 1996; Gigerenzer and Goldstein 1996). Moreover, it is also clear that once we address the issue of whether or not evolutionary psychologists and proponents of the heuristics and biases tradition disagree about the accuracy of our cognitive mechanisms, the same considerations apply *mutatis mutandis* to the putative disagreement over judgments. For this reason we will focus primarily on whether or not there is any genuine disagreement between evolutionary psychology and the heuristics and biases program over the accuracy of our cognitive mechanisms.

When applied to cognitive mechanisms, Gigerenzer's accuracy-based criterion for epistemic evaluation bears an intimate relationship to the reliabilist tradition in epistemology according to which (very roughly) a cognitive mechanism is rational just in case it tends to produce true beliefs and avoid producing false ones (Goldman 1986; Nozick 1993).[11] One frequently observed consequence of reliabilist and accuracy-based approaches to the evaluation of cognitive mechanisms is that assessments must be relativized to some environment or domain of information (Goldman 1986; Nozick 1993; Stich 1990). A visual system, for example, is not reliable or unreliable *simpliciter* but only reliable or accurate relative to a (set of) environment(s) or a domain of information.[12] Moreover, there is an indefinitely wide range of environments or domains to which evaluations might be relativized. For current purposes, however, let's focus on two that have been suggested by D. Sperber to be particularly relevant to understanding the evolutionary psychological approach to reasoning—what he calls the *actual domain* and the *proper*

---

10. Evolutionary psychologists often use the term *rational* in scare quotes. When they do so, it is clear that they intend to refer to judgments, mechanisms, or procedures that are construed as rational by the lights of the standard picture.

11. There are also interesting questions about the relationship between the accuracy-based criterion and the standard picture, but we do not have the space to discuss them here.

12. So, for example, the human visual system may well be accurate relative to the range of information that it processes in the environments in which we typically live. But as Gigerenzer (1998) notes, our color vision is singularly *un*-reliable in parking lots illuminated by mercury vapor lamps. And in the "world" of the psychophysicist with its array of exotic visual stimuli, other components of the visual system can be very unreliable indeed.

domain for a cognitive mechanism (1994). The actual domain for a given reasoning module is "all the information in the organism's environment that may (once processed by perceptual modules, and possibly by other conceptual modules) satisfy the module's input conditions" (51–52). By "input conditions" Sperber means those conditions that must be satisfied in order for the module to be able to process a given item of information. So, for example, if a module requires that a problem be stated in a particular format, then any information not stated in that format fails to satisfy the module's input conditions. By contrast, the proper domain for a cognitive mechanism is all the information that it is the mechanism's "biological function to process" (52). The proper domain is the information that the mechanism was designed to process by natural selection. In recent years, many philosophers of biology have come to regard the notion of a biological function as a particularly slippery one.[13] For current purposes we can rely on the following very rough characterization: the biological functions of a system are the activities or effects of the system in virtue of which the system has remained a stable feature of an enduring species.

Do evolutionary psychologists and proponents of the heuristics and biases tradition disagree about the accuracy of reasoning mechanisms in their *proper* domains? Clearly not. For while evolutionary psychologists have maintained that cognitive mechanisms will tend to perform accurately in their proper domains—on the kinds of information that they are designed to process—the heuristics and biases tradition has been entirely silent on the issue. Determining the accuracy of cognitive mechanisms *in the proper domain* is simply not the line of work that proponents of heuristics and biases are engaged in. So there could be no disagreement here.

It is similarly implausible to maintain that evolutionary psychologists and advocates of the heuristics and biases tradition disagree over the accuracy of our reasoning mechanisms in the *actual* domain. Clearly, evolutionary psychologists think that *some* of our reasoning mechanisms are accurate in the actual domain. But it is equally clear that they do not claim that *all* of these mechanisms are. They certainly cite no evidence that could support the claim that *all* of our reasoning mechanisms are accurate in the actual domain. And, what is more important, such a claim would be patently incompatible with their ameliorative project. If all our reasoning mechanisms are accurate in the actual domain, then there is little room for systematically *improving* human reasoning. So it must be the case that what evolutionary psychologists want to claim is that *some but not all* of our reasoning mechanisms are accurate in the actual domain.

Do proponents of the heuristics and biases tradition reject this claim? As far as we can see, the answer is no. They clearly think that *some* of our cognitive mechanisms are inaccurate in the actual domain. This, after all, is a central message of their research program. But they have been largely silent on the issue of whether or not we possess

13. See, for example, Godfrey-Smith 1994, Neander 1991, and Plantinga 1993.

other reasoning mechanisms that are accurate in the actual domain. And this is simply because, as we mentioned earlier on, proponents of the heuristics and biases tradition have primarily focused on explaining instances of incorrect judgment rather than explaining instances of successful inference. Nonetheless, as we saw earlier, theorists working within the heuristics and biases tradition are not averse to the idea that we have reasoning mechanisms other than the ones that employ normatively problematic heuristics and, to the extent that they say anything about these other mechanisms, they seem amenable to the idea that they may be accurate. So, for example, Kahneman and Tversky seem entirely comfortable with the idea that mechanisms that employ correct rules of probabilistic inference can produce highly accurate judgments in contexts where the problem is transparent and "extensional" cues are effective (Tversky and Kahneman 1983).

The situation is similar when we turn to the issue of whether or not evolutionary psychologists and advocates of the heuristics and biases approach disagree over the accuracy of our *judgments*. Evolutionary psychologists think that we tend to be accurate in the *proper* domain, whereas proponents of the heuristics and biases program are simply silent on the issue. And both parties appear to think that *many but not all* of our judgments are accurate in the *actual* domain. There are, of course, lots of issues of detail where the two research programs disagree. So, for example, Gigerenzer has challenged some of the interpretations that advocates of the heuristics and biases program have imposed on specific experiments. We will consider some of these cases in section 4. But we maintain that these disagreements are *merely* matters of detail and ought not to distract from the genuine consensus between evolutionary psychology and the heuristics and biases program. Both programs clearly accept that many of our judgments in the actual domain are inaccurate and that we are subject to systematic errors.

This is a central claim of the heuristics and biases program, and evolutionary psychology is similarly committed to this view by virtue of endorsing the ameliorative project. Moreover, neither program insists that *all* of our judgments are inaccurate. Both, for example, think that our judgments about frequency can be highly accurate. Again, there is no disagreement. So we can now replace Table 9.3 with Table 9.4.

TABLE 9.4

Kinds of epistemic dispute narrowed to two options

	Judgments	Mechanisms
"Standard picture"	*no dispute*	*no dispute*
Accuracy in the actual domain	*no dispute*	*no dispute*
Accuracy in the proper domain	*no dispute*	*no dispute*
Optimal given relevant constraints		

CONSTRAINED-OPTIMALITY ASSESSMENTS

A final normative standard that has been invoked by participants in the debate between evolutionary psychology and the heuristics and biases tradition is one that applies only to the evaluation of cognitive mechanisms and not to the judgments that these mechanisms produce. The standard in question maintains that a reasoning mechanism is normatively unproblematic to the extent that it is *optimal given the constraints to which it is subject*. This proposal is alluded to by Gigerenzer when he suggests that some reasoning mechanisms may be optimal in the way that Herman von Helmholtz and Richard Gregory propose that visual processing mechanisms are optimal: they are *the best systems available for acquiring an accurate picture of the world given the constraints under which they must operate*. One crucial point to stress is that the best system (given the constraints under which it operates) need not be a system that never makes mistakes. As Gigerenzer points out, such "systems can be fooled and may break down when stable, long-term properties of the environment to which they are adapted change" (1997, 10). So, for example, Gregory maintains that visual "illusions will be a necessary part of all efficiently designed visual machines"—even the *best-designed* visual systems (Gregory, quoted in Gigerenzer 1991a, 228). Similarly, Gigerenzer suggests that, given the constraints under which real cognitive systems must operate, "cognitive illusions" or "biases" will be a necessary part of an efficiently designed reasoning mechanism. Thus, the Helmholtzian view "allows both for optimal cognitive functioning and for systematic illusions" (Gigerenzer 1991a, 240).

Is there any disagreement between evolutionary psychologists and proponents of the heuristics and biases program on the issue of whether or not we possess mechanisms that are optimally well designed (given the appropriate constraints) for probabilistic reasoning? Once again, we maintain, the answer is no. While evolutionary psychologists have suggested that we possess mechanisms that are optimal in the relevant sense, proponents of the heuristics and biases program need not and do not deny this claim. To see why, it is important to note that when evolutionary psychologists suggest that we possess reasoning mechanisms that are optimal given the constraints, they typically appear to have in mind the claim that we possess cognitive mechanisms that are optimally well designed for processing information in their *proper domains* (and under conditions similar to those our evolutionary ancestors would have encountered) and not the claim that we possess mechanisms that are optimally well designed for processing information in their *actual domains*. Thus, for example, Cosmides and Tooby suggest that

> our minds come equipped with very sophisticated intuitive competences that are well-engineered solutions to the problems humans normally encountered in natural environments . . . and that ecologically valid input (e.g., frequency formats) may be necessary to activate these competences. (1996, 9)

But if the notion of optimality invoked by evolutionary psychologists is indexed to the proper domain, then, as we have already seen, proponents of the heuristics and biases program do not disagree. The heuristics and biases program simply is not concerned with the performance of cognitive mechanisms in their proper domains.

Suppose, however, that, contrary to appearances, evolutionary psychologists do wish to maintain that we possess reasoning mechanisms that are optimal relative to the actual domain. Even so, they clearly could not maintain that *all* of our reasoning mechanisms are optimal since, once again, such a view would render their ameliorative project impossible. If all our reasoning mechanisms were the best that they could be, then we *couldn't* make them better. Here the (dis)analogy between visual systems and reasoning systems is illuminating. It is plausible to claim that when functioning normally our visual systems are optimal in the sense that they simply cannot be improved. By contrast, we *can* improve our reasoning—hence the ameliorative project. So the most that evolutionary psychologists could be claiming is that some or perhaps many of our cognitive mechanisms are optimal relative to the actual domain. But this is not a claim that proponents of the heuristics and biases tradition either do or should reject. To the best of our knowledge, proponents of the heuristics and biases program have never denied that we possess some reasoning mechanisms that are optimal in this sense. What they do deny is that *all* of the cognitive mechanisms that subserve reasoning are optimal in the sense that they always produce judgments that are correct and/or accord with the principles of the probability calculus. This, however, is a very different notion of optimality—a notion of optimality that does not take into consideration the constraints under which our reasoning systems must operate.

There is no reason to suppose that the heuristics and biases program is committed to denying that we possess cognitive mechanisms that are optimal in the actual domain *given the constraints under which they operate*. For as we have already seen, the claim that a reasoning system is optimal (given the appropriate constraints) is perfectly consistent with the view that it is subject to lots of biases and cognitive illusions. Thus, proponents of the heuristics and biases program need not and do not deny that some or even many of our cognitive mechanisms may be optimal in the Helmholtzian sense that Gigerenzer and other evolutionary psychologists have in mind. And if this is correct, then we can replace Table 9.4 with Table 9.5.

4. Some Real Disagreements

The main burden of this chapter has been to dispel the illusion that there is any substantive disagreement between evolutionary psychologists and advocates of the heuristics and biases tradition concerning the extent of human rationality. We do not intend to suggest, however, that there is nothing left for evolutionary psychologists and proponents of the heuristics and biases program to disagree about. Clearly there is. Indeed, there are

TABLE 9.5

Kinds of epistemic dispute narrowed to one option

	Judgments	Mechanisms
"Standard picture"	*no dispute*	*no dispute*
Accuracy in the actual domain	*no dispute*	*no dispute*
Accuracy in the proper domain	*no dispute*	*no dispute*
Optimal given relevant constraints		*no dispute*

a number of different disputes that remain. One of these disputes focuses on the issue of how we ought to apply probability theory to specific problems in the heuristics and biases literature—for example, the lawyer/engineer problem and the Harvard Medical School problem—and whether or not probability theory provides a uniquely correct answer to these problems. Though authors in the heuristics and biases tradition often appear to assume that there is only one normatively correct answer to these problems, Gigerenzer has argued that there are typically a number of equally reasonable ways of applying probability theory to the problems and that these different analyses result in distinct but equally correct answers (1991a, 1994).

Another very real dispute concerns the adequacy of the explanations proposed by proponents of the heuristics and biases tradition—explanations that invoke heuristics, such as availability and representativeness, in order to explain cognitive phenomena. Evolutionary psychologists have maintained that these "heuristics are too vague to count as explanations" and that psychologists who work in the heuristics and biases tradition have failed to "specify precise and falsifiable process models, to clarify the antecedent conditions that elicit various heuristics, and to work out the relationship between heuristics" (Gigerenzer 1996, 593). Proponents of the heuristics and biases tradition have responded by arguing that evolutionary psychologists have "missed the point" (Kahneman and Tversky 1996). They maintain that representativeness and other heuristics "can be assessed experimentally" and that testing the hypothesis that probability judgments are mediated by these heuristics "does not require a theoretical model" (Kahneman and Tversky 1996).

On our view, both of these disputes raise deep and interesting questions, which we plan to address elsewhere. In this section we propose to focus on a third very real dispute between evolutionary psychologists and proponents of the heuristics and biases tradition, one that has often been center stage in the literature. This is the disagreement over what interpretation of probability theory to adopt.

There has been a long-standing disagreement between proponents of the heuristics and biases program and evolutionary psychologists over what we should recognize as the correct interpretation of probability theory. In contrast with psychologists in the heuristics and biases tradition, Gigerenzer has urged that probability theory ought to be given a frequentist interpretation according to which probabilities are construed as relative frequencies of events in one class to events in another. As Gigerenzer points out, according to "this frequentist view, one cannot speak of a probability unless a reference class is defined" (1993, 292–93). So, for example, "the relative frequency of an event such as death is only defined with respect to a reference class such as 'all male pub-owners fifty years old living in Bavaria'" (Gigerenzer 1993, 292). One consequence of this that Gigerenzer is particularly keen to stress is that according to frequentism, *it makes no sense* to assign probabilities to single events. Claims about the probability of a single event are *literally meaningless*: "For a frequentist . . . . the term 'probability,' when it refers to a *single event*, has no meaning at all for us" (1991a, 88). Moreover, Gigerenzer maintains that because of this "a strict frequentist" would argue that "the laws of probability are about frequencies and not about single events" and, hence, that "no judgment about single events can violate probability theory" (1993, 292–93).

In stark contrast with Gigerenzer's frequentism, Kahneman, Tversky, and their followers insist that probability theory *can* be meaningfully applied to single events and hence that judgments about single events (e.g., Jack being an engineer or, in another well-known problem, Linda being a bank teller)[14] can violate probability theory. This disagreement emerges very clearly in Kahneman and Tversky's 1996 work, where they argue that Gigerenzer's treatment of judgment under uncertainty "appears far too restrictive" because it "does not apply to events that are unique for the individual and, therefore, excludes some of the most important evidential and decision problems in people's lives" (589). Instead of adopting frequentism, Kahneman and Tversky suggest that some "subjectivist" or "Bayesian" account of probability may be preferable.

---

14. This problem was first studied by Tversky and Kahneman (1982), who presented subjects with the following task:

Linda is 31 years old, single, outspoken, and very bright. She majored in philosophy. As a student, she was deeply concerned with issues of discrimination and social justice, and also participated in anti-nuclear demonstrations.

Please rank the following statements by their probability, using 1 for the most probable and 8 for the least probable.

(a) Linda is a teacher in elementary school.
(b) Linda works in a bookstore and takes Yoga classes.
(c) Linda is active in the feminist movement.
(d) Linda is a psychiatric social worker.
(e) Linda is a member of the League of Women Voters.
(f) Linda is a bank teller.
(g) Linda is an insurance salesperson.
(h) Linda is a bank teller and is active in the feminist movement.

In a group of naive subjects with no background in probability and statistics, 89 percent judged that statement (h) was more probable than statement (f). For current purposes, the key point to notice is that subjects are asked to make judgments about a single event—e.g., that Linda is a bank teller—rather than a relative frequency. For this reason. Gigerenzer has insisted, contrary to the claims in the heuristics and biases literature, that ranking (h) as more probable than (f) "is not a violation of probability theory . . . [since] . . . for a frequentist, this problem has nothing to do with probability theory" (1991a, 91–92).

This disagreement over the interpretation of probability raises complex and important questions in the foundations of statistics and decision theory about the scope and limits of our formal treatment of probability. Moreover, the dispute between frequentists and subjectivists has been a central debate in the foundations of probability for much of the twentieth century (Mises 1957; Savage 1972). Needless to say, a satisfactory treatment of these issues is beyond the scope of this chapter. But we would like to comment briefly on what we take to be the central role that issues about the interpretation of probability theory play in the dispute between evolutionary psychologists and proponents of the heuristics and biases program. In particular, we will argue that Gigerenzer's use of frequentist considerations in this debate is deeply problematic.

Questions about the interpretation of probability entered the debate between evolutionary psychology and the heuristics and biases tradition primarily because it was realized by some theorists—most notably Gigerenzer—that these questions bear on the issue of whether or not human reasoning violates appropriate norms of rationality. As we have already seen, Gigerenzer argues that if frequentism is true, then statements about the probability of single events are meaningless and, hence, that judgments about single events *cannot* violate probability theory (1993, 292–93). Gigerenzer clearly thinks that this conclusion can be put to work in order to dismantle part of the evidential base for the claim that human judgments and reasoning mechanisms violate appropriate norms. For as we have seen, participants in the debate between evolutionary psychology and the heuristics and biases tradition typically view probability theory as the source of appropriate normative constraints on probabilistic reasoning. And if frequentism is true, then no probabilistic judgments about single events will be normatively problematic (by this standard), since they will not violate probability theory. In which case, Gigerenzer gets to exclude all experimental results that involve judgments about single events as evidence for the existence of normatively problematic, probabilistic judgments and reasoning mechanisms.

On the face of it, Gigerenzer's strategy is quite persuasive. Nevertheless, we think that it is subject to serious objections. Frequentism itself is a hotly contested view, but even if we grant, for argument's sake, that frequentism is correct, there are still serious grounds for concern. First, as we observed in note 6, there is a serious tension between the claim that subjects don't make errors in reasoning about single events and the ameliorative project that evolutionary psychologists are engaged in. The current point is not that frequentism is false but merely that evolutionary psychologists cannot comfortably maintain both (1) that we don't violate appropriate norms of rationality when reasoning about the probabilities of single events and (2) that reasoning improves when single-event problems are converted into a frequentist format.

A second and perhaps more serious problem with Gigerenzer's use of frequentist considerations is that it is very plausible to maintain that *even if* statements about the probabilities of single events really are meaningless and hence do not violate the probability calculus, subjects are still guilty of making *some sort of error* when they deal with problems about single events. For if, as Gigerenzer would have us believe, judgments about the probabilities of single events are meaningless, then surely the correct answer to a (putative) problem about the probability of a single event is not some numerical value or rank ordering but rather: "Huh?" or, "That's utter nonsense!" or, "What on earth are you talking about?" Consider an analogous case, in which you are asked to answer a question like "Is Linda taller than?" or "How much taller than is Linda?" Obviously these questions are nonsense because they are incomplete. In order to answer them you must be told what the other relatum of the "taller than" relation is supposed to be. Unless this is done, answering yes or no or providing a numerical value would surely be normatively inappropriate. Now according to the frequentist, the question "What is the probability that Linda is a bank teller?" is nonsense for much the same reason that "Is Linda taller than?" is. So when subjects answer the single-event probability question by providing a *number* they are doing something that is clearly normatively inappropriate. The normatively appropriate answer is "Huh?," not, "Less than ten percent."

It might be suggested that the answers that subjects provide in experiments that involve single-event probabilities are an artifact of the demand characteristics of the experimental context. Subjects (one might claim) know, if only implicitly, that single-event probabilities are meaningless. But because they are presented with forced choice problems that require a probabilistic judgment, they end up giving silly answers. So one might think that the take-home message is: "Don't blame the subject for giving a silly answer. Blame the experimenter for putting the subject in a silly situation in the first place!" But this proposal is implausible for two reasons. First, as a matter of fact, ordinary people use judgments about single-event probabilities in all sorts of circumstances outside of the psychologist's laboratory. So it is implausible to think that *they* view single-event probabilities as meaningless. But second, even if subjects really did think that single-event probabilities were meaningless, presumably we should expect them to provide more or less random answers and not the sorts of systematic responses that are observed in the psychological literature. Again, consider the comparison with the question "Is Linda taller than?" It would be a truly stunning result if everyone who was pressured to respond said yes.

5. Conclusion

The main aim of this chapter has been to dispel an illusion: the illusion that evolutionary psychology and the heuristics and biases tradition are deeply divided in their assessments of human reasoning. We started by outlining the two research programs and disentangling their core claims from the rhetorical flourishes that have obscured an emerging consensus between the two programs about the scope and limits of human rationality and about the cognitive architecture that supports it. We then showed that, contrary to appearances, there is no substantial disagreement between evolutionary psychologists and advocates of the heuristics and biases program over the extent of human rationality. On a number of different readings of what the dispute is supposed to be, *neither research program denies the core claims of the other* and, in many cases, it is clear that they should and do endorse each other's core claims. Finally, we briefly focused on some of the points of disagreement that remain once the illusory dispute has disappeared. Though there are some important issues that divide evolutionary psychologists and advocates of the heuristics and biases program, there is also a surprising degree of consensus. Moreover, and this has been our central theme, they do not really have any deep disagreement over the extent of human rationality.

REFERENCES

Bazerman, M., and M. Neale. 1986. Heuristics in Negotiation. In H. Arkes and K. Hammond, eds., *Judgment and Decision Making: An Interdisciplinary Reader*, 311–21. Cambridge: Cambridge University Press.

Bower, B. 1996. Rational Mind Design: Research into the Ecology of Thought Treads on Contested Terrain. *Science News* 150: 24–25.

Casscells, W., A. Schoenberger, and T. Grayboys. 1978. Interpretation by Physicians of Clinical Laboratory Results. *New England Journal of Medicine* 299: 999–1000.

Cosmides, L., and J. Tooby. 1996. Are Humans Good Intuitive Statisticians After All? Rethinking Some Conclusions from the Literature on Judgment Under Uncertainty. *Cognition* 58: 1–73.

Fodor, J. A. 1983. *Modularity of Mind: An Essay on Faculty Psychology*. Cambridge, MA: MIT Press.

Gigerenzer, G. 1991a. How to Make Cognitive Illusions Disappear: Beyond "Heuristics and Biases." *European Review of Social Psychology* 2: 83–115.

———. 1991b. On Cognitive Illusions and Rationality. *Poznan Studies in the Philosophy of the Sciences and the Humanities* 21: 225–49.

———. 1993. The Bounded Rationality of Probabilistic Mental Models. In K. Manktelow and D. Over, eds., *Rationality: Psychological and Philosophical Perspectives*, 284–313. London: Routledge.

———. 1994. Why the Distinction Between Single-Event Probabilities and Frequencies Is Important for Psychology (and Vice Versa). In G. Wright and P. Ayton, eds., *Subjective Probability*, 129–61. New York: Wiley.

———. 1996. On Narrow Norms and Vague Heuristics: A Reply to Kahneman and Tversky (1996). *Psychological Review* 103: 592–96.

———. 1997. The Modularity of Social Intelligence. In A. Whiten and R. Byrne, eds., *Machiavellian Intelligence II*, 264–80. Cambridge: Cambridge University Press.

———. 1998. Ecological Intelligence: An Adaptation for Frequencies. In D. Cummins and C. Allen, eds., *The Evolution of Mind*, 9–29. New York: Oxford University Press.

Gigerenzer, G., and D. G. Goldstein. 1996. Reasoning the Fast and Frugal Way: Models of Bounded Rationality. *Psychological Review* 103: 650–69.

Gigerenzer, G., and U. Hoffrage. 1995. How to Improve Bayesian Reasoning Without Instruction: Frequency Formats. *Psychological Review* 102: 684–704.

Gigerenzer, G., U. Hoffrage, and H. Kleinbölting. 1991. Probabilistic Mental Models: A

Brunswikian Theory of Confidence. *Psychological Review* 98: 506–28.

Godfrey-Smith, P. 1994. A Modern History Theory of Functions. *Nous* 28: 344–62.

Goldman, A. I. 1986. *Epistemology and Cognition*. Cambridge, MA: Harvard University Press.

Gould, S. 1992. *Bully for Brontosaurus: Further Reflections in Natural History*. London: Penguin.

Harman, G. H. 1986. *Change in View: Principles of Reasoning*. Cambridge, MA: MIT Press.

Hoffrage, U., and G. Gigerenzer. 2004. How to Improve the Diagnostic Inferences of Medical Experts. In E. Kurz-Milcke and G. Gigerenzer, eds., *Experts in Science and Society*, 249–68. New York: Kluwer/Plenum.

Kahneman, D., P. Slovic, and A. Tversky, eds. 1982. *Judgment Under Uncertainty: Heuristics and Biases*. Cambridge: Cambridge University Press.

Kahneman, D., and A. Tversky. 1972. Subjective Probability: A Judgment of Representativeness. *Cognitive Psychology* 3: 340–54.

———. 1973. On the Psychology of Prediction. *Psychological Review* 80: 237–51. Reprinted in D. Kahneman, P. Slovic, and A. Tversky, eds., *Judgment Under Uncertainty: Heuristics and Biases*, 48–68. Cambridge: Cambridge University Press, 1982.

———. 1996. On the Reality of Cognitive Illusions: A Reply to Gigerenzer's Critique. *Psychological Review* 103: 582–91.

Mises, R. von. 1957. *Probability, Statistics and Truth*. London: Allen and Unwin.

Neander, K. 1991. The Teleological Notion of "Function." *Australasian Journal of Philosophy* 59: 454–68.

Nisbett, R., and E. Borgida. 1975. Attribution and the Social Psychology of Prediction. *Journal of Personality and Social Psychology* 32: 932–43.

Nozick, R. 1993. *The Nature of Rationality*. Princeton: Princeton University Press.

Piattelli-Palmarini, M. 1994. *Inevitable Illusions: How Mistakes of Reason Rule Our Minds*. New York: John Wiley.

Pinker, S. 1997. *How the Mind Works*. New York: W. W. Norton.

Plantinga, A. 1993. *Warrant and Proper Function*. Oxford: Oxford University Press.

Samuels, R. 1998. Evolutionary Psychology and the Massive Modularity Hypothesis. *British Journal for the Philosophy of Science* 49: 575–602.

Samuels, R., S. Stich, and P. Tremoulet. 1999. Rethinking Rationality: From Bleak Implications to Darwinian Modules. In E. LePore and Z. Pylyshyn, eds., *What Is Cognitive Science?* Oxford: Basil Blackwell.

Savage, L. J. 1972. *The Foundations of Statistics*. London: Wiley.

Slovic, P., B. Fischhoff, and S. Lichtenstein. 1976. Cognitive Processes and Societal Risk Taking. In J. S. Carol and J. W. Payne, eds., *Cognition and Social Behavior*, 165–84. Hillsdale, NJ: Erlbaum.

Sperber, D. 1994. The Modularity of Thought and the Epidemiology of Representations. In L. A. Hirschfeld and S. A. Gelman, eds., *Mapping the Mind: Domain Specificity in Cognition and Culture*, 39–67. Cambridge: Cambridge University Press.

Stein, E. 1996. *Without Good Reason: The Rationality Debate in Philosophy and Cognitive Science*. Oxford: Clarendon Press.

Stich, S. 1990. *The Fragmentation of Reason*. Cambridge, MA: MIT Press.

Tooby, J., and L. Cosmides. 1992. The Psychological Foundations of Culture. In J. Barkow, L. Cosmides, and J. Tooby, eds., *The Adapted Mind: Evolutionary Psychology and the Generation of Culture*, 19–136. Oxford: Oxford University Press.

———. 1995. Foreword. In S. Baron-Cohen, *Mindblindness: An Essay on Autism and Theory of Mind*, xi–xviii. Cambridge, MA: MIT Press.

Tversky, A., and D. Kahneman. 1982. Judgments of and by Representativeness. In D. Kahneman, P. Slovic, and A. Tversky, eds., *Judgment Under Uncertainty: Heuristics and Biases*, 84–98. Cambridge: Cambridge University Press.

———. 1983. Extensional Versus Intuitive Reasoning: The Conjunction Fallacy in Probability Judgments. *Psychological Review* 90: 293–315.

10

META-SKEPTICISM

Meditations in Ethno-Epistemology[1]

Shaun Nichols, Stephen Stich, and Jonathan M. Weinberg

THROUGHOUT THE TWENTIETH CENTURY, an enormous amount of intellectual fuel was spent debating the merits of a class of skeptical arguments which purport to show that knowledge of the external world is not possible. These arguments, whose origins can be traced back to Descartes, played an important role in the work of some of the leading philosophers of the twentieth century, including Russell, Moore and Wittgenstein, and they continue to engage the interest of contemporary philosophers (for example, Cohen 1999; DeRose 1995; Hill 1996; Klein 1981; Lewis 1996; McGinn 1993; Nozick 1981; Schiffer 1996; Unger 1975; Williams 1991). Typically, these arguments make use of one or more premises which the philosophers proposing them take to be intuitively obvious. Beyond an appeal to intuition, little or no defense is offered, and in many cases it is hard to see what else *could* be said in support of these premises. A number of authors have suggested that the intuitions undergirding these skeptical arguments are *universal*—shared by everyone (or almost everyone) who thinks reflectively about knowledge. In this chapter we will offer some evidence indicating that they are *far* from universal. Rather, the evidence suggests that many of the intuitions epistemologists invoke vary with the cultural background, socio-economic status and educational background of the person offering the intuition. And this, we will argue, is bad news for the skeptical arguments that rely on those intuitions. The evidence may also be bad news for skepticism itself—not because it shows that skepticism is *false*, but rather because, if we accept one prominent account of the link between epistemic intuitions and epistemic concepts, it indicates that skepticism may be much less *interesting* and much less *worrisome* than philosophers have taken it to be.

1. We are grateful to Gary Barlett for helpful comments on earlier drafts of this chapter.

Here's how we propose to proceed. In Section 1, we'll begin by characterizing and offering a few examples of the sorts of skeptical arguments that are the targets of our critique. We will also assemble a few quotes from leading philosophers which suggest that they think the intuitions on which the arguments rely are, near enough, universal. In Section 2, we'll present some evidence indicating that intuitions of the sort that have loomed large in the philosophical literature for the last 40 years vary systematically with culture and socio-economic status. The examples we'll focus on in Section 2 typically do not play a role in skeptical arguments, and it might be suggested that intuitions which do play a role in skeptical arguments are less subject to cultural variation. Indeed, it might be thought that they form part of a universal core of epistemic intuitions. We think the hypothesis that there is such a universal core deserves to be explored seriously, and in Section 3 we will present some evidence that is compatible with that hypothesis. However, as we'll show in Section 4, there is good reason to think that if there is a universal core, it does not include a number of the intuitions that play a central role in skeptical arguments. In Section 5, we'll argue that the evidence we've presented suggests that the appeal of skeptical arguments is culturally local and that this fact justifies a kind of "meta-skepticism" since it suggests that crucial premises in the arguments for skepticism are not to be trusted. We'll also take up one possible response to our argument for meta-skepticism. This response maintains that differences in epistemic intuitions are evidence for differences in epistemic concepts. If that's right, then the fact that people in other cultures don't share our skeptical intuitions does not cast any doubt on the truth of our intuitions, since their intuitions aren't really about what we call "knowledge" at all. But this response, we'll argue, engenders another kind of meta-skepticism. For while it may fend off the challenge to the premises of skeptical arguments, it raises serious doubts about the importance of the conclusions.

1 Skeptical Arguments, Skeptical Intuitions and Universality

The kind of skeptical argument on which we'll be focusing might be called *Cartesian*.[2] These arguments rely essentially on an intuition that we do not, or perhaps even cannot, know that some skeptical hypothesis does not obtain.[3] What makes the hypothesis skeptical is that its truth is inconsistent with some propositions we ordinarily would take ourselves to know, although the hypothesis seems to be consistent with all our evidence for those propositions. The intuition serves as a major premise in a skeptical

---

2. Though we take no stand on what exactly Descartes had in mind. For some relevant discussion see Burnyeat 1982a.

3. As we use the notion, an *intuition* is simply a spontaneous judgment about the truth or falsity of a proposition—a judgment for which the person making the judgment may be able to offer little or no further justification. For ease of exposition, we will also often use the term "intuition" for the proposition judged to be true or false.

argument to the effect that we do not, or perhaps even cannot, have knowledge of the propositions that we ordinarily take ourselves to have. The ur-example of the sort of skeptical hypothesis we have in mind is the evil genius of *Meditations I*, while in contemporary epistemology the most widely discussed example may be the brain-in-vat hypothesis discussed below. We'll use the term *skeptical intuition* for an intuition that we do not know the falsity of such a skeptical hypothesis. We believe that these skeptical intuitions are the driving force behind the modern concern with this brand of skepticism.[4]

An example of the sort of skeptical argument we have in mind is stated with characteristic succinctness by Stephen Schiffer.

1. I don't know that I'm not a BIV (i.e., a bodiless brain in a vat who has been caused to have just those sensory experiences I've had).
2. If I don't know that I'm not a BIV, then I don't know that I have hands.
3. I don't know that I have hands. (Schiffer 1996, 317; numbering added)

Schiffer does not pause to offer any reasons to accept either of the premises, presumably because he thinks they are intuitively obvious. Keith DeRose, in his discussion of the argument, is only slightly more forthcoming. To convince us of the plausibility of the premises of the BIV argument, DeRose rephrases the premises and adds a pair of rhetorical questions aimed at bringing out the intuition that the premises are obviously true.

However improbable or even bizarre it may seem to suppose that I am a BIV, it also seems that I don't know that I'm not one. How *could* I know such a thing? ... it also seems that if, for all I know, I am a BIV, then I don't know that I have hands. How could I know that I have hands if, for all I know, I'm bodiless (and therefore handless)? (DeRose 1995, 2)

Elsewhere, DeRose's appeal to intuition is more explicit. In the Introduction to a collection of essays on skepticism, he sketches the *Argument from Skeptical Hypothesis* as follows:

---

4. Note that we are not here concerning ourselves with what has been called "Pyrrhonian" or "Agrippan" skepticism. Such skepticism does not rely on an intuition involving skeptical hypotheses, but rather generates a paradox through the three plausible-sounding principles that (i) we may not rationally stop reasoning at an arbitrary point; (ii) we may not rationally believe based on circular reasoning; and (iii) we may not rationally believe on the basis of an infinite regress of reasons. The upshot of this paradox is that we cannot believe rationally at all. Arguments like this also depend on intuitions to support each principle of the trilemma. But none of the data we will be presenting below is directly relevant to that type of intuition. Nonetheless, those concerned with this brand of skepticism may well want to worry that something similar to the argument we are about to launch against the Cartesian might at some later date find a Pyrrhonian target.

1. I don't know that not-H.
2. If I don't know that not-H, then I don't know that O.
   So,
C. I don't know that O.

And he goes on to say that "the skeptical argument really is powerful. . . . The argument is clearly valid . . . and *each of its premises, considered on its own, enjoys a good deal of intuitive support*" (DeRose 1999, 2–3; emphasis added).

The following passage from Stewart Cohen (1999) provides another example of the sort of skeptical argument we have in mind. It is also a clear illustration of the central role that appeal to intuition has played in recent discussions of skepticism.

> Suppose, to use Dretske's example, that you are at the zoo looking at the Zebra exhibit. Consider the possibility that what you see is not a zebra but rather a cleverly-disguised mule. Though you may have some reason to deny you are looking at a cleverly-disguised mule, it seems wrong to say you know you are not looking at a cleverly-disguised mule. After all, that's just how it would look if it were a cleverly-disguised mule.

The skeptic then appeals to a deductive closure principle for knowledge:

(C) If S knows P and S knows that P entails Q, then S knows Q.
    This principle has considerable intuitive force. Now, let P be some proposition I claim to know and let H be a skeptical alternative to P. Then from the closure principle, we can derive

(1) If I know P, then I know not-H
Put this together with
(2) I do not know not-H
and it follows that
(3) I know P.
is false. . . .

To respond to the deductive closure argument, a fallibilist must deny either premise (1) or premise (2). The problem . . . is that both of these premises are intuitively quite appealing. Then again, many instances of (3), the denial of the conclusion of the argument, seem intuitively compelling. This has led some to argue that we can reject one premise of the skeptical argument by appealing to the conjunction of (3) and the other premise. Some proponents of the relevant alternatives theory argue that our strong intuitions supporting (2) and (3) just show that (1) (and therefore the closure principle) is false. As Dretske has argued, the fact that it is very intuitive both that I know that I see a zebra, and that I fail to know I do not see a cleverly-disguised mule just shows that the closure principle is false. . . . *Each view we have considered attempts to exploit intuitions favorable to it. The skeptic appeals to (1) and (2) to deny (3). The relevant alternatives theorist appeals to (2) and (3) to deny (1). And the Moorean appeals to (1) and (3) to deny (2).*

(Cohen 1999, 62; emphasis added)

In the philosophical literature on skepticism, it is often suggested that both skeptical intuitions and the skeptical conclusions they apparently entail are universally shared. In *The Significance of Philosophical Skepticism*, Barry Stroud maintains that skepticism

appeals to something deep in our nature and seems to raise a real problem about the human condition. It is natural to feel that either we must accept the literal truth of the conclusion that we can know nothing about the world around us, or else we must somehow show that it is not true. (Stroud 1984, 39)

Similarly, Colin McGinn takes skepticism to be a universal feature lurking in human thought:

Common sense takes knowledge to be both possible and widespread, simply part of life. People (and some animals) are assumed to know a great many things across a broad range of subject-matters. . . . But it takes very little reflection, or prompting, to cast all this into serious doubt: we quickly come to feel that the concept lacks the kind of broad and ready application we earlier took for granted. Skeptical thoughts occur readily and with considerable force, soon leading us to declare that, after all, we know little or nothing. The concept strikes us as containing the seeds of its own destruction, by requiring the satisfaction of conditions that are palpably unsatisfied. Ontogenetically, the concept of knowledge comes into play during the first three or four years, but it is apt to lose its moorings during adolescence, when reflection intrudes. Then it is commonly asserted, with the air of the platitudinous, that of course nobody ever really *knows* anything. How could they, given the content of the concept and the facts of epistemic life? Philosophical scepticism thus seems endemic to the use of epistemic concepts: to reflect on the concept of knowledge is immediately to question its application. Not surprisingly, then, scepticism arose early in the history of philosophical thought and has continued to exercise a powerful hold on it. I hazard the anthropological conjecture that every culture has its sceptics, silent though they may be. There is something primitive and inevitable about sceptical doubt. It runs deep in human thought. The question is whether it can be overcome, and by what means.

(McGinn 1993, 107–8)

McGinn not only thinks that skepticism is "primitive and inevitable"; he also claims that the skeptical challenge is so overwhelming that we must be cognitively incapable of finding a satisfactory reply (see also Nagel 1986).[5] Clearly, many philosophers think that the epistemic intuitions that underlie skeptical arguments are widely shared, and this is an important part of the reason that the skeptical arguments are supposed to have such an enduring importance.

2 Epistemology as Ethnography

One of us has long been intrigued by the possibility that different groups of people *might* have very different epistemic intuitions (Stich 1988, 1990), and a few years ago we learned of two research projects in cross-cultural psychology which suggested that systematic diversity in epistemic intuitions was more than a mere possibility. In one of these projects, Richard Nisbett and his collaborators (Nisbett et al. 2001) have found large and systematic differences between East Asians and westerners[6] on a long list of quite basic cognitive processes including perception, attention and memory. These groups also differ in the way they go about describing, predicting and explaining events, in the way they categorize objects and in the way they revise beliefs in the face of new arguments and evidence. Nisbett and his colleagues maintain that these differences "can be loosely grouped together under the heading of holistic vs. analytic thought." Holistic thought, which predominates among East Asians, is characterized as "involving an orientation to the context or field as a whole, including attention to relationships between a focal object and the field, and a preference for explaining and predicting events on the basis of such relationships." Analytic thought, the prevailing pattern among westerners, is characterized as "involving detachment of the object from its context, a tendency to focus on attributes of the object in order to assign it to categories, and a preference for using rules about the categories to explain and predict the object's behavior" (Nisbett et al. 2001, 293). Westerners also have a stronger sense of agency and independence, while East Asians have a much stronger commitment to social harmony. In East Asian society, the individual feels "very much a part of a large and complex social organism . . . where behavioral prescriptions must be followed and role obligations adhered to scrupulously" (Nisbett et al. 2001,

---

5. Steven Pinker follows McGinn down this path (1997, 559).

6. The East Asian subjects were Chinese, Japanese and Korean. Some of the experiments were conducted in Asia, others used East Asian students studying in the USA or first- and second-generation East Asian immigrants to the USA. The western subjects were Americans of European ancestry.

292–93). As a result of these differences, Nisbett and his colleagues maintain, there is considerable cultural variation in the *epistemic practices* in these two cultural traditions— people in the two cultures form beliefs and categories, construct arguments and draw inferences in significantly different ways. Of course, this does not show that there are also cross-cultural differences in epistemic *intuitions*. But it does suggest that it is a serious empirical possibility, and that it might be worth finding out whether these differences in epistemic practices are associated with parallel differences in epistemic intuitions.

The second research project that attracted our attention looked explicitly at *intuitions*, though they were moral rather than epistemic intuitions. In an intriguing series of studies, Jonathan Haidt and his collaborators explored the extent to which moral intuitions about events in which no one is harmed track judgments about disgust in people from different cultural and socio-economic groups (Haidt et al. 1993). For their study they constructed a set of brief stories about victimless activities that were intended to trigger the emotion of disgust. They presented these stories to subjects using a structured interview technique designed to determine whether the subjects found the activities described to be disgusting and also to elicit the subjects' moral intuitions about the activities. For instance, in one story, a family's dog is run over and killed by a car, and the family decides to eat the dog. The interviews were administered to both high and low socio-economic status (SES) subjects in Philadelphia and in two cities in Brazil. Though the cultural differences were relatively small, Haidt and colleagues found large differences in moral intuitions between social classes. Low SES subjects tend to think that eating your dog is seriously morally wrong; high SES subjects don't. Much the same pattern was found with the other scenarios used in the study.

Though neither of these studies directly addresses the issue of group differences in epistemic intuition, the results they reported led us to think that the following pair of hypotheses might well be true:

Hypothesis 1: Epistemic intuitions vary from culture to culture.

Hypothesis 2: Epistemic intuitions vary from one socio-economic group to another.

Another hypothesis was suggested by anecdotal rather than experimental evidence. It has often seemed to us that students' epistemic intuitions change as they take more philosophy courses, and we have often suspected that we and our colleagues were, in effect, teaching neophyte philosophers to have intuitions that are in line with those of more senior members of the profession. Or perhaps we are not modifying intuitions at all but simply weeding out students whose intuitions are not mainstream. If either of these is the case, then the intuitions that we use in our philosophical work are not those of the man and woman in the street, but those of a highly trained and self-selecting community. These speculations led to:

Hypothesis 3: Epistemic intuitions vary as a function of how many philosophy courses a person has had.

For the last two years, we have been conducting a series of experiments designed to test these hypotheses. In designing our experiments, we wanted our intuition probes—the cases that we would ask subjects to judge—to be similar to cases that have actually been used in the recent literature in epistemology. Would different groups show significantly different responses to standard epistemic thought experiments? The answer, it seems, is yes. While the results we have so far are preliminary, they are sufficient, we think, to suggest that there are substantial and systematic differences in the epistemic intuitions of people in different cultures and socio-economic groups. In Weinberg, Nichols and Stich (2001), we present a detailed account of our studies and results. For present purposes, it will suffice to sketch a few of the highlights.

The internalism/externalism debate has been central to analytic epistemology for decades. Internalism with respect to some epistemically evaluative property (for example, knowledge) is the view that *only* factors within an agent's introspective grasp can be relevant to whether the agent's beliefs have that property. Other factors beyond the scope of introspection, such as the reliability of the psychological mechanisms that actually produced the belief, are epistemically external to the agent. In our experiments, we included a number of "Truetemp" cases inspired by Lehrer (2000), designed to explore whether externalist/internalist dimensions of our subjects' intuitions differed in subjects with different cultural backgrounds. Here is one of the questions we presented to our subjects:

> One day Charles is suddenly knocked out by a falling rock, and his brain becomes re-wired so that he is always absolutely right whenever he estimates the temperature where he is. Charles is completely unaware that his brain has been altered in this way. A few weeks later, this brain re-wiring leads him to believe that it is 71 degrees in his room. Apart from his estimation, he has no other reasons to think that it is 71 degrees. In fact, it is at that time 71 degrees in his room. Does Charles really know that it was 71 degrees in the room, or does he only believe it?
>
> REALLY KNOWS   ONLY BELIEVES

In this intuition probe, Charles' belief is produced by a reliable mechanism, but it is stipulated that he is completely unaware of this reliability. This makes his reliability epistemically external. Therefore, to the extent that a subject population is unwilling to attribute knowledge in this case, we have evidence that suggests that the group's "folk epistemology" is internalist. Since the mechanism that leads to Charles' belief is not shared by other members of his community, Nisbett's work suggests that East Asians (EAs), with their strong commitment to social harmony, might be less inclined than individualistic westerners (Ws) to count Charles' belief as knowledge. And, indeed, we found that while both EAs and Ws tended to deny knowledge, EA subjects were much more likely to deny knowledge than were Ws (Fisher Exact Test, p = .02). The results are shown in Figure 10.1.[7]

---

7. Our subjects in all the ethnic group studies were undergraduates at Rutgers University. All of them were fluent in English. In classifying subjects into ethnic groups we relied on the same ethnic identification questionnaire that Nisbett and his colleagues had used. We are grateful to Professor Nisbett for providing us with a copy of the questionnaire and for much helpful advice on its use.

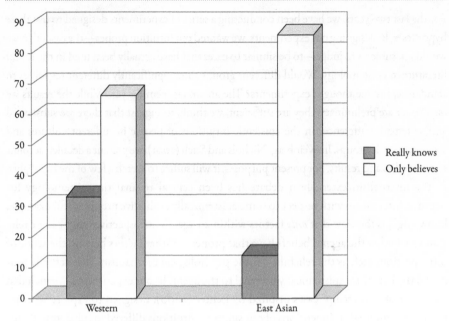

FIGURE 10.1 Individualistic Truetemp case

Another category of examples that has had a tremendous impact on analytic epistemology are "Gettier cases," in which a person has a true belief for which she has good evidence, though, as it happens, the evidence is false, or only accidentally true, or in some other way warrant-deprived. By their very construction, these cases are in many ways quite *similar* to unproblematic cases in which a person has good and true evidence for a true belief. Nisbett and his colleagues have shown that EAs are more inclined than Ws to make categorical judgments on the basis of similarity; Ws, on the other hand, are more disposed to focus on causation in describing the world and classifying things (Norenzayan et al. 1999; Watanabe 1998, 1999). In many Gettier cases, there is a break in the causal link from the fact that makes the agent's belief true to her evidence for that belief. This suggests that EAs might be much less inclined than Ws to withhold the attribution of knowledge in Gettier cases. And, indeed, they are.

The intuition probe we used to explore cultural differences on Gettier cases was the following:

Bob has a friend, Jill, who has driven a Buick for many years. Bob therefore thinks that Jill drives an American car. He is not aware, however, that her Buick has recently been stolen, and he is also not aware that Jill has replaced it with a Pontiac, which is a different kind of American car. Does Bob really know that Jill drives an American car, or does he only believe it?

REALLY KNOWS   ONLY BELIEVES

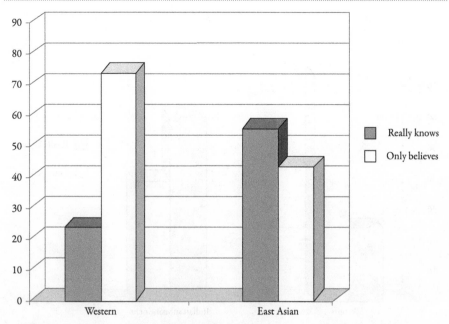

FIGURE 10.2 Gettier case: Western and East Asian

This probe produced a striking difference between the groups (Fisher Exact Test, p = .006). While a large majority of Ws give the standard answer in the philosophical literature, namely, "Only believes," a majority of EAs have the *opposite* intuition—they said that Bob really knows. The results are shown in Figure 10.2.

The data we've presented so far suggest that westerners and East Asians have significantly different epistemic intuitions. What about people in other cultures? We know of no experimental studies of cross-cultural differences in epistemic *practices* that are as rich and detailed as those of Nisbett and his colleagues. However, for some years Richard Shweder and his colleagues have been assembling evidence indicating that the thought processes of some groups of people on the Indian subcontinent are quite different from those of westerners (Shweder 1991). In some respects, the account of Indian thought that Shweder offers is rather similar to the account that Nisbett offers of East Asian thought—holism looms large in both accounts—though in other respects they are quite different. So one might suspect that the epistemic intuitions of people from the Indian subcontinent (SCs) would be in some ways similar to those of EAs. And indeed they are. Like the EA subjects, SC subjects were much more likely than W subjects to attribute knowledge in a Gettier case (Fisher Exact Test, p = .002). The SC results on the Gettier case are shown in Figure 10.3.

When we first analyzed these data, we found them quite unsettling, since it seemed perfectly obvious to us that the people in Gettier cases *don't* have knowledge. But the results from our studies suggest that an important part of the explanation of our own clear intuitions about these cases is the fact that we were raised in a western culture. Nisbett was likewise surprised by his findings of cross-cultural differences in epistemic practices. In a recent review article, Nisbett and colleagues write:

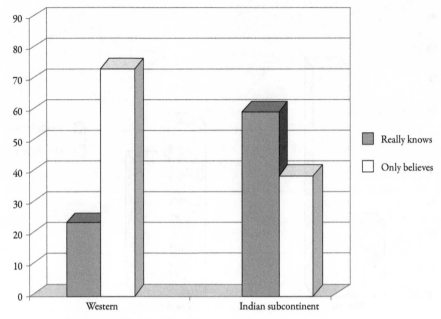

FIGURE 10.3 Gettier case: Western and Indian

Almost two decades ago, Richard E. Nisbett wrote a book with Lee Ross entitled, modestly, *Human Inference* (Nisbett and Ross, 1980). Roy D'Andrade, a distinguished cognitive anthropologist, read the book and told . . . Nisbett he thought it was a "good ethnography." The author was shocked and dismayed. But we now wholeheartedly agree with D'Andrade's contention about the limits of research conducted in a single culture. Psychologists who choose not to do cross-cultural psychology may have chosen to be ethnographers instead.

(Nisbett et al. 2001, 307)

Our results suggest that philosophers who rely on their own intuitions about matters epistemic, and those of their colleagues, may have inadvertently made a similar choice. They too have chosen to be ethnographers; what they are doing is *ethno-epistemology*.

3 The Core Epistemology Hypothesis

If epistemic intuitions are indeed culturally local, it poses a threat to the claim that skepticism is "primitive and inevitable." For, to the extent that western skepticism relies on culturally local intuitions, its appeal will also be culturally local. But the evidence reported in Section 2 poses only an indirect threat to arguments for skepticism, for while that evidence indicates that *some* epistemic intuitions may be culturally local, we have not yet offered any evidence about the sort of *skeptical intuitions* that play a crucial role in arguments for skepticism.

Philosophers who think that skepticism's appeal is universal might suggest that while Gettier intuitions and Truetemp intuitions are culturally local, skeptical intuitions are less variable. Indeed, for all we have said, skeptical intuitions might be part of a universal core of epistemic intuitions, a core shared by just about everyone.

The hypothesis that there may be a core set of universal epistemic intuitions is one that we think deserves careful empirical scrutiny. In our own studies, we found that on one crucial probe, there were no statistically significant differences among *any* of the groups we looked at. For all of our subject groups we included a question designed to determine whether subjects treat mere subjective certainty as knowledge. The question we used was the following:

> Dave likes to play a game with flipping a coin. He sometimes gets a "special feeling" that the next flip will come out heads. When he gets this "special feeling," he is right about half the time, and wrong about half the time. Just before the next flip, Dave gets that "special feeling," and the feeling leads him to believe that the coin will land heads. He flips the coin, and it does land heads. Did Dave really know that the coin was going to land heads, or did he only believe it?
>
> REALLY KNOWS   ONLY BELIEVES

As shown in Figure 10.4, there was no significant difference between the western and East Asian subjects on this question (Fisher Exact Test, p = .78); similarly, in our studies of socio-economic groups, we found no difference on this question between high and low SES groups (Fisher Exact Test, p = .294).[8] In all groups almost none of our subjects judged that this was a case of knowledge. Though obviously much more research is

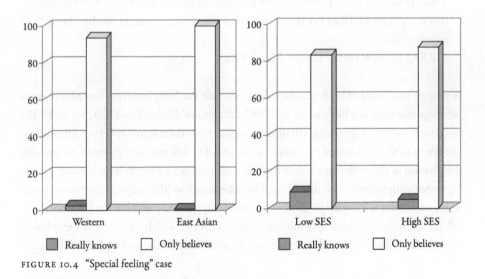

FIGURE 10.4 "Special feeling" case

---

8. The methods used in the SES studies are discussed in Section 4.

needed, these results are compatible with the hypothesis that *some* epistemic intuitions are universal.

4 The Ethnography of Skeptical Intuitions

If there is a universal core of epistemic intuitions, are skeptical intuitions among them? In this section we'll offer evidence suggesting that, for some skeptical intuitions at least, the answer is no. In Section 2, we set out three hypotheses about potential sources of diversity in epistemic intuitions. We proposed that epistemic intuitions might vary as a function of *culture, SES* and *philosophical training*. Data we have recently collected indicate that skeptical intuitions vary as a function of *all* of these factors.

We will begin with the data on different SES groups. For these studies, the experimenter approached adults near various commercial venues in downtown New Brunswick, New Jersey, and offered adults a fast-food restaurant gift certificate for participating in the study. Following Haidt (and much other research in social psychology), we used years of education to distinguish low and high SES groups. One of the probes given to these subjects was based on the example from Fred Dretske's work that Cohen mentions in the passage we quoted earlier.

> Pat is at the zoo with his son, and when they come to the zebra cage, Pat points to the animal and says, "That's a zebra." Pat is right—it is a zebra. However, given the distance the spectators are from the cage, Pat would not be able to tell the difference between a real zebra and a mule that is cleverly disguised to look like a zebra. And if the animal had really been a cleverly disguised mule, Pat still would have thought that it was a zebra. Does Pat really know that the animal is a zebra, or does he only believe that it is?
>
> REALLY KNOWS   ONLY BELIEVES

Although a majority of both groups maintained that Pat "only believes," low SES subjects were significantly more likely to say that Pat "really knows" (Fisher Exact Test, p = .038). The results are shown in Figure 10.5. This finding suggests that there is an important difference in the extent to which skeptical intuitions can be found in different SES groups. One possible explanation of this difference is that high SES subjects are willing to accept much weaker "knowledge-defeaters" than low SES subjects because low SES subjects have lower minimum standards for knowledge. This explanation is supported by another result we obtained. We presented low and high SES subjects with a scenario in which a person has a true belief, though the evidence he relied on might have been fabricated. The probe goes as follows:

> It's clear that smoking cigarettes increases the likelihood of getting cancer. However, there is now a great deal of evidence that just using nicotine by itself without

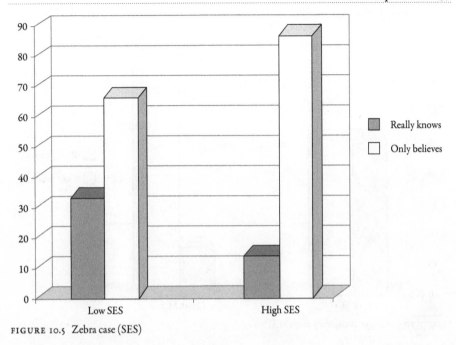

FIGURE 10.5 Zebra case (SES)

smoking (for instance, by taking a nicotine pill) does not increase the likelihood of getting cancer. Jim knows about this evidence and as a result, he believes that using nicotine does not increase the likelihood of getting cancer. It is possible that the tobacco companies dishonestly made up and publicized this evidence that using nicotine does not increase the likelihood of cancer, and that the evidence is really false and misleading. Now, the tobacco companies did not actually make up this evidence, but Jim is not aware of this fact. Does Jim really know that using nicotine doesn't increase the likelihood of getting cancer, or does he only believe it?

　　REALLY KNOWS　　ONLY BELIEVES

Once again, we found that responses vary significantly as a function of SES (Fisher Exact Test, p = .007). The results are shown in Figure 10.6. These data, like the data in Figure 10.5, indicate that there are significant differences between SES groups in their tendencies toward skeptical intuitions, and both findings are compatible with the hypothesis that high SES groups cleave to higher minimum standards of knowledge than low SES groups.

In our cross-cultural studies, we presented students with another variant of Dretske's zebra case:

Mike is a young man visiting the zoo with his son, and when they come to the zebra cage, Mike points to the animal and says, "That's a zebra." Mike is right—it is a zebra. However, as the older people in his community know, there are lots of ways that people can be tricked into believing things that aren't true. Indeed, the older

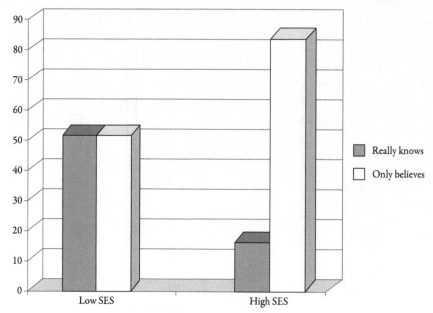

FIGURE 10.6 Cancer conspiracy case (SES)

people in the community know that it's possible that zoo authorities could cleverly disguise mules to look just like zebras, and people viewing the animals would not be able to tell the difference. If the animal that Mike called a zebra had really been such a cleverly painted mule, Mike still would have thought that it was a zebra. Does Mike really know that the animal is a zebra, or does he only believe that it is?

REALLY KNOWS   ONLY BELIEVES

Using this probe, we found a significant difference between western and subcontinental subjects (Fisher Exact Test, p = .049) (Figure 10.7). One possible explanation of these data is that SCs, like low SES westerners, regard knowledge as less demanding than do high SES westerners. And in fact we found that SC subjects were also more likely than Ws to attribute knowledge in the conspiracy case (Fisher Exact Test, p = .025). The results are shown in Figure 10.8. SC and low SES subjects thus appear to be significantly less susceptible to skeptical intuitions, at least in these cases. These findings contrast sharply with our evidence on EAs. We did *not* find significant differences between EAs and high SES Ws on either the zebra case or the conspiracy case.[9]

---

9. Note that our results in the zebra case and the conspiracy case do not *directly* demonstrate cross-cultural diversity with respect to skeptical intuitions. For the subjects were asked whether the characters in the stories knew, not the falsity of a skeptical hypothesis, but the truth of an ordinary claim inconsistent with that hypothesis. For example, we did not ask whether Mike really knew that the animal was not a painted mule— we only asked whether he knew that it was a zebra. The experimental materials, in suggesting the presence of

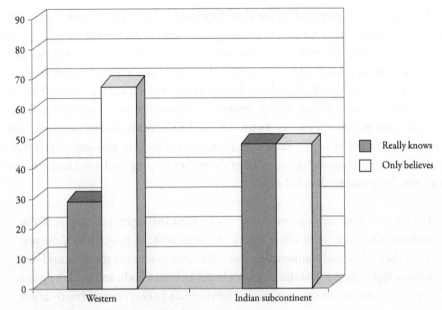

FIGURE 10.7 Zebra case: Western and Indian

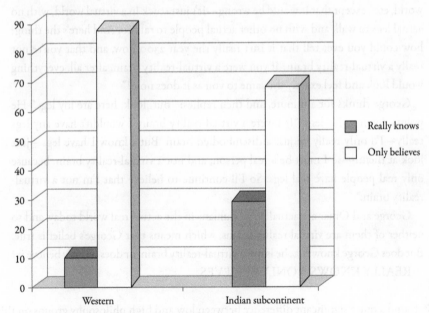

FIGURE 10.8 Conspiracy case: Western and Indian

uneliminated skeptical hypotheses, clearly invite the subjects to engage in skeptical reasoning, and our data strongly indicate significant diversity in the willingness of members of different groups to engage in such thinking. Further research is needed to determine *why* different groups tend to give different answers in the experiments we've reported. However, in the experiment we are about to recount, we *did* directly test a skeptical intuition—indeed, we tested the skeptical intuition *par excellence*.

In Section 2, we proposed, as our third hypothesis, that epistemic intuitions might vary as a function of the number of philosophy courses one had taken. Though no data relevant to this third hypothesis were presented in our earlier paper on epistemic intuitions (Weinberg, Nichols and Stich 2001) we have recently completed a study that provides some support for this hypothesis. In that study we presented subjects with a series of epistemic intuition probes, and we divided the subjects into two groups: subjects who had taken few philosophy courses (two or less) and subjects who had taken many philosophy courses (three or more). There were 48 students in the "low philosophy" group and 15 in the "high philosophy" group. One of the probes we presented was a brain-in-a-vat scenario. The probe reads as follows:

> George and Omar are roommates, and enjoy having late-night "philosophical" discussions. One such night Omar argues, "At some point in time, by, like, the year 2300, the medical and computer sciences will be able to simulate the real world very convincingly. They will be able to grow a brain without a body, and hook it up to a supercomputer in just the right way so that the brain has experiences exactly as if it were a real person walking around in a real world, talking to other people, and so on. And so the brain would believe it was a real person walking around in a real world, etc., except that it would be wrong—it's just stuck in a virtual world, with no actual legs to walk and with no other actual people to talk to. And here's the thing: how could you ever tell that it isn't really the year 2300 now, and that you're not really a virtual-reality brain? If you were a virtual-reality brain, after all, everything would look and feel exactly the same to you as it does now!"
>
> George thinks for a minute, and then replies: "But, look, here are my legs." He points down to his legs. "If I were a virtual-reality brain, I wouldn't have any legs really—I'd only really be just a disembodied brain. But I know I have legs—just look at them!—so I must be a real person, and not a virtual-reality brain, because only real people have real legs. So I'll continue to believe that I'm not a virtual-reality brain."
>
> George and Omar are actually real humans in the actual real world today, and so neither of them are virtual-reality brains, which means that George's belief is true. But does George know that he is not a virtual-reality brain, or does he only believe it?
> REALLY KNOWS   ONLY BELIEVES

We found a quite significant difference between low and high philosophy groups on this probe (Fisher Exact Test, $p = .016$). The evidence indicates that students with less philosophy are more likely to claim that the person knows he's not a brain in a vat. The results are presented in Figure 10.9. This suggests that the propensity for skeptical intuitions varies significantly as a function of exposure to philosophy. Indeed, so far this skeptical intuition case is the *only* probe on which we have found significant differences between students as a function of how many philosophy classes they have had.

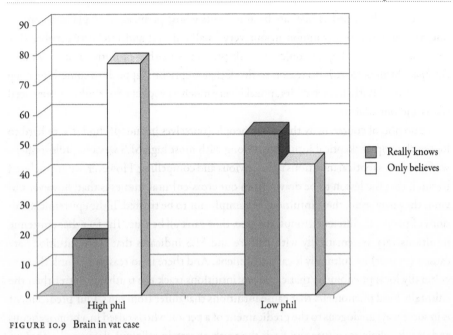

FIGURE 10.9 Brain in vat case

5 Some Meta-Skeptical Conclusions

What conclusions can be drawn from these studies? The first and most obvious conclusion is that, though the empirical exploration of epistemic intuitions, and of philosophical intuitions more generally, is still in its infancy, the evidence currently available suggests that all three of our initial hypotheses may well be true. Epistemic intuitions, including skeptical intuitions, appear to vary systematically as a function of the cultural background, the socio-economic status and the number of philosophy courses taken by the person whose intuitions are being elicited. We want to emphasize that all the results we have reported should be regarded as quite preliminary. To make a suitably rich and compelling case for our hypotheses, it will be important to replicate and extend the findings we have reported. But our data thus far certainly lend support to the claim that there is a great deal of diversity in epistemic intuitions, and that a substantial part of that diversity is due to differences in cultural background, SES and philosophical training.

If that's right, and if, as we contended in Section 1, the defense of many of the premises used in arguments for skepticism comes to rest on an explicit or implicit appeal to intuition, then we can also conclude that the appeal of these skeptical arguments will be much more local than many philosophers suppose. For if people in different cultural and SES groups and people who have had little or no philosophical training do not share *"our"* intuitions (that is, the intuitions of the typical analytic philosopher, who is white, western, high SES and has had *lots* of philosophical training) then they are unlikely to be as convinced or distressed as "*we*" are by arguments whose premises seem plausible only if one has the intuitions common in our very small cultural and intellectual tribe. *Pace* McGinn's "anthropological conjecture," skepticism is neither primitive nor inevitable. And *pace* Stroud, there is no reason to think that skepticism "appeals to something deep in our nature." Rather, it seems, its appeal is very much a product of our culture, our social status and our education!

We do not, of course, deny that some people (ourselves included!) find it very hard to loosen the grip of skeptical intuitions. Along with most high SES western philosophers, we find many skeptical intuitions to be obvious and compelling. However, we are inclined to think that the lesson to be drawn from our cross-cultural studies is that, however obvious they may seem, these intuitions are simply not to be trusted. If the epistemic intuitions of people in different groups disagree, they can't all be true. The fact that epistemic intuitions vary systematically with culture and SES indicates that these intuitions are caused (in part) by culturally local phenomena. And there is no reason to think that the culturally local phenomena that cause *our* intuitions track the truth any better than the culturally local phenomena that cause intuitions that differ from ours. Our predicament is in some ways analogous to the predicament of a person who is raised in a homogeneous and deeply religious culture and finds the truth of certain religious claims to be obvious or compelling. When such a person discovers that other people do not share his intuitions, he may well come to wonder why his intuitions are any more likely to be true than theirs. On second thought, our situation is a bit worse. The religious person might rest content with the thought that, for some reason or other, God has chosen to cause his group to have religious intuitions that track the truth. Few philosophers will rest content with the parallel thought about their epistemic intuitions.

We are not, we should stress, defending a generalized skepticism that challenges the use of *all* intuitions in philosophy. Rather, our skepticism is focused on those intuitions that differ systematically from one social group to another. There is, of course, a sense in which the philosophical literature on skepticism also supports the conclusion that some of our epistemic intuitions are not to be trusted, since, as the quote from Cohen in Section 1 illustrates, much of that literature is devoted to showing that our epistemic intuitions appear to support a logically inconsistent set of propositions, and to arguing about which of these intuitions should be ignored. But our findings raise a quite different problem. For even if some individual or group had a completely consistent set of intuitions, the fact that these intuitions are determined, to a significant degree, by one's cultural, SES and educational background, and the fact that people in other groups have systematically different intuitions, raises the question of why the folks who have these consistent intuitions should trust any of them.

One way in which a philosopher might resist our contention that the systematic cultural variation in epistemic intuitions indicates that these intuitions are not to be trusted would be to argue that intuitive differences of the sort that we've reported are an indication that the people offering the intuitions *have different epistemic concepts*. In his recent book, *From Metaphysics to Ethics*, Frank Jackson clearly endorses the view that people whose epistemic intuitions differ on philosophically important cases should be counted as having different epistemic concepts.

> I have occasionally run across people who resolutely resist the Gettier cases. Sometimes it has seemed right to accuse them of confusion . . . but sometimes it is clear that they are not confused; what we then learn from the stand-off is simply that they use the word "knowledge" to cover different cases from most of us. In these cases it is, it seems to me, misguided to accuse them of error (unless they go on to say that their concept of knowledge is ours).

> (Jackson 1998, 32)

So for Jackson (unconfused) East Asians or Indians who insist that the people described in Gettier cases *do* have knowledge are not disagreeing with those of us who think they don't. Rather, they are simply using the term "knowledge" to express a different concept. And, in all likelihood, an East Asian or Indian is *right* to insist that (as he uses the term) people in Gettier cases *do* have knowledge, just as, in all likelihood, we are right to insist that (as we use the term), they *don't*. Though Jackson focuses on the example of Gettier cases, we think it is clear that he would say much the same about people who react differently to the sorts of skeptical intuition probes discussed in Section 4. Those people, too, if they are not simply confused, should be viewed as having different epistemic concepts. Thus there is no real disagreement between people who react differently to skeptical intuition probes, and in all likelihood their intuitions are all true.

There is, of course, a substantial literature on concepts and concept individuation (see, for example, Margolis and Laurence 1999), and many of the leading contributors to that literature would strongly disagree with Jackson's claim that people who have different intuitions about Gettier cases have different concepts of knowledge (see, for example, Fodor 1998). We have no allegiance to any theory of concepts or to any account of concept individuation. But we think it is of considerable interest to simply *assume*, for argument's sake, that Jackson is right, and to ask what follows.

One important consequence of this assumption is that it undermines our attempt to argue from the results of our cross-cultural studies of epistemic intuitions to the conclusion that those intuitions are not to be trusted. Crucial to our argument was the claim that, since epistemic intuitions of people in different groups disagree, they can't all be true. But if Jackson is right about concepts, then our subjects are not really disagreeing at all; they are simply using the word "knowledge" (or "know") to express different concepts. So their intuitively supported claims about knowledge (or, to be more precise, about what *they* call "knowledge"), including those claims used in arguments for skepticism, *can* all be true, and as Jackson would have it, in all likelihood they *are*.

But while Jackson's account of concept individuation makes it easier to maintain that the premises of skeptical arguments are true, it makes it harder to see why the *conclusions* of those arguments are interesting or worrisome. To see the point, we need only note that, if Jackson is right about concepts and if we are right about the influence of culture, SES and philosophical training on epistemic intuitions, then it follows that the term "knowledge" is used to express *lots of concepts*. East Asians, Indians and high SES westerners all have different concepts; high and low SES westerners have different concepts; people who have studied lots of philosophy and people who have studied no philosophy have different concepts. And that, no doubt, is just the tip of the iceberg. Moreover, these concepts don't simply differ in *intension*, they differ in *extension*—they apply to different classes of actual and possible cases.

In the philosophical tradition, skepticism is taken to be worrisome because it denies that knowledge is possible, and that's bad because knowledge, it is assumed, is something very important. On Plato's view, "wisdom and knowledge are the highest of human things" (Plato 1892/1937, 352), and many people, both philosophers and ordinary folk, would agree. But obviously, if there are many concepts of knowledge, and if these concepts have different extensions, it can't be the case that *all* of them are the highest of human things. If Jackson is right about concepts, then the arguments for skepticism in the philosophical tradition pose a serious challenge to the possibility of having what high SES, white westerners with lots of philosophical training call "knowledge." But those arguments give us no reason to think that we can't have what other people—East Asians, Indians, low SES people, or scientists who have never studied philosophy—would call "knowledge." And, of course, those skeptical arguments give us no reason at all to think that what high SES white western philosophers call "knowledge" is any better, or more important, or more desirable, or more useful than what these other folks call "knowledge," or that it is any closer to "the highest of human things." Without some reason to think that what white, western, high SES philosophers call "knowledge" is any more valuable, desirable or useful than any of the other commodities that other groups call "knowledge" it is hard to see why we should care if we can't have it.

Let us close with a brief review of the main themes of the chapter. Arguments for skepticism have occupied a central place in western philosophy. And it's easy to see why. Skeptical arguments threaten dramatic conclusions from premises that are intuitively compelling to many philosophers, including the three of us. A number of western philosophers maintain that the intuitions invoked in skeptical arguments have nothing to do with being western or a philosopher. Rather, these intuitions are regarded as intrinsic to human nature and cross-culturally universal. We've argued that our evidence poses a serious challenge to this universalist stance. Our data suggest that some of the most familiar skeptical intuitions are far from universal—they vary as a function of culture, SES and educational background. We find that this evidence generates a nagging sense that our own skeptical intuitions are parochial vestiges of our culture and education. Had we been raised in a different culture or SES group or had a different educational background, we would have been much less likely to find these intuitions compelling. This historical arbitrariness of our skeptical intuitions leads us to be skeptical that we can trust these intuitions to be true; for we see no reason to think that our cultural and intellectual tribe should be so privileged. One might, as we've noted, maintain that different cultural, SES and educational groups simply have different concepts of knowledge, and that on our concept of knowledge, the skeptical intuitions are true. Although this response is available, it saps the drama from the skeptical conclusion. It's not clear that skepticism would have held such a grip over the minds of epistemologists if the skeptic is reduced to the claim that the external world can't be "known," according to the concept of knowledge used by the relatively small cultural group to which we happen to belong. As one of us wrote some years ago, "The best first response to the skeptic who maintains that we cannot achieve certainty, . . . knowledge or what have you, is not to argue that we can. Rather, it is to ask, so what?" (Stich 1990, 26).

REFERENCES

Burnyeat, M. 1982a. Idealism and Greek Philosophy: What Descartes Saw and Berkeley Missed. *Philosophical Review* 90: 3–40.
Cohen, S. 1999. Contextualism, Skepticism, and the Structure of Reasons. In J. Tomberlin, ed., *Philosophical Perspectives*, vol. 13: *Epistemology*, 57–89. Oxford: Blackwell.
DeRose, K. 1995. Solving the Skeptical Problem. *Philosophical Review* 104: 1–52.
DeRose, K., and T. A. Warfield. 1999. *Skepticism: A Contemporary Reader*. Oxford: Oxford University Press.
Fodor, J. 1998. *Concepts: Where Cognitive Science Went Wrong*. Oxford: Oxford University Press.
Haidt, J., S. Koller, and M. Dias. 1993. Affect, Culture and Morality. *Journal of Personality and Social Psychology* 65, 4: 613–28.
Hill, C. 1996. *Sensations*. Cambridge: Cambridge University Press.
Jackson, F. 1998. *From Metaphysics to Ethics: A Defense f Conceptual Analysis*. Oxford: Clarendon Press.
Klein, P. 1981. *Certainty: A Refutation of Skepticism*. Oxford: Clarendon Press.
Lehrer, K. 2000. *Theory of Knowledge*, 2nd ed. Boulder, CO: Westview Press.
Lewis, D. 1996. Elusive Knowledge. *Australasian Journal of Philosophy* 74: 549–67.
Margolis, E., and S. Laurence, eds. 1999. *Concepts*. Cambridge, MA: MIT Press.
McGinn, C. 1993. *Problems in Philosophy: The Limits of Inquiry*. Oxford: Blackwell.
Nagel, T. 1986. *The View from Nowhere*. Oxford: Oxford University Press.
Nisbett, R., K. Peng, I. Choi, and A. Norenzayan. 2001. Culture and Systems of Thought: Holistic Versus Analytic Cognition. *Psychological Review* 108, 2: 291–310.
Nisbett, R., and L. Ross. 1980. *Human Inference: Strategies and Shortcomings of Social Judgment*. Englewood Cliffs, NJ: Prentice-Hall.
Norenzayan, A., R. Nisbett, E. Smith, and B. J. Kim. 1999. Rules vs. Similarity as a Basis for Reasoning and Judgment in East and West. Ann Arbor: University of Michigan.
Nozick, R. 1981. *Philosophical Explanations*. Cambridge, MA: Harvard University Press.
Pinker, S. 1997. *How the Mind Works*. New York: Norton.

Plato. 1892/1937. *Dialogues*. Trans. B. Jowett. New York: Random House.

Schiffer, S. 1996. Contextualist Solutions to Skepticism. *Proceedings of the Aristotelian Society* 96: 317–33.

Shweder, R. 1991. *Thinking Through Cultures: Explorations in Cultural Psychology*. Cambridge, MA: Harvard University Press.

Stich, S. 1988. Reflective Equilibrium, Analytic Epistemology and the Problem of Cognitive Diversity. *Synthese* 74: 391–413.

———. 1990. *The Fragmentation of Reason*. Cambridge, MA: MIT Press.

Stroud, B. 1984. *The Significance of Philosophical Skepticism*. Oxford: Clarendon Press.

Unger, P. 1975. *Ignorance: A Case for Scepticism*. Oxford: Oxford University Press.

Watanabe, M. 1998. Styles of Reasoning in Japan and the United States: Logic of Education in Two Cultures. Paper presented at the American Sociological Association Annual Meeting, San Francisco, August.

———. 1999. Styles of Reasoning in Japan and the United States: Logic of Education in Two Cultures. PhD thesis, Columbia University.

Weinberg, J., S. Nichols, and S. Stich. 2001. Normativity and Epistemic Intuitions. *Philosophical Topics* 1–2: 429–60.

Williams, M. 1991. *Unnatural Doubts: Epistemological Realism and the Basis of Scepticism*. Oxford: Blackwell.

Too many moral philosophers and
commentators on moral philosophy...
have been content to invent their psychology
or anthropology from scratch....

S. DARWALL, A. GIBBARD, AND

P. RAILTON (1997, 34–35)

11

AS A MATTER OF FACT

Empirical Perspectives on Ethics

John M. Doris and Stephen Stich

1. Introduction

Regarding the assessment of Darwall and colleagues, we couldn't agree more: far too many moral philosophers have been content to *invent* the psychology or anthropology on which their theories depend, advancing or disputing empirical claims with little concern for empirical evidence. We also believe—and we expect Darwall, Gibbard, and Railton would agree—that this empirical complacency has impeded progress in ethical theory and discouraged investigators in the biological, behavioral, and social sciences from undertaking philosophically informed research on ethical issues.

We realize that some moral philosophers have taken there to be good reasons for shunning empirical inquiry. For much of the twentieth century, many working in analytic ethics—variously inspired by Hume's (1978, 469) pithy injunction against inferring *ought* from *is* and the seductive mysteries of Moore's (1903, esp. 10–17) "Open Question Argument"—maintained that descriptive considerations of the sort adduced in the natural and social sciences cannot constrain ethical reflection without vitiating its prescriptive or normative character (e.g., Stevenson 1944, 108–10; R. M. Hare 1952, 79–93). The plausibility of such claims is both debated and debatable, but it is clear that they have helped engender suspicion regarding "naturalism" in ethics, which we understand, broadly, as the view that *ethical theorizing should be an (in part) a posteriori inquiry richly informed by relevant empirical considerations.*[1] Relatedly, this anti-naturalist suspicion enables disciplinary xenophobia in philosophical ethics, a reluctance to engage research beyond the philosophical literature. The methodology we advocate here—a resolutely naturalistic approach to ethical theory squarely engaging the relevant biological, behavioral, and social sciences—flouts both of these anxieties.

Perhaps those lacking our equanimity suspect that approaches of the sort we endorse fail to heed Stevenson's (1963, 13) advice that "Ethics must not be psychology," and thereby lapse into a noxious "scientism" or "eliminativism." Notoriously, Quine (1969, 75) advocated eliminativism in his rendering of naturalized epistemology, urging philosophical "surrender of the epistemological burden to psychology." Quine was sharply rebuked for slighting the normative character of epistemology (e.g., Kim 1988; Stich 1993a), but we are not suggesting, in a rambunctiously Quinean spirit, "surrender of the *ethical* burden to psychology." And so far as we know, neither is anyone else. Ethics must not—indeed cannot—*be* psychology, but it does not follow that ethics should *ignore* psychology.

The most obvious, and most compelling, motivation for our perspective is simply this: It is not possible to step far into the ethics literature without stubbing one's toe on empirical claims. The thought that moral philosophy can proceed unencumbered by facts seems to us an unlikely one: there are just too many places where answers to important ethical questions require—and have very often presupposed—answers to empirical questions.

A small but growing number of philosophers, ourselves included, have become convinced that answers to these empirical questions should be informed by systematic empirical research.[2] This is not to say that relevant information is easy to come by: the science is not always packaged in forms that are easy on the philosophical digestion. As Darwall et al. (1997, 47 ff.) caution, one won't often find "a well-developed literature in the social sciences simply awaiting philosophical discovery and exploitation." Still, we are more optimistic than Darwall and colleagues about the help philosophers can expect from empirical literatures: science has produced much experimental and theoretical work that appears importantly relevant to ongoing debates in ethical theory, and some moral philosophers have lately begun to pursue empirical investigations. To explore the issues fully requires far more space than is available here; we must content ourselves with developing a few rather programmatic examples of how an empirically sensitive philosophical ethics might proceed.

Our point is not that reference to empirical literatures can be expected, by itself, to resolve debates in moral theory. Rather, we hope to convince the reader that these literatures are often deeply relevant to important debates, and it is therefore intellectually

---

1. Compare Railton's (1989, 155–56) "methodological naturalism."
2. See Gibbard 1990, 58–61; Flanagan 1991; Goldman 1993; Johnson 1993; Stich 1993b; Railton 1995; Blackburn 1998, 36–37; Bok 1996; Doris 1996, 1998, 2002; Becker 1998; Campbell 1999; Harman 1999, 2000; Merritt 1999, 2000; Doris and Stich 2001; Woolfolk and Doris 2002.

irresponsible to ignore them. Sometimes empirical findings seem to contradict what particular disputing parties assert or presuppose, while in other cases, they appear to reconfigure the philosophical topography, revealing that certain lines of argument must traverse empirically difficult terrain. Often, philosophers who follow these challenging routes will be forced to make additional empirical conjectures, and these conjectures, in their turn, must be subject to empirical scrutiny. The upshot, we conclude, is that an intellectually responsible philosophical ethics is one that continuously engages the relevant empirical literature.

2. Character

In the second half of the twentieth century the "ethics of virtue" became an increasingly popular alternative to the Kantian and utilitarian theories that had for some time dominated normative ethics. In contrast to Kantianism and utilitarianism, which despite marked differences share an emphasis on identifying morally obligatory actions, virtue-centered approaches emphasize the psychological constitution, or character, of actors. The central question for virtue ethics, so the slogan goes, is not what sort of action to do, but what sort of person to be.[3] As Bernard Williams (1985, 1) has eloquently reminded us, the "aims of moral philosophy, and any hopes it may have of being worth serious attention, are bound up with the fate of Socrates' question" How should one live?, and it has seemed to many philosophers, not least due to Williams's influence, that any prospects for a satisfying answer rest with the ethics of character. Allegedly, if ethical reflection is to help people understand and improve themselves and their relations to others, it must be reflection focused on the condition and cultivation of character (see Williams 1993, 91–95).

Virtue ethics, especially in the Aristotelian guises that dominate the field, typically presupposes a distinctive account of human psychology. Nussbaum (1999, 170), although she insists that the moniker "virtue ethics" has been used to tag such a variety of projects that it represents a "misleading category," observes that approaches so titled are concerned with the "settled patterns of motive, emotion, and reasoning that lead us to call someone a person of a certain sort (courageous, generous, moderate, just, etc.)." If this is a fair characterization—and we think it is—then virtue ethics is marked by a particular interest in moral psychology, an interest in the cognitive, affective, and emotional patterns that are associated with the attribution of character traits.[4] This interest looks to be an empirical interest, and it's natural to ask how successfully virtue ethics addresses it.

---

3. The notation that character is evaluatively independent of or prior to action is something thought to be the distinctive emphasis of virtue ethics (see Louden 1984, 29; Watson 1990, 451–52). But this is not plausibly understood to mean that virtue ethics is indifferent regarding questions of what to do; the question of conduct should be of substantial importance on both virtue and action-centered approaches (see Sher 1998, 15–17).

4. Nussbaum (1999, 170) observes that Kantian and utilitarian approaches may share virtue ethics' interest in character. Space prohibits discussion, but if Nussbaum were right, our argument would have more sweeping implications than we contemplate here.

The central empirical issue concerns, to borrow Nussbaum's phrase, "settled patterns" of functioning. According to Aristotle, genuinely virtuous action proceeds from "firm and unchangeable character" rather than from transient motives (1984, 1105a28–b1); while the good person may suffer misfortune that impairs his activities and diminishes happiness, he "will never [*oudepote*] do the acts that are hateful and mean" (1984, 1100b32–34; cf. 1128b29; cf. Cooper 1999, 299 ff.).[5] In an influential contemporary exposition, McDowell (1978, 26–27) argued that considerations favoring vicious behavior are "silenced" in the virtuous person; although such an individual may recognize inducements to vice, she will not count them as reasons for action. As we understand the tradition, virtues are supposed to be robust traits; if a person has a robust trait, she can be confidently (although perhaps not with absolute certainty) expected to display trait-relevant behavior across a wide variety of trait-relevant situations, even where some or all of these situations are not optimally conducive to such behavior (Doris 2002, 18).[6]

Additionally, some philosophers have supposed that character will be evaluatively integrated—traits with associated evaluative valences are expected to co-occur in personality (see Doris 2002, 22; Flanagan 1991, 283–90). As Aristotle (1984, 1144b30–1145a2; cf. Irwin 1988, 66–71) has it, the virtues are inseparable; given the qualities of practical reason sufficient for the possession of one virtue, one can expect to find the qualities of practical reason sufficient for them all.

While understandings of character and personality akin to those just described have been hotly contested in psychology departments at least since the critiques of Vernon (1964), Mischel (1968), and Peterson (1968), moral philosophers have not been especially quick in taking the matter up. Flanagan's (1991) careful discussion broached the issue in contemporary analytic ethics, while Doris (1998, 2002) and Harman (1999, 2000) have lately pressed the point less temperately: although they manifest some fraternal disagreements, Harman and Doris both insist that the conception of character presupposed by virtue ethics is empirically inadequate.

The evidence for this contention, often united under the theoretical heading of "situationism," has been developed over a period of some seventy years, and includes some of the most striking research in the human sciences.

- Mathews and Canon (1975, 574–75) found subjects were five times more likely to help an apparently injured man who had dropped some books when

---

5. In Aristotle's view, the virtues are *hexeis* (1984, 1106a10–12), and a *hexis* is a disposition that is "permanent and hard to change" (1984, 8b25–9a9). This feature of Aristotle's account is emphasized by commentators: Sherman (1989, 1) says that for Aristotle (as well as for us) character traits explain why "someone can be *counted on* to act in certain ways" (cf. Woods 1986, 149; Annas 1993, 51; Audi 1995, 451; Cooper 1999, 238).

6. This follows quite a standard theme in philosophical writings on virtue and character. For example, Blum (1994, 178–80) understands compassion as a trait of character typified by an altruistic attitude of "strength and duration," which should be "stable and consistent" in prompting beneficent action (cf. Brandt 1970, 27; Dent 1975; McDowell 1979, 331–33; Larmore 1987, 12).

ambient noise was at normal levels than when a power lawnmower was
running nearby (80 percent v. 15 percent).

- Darley and Batson (1973, 105) report that passers-by not in a hurry were
  six times more likely to help an unfortunate who appeared to be in
  significant distress than were passers-by in a hurry (63 percent vs.
  10 percent).
- Isen and Levin (1972, 387) discovered that people who had just found a
  dime were twenty-two times more likely to help a woman who had
  dropped some papers than those who did not find a dime (88 percent vs.
  4 percent).
- Milgram (1974) found that subjects would repeatedly "punish" a screaming
  "victim" with realistic (but simulated) electric shocks at the polite request of
  an experimenter.
- Haney, Banks, and Zimbardo (1973) describe how college students role-playing
  in a simulated prison rapidly descended to *Lord of the Flies* barbarism.

There apparently exists an alarming disproportion between situational input and morally
disquieting output; it takes surprisingly little to get people behaving in morally undesir-
able ways. The point is not that circumstances influence behavior, or even that seemingly
good people sometimes do lousy things. No need to stop the presses for that. Rather, the
telling difficulty is just how insubstantial the situational influences effecting troubling
moral failures seem to be; it is not that people fall short of ideals of virtue and fortitude,
but that they can be *readily* induced to *radically* fail such ideals.

The argument suggested by this difficulty can be outlined as follows: a large body of
research indicates that cognition and behavior are extraordinarily sensitive to the situations in which people are embedded. The implication is that individuals—on the altogether plausible assumption that most people will be found in a range of situations
involving widely disparate cognitive and behavioral demands—are typically highly variable in their behavior, relative to the behavioral expectations associated with familiar trait
categories such as honesty, compassion, courage, and the like. But if people's behavior
were typically structured by robust traits, one would expect quite the opposite: namely,
behavior consistent with a given trait—e.g., behavior that is appropriately and reliably
honest, compassionate, or courageous—across a diversity of situations. It follows, according to the argument, that behavior is not typically structured by the robust traits that
figure centrally in virtue-theoretic moral psychology. Analogous considerations are supposed to make trouble for notions of evaluative integration; the endemic lack of uniformity in behavior adduced from the empirical literature undermines expectations of
integrated character structures.

The situationist argument has sometimes been construed by philosophers as asserting
that character traits "do not exist" (Flanagan 1991, 302; Athanassoulis 2000, 219–20;

Kupperman 2001, 250), but this is a misleading formulation of the issue.[7] In so far as to deny the existence of traits is to deny the existence of persisting dispositional differences among persons, the claim that traits do not exist seems unsustainable, and the exercise of refuting such a claim idle. (Indeed, it is a claim that even psychologists with strong situationist sympathies, e.g., Mischel 1968, 8–9, seem at pains to disavow.) The real issue dividing the virtue theorist and the situationist concerns the appropriate characterization of traits, not their existence or nonexistence. The situationist argument that needs to be taken seriously, and which to our mind stands unrefuted, holds that the Aristotelian conception of traits as robust dispositions—the sort which lead to trait-relevant behavior across a wide variety of trait-relevant situations—is radically empirically undersupported. To put the ethical implications of this a bit aggressively, it looks as though attribution of robust traits like virtues may very well be unwarranted in most instances,[8] programs of moral education aimed at inculcating virtues may very well be futile, and modes of ethical reflection focusing moral aspirations on the cultivation of virtue may very well be misguided.

At this point, the virtue theorist may offer one of two responses. She can accept the critics' interpretation of the empirical evidence while denying that her approach makes empirical commitments of the sort the evidence indicates is problematic. Or she can allow that her approach makes commitments in empirical psychology of the sort that would be problematic if the critics' interpretations of the evidence were sustainable, but deny that the critics have interpreted the evidence aright. The first option, we might say, is "empirically modest" (see Doris 2002, 110–12): because such renderings make only minimal claims in empirical psychology, they are insulated from empirical threat. The second option, conversely, is "empirically vulnerable" (see Railton 1995, 92–96): it makes empirical claims with enough substance to invite empirically motivated criticism.

We shall first discuss empirically modest rejoinders to the situationist critique. Numerous defenders of virtue ethics insist that virtue is not expected to be widely instantiated, but is found in only a few extraordinary individuals, and these writers further observe that this minimal empirical commitment is quite compatible with the disturbing, but not exceptionlessly disturbing, behavior in experiments like Milgram's (see Athanassoulis 2000, 217–19; DePaul 1999; Kupperman 2001, 242–43). The critics are bound to concede the point, since the empirical evidence cannot show that the instantiation of virtue in actual human psychologies is impossible; no empirical evidence could secure so strong a result. But so construed, the aspirations of virtue ethics are not entirely clear; if

---

7. Part of the reason for this error may be some spirited rhetoric of Harman's (e.g., the title of Harman 2000: "The Nonexistence of Character Traits"). But Harman repeatedly offers qualifications that caution against it; he voices skepticism about the existence of "ordinary character traits of *the sort people think there are*" (1999, 316) and "character traits *as ordinarily conceived*" (2000, 223; our italics). This is to reject a particular conception of character traits, not to deny that character traits exist. For his part, Doris (1998, 507; 2002, 62–66) quite explicitly acknowledges the existence of traits, albeit traits with less generalized effects on behavior than is often supposed.

8. The difficulty is not limited to rival academic theories; there is a large body of empirical evidence indicating that everyday "lay" habits of person perception seriously overestimate the impact of individual dispositional differences on behavioral outcomes. For summaries, see Jones 1990; Ross and Nisbett 1991, 119–44; Gilbert and Malone 1995; Doris 2002, 92–106.

virtue is *expected* to be rare, it is not obvious what role virtue theory could have in a (generally applicable) program of moral education.[9] This rings a bit odd, given that moral education—construed as aiming for the development of the good character necessary for a good life—has traditionally been a distinctive emphasis in writing on virtue, from Aristotle (1984, 1099b9–32, 1103b3–26) to Bennett (1993, 11–16; cf. Williams 1985, 10). Of course, the rarity of virtue might be thought a contingent matter; given the appropriate modalities of moral education, the virtue ethicist might say, virtue can be widely inculcated. But philosophers, psychologists, and educators alike have tended to be a bit hazy regarding particulars of the requisite educational processes; theories of moral education, and character education in particular, are typically not supported by large bodies of systematic research adducing behavioral differences corresponding to differing educational modalities (Leming 1997a, b; Hart and Killen 1999, 12; Doris 2002, 121–27).

It is tempting to put the situationist point a bit more sharply. It is true that the evidence does not show that the instantiation of virtue in actual human psychologies is impossible. But it also looks to be the case that the available systematic empirical evidence is compatible with virtue being psychologically impossible (or at least wildly improbable), and this suggests that the impossibility of virtue is an empirical possibility that has to be taken seriously. So while the evidence doesn't refute an empirically modest version of virtue ethics, it is plausibly taken to suggest that the burden of argument has importantly shifted: The advocate of virtue ethics can no longer simply assume that virtue is psychologically possible. If she can't offer compelling evidence—very preferably, more than anecdotal evidence—favoring the claim that virtue is psychologically possible, then she is in the awkward position of forwarding a view that would be undermined if an empirical claim which is not obviously false were to turn out to be true, without offering compelling reason to think that it won't turn out to be true.

Suppose the realization of virtue were acknowledged to be impossible: it might yet be insisted that talk of virtue articulates ethical ideals that are well suited—presumably better suited than alternatives, if virtue ethics is thought to have distinctive advantages—to facilitating ethically desirable conduct (see Blum 1994, 94–96). Asserting such a practical advantage for virtue ethics entails an empirical claim: reflection on the ideals of virtue can help actual people behave better. For example, it might be claimed that talk of virtue is more compelling, or has more motivational "grip," than abstract axiological principles. We know of little systematic evidence favoring such claims, and we are unsure of what sort of experimental designs are fit to secure them, but the only point we need to insist on is that even this empirically modest rendering of virtue ethics may bear contentious empirical commitments. If virtue ethics is alleged to have practical implications, it cannot avoid empirical assertions regarding the cognitive and motivational equipment with which people navigate their moral world.

---

9. Of course, if the virtue theorist is an elitist, this need not trouble her. But while historical writers on the virtues have at times manifested elitist sympathies (Aristotle 1984, 1123a6–10,1124a17–b32; Hume 1975, 250–67), this is not a sensibility that is typically celebrated by contemporary philosophers.

Even without an answer to such practical questions, it might be thought that virtue ethics is fit to address familiar conceptual problems in philosophical ethics, such as rendering an account of right action. In Hursthouse's (1999, 28; cf. 49–51) account of virtue ethics, "An action is right if it is what a virtuous agent would characteristically (i.e., acting in character) do in the circumstances." Hursthouse (1999, 123–26, 136, 140) further insists that an action does not count as "morally motivated" simply by dint of being the sort of thing a virtuous person does, done for reasons of the sort the virtuous person does it for; it must proceed "from virtue," that is, "from a settled state of good character." If this requirement is juxtaposed with the observation that the relevant states of character are extremely rare, as an empirically modest rendering of virtue ethics maintains, we apparently get the result that "morally motivated" actions are also extremely rare (a virtue-theoretic result, interestingly, with which Kant would have agreed). This need not trouble Hursthouse (1999, 141–60); she seems to allow that very often—perhaps always—one sees only approximations of moral motivation. It does trouble us. We think that less than virtuous people, even smashingly less than virtuous people, sometimes do the right thing for the right reasons, and these actions are fit to be honored as "morally motivated." It may not happen as often as one would like, but morally motivated conduct seems to happen rather more frequently than one chances on perfect virtue. Oskar Schindler, the philandering war profiteer who rescued thousands of Jews from the Nazis, is a famous example of the two notions coming apart (see Kenneally 1982), but with a little attention to the history books, we can surely adduce many more. The burden of proof, it seems to us, is on those asserting that such widely revered actions are not morally motivated.

There are also serious questions about the competitive advantages enjoyed by empirically modest virtue ethics. It has seemed to many that a chief attraction of character-based approaches is the promise of a lifelike moral psychology—a less wooden depiction of moral affect, cognition, motivation, and education than that offered by competing approaches such as Kantianism and utilitarianism (Flanagan 1991, 182; Hursthouse 1999, 119–20). Proponents of virtue ethics, perhaps most prominently MacIntyre (1984) and Williams (1985, 1993), link their approach—as Anscombe (1958, 4–5) did in a paper widely regarded as the call to arms for contemporary virtue ethics—to prospects for more psychological realism and texture. We submit that this is where a large measure of virtue ethics' appeal has lain; if virtue ethicists had tended to describe their psychological project along the lines just imagined, as deploying a moral psychology only tenuously related to the contours of actual human psychologies, we rather doubt that the view would now be sweeping the field.

We contend that for virtue ethics to retain its competitive advantage in moral psychology it must court empirical danger by making empirical claims with enough substance to be seriously tested by the empirical evidence from psychology. For instance, the virtue theorist may insist that while perfect virtue is rare indeed, robust traits approximating perfect virtue—reliable courage, temperance, and the rest—may be widely inculcated, and perhaps similarly for robust vices—reliable cowardice, profligacy, and so on.[10] To defend such a position, the virtue theorist must somehow discredit the critic's empirical evidence. Various arguments might be thought to secure such a result: (i) The situationist experiments might be methodologically flawed; problems in experimental design or data analysis, for example, might undermine the results. (ii) The experiments might fail standards of ecological validity; the experimental contexts might be so distant from natural contexts as to preclude generalizations to the "real world." (iii) General conclusions from the experiments might be prohibited by limited samples; in particular, there appears to be a dearth of longitudinal behavioral studies that would help assess the role of character traits "over the long haul." (iv) The experiments may be conceptually irrelevant; for example, the conceptions of particular traits operationalized in the empirical work may not correspond to the related conceptions figuring in virtue ethics.

The thing to notice straight away is that motivating contentions like the four above require evaluating a great deal of psychological research; making a charge stick to one experiment or two, when there are hundreds, if not thousands, of relevant studies, is unlikely to effect a satisfying resolution of the controversy. The onus, of course, falls on both sides: just as undermining arguments directed at single experiments are of limited comfort to the virtue theorist, demonstrating the philosophical relevance of a lone study is not enough to make the critics' day. Newspaper science reporting notwithstanding, in science there is seldom, or never, a single decisive experiment or, for that matter, a decisive experimental failure. General conclusions about social science can legitimately be drawn only from encountering, in full detail, a body of research, and adducing patterns or trends. Doris (2002) has recently attempted to approximate this methodological standard in a book-length study, and he there concludes that major trends in empirical work support conclusions in the neighborhood indicated by the more programmatic treatments of Doris (1998) and Harman (1999, 2000). Whether or not one is drawn to this conclusion, we think it clear that the most profitable discussion of the empirical literature will proceed with detailed discussion of the relevant empirical work. If an empirically vulnerable virtue ethics is to be shown empirically defensible, defenders must provide much fuller consideration of the psychology. To our knowledge, extant defenses of virtue ethics in the face of empirical attack do not approximate the required breadth and depth.[11] Hopefully, future discussions will rectify this situation, to the edification of defenders and critics alike.

---

10. There is some question as to whether vices are expected to be robust in the way virtues are, but some philosophers seem to think so: Hill (1991, 130–32) apparently believes that calling someone weak-willed marks characteristic patterns of behavior.

11. For example, Kupperman 2001 refers to nine items in the empirical literature in responding to Harman, and Athanassoulis 2000, three.

3. Moral Motivation

Suppose a person believes that she ought to do something: donate blood to the Red Cross, say, or send a significant contribution to an international relief agency. Does it follow that she will be moved actually to act on this belief? Ethical theorists use internalism to mark an important cluster of answers to this question, answers maintaining that the motivation to act on a moral judgment is a necessary or intrinsic concomitant of the judgment itself, or that the relevant motivation is inevitably generated by the very same mental faculty that produces the judgment.[12] One familiar version of internalism is broadly Kantian, emphasizing the role of rationality in ethics. As Deigh (1999, 289) characterizes the position, "reason is both the pilot and the engine of moral agency. It not only guides one toward actions in conformity with one's duty, but it also produces the desire to do one's duty and can invest that desire with enough strength to overrule conflicting impulses of appetite and passion." A notorious difficulty for internalism is suggested by Hume's (1975, 282–84) "sensible knave," a person who recognizes that the unjust and dishonest acts he contemplates are wrong, but is completely unmoved by this realization. More recent writers (e.g., Nichols 2002) have suggested that the sensible knave (or, as philosophers often call him, "the amoralist") is more than a philosophical fiction, since clinical psychologists and other mental health professionals have for some time noted the existence of sociopaths or psychopaths, who appear to *know* the difference between right and wrong but quite generally lack motivation to *do* what is right. If this understanding of the psychopath's moral psychology is accurate, internalism looks to be suffering empirical embarrassment.[13]

Internalists have adopted two quite different responses to this challenge, one conceptual and the other empirical. The first relies on conceptual analysis to argue that a person couldn't really believe that an act is wrong if he has no motivation to avoid performing it. For example, Michael Smith claims it is "a conceptual truth that agents who make moral judgements are motivated accordingly, at least absent weakness of the will and the like" (Smith 1994, 66). Philosophers who adopt this strategy recognize that imaginary knaves and real psychopaths may *say* that something is "morally required" or "morally wrong" and that they may be expressing a judgment that they sincerely accept. But if psychopaths are not motivated in the appropriate way, their words do not mean what non-psychopaths mean by these words and the concepts they express with these words are not the

---

12. A stipulation: We refer to views in the neighborhood of what Darwall (1983, 54) calls "judgement internalism," the thesis that it is "a necessary condition of a genuine instance of a certain sort of judgement that the person making the judgement be disposed to act in a way appropriate to it." Space limitations force us to ignore myriad complications; for more detailed discussion see Svavarsdóttir 1999.

13. There is august precedent for supposing that the internalism debate has empirical elements. In his classic discussion, Frankena (1976, 73) observed that progress here requires reference to "the psychology of human motivation"—"The battle, if war there be, cannot be contained; its field is the whole human world." We hope that Frankena would have appreciated our way of joining the fight.

ordinary moral concepts that non-psychopaths use. Therefore psychopaths "do not *really* make moral judgements at all" (Smith 1994, 67).

This strategy only works if ordinary moral concepts require that people who *really* make moral judgments have the appropriate sort of motivation. But there is considerable disagreement in cognitive science about whether and how concepts are structured, and about how we are to determine when something is built into or entailed by a concept (Margolis and Laurence 1999). Indeed, one widely discussed approach maintains that concepts have no semantically relevant internal structure to be analyzed—thus there are no conceptual entailments (Fodor 1998). Obviously, internalists who appeal to conceptual analysis must reject this account, and in so doing they must take a stand in the broadly empirical debate about the nature of concepts.

Smith is one moral theorist who has taken such a stand. Following Lewis (1970, 1972), Jackson (1994), and others, Smith proposes that a concept can be analyzed by specifying the "maximal consistent set of platitudes" in which the concept is invoked; it is by "coming to treat those platitudes as platitudinous," Smith (1994, 31) maintains, that "we come to have mastery of that concept." If this is correct, the conceptual analysis defense of internalism requires that the maximally consistent set of platitudes invoking the notion of a moral judgment includes a claim to the effect that "agents who make moral judgements are motivated accordingly." Once again, this is an empirical claim. Smith appeals to his own intuitions in its support, but it is of course rather likely that opponents of internalism do not share Smith's intuitions, and it is difficult to say whose intuitions should trump.

In the interests of developing a non-partisan analysis, Nichols (2002) has been running a series of experiments in which philosophically unsophisticated undergraduates are presented with questions like these:

> John is a psychopathic criminal. He is an adult of normal intelligence, but he has no emotional reaction to hurting other people. John has hurt, and indeed killed, other people when he has wanted to steal their money. He says that he knows that hurting others is wrong, but that he just doesn't care if he does things that are wrong. Does John really understand that hurting others is morally wrong?
>
> Bill is a mathematician. He is an adult of normal intelligence, but he has no emotional reaction to hurting other people. Nonetheless, Bill never hurts other people simply because he thinks that it is irrational to hurt others. He thinks that any rational person would be like him and not hurt other people. Does Bill really understand that hurting others is morally wrong? (Nichols 2004, 74)

Nichols's preliminary results are exactly the opposite of what Smith would have one expect. An overwhelming majority of subjects maintained that John, the psychopath, did understand that hurting others is morally wrong, while a slight majority maintained that Bill, the rational mathematician, did not. The implication seems to be that the subjects' concept of moral judgment does not typically include a "motivational platitude." These results do not, of course, constitute a decisive refutation of Smith's conceptual analysis, since Smith can reply that responses like those Nichols reports would not be part of the maximally consistent set of platitudes that people would endorse after due reflection. But this too is an empirical claim; if Smith is to offer a compelling defense of it he should—with our enthusiastic encouragement—adduce some systematic empirical evidence.

A second internalist strategy for dealing with the problem posed by the amoralist is empirical: even if amoralists are conceptually possible, the internalist may insist, their existence is psychologically impossible. As a matter of psychological fact, this argument goes, people's moral judgments are accompanied by the appropriate sort of motivation.[14] A Kantian elaboration of this idea, on which we will focus, maintains that people's moral judgments are accompanied by the appropriate sort of motivation *unless their rational faculties are impaired*. (We'll shortly see that much turns on the fate of the italicized clause.) Recent papers by Roskies (2003) and Nichols (2002) set out important challenges to this strategy.

Roskies's argument relies on Damasio and colleagues' work with patients suffering injuries to the ventromedial (VM) cortex (Damasio, Tranel, and Damasio 1990; Saver and Damasio 1991; Bechara, Damasio, and Damasio 2000). On a wide range of standard psychological tests, including tests for intelligence and reasoning abilities, these patients appear quite normal. They also do as well as normal subjects on Kohlberg's tests of *moral* reasoning, and when presented with hypothetical situations they offer moral judgments that concur with those of normal subjects. However, these patients appear to have great difficulty acting in accordance with those judgments. As a result, although they often led exemplary lives prior to their injury, their post-trauma social lives are a shambles. They disregard social conventions, make disastrous business and personal decisions, and often engage in anti-social behavior. Accordingly, Damasio and his colleagues describe the VM patients' condition as "acquired sociopathy" (Saver and Damasio 1991).

Roskies maintains that VM patients do not act on their moral judgments because they suffer a *motivational* deficit. Moreover, the evidence indicates that these individuals do not have a *general* difficulty in acting on evaluative judgments; rather, Roskies (2003) maintains, action with respect to moral and social evaluation is differentially impaired. In addition to the behavioral evidence, this interpretation is supported by the anomalous pattern of skin-conductance responses (SCRs) that VM patients display.[15] Normal individuals produce an SCR when presented with emotionally charged or value-laden stimuli, while VM patients typically do not produce SCRs in response to such stimuli. SCRs are not entirely lacking in VM patients, however. SCRs are produced when VM patients are surprised or startled, for example, demonstrating that the physiological basis for these

---

14. We prescind from questions as to whether the motivation need be overriding, although we suspect formulations not requiring overridingness are more plausible.

15. SCR is a measure of physiological arousal, which is also sometimes called galvanic skin response, or GSR.

responses is intact. In addition, their presence is reliably correlated with cases in which patients' actions are consistent with their judgments about what to do, and their absence is reliably correlated with cases in which patients fail to act in accordance with their judgments. Thus, Roskies contends, the SCR is a reliable indicator of motivation. So the fact that VM patients, unlike normal subjects, do not exhibit SCRs in response to morally charged stimuli suggests that their failure to act in morally charged situations results from a motivational deficit.

On the face of it, acquired sociopathy confounds internalists maintaining that the moral judgments of rational people are, as a matter of psychological fact, always accompanied by appropriate motivation.[16] Testing indicates that the general reasoning abilities of these patients are not impaired, and even their moral reasoning seems to be quite normal. So none of the empirical evidence suggests the presence of a cognitive disability. An internalist might insist that these post-injury judgments are not *genuine* instances of moral judgments because VM patients no longer know the standard meaning of the moral words they use. But unless it is supported by an appeal to a conceptual analysis of the sort we criticized earlier, this is a rather implausible move; as Roskies notes, all tests of VM patients indicate that their language, their declarative knowledge structures, and their cognitive functioning are intact. There are, of course, many questions about acquired sociopathy that remain unanswered and much work is yet to be done. However these questions get answered, the literature on VM patients is one that moral philosophers embroiled in the internalism debate would be ill advised to ignore; once again, the outcome of a debate in ethical theory looks to be contingent on empirical issues.

The same point holds for other work on anti-social behavior. Drawing on Blair's (1995) studies of psychopathic murderers imprisoned in Great Britain, Nichols (2002) has recently argued that the phenomenon of psychopathy poses a deep and complex challenge for internalism. Again, the general difficulty is that psychopaths seem to be living instantiations of Hume's sensible knave: although they appear to be rational and can be quite intelligent, psychopaths are manipulative, remorseless, and devoid of other-regarding concern. While psychopaths sometimes acknowledge that their treatment of other people is wrong, they are quite indifferent about the harm that they have caused; they seem to have no motivation to avoid hurting others (R. D. Hare 1993).

Blair's (1995) evidence complicates this familiar story. He found that psychopaths exhibit surprising deficits on various tasks where subjects are presented with descriptions of "moral" transgressions like a child hitting another child and "conventional" transgressions like a child leaving the classroom without the teacher's permission. From early childhood, normal children distinguish moral from conventional transgressions on a number of dimensions: they view moral transgressions as more serious, they explain why the acts are wrong by appeal to different factors (harm and fairness for moral transgressions, social

---

16. Roskies herself does not offer acquired sociopathy as a counter-example to the Kantian version of empirical internalism, but we believe the evidence *is* in tension with the Kantian view we describe.

acceptability for conventional transgressions), and they understand conventional transgressions, unlike moral transgressions, to be dependent on authority (Turiel, Killen, and
Hedwig 1987; Nucci 1986).

For example, presented with a hypothetical case where a teacher says there is no rule
about leaving the classroom without permission, children think it is OK to leave without
permission. But presented with a hypothetical where a teacher says there is no rule against
hitting other children, children do not judge that hitting is acceptable. Blair has shown
that while autistic children, children with Down syndrome, and a control group of incarcerated non-psychopath murderers have relatively little trouble in drawing the moral-
conventional distinction and classifying cases along these lines, incarcerated psychopaths
are unable to do so.

This inability might be evidence for the hypothesis that psychopaths have a reasoning
deficit, and therefore do not pose a problem for internalists who maintain that a properly
functioning reasoning faculty reliably generates some motivation to do what one believes
one ought to do. But, as Nichols (2002) has pointed out, the issue cannot be so easily
resolved, because psychopaths have also been shown to have *affective* responses that are
quite different from those of normal subjects. When shown distressing stimuli (like slides
of people with dreadful injuries) and threatening stimuli (like slides of an angry man
wielding a weapon), normal subjects exhibit much the same suite of physiological responses. Psychopaths, by contrast, exhibit normal physiological responses to threatening
stimuli, but abnormally low physiological responses to distressing stimuli (Blair et al.
1997). Thus, Nichols argues, it may well be that the psychopath's deficit is not an abnormal reasoning system, but an abnormal affect system, and it is these affective abnormalities, rather than any rational disabilities, that are implicated in psychopaths' failure to
draw the moral-conventional distinction.[17] If his interpretation is correct, it looks as
though the existence of psychopaths does undermine the Kantian internalist's empirical
generalization: contra the Kantian, there exists a substantial class of individuals *without
rational disabilities* who are not motivated by their moral judgments.

We are sympathetic to Nichols's account, but as in the case of VM patients, the internalist is free to insist that a fuller understanding of psychopathy will reveal that the
syndrome does indeed involve rational disabilities. Resolving this debate will require
conceptual work on how to draw the boundary between reason and affect, and on what
counts as an abnormality in each of these domains. But it will also require much more
empirical work aimed at understanding exactly how psychopaths and non-psychopaths
differ. The internalist—or at least the Kantian internalist—who wishes to diffuse the difficulty posed by psychopathy must proffer an empirically tenable account of the psychopath's cognitive architecture that locates the posited rational disability. We doubt that

---

17. Here Nicholas offers support for the "sentimentalist" tradition, which maintains that emotions (or "sentiments") play a central role in moral judgment. For a helpful treatment of sentimentalism, see D'Arms and
Jacobson 2000.

such an account is forthcoming. But—to instantiate once more our take-home message—our present point is that if internalists are to develop such an account, they must engage the empirical literature.

4. Moral Disagreement

Numerous contemporary philosophers, including Brandt (1959), Harman (1977, 125–36), Railton (1986a, b), and Lewis (1989), have proposed dispositional theories of moral rightness or non-moral good, which "make matters of value depend on the affective dispositions of agents" (see Darwall et al. 1997, 28–29).[18] The various versions differ in detail,[19] but a rendering by Brandt is particularly instructive. According to Brandt (1959, 241–70), ethical justification is a process whereby initial judgments about particular cases and general moral principles are revised by testing these judgments against the attitudes, feelings, or emotions that would emerge under appropriately idealized circumstances. Of special importance on Brandt's (1959, 249–51, 261–64) view are what he calls "qualified attitudes"—the attitudes people would have if they were, *inter alia*, (1) impartial, (2) fully informed about and vividly aware of the relevant facts, and (3) free from any "abnormal" states of mind, like insanity, fatigue, or depression.[20]

As Brandt (1959, 281–84) noted, much depends on whether all people would have the same attitudes in ideal circumstances—i.e., on whether their attitudes would *converge* in ideal circumstances. If they would, then certain moral judgments—those where the idealized convergence obtains—are justified for all people, and others—those where such convergence fails to obtain—are not so justified. But if people's attitudes generally fail to converge under idealized circumstances, qualified attitude theory apparently lapses into a version of relativism, since any given moral judgment may comport with the qualified attitudes of one person, and thus be justified for him, while an incompatible judgment may comport with the attitudes of another person, and thus be justified for her.[21]

Brandt, who was a pioneer in the effort to integrate ethical theory and the social sciences, looked primarily to anthropology to help determine whether moral attitudes can

---

18. These views reflect a venerable tradition linking moral judgment to the affective states that people would have under idealized conditions; it extends back to Hutcheson (1738), Hume (1975, 1978), and Adam Smith (2002).

19. A particularly important difference concerns the envisaged link between moral claims and affective reactions. Firth (1952, 317–45) and Lewis (1989) see the link as a matter of meaning, Railton (1986b) as a synthetic identity, and Brandt (1959, 241–70) both as a matter of justification and, more tentatively, as a matter of meaning.

20. Brandt was a prolific and self-critical thinker, and the 1959 statement may not represent his mature views, but it well illustrates how empirical issues can impact a familiar approach to ethical theory. For a helpful survey of Brandt's career, see Rosati 2000.

21. On some readings, qualified attitude theories may end up a version of *skepticism* if attitudes don't converge under ideal circumstances. Suppose a theory holds "an action is morally right (or morally wrong) if all people in ideal conditions would judge that action is morally right (or morally wrong)." Then if convergence fails to obtain in ideal conditions, this theory entails that there are no morally right (or morally wrong) actions.

be expected to converge under idealized circumstances. It is of course well known that anthropology includes a substantial body of work, such as the classic studies of Westermarck (1906) and Sumner (1934), detailing the radically divergent moral outlooks found in cultures around the world. But as Brandt (1959, 283–84) recognized, typical ethnographies do not support confident inferences about the convergence of attitudes under *ideal* conditions, in large measure because they often give limited guidance regarding how much of the moral disagreement can be traced to disagreement about factual matters that are not moral in nature, such as those having to do with religious or cosmological views.

With this sort of difficulty in mind, Brandt (1954) undertook his own anthropological study of Hopi people in the American southwest, and found issues for which there appeared to be serious moral disagreement between typical Hopi and white American attitudes that could not plausibly be attributed to differences in belief about non-moral facts. A notable example is the Hopi attitude towards causing animals to suffer, an attitude that might be expected to disturb many non-Hopis: "[Hopi] children sometimes catch birds and make 'pets' of them. They may be tied to a string, to be taken out and 'played' with. This play is rough, and birds seldom survive long. [According to one informant:] 'Sometimes they get tired and die. Nobody objects to this'" (Brandt 1954, 213).

Brandt (1959, 103) made a concerted effort to determine whether this difference in moral outlook could be traced to disagreement about non-moral facts, but he could find no plausible explanation of this kind; his Hopi informants didn't believe that animals lack the capacity to feel pain, for example, nor did they believe that animals are rewarded for martyrdom in the afterlife. According to Brandt (1954, 245), the Hopi do not regard animals as unconscious or insensitive; indeed, they apparently regard animals as "closer to the human species than does the average white man." The best explanation of the divergent moral judgments, Brandt (1954, 245) concluded, is a "basic difference of attitude." Accordingly, although he cautions that the uncertainties of ethnography make confident conclusions on this point difficult, Brandt (1959, 284) argues that accounts of moral justification like his qualified attitude theory *do* end in relativism, since "groups do sometimes make divergent appraisals when they have identical beliefs about the objects."

Of course, the observation that persistent moral disagreement appears to problematize moral argument and justification is not unique to Brandt. While the difficulty is long familiar, contemporary philosophical discussion was spurred by Mackie's (1977, 36–38) "argument from relativity" or, as it is called by later writers, the "argument from disagreement" (Brink 1989, 197; Loeb 1998). Such "radical" differences in moral judgment as are frequently observed, Mackie (1977, 36) argued, "make it difficult to treat those judgments as apprehensions of objective truths." As we see it, the problem is not only that moral disagreement often persists, but also that for important instances of moral disagreement—such as the treatment of animals—it is obscure what sort of considerations, be they methodological or substantive, *could* settle the issues (see Sturgeon 1988, 229). Indeed, moral disagreement might be plausibly expected to continue even when the disputants are in methodological agreement concerning the appropriate standards for moral argument. One way of putting the point is to say that application of the same method may, for different individuals or cultures, yield divergent moral judgments that are equally acceptable by the lights of the method, even in reflective conditions that the method countenances as ideal.[22]

In contemporary ethical theory, an impressive group of philosophers are "moral realists" (see Railton 1986a, b; Boyd 1988; Sturgeon 1988; Brink 1989; M. Smith 1994). Adherents to a single philosophical creed often manifest doctrinal differences, and that is doubtless the case here, but it is probably fair to say that most moral realists mean to resist the argument from disagreement and reject its relativist conclusion. For instance, Smith's (1994, 9; cf. 13) moral realism requires the objectivity of moral judgment, where objectivity is construed as "the idea that moral questions have correct answers, that the correct answers are made correct by objective moral facts, that moral facts are determined by circumstances, and that, by engaging in moral argument, we can discover what these objective moral facts are." There's a lot of philosophy packed into this statement, but it looks as though Smith is committed to the thought, contra our relativist, that moral argument, or at least moral argument of the right sort, can settle moral disagreements. Indeed, for Smith (1994, 6), the notion of objectivity "signifies the possibility of a convergence in moral views," so the prospects for his version of moral realism depend on the argument from disagreement not going through.[23] But can realists like Smith bank on the argument's failure?

Realists may argue that, in contrast to the impression one gets from the anthropological literature, there already exists substantial moral convergence. But while moral realists have often taken pretty optimistic positions on the extent of actual moral agreement (e.g., Sturgeon 1988, 229; M. Smith 1994, 188), there is no denying that there is an abundance of persistent moral disagreement. That is, on many moral issues—think of abortion and capital punishment—there is a striking failure of convergence even after protracted argument. The relativist has a ready explanation for this phenomenon: moral judgment is not objective in Smith's sense, and moral argument cannot be expected to accomplish what Smith and other realists think it can.[24] Conversely, the realist's task is to *explain away*

---

22. This way of putting the argument is at once uncontentious and contentious. It is uncontentious because it does not entail a radical methodological relativism of the sort, say, that insists there is nothing to choose between consulting an astrologer and the method of reflective equilibrium as an approach to moral inquiry (see Brandt 1959, 274–75). But precisely because of this, the empirical conjecture that moral judgments will not converge is highly contentious, since a background of methodological agreement would appear to make it more likely that moral argument could end in substantive moral agreement.

23. Strictly speaking, a relativist need not be a "non-factualist" about morality, since, for example, she can take it to be a moral fact that it is right for Hopi children to engage in their fatal play with small animals, and also take it to be a moral fact that it is wrong for American white children to do so. But the factualist-relativist will probably want to reject Smith's (1994, 13) characterization of moral facts as "facts about the reasons that we all share."

24. See Williams 1985, 136: "In a scientific inquiry there should ideally be convergence on an answer, where the best explanation of the convergence involves the idea that the answer represents how things are; in the area of the ethical, at least at high level of generality, there is no such coherent hope."

failures of convergence; she must provide an explanation of the phenomena consistent with it being the case that moral judgment is objective and moral argument is rationally resolvable. For our purposes, what needs to be emphasized is that the relative merits of these competing explanations cannot be fairly determined without close discussion of actual cases. Indeed, as acute commentators with both realist (Sturgeon 1988, 230) and anti-realist (Loeb 1998, 284) sympathies have noted, the argument from disagreement cannot be evaluated by a priori philosophical means alone; what's needed, as Loeb observes, is "a great deal of further empirical research into the circumstances and beliefs of various cultures."

Brandt (1959, 101–2) lamented that the anthropological literature of his day did not always provide as much information on the exact contours and origins of moral attitudes and beliefs as philosophers wondering about the prospects for convergence might like. However, social psychology and cognitive science have recently produced research which promises to further discussion; the closing decades of the twentieth century witnessed an explosion of "cultural psychology" investigating the cognitive and emotional processes of different cultures (Shweder and Bourne 1982; Markus and Kitayama 1991; Ellsworth 1994; Nisbett and Cohen 1996; Nisbett 1998; Kitayama and Markus 1999). A representative finding is that East Asians are more sensitive than Westerners to the field or context as opposed to the object or actor in their explanations of physical and social phenomena, a difference that may be reflected in their habits of ethical judgment. Here we will focus on some cultural differences found rather closer to home, differences discovered by Nisbett and his colleagues while investigating regional patterns of violence in the American North and South. We argue that these findings support Brandt's pessimistic conclusions regarding the possibility of convergence in moral judgment.

The Nisbett group's research can be seen as applying the tools of cognitive social psychology to the "culture of honor," a phenomenon that anthropologists have documented in a variety of groups around the world. Although such peoples differ in many respects, they manifest important commonalties:

A key aspect of the culture of honor is the importance placed on the insult and the necessity to respond to it. An insult implies that the target is weak enough to be bullied. Since a reputation for strength is of the essence in the culture of honor, the individual who insults someone must be forced to retract; if the instigator refuses, he must be punished—with violence or even death. (Nisbett and Cohen 1996, 5)

According to Nisbett and Cohen (1996, 5–9), an important factor in the genesis of southern honor culture was the presence of a herding economy. Apparently, honor cultures are particularly likely to develop where resources are liable to theft, and where the state's coercive apparatus cannot be relied upon to prevent or punish thievery. These conditions often occur in relatively remote areas where herding is the main viable form of agriculture; the "portability" of herd animals makes them prone to theft. In areas where farming rather than herding is the principal form of subsistence, cooperation among neighbors is more important, stronger government infrastructures are more common, and resources—like decidedly unportable farmland—are harder to steal. In such agrarian social economies, cultures of honor tend not to develop. The American South was originally settled primarily by peoples from remote areas of Britain. Since their homelands were generally unsuitable for farming, these peoples have historically been herders; when they emigrated from Britain to the South, they initially sought out remote regions suitable for herding, and in such regions, the culture of honor flourished.

In the contemporary South police and other government services are widely available and herding has all but disappeared as a way of life, but certain sorts of violence continue to be more common than they are in the North. Nisbett and Cohen (1996) maintain that patterns of violence in the South, as well as attitudes towards violence, insults, and affronts to honor, are best explained by the hypothesis that a culture of honor persists among contemporary white non-Hispanic southerners. In support of this hypothesis, they offer a compelling array of evidence, including:

- demographic data indicating that (1) among southern whites, homicide rates are higher in regions more suited to herding than agriculture, and (2) white males in the South are much more likely than white males in other regions to be involved in homicides resulting from arguments, although they are *not* more likely to be involved in homicides that occur in the course of a robbery or other felony (Nisbett and Cohen 1996, ch. 2);
- survey data indicating that white southerners are more likely than northerners to believe that violence would be "extremely justified" in response to a variety of affronts, and that if a man failed to respond violently, he was "not much of a man" (Nisbett and Cohen 1996, ch. 3);
- legal scholarship indicating that southern states "give citizens more freedom to use violence in defending themselves, their homes, and their property" than do northern states (Nisbett and Cohen 1996, 63).

Two experimental studies—one in the field, the other in the laboratory—are especially striking.

In the field study (Nisbett and Cohen 1996, 73–75), letters of inquiry were sent to hundreds of employers around the United States. The letters purported to be from a hard-working 27-year-old Michigan man who had a single blemish on his otherwise solid record. In one version, the "applicant" revealed that he had been convicted for manslaughter. The applicant explained that he had been in a fight with a man who confronted him in a bar and told onlookers that "he and my fiancée were sleeping together. He laughed at me to my face and asked me to step outside if I was man enough." According to the letter, the applicant's nemesis was killed in the ensuing fray. In the other version of the letter, the applicant revealed that he had been convicted of motor vehicle theft, perpetrated at a time when he needed money for his family. Nisbett and his colleagues assessed 112 letters of response, and found that southern employers were significantly more likely to be cooperative and sympathetic in response to the manslaughter letter than were northern employers, while no regional differences were found in responses to the theft letter. One southern employer responded to the manslaughter letter as follows (Nisbett and Cohen 1996, 75):

> As for your problems of the past, anyone could probably be in the situation you were in. It was just an unfortunate incident that shouldn't be held against you. Your honesty shows that you are sincere. . . . I wish you the best of luck for your future. You have a positive attitude and a willingness to work. These are qualities that businesses look for in employees. Once you are settled, if you are near here, please stop in and see us.

No letters from northern employers were comparably sympathetic.

In the laboratory study (Nisbett and Cohen 1996, 45–48) subjects—white males from both northern and southern states attending the University of Michigan—were told that saliva samples would be collected to measure blood sugar as they performed various tasks. After an initial sample was collected, the unsuspecting subject walked down a narrow corridor where an experimental confederate was pretending to work on some filing. Feigning annoyance at the interruption, the confederate bumped the subject and called him an "asshole." A few minutes after the incident, saliva samples were collected and analyzed to determine the level of cortisol—a hormone associated with high levels of stress, anxiety, and arousal, and testosterone—a hormone associated with aggression and dominance behavior. As Figure 11.1 indicates, southern subjects showed dramatic increases in cortisol and testosterone levels, while northerners exhibited much smaller changes.

The two studies just described suggest that southerners respond more strongly to insult than northerners, and take a more sympathetic view of others who do so, manifesting just the sort of attitudes that are supposed to typify honor cultures. We think that the data assembled by Nisbett and his colleagues make a persuasive case that a culture of honor persists in the American South. Apparently, this culture affects people's judgments, attitudes, emotions, behavior, and even their physiological responses. Additionally, there is evidence that child-rearing practices play a significant role in passing the culture of honor on from one generation to the next, and also that relatively permissive laws regarding gun ownership, self-defense, and corporal punishment in the schools both reflect and reinforce southern honor culture (Nisbett and Cohen 1996, 60–63, 67–69). In short, it seems to us that the culture of honor is deeply entrenched in contemporary southern

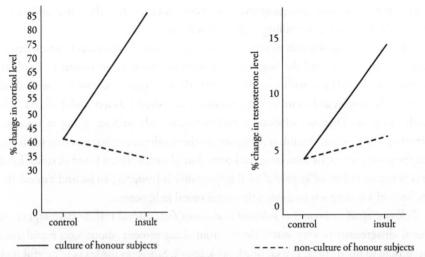

FIGURE 11.1 The results of an experiment by Nisbett and Cohen in which levels of cortisol and testosterone increased much more substantially in culture of honor subjects who were insulted by a confederate

culture, despite the fact that many of the material and economic conditions giving rise to it no longer widely obtain.[25]

We believe that the North-South cultural differences adduced by Nisbett and colleagues support Brandt's conclusion that moral attitudes will often fail to converge, even under ideal conditions. The data should be especially troubling for the realist, for despite the differences that we have been recounting, contemporary northern and southern Americans might be expected to have rather more in common—from circumstance to language to belief to ideology—than do, say, Yanomamö and Parisians. So if there is little ground for expecting convergence under ideal conditions in the case at hand, there is probably little ground in a good many others. To develop our argument a bit further, let us revisit the idealization conditions mentioned at the beginning of this section: impartiality, full factual information, and normality.

Impartiality. One strategy favored by moral realists concerned to explain away moral disagreement is to say that such disagreement stems from the distorting effects of individual interest (see Sturgeon 1988, 229–30); perhaps persistent disagreement doesn't so much betray deep features of moral argument and judgment as it does the doggedness with which individuals pursue their perceived advantage. For instance, seemingly moral disputes over the distribution of wealth may be due to perceptions—perhaps mostly inchoate—of individual and class interests rather than to principled disagreement about

---

25. The last clause is important, since realists (e.g., Brink 1989, 200) sometimes argue that apparent moral disagreement may result from cultures applying similar moral values to different economic conditions (e.g., differences in attitudes towards the sick and elderly between poor and rich cultures). But this explanation seems of dubious relevance to the described differences between contemporary northerners and southerners, who are plausibly interpreted as applying different values to similar economic conditions.

justice; persisting moral disagreement in such circumstances fails the impartiality condition, and is therefore untroubling to the moral realist.

But it is rather implausible to suggest that North-South disagreements over when violence is justified will fail the impartiality condition. There is no reason to think that southerners would be unwilling to universalize their judgments across relevantly similar individuals in relevantly similar circumstances, as indeed Nisbett and Cohen's "letter study" suggests. One can advocate a violent honor code without going in for special pleading.[26] We do not intend to denigrate southern values; our point is that while there may be good reasons for criticizing the honor-bound southerner, it is not obvious that the reason can be failure of impartiality, if impartiality is (roughly) to be understood along the lines of a willingness to universalize one's moral judgments.

Full and vivid awareness of relevant non-moral facts. Moral realists have argued that moral disagreements very often derive from disagreement about non-moral issues. According to Boyd (1988, 213; cf. Brink 1989, 202–3; Sturgeon 1988, 229), "careful philosophical examination will reveal ... that agreement on nonmoral issues would eliminate *almost all* disagreement about the sorts of moral issues which arise in ordinary moral practice." Is this a plausible conjecture for the data we have just considered? We find it hard to imagine what agreement on non-moral facts could do the trick, for we can readily imagine that northerners and southerners might be in full agreement on the relevant non-moral facts in the cases described. Members of both groups would presumably agree that the job applicant was cuckolded, for example, or that calling someone an "asshole" is an insult. We think it much more plausible to suppose that the disagreement resides in differing and deeply entrenched evaluative attitudes regarding appropriate responses to cuckolding, challenge, and insult.

Savvy philosophical readers will be quick to observe that terms like "challenge" and "insult" look like "thick" ethical terms, where the evaluative and descriptive are commingled (see Williams 1985, 128–30); therefore, it is very difficult to say what the extent of the factual disagreement is. But this is of little help for the expedient under consideration, since the disagreement-in-non-moral-fact response apparently *requires* that one *can* disentangle factual and moral disagreement.

It is of course possible that full and vivid awareness of the non-moral facts might motivate the sort of change in southern attitudes envisaged by the (at least the northern) moral realist; were southerners to become vividly aware that their culture of honor was implicated in violence, they might be moved to change their moral outlook. (We take this way of putting the example to be the most natural one, but nothing philosophical turns on it. If you like, substitute the possibility of bloody-minded northerners endorsing

---

26. The legal scholarship that Nisbett and Cohen (1996, 57–78) review makes it clear that southern legislatures are often willing to enact laws reflecting the culture of honor view of the circumstances under which violence is justified, which suggests there is at least some support among southerners for the idea that honor values should be universalizable.

honor values after exposure to the facts.) On the other hand, southerners might insist that the values of honor should be nurtured even at the cost of promoting violence; the motto "Death before dishonor," after all, has a long and honorable history. The burden of argument, we think, lies with the realist who asserts—culture and history notwith-standing—that southerners would change their mind if vividly aware of the pertinent facts.

Freedom from abnormality. Realists may contend that much moral disagreement may result from failures of rationality on the part of discussants (Brink 1989, 199–200). Obvi-ously, disagreement stemming from cognitive impairments is no embarrassment for moral realism; at the limit, that a disagreement persists when some or all disputing parties are quite insane shows nothing deep about morality. But it doesn't seem plausible that southerners' more lenient attitudes towards certain forms of violence are readily attrib-uted to widespread cognitive disability. Of course, this is an empirical issue, and we don't know of any evidence suggesting that southerners suffer some cognitive impairment that prevents them from understanding demographic and attitudinal factors in the genesis of violence, or any other matter of fact. What is needed to press home a charge of irratio-nality is evidence of cognitive impairment independent of the attitudinal differences, and further evidence that this impairment is implicated in adherence to the disputed values in the face of the (putatively) undisputed non-moral facts. In this instance, as in many others, we have difficulty seeing how charges of abnormality or irrationality can be made without one side begging the question against the other.

We are inclined to think that Nisbett and colleagues' work represents a potent coun-ter-example to any theory maintaining that rational argument tends to convergence on important moral issues; the evidence suggests that the North-South differences in atti-tudes towards violence and honor might well persist even under the sort of ideal condi-tions we have considered. Admittedly, our conclusions must be tentative. On the philosophical side, we have not considered every plausible strategy for "explaining away" moral disagreement and grounding expectations of convergence.[27] On the empirical side, we have reported on but a few studies, and those we do consider here, like any em-pirical work, might be criticized on either conceptual or methodological grounds.[28] Finally, we should make clear what we are *not* claiming: we do not take our conclusions here—even if fairly earned—to be a "refutation" of moral realism, in as much as there may be versions of moral realism that do not require convergence. Rather, we hope to have given an idea of the empirical work philosophers must encounter if they are to make defensible conjectures regarding moral disagreement. Our theme recurs: Responsible

---

27. In addition to the expedients we have considered, realists may plausibly appeal to, *inter alia*, requirements for internal coherence and the different "levels" of moral thought (theoretical versus popular, abstract versus concrete, general versus particular) at which moral disagreement may or may not be manifested. Brink (1989, 197–210) and Loeb (1998) offer valuable discussions with considerably more detail than we offer here, Brink manifesting realist sympathies and Loeb tending towards anti-realism.

28. We think Nisbett and Cohen will fare pretty well under such scrutiny. See Tetlock's (1999) favorable review.

treatment of the empirical issues requires reference to empirical science, whatever the science is ultimately taken to show.

5. Thought Experiments

Ethical reflection is often held to involve comparing general principles and responses to particular cases; commitment to a principle may compel the renunciation of a particular response, or commitment to a particular response may compel modification or renunciation of a general principle (Brandt 1959, 244–52; Rawls 1971, 20–21, 49). This emphasis on particular cases is not peculiar to ethics: "intuition pumps" or "thought experiments" have long been central elements of philosophical method (Dennett 1984, 17–18). In the instances we consider here, a thought experiment presents an example, typically a hypothetical example, in order to elicit some philosophically telling response; if a thought experiment is successful, it may be concluded that competing theories must account for the resulting response.[29] To extend the imagery of experimentation, responses to thought experiments are supposed to serve an evidential role in philosophical theory choice; the responses are data competing theories must accommodate.[30]

In ethics, one—we do not say the only—familiar rendering of the methodology is this: if an audience's ethical responses to a thought experiment can be expected to conflict with the response a theory prescribes for the case, the theory has suffered a counter-example. For instance, it is often claimed that utilitarian prescriptions for particular cases will conflict with the ethical responses many people have to those cases (e.g., Williams 1973, 99). The ethics literature is rife with claims to the effect that "many of us" or "we" would respond in a specified way to a given example, and such claims are often supposed to have philosophical teeth.[31] But who is this "we"? And how do philosophers know what this "we" thinks?

Initially, it doesn't look like "we" should be interpreted as "we philosophers." The difficulty is not that this approach threatens a sampling error, although it is certainly true that philosophers form a small and peculiar group. Rather, the problem is that philosophers can be expected to respond to thought experiments in ways that reflect their theoretical

---

29. There are substantive questions as to what sorts of responses to thought experiments may properly constrain philosophical theory choice. For example, what level of reflection or cognitive elaboration is required: are the responses of interest "pre-theoretical intuitions" or "considered judgments"? We will have something to say about this, but in terminology we will mostly favor the generic "responses," which we mean to be neutral regarding issues such as cognitive elaboration.

30. This analogy with science is not unique to our exposition. Singer (1974, 517; cf. 493) understands Rawls's (1971) method of reflective equilibrium as "leading us to think of our particular moral judgments as data against which moral theories are to be tested." As Singer (1974, 493 ff.) notes, in earlier treatments Rawls (1951) made the analogy with scientific theory choice explicit. We needn't hazard an interpretation of Rawls, but only observe that our analogy is not philosophically eccentric.

31. For appeals of this kind, see Blum 1994, 179; G. Strawson 1986, 87–89; P. Strawson 1982, 68; Wallace 1994, 81–82; Williams 1973, 99–100; 1981, 22.

predilections: utilitarians' responses to a thought experiment might be expected to plump for maximizing welfare, integrity and loyalty be damned, while the responses of Aristotelians and Kantians might plump in the opposite direction. If so, the thought experiment can hardly be expected to *resolve* the debate, since philosophers' responses to the example are likely to *reflect* their position in the debate.

The audience of appeal often seems to be some variant of "ordinary folk" (see Jackson 1998, 118, 129; Jackson and Pettit 1995, 22–29; Lewis 1989, 126–29). Of course, the relevant folk must possess such cognitive attainments as are required to understand the case at issue; very young children are probably not an ideal audience for thought experiments. Some philosophers may want to insist that the relevant responses are the "considered judgments" or "reflective intuitions" of people with the training required to see "what is philosophically at stake." But there is peril in insisting that the relevant cognitive attainments be some sort of "philosophical sophistication." Once again, if the responses are to help adjudicate between competing theories, the responders must be more or less theoretically neutral, but this sort of neutrality, we suspect, is rather likely to be vitiated by philosophical education. (Incredibly enough, informal surveys suggest that *our* students are overwhelmingly ethical naturalists!)

However exactly the philosophically relevant audience is specified, there are empirical questions that must be addressed in determining the philosophical potency of a thought experiment. In science, not all experiments produce data of evidentiary value; sampling errors and the failure of experimental designs to effectively isolate variables are two familiar ways in which experiments go wrong. Data resulting from such experiments are tainted, or without evidential value; analogously, in evaluating responses to a thought experiment, one needs to consider the possibility of taint. In particular, when deciding what philosophical weight to give a response to a thought experiment, philosophers need to determine the origins of the response. What features of the example are implicated in a response—are people responding to the substance of the case, or the style of exposition? What features of the audience are implicated in a response—do different demographic groups respond to an example differently? Such questions raise the following concern: ethical responses to thought experiments may be strongly influenced by ethically irrelevant characteristics of example and audience. Whether a characteristic is ethically relevant is a matter for philosophical discussion, but determining the status of a particular thought experiment also requires empirical investigation of its causally relevant characteristics; responsible philosophical discussion cannot rely on guesswork in this regard. We shall now give two examples illustrating our concerns about tainted origins, one corresponding to each of the two questions just asked.

Tversky and Kahneman presented subjects with the following problem:

Imagine that the U.S. is preparing for the outbreak of an unusual Asian disease, which is expected to kill 600 people. Two alternative programs to combat the disease have been proposed. Assume that the exact scientific estimate of the consequences of the programs are as follows:

If Program A is adopted, 200 people will be saved.

If Program B is adopted, there is a 1/3 probability that 600 people will be saved, and a 2/3 probability that no people will be saved.

A second group of subjects was given an identical problem, except that the programs were described as follows:

If Program C is adopted, 400 people will die.

If Program D is adopted, there is a 1/3 probability that nobody will die and a 2/3 probability that 600 people will die. (Tversky and Kahneman 1981, 453)

On the first version of the problem most subjects thought that Program A should be adopted. But on the second version most chose Program D, despite the fact that the outcome described in A is identical to the one described in C. The disconcerting implication of this study is that ethical responses may be strongly influenced by the manner in which cases are described or framed. Many effects of framing differences, such as that between 200 of 600 people being saved and 400 of 600 dying, we are strongly inclined to think, are ethically irrelevant influences on ethical responses (compare Horowitz 1998; Sinnott-Armstrong 2005). Unless this sort of possibility can be confidently eliminated, one should hesitate to rely on responses to a thought experiment for adjudicating theoretical controversies. Again, such possibilities can only be eliminated through systematic empirical work.[32]

Audience characteristics may also affect the outcome of thought experiments. Haidt and associates (Haidt, Koller, and Dias 1993, 613) presented stories about "harmless yet offensive violations of strong social norms" to men and women of high and low socioeconomic status (SES) in Philadelphia (USA), Porto Alegre, and Recife (both in Brazil). For example: ("A man goes to the supermarket once a week and buys a dead chicken. But before cooking the chicken, he has sexual intercourse with it. Then he cooks it and eats it") (Haidt et al. 1993, 617). Lower SES subjects tended to "moralize" harmless and offensive behaviors like that in the chicken story: these subjects were more inclined than their privileged counterparts to say that the actor should be "stopped or punished," and more inclined to deny that such behaviors would be "OK" if customary in a given country (Haidt et al. 1993, 618–19). The point is not that lower SES subjects are mistaken in their moralization of such behaviors while the urbanity of higher SES subjects represents the

---

32. Some authors—most notably Baron (1994)—have argued that the distorting influences of "heuristics and biases" like those uncovered in the recent psychological literature on reasoning, judgment, and decision-making are widespread in everyday ethical reflection. For overviews of the relevant psychological literature, see Nisbett and Ross 1980; Kahneman, Slovic, and Tversky 1982; Baron 2001.

most rationally defensible response. To recall our previous discussion of moral disagreement, the difficulty is deciding which of the conflicting responses to privilege, when both sorts of responses may be the function of more or less arbitrary cultural factors.

In presenting the Haidt group's work to philosophical audiences, our impression is that they typically decline to moralize the offensive behaviors, and we ourselves share their tolerant attitude. But of course philosophical audiences—by virtue of educational attainments if not stock portfolios—are overwhelmingly high SES. Haidt's work suggests that it is a mistake for a philosopher to say, as Jackson (1998, 32 ff.; cf. 37) does, that "my intuitions reveal the folk conception in as much as I am reasonably entitled, as I usually am, to regard myself as typical." The question is: Typical of what demographic? Are philosophers' ethical responses to thought experiments determined by the philosophical substance of the examples, or by cultural idiosyncrasies that are very plausibly thought to be ethically irrelevant? Once again, until such possibilities are ruled out by systematic empirical investigation, the philosophical heft of a thought experiment is open to question.[33]

The studies just described raise provocative questions about *how* responses to thought experiments are generated, but there may be equally provocative questions about *what* responses people actually have. And, to sound our now familiar theme, this question is one not credibly answered by guesswork. Indeed, we suspect that philosophical speculations about what responses to thought experiments are conventional may be wrong surprisingly often. We'll now report on one study conducive to such suspicions.

One of the most famous of philosophical conundrums, that of determinism and responsibility, can be derived—on one way of formulating the difficulty—from the juxtaposition of three claims that are individually quite plausible, but seem impossible to hold jointly:

(MRT) *Moral responsibility thesis*:	Human beings are sometimes morally responsible for their behavior.
(CT) *Causal thesis*:	All human behavior is linked to antecedent events by deterministic causal laws. (See Scanlon 1988, 152.)
(PAP) *Principle of alternate possibilities*:	A "person is morally responsible for what he has done only if he could have done otherwise." (See Frankfurt 1988, 1.)

---

33. We applaud Jackson's (1998, 36–37) advocacy of "doing serious public opinion polls on people's responses to various cases." However, we expect this may be necessary more often than Jackson imagines. According to Jackson (1998, 37), "Everyone who presents the Gettier cases [which are well-known epistemology thought experiments] to a class of students is doing their own bit of fieldwork, and we all know the answer they get in the vast majority of cases." Yet Weinberg et al. (Weinberg, Nichols, and Stich 2002) found that responses to epistemology thought experiments like the Gettier cases varied with culture and SES; this suggests that philosophers need to be more systematic in their fieldwork.

Here's one way of putting it: If CT is true, it looks as though it is never the case that people could have done otherwise, but then, given PAP, MRT must be false.[34] There are three standard responses to this trilemma. Two sorts of incompatibilists hold that MRT and CT cannot be held simultaneously: hard determinists (see Smart 1961, 303–6) reject MRT,[35] while libertarians (e.g., Kane 1996) insist that CT admits of exceptions in the case of human behavior, and are thus able to maintain MRT. Compatibilists, on the other hand, assert that MRT and CT can be simultaneously maintained; one well-known expedient is to reject PAP, and insist that people may be legitimately held responsible even when they could not have done otherwise (see Frankfurt 1988, 1–12).

The literature is voluminous, and the proffered solutions range from controversial to deeply unsatisfying; indeed, there is heated disagreement as to what exactly the problem is (Dennett 1984, 1–19). Discretion being the best part of valor, we won't review the arguments here. Given our present concerns, we instead consider objections to the effect that compatibilism is in some sense badly counter-intuitive. One way of forming this complaint is to say that people's "reactive attitudes"—ethical responses like anger, resentment, guilt, approbation, admiration, and the like—manifest a commitment to incompatibilism.[36] Here is Galen Strawson (1986, 88) on what he calls the "incompatibilist intuition":

> The fact that the incompatibilist intuition has such power for us is as much a natural fact about cogitative beings like ourselves as is the fact of our quite unreflective commitment to the reactive attitudes. What is more, the roots of the incompatibilist intuition lie deep in the ... reactive attitudes. ... The reactive attitudes enshrine the incompatibilist intuition.[37]

Let's do a little unpacking. On Strawson's (1986, 31; cf. 2, 84–88) rendering, incompatibilism is the view that the falsity of determinism is a necessary condition for moral responsibility. To suggest that the "incompatibilist intuition" is widespread, then, may be thought to imply that people's (possibly tacit) body of moral beliefs includes commitment to the

---

34. Our formulation is meant to be quite standard. Kane (2002a, 10) observes that statements of the difficulty in terms of alternative possibilities have dominated modern discussion. A recently prominent formulation proceeds not in terms of PAP, but by way of an "ultimacy condition," which holds that an actor is responsible for her behavior only if she is its "ultimate source" (see McKenna 2001, esp. 40–41). This does not impact the present discussion, however. First, notice that although some may maintain an ultimacy requirement and reject PAP, the two commitments need not be incompatible; Kane (1996, 2002b) holds them both. Secondly, as should become clear, the empirical work we describe below is relevant to both formulations.

35. As Kane (2002a, 27–32) observes, relatively few philosophers have been unqualifiedly committed to hard determinism; Smart's (1961) views on responsibility, for example, are complex.

36. Peter Strawson (1982) did the pioneering philosophical work on the reactive attitudes; he appears to reject the suggestion that such attitudes manifest a commitment to something in the spirit of incompatibilism.

37. G. Strawson puts the point rather emphatically, but similar observations are commonplace. Cf. Nagel 1986, 113, 125; Kane 1996, 83–85.

claim that CT is incompatible with MRT.[38] This is an empirical claim. Moreover, it is an empirical claim that looks to entail predictions about people's moral responses. What are the responses in question?

Like many other philosophers making empirical claims about human cognition and behavior, Strawson says relatively little about what predictions he thinks his claims entail. We won't put predictions in Strawson's mouth; instead, we'll consider one prediction that looks to follow from positing an incompatibilist intuition, at least on the familiar rendering of incompatibilism we've followed. Attributing a widespread commitment to an incompatibilist intuition is plausibly thought to involve the following prediction: for cases where the actor is judged unable to have done otherwise, people will not hold the actor responsible for what she has done.[39] In as much as this prediction is a good one, people should respond to thought experiments depicting an actor unable to do otherwise by abjuring attributions of responsibility and the associated reactive attitudes.

In a compatibilist spirit inspired by the work of Harry Frankfurt (1988), Woolfolk, Doris, and Darley (2006) hypothesized that observers may hold actors responsible even when the observers judge that the actors could not have done otherwise, at least in cases where the actors appear to manifest "identification." Very roughly, the idea is that the actor is identified with a behavior—and is therefore responsible for it—to the extent she "embraces" the behavior (or its motive), or performs it "wholeheartedly."[40] Woolfolk et al.'s suspicion was, in effect, that people's (possibly tacit) theory of responsibility is, contra Galen Strawson and others, compatibilist.

In one of the Woolfolk et al. studies, subjects read a story about two married couples vacationing together. According to the story, one of the vacationers has discovered that his wife is having an affair with his opposite number in the foursome; on the flight home, the vacationers' plane is hijacked, and armed hijackers order the cuckold to shoot the man who has been having an affair with his wife. In a "low identification" variation, the story contained the following material:

> Bill was horrified. At that moment Bill was certain about his feelings. He did *not* want to kill Frank, even though Frank was his wife's lover. But although he was appalled by the situation and beside himself with distress, he reluctantly placed the pistol at Frank's temple and proceeded to blow his friend's brains out.

---

38. There is again a question about the scope of "people"; Strawson's reference to "natural facts" may suggest that he is making a boldly pancultural attribution, but he might be more modestly attributing the theory only to those people who embody something like the "Western ethical tradition." We will not attempt to decide the interpretative question, because the empirical work we describe troubles even the more modest claim.

39. G. Strawson (1986, 25–31; 2002) may favor formulations in terms of ultimacy rather than PAP (see n. 33 above). This doesn't affect our argument, since the empirical work we recount below looks to trouble a prediction formulated in terms of ultimacy as well as the alternative possibilities formulation we favor.

40. For some discussion, see Velleman 1992; Bratman 1996; Watson 1996; Doris 2002, 140–46.

Conversely, in a "high identification" variation, the embittered cuckold embraces his opportunity:

> Despite the desperate circumstances, Bill understood the situation. He had been presented with the opportunity to kill his wife's lover and get away with it. And at that moment Bill was certain about his feelings. He wanted to kill Frank. Feeling no reluctance, he placed the pistol at Frank's temple and proceeded to blow his friend's brains out.

Consistent with Woolfolk and colleagues' hypothesis, the high-identification actor was judged more responsible, more appropriately blamed, and more properly subject to guilt than the low-identification actor.[41]

It is tempting to conclude that at least for the Woolfolk group's subjects (philosophy and psychology undergraduates at the University of California and Rutgers University), the incompatibilist intuition does not appear to be deeply entrenched. But at this point the incompatibilist will be quick to object: the above study may suggest that responsibility attributions are influenced by identification, but it says nothing about commitment to the incompatibilist intuition, because subjects may not have believed that the actor could not have done otherwise, and subjects therefore cannot be interpreted as attributing responsibility in violation of PAP. People may think that even when coerced, actors "always have a choice"; in the classic "your money or your life" scenario, the person faced with this unpleasant dilemma can always opt for her life. (We hasten to remind anyone tempted in such a bull-headed direction that the disjunct need not be exclusive!)

To address this objection, Woolfolk et al. attempted to elevate perceived constraint to the "could not have done otherwise" threshold:

> The leader of the kidnappers injected Bill's arm with a "compliance drug"—a designer drug similar to sodium pentothal, "truth serum." This drug makes individuals unable to resist the demands of powerful authorities. Its effects are similar to the impact of expertly administered hypnosis; it results in total compliance. To test the effects of the drug, the leader of the kidnappers shouted at Bill to slap himself. To his amazement, Bill observed his own right hand administering an open-handed blow to his own left cheek, although he had no sense of having willed his hand to move. The leader then handed Bill a pistol with one bullet in it. Bill was ordered to shoot Frank in the head. . . . when Bill's hand and arm moved again, placing the pistol at his friend's temple, Bill had no feeling that he had moved his arm to point the gun; it felt as though the gun had moved itself into position. Bill thought he noticed his finger moving on the trigger, but could

---

41. Woolfolk et al. (2006) obtained similar results for the prosocial behavior of kidney donation: an identified actor was credited for making a donation even when heavily constrained.

not feel any sensations of movement. While he was observing these events, feeling like a puppet, passively observing his body moving in space, his hand closed on the pistol, discharging it and blowing Frank's brains out.

Strikingly, subjects appeared willing to attribute responsibility to the shooter even here: once again, a high-identification actor was judged more responsible, more appropriately blamed, and more properly subject to guilt than a low-identification actor. No doubt this is not the most "naturalistic" scenario, but neither is it outlandish by philosophical standards. And it certainly looks to be a case where the actor would be perceived to fail the standard for responsibility set by PAP.[42] Indeed, Woolfolk et al. found that subjects were markedly less likely to agree to statements asserting that the actor "was free to behave other than he did," and "could have behaved differently than he did," than they were in the case of simple coercion described above. These results look to caution against positing a widespread commitment to the incompatibilist intuition. Deciding empirical issues concerning habits of responsibility attribution will not, of course, decide the philosophical dispute between compatibilists and incompatibilists. Yet in so far as the incompatibilist is making claims to the effect that compatibilists cannot accommodate entrenched habits of moral response, the empirical evidence is entirely relevant.

Once more, some philosophers may insist that the responses of interest are not the relatively unschooled or intuitive responses of experimental subjects like the Woolfolk group's undergraduates, but the tutored judgments of philosophers. We've already given some reasons for regarding this strategy with suspicion, but it seems to us especially problematic for the particular case of responsibility. Philosophical arguments about responsibility, it seems to us, often lean heavily on speculation about everyday practice. For example, Peter Strawson's (1982, 64, 68) extremely influential exposition repeatedly stresses the importance of reactive attitudes in "ordinary inter-personal relationships." While it may not be too much of a stretch to imagine that philosophers sometimes indulge in such relationships, it *is* a stretch to suppose that they are the only folk who do so. It is very plausible to argue—as indeed those who have deployed something like the incompatibilist intuition have done—that the contours of the everyday practice of responsibility attribution serve as a (defeasible) constraint on philosophical theories of responsibility: if the theory cannot accommodate the practice, it owes, at a bare minimum, a debunking account of the practice. One might insist that philosophical theorizing about responsibility is not accountable to ordinary practice, but this is to make a substantial break with important elements of the tradition.

There are a couple of ways in which philosophers can avoid the sorts of empirical difficulties we have been considering. First, they can deny that responses to particular cases have evidential weight in ethical theory choice, as some utilitarians—unsurprisingly,

---

42. It also looks as though the actor fails an ultimacy condition (see nn. 34 and 39 above).

given the rather startling implications of their position—have been inclined to do (e.g., Kagan 1989, 10–15; Singer 2000, xviii). Alternatively, they can appeal to the results of thought experiments in an expository rather than an evidential role; for example, a thought experiment might be used by an author to elucidate her line of reasoning without appealing to the responses of an imagined audience like "many of us." To some philosophers, such solutions will seem rather methodologically draconian, threatening to isolate ethical theory from the experience of ethical life (see Williams 1985, 93–119, esp. 116–19). But our point here is less grand: many users of thought experiments in ethics apparently have been—and we strongly suspect will continue to be—in the business of forwarding an imagined consensus on their thought experiments as evidence in theory choice. For these philosophers we offer the following methodological prescription: a credible philosophical methodology of thought experiments must be supplemented by a cognitive science of *thought* experiments that involves systematic investigation with *actual* experiments. There are just too many unanswered questions regarding the responses people have, and the processes by which they come to have them. We've no stake in any particular answers to such questions. What we do have a stake in, as we have throughout, is the observation that responsible answers to such questions will be informed by systematic empirical investigation.

6. Conclusion

We needn't linger on goodbyes; the main contours of our exposition should by now be tolerably clear. We have surveyed four central topics in ethical theory where empirical claims are prominent: character, moral motivation, moral disagreement, and thought experiments. We have argued that consideration of work in the biological, behavioral, and social sciences promises substantive philosophical contributions to controversy surrounding such topics as virtue ethics, internalism, moral realism, and moral responsibility. If our arguments are successful, we have also erected a general methodological standard: philosophical ethics can, and indeed must, interface with the human sciences.[43]

REFERENCES

Annas, J. 1993. *The Morality of Happiness*. New York: Oxford University Press.
Anscombe, G. E. M. 1958. Modern Moral Philosophy. *Philosophy* 33: 1–19.

---

43. For much valuable feedback, we are grateful to audiences at the Moral Psychology Symposium at the 2001 Society for Philosophy and Psychology meetings, the Empirical Perspectives on Ethics Symposium at the 2001 American Philosophical Association Pacific Division meetings, and a series of lectures on philosophy and cognitive science held at the Australian National University in July 2002—especially Louise Antony, Daniel Cohen, Frank Jackson, Michael Smith, and Valerie Tiberius. Thanks to Daniel Guevara, Jerry Neu, Alva Noë, and especially Don Loeb, Shaun Nichols, and Adina Roskies for comments on earlier drafts.

Aristotle. 1984. *The Complete Works of Aristotle*. Ed. J. Barnes. Princeton: Princeton University Press.

Athanassoulis, N. 2000. A Response to Harman: Virtue Ethics and Character Traits. *Proceedings of the Aristotelian Society* 100: 215–22.

Audi, R. 1995. Acting from Virtue. *Mind* 104: 449–71.

Baron, J. 1994. Nonconsequentialist Decisions. *Behavioral and Brain Sciences* 17: 1–42.

——. 2001. *Thinking and Deciding*. 3rd ed. Cambridge: Cambridge University Press.

Bechara, A., H. Damasio, and A. R. Damasio. 2000. Emotion, Decision Making and the Orbito-frontal Cortex. *Cerebral Cortex* 10: 295–307.

Becker, L. C. 1998. *A New Stoicism*. Princeton: Princeton University Press.

Bennett, W. J. 1993. *The Book of Virtues: A Treasury of Great Moral Stories*. New York: Simon and Schuster.

Blackburn, S. 1998. *Ruling Passions: A Theory of Practical Reasoning*. Oxford: Oxford University Press.

Blair, R. J. 1995. A Cognitive Developmental Approach to Morality: Investigating the Psychopath. *Cognition* 57: 1–29.

Blair, R. J., L. Jones, F. Clark, and M. Smith. 1997. The Psychopathic Individual: A Lack of Responsiveness to Distress Cues? *Psychophysiology* 34: 192–98.

Blum, L. A. 1994. *Moral Perception and Particularity*. Cambridge: Cambridge University Press.

Bok, H. 1996. Acting Without Choosing. *Noûs* 30: 174–96.

Boyd, R. N. 1988. How to Be a Moral Realist. In C. Sayre-McCord, ed., *Essays on Moral Realism*. Ithaca, NY: Cornell University Press.

Brandt, R. B. 1954. *Hopi Ethics: A Theoretical Analysis*. Chicago: University of Chicago Press.

——. 1959. *Ethical Theory: The Problems of Normative and Critical Ethics*. Englewood Cliffs, NJ: Prentice-Hall.

——. 1970. Traits of Character: A Conceptual Analysis. *American Philosophical Quarterly* 7: 23–37.

Bratman, M. E. 1996. Identification, Decision, and Treating as a Reason. *Philosophical Topics* 24: 1–18.

Brink, D. O. 1989. *Moral Realism and the Foundations of Ethics*. Cambridge: Cambridge University Press.

Campbell, J. 1999. Can Philosophical Accounts of Altruism Accommodate Experimental Data on Helping Behaviour? *Australasian Journal of Philosophy* 77: 26–45.

Cooper, J. M. 1999. *Reason and Emotion: Essays on Ancient Moral Psychology and Ethical Theory*. Princeton: Princeton University Press.

Damasio, A. R., D. Tranel, and H. Damasio. 1990. Individuals with Sociopathic Behavior Caused by Frontal Damage Fail to Respond Autonomically to Social Stimuli. *Behavioral Brain Research* 41: 81–94.

Daniels, N. 1979. Wide Reflective Equilibrium and Theory Acceptance in Ethics. *Journal of Philosophy* 76: 256–84.

Darley, J. M., and C. D. Batson. 1973. From Jerusalem to Jericho: A Study of Situational and Dispositional Variables in Helping Behavior. *Journal of Personality and Social Psychology* 27: 100–108.

D'Arms, J., and D. Jacobson. 2000. Sentiment and Value. *Ethics* 110: 722–48.

Darwall, S. L. 1983. *Impartial Reason*. Ithaca, NY: Cornell University Press.

———. 1989. Moore to Stevenson. In Robert Cavalier, James Gouinlock, and James Sterba, eds., *Ethics in the History of Philosophy*. London: Macmillan.

Darwall, S. L., A. Gibbard, and P. Railton, eds. 1997. *Moral Discourse and Practice: Some Philosophical Approaches*. New York: Oxford University Press.

Deigh, J. 1999. Ethics. In R. Audi, ed., *The Cambridge Dictionary of Philosophy*. Cambridge: Cambridge University Press.

Dennett, D. C. 1984. *Elbow Room: The Varieties of Free Will Worth Wanting*. Cambridge, MA: MIT Press.

Dent, N. J. H. 1975. Virtues and Actions. *Philosophical Quarterly* 25: 318–35.

DePaul, M. 1999. Character Traits, Virtues, and Vices: Are There None? In *Proceedings of the 20th World Congress of Philosophy*, i. Bowling Green, OH: Philosophy Documentation Center.

Doris, J. M. 1996. People Like Us: Morality, Psychology, and the Fragmentation of Character. Ph.D. diss., University of Michigan, Ann Arbor.

———. 1998. Persons, Situations, and Virtue Ethics. *Noûs* 32: 504–30.

———. 2002. *Lack of Character: Personality and Moral Behavior*. New York: Cambridge University Press.

Doris, J. M., and S. P. Stich. 2001. Ethics. In L. Nadel, gen. ed., D. Chalmers, philosophy ed., *The Encyclopedia of Cognitive Science*. London: Macmillan Reference.

Ellsworth, P. C. 1994. Sense, Culture, and Sensibility. In H. Markus and S. Kitayama, eds., *Emotion and Culture: Empirical Studies in Mutual Influence*. Washington, DC: American Psychological Association.

Firth, R. 1952. Ethical Absolutism and the Ideal Observer Theory. *Philosophy and Phenomenological Research* 12: 317–45.

Flanagan, O. 1991. *Varieties of Moral Personality: Ethics and Psychological Realism*. Cambridge, MA: Harvard University Press.

Fodor, J. 1998. *Concepts: Where Cognitive Science Went Wrong*. Oxford: Oxford University Press.

Frankena, W. K. 1976. Obligation and Motivation in Recent Moral Philosophy. In K. E. Goodpaster, ed., *Perspectives on Morality: Essays of William K. Frankena*. Notre Dame, IN: University of Notre Dame Press.

Frankfurt, H. 1988. *The Importance of What We Care About: Philosophical Essays*. Cambridge: Cambridge University Press.

Gibbard, A. 1990. *Wise Choices, Apt Feelings: A Theory of Normative Judgment*. Cambridge, MA: Harvard University Press.

Gilbert, D. T., and P. S. Malone. 1995. The Correspondence Bias. *Psychological Bulletin* 117: 21–38.

Goldman, A. I. 1993. Ethics and Cognitive Science. *Ethics* 103: 337–60.

Haidt, J., S. Koller, and M. Dias. 1993. Affect, Culture, and Morality; or, Is It Wrong to Eat Your Dog? *Journal of Personality and Social Psychology* 65: 613–28.

Haney, C., W. Banks, and P. Zimbardo. 1973. Interpersonal Dynamics of a Simulated Prison. *International Journal of Criminology and Penology* 1: 69–97.

Hare, R. D. 1993. *Without Conscience: The Disturbing World of the Psychopaths Among Us*. New York: Pocket Books.

Hare, R. M. 1952. *The Language of Morals*. Oxford: Oxford University Press.

Harman, G. 1977. *The Nature of Morality*. New York: Oxford University Press.

———. 1999. Moral Philosophy Meets Social Psychology: Virtue Ethics and the Fundamental Attribution Error. *Proceedings of the Aristotelian Society* 99: 315–31.

———. 2000. The Nonexistence of Character Traits. *Proceedings of the Aristotelian Society* 100: 223–26.

Hart, D., and M. Killen. 1999. Introduction: Perspectives on Morality in Everyday Life. In M. Killen and D. Hart, eds., *Morality in Everyday Life: Developmental Perspectives.* Cambridge: Cambridge University Press.

Hill, T. E. 1991. *Autonomy and Self-Respect.* Cambridge: Cambridge University Press.

Horowitz, T. 1998. Philosophical Intuitions and Psychological Theory. In M. DePaul and W. Ramsey, eds., *Rethinking Intuition: The Psychology of Intuition and Its Role in Philosophical Inquiry.* Lanham, MD: Rowman and Littlefield.

Hume, D. 1975. *Enquiries Concerning Human Understanding and Concerning the Principles of Morals.* 3rd ed. Oxford: Oxford University Press.

———. 1978. *A Treatise of Human Nature.* 2nd ed. Oxford: Oxford University Press.

Hursthouse, R. 1999. *On Virtue Ethics.* Oxford: Oxford University Press.

Hutcheson, F. 1738. *An Enquiry into the Original of Our Ideas of Beauty and Virtue, in Two Treatises.* London: D. Midwinter.

Irwin, T. H. 1988. Disunity in the Aristotelian Virtues. *Oxford Studies in Ancient Philosophy,* supp., 61–78.

Isen, A. M., and P. F. Levin. 1972. Effect of Feeling Good on Helping: Cookies and Kindness. *Journal of Personality and Social Psychology* 21: 384–88.

Jackson, F. 1994. Armchair Metaphysics. In J. O'Leary Hawthorne and M. Michael, eds., *Philosophy in Mind.* Dordrecht: Kluwer.

———. 1998. *From Metaphysics to Ethics: A Defense of Conceptual Analysis.* New York: Oxford University Press.

Jackson, F., and P. Pettit. 1995. Moral Functionalism and Moral Motivation. *Philosophical Quarterly* 45: 20–40.

Johnson, M. 1993. *Moral Imagination: Implications of Cognitive Science for Ethics.* Chicago: University of Chicago Press.

Jones, E. E. 1990. *Interpersonal Perception.* New York: W. H. Freeman.

Kagan, S. 1989. *The Limits of Morality.* Oxford: Oxford University Press.

Kahneman, D., P. Slovic, and A. Tversky. 1982. *Judgment Under Uncertainty: Heuristics and Biases.* Cambridge: Cambridge University Press.

Kane, R. 1996. *The Significance of Free Will.* Oxford: Oxford University Press.

———. 2002a. Introduction: The Contours of Contemporary Free Will Debates. In R. Kane, ed., *The Oxford Handbook of Free Will.* New York: Oxford University Press.

———. 2002b. Some Neglected Pathways in the Free Will Labyrinth. In R. Kane, ed., *The Oxford Handbook of Free Will.* New York: Oxford University Press.

Keneally, T. 1982. *Schindler's List.* New York: Simon and Schuster.

Kim, J. 1988. What Is "Naturalized Epistemology"? In J. Tomberlin, ed., *Philosophical Perspectives,* vol. 2: *Epistemology.* Atascadero, CA: Ridgeway.

Kitayama, S., and H. R. Markus. 1999. Yin and Yang of the Japanese Self: The Cultural Psychology of Personality Coherence. In D. Cervone and Y. Shoda, eds., *The Coherence of Personality: Social-Cognitive Bases of Consistency, Variability, and Organization.* New York: Guilford Press.

Kupperman, J. J. 2001. The Indispensability of Character. *Philosophy* 76: 239–50.

Larmore, C. E. 1987. *Patterns of Moral Complexity.* Cambridge: Cambridge University Press.

Leming, J. S. 1997a. Research and Practice in Character Education: A Historical Perspective. In A. Molnar, ed., *The Construction of Children's Character: Ninety-Sixth Yearbook of the National Society for the Study of Education*, 11. Chicago: University of Chicago Press.

———. 1997b. Whither Goes Character Education? Objectives, Pedagogy, and Research in Character Education Programs. *Journal of Education* 179: 11–34.

Lewis, D. 1970. How to Define Theoretical Terms. *Journal of Philosophy* 67: 427–46.

———. 1972. Psychophysical and Theoretical Identifications. *Australasian Journal of Philosophy* 50: 249–58.

———. 1989. Dispositional Theories of Value. *Proceedings of the Aristotelian Society*, supp., 63: 113–37.

Loeb, D. 1998. Moral Realism and the Argument from Disagreement. *Philosophical Studies* 90: 281–303.

Louden, R. B. 1984. On Some Vices of Virtue Ethics. *American Philosophical Quarterly* 21: 227–36.

MacIntyre, A. 1984. *After Virtue*. 2nd ed. Notre Dame, IN: University of Notre Dame Press.

Mackie, J. L. 1977. *Ethics: Inventing Right and Wrong*. New York: Penguin.

Margolis, E., and S. Laurence. 1999. *Concepts*. Cambridge, MA: MIT Press.

Markus, H. R., and S. Kitayama. 1991. Culture and the Self: Implications for Cognition, Emotion, and Motivation. *Psychological Review* 98: 224–53.

Mathews, K. E., and Cannon, L. K. 1975. Environmental Noise Level as a Determinant of Helping Behavior. *Journal of Personality and Social Psychology* 32: 571–77.

McDowell, J. 1978. Are Moral Requirements Hypothetical Imperatives? *Proceedings of the Aristotelian Society*, supp., 52: 13–29.

———. 1979. Virtue and Reason. *Monist* 62: 331–50.

———. 1987. *Projection and Truth in Ethics (Lindley Lecture)*. Lawrence: University of Kansas.

McKenna, M. 2001. Source Incompatibilism, Ultimacy, and the Transfer of Non-Responsibility. *American Philosophical Quarterly* 38: 37–51.

Merritt, M. 1999. Virtue Ethics and the Social Psychology of Character. Ph.D. diss., University of California, Berkeley.

———. 2000. Virtue Ethics and Situationist Personality Psychology. *Ethical Theory and Moral Practice* 3: 365–83.

Milgram, S. 1974. *Obedience to Authority*. New York: Harper and Row.

Mischel, W. 1968. *Personality and Assessment*. New York: Wiley.

Moore, G. E. 1903. *Principia Ethica*. Cambridge: Cambridge University Press.

Nagel, T. 1986. *The View from Nowhere*. New York: Oxford University Press.

Nichols, S. 2002. How Psychopaths Threaten Moral Rationalism; or, Is it Irrational to Be Amoral? *Monist* 85: 285–304.

———. 2004. *Sentimental Rules: On the Natural Foundations of Moral Judgment*. Oxford: Oxford University Press.

Nisbett, R. E. 1998. Essence and Accident. In J. M. Darley and J. Cooper, eds., *Attribution and Social Interaction: The Legacy of Edward E. Jones*. Washington, DC: American Psychological Association.

Nisbett, R. E., and D. Cohen. 1996. *Culture of Honor: The Psychology of Violence in the South*. Boulder, CO: Westview Press.

Nisbett, R. E., and L. Ross. 1980. *Human Inference: Strategies and Shortcomings of Social Judgment*. Englewood Cliffs, NJ: Prentice-Hall.

Nucci, L. 1986. Children's Conceptions of Morality, Social Conventions and Religious Prescription. In C. Harding, ed., *Moral Dilemmas: Philosophical and Psychological Reconsiderations of the Development of Moral Reasoning*. Chicago: Precedent Press.

Nussbaum, M. C. 1999. Virtue Ethics: A Misleading Category? *Journal of Ethics* 3: 163–201.

Peterson, D. R. 1968. *The Clinical Study of Social Behavior*. New York: Appleton-Century-Crofts.

Quine, W. V. O. 1969. Epistemology Naturalized. In *Quine, Ontological Relativity and Other Essays*. New York: Columbia University Press.

Railton, P. 1986a. Facts and Values. *Philosophical Topics* 14: 5–31.

———. 1986b. Moral Realism. *Philosophical Review* 95: 163–207.

———. 1989. Naturalism and Prescriptivity. *Social Philosophy and Policy* 7: 151–74.

———. 1995. Made in the Shade: Moral Compatibilism and the Aims of Moral Theory. *Canadian Journal of Philosophy*, supp., 21: 79–106.

Rawls, J. 1951. Outline of a Decision Procedure for Ethics. *Philosophical Review* 60: 167–97.

———. 1971. *A Theory of Justice*. Cambridge, MA: Harvard University Press.

Rosati, C. S. 2000. Brandt's Notion of Therapeutic Agency. *Ethics* 110: 780–811.

Roskies, A. 2003. Are Ethical Judgments Intrinsically Motivational? Lessons from "Acquired Sociopathy." *Philosophical Psychology* 16: 51–66.

Ross, L., and R. E. Nisbett. 1991. *The Person and the Situation: Perspectives of Social Psychology*. Philadelphia: Temple University Press.

Saver, J. L., and A. R. Damasio. 1991. Preserved Access and Processing of Social Knowledge in a Patient with Acquired Sociopathy Due to Ventromedial Frontal Damage. *Neuropsychologia* 29: 1241–9.

Scanlon, T. M. 1988. The Significance of Choice. In S. M. McMurrin, ed., *The Tanner Lectures on Human Values*, viii. Salt Lake City: University of Utah Press.

Sher, G. 1998. Ethics, Character, and Action. In E. F. Paul, F. D. Miller, and J. Paul, eds., *Virtue and Vice*. Cambridge: Cambridge University Press.

Sherman, N. 1989. *The Fabric of Character: Aristotle's Theory of Virtue*. New York: Oxford University Press.

Shweder, R. A., and E. J. Bourne. 1982. Does the Concept of the Person Vary Cross-Culturally? In A. J. Marsella and G. M. White, eds., *Cultural Conceptions of Mental Health and Therapy*. Boston, MA: Reidel.

Singer, P. 1974. Sidgwick and Reflective Equilibrium. *Monist* 58: 490–517.

———. 2000. *Writings on an Ethical Life*. New York: HarperCollins.

Sinnott-Armstrong, W. P. 2005. Moral Intuitionism Meets Empirical Psychology. In T. Horgan and M. Timmons, eds., *Metaethics After Moore*. New York: Oxford University Press.

Smart, J. J. C. 1961. Free-Will, Praise and Blame. *Mind* 70: 291–306.

Smith, Adam. 2002. *The Theory of Moral Sentiments*. New York: Cambridge University Press.

Smith, M. 1994. *The Moral Problem*. Oxford: Blackwell.

Stevenson, C. L. 1944. *Ethics and Language*. New Haven: Yale University Press.

———. 1963. *Facts and Values*. New Haven: Yale University Press.

Stich, S. 1993a. Naturalizing Epistemology: Quine, Simon and the Prospects for Pragmatism. In C. Hookway and D. Peterson, eds., *Philosophy and Cognitive Science*, Royal Institute of Philosophy, suppl. 34. Cambridge: Cambridge University Press.

———. 1993b. Moral Philosophy and Mental Representation. In M. Hechter, L. Nadel, and R. E. Michod, eds., *The Origin of Values*. New York: de Gruyter.

Strawson, G. 1986. *Freedom and Belief.* Oxford: Oxford University Press.

———. 2002. The Bounds of Freedom. In R. Kane, ed., *The Oxford Handbook of Free Will.* New York: Oxford University Press.

Strawson, P. 1982. Freedom and Resentment. In G. Watson, ed., *Free Will.* New York: Oxford University Press.

Sturgeon, N. L. 1988. Moral Explanations. In G. Sayre-McCord, ed., *Essays on Moral Realism.* Ithaca, NY: Cornell University Press.

Sumner, W. G. 1934. *Folkways.* Boston: Ginn.

Svavarsdóttir, S. 1999. Moral Cognitivism and Motivation. *Philosophical Review* 108: 161–219.

Tetlock, P. E. 1999. Review of Culture of Honor: The Psychology of Violence in the South. *Political Psychology* 20: 211–13.

Turiel, E., M. Killen, and C. Helwig. 1987. Morality: Its Structure, Functions, and Vagaries. In J. Kagan and S. Lamb, eds., *The Emergence of Morality in Young Children.* Chicago: University of Chicago Press.

Tversky, A., and D. Kahneman. 1981. The Framing of Decisions and the Psychology of Choice. *Science* 211: 453–63.

Velleman, J. D. 1992. What Happens When Someone Acts? *Mind* 101: 461–81.

Vernon, P. E. 1964. *Personality Assessment: A Critical Survey.* New York: Wiley.

Wallace, R. J. 1994. *Responsibility and the Moral Sentiments.* Cambridge, MA: Harvard University Press.

Watson, G. 1990. On the Primacy of Character. In Owen Flanagan and Amélie Oksenberg Rorty, eds., *Identity, Character, and Morality: Essays in Moral Psychology.* Cambridge, MA: MIT Press.

———. 1996. Two Faces of Responsibility. *Philosophical Topics* 24: 227–48.

Weinberg, J., S. Nichols, and S. Stich. 2002. Normativity and Epistemic Intuitions. *Philosophical Topics* 29: 429–60.

Westermarck, E. 1906. *Origin and Development of the Moral Ideas.* 2 vols. New York: Macmillan.

Williams, B. A. O. 1973. A Critique of Utilitarianism. In J. J. C. Smart and B. A. O. Williams, *Utilitarianism: For and Against.* Cambridge: Cambridge University Press.

———. 1981. *Moral Luck: Philosophical Papers 1973–1980.* Cambridge: Cambridge University Press.

———. 1985. *Ethics and the Limits of Philosophy.* Cambridge, MA: Harvard University Press.

———. 1993. *Shame and Necessity.* Berkeley: University of California Press.

Woods, M. 1986. Intuition and Perception in Aristotle's Ethics. *Oxford Studies in Ancient Philosophy* 4: 145–66.

Woolfolk, R. L., and J. M. Doris. 2002. Rationing Mental Health Care: Parity, Disparity, and Justice. *Bioethics* 16: 469–85

Woolfolk, R. L., J. M. Doris, and J. M. Darley. 2006. Identification, Situational Constraint, and Social Cognition: Studies in the Attribution of Moral Responsibility. *Cognition* 100: 283–301.

No concept is invoked more often by social
scientists in the explanations of human
behavior than norm.
—*ENCYCLOPEDIA OF*
THE SOCIAL SCIENCES

12

A FRAMEWORK FOR THE PSYCHOLOGY OF NORMS

Chandra Sekhar Sripada and Stephen Stich

HUMANS ARE UNIQUE in the animal world in the extent to which their day-to-day behavior is governed by a complex set of rules and principles commonly called *norms*. Norms delimit the bounds of proper behavior in a host of domains, providing an invisible web of normative structure embracing virtually all aspects of social life. People also find many norms to be deeply meaningful. Norms give rise to powerful subjective feelings that, in the view of many, are an important part of what it is to be a human agent. Despite the vital role of norms in human lives and human behavior, and the central role they play in explanations in the social sciences, very little systematic attention has been devoted to norms in cognitive science. Much existing research is partial and piecemeal, making it difficult to know how individual findings cohere into a comprehensive picture. Our goal in this essay is to offer an account of the psychological mechanisms and processes underlying norms that integrates what is known and can serve as a framework for future research.

In section 1, we'll offer a preliminary account of what norms are. In sections 2 and 3, we'll assemble an array of facts about norms and the psychology that makes them possible, drawn from a variety of disciplines. Though the distinction is not a sharp one, in section 2, we'll focus on social level facts, while in section 3, our focus will be on how norms affect individuals. In section 4, we'll offer a tentative hypothesis about the innate psychological architecture subserving the acquisition and implementation of norms, and explain why we believe an architecture like the one we propose can explain many of the facts assembled in sections 2 and 3. Section 5, the last and longest section, focuses on open questions—important issues about the cognitive science of norms that our account in section 4 does not address. In some cases, we've left these issues open because little is known about them; in other cases, more is known but crucial questions are still very much in dispute. Though we are acutely aware that our account of the psychology of norms leaves many important questions unanswered, we hope that the framework we provide will contribute to future research by clarifying some of those questions and offering an overview of how they are related.[1]

1. A Preliminary Characterization of Norms

We'll begin with an informal and provisional account of what we mean when we talk of *norms*. As we use the term, a norm is a rule or principle that specifies actions that are required, permissible, or forbidden independently of any legal or social institution. Of course, some norms are *also* recognized and enforced by social institutions and laws, but the crucial point is that they needn't be. To emphasize this fact, we'll sometimes say that norms have *independent normativity*. Closely linked to the independent normativity of norms is the fact that people are motivated to comply with norms in a way that differs from their motivation to comply with other kinds of social rules. Very roughly, people are motivated to comply with norms as *ultimate ends*, rather than as a means to other ends; we'll refer to this type of motivation as *intrinsic motivation*, and we'll have much more to say about it in section 3. People can *also* be motivated to comply with a norm for instrumental reasons, though intrinsic compliance motivation adds a substantial additional motivational force. Violations of norms, when they become known, typically engender *punitive attitudes*, like anger, condemnation, and blame, directed at the norm violator, and these attitudes sometimes lead to punitive behavior.

We believe that norms, as we've characterized them, are an important and theoretically useful subcategory of social rules, and that our characterization is broadly in line with other accounts, both historical and more recent (see Durkheim 1903/1953; McAdams 1997; Parsons 1952; Petit 1991). However, it is worth emphasizing that our account of norms is *not* intended as a *conceptual analysis* or an account of what the term "norm" means to ordinary speakers. Nor do we offer our characterization of norms as a formal definition. At best, it gives a rough-and-ready way to pick out what we believe is a theoretically interesting *natural kind* in the social sciences. If the framework for a psychological theory of norms set out in section 4 is on the right track, then a better account of the crucial features of norms can be expected to emerge as that theory is elaborated. One of

---

1. One issue we won't consider is how the psychological mechanisms we'll posit might have evolved. We believe that one of the advantages of the account we'll offer is that there is a plausible account of the evolution of these mechanisms. But assembling this evolutionary story is a substantial project which we won't attempt to undertake here.

the components of our framework is a "norm database," and it is the theory's job to tell us what can and cannot end up in that database.

Though there are a substantial number of empirically well-supported generalizations about norms, those generalizations and the evidence for them are scattered in the literatures of a number of different disciplines. In the next two sections, we'll assemble some of these generalizations and say a bit about the evidence for each. We'll begin with social-level features of norms, and then turn to individual-level facts about the ways norms are acquired and how they influence behavior.

2. Some Social-Level Facts About Norms

Norms are a *cultural universal*. The ethnographic database strongly suggests that norms and sanctions for norm violations are universally present in all human societies (Brown 1991; Roberts 1979; Sober and Wilson 1998). Moreover, there is reason to think that the universal presence of norms is very *ancient*. There is no evidence that norms originated in some society and spread by contact to other societies in the relatively recent past. Rather, norms are reliably present and are highly elaborated in all human groups, including hunter-gatherer groups and groups that are culturally isolated. This is just what we would expect on the hypothesis that norms are very ancient. All of this, we think, suggests that there are innate psychological mechanisms specialized for the acquisition and implementation of norms, since the existence of these mechanisms would help explain the universal presence of norms in all human groups.

In addition to being present in all cultures, norms tend to be ubiquitous in the lives of people in those cultures. They govern a vast array of activities, ranging from worship to appropriate dress to disposing of the dead. And while some norms deal with matters that seem to be of little importance, others regulate matters like status, mate choice, food, and sex that have a direct impact on people's welfare and their reproductive success.

Although norms are present in all human groups, one of the most striking facts about them is that the *contents* of the norms that prevail in different groups are quite variable. Moreover, these differences follow a characteristic pattern in which there is substantial homogeneity in the norms that prevail *within* groups and both commonalities and differences in the norms that prevail *across* groups. We believe that the distributional pattern of norms is an important source of evidence about the psychological mechanisms that underlie them. For this reason, we'll spend some time discussing the issue in more detail.

In assessing the distribution of norms across human groups, one question that immediately arises is: Are there any norms that are universally present in all human groups? The question must be handled with some care, since many candidate norm universals are problematic because they verge on being *analytic*—true in virtue of meaning alone. For example "Murder is wrong" or "Theft is wrong" don't count as legitimate universals since, roughly speaking, "murder" simply means killing someone else in a way that is not permissible, and "theft" simply means taking something from another in a way that is not permissible. For this reason, it is important, wherever possible, to frame the contents of norms in a nonnormative vocabulary. While analytic principles like "Murder is wrong" and "Theft is wrong" may be universals, the *specific* rules that regulate the *circumstances* under which killing or taking an item in the possession of another person is permitted are not so nearly uniform across groups.

With this caveat in mind, we return to the question of the distributional pattern of norms across human groups. One important fact is that there *is* a pattern to be discerned; norms are not indefinitely variable or randomly distributed across human groups. Rather, there are certain kinds of norms one sees again and again in almost all human societies, though in order to discern these commonalities, one has to stay at a fairly high level of generality. For example, most societies have rules that prohibit killing, physical assault, and incest (or sexual activity with one's kin). In addition, most societies have rules promoting sharing, reciprocating, and helping, at least under some circumstances (Cashdan 1989). Most societies have rules regulating sexual behavior among various members of society, and especially among adolescents (though the content of these rules varies considerably) (Bourguignon and Greenbaum 1973). And most societies have at least some rules that promote egalitarianism and social equality. For example, in nearly all hunter-gatherer groups, attempts by individuals to garner a disproportionate share of resources, women, or power are disapproved of sharply (Boehrn 1999). Examples like these could be multiplied easily in domains such as social justice, kinship, marriage, and many others.

While there is no doubt that there are certain high-level commonalities in the norms that prevail across groups, as one looks at norms in more detail, it is clear that there is tremendous variability in the *specific rules* one finds in different groups. Consider, for example, norms dealing with *harms*. While some kind of harm norm or other is found in virtually all human groups, the specific harm norms that prevail across groups are quite variable. In some simple societies, almost all harm-causing behaviors are strongly prohibited. Among the Semai, an aboriginal people of the Malaysian rain forest, for example, hitting and fighting, as well as more mundane behaviors such as insulting or slandering, are all impermissible, and Semai groups have among the lowest levels of violence of any human societies (Robarchek and Robarchek 1992). But other groups permit a much wider spectrum of harm-causing behaviors. In groups such as the Yanomamö of South America, the use of violence to settle conflicts is permitted (and indeed extremely common), and displays of fighting bravado are prized rather than condemned (Chagnon 1992). Among the Yanomamö, mortality due to intra- and intertribe conflict is extremely high, and some ethnographers have suggested that the level of mortality due to violence found among the Yanomamö is not at all uncommon in simple societies (Keeley 1996). In addition to variability in the kinds of harm and level of harm that are permitted, harm norms also differ with respect to the class of individuals a person is permitted to harm. Many groups draw a sharp distinction between harms committed against individuals within one's own community and individuals outside the group (though many groups do *not* draw such a sharp distinction; LeVine and Campbell 1972). Moreover, some societies permit some kinds of violence directed against women, children, animals, and also certain marginalized subgroups or castes (Edgerton 1992). The variability in harm norms is also evidenced by the manner in which they change over time. The philosopher Shaun Nichols (2004, ch. 7) provides a fascinating description of the gradual change in harm norms in Western societies over the last 400 years.

Incest prohibitions are another case in which high-level commonalities are found in conjunction with variability at the level of specific rules. It appears that almost all societies have norms prohibiting sexual intercourse between members of the nuclear family (we'll call these nearly universal rules *core incest prohibitions*). But incest prohibitions almost always extend beyond this core. In particular, incest prohibitions almost always extend to *other kinds* of sexual activity, and they almost always extend beyond just the *nuclear family*; they prohibit sexual activity with at least some members of one's nonnuclear kin. But the details of how incest prohibitions extend beyond core incest prohibitions are, as numerous studies have revealed, tremendously variable (Murdock 1949). For example, at one extreme are *exogamous groups*, in which marriage with *anyone* within one's own tribal unit is considered incestuous, though the offense is seldom seen as being of the same level of severity as intercourse within one's nuclear family.

Another feature of the distributional pattern of norms is that while most groups have some rule or other that falls under certain high-level themes, generalizations about commonalities in the norms found across groups typically have *exceptions*. For example, the incest prohibition is sometimes cited as the best example of a norm that is a universal feature of all human groups. And while it is true that core incest prohibitions can be found in virtually all groups, even this generalization may not be exceptionless. There is good evidence that brother-sister marriage (including sexual relations) occurred with some frequency in Egypt during the Roman period, and was practiced openly and unabashedly. In addition, brother-sister marriage is known to have occurred in a number of royal lineages, including those of Egypt, Hawaii, and the Inca empire (Durham 1991).

To sum up, we've identified three key features of the distributional pattern of norms. First, norms tend to cluster under certain general *themes*. Second, the specific rules that fall under these general themes are quite *variable*, though clearly thematically connected. And third, there are typically at least some *exceptions* that diverge from the general trend.

3. Some Individual-Level Facts About Norms

We turn now to some facts about how norms emerge within individuals, and how individuals are affected by the norms they acquire. There is excellent evidence indicating that norms exhibit a *reliable pattern of ontogenesis*. Regardless of their biological heritage, almost everyone (excepting those with serious psychological deficits) acquires the norms that prevail in the local cultural group in a highly reliable way. In no human group is it the case that some individuals reliably acquire the prevailing norms while many others don't. It also appears that all individuals acquire at least some norms of their group relatively *early* in life. All normal children appear to have knowledge of rules of a distinctly normative type between three and five years of age, and can distinguish these normative rules from other social rules (Nucci 2001; Turiel 1983). In addition, some competences associated with norms, such as the ability to reason about normative rules and rule violations, appears very early. Denise Cummins has shown that children as young as three to four perform substantially better on deontic rule reasoning tasks than they do on similar indicative reasoning tasks (Cummins 1996).

Further evidence about the ontogenesis of norms comes from a major crosscultural study in which Henrich and his colleagues investigated norms of cooperation and fairness in 15 small-scale societies using standard experimental game paradigms. (We'll discuss these games more fully later.) While this study found considerable diversity in the norms of cooperation and fairness prevailing in these societies, it also found that much of the crosscultural variation in norms among adults was already present by the time subjects reached the age of nine, and it persists thereafter (Henrich et al. 2001). In another crosscultural experimental study, Shweder and his colleagues examined moral norms in children and adults in Hyde Park, Illinois, and Bhubaneswar, India (Shweder, Mahapatra, and Miller 1987). As in Henrich and colleagues' study, there were lots of differences in the norms that prevailed in the two communities, and most of the differences were already established by the time subjects reached the age of seven.

Perhaps the most striking (and most overlooked) feature of norms is that they have powerful *motivation effects* on the people who hold them. Philosophers have long emphasized that from a subjective perspective, moral norms present themselves with a unique kind of subjective authority that differs from standard instrumental motivation. We believe that this philosophical intuition reflects a deep empirical truth about the psychology of norms, and we refer to the type of motivation associated with norms as *intrinsic motivation*. Our claim is that people are disposed to comply with norms even when there is little prospect for instrumental gain, future reciprocation, or enhanced reputation, and when the chance of being detected for failing to comply with the norm is very small. The claim we are making must be treated with care, however. At any given time, a person may be subject to multiple sources of motivation. So in some cases in which people are intrinsically motivated to comply with a norm, they may *also* be instrumentally motivated to comply with the norm. In other cases in which people are intrinsically motivated to comply with norms, they may nonetheless fail to comply for instrumental reasons. So our claim is not that people always *follow* norms or that when they follow norms they do so *only* because of intrinsic motivation. Rather, our claim is that humans display an independent intrinsic source of motivation for norm compliance, and thus that people are motivated to comply with norms *over and above* (and *to a substantial degree* over and above) what would be predicted from instrumental reasons alone.

There is an implication of our claims about intrinsic motivation that is worth emphasizing. Many norms, though by no means all, direct individuals to behave *unselfishly*. More precisely, many norms direct individuals to behave in ways that are contrary to what would in fact maximize satisfaction of their selfish preferences. Thus, in saying that people are intrinsically motivated to comply with norms, we are committed to the claim that people are motivated to comply in a way that frequently leads them to behave genuinely unselfishly. While philosophers have taken the claim that people are intrinsically motivated to comply with norms to be obvious and platitudinous, economic theorists and evolutionary-minded scientists have often argued that such behavior is very implausible from the perspective of selfish rationality (see Barash 1979, 135, 167; Downs 1957). We believe the arguments used by these theorists are deeply flawed. But a full rebuttal would take us far from the current topic, and here we instead emphasize that the claim that people are intrinsically motivated to follow norms has substantial *direct* empirical justification.

Some of this evidence comes from anthropology and sociology. A central principle of these disciplines is that people *internalize* the norms of their group. According to the internalization hypothesis, individuals exhibit a characteristic style of motivation in which the individual intrinsically values compliance with moral rules even when there is no possibility of sanction from an external source (Durkheim 1912/1968; Scott 1971). Internalization is invoked to explain a seemingly obvious and ubiquitous fact: having been taught to comply with the moral rules of their group, people exhibit a *lifelong* pattern of *highly reliable* compliance with the rule. Furthermore, this pattern of compliance does not seem to depend on overt coercion, or even the threat of coercion, at each particular instance in which compliance is displayed. Consistent with the internalization hypothesis, the ethnographic record routinely reports that people view norms as being distinctive because of their absoluteness, their authority, and the manner in which people regard them as deeply meaningful (see Edel and Edel 2000). These features of norms suggest that norm compliance is based on something over and above instrumental motivation.

Closer to home, the economist Robert Frank (1988) has pointed out a number of cases of norm compliance in day-to-day life that are not plausibly viewed as the product of instrumental rationality. His examples include tipping at a highway restaurant one will never revisit, jumping in a river to save a drowning person, refraining from littering on a lonely beach, returning a lost wallet containing a substantial amount of cash, and many others.

Though descriptive data of this sort is compelling enough, a problem for those who wish to defend the claim that people intrinsically comply with norms is that it is easy for skeptics to concoct a selfish instrumental motive for what superficially appears to be intrinsic compliance behavior. For this reason, experimental data that can distinguish the competing hypotheses is crucial. The social psychologist C. Daniel Batson has, over the course of a number of years, extensively studied the motivational structure of helping behavior using a number of ingenious experimental paradigms. Batson finds that helping behavior is best accounted for on the hypothesis that people promote the welfare of others as an ultimate end (especially when their empathy is engaged) and not on alternative

hypotheses that treat helping as instrumental toward ulterior benefits such as future reciprocation, or gaining social approval (Batson 1991). There is now a large literature in sociology and social psychology that reaches a similar conclusion. Reviewing this literature,
Pilliavin and Charng note:

> There appears to be a paradigm shift away from the earlier position that behavior
> that appears to be altruistic must, under closer scrutiny, be revealed as reflecting
> egoistic motives. Rather, theory and data now being advanced are more compatible
> with the view that true altruism—acting with the goal of benefiting another—does
> exist and is part of human nature. (1990, 27)

But perhaps the most compelling data indicating that people follow norms as ultimate
ends comes from experimental economics, where people's motivations to comply with
norms of fairness and reciprocity can be precisely detected and quantified. There is now
abundant evidence that in experimental games, subjects cooperate at levels *far* higher
than instrumental rationality alone would predict. For example, subjects routinely cooperate in *one-time-only, anonymous* prisoner's dilemma games (Marwell and Ames 1981).
In such games, choosing to cooperate is the "fair" thing to do, while choosing to defect
will earn the subject a higher payoff, regardless of what the other person chooses. Furthermore, these results are obtained even when subjects are *explicitly told* that they will
play the game only once, and their identity will remain anonymous. The fact that subjects
still routinely choose to cooperate suggests that that they are complying with norms of
fairness and reciprocity as an ultimate end, rather than pursuing what would satisfy their
selfish preferences. There are a large number of other kinds of games, such as public goods
games, the ultimatum game, the centipede game, and others in which similar results have
been obtained (see Thaler 1992, especially chaps. 2 and 3, for a review).

In addition to emphasizing the intrinsic nature of motivations to comply with moral
norms, philosophers have also recognized the intrinsic nature of motivation to *punish
norm violations*. Kant, famously, was a retributivist who held that punishment for violations of moral norms is a moral duty and is intrinsically valuable, and a substantial
number of other philosophers have endorsed the retributivist position (Kant 1887/1972,
102–7; see Ezorsky 1972, ch. 2, sec. 2). Other philosophers associated with distinct moral
traditions have also recognized the important role of duties to punish in the moral
domain. Mill, for example, maintains that moral violations are the ones that we feel that
society *ought to punish* (Mill 1863/1979, ch. 5). And a number of other philosophers have
advanced similar claims (Gibbard 1990, ch. 3; Moore 1987). Here, again, we believe that
these philosophical intuitions reflect a deep descriptive truth.

Before discussing the empirical literature on intrinsic motivation to punish, it's worth
reemphasizing some of the caveats made earlier. In claiming that people are intrinsically
motivated to punish norm violations, we are not claiming that these motivations *always*
translate into punitive behaviors. Human motivations are multifaceted and complex, and

people with intrinsic motivations to punish a norm violator may also have instrumental motivations not to punish. Thus motivations to punish serve to raise the probability of punitive behaviors, though they needn't translate into punitive behaviors in every instance. Furthermore, we are not claiming that *every* norm violation generates intrinsic motivations to punish. Rather, our claim is that norm violations that have the appropriate salience and severity generate motivations to punish. So while there is a *reliable connection* between norm violations and motivations to punish, this connection need not be realized in every occurrence of a norm violation.

There is a large anthropological and sociological literature attesting to the fact that norm violations elicit both punitive emotions like anger and outrage—and punitive behaviors like criticism, condemnation, avoidance, exclusion, or even physical harm—from most people within a society, and that these attitudes and behaviors are directed at rule violators (Roberts 1979; Sober and Wilson 1998). Furthermore, many social scientists have explicitly noted that punishment for norm violation, of this informal type, is *universally present in all societies.* For example, ostracism is a human universal (Brown 1991); gossip and criticism are human universals (Dunbar 1996; Wilson et al. 2000); and in all human groups, systems of sanctions, which utilize ostracism and gossip, as well as other informal sanctions, are applied to those who violate moral norms (Black 1998; Boehm 1999).

But here, again, it might be argued that, though there is ample evidence that people are disposed to punish norm violators, they do so for strictly selfish instrumental reasons. For example, people may punish to send a message to the violator, which produces a selfish gain for the punisher because the violator is deterred from repeating the offense. However, there is good evidence that motivations to punish are often truly intrinsic, and that punishment is not inflicted for selfish instrumental reasons alone.

One particularly striking finding is reported in Haidt et al. (submitted). In this study, subjects were shown films in which a normative transgression occurs. Subjects were offered various alternative endings; they preferred endings in which the perpetrators of the transgression were made to suffer, knew the suffering was repayment for the transgression, and suffered in a way that involved public humiliation. More revealingly, though, subjects were also offered an alternative ending in which the perpetrator realized what he did was wrong, showed genuine remorse, and grew personally as a result. Subjects' *rejection* of this ending suggests that their motivation to punish is not based on selfish instrumental ends, such as avoiding being harmed by the perpetrator in the future. Rather, they appear to be motivated by intrinsic motivations to punish the violator.

The most powerful evidence for intrinsic motivation to punish norm violations comes from experimental economics. Since the early 1990s, there has been a surge of interest in experimental economics in studying people's motivations to punish in controlled laboratory conditions. A large number of studies show that in various experimental situations and experimental games, people will punish others—*at substantial costs to themselves*—for violations of normative rules or a normative conception of fairness. This data is particularly powerful because it permits quantitative measures of the extent to which motivations to punish are unselfish and instrumentally irrational.

To illustrate the pattern of results in the literature, we'll describe a study by Fehr and Gachter (2002). In this study, 240 subjects played a public goods game in groups of four. Each member of the group was given 20 monetary units (MUs) and could either invest in a group project or keep the money for himself. For each unit invested, each of the four group members received four-tenths of an MU back. If a subject chose not to invest, he kept the full one unit. Given these payoffs, if all the subjects invest fully, each receives 32 units. If all subjects choose not to invest, each receives 20 units. Of course, if one subject chooses not to invest but the others invest fully, the "free-riding" subject receives the highest payoff, 44 MUs. Thus, the public goods game sets up a conflict between collective benefit and selfish interest.

Fehr and Gachter studied behavior in the public goods game under two conditions—a "punishment" condition and a "no punishment" condition. In the punishment condition, after each period of the game (a period consisted of one round of investment), subjects were informed of others' contributions and given an opportunity to punish any other player. Punishment cost 1 MU for the punisher and subtracted 3 MUs from the punished person's payoffs. Thus punishment was a costly act, but it created an even more substantial harm for the person being punished. Fehr and Gachter changed the composition of the group after each period, and ran the game for a total of six periods. Subjects did not know the identity of the members of the group in which they were placed (and all participants knew this fact), so a person could not personally benefit from the act of punishing, nor could a person build a reputation for contributing or punishing. Thus, to the extent that punishment deterred free-riding, the deterrence benefit was enjoyed by others. In the no-punishment condition, subjects played an identical game except for the fact that there was no opportunity to punish (Fehr and Gachter 2002).

The results of this study are quite striking, because they seem to violate a number of canons of self-interested economic rationality. First of all, Fehr and Gachter found that subjects in the no-punishment condition invested at much higher levels than self-interested rationality predicts, consistent with our previous claim that people follow norms of fairness as ultimate ends. In addition, in the punishment condition, Fehr and Gachter found that subjects punished, punished reliably, and punished severely. In the six periods of the experiment, 84.3 percent of the subjects punished at least once, and 34.3 percent punished five or more times during the six periods. Since subjects knew that they switched groups after every period and that their identity remained anonymous after every switch, their motivations to punish cannot be explained in terms of selfish rationality.

A number of more recent studies have shown an even more striking result. In various experimental situations and games, people will punish others at some cost to themselves even if they are *merely observers* of violations of normative rules or some normative conception of fairness, and they themselves are not directly affected by the norm violation (Fehr and Fischbacher 2004; Carpenter, Matthews, and Okomboli 2004). In a way, the existence of "third-party punishment" of this sort is actually fairly obvious and unsurprising (though it is very surprising from the standpoint of selfish rationality). Our everyday experience with human beings in a social context reveals that norm violations elicit powerful feelings of outrage from third parties who aren't directly harmed by the violation. In our view, the existence of third-party punishment of this sort shows, rather decisively, that punishment is not performed for mere instrumentally selfish reasons but rather is performed for intrinsic reasons.

One final point to make about punitive motivation is that, while children are given instruction (or at least some kind of social input) with respect to the *contents* of the norms of their social group, they are seldom, if ever, given input about the need to punish violations of norms. Thus it is remarkable that children who acquire normative rules systematically exhibit punitive attitudes toward those who violate the rules *without having been taught to exhibit these punitive attitudes*. For example, children who learn that hitting babies is wrong do not need to be taught that one should exhibit anger, hostility, and other punitive attitudes toward those who hit babies (Edwards 1987).

4. The Psychological Architecture Subserving Norms

In this section, we briefly sketch a theory about the psychological mechanisms underlying the acquisition and implementation of norms. The theory posits two closely linked *innate mechanisms*, one responsible for norm acquisition, the other for norm implementation. The function of the acquisition mechanism is to identify behavioral cues indicating that a norm prevails in the local cultural environment, to infer the content of that norm, and to pass information about the content of the norm on to the implementation system, where it is stored and used. The acquisition mechanism, we maintain, begins to operate quite early in development, and its operation is both automatic and involuntary. People do not need to turn it on, and they cannot turn it off—though it *may* be the case that the acquisition mechanism gradually turns itself off starting at some point after adolescence. The implementation mechanism performs a suite of functions, including maintaining a database of normative rules acquired by the acquisition mechanism, generating *intrinsic* motivation to comply with those rules as ultimate ends, detecting violations of the rules, and generating intrinsic motivation to punish rule violators. Figure 12.1 is a "boxological" rendition of the mechanisms we're positing.

The cluster of mechanisms we've sketched provides what we think is a plausible first pass at explaining many of the facts assembled in the previous two sections. The innate component dedicated to norm acquisition explains the fact that norms are universally present, that people acquire the norms of their own group, and that norm acquisition follows a reliable pattern of ontogenesis that starts quite early in life. The innate execution component explains why people are intrinsically motivated to comply with norms and intrinsically motivated to punish norm violators; it also explains why children manifest punitive attitudes toward norm violators without having been taught to do so. Of course, positing mechanisms that perform the functions we've described is only the first step in theory building. Nonetheless, for two quite different reasons, we think it is an important step. First, it makes substantive claims about innate mechanisms subserving the acquisition and implementation of norms, and it is hard to see how the facts we've assembled in sections 2 and 3 *could* be explained without positing innate psychological mechanisms that perform the functions we've sketched. Second, while our boxology raises more questions than it answers, it also provides a systematic framework in which those questions can be addressed. In the section that follows, we'll discuss *some* of the questions we think our theoretical framework brings into sharper focus. But before getting on to that, we should emphasize that the psychological mechanisms we've described are only *part* of what will inevitably be a much more complicated account of the way the mind deals with normative rules. Some of those further complications will be noted in section 5.

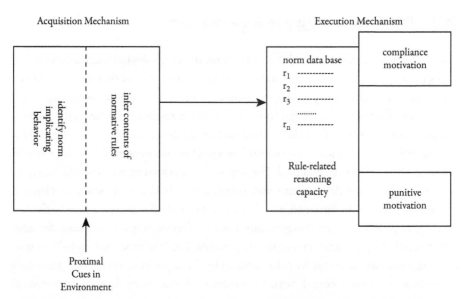

FIGURE 12.1 A first pass at a "boxological" sketch of the innate mechanisms underlying the acquisition and implementation of norms.

5. Some Open Questions

Obviously, there are *lots* of questions that the theoretical framework sketched in section 4 leaves unanswered. In this section, we'll only have space to discuss six of them.

5.1 NORMS VERSUS MORAL NORMS

In assembling our catalogue of social- and individual-level facts about norms, some of our claims were quite explicitly about *moral* norms, while others were about norms more generally. What is the relation between these two? As we noted in section 1, we think that norms, as we've characterized them, are a theoretically important *natural kind* in the social sciences. It also strikes us as quite likely that the *intuitive* category of *moral* norms is not coextensive with the class of norms that can end up in the norm database posited by our theory. Perhaps the most obvious mismatch is that the norm database, for many people in many cultures, will include lots of rules governing what food can be eaten, how to dispose of the dead, how to show deference to high-ranking people, and a host of other matters that our commonsense intuition does not count as moral. So what *is* our commonsense intuition picking out? One possibility that might find encouragement in the influential literature on the "moral/conventional distinction" (Nucci 2001; Turiel 1983) is that moral rules or norms are *another natural kind*—either a subset of the norms in the norm database or a class of rules that includes some rules *that are in the* norm database and some that are not. Kelly and Stich (2007) have argued that experimental studies of the moral/conventional distinction do not support the claim that moral rules are a natural kind. But perhaps that conclusion can be reached by a different route. Another option is that our intuitions about which rules are moral are guided by a culturally local collection of prototypes or exemplars that have been heavily influenced by the Western religious and philosophical tradition, and that do not pick out a natural kind at all. A third possibility is that moral rules might turn out to constitute a natural kind that is identical with the norms characterized by our theory. On this view, our intuitions about which rules are moral are sometimes simply mistaken, in much the same way that the folk intuition that whales are a kind of fish was mistaken (Sripada, unpublished manuscript). Though empirical work on how people go about deciding that a rule is (or is not) a *moral* rule will surely be relevant to the debate among these three options, the debate also implicates contested issues on the border between semantics and metaphysics. And since progress in *those* areas is often hard to discern, we don't expect the matter to be settled anytime soon.

5.2 PROXIMAL CUES

One of the jobs of the norm acquisition mechanism is to identify behavioral cues indicating that a norm prevails in the local cultural environment. What are those cues? Since norms, as we've characterized them, are rules whose violation is punished, it might be thought that the proximal cues for the acquisition processes must involve punishment. But we doubt that can be correct, because it is clear that some normative rules are acquired *before* the child observes a violation being punished, or even though the child *never* observes a rule violation at all. Another hypothesis about the proximal cues for norm acquisition comes from cognitive psychologist James Blair. Blair proposes that it is the display of *sad faces* by caretakers and others that, when paired with specific actions performed by the child, signals to the child that these actions count as normative transgressions. Evidence for this claim comes from the finding that psychopaths show abnormal emotional reaction to sad faces when compared with normal subjects, and psychopaths also display specific deficits in moral reasoning, suggesting that they have failed to acquire normative rules appropriately (Blair 1995; Blair et al. 1997). However, in a convincing critique, Nichols (2004, ch. 1) argues that Blair's hypothesis is twice mistaken: sad faces are neither necessary nor sufficient to trigger norm acquisition.

There is intriguing evidence from the anthropological literature suggesting that the proximal cues facilitating norm acquisition at least partially consist of *explicit verbal instruction*. The psychologist Carolyn Pope Edwards analyzed records of day-to-day norm transgressions among children in a Luo-speaking community in Southern Kenya and in a toddler classroom in Poughkeepsie, New York. She found that children frequently receive repeated, *explicit verbal instruction* (and also verbal commands and threats) during the course of norm acquisition and development (Edwards 1987). However, the question of what proximal cues trigger the acquisition of norms is still very much open, and much further research is needed (see Nichols 2005 and Dwyer 2006 for further discussion).

5.3 REPRESENTATIONAL FORMAT: HOW ARE NORMS STORED?

Many philosophers and psychologists who study norm-related reasoning assume that norms are stored in a sentence-like format regimented, perhaps, with the formalism of a deontic logic. However, we believe it is very much an open question whether this is the way norms are typically stored. The recent literature on the psychology of categorization suggests a number of plausible alternatives.

Exemplar theory (Murphy 2002; Smith and Medin 1981) offers a particularly intriguing option. On this account, norms might be stored as a cluster of exemplars, which can be thought of as representations of concrete, paradigmatic examples of actions that are required or prohibited by the norm. For example, people might store scenarios involving *hitting a defenseless child* and *stealing from the church collection plate* as exemplars of actions that are prohibited, and scenarios involving *keeping a deathbed promise* or *helping a stranger in distress* as exemplars of actions that are required. An exemplar-based theory of norm-guided judgment would propose that people judge novel actions in terms of their *similarity* to these stored exemplars—if an action is sufficiently similar to exemplars of prohibited actions, the action will be judged to be impermissible.[2] One way the exemplar-based account might work is that, in arriving at judgments of permissibility

---

2. The notion of "similarity" used in an exemplar-based account can be made precise in a number of different ways (see Murphy 2002 for a review). For our purposes, an intuitive notion of similarity will suffice.

or impermissibility, people search *exhaustively* through all of their stored exemplars, comparing each exemplar to the action being evaluated. On more complex (and in our view more plausible) versions of the exemplar-based account, it is not the case that *all* stored exemplars are accessed when making permissibility judgments. Rather, recent cognitive and emotional history serves to "prime," or activate, a subset of the relevant exemplars, and it is only this subset that is utilized in generating the judgments. On this version of the exemplar-based account, a person may make different judgments about the same case on different occasions, because recent circumstances have primed different subsets of her stored exemplars. Stich (1993) has speculated that the exemplar-based account provides a plausible explanation for many aspects of moral judgment. For example, the account helps explain the importance of myths and parables in moral pedagogy, since these stories can help build a rich stock of exemplars of morally praiseworthy and morally blameworthy conduct. The exemplar-based account also provides a ready explanation of the fact that moral judgment seems so sensitive to factors (such as the emotional "spin" used in describing a case) that might prime one or another exemplar.

In addition to exemplar-based approaches, the literature on the psychology of categorization suggests a number of other ways of understanding the processes that underlie judgments of permissibility and impermissibility. The representational structures invoked might include prototypes, stereotypes, theories, and narratives among others (see Murphy 2002 for a comprehensive review). In addition, theorists have proposed connectionist-inspired theories of permissibility judgment (Casebeer 2003). An intriguing possibility is that different kinds of processes underlie permissibility judgments in different contexts, in much the same way that different exemplars might be activated in different contexts. For example, people might utilize an exemplar-based process for forming permissibility judgments in the context of day-to-day norm-related cognition, especially when such judgments are made rapidly and "on the fly." However, when there is ample time for reflection, they may seek to form permissibility judgments by carefully and deliberately assessing actions in terms of their relationship with stored general rules and principles. But all of this, we hasten to add, is no more than speculation. The empirical study of the representational format of norms has barely begun.

5.4 THE ROLE OF THE EMOTIONS

There is a long tradition in philosophy suggesting that emotions play a central role in the processes underlying moral judgment and moral behavior (Gibbard 1990; Hume 1739/1964). While there are many different ways that emotions might interact with the norm psychology we've sketched, we are inclined to think that the evidence is clearest for the involvement of emotions in the generation of punitive motivation directed at those who violate norms. Indeed, there is a substantial body of data suggesting that humans have universal, species-typical emotional structures that mediate motivations to punish. This evidence indicates that three phenomena are closely linked: normative rule violations, the experience of certain emotions—including disgust and contempt, but in particular anger—and the experience of strong motivations to punish the elicitor of the emotion (see Haidt 2003 for a review). Though the relevant literature is enormous, it is not very cohesive. We'll give just a few illustrative examples.

Klaus Sherer and his colleagues undertook a large crosscultural study of emotions using a questionnaire method, and they found that subjects rate unfairness and immorality most highly as elicitors for the emotion of anger (Sherer 1997). David Sloan Wilson and Rick O'Gorman used a fictional scenario method and found that subjects invited to take the perspective of someone who is "wronged" experience anger, and that the strength of their anger is dependent on the importance of the fairness norm being violated (Wilson and O'Gorman 2003). In another study, Lawrence and his colleagues found that low doses of the dopamine receptor antagonist sulpiride produce selective deficits in a number of measures of anger, and also produce selective deficits in motivations to punish, as measured by subjects' willingness to punish others for violations of fairness norms (Lawrence et al. 2002; Lawrence, personal communication). We believe that these studies demonstrate a tight relationship between norm violations, emotional reactions, and motivations to punish, which in turn suggests that intrinsic motivations to punish norm violations are mediated by emotions.

In a particularly ingenious recent experiment, Wheatley and Haidt (2005) showed that emotion also seems to play a role in the production of moral *judgment*. The subjects in this experiment were hypnotized and told to feel disgust when they encountered the emotionally neutral words "take" or "often." Subjects were then asked to judge scenarios in which people behaved in morally problematic ways or in entirely unproblematic ways. Half of the subjects were given versions of the scenarios with the hypnotic cue word included, while the other half received nearly identical versions of the scenarios with the hypnotic cue word omitted. The presence of the hypnotic cue word in morally problematic scenarios led the subjects to asses the transgressions more harshly, while in the unproblematic scenarios, the presence of the word led a significant number of subjects to judge that the agent's actions were morally questionable. Findings like these suggest that emotions may play a role in producing moral judgments that subjects are aware of and can report. However, it is far from clear whether emotions *always* play a role in the generation of moral judgments. On the basis of neural imaging studies, Greene (2004) has suggested that there may be a second pathway leading to moral judgments—perhaps one in which explicit reasoning plays a role—that may not involve the emotions at all.

We are heartened by the fact that serious empirical work on these issues has blossomed in recent years, though clearly there is still a great deal we do not know. It is tempting to speculate that, in addition to playing a role in generating punitive motivation, emotions also play a role in *compliance* motivation, though we have been unable to find any very persuasive evidence in support of this conjecture. In addition, since the emotion systems that are involved in the generation of moral judgments can be triggered by components

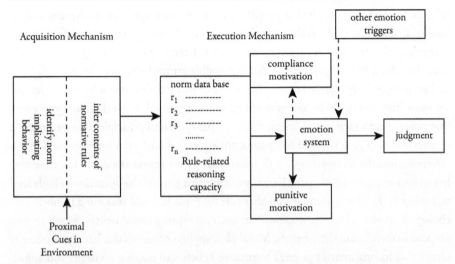

FIGURE 12.2 A more detailed sketch of the mechanisms underlying the acquisition and implementation of norms that includes the role of the emotion system. Solid lines indicate links that we take to be well supported by evidence; dotted lines indicate more speculative links.

of the mind other than the norm system, it would be very interesting, indeed, to know more about how that process works and how it influences moral judgment. In figure 12.2, we've added some components of the emotion system to the bare-bones boxology of figure 12.1.

5.5 THE ROLE OF EXPLICIT REASONING

Some of the most interesting and important questions about the psychology of norms focus on the role of explicit reasoning in shaping and justifying people's judgments and their behavior. Historically, philosophers, especially those in the Kantian tradition, and psychologists, especially those in the Kohlbergian tradition, have emphasized the role of explicit moral reasoning in the identification and acceptance of new normative rules and principles (Kohlberg, Levine, and Hewer 1983). Kohlbergians maintain that people pass through a sequence of *moral stages*. Earlier stages are characterized by egoistic kinds of thinking, while later stages are characterized by more objective and detached thought. According to Kohlberg, it is through a process of reasoning and reflection that people move away from earlier egoistic stages and come to adopt more objective perspectives that are supposed to be more acceptable from the standpoint of rationality.

The Kohlbergian picture seems to imply that reasoning or rationality can play a role in discovering *genuinely novel* moral principles, though we're inclined to be skeptical of this claim, since it is hard to see how pure rationality might discover novel moral principles *ex nihilo*. But there is another, more plausible way to interpret Kohlberg. Kohlberg frequently emphasizes the importance of "ideal perspective-taking" in moral reasoning

(Kohlberg 1981). The idea is that people strive to find principles for resolving moral dilemmas that are *reversible*, in the sense that the principles apply irrespective of the particular role in the dilemma occupied by the subject. Kohlberg seems to suggest that it is a brute fact about human psychology that irreversible principles are seen as unsatisfactory, and are progressively replaced during the course of moral development by principles that are more fully reversible. So one way of understanding Kohlberg is that he is proposing that people hold a tacit moral "metaprinciple": Accept moral principles that pass the test of reversibility in preference to competing principles that are less fully reversible. On this interpretation, the metaprinciple isn't prescribed by pure reason alone, but it is nevertheless an important, and perhaps universal, principle that governs the operation of high-level reasoning in the moral domain. Another role for explicit moral reasoning in norm psychology is in *identifying inconsistencies* in one's preexisting moral beliefs, which in turn can lead to revisions in these beliefs. Moral philosophers often call this basic procedure of identifying inconsistencies in one's normative beliefs and making revisions and adjustments that enhance their overall consistency "the method of reflective equilibrium."

In the last two paragraphs, we've referred rather loosely to people's *moral beliefs* and the *moral principles* they accept. But how are these beliefs and principles related to the norms stored in the norm database our theory posits? One possibility is that they are *identical*—that moral beliefs and principles just are the entries (or perhaps a subset of the entries) in the norm database. If that is the case, and if explicit reasoning can modify moral beliefs in the ways we've described, then this sort of reasoning can modify the contents of the norm database. But, as we noted in section 4, we suspect that the norm psychology we've been elaborating is only one part of the complex system the mind exploits when dealing with normative rules. Thus it is entirely possible that the moral beliefs and principles that Kohlberg and others are concerned with are stored somewhere else in the mind. They might, for example, be stored in the "belief box," along with factual beliefs, or they might reside in a dedicated system that is distinct from the norm system. These two options, both of which are versions of what we call *the two sets of books hypothesis*, are broadly consonant with "dual attitude" and "dual processing" theories that have been proposed for a number of other psychological capacities (Chaiken and Trope 1999; Stanovich 1999; Wilson, Lindsey, and Schooler 2000). We suspect that some version of the two sets of books hypothesis is correct, though we would be the first to admit that evidence for the hypothesis is not thick on the ground. If the hypothesis is true, it would go a long way toward explaining the commonplace observation that while people do recognize inconsistencies in their moral beliefs and rationally revise certain of them, those changes are often superficial; automatic, intuitive reactions to real-world cases are still governed by the old, inconsistent norms.

Wherever moral beliefs are stored, both the Kohlbergian and reflective equilibrium accounts of moral reasoning allow explicit moral reasoning and explicit moral beliefs to play an important causal role in determining the contents of people's moral judgments. For this reason, we can call both theories *rationalist* accounts of moral judgment.

Recently, however, the rationalist view has been challenged by the social psychologist Jonathan Haidt. According to Haidt, the casual relationship is often the reverse of that proposed in rationalist theories—rather than moral reasoning contributing to the formation of moral judgments, much moral reasoning is actually *post hoc justification*. Haidt argues that people's moral judgments are typically determined by their affective reactions to the case at hand, and they then use explicit reasoning processes to justify these antecedently arrived-at emotionally driven judgments.

In defending this "emotional dog and rational tail" picture, Haidt demonstrates the phenomenon he calls "moral dumbfounding" (Haidt 2001). Subjects are confronted with scenarios describing actions that most people consider to be unacceptable, but the scenarios are carefully contrived so that the typical reasons one might offer when asked why the action is wrong are not available. For example, one scenario is as follows.

Julie and Mark are brother and sister. They are traveling together in France on summer vacation from college. One night, they are staying alone in a cabin near the beach. They decide that it would be interesting and fun if they tried making love. At the very least it would be a new experience for each of them. Julie was already taking birth control pills, but Mark uses a condom just to be safe. They both enjoy making love, but they decide not to do it again. They keep that night as a special secret, which makes them feel even closer to each other. What do you think about that, was it OK for them to make love? (814)

Subjects immediately say that it was wrong for the siblings to make love. However, the typical reasons one might offer for this judgment—the danger of inbreeding, long-term emotional harm—don't apply in this case. Subjects nevertheless persist in their judgment that what the siblings did was wrong, saying something like "I don't know why, I can't explain it, I just know it's wrong" (Haidt 2001). According to Haidt, the phenomenon of moral dumbfounding suggests that quick emotion-driven systems play the primary role in generating at least some moral judgments. Explicit moral reasoning, by contrast, may often play the role of merely identifying socially acceptable justifications for these emotion-driven judgments.

In figure 12.3, we've supplemented figure 12.2 with various proposals about the role of explicit reasoning in moral judgment and moral belief formation.

5.6 INNATE CONSTRAINTS AND BIASES

On the theory we've sketched, the function of the norm acquisition mechanism is to identify norms in the surrounding cultural environment, infer their content, and pass that information along to the implementation component. One way to gain a deeper understanding of the norm acquisition process—and of the pattern of distribution of norms across cultures—is to explore the ways the acquisition system may be innately

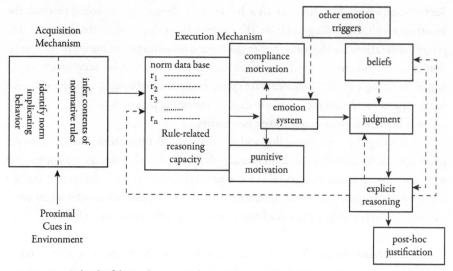

FIGURE 12.3 A sketch of the mechanisms underlying the acquisition and implementation of norms that includes various proposals about the role of explicit reasoning in moral judgment and moral belief formation. Solid lines indicate links that we take to be well supported by evidence; dotted lines indicate more speculative links with little empirical support.

constrained or biased. As a backdrop for thinking about these matters, we've found it useful to consider a *null hypothesis* that claims that the acquisition system exhibits no constraints or biases, and that it will acquire *all* and *only* those norms that are present in the child's cultural environment.[3] We've dubbed this "the Pac-Man thesis," inspired by the video game character that gobbles up everything it gets close to. If the Pac-Man thesis is true, then the norm acquisition system is equally unselective and unconstrained. There are, however, at least four ways in which the Pac-Man thesis *might* turn out to be false, and each of these corresponds to a distinct type of constraint or bias on norm acquisition.

Perhaps the most obvious way for the Pac-Man thesis to be mistaken is for some normative rules to be *innate*. Though there is a large philosophical literature debating the best interpretation of innateness claims in psychology (Cowie 1999; Griffiths 2002; Samuels 2002), for our purposes, we can consider a normative rule to be innate if various genetic and developmental factors make it the case that the rule would emerge in the norm database in a wide range of environmental conditions, even if (as a result of some extraordinary set of circumstances) the child's "cultural parents"—the people she encounters during the norm acquisition process—do *not* have the norm in *their* norm database. If there were innate norms of this sort, then they would almost certainly be cultural universals. Barring extraordinary circumstances, we should expect to find them in all human

---

3. Though we'll usually describe the norm acquirer as a "child," this is just a stylistic convenience—"norm acquirer" is a singularly awkward term. Whether and when the norm acquisition system shuts down, or slows down, as people mature, are open questions.

groups. However, as we noted in section 2, the ethnographic and historical evidence does not support the existence of such exceptionless universals. So, while there is still much to be learned, we're inclined to think that the available evidence does not support the existence of innate norms.

Another way the Pac-Man thesis might be false is that there might be an innately restricted set of possibilities from which all norms must be drawn during the course of acquisition. One way to unpack the idea of an innately restricted space of possibilities is by analogy with Noam Chomsky's *principles and parameters* approach to language learning (Chomsky 1988). According to Chomsky, the language faculty is associated with a set of parameters that can be set in various permissible ways. The child's linguistic experience serves to "toggle" the parameters associated with the language faculty, thus accounting for important aspects of the child's mature language competence. The parameters implicitly define the class of humanly learnable languages, so if a child were to be confronted with a language outside this class, the child would not learn it. A number of theorists have proposed that a broadly Chomskian principles and parameters model might provide a useful way to understand moral norm acquisition, and also serves to explain how norm variability is compatible with the existence of universal innate constraints (Harman 1999; Mikhail, Sorentino, and Spelke 1998; Nichols 2005; Stich 1993; Dwyer 2006), and recent experimental work by Marc Hauser and his colleagues suggests that there might indeed be universal constraints of a broadly Chomskian sort in the domain of harm norms (Hauser et al. 2007).

But there are other ways to understand the idea that norm acquisition is constrained by an innately restricted set of possibilities, ways that appear to be importantly distinct from the Chomskian principles and parameters model. For example, Alan Page Fiske has proposed that there are *four relational models* that structure all human social exchanges: communal sharing, equality matching, authority ranking, and market pricing (Fiske 1991). Fiske argues that the diversity of social arrangements and relationships found across human groups can ultimately be understood in terms of the operation of these four relational models. In addition, Richard Shweder and his colleagues have maintained that moral systems in all human societies are structured under one of the so-called big three families: community, authority, and divinity (Shweder et al. 1998). Paul Rozin and his colleagues expand on this idea with the proposal that each member of the big three family of moralities has an associated emotion that plays a primary role in mediating people's moral reactions—these emotions being contempt, anger, and disgust, respectively (Rozin et al. 1999). Though the ideas proposed by Fiske, Shweder and colleagues, and Rozin and colleagues are intriguing, it is not clear whether they are best understood as positing innate structures that serve to constrain or otherwise limit the space of moral norms that can be acquired, or whether they are positing some other kinds of psychological structures.

A third way for the Pac-Man thesis to be false would be as a result of the operation of what we call "Sperberian biases," which we name after anthropologist Dan Sperber, who has probably done more than anyone else to emphasize their importance (Sperber 1996). The Pac-Man thesis maintains that a child will always end up with an accurate copy of the norms of her cultural parents. But since no transmission process is error free, this sort of flawless copying is at best an idealization. Sometimes copying errors are random, but there are a variety of ways in which copying processes can give rise to *systematic* errors. For example, some sorts of normative rules may be more or less "attractive," due to the way they interact with one's preferences, aversions, emotions, and other elements of one's psychology. For the same reasons, or for other reasons, some normative rules might be easier to detect (i.e., they may be more salient), easier to infer, or easier to remember, store, or recall. The transmission process will be influenced systematically by all these factors. When copying errors change less attractive rules into more attractive ones, the new rules will be more likely to be retained and transmitted, but when copying errors change more attractive rules into less attractive ones, the new rules will be more likely to be eliminated. It is these systematic processes affecting norm transmission that we call "Sperberian biases." Sperberian biases are typically *weak*. They need not play a role in every instance of transmission from a cultural parent to a child, and often they will affect very few. Nevertheless, when their effects are summated over populations and over time, they generate a fairly strong population-level force that can have the effect of changing the distribution of norms in the direction favored by the Sperberian bias.

We can illustrate the operation of Sperberian biases by considering an example. Shaun Nichols has proposed that disgust acts as a Sperberian bias in the cultural transmission of etiquette norms (Nichols 2002). According to Nichols, *disgust* generates this bias by making certain kinds of etiquette rules more salient and more easily stored and recalled, and he marshals some intriguing evidence for these claims. Using data from sixteenth-century etiquette manuals from northern Europe, Nichols shows that etiquette rules whose violation engenders disgust are more likely to be part of today's etiquette codes than rules whose violation fails to do so. This finding suggests that the cumulative operation of disgust as a bias on the transmission of etiquette rules has had the long-term effect of shifting the distribution of etiquette rules over time in the direction favored by the bias. In the same way that disgust might engender a Sperberian bias in the case of etiquette norms, it's plausible that other cognitive structures, including various beliefs, preferences, aversions, and emotions, might engender Sperberian biases in the cultural transmission of other sorts of norms. We are inclined to think that the crosscultural distribution pattern of norms described in section 2 suggests that Sperberian biases have played a very powerful role in the transmission and evolution of norms. But making the case for this conjecture is a substantial project that will have to wait for another occasion (see Sripada 2008).

A final way the Pac-Man thesis might be mistaken turns on the operation of biases of a very different sort. Thus far, we have been tacitly assuming that the cultural parents to whom a child is exposed all share the same norms. But obviously this is not always the case. Often a child will be exposed to cultural parents who have themselves internalized significantly different norms. When this happens, the norm acquisition mechanism may utilize various selection principles, or *model selection biases*, in order to determine which cultural parent to copy. Various selection principles have been described in the literature (Boyd and Richerson 1985). These include a prestige bias leading the acquisition system to focus on a high-prestige person as a model, and age and gender biases that might, for example, focus the system on a model of the same sex who is slightly older. Alternatively, the acquisition system might rely on a conformity bias, adopting the cultural variant that is the most common. There is some evidence for age and gender biases in the transmission of norms (Harris 1998), and lots of evidence for prestige and conformity biases in the transmission of other cultural variants (Henrich and Boyd 1998; Henrich and Gil-White 2001). But how, exactly, this aspect of norm acquisition works is very much an open question.

6. Conclusion

Norms exert a powerful and pervasive influence on human behavior and human culture. Thus, the psychology of norms deserves to be a central topic of investigation in cognitive science. Our goal in this essay has been to provide a systematic framework for this endeavor. We've sketched the broad contours of a cluster of psychological mechanisms that can, we think, begin to explain some of the important facts about norms that have been recounted in various disciplines. Against the backdrop of the psychological architecture we've proposed, we've assembled a collection of open questions that the cognitive science of norms will have to address in the future. Clearly, in the study of the psychological processes that subserve norms, there is *lots* of work still to do. We will be very well satisfied indeed if our efforts provide a useful framework for organizing and integrating this work.

REFERENCES

Barash, D. 1979. *The Whisperings Within*. Harper and Row.
Batson, C. D. 1991. *The Altruism Question*. Lawrence Erlbaum Associates.
Black, D. 1998. *The Social Structure of Right and Wrong*. Academic Press.
Blair, J. 1995. A Cognitive Developmental Approach to Morality. *Cognition* 57.
Blair, R., L. Jones, F. Clark, and M. Smith. 1997. The Psychopathic Individual: A Lack of Responsiveness to Distress Cues? *Psychophysiology* 34.
Boehm, C. 1999. *Hierarchy in the Forest*. Harvard University Press.
Bourguignon, E., and L. Greenbaum. 1973. *Diversity and Homogeneity in World Societies*. HRAF Press.
Boyd, R., and P. Richerson. 1985. *Culture and the Evolutionary Process*. University of Chicago Press.

Brown, D. 1991. *Human Universals*. McGraw-Hill.

Carpenter, J., P. Matthews, and O. Okomboli. 2004. Why Punish? Social Reciprocity and the Enforcement of Prosocial Norms. *Journal of Evolutionary Economics* 14, 4.

Casebeer, W. 2003. *Natural Ethical Facts*. MIT Press.

Cashdan, E. 1989. Hunters and Gatherers: Economic Behavior in Bands. In S. Plattner, ed., *Economic Anthropology*. Stanford University Press.

Chagnon, N. 1992. *Yanomamö*. 4th ed. Harcourt Brace Jovanovich.

Chaiken, S., and Y. Trope. 1999. *Dual Process Theories in Social Science*. Guilford Press.

Chomsky, N. 1988. *Language and Problems of Knowledge*. MIT Press.

Cowie, F. 1999. *What's Within? Nativism Reconsidered*. Oxford University Press.

Cummins, D. 1996. Evidence for Deontic Reasoning in 3- and 4-year olds. *Memory and Cognition* 24.

Downs, A. 1957. *An Economic Theory of Democracy*. Harper Collins Publishers.

Dunbar, R. 1996. *Grooming, Gossip and the Evolution of Language*. Harvard University Press.

Durham, W. 1991. *Coevolution*. Stanford University Press.

Durkheim, E. 1903/1953. *Sociology and Philosophy*. Free Press.

———. 1912/1968. *The Elementary Forms of the Religious Life*. Allen and Unwin.

Dwyer, S. 2006. How Good Is the Linguistic Analogy? In P. Carruthers, S. Laurence, and S. Stich, eds., *The Innate Mind: Culture and Cognition*. Oxford University Press.

Edel, M., and A. Edel. 2000. *Anthropology and Ethics*. Transaction Publishers.

Edgerton, R. B. 1992. *Sick Societies*. Free Press.

Edwards, C. P. 1987. Culture and the Construction of Moral Values: A Comparative Ethnography of Moral Encounters in Two Cultural Settings. In J. Kagan and S. Lamb, eds., *The Emergence of Morality in Young Children*. University of Chicago Press.

Ezorsky, G., ed. 1972. *Philosophical Perspectives on Punishment*. State University of New York Press.

Fehr, E., and U. Fischbacher. 2004. Third Party Punishment and Social Norms. *Evolution and Human Behavior* 25, 2.

Fehr, E., and S. Gachter. 2002. Altruistic Punishment in Humans. *Nature* 415.

Fiske, A. P. 1991. *Structures of Social Life*. Free Press.

Frank, R. 1988. *Passion Within Reason*. W. W. Norton and Company.

Gibbard, A. 1990. *Wise Choices, Apt Feelings*. Harvard University Press.

Greene, G. 2004. fMRI Studies of Moral Judgment. Unpublished lecture given at the Dartmouth College Conference on the Psychology and Biology of Morality, Hanover, New Hampshire.

Griffiths, P. E. 2002. What Is Innateness? *Monist* 85, 1.

Haidt, J. 2001. The Emotional Dog and Its Rational Tail. *Psychological Review* 108, 4.

———. 2003. The Moral Emotions. In R. J. Davidson, K. Scherer, and H. H. Goldsmith, eds., *Handbook of Affective Sciences*. Oxford University Press.

Haidt, J., J. Sabini, D. Gromet, and J. Darley. Submitted. What Exactly Makes Revenge Sweet?

Harman, G. 1999. Moral Philosophy and Linguistics. In K. Brinkmann, ed., *Proceedings of the 20th World Conference of Philosophy*, vol. 1: *Ethics*. Reprinted in G. Harman, *Explaining Value and Other Essays in Moral Philosophy*. Clarendon Press, 2000.

Harris, J. R. 1998. *The Nurture Assumption: Why Children Turn Out the Way They Do*. Free Press.

Hauser, M., F. Cushman, L. Young, R. Kang-Xing Jin, and J. Mikhail. 2007. A Dissociation Between Moral Judgments and Justifications. *Mind and Language* 22: 1–21.

Henrich, J., and R. Boyd. 1998. The Evolution of Conformist Transmission and the Emergence of Between Group Differences. *Evolution and Human Behavior* 19.

Henrich, J., R. Boyd, S. Bowles, C. Camerer, E. Fehr, and H. Gintis. 2001. *Foundations of Human Sociality*. Oxford University Press.

Henrich, J., and F. Gil-White. 2001. The Evolution of Prestige: Freely Conferred Deference as a Mechanism for Enhancing the Benefits of Cultural Transmission. *Evolution and Human Behavior* 22.

Hume, D. 1739/1964. *A Treatise of Human Nature*. Clarendon Press.

Kant, I. 1887/1972. Justice and Punishment (from *Critique of Practical Reason*). In G. Ezorsky, ed., *Philosophical Perspectives on Punishment*. State University of New York Press.

Keeley, L. 1996. *War Before Civilization: The Myth of the Peaceful Savage*. Oxford University Press.

Kelly, D., and S. Stich. 2007. Two Theories About the Cognitive Architecture Underlying Morality. In P. Carruthers, S. Laurence, and S. Stich, eds., *The Innate Mind: Foundations and the Future*. Oxford University Press.

Kohlberg, L. 1981. Justice and Reversibility. In L. Kohlberg, *Essays on Moral Development*, vol. 1. Harper and Row.

Kohlberg, L., C. Levine, and A. Hewer. 1983. *Moral Stages: A Current Formulation and a Response to Critics*. Karger.

Lawrence, A. D., A. J. Calder, S. M. McGowan, and P. M. Grasby. 2002. Selective Disruption of the Recognition of Facial Expressions of Anger. *NeuroReport* 13, 6.

LeVine, R. A., and D. Campbell. 1972. *Ethnocentrism: Theories of Conflict, Ethnic Attitudes and Group Behavior*. John Wiley.

Marwell, G., and R. E. Ames. 1981. Economists Free Ride: Does Anyone Else? *Journal of Public Economics*.

McAdams, R. H. 1997. The Origin, Development, and Regulation of Social Norms. *Michigan Law Review* 96.

Mikhail, J., C. Sorentino, and E. Spelke. 1998. Towards a Universal Moral Grammar. In M. Gernsbacher and S. Derry, eds., *Proceedings, Twentieth Annual Conference of the Cognitive Science Society*. Lawrence Erlbaum and Associates.

Mill, J. S. 1863/1979. *Utilitarianism*. Hackett.

Moore, M. S. 1987. The Moral Worth of Retribution. In F. Schoeman, ed., *Responsibility, Character and the Emotions*. Cambridge University Press.

Murdock, G. P. 1949. *Social Structure*. Free Press.

Murphy, G. L. 2002. *The Big Book of Concepts*. MIT Press.

Nichols, S. 2002. On the Genealogy of Norms: A Case for the Role of Emotion in Cultural Evolution. *Philosophy of Science* 69.

———. 2004. *Sentimental Rules: On the Natural Foundations of Moral Judgment*. Oxford University Press.

———. 2005. Innateness and Moral Psychology. In P. Carruthers, S. Laurence, and S. Stich, eds., *The Innate Mind: Structure and Contents*. Oxford University Press.

Nucci, L. P. 2001. *Education in the Moral Domain*. Cambridge University Press.

Parsons, T. 1952. *The Social System*. Free Press.

Petit, P. 1991. Virtus Normativa: Rational Choice Perspectives. *Ethics* 100, 4.

Pilliavin, J. A., and H. W. Charng. 1990. Altruism: A Review of Recent Theory and Research. *American Sociological Review* 16.

Robarchek, C. A., and C. J. Robarchek. 1992. Cultures of War and Peace: A Comparative Study of Waorani and Semai. In J. Silverberg and P. Gray, eds., *Aggression and Peacefulness in Humans and Other Primates*. Oxford University Press.

Roberts, S. 1979. *Order and Dispute: An Introduction to Legal Anthropology*. St. Martin's Press.

Rozin, P., L. Lowery, S. Imada, and J. Haidt. 1999. The CAD Triad Hypothesis: A Mapping Between Three Moral Emotions (Contempt, Anger, Disgust) and Three Moral Codes (Community, Autonomy, Divinity). *Journal of Personality and Social Psychology* 76.

Samuels, R. 2002. Nativism in Cognitive Science. *Mind and Language* 17.

Scott, J. F. 1971. *The Internalization of Norms*. Prentice-Hall.

Sherer, K. 1997. The Role of Culture in Emotion-Antecedent Appraisal. *Journal of Personality and Social Psychology* 73.

Shweder, R., M. Mahapatra, and J. Miller. 1987. Culture and Moral Development. In J. Kagan and S. Lamb, eds., *The Emergence of Morality in Young Children*. University of Chicago Press.

Shweder, R., N. Much, M. Mahapatra, and L. Park. 1998. The "Big Three" of Morality (Autonomy, Community, And Divinity), and the "Big Three" Explanations of Suffering. In A. Brandt and P. Rozin, eds., *Morality and Health*. Routledge.

Smith, E., and D. Medin. 1981. *Categories and Concepts*. Harvard University Press.

Sober, E., and D. S. Wilson. 1998. *Unto Others*. Harvard University Press.

Sperber, D. 1996. *Explaining Culture*. Blackwell Publishers.

Sripada, C. S. 2008. Nativism and Moral Psychology. In W. Sinnott-Armstrong, ed., *Moral Psychology*, vol. 1: *The Evolution of Morality: Adaptations and Innateness*. MIT Press.

———. Unpublished manuscript. Carving the Social World at Its Joints: Conventions and Moral Norms as Natural Kinds.

Stanovich, K. 1999. *Who Is Rational?* Lawrence Erlbaum.

Stich, S. P. 1993. Moral Philosophy and Mental Representation. In M. Hechter, L. Nadel, and R. Michod, eds., *The Origin of Values*. De Gruyter.

Thaler, R. H. 1992. *The Winners' Curse: Paradoxes and Anomalies in Economic Life*. Free Press.

Turiel, E. 1983. *The Development of Social Knowledge: Morality and Convention*. Cambridge University Press.

Wheatley, T., and J. Haidt. 2005. Hypnotically Induced Disgust Makes Moral Judgments More Severe. *Psychological Science* 16: 780–84.

Wilson, D. S., and R. O'Gorman. 2003. Emotions and Actions Associated with Norm Breaking Events. *Human Nature* 14, 3.

Wilson, D. S., C. Wilczynski, A. Wells, and L. Weiser. 2000. Gossip and Other Aspects of Language as Group-Level Adaptations. In C. Heyes and L. Huber, eds., *The Evolution of Cognition*. MIT Press.

Wilson, T. D., S. Lindsey, and T. Schooler. 2000. A Model of Dual Attitudes. *Psychological Review* 107.

13

HARM, AFFECT, AND THE MORAL/CONVENTIONAL DISTINCTION

Daniel Kelly, Stephen Stich, Kevin J. Haley, Serena J. Eng,

and Daniel M. T. Fessler

1. Introduction

Commonsense intuition seems to recognize a distinction between two quite different sorts of rules governing behavior, namely *moral rules* and *conventional rules*. Prototypical examples of moral rules include those prohibiting killing or injuring other people, stealing their property, or breaking promises. Prototypical examples of conventional rules include those prohibiting wearing gender-inappropriate clothing (e.g., men wearing dresses), licking one's plate at the dinner table, and talking in a classroom when one has not been called on by the teacher. Philosophers approaching this issue from many different perspectives have tried to specify the features that a rule must have if it is to count as moral or conventional, though no consensus has emerged (Mill 1863; Rawls 1971; Gewirth 1978; Dworkin 1978; Searle 1995). Starting in the mid-1970s, however, a number of psychologists, following the lead of Elliott Turiel, have offered characterizations of the distinction between moral and conventional rules, and have gone on to argue that the distinction is both psychologically real and psychologically important (Turiel 1979; Turiel 1983; Turiel, Killen, and Helwig 1987; Smetana 1993; Nucci 2001). Though the details have varied over time and from one author to another, the core ideas that researchers in this tradition have advanced about moral rules are as follows:

- Moral rules have an objective, prescriptive force; they are not dependent on the authority of any individual or institution.

- Moral rules hold generally, not just locally; they not only proscribe behavior here and now, they also proscribe behavior in other countries and at other times in history.
- Violations of moral rules typically involve a victim who has been harmed, whose rights have been violated, or who has been subject to an injustice.
- Violations of moral rules are typically more serious than violations of conventional rules.

By contrast, the following are the core features of conventional rules according to the account proposed by researchers in this tradition:

- Conventional rules are arbitrary, situation-dependent rules that facilitate social coordination and organization; they do not have an objective, prescriptive force, and they can be suspended or changed by an appropriate authoritative individual or institution.
- Conventional rules are often local; the conventional rules that are applicable in one community often will not apply in other communities or at other times in history.
- Violations of conventional rules do not involve a victim who has been harmed, whose rights have been violated, or who has been subject to an injustice.
- Violations of conventional rules are typically less serious than violations of moral rules.

To make the case that the moral/conventional distinction characterized in this way is both psychologically real and psychologically important, Turiel and his associates developed an experimental paradigm (sometimes called the "moral/conventional task") in which subjects are presented with prototypical examples of moral and conventional rule transgressions and asked a series of questions aimed at determining:

(i) whether the subjects consider the transgressive action to be wrong, and if so, how serious it is;
(ii) whether the subjects think that the wrongness of the transgression is "authority dependent," i.e., does it depend on the existence of a socially sanctioned rule or the pronouncement of an authority figure (for example, a subject who has said that a specific rule-violating act is wrong might be asked: "What if the teacher said there is no rule in this school about [that sort of rule violating act], would it be right to do it then?)";
(iii) whether the subjects think the rule is general in scope; is it applicable to everyone, everywhere, or just to a limited range of people, in a restricted set of circumstances?

(iv) how the subjects would justify the rule; in justifying the rule, do subjects invoke harm, justice, or rights, or do they invoke the fact that the rule prevails locally and/or that it fosters the smooth running of some social organization?

Early findings using this paradigm indicated that subjects' responses to prototypical moral and conventional transgressions did indeed differ systematically (Nucci and Turiel 1978; Smetana 1981; Nucci and Nucci 1982). Transgressions of prototypical moral rules (almost always involving a victim who has clearly been harmed) were judged to be more serious, the wrongness of the transgression was not "authority dependent," the violated rule was judged to be general in scope, and these judgments were justified by appeal to harm, justice, or rights. Transgressions of prototypical conventional rules, by contrast, were judged to be less serious, the rules themselves were authority dependent and not general in scope, and the judgments were not justified by appeal to harm, justice, and rights. During the last twenty-five years, much the same pattern has been found in an impressively diverse set of subjects ranging in age from toddlers (as young as three and a half years) to adults, with a substantial array of different nationalities and religions (e.g., Nucci, Turiel, and Encarnacion-Gawrych 1983; Hollos, Leis, and Turiel 1986; Yau and Smetana 2003; for reviews, see Smetana 1993; Tisak 1995; Nucci 2001). The pattern has also been found in children with a variety of cognitive and developmental abnormalities, including autism (Blair 1996; Blair, Monson, and Frederickson 2001; Nucci and Herman 1982; Smetana, Kelly, and Twentyman 1984; Smetana et al. 1999). Much has been made of the intriguing fact that the pattern is not found in psychopaths or in children exhibiting psychopathic tendencies (Blair 1995, 1997).

What conclusions have been drawn from this impressive array of findings? Here again, the details have varied over time and from one author to another, and some of the crucial notions invoked have not been explained as clearly as one might like. Nevertheless, it is clear that a majority of investigators in this research tradition would likely endorse something like the following collection of conclusions:

(C-1) In moral/conventional task experiments subjects typically exhibit one of two *signature response patterns*. In the *signature moral pattern* rules are judged to be authority independent and general in scope; violations are more serious, and rules are justified by appeal to harm, justice, and rights. In the *signature conventional pattern* rules are judged to be authority dependent and not general in scope; violations are less serious, and rules are not justified by appeal to harm, justice, or rights. Moreover, these signature response patterns are what philosophers of science sometimes call "nomological clusters"—there is a strong ("lawlike") tendency for the members of the cluster to occur together.

(C-2) (a) Transgressions involving harm, justice, or rights evoke the signature moral pattern.

(b) Transgressions that do not involve harm, justice, or rights evoke the signature conventional pattern.

(C-3) The regularities described in (C-1) and (C-2) are pan-cultural, and they emerge quite early in development.

In recent years, both the moral/conventional task and the conclusions based on it have become widely influential among naturalistically-oriented philosophers interested in understanding the nature of moral judgment. Though Turiel and his followers maintain that the moral/conventional distinction is constructed by children as they interact with their social environment (Turiel 1979, 1983; Nucci 2001), some philosophers have argued that (C-3) suggests that knowledge of the moral/conventional distinction is innate (Dwyer 1999, 2006). In an influential article and an important recent book, Shaun Nichols (2002, 2004) builds on suggestions made by researchers who emphasize the link between morality and emotions, such as Kagan (1984), Damasio (1994), and Haidt (Haidt, Koller, and Dias 1993; see also Greene and Haidt 2002). In developing his "senti-mental rules" hypothesis, Nichols draws out the implications of this link for work on the moral/conventional distinction. On Nichols' view, the content of both moral and conventional rules is acquired via social transmission. However, people are innately disposed to have affective responses to actions with certain sorts of consequences, and transgressions of rules proscribing such actions evoke the signature moral pattern, while transgressions of rules governing actions that do not trigger affective responses evoke the signature conventional pattern.

Not everyone, however, has been persuaded by conclusions (C-1)–(C-3). For the most part, the dissenters have focused on rules and transgressions that do not deal with harm, justice, or rights. (C-2b) predicts that such transgressions should evoke the signature conventional response pattern. But, the dissenters maintain, there are many societies in which such transgressions evoke one or more of the signature moral responses, and thus, contrary to (C-3), the regularities described in (C-1) and (C-2) are not pan-cultural. For example, Haidt et al. (1993) cleaved closely to the paradigm established by Turiel, and showed that low SES groups in both Brazil and the USA judged transgressions such as privately washing the toilet bowl with the national flag and privately masturbating with a dead chicken to be serious moral transgressions. Other researchers employing the moral/conventional task methodology have reported similar results. In a study of children in traditional Arab villages in Israel, Nisan (1987) found that all transgressions tested evoked most of the signature moral response pattern, including such transgressions as mixed-sex bathing and addressing a teacher by his first name, behaviors that do not involve harm, justice, or rights. In another study, Nucci and Turiel reported that Orthodox Jewish children in the USA judged a number of religious rules to be authority independent even though the rules did not deal with harm, justice, or rights (Nucci and Turiel 1993; see also Nucci 2001, chapter 2, for discussion). Perhaps most interestingly, Nichols (2002, 2004) showed that for a particular subset of etiquette rules, namely those that prohibit disgust-inducing actions, American children judged transgressions to be serious, authority independent, and general in scope. American college students judged those same etiquette rules to be serious and authority independent, though not general in scope. Nichols' results pose a clear challenge to both (C-1) and (C-2b). In his study, the putative nomological clusters posited in (C-1) come apart in two different ways and, contrary to what (C-2b) predicts, transgressions that do not involve harm, justice, or rights evoke most of the elements of the signature moral response pattern.

Taken together, the findings cited above pose a significant challenge to (C-1)–(C-3). However, none of these results involve transgressions that deal with harm, justice, or rights. Nor have we been able to find any other study in the literature that contradicts (C-2a) by demonstrating that transgressions involving harm, justice, or rights do not evoke the signature moral pattern. One possible explanation for the absence of such studies in the literature is that (C-2a) is both true and pan-cultural. Perhaps transgressions involving harm, justice, or rights do reliably and cross-culturally evoke the signature moral response pattern. However, we think there are at least three reasons to be skeptical of this explanation. First, though there are many studies employing the moral/conventional task paradigm, the range of transgressions involving harm that has been included in these studies is remarkably narrow. Early work using the paradigm was done by developmental psychologists who focused on young children; accordingly, the examples of harmful transgressions studied were all behaviors that would be familiar to youngsters, such as pulling hair or pushing someone off a swing. In the intervening years, the moral/conventional task has been used with many different subject populations, and as the range of subject populations has broadened, so has the set of transgressions that do not involve harm, justice, or rights. Some of these newer transgressions were behaviors that might not be familiar to young children. Oddly, however, all of the harmful transgressions studied have been of the "schoolyard" variety, even when the experimental subjects were incarcerated psychopathic murderers (Blair 1995)! As a result, little is known about how people respond to a broader range of harmful transgressions in the moral/conventional task. Second, philosophical views like Bernard Williams' "relativism of distance" and the sophisticated version of moral relativism defended by Gilbert Harman encourage the speculation that there may be many moral rules—including those prohibiting slavery, corporal punishment, and treating women as chattel—that people do not generalize to other cultures or other historical periods (Williams 1985; Harman 2000). Though no systematic evidence has been offered, we think these speculations have considerable intuitive plausibility. Third, our informal sampling of public discussion about recent news stories dealing with issues such as the treatment of detainees at the US military base in Guantanamo Bay suggests that a significant number of people do not consider moral rules prohibiting harmful treatment in such cases to be authority independent.

In light of the above considerations, we sought to explore whether there are harmful transgressions that, contrary to (C-2a), do not evoke the signature moral responses. To this end, we assembled a collection of brief scenarios describing a variety of harmful transgressions. We then created multiple versions of these scenarios: in some we varied the time and/or location of the transgression, in others we varied whether or not the transgression had been sanctioned by an appropriate authority. In order to test the hypothesis suggested by Nichols, Haidt, and others that negative affect plays a central role in generating most of the signature moral responses even when the transgression does not involve harm, we also included one non-harmful transgression that was intended to evoke strong affect. These scenarios were grouped into pairs, designed to determine whether subjects thought that the transgressions at issue were general in scope or authority dependent.

2. Methods

2.1 PARTICIPANTS

Participation took place via a website titled "Four Minute Morality Survey." Participants were recruited with the aid of links using this title posted on websites that serve as clearinghouses for online psychological research (Amoeba Web [http://www.vanguard.edu/faculty/ddegelman/amoebaweb/index.cfm?doc_id=2751], Online Social Psychology Studies [http://www.socialpsychology.org/expts.htm], and Psychology Research on the Net [http://psych.hanover.edu/Research/exponnet.html]); brief requests for participation were also posted under the Volunteers section of the community forum website Craigslist.org. Participation was wholly anonymous, and no compensation was offered. In order to ensure that participants were capable of granting informed consent, participation was restricted to those 18 years of age and over. After removing responses from individuals who did not answer all parts of the survey, we were left with 1635 participants (50.3% male; mean age = 28.09, SD 9.65), 16.1% of whom identified themselves as living outside of the United States.

2.2 MATERIALS AND PROCEDURE

Following an introductory web page outlining the nature of participation in the study, participants viewed a web page presenting a short scenario and two questions. The first question, utilizing a binary Yes/No response, asked participants whether it was OK for the protagonist in the scenario to engage in the action described. The second question, utilizing a Likert-type scale anchored by "Not at all bad" and "Very bad," asked participants "On a scale from 0 to 9, how would you rate [the protagonist's] behavior?." Clicking on a link labeled "Continue" led to a second web page containing information that modified or reframed the scenario presented on the previous page (for example, some of the second web pages contained the statement "Suppose that [an authority figure had previously stated that the given behavior was not acceptable]," etc.), followed by the same two questions. Finally, participants completed a brief demographic questionnaire including a question about current country of residence, followed by a final "Thank You" page that displayed contact information for the investigators.

The stimulus materials consisted of 18 distinct ordered pairs of scenarios derived from 9 scenario sets. Each scenario set consisted of two related scenarios, A and B, which could be presented in two orders: A followed by B, or B followed by A. Each participant was randomly assigned to view one of the 18 ordered pairs of scenarios. Below, we describe the scenarios and the rationales behind them in greater detail.

2.3 DO HARM NORMS GENERALIZE?

According to (C-2a), transgressions involving harm evoke the signature moral pattern, and one component of that pattern is generality: actions judged wrong here and now should also be judged wrong at other times and in other cultures. So if transgressions involving harm are regarded as wrong if they are committed now (or in recent history) but are not judged to be wrong if they were committed long ago, this poses a direct challenge to (C-2a). Two of the scenario sets were designed to explore whether participants generalize their responses to transgressions of harm norms that are quite different from the schoolyard harm norms and transgressions typically used in moral/conventional task studies. An ordered pair of scenarios derived from one of those sets, which we will refer to as the "Whipping/Time" set, read as follows:

Screen 1:

Three hundred years ago, whipping was a common practice in most navies and on cargo ships. There were no laws against it, and almost everyone thought that whipping was an appropriate way to discipline sailors who disobeyed orders or were drunk on duty.

Mr. Williams was an officer on a cargo ship 300 years ago. One night, while at sea, he found a sailor drunk at a time when the sailor should have been on watch. After the sailor sobered up, Williams punished the sailor by giving him 5 lashes with a whip.

Is it OK for Mr. Williams to whip the sailor?

  YES   NO

On a scale from 0 to 9, how would you rate Mr. Williams' behavior?

Not at all bad   Very bad

0 1 2 3 4 5 6 7 8 9

Screen 2:

Mr. Adams is an officer on a large modern American cargo ship in 2004. One night, while at sea, he finds a sailor drunk at a time when the sailor should have been monitoring the radar screen. After the sailor sobers up, Adams punishes the sailor by giving him 5 lashes with a whip.

[For purposes of brevity, we hereafter omit the questions presented.]

The other scenario set that focused on generalization of harm norms was explicitly inspired by the Williams-Harman conjecture. We will refer to it as the "Slavery/Spatio-Temporal" set. One of the ordered pairs of scenarios derived from this set was the following:

Screen 1:

In ancient Greece and Rome, slaves were an important part of the economic and social system. Greek and Roman slaves were used as oarsmen, as soldiers, to maintain households, and to supply agricultural labor.

Screen 2:

In the United States, slaves were an important part of the economy of the South 200 years ago. American slaves were used mainly to maintain households, and to supply agricultural labor.

2.4 ARE HARM NORMS AUTHORITY INDEPENDENT?

Authority independence is another component of the signature moral profile, which according to (C-2a) is evoked by transgressions involving harm. So if transgressions that are clearly harmful are not judged to be authority independent, once again this will pose a direct challenge to (C-2a). Six additional scenario sets, including four that were far removed from the schoolyard transgressions used in earlier studies, were designed to explore whether participants judged harm norms to be authority independent. An example, derived from what we will refer to as the "Spank/Authority" set, reads as follows:

Screen 1:

It is against the law for teachers to spank students. Ms. Williams is a third grade teacher, and she knows about the law prohibiting spanking. She has also received clear instructions from her Principal not to spank students. But when a boy in her class is very disruptive and repeatedly hits other children, she spanks him.

Screen 2:

Now suppose that it was not against the law for teachers to spank students, and that Ms. Williams' Principal had told her that she could spank students who misbehave if she wanted to.

As mentioned earlier, the scenarios comprising each set were presented in one of two orders. In some cases, the order of the questions could simply be reversed. However, in scenario sets exploring authority independence, the relation between the two pairs had to be a bit more complicated. To illustrate the point, here is the other, reverse-ordered pair of scenarios derived from the Spank/Authority set:

Screen 1:

Ms. Williams is a third grade teacher. Her Principal has told her that she can spank students who misbehave if she wants to, and in their state there is no law against spanking students. When a boy in her class is very disruptive and repeatedly hits other children, she spanks him.

Screen 2:

Now suppose that there was a law against spanking students in their state, and that Ms. Williams' Principal had given her clear instructions not to spank students.

A second set of scenarios designed to determine whether participants judged harm transgressions to be authority independent was the "Military/Authority" set. One of the ordered pairs derived from this set was:

Screen 1:

For many years, the military training of elite American commandos included a simulated interrogation by enemy forces in which the trainees were threatened and physically abused. Most people in the military believe that these simulated interrogations were helpful in preparing trainees for situations they might face later in their military careers. Though no one was ever killed or permanently disabled by the physical abuse they received during these simulated interrogations, the trainees often ended up with bruises or injuries that lasted for a week or more.

Recently, the Pentagon issued orders prohibiting physical abuse in military training. Sergeant Anderson is a soldier who trains elite American commandos. He knows about the orders prohibiting physical abuse and his immediate superiors have ordered him not to do it. Nonetheless, he regularly threatens and physically abuses trainees during the simulated interrogations that he conducts.

Screen 2:

Now suppose that the Pentagon had never issued orders prohibiting physical abuse in military training, and that Sergeant Anderson's superiors had told him that the use of physical abuse was acceptable in simulated interrogations.

2.5 DOES NEGATIVE AFFECT GENERATE SIGNATURE MORAL RESPONSES?

As we noted earlier, paralleling work by Haidt (Haidt et al. 1993; see also Greene and Haidt 2002), Nichols (2002, 2004) has proposed that negative affect plays a central role in generating most of the components of the signature moral response. More specifically, Nichols maintains that subjects will be more inclined to generalize the applicability of norms and to regard them as authority independent if transgressions of the norms evoke negative affect. To test Nichols' hypothesis about the role of negative affect in generating judgments of generality, we used scenarios involving mortuary cannibalism, on the assumption that this activity would be likely to generate strong affect among our sample of internet users. Here is an ordered pair derived from what we will call the "Cannibalism/Spatial" set:

Screen 1:

A number of cultures in various parts of the world traditionally engaged in the practice of eating parts of their deceased relatives' bodies as part of elaborate funeral rituals. Suppose you came upon such a funeral where people in one of these groups were eating parts of their deceased relatives' bodies.

Screen 2:

Now suppose there is a small group of Americans living in Northern California who have the ritual practice of eating parts of their deceased relatives' bodies as part of funeral rituals. Suppose you came upon a group of these Americans at a funeral where people were eating parts of the bodies of their deceased relatives.

3. Results

In this section, we will present an overview of some of the more interesting results. For the complete text of all the scenario pairs and full details on the results, go to: http://www.rci.rutgers.edu/~stich/Data/Data.htm.

In the Whipping/Temporal set we found a dramatic difference in subjects' judgments on the two members of the set. The results for the "Is it OK . . ." question are presented on the left in Figure 13.1; the scalar results are on the right. Clearly, many subjects think whipping was OK 300 years ago though they do not think it is OK now.

In the Slavery scenarios (in which both spatial and temporal distance varied), we again found a dramatic difference, confirming the Williams-Harman conjecture. Combining responses from the two versions, 11% of subjects reported that slavery was OK in Greco-Roman societies, but only 7% reported that it was OK in the American South (p = 0.021). This same pattern of results held for responses to the scalar "how bad" questions.[1]

The results from the Spank/Authority set were also quite dramatic. Pooling data from the two orders, we find that 44% of subjects responded that it is OK to spank when spanking is not prohibited, but only 5% said it was OK when spanking is prohibited (χ^2 = 63.02, p = 0.000). In the Military/Authority set, pooling the data from both orders, 58% of subjects responded that physical abuse is OK when it is not prohibited, while a mere 9% responded that it is OK when it is prohibited (χ^2 = 71.01, p = 0.000).

---

1. Significant order of presentation effects were found in all but three of our scenarios. It is not clear how this finding should be interpreted. For details, see the results available online at http://www.rci.rutgers.edu/~stich/Data/Data.htm.

%

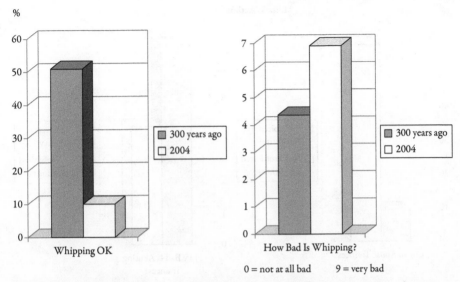

FIGURE 13.1 Judgments about the acceptability of whipping a derelict sailor 300 years ago and in 2004. The bar graph on the left shows the percent of YES responses to the binary "Is it OK?" question (χ^2 = 79.01; p = 0.000). The bar graph on the right represents responses to the question: How would you rate Mr. X's behavior? (t(198) = 13.55; p = 0.000). In both bar graphs, data from the two orders of presentation are pooled.

The results for both the "Is it OK" question and the scalar question in the Military/Authority set are presented in Figure 13.2. In sum, in both the Military/Authority set and the Spank/Authority set many subjects do not judge the harmful transgression to be authority independent.

In addition to the Spank/Authority and the Military/Authority sets, four other scenario sets were used to explore whether subjects treat harm transgressions as authority dependent. The pattern in all of these was similar to the patterns in the Spank/Authority and Military/Authority sets. The full text of the scenarios and all of the results are available at http://www.rci.rutgers.edu/~stich/Data/Data.htm; to give the reader a rough idea of the consistent pattern that we found, here is a quick overview of the responses for the "Is it OK" question, in each case pooled over the two orders of presentation:

- Whipping/Authority: OK when not prohibited: 22%; OK when prohibited: 6% (χ^2 = 25.26, p = 0.000).
- Prisoner Abuse/Authority: OK when not prohibited: 15%; OK when prohibited: 1% (χ^2 = 20.35, p = 0.000).
- Hair Pulling/Authority: OK when not prohibited: 14%; OK when prohibited: 4% (χ^2 = 12.89, p = 0.000).
- Hitting/Authority: OK when not prohibited: 52%; OK when prohibited: 14% (χ^2 = 62.35, p = 0.000).

%   Military/Authority

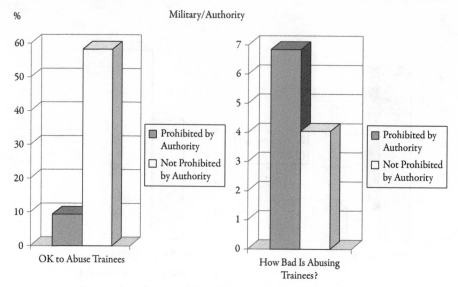

FIGURE 13.2 Judgments about the acceptability of abusing military trainees when prohibited and not prohibited by authority. The bar graph on the left shows the percent of YES responses to the binary "Is it OK?" question ($\chi^2 = 71.01$; p = 0.000). The bar graph on the right represents responses to the question: How would you rate Sgt. Anderson's behavior? (t(150) = 12.91; p = 0.000). In both bar graphs, data from the two orders of presentation are pooled.

In the Cannibalism/Spatial set, in the pooled data on the "Is it OK" question, 74% reported that eating human flesh is OK in foreign cultures, but only 56% reported that it is OK in Northern California ($\chi^2 = 26.68$, p = 0.000). If, as we have plausibly assumed, cannibalism evokes negative affect among our subjects, then this difference poses a problem for Nichols' claim that negative affect leads people to generalize their judgments.

4. Discussion

Much of the significance of the extensive literature using the moral/conventional task paradigm derives from the support this paradigm appears to provide for the central hypotheses of the Turiel School, namely: (C-1) the signature moral response pattern and the signature conventional response pattern are *nomological clusters*; (C-2a) transgressions involving harm, justice, or rights evoke the former pattern; (C-2b) transgressions not involving harm, justice, or rights evoke the latter pattern; and (C-3) the generalizations in (C-1), (C-2a), and (C-2b) are valid across cultures. As noted in the Introduction, previous work has cast doubt on (C-1), (C-2b), and (C-3), as investigators have reported a number of cases of transgressions that do not involve harm, justice, or rights but which nonetheless evoke components of the signature moral response pattern. However, the work reviewed in the Introduction offers no reason to doubt that (C-2a) is true.

Prompted by this earlier work, Nichols proposed that important elements of the signature moral response pattern are produced by transgressions that evoke significant negative affect (Nichols 2002, 2004). This hypothesis enables Nichols to explain why etiquette transgressions that evoke disgust are judged to be authority independent; it also leads him to predict that harm transgressions, which evoke distress, will also be judged to be authority independent and general in scope.

Six of the nine scenario sets used in our study were designed to determine whether there are harm transgressions that are not judged to be authority independent. In all six cases, the response patterns indicated that a substantial number of subjects did not judge harm transgressions to be authority independent. This casts doubt on both (C-2a) and on Nichols' prediction. Two other scenario sets in our study were designed to determine whether there are harm transgressions that people do not generalize to cultures that are distant in time and/or space. In both cases, a substantial number of subjects did not generalize, a result which casts further doubt on (C-2a). Our final scenario set was designed to directly test Nichols' hypothesis that affect plays a central role in generating judgments of generality in scope. The results give reason to doubt that hypothesis as well.

In the Introduction we cited a number of studies that call into question (C-1), (C-2b), and (C-3), three of the major conclusions that have been drawn from work in the Turiel tradition. The one conclusion on our list that was not challenged by those studies was (C-2a). Though additional studies using non-schoolyard transgressions are surely needed, our findings indicate that (C-2a) may also be mistaken. Thus our work adds to what we think is a growing body of evidence justifying substantial skepticism about *all* the major conclusions that have been drawn from studies using the moral/conventional task.

We believe that our findings raise two important questions that must be addressed in future research. First, why did previous research on schoolyard harm transgressions appear to support (C-2a)? Is there something special about these simple harm transgressions that is not shared by the more "grown-up" transgressions that we also used in our study? Second, if (C-1), (C-2a), (C-2b), and (C-3) are all mistaken, what are the implications for studies, such as Blair's work on psychopaths and individuals with autism (1995, 1996, 1997), which have used results on the moral/conventional task as the basis for drawing important conclusions about the processes underlying moral judgment? If, as our results suggest, the moral/conventional task is not a good assay for the existence of a psychologically important distinction, then the reasoning behind those conclusions merits careful scrutiny indeed.

ACKNOWLEDGEMENTS

We are grateful to Jonathan Haidt and to an anonymous referee for *Mind and Language* for many helpful suggestions on an earlier draft of this paper.

REFERENCES

Blair, R. 1995. A Cognitive Developmental Approach to Morality: Investigating the Psychopath. *Cognition* 57: 1–29.

———. 1996. Brief Report: Morality in the Autistic Child. *Journal of Autism and Developmental Disorders* 26: 571–79.

———. 1997. Moral Reasoning and the Child with Psychopathic Tendencies. *Personality and Individual Differences* 26: 731–39.

Blair, R., J. Monson, and N. Frederickson. 2001. Moral Reasoning and Conduct Problems in Children with Emotional and Behavioural Difficulties. *Personality and Individual Differences* 31: 799–811.

Damasio, A. R. 1994. *Descartes' Error: Emotion, Reason, and the Human Brain.* New York: Avon Books.

Dworkin, R. 1978. *Taking Rights Seriously.* Cambridge, MA: Harvard University Press.

Dwyer, S. 1999. Moral Competence. In K. Murasugi and R. Stainton, eds., *Philosophy and Linguistics.* Boulder, CO: Westview Press.

———. 2006. How Good Is the Linguistic Analogy? In P. Carruthers, S. Laurence, and S. Stich, eds., *The Innate Mind,* vol. II: *Culture and Cognition.* New York: Oxford University Press.

Gewirth, A. 1978. *Reason and Morality.* Chicago: University of Chicago Press.

Greene, J., and J. Haidt. 2002. How (and Where) Does Moral Judgment Work? *Trends in Cognitive Science* 612: 517–23.

Haidt, J., S. Koller, and M. Dias. 1993. Affect, Culture and Morality, or Is It Wrong to Eat Your Dog? *Journal of Personality and Social Psychology* 65: 613–28.

Harman, G. 2000. *Explaining Value.* Oxford: Clarendon Press.

Hollos, M., P. Leis, and E. Turiel. 1986. Social Reasoning in Ijo Children and Adolescents in Nigerian Communities. *Journal of Cross-Cultural Psychology* 17: 352–76.

Kagan, J. 1984. *The Nature of the Child.* New York: Basic Books.

Mill, J. S. 1863 [1963]. *Utilitarianism.* New York: Washington Square Press.

Nichols, S. 2002. Norms with Feeling: Toward a Psychological Account of Moral Judgment. *Cognition* 84: 223–36.

———. 2004. *Sentimental Rules: On the Natural Foundations of Moral Judgment.* Oxford: Oxford University Press.

Nisan, M. 1987. Moral Norms and Social Conventions: A Cross-Cultural Comparison. *Developmental Psychology* 23: 719–25.

Nucci, L. 2001. *Education in the Moral Domain.* Cambridge: Cambridge University Press.

Nucci, L., and S. Herman. 1982. Behavioral Disordered Children's Conceptions of Moral, Conventional, and Personal Issues. *Journal of Abnormal Child Psychology* 10: 411–25.

Nucci, L., and M. Nucci. 1982. Children's Social Interactions in the Context of Moral and Conventional Transgressions. *Child Development* 53: 403–12.

Nucci, L., and E. Turiel. 1978. Social Interactions and the Development of Social Concepts in Preschool Children. *Child Development* 49: 400–407.

———. 1993. God's Word, Religious Rules, and Their Relation to Christian and Jewish Children's Concepts of Morality. *Child Development* 64, 1475–1491.

Nucci, L., E. Turiel, and G. Encarnacion-Gawrych. 1983. Children's Social Interactions and Social Concepts in the Virgin Islands. *Journal of Cross-Cultural Psychology* 14: 469–87.

Rawls, J. 1971. *A Theory of Justice*. Cambridge, MA: Harvard University Press.

Searle, J. R. 1995. *The Construction of Social Reality*. New York: Free Press.

Smetana, J. 1981. Preschool Children's Conceptions of Moral and Social Rules. *Child Development* 52: 1333–6.

———. 1993. Understanding of Social Rules. In M. Bennett, ed., *The Development of Social Cognition: The Child as Psychologist*. New York: Guilford Press.

Smetana, J., M. Kelly, and C. Twentyman. 1984. Abused, Neglected, and Nonmaltreated Children's Conceptions of Moral and Social-Conventional Transgressions. *Child Development* 55: 277–87.

Smetana, J., S. Toth, D. Cicchetti, J. Bruce, P. Kane, and C. Daddis. 1999. Maltreated and Nonmaltreated Preschoolers' Conceptions of Hypothetical and Actual Moral Transgressions. *Developmental Psychology* 35: 269–81.

Tisak, M. 1995. Domains of Social Reasoning and Beyond. In R. Vasta, ed., *Annals of Child Development*, vol. 11. London: Jessica Kingsley.

Turiel, E. 1979. Distinct Conceptual and Developmental Domains: Social Convention and Morality. In H. Howe and C. Keasey, eds., *Nebraska Symposium on Motivation, 1977: Social Cognitive Development*. Lincoln: University of Nebraska Press.

———. 1983. *The Development of Social Knowledge*. Cambridge: Cambridge University Press.

Turiel, E., M. Killen, and C. Helwig. 1987. Morality: Its Structure, Functions, and Vagaries. In J. Kagan and S. Lamb, eds., *The Emergence of Morality in Young Children*. Chicago: University of Chicago Press.

Williams, B. 1985. *Ethics and the Limits of Philosophy*. Cambridge, MA: Harvard University Press.

Yau, J., and J. Smetana. 2003. Conceptions of Moral, Social-Conventional, and Personal Events Among Chinese Preschoolers in Hong Kong. *Child Development* 74: 1647–58.

14

TWO THEORIES ABOUT THE COGNITIVE ARCHITECTURE

UNDERLYING MORALITY

Daniel Kelly and Stephen Stich

IN THIS CHAPTER we compare two theories about the cognitive architecture underlying morality. One theory, proposed by Sripada and Stich (2006), posits an interlocking set of innate mechanisms that internalize moral norms from the surrounding community and generate intrinsic motivation to comply with these norms and to punish violators. The other theory, which we call the M/C model, was suggested by the widely discussed and influential work of Elliot Turiel, Larry Nucci, and others on the "moral/conventional task." This theory posits two distinct mental domains, the moral and the conventional, each of which gives rise to a characteristic suite of judgments about rules in that domain and about transgressions of those rules. We give an overview of both theories and of the data each was designed to explain. We go on to consider a growing body of evidence that suggests the M/C model is mistaken. That same evidence, however, is consistent with the Sripada and Stich theory. Thus, we conclude that the M/C model does not pose a serious challenge for the Sripada and Stich theory.

1. Introduction

In recent years, many cognitive scientists and empirically oriented philosophers have turned their attention to questions about morality.[1] Among the issues that have been actively discussed are the nature of the cognitive mechanisms subserving various aspects of moral cognition, and whether or to what extent those mechanisms are innately specified

---

1. For overviews of this work, see Doris and Stich 2005, 2006.

(Dwyer 1999, 2006; Greene and Haidt 2002; Haidt 2001; Hauser 2006; Nichols 2004; Prinz 2007; Sripada and Stich 2006). In this chapter we will compare two accounts of the cognitive architecture underlying morality. The first of these, which was proposed by Sripada and Stich (2006), posits an interlocking set of innate mechanisms that underlie the acquisition of moral norms from the surrounding community and the generation of characteristic motivations to comply with those norms and to punish others who violate them. In section 2 we'll give a brief sketch of the Sripada and Stich (S&S) model.

The second account has a more complicated provenance. Since the mid-1970s, some of the most influential work in moral psychology has been aimed at exploring and explaining the distinction between moral and conventional rules. Inspired by the pioneering work of Elliot Turiel, researchers in this tradition have published over 60 papers in which they investigate the emergence of the distinction in children and study its contours in an impressive range of subject populations. In section 3, we'll present an overview of this research and some of the important conclusions that have been drawn from it. Researchers in this tradition have devoted relatively little effort to proposing explicit accounts of the psychological mechanisms and processes that underlie people's ability to draw the moral/conventional distinction. So, in section 4, we will suggest one sort of psychological model that might be posited to explain the experimental results described in section 3 and the conclusions drawn from them. That model, which we'll call the M/C model, is dramatically different from the S&S model and, as we will argue in section 4, the two models lead to very different predictions. Since it promises to explain a vast array of empirical findings, the M/C model is also, arguably, the best-supported competitor to the S&S theory.

In section 5, our stance turns critical. Though there are many studies compatible with the conclusions about the moral/conventional distinction assembled in section 3, we believe there is mounting evidence that points in the other direction, suggesting that those conclusions are in fact false and thus that the M/C model, which is designed to explain those conclusions, is untenable. However, as we'll argue in section 5, this evidence is all comfortably compatible with the S&S model. So the conclusion for which we'll be arguing is that the M/C model does not pose a serious challenge to the S&S theory.

2. The S&S Theory of the Psychological Mechanisms Underlying Norms

Norms are a ubiquitous and important element of morality and of social life in general. In "A Framework for the Psychology of Norms," Sripada and Stich (2006) offer a theory about the innate cognitive architecture that gives rise to many of the individual and social level facts about norms. In this section we'll begin by recounting some of those facts. We'll then sketch some of the central elements of the S&S model, focusing on those that are most important when comparing the S&S model with the M/C model.[2]

---

2. For further details, along with an extended discussion of the evidence supporting the empirical claims made in this section, which is drawn from a number of different disciplines, see Sripada and Stich 2006.

S&S argue that norms are a theoretically important class of behavior-regulating social rules characterized by the following features:

- *Independent normativity:* Norms are rules which specify behaviors that are required or forbidden independently of any legal or social institution or authority, though of course some norms are also enforced by laws or other social institutions.
- *Punishment-supported stability:* Violations of norms result in a variety of punitive attitudes—including anger, condemnation, and blame—directed at rule violators, and these attitudes sometimes lead to punitive behavior; the presence of these punitive attitudes in members of the community contributes to a norm's long-term stability.
- *Universal presence:* All human societies have norms and sanctions for norm violations; this includes human groups that have been in long-standing isolation from other groups.
- *Ubiquity and importance:* In virtually all societies, norms regulate a vast array of day-to-day behaviors, including behavior in a large number of quite important domains, such as social exchanges, status relationships, sexual behavior, mate choice, diet, and a host of others.
- *Reliable pattern of ontogenesis:* All normal children appear to have knowledge of some norms by the age of three to five, and much of the cross-cultural diversity of normative rules among adults in different societies is already present and stable by the age of nine.
- *Cultural conformity:* Children typically acquire the normative rules which prevail in their cultural group, regardless of their own biological heritage.
- *Substantial cross-cultural diversity:* The specific behaviors required or forbidden by norms vary dramatically from culture to culture.

Together, these last two features of norms—cultural conformity and substantial cross-cultural diversity—strongly suggest that norm development is significantly culturally determined. Another important pair of properties of norms involves the motivational effects they have on agents. Philosophers have long emphasized that from a subjective perspective, norms present themselves with a unique kind of authority that differs from standard instrumental motivation. Sripada and Stich argue that this philosophic tradition is largely correct. More specifically, they maintain that an internalized norm generates robust and reliable motivation to comply with that norm and to punish those who violate it. Moreover, this motivation does not depend on the agent's beliefs about the social or personal consequences of compliance or non-compliance.

Let's now consider what sort of psychological architecture might explain the features of norms that we've assembled. The facts that norms are universally present in all societies, that they differ dramatically from one society to another, and that they exhibit a reliable pattern of ontogenesis suggest the existence of *innate mechanisms dedicated to norm acquisition*. The function of these mechanisms is to locate and internalize the norms prevailing in the surrounding society. Once a normative rule is acquired, it gives rise to reliable and robust intrinsic motivation to comply with the norm and to punish those who violate it. It is worth emphasizing that this pair of motivations sharply distinguishes norms from other rules or information that may be mentally represented elsewhere in an agent's cognitive system. This suggests that *norm utilization is subserved by its own, dedicated "execution" mechanism, and that this mechanism, too, is innate*. Thus a first pass at characterizing the psychological architecture subserving the acquisition and utilization of norms might look like the system labeled with black type in figure 14.1.[3]

The mechanism for acquiring norms depicted in figure 14.1 performs a cluster of functions that includes identifying behavioral cues which indicate that a punishment-enforced normative rule prevails in the local cultural environment, inferring the content of the rule, and passing that information on to other cognitive mechanisms for storage and utilization. On the S&S account, the acquisition mechanism operates automatically—a person does not decide to turn it on and cannot decide to turn it off, though it *may* be the case that the acquisition mechanism gradually turns itself off starting at some point late in adolescence. The mechanism for executing norms performs a set of functions that includes maintaining a database of the normative rules that were identified and passed along by the acquisition

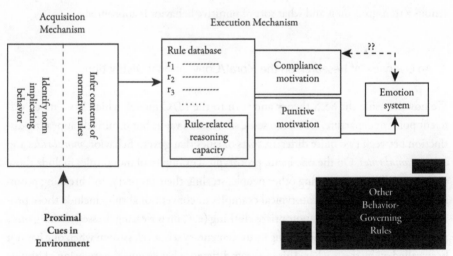

FIGURE 14.1 The S&S model. A first pass at characterizing the cognitive architecture underlying the acquisition and utilization of norms.

---

3. Figure 14.1, we should stress, is only a first pass. In the last section of their paper, S&S develop a much more complicated model, aimed at accommodating a significantly larger collection of empirical findings. We focus on the simplified model in figure 14.1 because it makes it easier to see the differences between S&S's model and the M/C model that we'll elaborate in section 4.

mechanism, generating intrinsic motivation to comply with those rules, detecting violations of the rules, and generating intrinsic motivation to punish the violators.

Of course, people also accept and follow many behavior-governing rules that they do not treat as norms, in the robust sense just described. The motivation for following these other types of rules varies, and can include considerations of prudence, fear of social sanctions, and a variety of other factors. These rules, it is plausible to assume, are stored and executed by a variety of different mental mechanisms, represented by the black boxes in the lower right of figure 14.1. What distinguishes this heterogeneous set of rules from norms, according to the S&S theory, is that they are not acquired by the innate norm acquisition mechanism and they *do not* automatically engender either the compliance motivation or the punitive motivation associated with norms.

It is important to note that the architecture depicted in figure 14.1 allows considerable variation with respect to the sorts of rules that the norm system can acquire and the sorts of punishments these rules can motivate.[4] The normative rule database can contain rules governing a wide variety of behaviors including harming others, sexual practices, food preparation and consumption, burial rituals, and so on. Moreover, rules can include information about the people to whom they apply, and different rules can apply to different groups of people. Some might apply to everyone, while others might apply only to more narrowly circumscribed groups such as adult women, or unmarried men, or members of a specific religion or caste, or even menstruating women in one's own tribe or village. And while all rule violations lead to punitive attitudes, the rules themselves can specify how serious a transgression is and what sort of punitive behavior is appropriate.

3. An Overview of Research on the Moral/Conventional Distinction

We now set aside the S&S theory and turn to the M/C model, which has a much different point of departure. Common sense sanctions a vague but intuitively appealing distinction between two quite different sorts of rules that govern behavior: *moral rules* and *conventional rules*. On the one hand, prototypical examples of moral rules include those prohibiting killing or injuring other people, stealing their property, and breaking promises. On the other hand, prototypical examples of conventional rules include those prohibiting wearing gender-inappropriate clothing (e.g., men wearing dresses), licking one's plate at the dinner table, and talking in an elementary school classroom when one has not been called on by the teacher. This intuitive difference has caught the attention of philosophers of various orientations. Many have attempted to clarify the distinction, some by specifying those features that are distinctive of moral rules (Mill 1863/1963; Rawls 1971; Gewirth 1978; Dworkin 1978; Gert 2005), and others by giving an account of systems of

---

4. See, however, Sripada and Stich 2006, sec. 5.6, for a discussion of the various ways in which the contents of the database might be constrained or biased.

conventions and the rules that are embedded within them (Lewis 1969; Searle 1995). Despite (or perhaps due to) the wide range of approaches philosophers have taken to this issue, no single account has been widely accepted.

Psychologists have taken an interest in the distinction as well. Starting in the mid-1970s, a number of developmental psychologists, following the lead of Elliot Turiel, have offered their own characterization(s) of the intuitive distinction between moral and conventional rules. Moreover, they have gone on to argue that the distinction, as they characterize it, is both psychologically real and psychologically important (Turiel 1979, 1983; Turiel, Killen, and Helwig 1987; Smetana 1993; Nucci 2001). Let us start with the proposed characterization of the distinction. Though the details have varied over time and from one author to another, the core ideas that researchers in this tradition have advanced about moral rules are as follows:

- Moral rules have an objective, prescriptive force; they are not dependent on the authority of any individual or institution.
- Moral rules hold generally, not just locally; they not only proscribe behavior here and now, they also proscribe behavior in other countries and at other times in history.
- Violations of moral rules involve a victim who has been harmed, whose rights have been violated, or who has been subjected to an injustice.
- Violations of moral rules are typically more serious than violations of conventional rules.

By contrast, the following are the core features of conventional rules according to the account proposed by researchers in this tradition:

- Conventional rules are arbitrary, situation-dependent rules that facilitate social coordination and organization; they do not have an objective, prescriptive force, and they can be suspended or changed by an appropriate authoritative individual or institution.
- Conventional rules are often local; the conventional rules that are applicable in one community often will not apply in other communities or at other times in history.
- Violations of conventional rules do not involve a victim who has been harmed, whose rights have been violated, or who has been subjected to an injustice.
- Violations of conventional rules are typically less serious than violations of moral rules.[5]

---

5. Although there seems to be general agreement that violations of moral rules are *typically* more serious than violations of conventional rules, some authors downplay the importance of seriousness in their formal characterization of the moral/conventional distinction. For example, Smetana (1993, 117) maintains that "severity of the transgression is not considered to be a formal criterion for distinguishing moral and conventional rules and transgressions."

Having offered a characterization of the distinction between moral and conventional rules, Turiel and his associates then set about developing an experimental paradigm to explore the psychological status of the distinction they had described. Experiments were designed to test the hypothesis that the moral/conventional distinction, characterized in this way, is both psychologically real and psychologically important. In these experiments (employing what has come to be called the "moral/conventional task"), subjects are presented with examples of transgressions of both prototypical moral rules and prototypical conventional rules, and are then asked a series of probe questions. These questions are designed to elicit subjects' judgments about the transgressions along a number of significant dimensions, often called criteria. More specifically, "criterion judgments" were elicited from subjects to determine the following:

1. whether the subjects consider the transgressive action to be wrong, and if so, how serious it is;

2. whether the subjects think that the wrongness of the transgression is "authority dependent" (i.e., does it depend on the existence of a socially sanctioned rule or on the pronouncement or endorsement of an authority figure?). For example, a subject who has said that a specific rule-violating act is wrong might be asked: "What if the teacher said there is no rule in this school about [that sort of rule-violating act]? Would it be right to do it then?";

3. whether the subjects think the rule is general in scope; whether it is applicable to everyone, everywhere, or just to a limited range of people, in a restricted set of circumstances;

4. how the subjects would justify the rule; in justifying the rule, do subjects invoke harm, justice, or rights, or do they invoke the fact that the rule prevails locally and/or that it fosters the smooth running of some social organization?

Results from the initial experiments using this paradigm supported the claim that the moral/conventional distinction, as characterized by Turiel and his associates, is indeed psychologically significant. They indicated that subjects' responses to prototypical moral and conventional transgressions differed systematically, and in just the way suggested by the characterization given above (Nucci and Turiel 1978; Smetana 1981; Nucci and Nucci 1982). More specifically, transgressions of prototypical moral rules (almost always involving a victim who has clearly been harmed) were judged to be wrong and to be more serious than transgressions of prototypical conventional rules; the wrongness of the transgression was judged not to be "authority dependent"; the violated rule was judged to be general in scope; and these judgments were justified by appeal to harm, justice, or rights. Subjects judged transgressions of prototypical conventional rules quite differently. They were judged to be wrong but usually less serious; the rules themselves were judged to be authority-dependent and not general in scope; and the judgments were not justified by appeal to harm, justice, or rights. Adding to the case that the distinction thus characterized is psychologically real was the fact that the pattern of replies appeared to be quite robust. The pattern was not significantly affected, for instance, by the way in which transgressions were presented to subjects, the wording of the questions, or the order in which the questions were asked.

Supporting the contention that this pattern of results—along with the moral/conventional distinction as characterized by Turiel and his followers—is psychologically important is the prevalence of the pattern across a wide range of subject populations. Since the mid-1970s, the same pattern reported in the initial studies has been found in an impressively diverse set of subjects ranging in age from toddlers (as young as three and a half years) to adults, with a substantial array of different nationalities and religions.[6] The pattern has also been found in children with a variety of cognitive and developmental abnormalities, including autism (Blair 1996; Blair, Monson, and Frederickson 2001; Nucci and Herman 1982; Smetana, Kelly, and Twentyman 1984; Smetana et al. 1999). The pattern is notably absent, however, in both psychopaths and children exhibiting psychopathic tendencies (Blair 1995, 1997). Though many researchers see significance in this latter finding, no single explanation yet enjoys a consensus.

This large and prima facie striking set of experimental results seems laden with psychological implications. So it is hardly surprising that researchers in the moral/conventional tradition have drawn ambitious conclusions from their work. Here again the details of those conclusions have varied over time and from one author to another, and unfortunately, some of the crucial notions appealed to in those conclusions have not been explained as carefully as one might like. Nevertheless, it is clear that a majority of investigators in this research tradition would likely endorse something like the following collection of conclusions:

(C-1) The Clustering of Criterion Judgments: In moral/conventional task experiments, subjects typically exhibit one of two *signature response patterns*. In the first signature pattern, rules are judged to be authority-independent and general in scope; violations are wrong and typically judged to be serious; and judgments are justified by appeal to harm, justice, or rights. We call this the *signature moral pattern*. In the second signature pattern, rules are judged to be authority-dependent and not general in scope; violations are wrong but usually less serious; and judgments are not justified by appeal to harm, justice, or rights. We call this the *signature conventional pattern*. Moreover, these signature response patterns are what philosophers of

6. For a study that included three-and-a-half-year-old children, see Smetana and Braeges 1990. Among the cultural and religious groups studied were Chinese preschoolers (Yau and Smetana 2003), Korean children (Song, Smetana, and Kim 1987), Ijo children in Nigeria (Hollos, Leis, and Turiel 1986), Virgin Islander children, teens, and adults (Nucci, Turiel, and Encarnacion-Gawrych 1983), Roman Catholic high school and university students (Nucci 1985), Amish and Mennonite children and teens, and Dutch Reformed Calvinist children and teens (Nucci and Turiel 1993). For reviews, see Smetana 1993, Tisak 1995, and Nucci 2001.

science sometimes call "nomological clusters"—there is a strong (lawlike) tendency for the members of the cluster to occur together.

(C-2) Response Patterns and Transgression Types: Not only do criterion judgments cluster into two distinct response patterns, but each pattern is reliably evoked by a certain *type* of transgression. Specifically, (a) transgressions involving harm, justice, or rights evoke the *signature moral pattern*, while (b) transgressions that do not involve harm, justice, or rights evoke the *signature conventional pattern*.

(C-3) Universality: The regularities described in (C-1) and (C-2) are pancultural, and they emerge quite early in development.

4. Explaining the Results: The M/C Model

As we noted in the Introduction, we are skeptical about these conclusions, but in this section we propose to bracket that skepticism. Instead, we will assume that (C-1), (C-2), and (C-3) are true and ask what sort of cognitive architecture could explain such (putative) facts. Researchers who work on the moral/conventional distinction maintain that their results can be explained by the hypothesis that moral rules and conventional rules belong to two quite different conceptual "domains." By way of clarifying this hypothesis, these researchers highlight several important characteristics of the domains, maintaining that they are *distinct* and *independent* from each other, that they *underlie* subjects' capacity to differentiate between different types of rules, and that they are *present cross-culturally* and *in place quite early in development*.

According to Nucci, for example, "[t]hese two forms of social regulation, morality and convention, are both part of the social order. Conceptually, however, they are not reducible to one another and are understood within distinct conceptual frameworks or domains" (Nucci 2001, 7). Turiel similarly claims that "social convention and morality a) constitute two distinct conceptual domains, which b) develop independently of each other" (Turiel 1979, 77). While they are sometimes hard to interpret, advocates of the domain hypothesis also suggest that the differences between the conceptual domains have an important role to play in explaining the criterion judgments elicited from subjects on the moral/conventional task. The nature of that role is often left vague because advocates emphasize subjects' *ability* to differentiate different kinds of social rules, rather than spelling out the alleged role of the domains in *explaining* the ability. For example, Smetana remarks: "Children have been asked to make judgments along a set of dimensions that are hypothesized to differentiate moral and conventional rules. . . . In general, this research has indicated that children across a wide age range distinguish between moral and social-conventional rules and transgressions in their reasoning and judgments" (Smetana 1993, 114–15). Nucci more directly connects this ability to the domains, and to the specific criterion judgments elicited in the M/C task experiments: "[w]hat we have learned through research over the past twenty-five years is that people in general . . . reason very differently about matters of morality, convention and personal choice. More specifically, these conceptual differences become apparent when people are asked to evaluate different actions in terms of criteria [like those set out above]" (Nucci 2001, 6). Nucci also makes the following remarks regarding the explanatory link between the domains and performance on the M/C task experiments:

> In order to gain clear-cut answers to whether or not people make distinctions between morality and convention, researchers have asked people to make judgments that would constitute prototypical examples of moral or conventional issues [*sic*]. . . . Consistent with the assumptions of domain theory, children and adults distinguish between morality and convention *on the basis of these criteria*. (2001, 10; emphasis added)

In elucidating the (putative) relationship between subjects' performances on the M/C task and the hypothesized conceptual domains, comments such as these suggest a cognitive architecture like the one we are about to propose. Finally, advocates of the moral/conventional domain theory hold that these domains are cross-cultural, and in place early in psychological development. Nucci maintains that "in all cases, children and adolescents have been found to treat moral issues entailing harm and injustice in much the same way" (2001, 12) and that "the domain of morality is structured around issues that are universal and non-arbitrary" (19). Yau and Smetana hold that "[r]esearch in diverse cultures has shown that children across a wide age range differentiate morality from social convention" (2003, 654).

While the moral/conventional domain theorists do not go on to offer explicit cognitive models like those proposed by S&S, the details of their domain hypothesis suggest what such a model might look like. For if the fact that a rule belongs to a particular domain is to *explain* the pattern of responses that subjects offer when presented with questions about the rule and transgressions of the rule, then a domain is best thought of as a *functionally distinct component of the mind* that stores rules (or representations of rules). In addition to its proprietary set of rules, each distinct domain would also contain a proprietary body of information. The information stored in each domain would lead subjects to respond as they do to questions about the rules stored in that domain, and also to questions about transgressions of those rules. The information stored in the moral domain, for example, would indicate that rules stored therein are authority-independent and general in scope; it would also indicate that those rules can be justified by appeal to harm, justice, or rights, and that transgressions of those rules are typically serious. Furthermore, in order to explain facts such as those described in (C-2a), which claims that the signature moral response pattern is evoked only by rules that deal with harm, justice, or rights, the domain hypothesis must also insist that the component of the mind that we're calling the moral domain is restricted in such a way that it contains only rules of that sort. Figure 14.2 is our attempt to capture the essential features of the domain hypothesis. We will call it the M/C model.

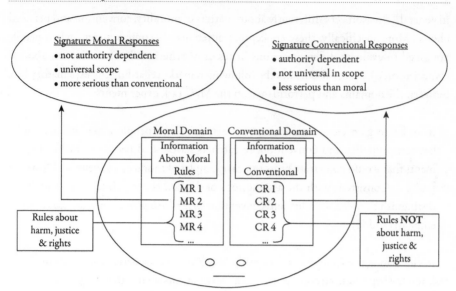

FIGURE 14.2 The M/C model of the psychological mechanisms underlying performance on the moral/conventional task.

The M/C model depicted in figure 14.2 raises two important questions. First, where does the information in the domains come from? Second, what explains the fact that only rules dealing with harm, justice, or rights end up being stored in the moral domain, while only rules dealing with things other than harm, justice, or rights are stored in the conventional domain? Several answers to these questions have been proposed. First, though they are often hard to interpret, many researchers in the Turiel tradition suggest that the information about moral and conventional rules in the two domains is "constructed," by which they seem to mean that it is not conveyed by other people. Rather, that information is acquired via individual learning as the child interacts with the social environment. Researchers in this tradition also apparently believe that particular features of these interactions with the social environment enable the child to figure out which rules belong in which domain.[7] Others, most notably Susan Dwyer (1999, 2006), impressed by the claim that the information contained in the domains is both pancultural and available early in

---

7. For instance, Turiel (1983, 9) says that "thought is organized and . . . it is constructed out of the child's interactions with the environment." See also Turiel 1979, 108: "the child's conceptual knowledge is formed out of his actions upon the environment. To form concepts about objects and events the child must act upon them. Thus conceptual development is a constructive process stemming from individual-environment interactions." In response to the second question, what explains the fact that only rules dealing with harm, justice, or rights come to be stored in the moral domain, while only rules not dealing with harm, justice, or rights come to be stored in the conventional domain, domain theorists appeal to the (putatively) distinctive and intrinsic features of actions that violate moral rules. Rules dealing with harm, justice, or rights end up in the moral domain because transgressions of those rules, in contrast to transgressions of conventional rules, are marked by distinctive and intrinsic features, namely, "consequences such as harm inflicted upon others, violation of rights, effect on general welfare" (Turiel 1979, 80).

development, argue that the information is innately specified. Dwyer may also believe that some of the rules in the moral domain are innately specified as well. In support of this view, she offers a version of the "poverty of the stimulus" argument commonly found in discussions of linguistic knowledge. It is hard to see how the information that the child ends up with could possibly be inferred from the limited information available in the child's physical and social environment.[8] Finally, Shaun Nichols (2002, 2004) has offered a rather different account in which both social transmission and innate predispositions play a role. On Nichols's hypothesis, the *content* of both moral and conventional rules is acquired via social transmission. However, people are innately disposed to have affective responses to actions with certain sorts of consequences, and rules proscribing those actions evoke the signature moral response.

Obviously, each of these alternatives needs to be spelled out in greater detail. That's not a project we propose to undertake here, however. Nor need we take a stand on which alternative is more plausible. For it is our view that the architecture proposed in the M/C model is seriously mistaken. To put the point bluntly, we don't believe that the psychological domains posited by the M/C model exist. If we are right, then questions about where the information in the domains comes from and how particular rules get assigned to one domain or the other are otiose.

Before setting out our case against the M/C model, it will be useful to underscore the differences between that model and the S&S model, and to draw out some of the ways in which the models lead to quite different predictions. Since the M/C model was designed to explain (C-1), (C-2), and (C-3)—the major conclusions that researchers in the Turiel tradition have drawn from moral/conventional task experiments—it is no surprise that the M/C model is comfortably compatible with those conclusions. But if the S&S model is correct, we should expect each of those conclusions to be false.

To see why, let's focus first on (C-1), the clustering of criterion judgments. The claim here is that the two signature response patterns in moral/conventional task experiments are *nomological clusters*, and thus that the members of each cluster will typically occur together. On the M/C model, this is just what we should expect, since responses to moral/conventional task questions are guided by the information in the domain where the rule being investigated is stored. On the S&S theory, on the other hand, no such nomological clustering is to be expected. According to the S&S theory, any rule in the normative rule database will generate reliable and robust intrinsic motivation to comply and to punish violators. Since these motivations are intrinsic, they do not depend on authority, or on the existence of social rules, or on fear of social sanctions. So, for any rule stored in a subject's normative rule database, we would expect the subject to judge the rule to be authority-independent when given the moral/conventional task, since the subject feels motivated to comply and to punish violations whether or not the rule is

---

8. For more on poverty of the stimulus arguments, see Segal 2007 and Baker 2007. For another discussion of the innateness of the moral/conventional/distinction, see Wilson 1993, 141ff.

sanctioned by an authority. However, the S&S theory gives no reason to think authority independence will regularly be accompanied by any other specific criterion judgment. On the contrary, rules stored in the normative rule database can vary in how general they are, how serious transgressions are, and what their justification is. Thus, we should *not* expect that rules judged to be authority-independent will also be judged to be applicable to everyone, that their transgressions will be judged to be serious, or that they will be justified by appeal to harm, justice, or rights.

The S&S theory also maintains that lots of different sorts of behavior regulating rules will be stored outside the normative rule database—in the black boxes in figure 14.1. Though some rules stored there might evoke an authority-independent response, many will not. Moreover, rules stored outside the normative rule database may evoke any pattern of answers on the seriousness and generality questions. So if the S&S model is on the right track, there should be no nomological clustering of the signature response patterns. Indeed, the S&S theory leads us to expect that responses in the moral/conventional task could occur in just about any combination.

(C-2) deals with the alleged correlation between response patterns and transgression types. More specifically, it maintains that transgressions involving harm, justice, or rights will evoke the signature moral pattern, while transgressions not involving harm, justice, or rights will evoke the signature conventional pattern. And here again, of course, this is just what the M/C model would predict, since on that model only rules involving harm, justice, or rights can be stored in the moral domain, and only rules not involving harm, justice, or rights can be stored in the conventional domain. On the S&S model, by contrast, neither rules involving harm, justice, or rights nor rules *not* involving harm, justice, or rights constitute a distinctive psychological category. Some rules from each group may find their way into the normative rule database, and others may be stored in other components of the mind. So, for example, on the S&S account, it is entirely possible that a rule prohibiting harm of a certain sort would be stored outside the normative rule database, and thus that a transgression of that rule would evoke an authority-*dependent* response. It is also possible that a rule prohibiting behavior that does not involve harm, justice, or rights would be included in the normative rule database, and thus that a transgression of that rule would evoke an authority-*independent* response.

Finally, according to (C-3), the regularities described in (C-1) and (C-2) are both pancultural and early emerging. The M/C model, as we have developed it, predicts that the patterns will be pancultural, though it does not explain why they emerge early in development.[9] The S&S theory need not worry about the patterns being pancultural or early emerging, since, as we've just seen, the S&S theory predicts that the patterns do not exist at all!

Clearly, there is no shortage of empirically testable disagreements between the two models. Let's now ask which one fares better in accommodating the data.

---

9. To the best of our knowledge, advocates of moral/conventional domain theory have never offered an explanation of the (putative) fact that the patterns emerge early in development.

5 The Models and the Evidence

In section 3 we gave an overview of some of the findings that have led many researchers in the Turiel tradition to advocate conclusions (C-1) through (C-3). Not everyone has been persuaded by these conclusions, however. Most of the dissenters have been impressed with the diversity in the sorts of behaviors that different cultures "moralize" by treating them as wrong in an authority-independent way. These researchers have focused on rules and transgressions that do not involve harm, justice, or rights. (C-2b) predicts that such transgressions should evoke the signature conventional response pattern. But, the dissenters maintain, there are many societies in which such transgressions evoke one or more of the signature *moral* responses. If this is correct, then not only is (C-2b) false, but so is (C-3)—the claim that the regularities described in (C-1) and (C-2) are pancultural.

For example, in a pioneering and influential study Haidt et al. (Haidt, Koller, and Dias 1993) employed much of standard moral/conventional task methodology, and showed that low socioeconomic status (SES) groups in both Brazil and the United States judged activities such as privately washing the toilet bowl with the national flag and privately masturbating with a dead chicken to be generally and seriously wrong, and that this judgment did not depend on any authority figure or explicit rule prohibiting these activities. In addition to the standard probe questions, Haidt et al. added another question that allowed subjects to explicitly specify which transgressions they took to be harmless. Even when the low SES groups acknowledged that no one was harmed by a particular sort of behavior, those groups still judged many of the harmless transgressions to have most of the features of the signature moral response pattern. Other researchers employing the moral/conventional task methodology have reported similar results. In a study of children in traditional Arab villages in Israel, Nisan (1987) found that all of the transgressions tested evoked most of the signature moral response pattern, including such transgressions as mixed-sex bathing and addressing a teacher by his first name—behaviors that clearly do not involve harm, justice, or rights. In another study, Nucci and Turiel reported that Orthodox Jewish children in the United States judged a number of religious rules to be authority-independent even though the rules did not deal with harm, justice, or rights (Nucci and Turiel 1993; see also Nucci 2001, chap. 2, for discussion).

Perhaps most interestingly, Nichols (2002, 2004) showed that for a particular subset of etiquette rules, namely, those that prohibit disgust-inducing actions, American children judged transgressions to be serious, authority-independent, and general in scope. American college students judged transgression of those same etiquette rules to be serious and authority-independent, though they did not regard the rules as general in scope. Like the other studies just described, Nichols's work clearly raises problems for claim (C-2b). However, his results are unique in that they also pose a particularly clean challenge to (C-1), the claim about the clustering of criterion judgments. In

Nichols's study, not only do transgressions that do not involve harm, justice, or rights evoke most of the elements of the signature moral response pattern, contrary to what (C-2b) predicts, but the putative nomological clusters posited in (C-1) come apart in two different ways. Indeed, Nichols finds three different sets of responses to rules that do not involve harm, justice, or rights,[10] and finds that adults and children respond differently to the same rules.

Taken together, we think the findings just cited pose a significant challenge to (C-1) through (C-3), and thus to the M/C model which predicts those conclusions. Since the S&S theory does not predict that transgressions not involving harm, justice, or rights will exhibit the signature conventional response pattern, and does not expect criterion judgments to exhibit any systematic pattern or nomological clustering, all of the findings we've just cited are comfortably compatible with the S&S theory. Moreover, we suspect that the results described in the previous two paragraphs may be only the tip of the iceberg. For a variety of reasons, researchers using the moral/conventional task have looked only at a relatively narrow range of transgressions that do not involve harm, rights, or justice. However, the literature in cultural psychology and anthropology, as well as reports in the popular press, lead us to expect that if researchers using the moral/conventional task were to study a more extensive range of transgressions in a wider range of cultural groups, they would find (C-1) through (C-3) *massively* disconfirmed. For example, we would expect that a vast majority of Americans, along with people in many other cultures, would judge that consensual sibling incest is wrong, and that the wrongness of incest is authority-independent.[11] We would expect much the same judgment about homosexual sex from the 55 percent of the American public who tell opinion researchers that homosexual behavior is a sin.[12] We are also prepared to bet that in traditional societies where taboo violations and failure to respond appropriately to "polluting" acts such as being touched by a low-caste person are taken very seriously, these violations would not lead to the full set of signature conventional responses that would be predicted by the M/C model.[13]

It is noteworthy that none of the studies we have described as posing a challenge to (C-1) through (C-3) use transgressions involving harm, justice, or rights. Nor have we been able to find any other study in the literature that contradicts (C-2a) by demonstrating that transgressions involving harm, justice, or rights do not evoke the signature

---

10. The third pattern that Nichols found was the only one predicted by (C-2b): Etiquette rules prohibiting actions that are not disgust-inducing evoke the signature conventional pattern.

11. Haidt (2001) reports a study in which university-age subjects could not justify their strong moral condemnation of a case of consensual sibling incest in which the couple used two forms of birth control. Though Haidt did not ask questions designed to gauge subjects' views about authority independence, the tapes of some of the interviews in that study make it hard to believe that the subjects thought the wrongness of incest was authority-dependent.

12. The Pew Forum on Religion and Public Life, http://pewforum.org/docs/index.php?DocID=38#4.

13. See Shweder, Mahapatra, and Miller 1987 and Shweder et al. 1997 for some suggestive discussion of norms governing polluting acts, and Fessler and Navarrete 2003 for very useful material on taboos.

moral pattern. One possible explanation for the absence of such studies in the literature is that (C-2a) is both true and pancultural. Perhaps transgressions involving harm, justice, or rights do reliably and cross-culturally evoke the signature moral response pattern. However, we think there are at least three reasons to be skeptical of this explanation. First, though there are many studies employing the moral/conventional task paradigm, the range of transgressions involving harm that have been included in these studies is remarkably narrow. Early work using the paradigm was done by developmental psychologists and was focused on young children. Thus the examples of harmful transgressions studied were all behaviors that would be familiar to youngsters, such as pulling hair and pushing someone off a swing. In the intervening years, the moral/conventional task has been used with a number of different subject populations, and the set of transgressions that do not involve harm, justice, or rights has broadened somewhat as well. Though we know of no study that asked subjects to consider incest, homosexuality, or taboo violations, some of the transgressions described in more recent work were behaviors that might not be familiar to young children. Oddly, however, all of the *harmful* transgressions studied have been of the "schoolyard" variety, even when the experimental subjects were incarcerated psychopathic murderers (Blair 1995)! As a result, little is known about how people respond to a broader range of harmful transgressions in the moral/conventional task. Second, philosophical views such as Bernard Williams's "relativism of distance" and the sophisticated version of moral relativism defended by Gilbert Marinali encourage the speculation that there may be many moral rules—including those prohibiting slavery, corporal punishment, and treating women as chattel—that people do not generalize to other cultures or other historical periods (Williams 1985; Harman 2000). Though these philosophers offer only anecdotal evidence, we think these speculations have considerable intuitive plausibility. Third, our informal sampling of public discussion about recent news stories dealing with issues such as the treatment of detainees at the U.S. military base in Guantanamo Bay, Cuba, suggests that a significant number of people do not consider rules prohibiting harmful treatment in such cases to hold independently of authority.

In order to explore the possibility that many harmful transgressions that are not of the schoolyard variety would *not* evoke the signature moral response pattern, we designed a Web-based study, in collaboration with Kevin Haley, Serena Eng, and Daniel Fessler, in which participants were asked about a number of such transgressions (Kelly et al. 2007). For example, to explore whether rules prohibiting use of corporal punishment are judged to be authority-independent, participants were presented with the pair of questions in box 14.1. The results were quite dramatic: 8 percent of participants said it was OK to spank the boy in response to question (A), and 48 percent said it was OK to spank the boy in response to question (B). Similar results were found when the questions, appropriately modified, were asked in the opposite order.[14] So for a very substantial number of

---

14. Pooling the two orders, 5 percent judged that spanking was OK in response to question (A) and 44 percent judged that it was OK in response to question (B), p = 0.000.

respondents, it appears that the rule against spanking is not authority-independent. Five other scenarios were used to explore whether rules prohibiting serious harms would be judged to be authority-independent, and in each case the results indicated that for a significant number of subjects, they were not.[15]

BOX 14.1

A PAIR OF QUESTIONS DESIGNED TO DETERMINE WHETHER
PARTICIPANTS JUDGED A RULE AGAINST CORPORAL PUNISHMENT TO BE
AUTHORITY-INDEPENDENT

(A) It is against the law for teachers to spank students. Ms. Williams is a third grade teacher, and she knows about the law prohibiting spanking. She also has received clear instructions from her principal not to spank students. But when a boy in her class is very disruptive and repeatedly hits other children, she spanks him.

Is it OK for Ms. Williams to spank the boy?

YES   NO

On a scale from 0 to 9, how would you rate Ms. Williams' behavior?

Not at all bad   Very bad

   0   1   2   3   4   5   6   7   8   9

(B) Now suppose that it was not against the law for teachers to spank students and that Ms. Williams' principal had told her that she could spank students who misbehave if she wanted to.

Is it OK for Ms. Williams to spank the boy?

YES   NO

On a scale from 0 to 9, how would you rate Ms. Williams' behavior?

Not at all bad   Very bad

   0   1   2   3   4   5   6   7   8   9

The pair of questions in box 14.2 was designed to determine whether participants judged rules prohibiting harmful behavior to be temporally universal. Are actions that are judged to be wrong now also judged to be wrong in the past? Once again the results were quite dramatic, clearly confirming Williams's claims about the "relativism of distance." In response to question (A), 52 percent of participants said that it was OK to whip a drunken sailor 300 years ago, but only 6 percent said it was OK to do it today![16] A second pair of questions asked subjects to judge the wrongness of slavery in the American South and in ancient Greece and Rome. In this case, too, significantly fewer subjects judged slavery to be wrong long ago and far away.

---

15. The full text of all questions used in this study, along with all of the data, are available online at http://www.rci.rutgers.edu/~stich/Data/Scenarios%20&%20Results.rtf.

16. Asking the questions in the opposite order had no significant effect. When the results from the two orders were pooled, 51 percent said whipping was OK in response to (A) and 10 percent said it was OK in response to (B), $p = 0.000$.

BOX 14.2

A PAIR OF QUESTIONS DESIGNED TO DETERMINE WHETHER
PARTICIPANTS JUDGED A RULE AGAINST CORPORAL PUNISHMENT TO BE
TEMPORALLY GENERAL

(A) Three hundred years ago, whipping was a common practice in most navies and
on cargo ships. There were no laws against it, and almost everyone thought that
whipping was an appropriate way to discipline sailors who disobeyed orders or
were drunk on duty. Mr. Williams was an officer on a cargo ship 300 years ago.
One night while at sea, he found a sailor drunk at a time when the sailor should
have been on watch. After the sailor sobered up, Williams punished the sailor
by giving him five lashes with a whip.

Is it OK for Mr. Williams to whip the sailor?

YES   NO

On a scale from 0 to 9, how would you rate Mr. Williams' behavior?

Not at all bad   Very bad

0   1   2   3   4   5   6   7   8   9

(B) Mr. Adams is an officer on a large modern American cargo ship in 2004. One
night while at sea, he finds a sailor drunk at a time when the sailor should have
been monitoring the radar screen. After the sailor sobers up, Adams punishes the
sailor by giving him five lashes with a whip.

Is it OK for Mr. Adams to whip the sailor?

YES   NO

On a scale from 0 to 9, how would you rate Mr. Adams' behavior?

Not at all bad   Very bad

0   1   2   3   4   5   6   7   8   9

We believe that the Kelly et al. experiment poses a serious challenge to (C-2a),
which claims that harm norms evoke the signature moral pattern. Rather, it seems,
when we go beyond the narrow range of schoolyard transgressions that have been
used in previous studies, many subjects think that rules prohibiting harmful actions
are neither authority-independent nor general in scope. In directly challenging the
conclusion (C-2a), these findings significantly add to the case against the M/C
model, which was designed to predict that conclusion and explain why it was true.
As we noted earlier, the S&S model, in contrast with the M/C model, accords harm
norms no special status. According to the S&S theory, some harm norms may be
stored in the normative rule database, and those that are will be judged to be authority-independent, though they may be of limited generality. Others may be stored
in other components of the mind, and those may be judged to be both authority-
dependent and of limited generality. So the Kelly et al. results are fully compatible
with the S&S theory.

6. Conclusion

Our goal, in this chapter, has been to assess the merits of two competing accounts of the cognitive architecture underlying morality: the S&S model, which was designed to account for a range of findings in a variety of disciplines, and the M/C model, which was designed to explain the main conclusions drawn from a large body of work using the moral/conventional task. We've tried to shape the discussion in a way that emphasizes the differences between these two models and highlights the fact that they are incompatible with one another: they make divergent predictions about a wide range of moral judgments, including the sorts of judgments that are central to the M/C task. The view we've been arguing for is that the S&S model is clearly superior, especially in light of the growing body of evidence indicating that the conclusions (C-1), (C-2), and (C-3), which the M/C model was designed to explain, are themselves very problematic. A leitmotif in our critique of the conclusions drawn from moral/conventional task studies is that these studies have focused on a very narrow range of rules and transgressions. As researchers have begun to explore people's judgments about a broader and more varied class of rules and transgressions, the shortcomings of the conclusions drawn from earlier work using the moral/conventional task have become increasingly apparent.

While the focus of this chapter has been largely restricted to two specific accounts of cognitive architecture, there is reason to think that, if correct, our grim assessment of the conclusions drawn from studies using the moral/conventional task has implications of much wider relevance. In recent years, a number of psychologists and philosophers have assumed that the moral/conventional task tells us something important about moral psychology, and they have used this assumption in arguing for a variety of important claims. For example, the philosopher Shaun Nichols (2004) has claimed that the capacity to draw the moral/conventional distinction "reflects the ability to appreciate the distinctive status of morality" (4), that it "plumbs a fairly deep feature of moral judgment" (6), and that it can be used "as a measure of moral cognition" (196). And the psychologist James Blair (1995, 1996, 1997; Blair, Monson, and Frederickson 2001) has used the task to draw conclusions about the moral capacities of psychopaths and individuals with autism. We've argued that the evidence reviewed above shows the M/C model of cognitive architecture is false. That evidence also suggests that the moral/conventional task itself is not a good assay for the existence of a psychologically important distinction. If that's right, then the reasoning behind claims like Nichols's and Blair's merits very careful scrutiny.

We are often asked whether we think that our critique of work in the Turiel tradition indicates that there is no moral/conventional distinction at all. Our answer is that the question itself is far from clear. If what is being asked is "Do the commonsense concepts of *moral rule* (or *moral transgression*) and *conventional rule* (or *conventional transgression*) pick out different sets of rules (or transgressions)?" the answer is almost certainly yes. But if what is being asked is "Are the sets of rules picked out by these commonsense concepts *disjoint?*" the answer is that we don't know, since no one has done the sort of careful work that would be required to answer this question in a convincing way. We suspect, however, that the answer is no, since lots of transgressions strike us as both moral and conventional. In our culture, for example, it would be both a moral transgression and a violation of convention to wear a clown suit to one's father's funeral. But whatever the facts may be about the ordinary concepts of moral rule and conventional rule, they won't get researchers like Nichols and Blair off the hook. For when Nichols says that the capacity to draw the moral/convention distinction "reflects the ability to appreciate the distinctive status of morality," and when Blair uses the inability to draw the distinction as evidence about the moral cognition of psychopaths, what they have in mind is the distinction as drawn by *Turiel and his followers*. And if we are right, that ability cannot be used "as a measure of moral cognition" (Nichols 2004, 196) or of anything else of psychological interest.

REFERENCES

Baker, M. 2007. The Creative Aspect of Language Use and Nonbiological Nativism. In P. Carruthers, S. Laurence, and S. Stich, eds., *The Innate Mind: Foundations and the Future*. Oxford: Oxford University Press.

Blair, R. 1995. A Cognitive Developmental Approach to Morality: Investigating the Psychopath. *Cognition* 57.

———. 1996. Brief Report: Morality in the Autistic Child. *Journal of Autism and Developmental Disorders* 26.

———. 1997. Moral Reasoning and the Child with Psychopathic Tendencies. *Personality and Individual Differences* 26.

Blair, R., J. Monson, and N. Frederickson. 2001. Moral Reasoning and Conduct Problems in Children with Emotional and Behavioural Difficulties. *Personality and Individual Differences* 31.

Doris, J., and S. Stich. 2005. As a Matter of Fact: Empirical Perspectives on Ethics. In F. Jackson and M. Smith, eds., *The Oxford Handbook of Contemporary Philosophy*. Oxford: Oxford University Press.

———. 2006. Moral Psychology: Empirical Approaches. In Edward N. Zalta, ed., *The Stanford Encyclopedia of Philosophy*, summer 2006 edition, http://plato.stanford.edu/archives/sum2006/entries/moral-psych-emp.

Dworkin, R. 1978. *Taking Rights Seriously*. Cambridge, MA: Harvard University Press.

Dwyer, S. 1999. Moral Competence. In K. Murasugi and R. Stainton, eds., *Philosophy and Linguistics*. Boulder, CO: Westview Press.

———. 2006. How Good Is the Linguistic Analogy? In P. Carruthers, S. Laurence, and S. Stich, eds., *The Innate Mind: Culture and Cognition*. Oxford: Oxford University Press.

Fessler, D. M. T., and C. D. Navarrete. 2003. Meat Is Good to Taboo: Dietary Proscriptions as a Product of the Interaction of Psychological Mechanisms and Social Processes. *Journal of Cognition and Culture* 3.

Gert, B. 2005. The Definition of Morality. In Edward N. Zalta, ed., *The Stanford Encyclopedia of Philosophy*, fall 2005 edition, http://plato.stanford.edu/archives/fall2005/entries/morality-definition.

Gewirth, A. 1978. *Reason and Morality*. Chicago: University of Chicago Press.

Greene, J., and J. Haidt. 2002. How (and Where) Does Moral Judgment Work? *Trends in Cognitive Science* 6.

Haidt, J. 2001. The Emotional Dog and Its Rational Tail. *Psychological Review* 108.

Haidt, J., S. Koller, and M. Dias. 1993. Affect, Culture and Morality, or Is It Wrong to Eat Your Dog? *Journal of Personality and Social Psychology* 65.

Harman, G. 2000. *Explaining Value*. Oxford: Clarendon Press.

Hauser, M. 2006. *Moral Minds: How Nature Designed Our Universal Sense of Right and Wrong*. New York: HarperCollins.

Hollos, M., P. Leis, and E. Turiel. 1986. Social Reasoning in Ijo Children and Adolescents in Nigerian Communities. *Journal of Cross-Cultural Psychology* 17.

Kelly, D., S. Stich, K. Haley, S. Eng, and D. Fessler. 2007. Harm, Affect and the Moral/Conventional Distinction. *Mind and Language* 22.

Mill, J. S. 1863/1963. *Utilitarianism*. New York: Washington Square Press.

Nichols, S. 2002. Norms with Feeling: Toward a Psychological Account of Moral Judgment. *Cognition* 84.

———. 2004. *Sentimental Rules: On the Natural Foundations of Moral Judgment*. Oxford: Oxford University Press.

Nisan, M. 1987. Moral Norms and Social Conventions: A Cross-Cultural Comparison. *Developmental Psychology* 23.

Nucci, L. 1985. Children's Conceptions of Morality, Societal Convention, and Religious Prescription. In C. Harding, ed., *Moral Dilemmas: Philosophical and Psychological Issues in the Development of Moral Reasoning*. Chicago: Precedent.

———. 2001. *Education in the Moral Domain*. Cambridge: Cambridge University Press.

Nucci, L., and S. Herman. 1982. Behavioral Disordered Children's Conceptions of Moral, Conventional, and Personal Issues. *Journal of Abnormal Child Psychology*, 10.

Nucci, L., and M. Nucci. 1982. Children's Social Interactions in the Context of Moral and Conventional Transgressions. *Child Development* 53.

Nucci, L., and E. Turiel. 1993. God's Word, Religious Rules, and Their Relation to Christian and Jewish Children's Concepts of Morality. *Child Development* 64.

Nucci, L., E. Turiel, and G. Encarnacion-Gawrych. 1983. Children's Social Interactions and Social Concepts in the Virgin Islands. *Journal of Cross-Cultural Psychology* 14.

Prinz, J. 2007. *The Emotional Construction of Morals*. Oxford: Oxford University Press.

Rawls, J. 1971. *A Theory of Justice*. Cambridge, MA: Harvard University Press.

Searle, J. R. 1995. *The Construction of Social Reality*. New York: Free Press.

Segal, G. 2007. Poverty of Stimulus Arguments Concerning Language and Folk Psychology. In P. Carruthers, S. Laurence, and S. Stich, eds., *The Innate Mind: Foundations and the Future*. Oxford: Oxford University Press.

Shweder, R., M. Mahapatra, and J. Miller. 1987. Culture and Moral Development. In J. Kagan and S. Lamb, eds., *The Emergence of Morality in Young Children*. Chicago: University of Chicago Press.

Shweder, R., N. Much, M. Mahapatra, and L. Park. 1997. The "Big Three" of Morality (Autonomy, Community, and Divinity) and the "Big Three" Explanations of Suffering. In A. Brandt and P. Rozin, eds., *Morality and Health*. New York: Routledge.

Smetana, J. 1981. Preschool Children's Conceptions of Moral and Social Rules. *Child Development* 52.

———. 1993. Understanding of Social Rules. In M. Bennett, ed., *The Development of Social Cognition: The Child as Psychologist*. New York: Guilford Press.

Smetana, J., and J. Braeges. 1990. The Development of Toddlers' Moral and Conventional Judgments. *Merrill-Palmer Quarterly* 36.

Smetana, J., M. Kelly, and C. Twentyman. 1984. Abused, Neglected, and Nonmaltreated Children's Conceptions of Moral and Social-Conventional Transgressions. *Child Development* 55.

Smetana, J., S. Toth, D. Cicchetti, J. Bruce, P. Kane, and C. Daddis. 1999. Maltreated and Nonmaltreated Preschoolers' Conceptions of Hypothetical and Actual Moral Transgressions. *Developmental Psychology* 35.

Song, M., J. Smetana, and S. Kim. 1987. Korean Children's Conceptions of Moral and Conventional Transgressions. *Developmental Psychology* 23.

Sripada, C., and S. Stich. 2006. A Framework for the Psychology of Norms. In P. Carruthers, S. Laurence, and S. Stich, eds., *The Innate Mind: Culture and Cognition*. Oxford: Oxford University Press.

Tisak, M. 1995. Domains of Social Reasoning and Beyond. In R. Vasta, ed., *Annals of Child Development*, vol. 11. London: Jessica Kingsley.

Turiel, E. 1979. Distinct Conceptual and Developmental Domains: Social Convention and Morality. In H. Howe and C. Keasey, eds., *Nebraska Symposium on Motivation, 1977: Social Cognitive Development*. Lincoln: University of Nebraska Press.

———. 1983. *The Development of Social Knowledge*. Cambridge: Cambridge University Press.

Turiel, E., M. Killen, and C. Helwig. 1987. Morality: Its Structure, Functions, and Vagaries. In J. Kagan and S. Lamb, eds., *The Emergence of Morality in Young Children*. Chicago: University of Chicago Press.

Turiel, E., and L. Nucci. 1978. Social Interactions and the Development of Social Concepts in Preschool Children. *Child Development* 49.

Williams, B. 1985. *Ethics and the Limits of Philosophy*. Cambridge, MA: Harvard University Press.

Wilson, J. 1993. *The Moral Sense*. New York: Free Press.

Yau, J., and J. Smetana. 2003. Conceptions of Moral, Social-Conventional, and Personal Events Among Chinese Preschoolers in Hong Kong. *Child Development* 74.

15

ALTRUISM

Stephen Stich, John M. Doris, and Erica Roedder

1. Philosophical Background

People sometimes behave in ways that benefit others, and they sometimes do this while knowing that their helpful behavior will be costly, unpleasant, or dangerous. But at least since Plato's classic discussion in the second book of the *Republic*, debate has raged over *why* people behave in these ways. Are their motives altruistic, or is their behavior ultimately motivated by self-interest? According to Thomas Hobbes, who famously advocated the latter option,

> No man giveth but with intention of good to himself, because gift is voluntary; and of all voluntary acts, the object is to every man his own good; of which, if men see they shall be frustrated, there will be no beginning of benevolence or trust, nor consequently of mutual help. (Hobbes 1981, ch. 15)

This selfish or egoistic view of human motivation has had no shortage of eminent advocates, including La Rochefoucauld (2007), Bentham (1824, 392–93), and Nietzsche (1997, 148).[1] Egoism is also arguably the dominant view of human motivation in much

---

1. Interpretation of historical texts is, of course, often less than straightforward. While there are passages in the works of each of these philosophers that can be interpreted as advocating egoism, scholars might debate whether these passages reflect the author's considered option. Much the same is true for the defenders of altruism mentioned below.

contemporary social science, particularly in economics (see Grant 1997; Miller 1999). Dissenting voices, though perhaps fewer in number, have been no less eminent. Butler (1726, esp. Sermon XI), Hume (1975, 272, 298), Rousseau (1985), and Adam Smith (1853) have all argued that, sometimes at least, human motivation is genuinely *altruistic*.

Although the issue that divides egoistic and altruistic accounts of human motivation is substantially empirical, competing answers may have profound consequences for moral theory.[2] For example, Kant (1785, sec. 1, para. 12) famously argued that a person should act "not from inclination but from duty, and by this would his conduct first acquire true moral worth." But egoism maintains that *all* human motivation is ultimately self-interested, and if so, people *can't* act "from duty" in the way that Kant urged. Thus, if egoism were true, Kant's account would entail that *no* conduct has "true moral worth."[3] The same difficulty obtains for Aristotle's insistence, in *Nicomachean Ethics*, ii 4, that acting virtuously requires choosing the virtuous action "for its own sake." Once again, if all actions are ultimately self-interested, it is unclear how any action can meet Aristotle's criterion, and we must consider the possibility of skepticism about virtuous action.

Whether or not such difficulties can be ameliorated, there can be little doubt that they resonate widely. It is easy to find philosophers who suggest that altruism is required for morality or that egoism is incompatible with morality—and easier still to find philosophers who claim that *other* philosophers think this. In the standard reference work we consulted (LaFollette 2000a), examples abound:

> Moral behavior is, at the most general level, altruistic behavior, motivated by the desire to promote not only our own welfare but the welfare of others. (Rachels 2000, 81)
>
> [O]ne central assumption motivating ethical theory in the Analytic tradition is that the function of ethics is to combat the inherent egoism or selfishness of individuals. Indeed, many thinkers define the basic goal of morality as "selflessness" or "altruism." (Schroeder 2000, 396)
>
> Philosophers since Socrates worried that humans might be capable of acting only to promote their own self-interest. But if that is all we can do, then it seems morality is impossible. (LaFollette 2000b, 5)

---

2. A note on terminology: we shall use the terms "egoism" and "altruism" for views about the nature of human motivation that will be explained in more detail below. Other authors prefer to call these views "psychological egoism" and "psychological altruism" to distinguish them from normative claims about how people should behave, and from an evolutionary notion of altruism that we'll discuss in Section 3. Since both evolutionary altruism and psychological altruism will be considered in Section 3, we'll use "psychological altruism" for the latter notation in that section.

3. Kant appears to consider this possibility: "A cool observer, one that does not mistake the wish for good, however lively, for its reality, may sometimes doubt whether true virtue is actually found anywhere in the world" (Kant 1785, sec. 2)

If these philosophers are right, and egoism is true, moral skepticism may be in order.

Additionally, if egoism is true, then we face a dilemma in answering the venerable question, "Why should I be moral?" If this question requests a justification that can actually motivate an agent to act morally, then egoism poses strong constraints on how it can be answered: the answer will have to ground moral motivation in the agent's self-interest. On the other hand, the question "Why should I be moral?" might be construed as inquiring after a merely theoretic justification—one that might or might not motivate a person to act morally. If the question is construed in this way, and if egoism is true, then there may well be a disconnect between moral theory and moral motivation. Our best moral theories may well answer the question "Why be moral?" by appealing to symmetry between the self and other or ideals of social harmony. Unfortunately, these appeals— while perhaps enlightening—will be motivationally moot.

Yet another cluster of issues surrounds the principle *"ought" implies "can."* Depending on the modal strength of egoism, it could turn out that persons simply cannot be motivated by anything other than self-interest. If this is true, and if "ought" implies "can," then it cannot be said that humans *ought* to be motivated by anything other than self-interest.

There are related implications for political philosophy. If the egoists are right, then the *only* way to motivate prosocial behavior is to give people a selfish reason for engaging in such behavior, and this constrains the design of political institutions intended to encourage civic-minded behavior. John Stuart Mill, who like Bentham before him was both a utilitarian and an egoist, advocated a variety of manipulative social interventions to engender conformity with utilitarian moral standards.[4]

Since the empirical debate between egoists and altruists appears to have such striking implications, it should come as no surprise that psychologists and other scientists have done a great deal of work aimed at determining which view is correct. But before we turn to the empirical literature, it is important to get clearer on what the debate is really about. We shall begin, in Section 2, with a brief sketch of a cluster of assumptions about human desires, beliefs, actions, and motivation that are widely shared by historical and contemporary authors on both sides in the debate. With this as background, we'll be able to offer a more sharply focused account of the debate.[5] In Section 3, our focus will be on links between evolutionary theory and the egoism/altruism debate. There is a substantial literature employing evolutionary theory on each side of the issue. However, it is our contention that neither camp has offered a convincing case. We are much more sanguine about recent research on altruism in social psychology, which will be our topic in Section 4.

---

4. For example, Mill suggests instilling "hope of favor and the fear of displeasure from our fellow creatures or from the Ruler of the Universe" (Mill 1861/2001, ch. 3). Another proposal was to instill a feeling of conscience: "a pain, more or less intense, attendant on violation of duty.... This feeling [is] all encrusted over with collateral associations . . . derived from . . . fear; from all the forms of religious feeling; from self-esteem . . . and occasionally even self-abasement" (ibid.).

5. For more on the history of the debate between egoists and altruists, see Broad 1930; MacIntyre 1967; Nagel 1970; Batson 1991, chs. 1–3; Sober and Wilson 1998, ch. 9.

Although we don't think this work has resolved the debate, we shall argue that it has made illuminating progress—progress that philosophers interested in the question cannot afford to ignore.

2. Desires and Practical Reasoning

As we understand it, the egoism/altruism debate is typically structured by three familiar assumptions about the nature of desire and practical reasoning. First, parties to the debate typically assume that genuine actions are caused by desires. If Albert wants (or desires) to raise his hand, and if this desire causes his hand to go up, then this behavior counts as an *action*.[6] If, by contrast, Beth has no desire to raise her hand but it goes up anyway because of a nervous tic, or because Albert lifts it, then this behavior does not count as an action. Within this debate the term "desire" is used in a very inclusive way; it is a general term covering many motivational states. Donald Davidson (1963, 685–86) famously character-ized all such motivational states as *pro-attitudes* (we prefer the term *desires*) and empha-sized that this was meant to include states such as warnings, urges, promptings, and yens, enduring character traits like a taste for loud company, and passing fancies like a sudden desire to touch a woman's elbow!

A second assumption is that desires and beliefs can interact to generate a chain of new desires via a process that is often called *practical reasoning*. Thus, for example, if Cathy wants an espresso, and if she acquires the belief that the Starbucks on Main Street is the best place to get an espresso, this may cause her to desire to go to the Starbucks on Main Street. If she believes that the best way to get to Main Street is to take the number 43 bus, this, along with the newly formed desire to go to Starbucks, may cause a desire to take the number 43 bus. And so on.[7] Cathy's desire to take the bus and her desire to go to Star-bucks are *instrumental* desires. She has them only because she wants that espresso.

But, and this is the final assumption, not all desires can be instrumental desires. If we are to avoid circularity or an infinite regress, there must be some desires that are not generated by our belief that satisfying them will facilitate satisfying some other desire. These are our "ultimate" desires; the states of affairs that will satisfy them are desired, as is often said, *for their own sake*. Figure 15.1 depicts all this in a format that will come in handy later on.

With this background in place, it can be seen that the debate between egoists and al-truists is a debate about *ultimate* desires. Egoists maintain that *all* of our ultimate desires are selfish, and although altruists concede that some of our ultimate desires are selfish,

---

6. Actually, not just any causal link between the desire and the behavior will do, and a great deal of philosophical work has been devoted to specifying the appropriate connection. See Grice 1971; Davidson 1980; Bratman 1987; Velleman 1989; Wilson 2002.

7. For a classic statement of this conception of action, see Goldman 1970.

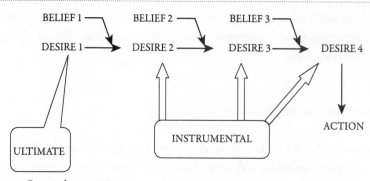

FIGURE 15.1 Practical reasoning
A causal process in which pre-existing desires and beliefs interact to generate a chain of new instrumental desire.

they insist that people can and do have ultimate desires for the well-being of others. However, this account of the debate leaves a number of sticky issues yet to be addressed.[8]

One of these concerns the distinction between ultimate and instrumental desires. Our explanation of the distinction suggests that all desires fall into one category or the other, but it certainly seems to be possible for some desires to be both. Consider, for example, the desire to avoid pain. This is often cited as a paradigm case of an ultimate desire. But now suppose that David is in pain and desires not to be. Suppose too that David believes his mother is deeply distressed by the fact that he is in pain, and that David *also* wants his pain to end in order to alleviate his mother's distress. Should we count this desire as ultimate or instrumental? It seems to be both. In the context of the egoism/altruism debate we think that both sides should agree that a desire counts as ultimate if it has *any* ultimate "component" and that desires like David's clearly have an ultimate component. So if people's desires for the well-being of others ever have an ultimate component, then the altruist wins. But this still leaves us with the problem of saying more precisely what this talk about "ultimate components" amounts to.

Some progress can be made by appealing to counterfactuals: a person's desire has an ultimate component if she would continue to have the desire even if she no longer believed that satisfying the desire would lead to the satisfaction of some other desire. This is only a first pass, since, as clever philosophy majors know, it is easy to construct counterexamples to simple counterfactual analyses like this one.[9] For our purposes, however, no more nuanced account is required.

Another issue is how we are to interpret the notion of *self-interested* desires and desires *for the well-being of others*. According to one influential version of egoism, often called

8. This account of the debate raises interesting questions about the role of emotions. There are complex issues here. However, in this chapter we shall be assuming that, for any emotion, if that emotion is to serve as the origin of action, it must cause some ultimate motivational state (i.e., an ultimate desire) or include some motivational component (again, an ultimate desire). We can then ask whether that ultimate desire is self- or other-oriented. This, in turn, will determine whether the action is egoistic or altruistic.

9. Martin 1994; Lewis 1997.

hedonism, there are only two sorts of ultimate desires: the desire for pleasure and the desire to avoid pain.[10] Another, less restrictive, version of egoism allows that people may have a much wider range of ultimate self-interested desires, including desires for their own survival, power, and prestige.[11] While these desires are unproblematically self-interested, there are lots of other examples whose status is less clear. Is a desire for friendship self-interested? How about a desire to be involved in a mutually loving relationship? Or a desire to discover the cure for AIDS? Whether or not people have ultimate desires for any of these things is an open question. If they do, then hedonism is simply mistaken, since hedonism claims that there are only two sorts of ultimate desires. But what about non-hedonistic egoism; would it be refuted if people have ultimate desires like these? Given the conceptual uncertainties, we're inclined to think that egoism is vague. And similarly for altruism: if Albert has an ultimate desire that Beth be happy or that Cathy be cured of AIDS, then clearly the altruists are right and the egoists are wrong, since ultimate desires like these, if they exist, surely count as desires for the well-being of others. But suppose Albert has the ultimate desire that he and Beth be involved in a mutually loving relation-ship, or that *he* (as opposed to his rival in the next lab) cure Cathy of AIDS. Would *these* ultimate desires suffice to show that altruism is right and egoism is wrong? Here again there is no clear and well-motivated answer. So altruism, like egoism, is vague. Fortunately, this vagueness need not be an insuperable problem in evaluating the competing theories, since there is no shortage of clear cases on both sides. If all ultimate desires are *clearly* self-interested, then the egoists are right. But if there are any ultimate desires that are clearly for the well-being of others, then the altruists are right and the egoists are wrong.

Before we turn to the empirical literature, there is one final complication that needs to be discussed. Despite the vagueness of the categories of self-interested desires and desires for the well-being of others, there seems to be a wide range of desires that clearly fall into *neither* category. Examples include the desire that great works of art be preserved and the desire that space exploration be pursued. Perhaps more interesting for moral theory are examples like the desire to do one's moral duty and the desire to obey God's command-ments. Whether anyone holds these as *ultimate* desires is debatable. But if people do, then egoism is mistaken, since these desires are not self-interested. Interestingly, however, if ultimate desires like these exist, it would *not* show that altruism is true, since these desires are not desires for the well-being of others. Of course, a person who held the ulti-mate desire to do his moral duty might also believe that it was his duty to alleviate the suffering of the poor, and that belief might generate a desire to alleviate the suffering of

---

10. Perhaps the most famous statement of hedonism is found in the first two sentences of Jeremy Bentham's *An Introduction to the Principles of Morals and Legislation* (1798/1996, 11): "Nature has placed mankind under the governance of two sovereign masters, pain and pleasure. It is for them alone to point out what we ought to do, as well as to determine what we shall do."

11. Hedonists do not deny that many people desire such things, but they insist that these are not ultimate desires. According to the hedonist, people want wealth, power, and the rest only because they believe that being wealthy, powerful, etc. will lead to more pleasure and less pain.

the poor, which *is* a clear example of a desire for the well-being of others. But this lends no support to altruism, because the *ultimate* desire, in this case, is not for the well-being of others.

The topography has gotten a bit complicated; Figure 15.2 may help keep the contours clear. In that figure, we've distinguished four sorts of desires. Hedonism maintains that all ultimate desires fall into category 1. Egoism maintains that all ultimate desires fall into category 2, which has category 1 as a subset. Altruism claims that some ultimate desires fall into category 4. Finally, if there are ultimate desires that fall into category 3 but none that fall into category 4, then both egoism and altruism are mistaken.

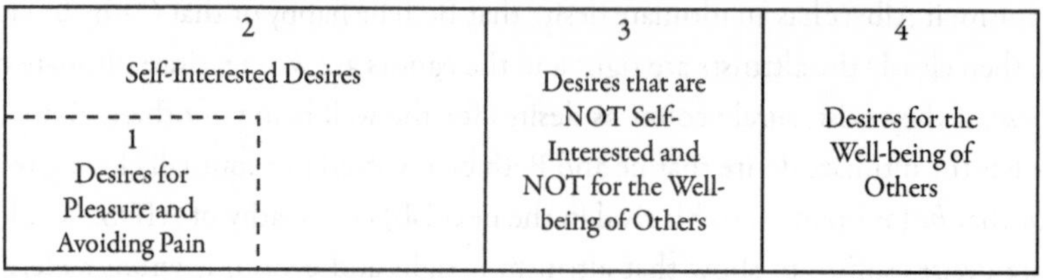

2 Self-Interested Desires	3	4
1 Desires for Pleasure and Avoiding Pain	Desires that are NOT Self-Interested and NOT for the Well-being of Others	Desires for the Well-being of Others

FIGURE 15.2 Four sorts of desires
Hedonism maintains that all ultimate desires are in category 1; egoism maintains that all ultimate desires are in category 2; altruism maintains that some ultimate desires are in category 4.

3. Altruism and Evolution

Readers familiar with some of the popular literature on the evolution of morality that has appeared in the last few decades might suspect that contemporary evolutionary biology has resolved the debate between egoists and altruists. For some readers—and some writers—seem to interpret evolutionary theory as showing that altruism is "biologically impossible." However, we maintain that the large literature on evolution and altruism has done very little to advance the philosophical debate. In this section, we shall make the case for this claim. We'll begin with arguments that purport to show that considerations drawn from evolutionary theory make altruism unlikely or impossible (except, perhaps, in a very limited range of cases). We'll then turn to a cluster of arguments, offered by Elliott Sober and David Sloan Wilson, that try to establish the opposite conclusion: evolutionary theory makes it appear quite likely that psychological altruism is true.

3.1. EVOLUTIONARY ARGUMENTS AGAINST ALTRUISM

In discussions of evolution and altruism it is important to bear in mind a crucial distinction between two very different notions of altruism, which (following Sober and Wilson) we'll call *evolutionary altruism* and *psychological altruism*. Psychological altruism is the notion that has been at center stage in philosophical debates since antiquity. In most of this chapter, when we use the word "altruism," we are referring to psychological altruism. But in this section, to avoid confusion, we'll regularly opt for the longer label "psychological altruism." As we explained in Section 2, an organism is psychologically altruistic if and only if it has ultimate desires for the well-being of others, and a behavior is psychologically altruistic if and only if it is motivated by such a desire. By contrast, a behavior (or a behavioral disposition) is *evolutionarily altruistic* if and only if it reduces the inclusive fitness of the organism exhibiting the behavior and increases the inclusive fitness of some other organism. Roughly speaking, inclusive fitness is a measure of how many copies of an organism's genes will exist in subsequent generations.[12] Since an organism's close kin share many of its genes, an organism can increase its inclusive fitness either by reproducing or by helping close kin to reproduce. Thus many behaviors that help kin to reproduce are *not* evolutionarily altruistic, even if they are quite costly to the organism doing the helping.[13]

It is important to see that evolutionary altruism and psychological altruism are logically independent notions—neither one entails the other. It is logically possible for an organism to be evolutionarily altruistic even if it is entirely devoid of mental states and thus can't have any ultimate desires. Indeed, since biologists interested in evolutionary altruism use the term "behavior" very broadly, it is possible for paramecia, or even plants, to exhibit evolutionarily altruistic behavior. It is also logically possible for an organism to be a psychological altruist without being an evolutionary altruist. For example, an organism might have ultimate desires for the welfare of its own offspring. Behaviors resulting from that desire will be psychologically altruistic but not evolutionarily altruistic, since typically such behaviors will increase the inclusive fitness of the parent.

Evolutionary altruism poses a major puzzle for evolutionary theorists, since if an organism's evolutionarily altruistic behavior is heritable, we might expect that natural selection would replace the genes implicated in evolutionarily altruistic behavior with genes that did not foster evolutionarily altruistic behavior, and thus the evolutionarily altruistic behavior would disappear. In recent years, there has been a great deal of discussion of this problem. Some theorists have offered sophisticated models purporting to show how, in appropriate circumstances, evolutionary altruism could indeed evolve,[14] while others have maintained that evolutionary altruism is extremely unlikely to evolve in a species like ours, and that under closer examination all putative examples of altruistic behavior will turn out not to be altruistic at all. In the memorable words of biologist Michael Ghiselin (1974, 247), "Scratch an 'altruist' and watch a 'hypocrite' bleed."

---

12. Attempting a more precise account raises difficult issues in the philosophy of biology (e.g., Beatty 1992); fortunately our purposes do not require greater precision.

13. Some writers, including Sober and Wilson, define evolutionary altruism in terms of individual fitness (a measure of how many descendants an individual has) rather than inclusive fitness. For present purposes, we prefer the inclusive fitness account, since it facilitates a more plausible statement of the evolutionary argument aimed at showing that psychological altruism is possible only in very limited domains.

14. See, for example, Sober and Wilson 1998, Part I.

What is important for our purposes is that, even if the skeptics who doubt the existence of evolutionary altruism are correct, this would not resolve the philosophical debate over egoism and altruism since, as we have noted above, it entails nothing at all about the existence of psychological altruism. Unfortunately, far too many writers, including perhaps Ghiselin himself, have made the mistake of assuming that the arguments against evolutionary altruism show that the sort of altruism that is of interest to moral theorists does not exist.

Although these considerations show that evolutionary theorists have no reason to deny that organisms can be psychological altruists, some authors have suggested that evolutionary theory permits psychological altruism only in very limited domains. The reasoning proceeds as follows: there are only two ways that a disposition to engage in behavior that helps other organisms but lowers one's own chance of survival and reproduction can evolve. One of these is the case in which the recipients of help are one's own offspring, or other close kin. Kin selection theory, pioneered by W. D. Hamilton (1963, 1964a, 1964b), makes it clear that in appropriate circumstances, genes leading to costly helping behavior will tend to spread throughout a population, provided that the recipients of the help are relatives, since this sort of helping behavior increases the number of copies of those genes that will be found in future generations. The other way in which a disposition to help can evolve requires that episodes of helping behavior are part of a longer-term reciprocal strategy in which the organism that is the beneficiary of helping behavior is subsequently disposed to help its benefactor. Building on ideas first set out in Trivers's (1971) classic paper on "reciprocal altruism," Axelrod and Hamilton (1981) described a simple "tit-for-tat" strategy, in which an organism helps on the first appropriate opportunity and then helps on subsequent opportunities if and only if the partner helped on the previous appropriate opportunity. They showed that tit-for-tat would be favored by natural selection over many other strategies, including a purely selfish strategy of never offering help but always accepting it. Since psychological altruism will lead to helping behavior, it is argued, psychological altruism can evolve only when a disposition to helping behavior can. So it is biologically possible for organisms to have ultimate desires to help their kin, and to help non-kin with whom they engage in ongoing reciprocal altruism. But apart from these special cases, psychological altruism can't evolve.

Versions of this influential line of thought can be found in many places (see, e.g., Nesse 1990; Wright 1994, chs. 8, 9; Rachels 1990, ch. 4). However, we think there is good reason to be very skeptical about the crucial assumption, which maintains that dispositions to helping behavior can evolve *only* via kin selection or reciprocal altruism. It has long been recognized that various sorts of group selection, in which one group of individuals leaves more descendants than another group, can lead to the evolution of helping behavior. Until recently, though, the reigning orthodoxy in evolutionary biology has been that the conditions under which group selection can act are highly unlikely to occur in natural breeding populations, and thus group selection is unlikely to have played a substantial role in human evolution. This view has been boldly challenged by Sober and Wilson

(1998), and while their views are very controversial, we think that the extent to which group selection played a role in human evolution is very much an open question.

Much less controversially, Boyd and Richerson (1992) have developed models demonstrating that helping behavior (and, indeed, just about *any* sort of behavior) can evolve if informal punishment is meted out to individuals who do not help in circumstances when they are expected to. In such circumstances, psychological altruism could be favored by natural selection. More recently, Sripada (2007) has argued that ultimate desires for the well-being of others could evolve via a rather different route. As Sripada observes, there are many situations in which people are better off if they act in a coordinated way, but where no specific way of acting is best. Driving on the right (or the left) is an obvious example: it matters not a whit whether the convention is to drive on the right or left, but failure to adopt *some* convention would be a disaster. In these situations several different "coordination equilibria" may be equally adaptive. To enable groups to reap the benefits of acting in a coordinated way, Sripada argues, natural selection may well have led to the evolution of a psychological mechanism that generates ultimate desires to adhere to locally prevailing customs or practices. And since some of those locally prevailing customs may require helping others, some of the ultimate desires produced by that psychological mechanism might well be psychologically altruistic. If Boyd and Richerson and Sripada are right, and we believe they are, then evolutionary theory gives us no reason to suppose that psychological altruism must be restricted to kin or to individuals involved in reciprocal exchanges. So, contrary to the frequently encountered presumption that evolutionary biology has resolved the debate between psychological egoists and psychological altruists in favor of egoism, it appears that evolutionary theory offers little succor to the egoists.

3.2. EVOLUTIONARY ARGUMENTS FOR ALTRUISM[15]

In stark contrast with writers who think that evolutionary arguments show that psychological altruism is unlikely or impossible, Sober and Wilson (1998) believe that there are evolutionary arguments *for* the existence of psychological altruism. "Natural selection," they maintain, "is unlikely to have given us purely egoistic motives."[16] While granting that their case is "provisional" (8), they believe that their "analysis . . . provides evidence for the existence of psychological altruism" (12).

In setting out their arguments, Sober and Wilson adopt the wise strategy of focusing on the case of parental care. Since the behaviors that organisms exhibit in taking care of their offspring are typically *not* altruistic in the evolutionary sense, we can simply put aside whatever worries there may be about the existence of evolutionary altruism. Given

---

15. Much of this section is based on Stich 2007. We are grateful to Elliott Sober and Edouard Machery for helpful comments on this material.

16. Sober and Wilson 1998, 12. For the remainder of this section, all quotes from Sober and Wilson 1998 will be identified by page numbers in parentheses.

the importance of parental care in many species, it is all but certain that natural selection played a significant role in shaping that behavior. And while different species no doubt utilize very different processes to generate and regulate parental care behavior, it is plausible to suppose that in humans *desires* play an important role in that process. Sober and Wilson believe that evolutionary considerations can help us determine the nature of these desires:

> Although organisms take care of their young in many species, human parents provide a great deal of help, for a very long time, to their children. We expect that when parental care evolves in a lineage, natural selection is relevant to explaining why this transition occurs. Assuming that human parents take care of their children because of the desires they have, we also expect that evolutionary considerations will help illuminate what the desires are that play this motivational role. (301)

Of course, as Sober and Wilson note, we hardly need evolutionary arguments to tell us about the content of some of the desires that motivate parental care. But it is much harder to determine whether these desires are instrumental or ultimate, and it is here, they think, that evolutionary considerations can be of help.

> We conjecture that human parents typically *want* their children to do well—to live rather than die, to be healthy rather than sick, and so on. The question we will address is whether this desire is merely an instrumental desire in the service of some egoistic ultimate goal, or part of a pluralistic motivational system in which there is an ultimate altruistic concern for the child's welfare. We will argue that there are evolutionary reasons to expect motivational pluralism to be the proximate mechanism for producing parental care in our species. (302)

Since parental care is essential in humans, and since providing it requires that parents have the appropriate set of desires, the processes driving evolution must have solved the problem of how to assure that parents would have the requisite desires. There are, Sober and Wilson maintain, three kinds of solutions to this evolutionary problem.

> A relatively direct solution to the design problem would be for parents to be psychological altruists—let them care about the well-being of their children as an end in itself. A more indirect solution would be for parents to be psychological hedonists[17]—let them care only about attaining pleasure and avoiding pain, but let them be so constituted that they feel good when their children do well and feel bad when

---

17. Sober and Wilson cast their argument as a contest between altruism and hedonism because "[b]y pitting altruism against hedonism, we are asking the altruism hypothesis to reply to the version of egoism that is most difficult to refute" (297). For expository purposes, we shall follow their lead here, although we are not committed to their evaluation of hedonism.

their children do ill. And of course, there is a pluralistic solution to consider as well—let parents have altruistic *and* hedonistic motives, both of which motivate them to take care of their children. (305)

"Broadly speaking," they continue, "there are three considerations that bear on this question" (ibid.). The first of these is *availability*; for natural selection to cause a trait to increase in frequency, the trait must have been available in an ancestral population. The second is *reliability*. Since parents who fail to provide care run a serious risk of never having grandchildren, we should expect that natural selection will prefer a more reliable solution over a less reliable one. The third consideration is *energetic efficiency*. Building and maintaining psychological mechanisms will inevitably require an investment of resources that might be used for some other purpose. So, other things being equal, we should expect natural selection to prefer the more efficient mechanism. There is, Sober and Wilson maintain, no reason to think that a psychologically altruistic mechanism would be less energetically efficient than a hedonist mechanism, nor is there any reason to think that an altruistic mechanism would have been less likely to be available. When it comes to reliability, on the other hand, they think there is a clear difference between a psychologically altruistic mechanism and various possible hedonistic mechanisms: an altruistic mechanism would be more reliable, and thus it is more likely that the altruistic mechanism would be the one that evolved.

To make their case, Sober and Wilson offer a brief sketch of how hedonistic and altruistic mechanisms might work, and then set out a variety of reasons for thinking that the altruistic mechanism would be more reliable. However, we believe that in debates about psychological processes, the devil is often in the details. So rather than relying on Sober and Wilson's brief sketches, we shall offer somewhat more detailed accounts of the psychological processes that might support hedonistic and psychologically altruistic parental behavior. After setting out these accounts, we'll go on to evaluate Sober and Wilson's arguments about reliability.

Figure 15.3 is a depiction of the process underlying psychologically altruistic behavior. In Figure 15.3, the fact that the agent's child needs help (represented by the unboxed token of "My child needs help" in the upper left) leads to the belief *My child needs help*. Of course, formation of this belief requires complex perceptual and cognitive processing, but since this part of the story is irrelevant to the issue at hand, it has not been depicted. The belief *My child needs help*, along with other beliefs the agent has, leads to a belief that a certain action, A*, is the best way to help her child. Then, via practical reasoning, this belief and the *ultimate* desire, *I do what will be most helpful for my child*, leads to the desire to do A*. Since in this altruistic account the desire, *I do what will be most helpful for my child*, is an ultimate desire, it is not itself the result of practical reasoning.

The hedonistic alternatives we shall propose retain all of the basic structure depicted in Figure 15.3, but they depict the desire that *I do what will be most helpful for my child*

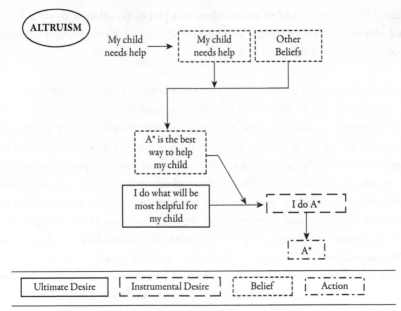

FIGURE 15.3 The process underlying psychologically altruistic behavior.

as an instrumental rather than an ultimate desire. The simplest way to do this is via what we shall call *future pain hedonism*, which maintains that the agent believes she will feel bad in the future if she does not help her child now. Figure 15.4 is our sketch of future pain hedonism. In it, the content of the agent's ultimate desire is hedonistic: *I maximize my pleasure and minimize my pain*. The desire, *I do what is most helpful for my child*, is an instrumental desire, generated via practical reasoning from the ultimate hedonistic desire along with the belief that *If I don't do what is most helpful for my child I will feel bad*.

Figure 15.5 depicts another, more complicated, way in which the desire, *I do what is most helpful to my child*, might be the product of hedonistic practical reasoning, which we'll call *current pain hedonism*. On this account, the child's need for help causes the parent to feel bad, and the parent believes that if she feels bad because her child needs help and she does what is most helpful, she will stop feeling bad. This version of hedonism is more complex than the previous version, since it includes an affective state—feeling bad—in addition to various beliefs and desires, and in order for that affective state to influence practical reasoning, the parent must not only experience it, but know (or at least believe) that she is experiencing it, and why.

In their attempt to show that natural selection would favor an altruistic process over the hedonistic alternatives, Sober and Wilson offer a number of arguments, all of them focused on the more complicated current pain hedonism, although they think that "the argument would remain the same if we thought of the hedonist as acting to avoid future pain" (318). In discussing these arguments, we shall start with three that we don't find very

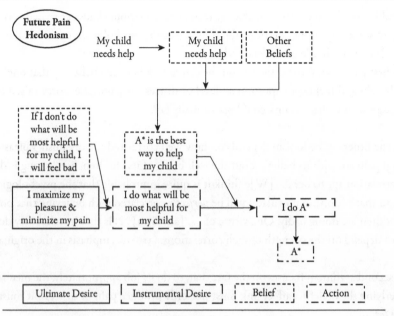

FIGURE 15.4 The process underlying future pain hedonism.

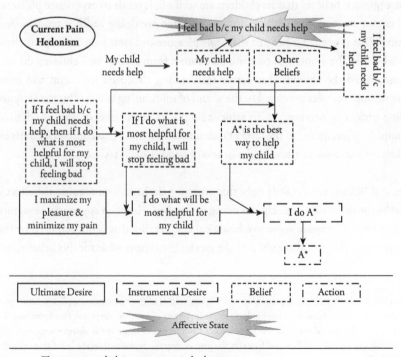

FIGURE 15.5 The process underlying current pain hedonism.

plausible; we'll then take up one that we think poses a serious challenge to hedonism and leads to some important questions about how, exactly, psychological egoism and psychological altruism should be understood.

A first pair of arguments focuses on the causal link between believing that one's child needs help and feeling an appropriate level of distress or pain. The worry raised by the first argument is that the link could occasionally fail.

> If the fitness of hedonism depends on how well correlated the organism's pleasure and pain are with its beliefs about the well-being of its children, how strong is this correlation apt to be? . . . [W]e think it is quite improbable that the psychological pain that hedonism postulates will be *perfectly* correlated with believing that one's children are doing badly. One virtue of . . . [altruism] . . . is that its reliability does not depend on the strength of such correlations. (315–16, emphasis in the original)

The second argument focuses on the fact that, to do its job appropriately, the mechanism underlying the belief-to-affect link must not only produce pain or distress; it must produce *lots* of it.

> Hedonism assumes that evolution produced organisms—ourselves included—in which psychological pain is strongly correlated with having beliefs of various kinds. In the context of our example of parental care, the hedonist asserts that whenever the organism believes that its children are well off, it tends to experience pleasure; whenever the organism believes that its children are doing badly, it tends to feel pain. What is needed is not just that *some* pleasure and *some* pain accompany these two beliefs. The amount of pleasure that comes from seeing one's children do well must exceed the amount that comes from eating chocolate ice cream and from having one's temples massaged to the sound of murmuring voices. This may require some tricky engineering. . . . To achieve simplicity at the level of ultimate desires, complexity is required at the level of instrumental desires. This complexity must be taken into account in assessing the fitness of hedonism.[18] (315)

Sober and Wilson are certainly right that current pain hedonism requires the affect generated by the belief that one's child is doing well or badly be of an appropriate magnitude, and that this will require some psychological engineering that is not required by the altruist process. They are also right that the mechanism responsible for this belief-to-affect

---

18. It is perhaps worth noting that, pace Sober and Wilson, neither of these arguments applies to future pain hedonism, since that version of hedonism does not posit the sort of belief-to-affect link that Sober and Wilson find suspect. We should also note that for the sake of simplicity, we'll ignore the pleasure engendered by the belief that one's child is well off and focus on the pain or distress engendered by the belief that one's child is doing badly.

link will not establish a perfect correlation between belief and affect; like just about any psychological mechanism, it is bound to fail now and then.

However, we don't think that either of these facts offers much reason to believe that natural selection would favor the altruistic process. To see why, let's first consider the fact that the belief-to-affect link will be less than perfectly reliable. It seems that natural selection has built lots of adaptively important processes by using links between categories of belief and various sorts of affective states. Emotions like anger, fear, and disgust, which play crucial roles in regulating behavior, are examples of states that are often triggered by different sorts of beliefs. And in all of these cases, it seems (logically) possible to eliminate the pathway that runs via affect, and replace it with an ultimate desire to behave appropriately when one acquires a triggering belief. Fear, for example, might be replaced by an ultimate desire to take protective action when you believe that you are in danger. Since natural selection has clearly opted for an emotion mediation system in these cases rather than relying on an ultimate desire that avoids the need for a belief-to-affect link, we need some further argument to show that natural selection would not do the same in the case of parental care, and Sober and Wilson do not offer any.

The second argument faces a very similar challenge. It will indeed require some "tricky engineering" to be sure that beliefs about one's children produce the right amount of affect. But much the same is true in the case of other systems involving affect. For the fear system to work properly, seeing a tiger on the path in front of you must generate quite intense fear—a lot more than would be generated by your belief that if you ran away quickly you might stub your toe. While it no doubt takes some tricky engineering to make this all work properly, natural selection was up to the challenge. Sober and Wilson give us no reason to think natural selection was not up to the challenge in the case of parental care as well. Edouard Machery has pointed out to us another problem with the "tricky engineering" argument. On Sober and Wilson's account, altruists will have many ultimate desires in addition to the desire to do what will be most helpful for their children. So to ensure that the ultimate desire leading to parental care usually prevails will *also* require some tricky engineering.

A third argument offered by Sober and Wilson is aimed at showing that natural selection would likely have preferred a system for producing parental care, which they call "PLUR" (for *pluralism*), in which *both* hedonistic motivation and altruistic motivation play a role, over a "monistic" system that relies on hedonism alone. The central idea is that, in many circumstances, two control mechanisms are better than one.

> PLUR postulates two pathways from the belief that one's children need help to the act of providing help. If these operate at least somewhat independently of each other, and each on its own raises the probability of helping, then the two together will raise the probability of helping even more. Unless the two pathways postulated by PLUR hopelessly confound each other, PLUR will be more reliable than HED [hedonism]. PLUR is superior because it is a *multiply connected control device*. (320, emphasis in the original)

Sober and Wilson go on to observe that "multiply connected control devices have often evolved." They sketch a few examples, then note that "further examples could be supplied from biology, and also from engineering, where intelligent designers supply machines (like the space shuttle) with backup systems. Error is inevitable, but the chance of disastrous error can be minimized by well-crafted redundancy" (ibid.).

Sober and Wilson are surely right that well-crafted redundancy will typically improve reliability and reduce the chance of disastrous error. They are also right that both natural selection and intelligent human designers have produced lots of systems with this sort of redundancy. But, as the disaster that befell the *Columbia* space shuttle and a myriad of other technical catastrophes vividly illustrate, human engineers also often design crucial systems *without* backups. So too does natural selection, as people with damaged hearts or livers, or with small but disabling strokes, are all too well aware. One reason for lack of redundancy is that redundancy almost never comes without costs, and those costs have to be weighed against the incremental benefits that a backup system provides. Since Sober and Wilson offer us no reason to believe that, in the case of parental care, the added reliability of PLUR would justify the additional costs, their redundancy argument lends no support to the claim that natural selection would prefer PLUR to a monistic hedonism, or, for that matter, to a monistic altruism.[19]

Sober and Wilson's fourth argument raises what we think is a much more troublesome issue for the hedonistic hypothesis.

> Suppose a hedonistic organism believes on a given occasion that providing parental care is the way for it to attain its ultimate goal of maximizing pleasure and minimizing pain. What would happen if the organism provides parental care, but then discovers that this action fails to deliver maximal pleasure and minimal pain? If the organism is able to learn from experience, it will probably be less inclined to take care of its children on subsequent occasions. Instrumental desires tend to diminish and disappear in the face of negative evidence of this sort. This can make hedonistic motivation a rather poor control device. . . . [The] instrumental desire will remain in place only if the organism . . . is trapped by an unalterable illusion. (314–15)

Sober and Wilson might have been more careful here. When it turns out that parental care does not produce the expected hedonic benefits, the hedonistic organism needs to have some beliefs about why this happened before it can effectively adjust its beliefs and instrumental desires. If, for example, the hedonist portrayed in Figures 15.4 or 15.5 comes to believe (perhaps correctly) that it was mistaken in inferring that A* was the best way to help, then it

---

19. Even if there were some reason to think that natural selection would prefer a redundant system, this would not, by itself, constitute an argument for altruism. Redundancy can exist in an entirely hedonistic system, for instance one that includes both current and future pain hedonism.

will need to adjust some of the beliefs that led to that inference, but the beliefs linking helping to the reduction of negative affect will require no modification. But despite this slip, we think that Sober and Wilson are on to something important. Both versions of hedonism that we've sketched rely quite crucially on beliefs about the relation between helping behavior and affect. In the case of future pain hedonism, as elaborated in Figure 15.4, the crucial belief is: *If I don't do what will be most helpful for my child, I will feel bad*. In the version of current pain hedonism sketched in Figure 15.5, it's: *If I feel bad because my child needs help, then if I do what is most helpful for my child, I will stop feeling bad*. These beliefs make empirical claims, and like other empirical beliefs they might be undermined by evidence (including misleading evidence) or by more theoretical beliefs (rational or irrational) that a person could acquire by a variety of routes. This makes the process underlying parental care look quite vulnerable to disruption and suggests that natural selection would likely opt for some more reliable way to get this crucial job done.[20] The version of altruism depicted in Figure 15.3 fits the bill nicely. By making the desire, *I do what will be most helpful for my child* an ultimate desire, it sidesteps the need for empirical beliefs that might all too easily be undermined.

We think this is an original and powerful argument for psychological altruism. Ultimately, however, we are not persuaded. To explain why, we'll have to clarify what the altruist and the egoist are claiming. Psychological altruists, recall, maintain that people have ultimate desires for the well-being of others, while psychological egoists believe that all desires for the well-being of others are instrumental, and that all of our ultimate desires are self-interested. As depicted in Figure 15.1, an instrumental desire is a desire that is produced or sustained entirely by a process of practical reasoning in which a desire and a belief give rise to or sustain another desire. In our discussion of practical reasoning (in Section 2), while a good bit was said about desire, nothing was said about the notion of *belief*; it was simply taken for granted. At this point, however, we can no longer afford to do so. Like other writers in this area, including Sober and Wilson, we tacitly adopted the standard view that beliefs are inferentially integrated representational states that play a characteristic role in an agent's cognitive economy. To say that a belief is *inferentially integrated* is to say (roughly) that it can be both generated and removed by inferential processes that can take any (or just about any) other beliefs as premises.

While inferentially integrated representational states play a central role in many discussions of psychological processes and cognitive architecture, the literature in both cognitive science and philosophy also often discusses belief-like states that are "stickier" than this. Once they are in place, these "stickier" belief-like states are hard to modify by

---

20. Note that the vulnerability to disruption we're considering now is likely to be a much more serious problem than the vulnerability that was at center stage in Sober and Wilson's first argument. In that argument, the danger posed for the hedonistic parental care system was that "the psychological pain that hedonism postulates" might not be "*perfectly* correlated with believing that one's children are doing badly" (316, emphasis in the original). But, absent other problems, a hedonistic system in which belief and affect were highly—though imperfectly—correlated would still do quite a good job of parental care. Our current concern is with the stability of the crucial belief linking helping behavior and affect. If that belief is removed, the hedonistic parental care system simply crashes, and the organism will not engage in parental care except by accident.

acquiring or changing other beliefs. They are also often unavailable to introspective access. In Stich (1978), they were termed *sub-doxastic states*.

Perhaps the most familiar example of sub-doxastic states are the grammatical rules that, according to Chomsky and his followers, underlie speech production, comprehension, and the production of linguistic intuitions. These representational states are clearly not inferentially integrated, since a speaker's explicit beliefs typically have no effect on them. A speaker can, for example, have thoroughly mistaken beliefs about the rules that govern his linguistic processing without those beliefs having any effect on the rules or on the linguistic processing that they subserve. Another important example is the *core beliefs* posited by Carey and Spelke (Carey and Spelke 1996; Spelke 2000, 2003). These are innate representational states that underlie young children's inferences about the physical and mathematical properties of objects. In the course of development, many people acquire more sophisticated theories about these matters, some of which are incompatible with the innate core beliefs. But, if Carey and Spelke are correct, the core beliefs remain unaltered by these new beliefs and continue to affect people's performance in a variety of experimental tasks.

Although sub-doxastic states are sticky and hard to remove, they do play a role in *inference-like* interactions with other representational states, although their access to other representational premises and other premises' access to them is limited. In *The Modularity of Mind*, Fodor (1983) notes that representational states stored in the sorts of mental modules he posits are typically sub-doxastic, since modules are "informationally encapsulated." But not all sub-doxastic states need reside in Fodorian modules.

Since sub-doxastic states can play a role in inference-like interactions, and since practical reasoning is an inference-like interaction, it is possible that sub-doxastic states play the belief-role in some instances of practical reasoning. So, for example, rather than the practical reasoning structure illustrated in Figure 15.1, some examples of practical reasoning might have the structure shown in Figure 15.6. What makes practical reasoning structures like this important for our purposes is that, since SUB-DOXASTIC STATE 1 is difficult or impossible to remove using evidence or inference, DESIRE 2 will be reliably correlated with DESIRE 1.

Let's now consider whether DESIRE 2 in Figure 15.6 is instrumental or ultimate. As we noted in Section 1, the objects of ultimate desires are typically characterized as "desired for their own sakes" while instrumental desires are those that agents have only because they think that satisfying the desire will lead to the satisfaction of some other desire. In Figure

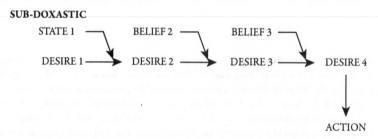

FIGURE 15.6 An episode of practical reasoning in which a sub-doxastic state plays a role.

15.6, the agent has DESIRE 2 only because he thinks that satisfying the desire will lead to the satisfaction of DESIRE 1. So it looks as if the natural answer to our question is that DESIRE 2 is instrumental; the only ultimate desire depicted in Figure 15.6 is DESIRE 1.

If this is right, if desires like DESIRE 2 are instrumental rather than ultimate, then Sober and Wilson's evolutionary argument for psychological altruism is in trouble. The central insight of that argument was that both versions of hedonism rely on empirical beliefs that might all too easily be undermined by other beliefs the agent might acquire. Suppose, however, that in Figures 15.4 and 15.5, the representations

> *If I don't do what will be most helpful for my child, I will feel bad*

and

> *If I feel bad because my child needs help, then if I do what is most helpful for my child, I will stop feeling bad*

are not beliefs but sticky sub-doxastic states. If we grant that desires like DESIRE 2 in Figure 15.6, which are produced or sustained by a desire and a sub-doxastic state, count as instrumental desires, not ultimate desires, then the crucial desire whose presence Sober and Wilson sought to guarantee by making it an ultimate desire, i.e.,

> *I do what will be most helpful for my child*

is no longer at risk of being undermined by other beliefs. Since the crucial desire is reliably present in both the altruistic model and in both versions of the hedonist model, natural selection can't prefer altruism because of its greater reliability in getting a crucial job done.

As we've seen, Sober and Wilson contend that when an instrumental desire does not lead to the expected hedonic payoff, the "desire will remain in place only if the organism . . . is trapped by an unalterable illusion" (315). But as a number of authors have noted, some illusions—or as we would prefer to put it, some belief-like representational states that are not strictly true—are conducive to fitness (Stich 1990; Plantinga 1993; Sober 1994; Godfrey-Smith 1996). In a variety of domains, it appears that natural selection has used sub-doxastic states and processes that have some of the features of mental modules to ensure that those representations stay put and are not undermined by the systems that revise beliefs. Since natural selection often exploits the same trick over and over again, it is entirely possible that, when faced with the problem of assuring that parents were motivated to care for their children, this was the strategy it selected. Our conclusion, of course, is *not* that parental care is subserved by an egoistic psychological process, but rather that Sober and Wilson's argument leaves this option quite open. Their analysis does not "provide . . . evidence for the existence of psychological altruism" (12).

Our central claim in this section has been that evolutionary theory offers little prospect for movement in philosophical debates between psychological egoism and psychological altruism. In 3.1 we saw that evolutionary considerations don't rule out psychological altruism or restrict its scope, and in 3.2 we've argued that Sober and Wilson's arguments—by far the most sophisticated attempt to make an evolutionary case *for* psychological altruism—are not convincing.

4. The Social Psychology of Altruism

We now turn from theoretical considerations purporting to make the existence of altruism seem likely (or unlikely) to attempts at directly establishing the existence of altruism through experimental observation. The psychological literature relevant to the egoism vs. altruism debate is vast, but in this section we shall focus primarily on the work of Daniel Batson and his associates, who have done some of the most important work in this area.[21] Batson, along with many other researchers, begins by borrowing an idea that has deep roots in philosophical discussions of altruism. Although the details and the terminology differ significantly from author to author, the central idea is that altruism is often the product of an emotional response to another's distress.

For example, Aquinas maintains that "mercy is the heartfelt sympathy for another's distress, impelling us to succour him if we can."[22] And Adam Smith tells us that "pity or compassion [is] the emotion we feel for the misery of others, when we either see it, or are made to conceive it in a very lively manner" and these emotions "interest [man] in the fortunes of others, and render their happiness necessary to him, though he derives nothing from it except the pleasure of seeing it."[23] While different writers have used different terms for the emotional response in question, Batson (1991, 58) labels it "empathy," which he characterizes as "an other-oriented emotional reaction to seeing someone suffer," and he calls the traditional idea that empathy leads to altruism the *empathy-altruism hypothesis*.

In this section we shall begin, in 4.1, by introducing Batson's account of empathy, and discussing some problems with that account. In 4.2, we'll evaluate Batson's claims about the causal pathway leading from perspective taking to empathy and from empathy to helping behavior. In the remainder of the section, we'll look carefully at some of Batson's experiments that are designed to test the empathy-altruism hypothesis against a variety of egoistic alternatives. In a number of cases, we believe, the experiments have made important progress by showing that versions of egoism that have loomed large in philosophical discussion are not very promising. But in other cases we'll argue that Batson's experiments have not yet succeeded in undermining an egoistic alternative.

---

21. For useful reviews of the literature see Piliavin and Charng 1990; Batson 1991, 1998; Schroeder et al. 1995; Dovidio et al. 2006. We are grateful to Daniel Batson for helpful discussion of the material in this section.

22. Aquinas (1270/1917, II–II, 30, 3).

23. Smith (1759/1853, I, I, 1. 1).

While the Batson group's experimental program is novel, the dialectical space is one, we dare say, that has exercised generations of introductory philosophy students: for many examples of helping behavior, the egoist and altruist can both offer psychological explanations consistent with their hypothesis, and the ensuing arguments concern which explanation is most plausible. Unfortunately, as generations of introductory philosophy students have found out, such arguments are bound to end in inconclusive speculation—so long as the competing explanations are not empirically evaluated. By showing how such evaluation may proceed, the Batson group has enabled progress in a shopworn debate.

4.1. EMPATHY AND PERSONAL DISTRESS

Since there is no standardized terminology in this area, Batson's choice of the term "empathy" to label the emotion, or cluster of emotions, that plays a central role in his theory is inevitably somewhat *stipulative*—he might have chosen "compassion" or "sympathy" or even "pity" for the term of art he needs. Because of this, we are not concerned with the question of whether he uses "empathy" in ways consistent with common usage. However, we do think his characterization of empathy is neither as clear nor as detailed as one might hope. Much of what Batson says is aimed at contrasting empathy with a different cluster of affective responses to other people's suffering, which Batson calls "personal distress." According to Batson, empathy "includes feeling sympathetic, compassionate, warm, softhearted, tender, and the like, and according to the empathy-altruism hypothesis, it evokes altruistic motivation" (1991, 86). Personal distress, by contrast, is "made up of more self-oriented feelings such as upset, alarm, anxiety, and distress" (ibid., 117). Elsewhere, he tells us that personal distress "includes feeling anxious, upset, disturbed, distressed, perturbed, and the like, and evokes egoistic motivation to have the distress reduced" (ibid., 86). While these characterizations may suffice for designing experiments aimed at testing the view that empathy leads to altruistic motivation, they leave a number of important issues unaddressed.

One of these issues is often discussed under the heading of "congruence" or "homology." Sometimes when an observer becomes aware that another person (the "target," as we'll sometimes say) is experiencing an emotion, this awareness can cause a similar emotion in the observer. If, for example, you are aware that Ellen is frightened of the man walking toward her, you may also become frightened of him; if you learn that your best friend is sad because of the death of his beloved dog, this may make you sad as well. In these cases, the emotion evoked in the observer is said to be *congruent* or *homologous* to the emotion of the target. Since Batson describes empathy as a "vicarious emotion that is congruent with but not necessarily identical to the emotion of another" (1991, 86), it is tempting to suppose that he thinks empathic emotions are always at least similar to an emotion the target is experiencing (or similar to what the observer believes the target's emotion to be). But as both Sober and Wilson (1998, 234–35) and Nichols (2004, 32) have noted, *requiring* congruence in the emotion that allegedly gives rise to altruistic motivation may be unwise. Accident victims who are *obviously* unconscious sometimes evoke an "other-oriented emotional reaction" that might be characterized as "compassionate, warm, softhearted, tender, and the like," and people who feel this way are sometimes motivated to help the unconscious victim. But if empathy requires congruence, then the emotion that motivates people to help in these cases *can't* be empathy, since unconscious people aren't experiencing any emotions. We're inclined to give Batson the benefit of the doubt here, and interpret him—charitably, we believe—as holding that empathy is sometimes, or often, a congruent emotion, but that it need not always be. Presumably personal distress is also sometimes congruent, as when one person's anxiety or alarm evokes anxiety or alarm in an observer. So empathy and personal distress cannot be distinguished by reference to congruence.

Another issue of some importance is whether empathy is always unpleasant or, as psychologists often say, aversive. According to Batson (1991, 87), "empathy felt for someone who is suffering will likely be an unpleasant, aversive emotion," and of course this is just what we would expect if empathy were often a congruent emotion. But as Sober and Wilson (1998, 235) note, we sometimes talk about empathizing with another person's pleasant emotions, and when the term is used in this way, one can have empathic joy as well as empathic sadness. Although Sober and Wilson are certainly right that ordinary language allows us to talk of empathizing with people's positive emotions as well as with their negative emotions, we think Batson is best understood as *stipulating* that, as he uses the term, empathy is a response to the belief that the target is suffering, and that it is typically aversive. Since personal distress is typically—or perhaps always—unpleasant, the distinction between them cannot be drawn by focusing on aversiveness.

That leaves "self-orientedness" vs. "other-orientedness" as the principal dimension on which personal distress and empathy differ. Thus the distinction is doing important theoretical work for Batson, although he does not tell us much about it. We believe that the distinction Batson requires becomes sufficiently clear when operationalized in his experimental work, and we shall not further tarry on the conceptual difficulty. But more conceptual and empirical work aimed at clarifying just what empathy and personal distress are would certainly be welcome.[24]

4.2 EMPATHY, PERSPECTIVE-TAKING AND HELPING BEHAVIOR

In order to put the empathy-altruism hypothesis to empirical test, it is important to have ways of inducing empathy in the laboratory. There is, Batson maintains, a substantial body of literature suggesting that this can indeed be done. For example, Stotland (1969) showed that subjects who were instructed to imagine how a target person felt when undergoing

---

24.Both Sober and Wilson (1998, 231–37) and Nichols (2004, ch. 2) have useful discussions, though we think much more remains to be done.

what subjects believed to be a painful medical procedure reported stronger feelings of empathy and showed greater physiological arousal than subjects who were instructed to watch the target person's movements. Krebs (1975) demonstrated that subjects who observe someone *similar to themselves* undergo painful experiences show more physiological arousal, report identifying with the target more strongly, and report feeling worse while waiting for the painful stimulus to begin than do subjects who observe the same painful experiences administered to someone who is not similar to themselves. Additionally, Krebs (1975) found subjects more willing to help at some personal cost when the sufferer was similar to themselves.

There is also evidence that the effects of empathy are focused on the specific distress that evokes it. Stotland's technique for manipulating empathy by instructing subjects to take the perspective of the person in distress was used by Dovidio et al. (1990) to induce empathy for a young woman, with subjects focusing on one of two quite different problems that the young woman faced. When given an opportunity to help the young woman, subjects in whom empathy had been evoked were more likely to help than subjects in a low empathy condition, and the increase in helping was specific to the problem that had evoked the empathy.

On the basis of these and other experiments, Batson concludes that the process of perspective-taking plays a central role in arousing empathy. According to Batson, "adopting the needy person's perspective involves imagining how that person is affected by his or her situation" (1991, 83), and "adopting the needy person's perspective seems to be a *necessary condition* for arousal of empathetic emotion" (ibid., 85, emphasis added). He goes on to assemble a list of ways in which perspective-taking, and thus empathy, can be induced.

[A] perspective-taking set, that is, a set to imagine how the person in need is affected by his or her situation ... may be induced by prior experience in similar situations, by instructions, or by a feeling of attachment to the other. In the psychology laboratory perspective taking has often been induced by instructions. . . . In the natural stream of behavior also, perspective taking may be the result of instructions, including self-instructions (e.g., "I should walk a mile in his moccasins"), but it is more often the result either of prior similar experience ("I know just how you must feel") or of attachment. (Ibid., 84)

Figure 15.7 is a sketch of the causal pathways that, on Batson's account, can lead to empathy.

Although we are prepared to believe that Figure 15.7 depicts a number of possible routes to empathy, we are, for two reasons, skeptical about Batson's claim that perspective-taking is a *necessary condition* for arousing empathy. First, while the experimental evidence Batson cites makes it plausible that attachment and similarity to self can indeed lead to empathy, it does not rule out the possibility that these processes bypass perspective-taking and lead *directly* to empathy. Second, we know of no literature that takes on

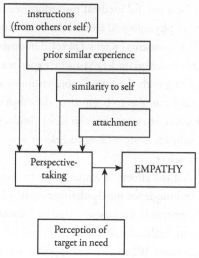

FIGURE 15.7 Batson's account of the causal pathways that can lead to empathy.

the task of showing that there are no *other* routes to empathy, so the existence of quite different causal pathways leading to empathy is largely unexplored. Neither of these reservations poses a major challenge to Batson's project, however, since what he really needs is the claim that—whatever the mechanism may be—the four factors at the top of Figure 15.7 can be used to induce empathy in experimental subjects. And we think that both the pre-existing literature and many of Batson's own experiments provide compelling support for that claim.

With this element in place, Batson's next step is to make the case that empathy leads to helping behavior. Here again, he relies in part on work by others, including the Krebs (1975) and Dovidio et al. (1990) studies cited earlier. Many of Batson's own experiments, some of which we'll describe below, also support the contention that empathy and empathy-engendering experimental manipulations increase the likelihood of helping behavior. Another important source of support for this conclusion is a meta-analysis of a large body of experimental literature by Eisenberg and Miller (1987). On the basis of these and other studies, Batson (1991, 95) concludes that "there is indeed an empathy-helping relationship; feeling empathy for a person in need increases the likelihood of helping to relieve that need."

4.3. THE EMPATHY-ALTRUISM HYPOTHESIS

It might be thought that establishing a causal link between empathy and helping behavior would be bad news for egoism. But, as Batson makes clear, the fact that empathy leads to helping behavior does not resolve the dispute between egoists and altruists, since it does not address the nature of the motivation for the helping behavior that empathy evokes. Egoists, of course, do not deny that people engage in helping behavior. Nor need they deny that seeing other people in distress can cause emotions like empathy or that these emotions can lead to helping behavior. The crucial question dividing egoists from altruists is: how does the emotion engender helping behavior?

The empathy-altruism hypothesis asserts that empathy causes a genuinely altruistic desire to help—an ultimate desire for the well-being of the sufferer. It is important to note that the empathy-altruism hypothesis does not predict that agents who feel empathy for a target person will always help the target; people typically have various and conflicting desires, and not all conflicts are resolved in favor of empathy's urgings. Moreover, even when there are no conflicting desires, it will sometimes be the case that the agent simply does not know how to help. What the empathy-altruism hypothesis claims is that empathy evokes an ultimate desire that the target's distress be reduced. In favorable cases, this ultimate desire, along with the agent's background beliefs, will generate a plan of action. That plan will compete with other plans generated by competing, non-altruistic desires. When the altruistic desire is stronger than the competing desires, the altruistic plan is chosen and the agent engages in helping behavior. It is also important to keep in mind that the empathy-altruism hypothesis does not entail that people who feel little or no empathy will not want to help and will not engage in helping behavior, since an instrumental desire to help can be produced by a variety of processes in which empathy plays no role.

So the empathy-altruism hypothesis offers one account of the way in which empathy can lead to helping behavior. But there is also a variety of egoistic alternatives by which empathy might lead to helping behavior without generating an ultimate desire to help. Perhaps the most obvious of these is that empathy might simply be (or cause) an unpleasant experience, and that people are motivated to help because they believe that helping is the best way to stop the unpleasant experience that is caused by someone else's distress. Quite a different family of egoistic possibilities focuses on the rewards to be expected for helping and/or the punishments to be expected for withholding assistance. If people believe that others will sanction them if they fail to help in certain circumstances, or reward them if they do help, and if they believe that the feeling of empathy marks those cases in which social sanctions or rewards are most likely, then we would expect people to be more helpful when they feel empathy, even if their ultimate motivation is purely egoistic. A variation on this theme focuses on rewards or punishments that are self-generated or self-administered. If people believe that helping may make them feel good, or that failing to help may make them feel bad, and that these feelings will be most likely to occur in cases where they feel empathy, then once again we would expect people who empathize to be more helpful, although their motives may be not at all altruistic.

For more than twenty-five years, Batson and his associates have been systematically exploring these and other options for explaining the link between empathy and helping behavior. Their strategy is to design experiments in which the altruistic explanation, which maintains that empathy leads to an ultimate desire to help, can be compared to one or another specific egoistic alternative. If the strategy succeeds, it does so by eliminating plausible egoistic competitors one at a time and by generating a pattern of evidence that is best explained by the empathy-altruism hypothesis. Batson (1991, 174) concludes, albeit tentatively, that the empathy-altruism hypothesis is correct.

> In study after study, with no clear exceptions, we find results conforming to the pattern predicted by the empathy-altruism hypothesis, the hypothesis that empathic emotion evokes altruistic motivation. At present, there is no egoistic explanation for the results of these studies. . . . Pending new evidence or a plausible new egoistic explanation for the existing evidence, the empathy-altruism hypothesis, however improbable, seems to be true.

Reviewing all of these studies would require a very long chapter indeed.[25] Rather than attempt that, we shall take a careful look at some of the best known and most influential experiments aimed at putting altruism to the test in the psychology laboratory. These will, we hope, illustrate both the strengths and the challenges of this approach to the egoism vs. altruism debate.

4.4. THE EMPATHY-ALTRUISM HYPOTHESIS VS. THE AVERSIVE-AROUSAL REDUCTION HYPOTHESIS

Of the various egoistic strategies for explaining helping behavior, among the most compelling is what Batson calls the "aversive-arousal reduction hypothesis." The simplest version of this idea claims that seeing someone in need causes an aversive emotional reaction—something like Batson's personal distress—and this leads to a desire to eliminate the aversive emotion. Sometimes the agent will believe that helping is the easiest way to eliminate the aversive emotion, and this will lead to an instrumental desire to help, which then leads to helping behavior.[26] However, this simple version of the aversive-arousal reduction hypothesis cannot explain the strong effect that empathy-inducing factors have on helping behavior (as discussed in Section 4.2). To accommodate that effect, a more sophisticated version of the hypothesis must be constructed. A plausible suggestion is that the distress felt when we see someone in need is significantly greater when we also feel empathy. This increased distress might be explained by the fact that empathy itself is aversive, or it might be because personal distress is increased when we feel empathy, or perhaps both factors play a part. Whatever the cause, the egoist will insist that the increased helping in situations that evoke empathy is due to an ultimate desire to alleviate

---

25. For excellent overviews of this research, see Batson 1991, 1998.

26. This idea, which is widely discussed in the social sciences, has venerable philosophical roots. In *Brief Lives*, written between 1650 and 1695, John Aubrey (1949) describes an occasion on which Thomas Hobbes gave alms to a beggar. Asked why, Hobbes replied that by giving alms to the beggar, he not only relieved the man's distress but he also relieved his own distress at seeing the beggar's distress.

the increased distress. By contrast, the empathy-altruism hypothesis maintains that when people feel empathy, this evokes an ultimate desire to help, and that, in turn, sometimes leads to genuinely altruistic behavior.

Batson argues that manipulating difficulty of escape allows us to compare these two hypotheses experimentally. The central idea is that if a subject is motivated by an ultimate desire to help the target, that desire can be satisfied only by helping. However, if a subject is motivated by a desire to reduce his own distress, that desire can be satisfied either by helping or by merely escaping from the distress-inducing situation—for example, by leaving the room so that one is no longer confronted by the needy target. Assuming that subjects do whatever is easier and less costly, the aversive-arousal reduction hypothesis thus predicts that even subjects experiencing empathy will simply leave the needy target, provided escape is made easy enough.

Since the experimental designs are rather complex, it will be helpful to graphically illustrate the claims made by both the empathy-altruism hypothesis and the aversive-arousal reduction hypothesis. If a subject feels little or no empathy for a target, then Figure 15.8 depicts the processes underlying the subject's behavior according to both the aversive-arousal reduction hypothesis and the empathy-altruism hypothesis. In this low-empathy situation, personal distress is the only emotional reaction engendered by the perception of the target in need, and both helping and leaving are live options for reducing this distress.

Although the empathy-altruism hypothesis and the aversive-arousal reduction hypothesis agree about the case in which a subject feels no empathy for a target, the two hypotheses differ where a subject feels a significant amount of empathy for a target.

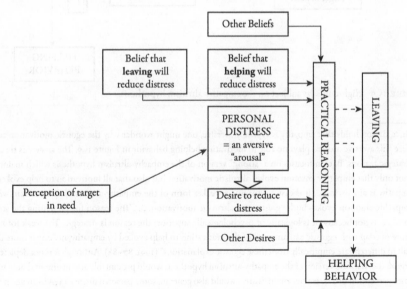

FIGURE 15.8 Low-empathy subject on both the empathy-altruism hypothesis and the aversive-arousal reduction hypothesis.

Figure 15.9 depicts the processes underlying the subject's behavior according to Batson's version of the empathy-altruism hypothesis.

Here, perception of the target's need leads to empathy and that produces an ultimate desire to help. Since leaving is not an effective strategy for satisfying this desire, helping is the likely behavior—although, of course, the subject might have some other desire that is stronger than the ultimate desire to help, so helping is not the only possible outcome.[27] The aversive-arousal reduction hypothesis, by contrast, depicts the processes underlying a high-empathy subject as in Figure 15.10. While the perception of the target in distress leads to empathy in this case too, the empathy simply heightens the subject's personal distress and thus strengthens his desire to reduce the distress. Since the subject believes

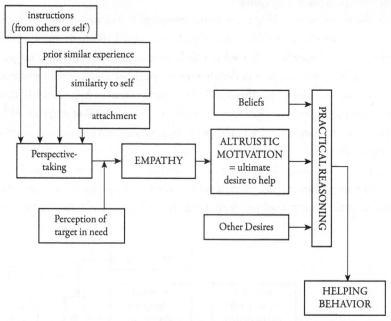

FIGURE 15.9 High-empathy subject on the empathy-altruism hypothesis.

---

27. Since Batson holds that empathy is typically aversive, one might wonder why the egoistic motivation to reduce this aversive arousal plays no role in motivating helping behavior in Figure 15.9. The answer is that, for strategic reasons, Batson focuses on a "strong" version of the empathy-altruism hypothesis which maintains "not only that empathic emotion evokes altruistic motivation but also that all motivation to help evoked by empathy is altruistic. . . . It is easy to imagine a weaker form of the empathy-altruism hypothesis, in which empathic emotion evokes both egoistic and altruistic motivation. . . . The reason for presenting the strong form . . . is not because it is logically or psychologically superior; the reason is strategic. The weak form has more overlap with egoistic explanations of the motivation to help evoked by empathy, making it more difficult to differentiate empirically from these egoistic explanations" (1991, 87–88). Although it is not depicted in Figure 15.9, Batson's version of the empathy-altruism hypothesis would presumably also maintain that in many cases perception of a target person in distress would also generate some personal distress even in an agent who strongly empathizes with the target. And when the agent believes that leaving is the easiest way to reduce that personal distress, this will generate some motivation to leave.

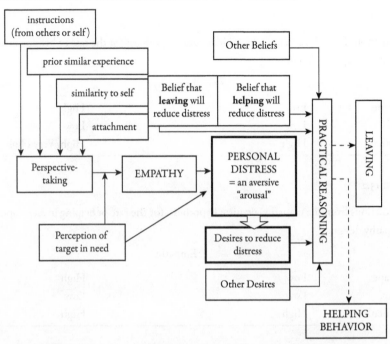

FIGURE 15.10 High-empathy subject on the aversive-arousal reduction hypothesis.

that either helping or leaving will reduce distress, both of these actions are live options, and the subject will select the one that he believes to be easiest.

In designing experiments to compare the empathy-altruism hypothesis with the aversive-arousal reduction hypothesis, Batson must manipulate two distinct variables. To determine whether empathy is playing a role in producing helping behavior, he has to compare the behavior of low-empathy and high-empathy subjects. To determine whether ease of escape has any effect on the likelihood of helping behavior, he must arrange things so that leaving is significantly more costly for some subjects than for others. So there are four experimental conditions: low-empathy subjects where escape is either (1) easy or (2) hard, and high-empathy subjects where leaving is either (3) easy or (4) hard. Batson summarizes what he takes to be the predictions made by the aversive-arousal reduction hypothesis and by the empathy-altruism hypothesis in Tables 15.1 and 15.2 (Batson 1991, 111). The crucial difference is in the upper-right quadrants, where escape is easy and empathy is high. Under these conditions, Batson maintains, the egoistic aversive-arousal reduction hypothesis predicts a low level of helping behavior, while the empathy-altruism hypothesis predicts that the rate of helping will be high.

To test these predictions, Batson and his colleagues conducted a total of six experiments. In one of these (Batson et al. 1981, experiment 1), student subjects were required to watch, via what they believed to be closed-circuit TV, as another student subject,

TABLE 15.1

Predictions from the aversive-arousal reduction hypothesis for the rate of helping in an escape × empathy design

	Empathy	
Escape	Low	High
Easy	Low	Low
Difficult	High	High/Very High

TABLE 15.2

Predictions from the empathy-altruism hypothesis for the rate of helping in an escape × empathy design

	Empathy	
Escape	Low	High
Easy	Low	Low
Difficult	High	High

Elaine, attempted to perform a task while receiving electric shocks at random intervals. Observer subjects were told that their task would be to form and report an impression of how Elaine performs under aversive conditions. Actually, what the subjects were viewing was a videotape. On the tape, Elaine is clearly finding the shocks very uncomfortable, and after her second trial at doing the task, she explains to Martha, the assistant overseeing the experiment, that she is unusually sensitive to mild electric shocks because of a childhood trauma. Martha then suggests that perhaps the observer subject might be willing to help Elaine by taking her place, and the experimenter asks whether the subject is willing to do that. To manipulate ease of escape, some subjects are told that if they decide not to take Elaine's place, they will be required to watch eight additional trials, while other subjects are told that if they decide not to take Elaine's place, they will be free to go, although Elaine will have to endure eight more trials. To manipulate the level of empathy that subjects feel for Elaine, subjects are given a copy of a personal values and interests questionnaire, allegedly filled out by Elaine, in order to help them form an impression of her performance. In the high-empathy condition, Elaine's values and interests are very similar to the subject's (which had been determined in a screening session several weeks before), while in the low-empathy condition, they are very different. The results, given in Table 15.3, clearly exhibit the pattern that Batson thinks is predicted by the empathy-altruism hypothesis, not the pattern that Batson thinks is predicted by the aversive-arousal reduction hypothesis.

In four additional experiments, Batson and his associates used a total of four different techniques to create the low- and high-empathy conditions, two techniques for

TABLE 15.3

Proportion of subjects agreeing to take shocks for Elaine (Batson et al. 1981, experiment 1)

Escape Condition	Empathy Condition	
	Low (Dissimilar Victim)	High (Similar victim)
Easy	.18	.91
Difficult	.64	.82

manipulating ease of escape, and two different need situations.[28] The results in all of these experiments exhibited the same pattern. Intriguingly, in a sixth experiment, Batson attempted to break the pattern by telling the subjects that the shock level they would have to endure was the highest of four options, "clearly painful but not harmful." They reasoned that, in these circumstances, even if high-empathy subjects had an ultimate desire to help, this desire might well be overridden by the desire to avoid a series of very painful shocks. As expected, the pattern of results in this experiment fit the pattern in Table 15.1.

These are, we think, truly impressive findings. Over and over again, in well-designed and carefully conducted experiments, Batson and his associates have produced results that are clearly compatible with what Batson has argued are the predictions of the empathy-altruism hypothesis, as set out in Table 15.2, and clearly incompatible with the predictions of the aversive-arousal reduction hypothesis, as set out in Table 15.1. Even the "clearly painful shock" experiment, which produced results in the pattern of Table 15.1, is comfortably compatible with the empathy-altruism hypothesis since, as we noted in our discussion of Figure 15.9, the empathy-altruism hypothesis allows that high-empathy subjects may have desires that are stronger than their ultimate desire to help the target, and the desire to avoid a painful electric shock is a very plausible candidate.

There is, however, a problem to be overcome before we conclude that the aversive-arousal reduction hypothesis cannot explain the findings that Batson has reported. In arguing that Table 15.1 reflects the predictions made by the aversive-arousal reduction hypothesis, Batson assumes that escape will alleviate personal distress (and the aversive component of empathy) in both low- and high-empathy situations, and that subjects believe this, although the belief, along with many other mental states and processes posited in Figures 15.8, 15.9, and 15.10, may not be readily available to introspection. We might call this the out of sight, out of mind assumption.[29] But, elaborating on an idea suggested by Hoffman (1991) and Hornstein (1991), an advocate of egoism might propose that

28. The experiments are reported in Batson el al. 1981, Toi and Batson 1982, and Batson et al. 1983.

29. As Batson himself remarks, "[T]he old adage, 'Out of sight, out of mind,' reminds us that physical escape often permits psychological escape as well" (1991, 80).

although subjects do believe this when they have little empathy for the target, they do not believe it when they have high empathy for the target. Perhaps high-empathy subjects believe that if they leave the scene they will continue to be troubled by the thought or memory of the distressed target and thus that physical escape will not lead to psychological escape. Indeed, in cases where empathy is strong and is evoked by attachment, this is just what common sense would lead us to expect. (Do you suppose that if you abandoned your mother when she was in grave distress, you would no longer be troubled by the knowledge of her plight?) But if the high-empathy subjects in Batson's experiments believe that they will continue to be plagued by distressing thoughts about the target even after they depart, then the egoistic aversive arousal reduction hypothesis predicts that these subjects will be inclined to help in both the easy physical escape and the difficult physical escape conditions, since helping is the only strategy they believe will be effective for reducing the aversive arousal.[30] So neither the findings reported in Table 15.3 nor the results of any of Batson's other experiments would give us a reason to prefer the empathy-altruism hypothesis over the aversive-arousal reduction hypothesis, because both hypotheses would make the same predictions.

Is it the case that high-empathy subjects in experiments like Batson's believe that unless they help they will continue to think about the target and thus continue to feel distress, and that this belief leads to helping because it generates an egoistic instrumental desire to help? This is, of course, an empirical question, and until recently there was little evidence bearing on it. But a cleverly designed experiment by Stocks and his associates (Stocks et al. 2009) suggests that, in situations like those used in Batson's experiments, a belief that they will continue to think about the target does not play a significant role in causing the helping behavior in high-empathy subjects. The first phase of the experiment was a "psychological escape" manipulation. Half the subjects were told that they would soon be participating in a "deleting memories" training session that would permanently delete their memories of an audiotaped news segment that they were about to hear. The remaining subjects were told that they would soon be participating in a "saving memories" training session designed to permanently enhance the memories of the news segment they were about to hear. Then, using stimulus materials that we shall see in various of Batson's experiments, the experimenters played subjects a fictional college radio news segment about the plight of a fellow student, Katie Banks, whose parents have recently been killed in an automobile accident, leaving her to care for her younger brother and sister. In the interview, Katie mentions that she has begun a fund-raising campaign to raise money for her college tuition and for living expenses for her siblings. If she is not successful, she will be forced to drop out of school and put her brother and sister up for adoption. Empathy for Katie was manipulated by using the Stotland-inspired technique—instructing

---

30. The point emerges clearly in Figure 15.10. If the belief that leaving will reduce distress is eliminated, then LEAVING is no longer a way to satisfy the desire to reduce distress. So HELPING BEHAVIOR is the only way to satisfy this desire.

some participants to imagine how Katie felt and others to try to remain as objective and detached as possible. After hearing the tape, subjects completed two questionnaires, one designed to assess the success of the empathy manipulation, the other designed to test the effectiveness of the psychological escape manipulation. Both manipulations were successful: crucially, subjects reported being quite confident that the memory training session would enhance or delete their memory of the Katie Banks interview they had just heard. Finally, subjects were given an unexpected opportunity to help Katie with her child care and home maintenance chores.

Stocks and his associates reasoned that if high-empathy subjects in the Batson experiments recounted earlier are egoists who help because they believe that they will continue to have distressing thoughts about the victim, then in this experiment high-empathy subjects who believed their memories of Katie would be enhanced by the training session would be highly motivated to help, while subjects who believed that their memories of Katie would soon be deleted would have little motivation to help. If, by contrast, empathy generates altruistic motivation, there should be little difference between those high-empathy subjects who believe their memories of Katie will be enhanced and those who believe that their memories of her will soon be deleted. The results, shown in Table 15.4, provide impressive confirmation of the prediction based on the empathy-altruism hypothesis.[31]

We believe that Batson's work on the aversive-arousal reduction hypothesis, buttressed by the Stocks et al. finding, is a major advance in the egoism vs. altruism debate. No thoughtful observer would conclude that these experiments show that altruism is true, since, as Batson himself emphasizes, the aversive-arousal reduction hypothesis is just one among many egoistic alternatives to the empathy-altruism hypothesis, although it has been one of the most popular egoistic strategies for explaining helping behavior. But the

TABLE 15.4

Proportion of subjects agreeing to help Katie Banks (Stocks et al., under review: experiment 1)

Psychological Escape	Empathy	
	Low	High
Easy—memory deleted	.08	.67
Difficult—memory enhanced	.42	.58

31. Both the aversive-arousal reduction hypothesis and the empathy-altruism hypothesis predict that low-empathy subjects will behave egoistically, and thus that they will be less inclined to help when they believe that their memories of Katie will be deleted than when they believe their memories will linger. The fact that this prediction is confirmed is a further indication that the psychological escape manipulation was successful.

experimental findings strongly suggest that in situations like those that Batson has studied, the empathy-altruism hypothesis offers a much better explanation of the subjects' behavior than the aversive-arousal reduction hypothesis (Batson 1991, 127).

4.5 THE EMPATHY-ALTRUISM HYPOTHESIS VS. THE EMPATHY-SPECIFIC PUNISHMENT HYPOTHESIS

As noted earlier, thinkers in the egoist tradition have proposed many alternatives to the hypothesis that empathy engenders genuine altruism. Although aversive-arousal reduction may be the most popular of these, another familiar proposal maintains that people engage in helping behavior because they fear they will be punished if they do not help. On one version of this view, the punishments are socially administered. *If I don't help*, the agent worries, *people will think badly of me, and this will have negative effects on how they treat me.* On another version, which to our mind is both more plausible and more difficult to assess experimentally, the punishments that people are worried about are self-administered. If she doesn't help, the agent believes, she will suffer the pangs of guilt, or shame, or some other aversive emotion. As they stand, neither of these egoist accounts can explain the fact that empathy increases the likelihood of helping, but more sophisticated versions are easy to construct.[32] They need only add the assumption that people think either social sanctions or self-administered sanctions for not helping are more likely when the target engenders empathy. We'll take up the social and self-administered variants in turn. We believe that currently available evidence supports the conclusion that the social version is incorrect, but we shall argue that the evidence regarding the self-administered version is inconclusive.

Following Batson, let's call the social variant of this hypothesis (the one that maintains that subjects believe socially administered sanctions to be more likely when the target engenders empathy) the *socially administered empathy-specific punishment hypothesis*. To test it against the empathy-altruism hypothesis, Batson and his associates designed an experiment in which they manipulated both the level of empathy that the subject felt for the target and the likelihood that anyone would know whether or not the subject had opted to help a person in need. Obviously, if your decision is secret, you need have no fear of social sanctions. Thus the socially administered empathy-specific punishment hypothesis predicts that high-empathy subjects will be more likely to help when others will know whether or not they decide to help. On the empathy-altruism hypothesis, by contrast, high-empathy subjects are motivated by an ultimate desire to help, and thus their helping levels should be high whether or not others will know if they decided not to help. In the low-empathy condition, both hypotheses predict that levels of helping will be low. These predictions are summarized in Tables 15.5 and 15.6.

---

32. The problem is similar to the one confronting the simple version of the aversive-arousal reduction hypothesis discussed at the beginning of 4.4, as is the solution.

TABLE 15.5

Predictions about the amount of helping on the socially administered empathy-specific punishment hypothesis

	Empathy	
Would the helping choice be private or public?	Low	High
Public	Low	High
Private	Low	Low

TABLE 15.6

Predictions about the amount of helping on the empathy-altruism hypothesis

	Empathy	
Would the helping choice be private or public?	Low	High
Public	Low	High
Private	Low	High

Subjects in the experiment were told that they were participating in an impression-formation study, and that they had been randomly assigned to the role of "listener" who would read confidential notes from another student participant, the "communicator." The listeners were given two notes from a fictional communicator, "Janet Arnold," an out-of-state freshman who reveals that she is very lonely and hoping to find a friend. After completing a form on which subjects indicated their impressions of Janet and their emotional responses to her note, they were presented with an unexpected opportunity to befriend Janet by volunteering to take part in a study of long-term relationships which would involve an initial meeting with Janet and periodic phone interviews about the development of their friendship. Participants who were willing to help were asked how much time they were willing to spend with Janet during the next month.

To manipulate empathy, Batson and his associates used the Stotland technique. Subjects assigned to the low-empathy condition were instructed to "Read the information in the communicator's notes carefully, trying to be as objective as possible. Try to focus on the techniques used to get the communicator's message across." Subjects assigned to the high-empathy condition were instructed to "Read the information in the communicator's notes carefully, trying to take the perspective of the individual writing the notes. Try to imagine how this individual feels about what he or she writes" (1991, 132).

Four steps were taken to manipulate the perceived potential for negative social evaluation. In the low-potential condition, where the subjects' choices were private (Batson 1991, 132):

(1) Subjects were told that they would be the only person ever to read the communicator's notes, and the notes were delivered in a sealed envelope.

(2) Subjects were assured that the questionnaires reporting their reactions to Janet's note would be anonymous.

(3) Subjects' responses to the invitation to participate in the long-term relationship study were returned to the professor in a sealed envelope, so no one would know if they did not want to help Janet. (Since they believed the professor had not read Janet's note, they could be expected to surmise that he would not know that Janet needed a friend.)

(4) In the letter inviting them to participate in the relationship study, subjects were told that Janet would be contacted "only if you want a meeting; if you do not, then we will not contact the communicator and he or she will not know that you were ever asked about actually meeting."

In the high-potential condition where the subjects' choices were public (Batson 1991, 133):

(1) Subjects were told that the experimenter would (a) read the communicator's notes, (b) collect the subject's completed questionnaire, and (c) compare the content of the notes with the content of the questionnaire.

(2) No envelope was provided for their response to the invitation to participate in the long-term relationship study, so subjects could infer that the experimenter would know about Janet's need for a friend, about their emotional reaction to Janet, and would also know whether or not they had agreed to help Janet.

(3) Subjects were told that Janet would know if they decided not to help.

As Batson states, or perhaps understates, procedures in the high-potential (public) condition "were designed to highlight the possibility of negative social evaluation if the participant decided not to volunteer to spend time with Janet" (1991, 133).

The results, given in Table 15.7, indicate that the socially administered empathy-specific punishment hypothesis did not fare well. On the basis of this experiment and a similar experiment in which empathy for Janet was not manipulated but was measured by

TABLE 15.7

Amount of help offered Janet (Fultz et al. 1986, study 2)

Would the helping choice be private or public?	Empathy	
	Low	High
Public	.67	1.71
Private	1.29	2.44

self-report, Batson concludes that the socially administered empathy-specific punishment hypothesis is not consistent with the experimental findings.

> Contrary to what the social-evaluation version of the empathy-specific punishment hypothesis predicted, eliminating anticipated negative social evaluation in these two studies did not eliminate the empathy-helping relationship. Rather than high empathy leading to more help only under high social evaluation, it led to more helping under both low and high social evaluation. This pattern of results is not consistent with what would be expected if empathically aroused individuals are egoistically motivated to avoid looking bad in the eyes of others; it is quite consistent with what would be expected if empathy evokes altruistic motivation to reduce the victim's need. (1991, 134)

Although two experiments hardly make a conclusive case, we are inclined to agree with Batson that these studies make the socially administered empathy-specific punishment hypothesis look significantly less plausible than the empathy-altruism hypothesis. High-empathy subjects were more likely to help whether or not they could expect their behavior to be socially scrutinized. So another popular egoist hypothesis has been dealt a serious blow. At least in some circumstances, empathy appears to facilitate helping independently of the threat of social sanction.[33]

There is, however, another version of the empathy-specific punishment hypothesis that must be considered, and we are less sanguine about Batson's attempts to defend the empathy-altruism hypothesis against this version. According to the self-administered empathy-specific punishment hypothesis, people are motivated to help because they believe that if they don't help they will experience some negative self-regarding emotion, such as guilt or shame. As Batson (1991, 98) explicates the view, "we learn through socialization that empathy carries with it a special obligation to help and, as a result, an extra dose of self-administered shame or guilt if we do not. When we feel empathy we think of the impending additional self-punishments and help in order to avoid them. . . . To test whether self-punishment underlies the empathy-helping relationship," Batson (1991, 134–35) notes, "high-empathy individuals must anticipate being able to escape . . . from negative self-evaluation." But, one might wonder, how is that possible? Here is the crucial passage in which Batson addresses the question and sets out his strategy.

---

33. These studies do not address a variant of the socially administered empathy-specific punishment hypothesis that might be called the "divinely administered empathy-specific punishment hypothesis." It is very plausible that subjects in the private low potential for social evaluation condition believed that no ordinary person would know if they declined to help someone in need. But these subjects might believe that God would know, that He would punish them for their failure to help, and that God's punishment would be particularly severe when they failed to help someone for whom they felt empathy. To the best of our knowledge, the divinely administered empathy-specific punishment hypothesis is a version of egoism that has not been explored empirically.

[I]f expectations of self-punishment have been internalized to the degree that they are automatic and invariant across all helping situations, then providing escape seems impossible. It seems unlikely, however, that many people—if any—have internalized procedures for self-punishment to such a degree. Even those who reflexively slap themselves with guilt and self-recrimination whenever they do wrong are likely to be sensitive to situational cues in determining when they have done wrong. . . . And given the discomfort produced by guilt and self-recrimination, one suspects that most people will not reflexively self-punish but will, if possible, overlook their failures to help. They will dole out self-punishments only in situations in which such failures are salient and inescapable.

   If there is this kind of leeway in interpreting failure to help as unjustified and hence deserving of self-punishment, then expectation of self-punishment may be reduced by providing some individuals with information that justifies not helping in some particular situation. The justifying information probably cannot be provided directly by telling individuals not to feel guilty about not helping. Calling direct attention to the failure may have the reverse effect; it may highlight the associated punishments. The information needs to be provided in a more subtle, indirect way. (1991, 135)

Before considering how Batson and his associates designed experiments that attempt to implement this strategy, we want to emphasize a subtle but very important concern about the passage we've just quoted. In that passage, Batson slips back and forth between claims about people's expectations about self-punishment and their internalized procedures for administering it. The latter are claims about what people will actually feel if they fail to help in various circumstances, while the former are claims about what people believe they will feel. The distinction is an important one because in the debate between egoists and altruists it is the beliefs that are crucial. To see this, recall what is at issue. Both egoists and altruists agree that people sometimes desire to help others, but egoists insist that these desires are always instrumental desires, while altruists maintain that, sometimes at least, these desires are not instrumental but ultimate. As we saw in Section 1, instrumental desires are desires that are produced or sustained via practical reasoning, a process in which desires and beliefs lead to new desires. So an egoist who advocates the self-administered empathy-specific punishment hypothesis would maintain that the desire to help is generated by an episode of practical reasoning something like the one in Figure 15.11. In that diagram, BELIEF 2 (*If I feel empathy and don't help, then I will feel guilty*) plays a central role, since it is this belief that is supposed to capture the agent's expectations about self-punishment. That belief may or may not be accurate—perhaps the agent won't actually feel guilty. But the accuracy of the belief is not relevant to the debate between egoists and altruists. What is crucial is just that the subject has some belief that, together with her desire not to feel guilt (DESIRE 2), will generate DESIRE 3 (*I help when I feel empathy*). The importance of all this will emerge as we review Batson's experiments and how he interprets them.

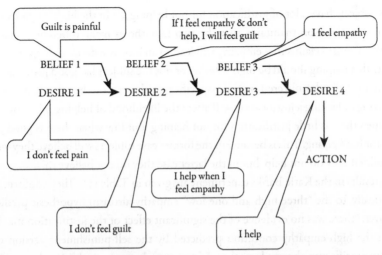

FIGURE 15.11 The self-administered empathy-specific punishment account of the practical reasoning leading to the instrumental desire to help.

In designing experiments to test the empathy-altruism hypothesis against the self-administered empathy-specific punishment hypothesis, Batson's strategy is to provide some subjects with a justification for not helping. By doing this, Batson's goal is to alter his subjects' beliefs; he expects that subjects who have been given a justification for not helping will be less likely to believe that they will feel guilty if they do not help. In one experiment, subjects were asked to listen to a tape of what they were told was a pilot broadcast of a campus radio show. The show is an interview with Katie Banks, whom we met earlier in our discussion of the Stocks et al. experiment. She is a student on their campus struggling to stay in school and keep her family together after her parents are killed in an automobile accident. To manipulate levels of empathy, the investigators again used the Stotland procedure. After listening to the tape, subjects are given an opportunity to pledge time to help Katie. To manipulate the justification that subjects have for not helping, some are given a sign-up sheet on which five of seven previous "participants" in the study have agreed to help, while others are given a sign-up sheet on which only two of the previous seven participants have agreed to help. By getting the second group to believe that most previous participants had not been willing to help, Batson and his associates intend to be providing just the sort of "subtle, indirect" justification for not helping that their strategy requires.[34]

According to Batson, in the low-empathy condition, both the empathy-altruism hypothesis and the self-administered empathy-specific punishment hypothesis will make the same prediction: helping will be high in the low-justification condition (where subjects have little justification for not helping) and low in the high-justification condition

---

34. One might worry, here, that the sign up-sheet manipulation could have just the opposite effect. If lots of other people have already signed up to help Katie, some subjects might come to believe that they are justified in not helping, since she already has plenty of help.

(where subjects have a lot of justification for not helping).[35] In the high-empathy condition, however, Batson maintains that the two hypotheses make different predictions. Empathy-altruism claims that empathy will lead to an ultimate desire to help, and thus it predicts that helping should be high whether or not the subject has good justification for not helping. Self-administered empathy-specific punishment, on the other hand, predicts that having or lacking a justification will affect the likelihood of helping. Helping will be high when there is little justification for not helping, but low when there is good justification for not helping. This is because in the former case subjects will believe they will feel very guilty if they do not help, but in the latter case they do not believe this.

The results in the Katie Banks experiment are given in Table 15.8. They conform, quite dramatically, to the "three high and one low" empathy-altruism hypothesis prediction. Moreover, "there was no evidence of the significant effect of the justification manipulation in the high-empathy condition predicted by the self-punishment version of the empathy-specific punishment hypothesis" (1991, 138). In a pair of additional experiments, Batson and his associates varied the helping opportunity, the justification manipulation and the empathy manipulation. In those experiments, too, "the pattern of helping was very much as predicted by the empathy-altruism hypothesis" (ibid., 140). Once again, it appears there is good reason to prefer the empathy-altruism hypothesis over an egoistic empathy-specific punishment alternative. But we are not convinced.

Our concerns are not focused on the details of Batson's experiments, but on his account of what the self-administered empathy-specific punishment hypothesis predicts. To make the point, let's return to the practical reasoning diagram in Figure 15.11. In that diagram, BELIEF 2 portrays the agent believing: *If I feel empathy and don't help, I will feel guilt*. But if Batson is right, that account of BELIEF 2 needs to be modified, since if the agent really believed that, then the justification manipulation would have no effect. In order for the justification manipulation to disrupt the process portrayed in Figure 15.11,

TABLE 15.8

Proportion of participants volunteering to help Katie Banks (Batson et al. 1988, study 3)

Justification condition	Empathy Condition	
	Low	High
Low justification for not helping	.55	.70
High justification for not helping	.15	.60

35. In order to derive this prediction for the low-justification condition. Batson must assume that, even without empathy, subjects "should be egoistically motivated to avoid general shame and guilt associated with a failure to help" (1991, 136). So, as Batson is interpreting the self-administered empathy-specific punishment hypothesis, it maintains that even low-empathy individuals believe they will feel some guilt if they fail to help without justification, and high-empathy individuals believe they will feel significantly more guilt if they fail to help without justification.

BELIEF 2 would have to be something like: *If I feel empathy and don't help, I will feel guilt UNLESS there is justification for not helping.* That belief, along with DESIRE 2 (I don't feel guilt), would lead to DESIRE 3 with the content: *I help when I feel empathy UNLESS there is justification for not helping,* and that is just what Batson needs to derive his predictions about what agents are likely to do in high-empathy situations, if the self-administered empathy-specific punishment hypothesis is correct. Suppose, however, that instead of this candidate for BELIEF 2, what agents actually believe is: *If I feel empathy and don't help, I will feel guilt EVEN IF there is justification for not helping.* In that case, DESIRE 3 would be: *I help when I feel empathy EVEN IF there is justification for not helping,* and the self-administered empathy-specific punishment hypothesis would predict high levels of helping in high-empathy subjects whether or not there is justification for not helping. Since this is just what the empathy-altruism hypothesis predicts, Batson's experiments would not be able to distinguish between the two hypotheses. So clearly the content of agents' beliefs about the link between empathy and guilt is playing a crucial role in Batson's argument.

What grounds does Batson offer for assuming that subjects believe: *If I feel empathy and don't help, I will feel guilt UNLESS there is justification for not helping,* rather than: *If I feel empathy and don't help, I will feel guilt EVEN IF there is justification for not helping*? As best we can tell, the long passage we quoted earlier is his only attempt to justify the assumption. But that passage offers no evidence for the claims it makes about people's "internalized procedures for self-punishment." Moreover, even if Batson's speculations about those procedures are true, it would not justify the claim he really needs, namely that people have accurate beliefs about these internalized procedures. The prediction that Batson derives from the egoistic hypothesis requires assuming that people typically have a specific sort of belief about what they will feel if they fail to help when there is justification for not helping. That is an empirical assumption, of course, but it is one for which Batson offers no evidence. Batson might be able to protect his argument from our critique by showing that subjects really do have the belief that his prediction assumes. But until that is done, the experiments we have discussed give us no good reason to reject the self-administered empathy-specific punishment hypothesis.

The findings we have discussed so far are not, however, the only ones that Batson relies on in his critique of the self-administered empathy-specific punishment hypothesis. In another version of the Katie Banks experiment, Batson and his associates attempted to determine what participants were thinking when they made their decisions about whether to offer help. Here is Batson's explanation of the motivation for this experiment:

> The empathy-specific punishment hypothesis and the empathy-altruism hypothesis each postulate a different goal for the helping associated with feeling empathy: The goal is avoiding punishment in the former; the goal is relieving the victim's need for the latter. Each hypothesis assumes that the empathically aroused individual, when deciding to help, has one of these goals in mind. If this is true, then cognitions relevant to one of these goals should be associated with empathy-induced helping. (1991, 143)

So if we can find some way to determine what empathically engaged individuals are thinking about, Batson argues, we may be able to provide evidence for one or another of these hypotheses. Simply asking subjects what they were thinking about is methodologically problematic, first because the relevant thoughts might not have been fully conscious, and second because subjects might be unwilling, or otherwise unable, to provide accurate self-reports. But, as it happens, the well-known Stroop procedure provides a way of determining what people are thinking about without directly asking them. In the Stroop procedure, subjects are shown words typed in various colors. Their task is to name the color of the type, and to do so as quickly as possible. Previous research had shown that the time taken to respond for a particular word (the "latency," in psychologists' jargon) will increase whenever a subject has been thinking about something related to that word (Geller and Shaver 1976).

In the experiment, which for the most part repeated the Katie Banks procedure, the experimenter paused after telling subjects that they would be given an opportunity to sign up to help Katie, and administered a Stroop test. Some of the words used, like DUTY, GUILT, SHAME, SHOULD, were taken to be "punishment-relevant"; other words, including HOPE, CHILD, NEEDY, FRIEND, were classified as "victim-relevant"; and still other words, LEFT, RAPID, LARGE, BREATH, were classified as neutral. Here is Batson's account of the results and his interpretation of them:

> [T]he only positive association in the high-empathy condition was a correlation between helping and color-naming latency for the victim-relevant words. . . . This was the correlation predicted by the empathy-altruism hypothesis. Contrary to the prediction of the empathy-specific punishment hypothesis, there was no evidence of a positive correlation in the high-empathy condition between helping and color-naming latency for the punishment-relevant words.
>
> In the low-empathy condition, in which empathic feelings had not been explicitly aroused, there was not a positive correlation between helping and latency for the victim-relevant words. This finding suggests that the positive correlation for victim-relevant words in the high-empathy condition was not due to some general characteristic of these words or their association with helping. The relationship seemed to be empathy specific. (1991, 147)

Although this is an ingenious experiment with intriguing results, we are again skeptical that the results favor one hypothesis over the other. To make the case for our skepticism, we'll argue that the self-administered empathy-specific punishment hypothesis can be plausibly construed in a way that it does not predict, of the agent, that she will be thinking punishment-relevant thoughts. Instead, it predicts exactly what Batson found: the agent thinks only victim-relevant thoughts.

Let's begin by returning to the quotation, two paragraphs back, in which Batson explains the motivation for the experiment. According to Batson, "The empathy-specific punishment hypothesis and the empathy-altruism hypothesis each postulate a different goal for the helping associated with feeling empathy: The goal is avoiding punishment in the former; the goal is relieving the victim's need for the latter" (1991, 143). It is important to see that this claim is plausible only if "goal" is understood to mean ultimate desire, and is clearly false if "goal" refers to any desire that may play a role in the process leading to helping behavior. On the empathy-specific punishment hypothesis, although the ultimate desire is avoiding punishment (or the pain that punishment engenders), this leads to an instrumental desire to relieve the victim's need. So it is misleading for Batson to claim that "each hypothesis assumes that the empathically aroused individual, when deciding to help, has one of these goals in mind" (1991, 143), since the empathy-specific punishment hypothesis maintains that the empathically aroused individual has both desires in mind—one as an ultimate desire and the other as an instrumental desire. This suggests that the empathy-specific punishment hypothesis should predict that high-empathy subjects have a longer latency for both punishment-relevant words and victim-relevant words.

If this is right, then we've located a slip in what Batson claims about the prediction of the empathy-specific punishment hypothesis. However, it might be thought that this does no serious harm to Batson's case, since the experimental results also contradict this new prediction. On the new prediction, high-empathy subjects should be thinking both punishment-relevant and victim-relevant thoughts. But they aren't. They are thinking only victim-relevant thoughts, which is what the empathy-altruism hypothesis predicts.

This is not the end of the story, however. For we believe that on one very natural interpretation of the empathy-specific punishment hypothesis, it will not predict that agents think punishment-relevant thoughts. To set out this interpretation, we'll need to introduce the idea of a long-standing instrumental desire. Consider what happens when you get your monthly electric bill. Typically, we'll assume, you pay it. Why? Well, because you have a desire to pay it. This is, to be sure, an instrumental desire, not an ultimate desire. You want to pay your electric bill because you believe that if you don't, they will turn off your electricity, and that would lead to lots of other unpleasant consequences which you want to avoid. The lights would go out; the heat or air-conditioning would go off; your computer would stop working; it would be a real pain in the neck. But are any of these consequences on your mind when you reach for the checkbook to pay the electricity bill? Quite typically, we think, the answer is no. Rather, what happens is that you have a long-standing desire to pay the electric bill on time whenever it comes. This is an instrumental desire; there is nothing intrinsically desirable about paying the bill. So, like other instrumental desires, it was formed via a process of practical reasoning. But that was a long time ago, and there is no need to revisit that process every time you pay your bill. Most people, we think, have lots of desires like that. They are enduring desires that were formed long ago via practical reasoning. When the circumstances are appropriate, they are activated, they generate further instrumental desires, and ultimately they lead to action. And all of this happens without either consciously or unconsciously revisiting the practical reasoning that led to the formation of the long-standing desire.

Let's return, now, to Figure 15.11, which sketches the motivational structure underlying helping behavior on one version of the empathy-specific punishment hypothesis. On the interpretation of the hypothesis that we are proposing, DESIRE 3 is a long-standing instrumental desire. It was originally formed via the egoistic process of practical reasoning sketched on the left side of Figure 15.11. But there is no need to repeat that process every time the desire is activated, any more than there is a need to reflect on the lights going out every time you pay your electric bill. On this interpretation of the empathy-specific punishment hypothesis, the agent will not activate thoughts about guilt and punishment when she decides to help. Instead, the only thoughts that need be activated are thoughts about the victim and how to help her. So, on this interpretation, the results of Batson's Stroop experiment are just what the empathy-specific punishment hypothesis would predict. Thus the experiment gives us no reason to prefer empathy-altruism over empathy-specific punishment.

In this section we have looked at two versions of the egoistic empathy-specific punishment hypothesis. We've argued that Batson's work poses a serious challenge to the version on which the punishment is delivered by others. But Batson's experiments do not make a convincing case against the version on which the punishment is self-inflicted, via guilt or some other aversive emotion. To address the problems we've elaborated, Batson needs to provide more convincing evidence about the beliefs that subjects invoke when they are making their decision about helping Katie Banks, and about the processes that generate and sustain the desires involved in that decision. This is a tall order, since it is no easy matter to get persuasive evidence about either of these. The need for such evidence makes it clear how challenging empirical work in this area can be. But, as illustrated by Batson's own work, as well as the Stocks et al. study discussed in the previous section, cleverly designed experiments can go a long way toward resolving issues that at first appear intractable. So the gap in Batson's case against the empathy-specific punishment hypothesis certainly gives us no reason to be skeptical about the experimental approach to the egoism vs. altruism debate.

4.6. THE EMPATHY-ALTRUISM HYPOTHESIS VS. THE EMPATHY-SPECIFIC REWARD HYPOTHESIS

In the previous section our focus was on the venerable idea that helping is motivated by fear of punishment. In this section, we'll take a brief look at the equally venerable idea that helping is motivated by the expectation of reward. Like punishment, reward can come from two sources: others can reward us in various ways for our helpful actions, or we can reward ourselves—helping others can make us feel good. But just as in the case of punishment, the simple theory that people help others because they believe they will be rewarded offers no explanation for the fact that empathy increases helping behavior. To remedy this problem, the egoist can propose that "helping is especially rewarding when the helper feels empathy for the person in need" (Batson 1991, 97). This is the view that Batson calls the empathy-specific reward hypothesis. Although the idea can be spelled out in a variety of ways, we'll begin with the version that claims "that we learn through socialization that additional rewards follow helping someone for whom we feel empathy; these rewards most often take the form of extra praise from others or a special feeling of pride in ourselves. When we feel empathy, we think of these additional rewards, and we help in order to get them" (ibid.).

To motivate an ingenious experiment designed to test this hypothesis against the empathy-altruism hypothesis, Batson notes that it is only one's own helping, or attempts to help, that make one eligible for the rewards that helping engenders; if someone else helps the target before you get around to it, the rewards are not forthcoming. This is plausible both in the case where the rewards are provided by others and in the case where the rewards are provided by our own self-generated feeling of pride. For surely we don't typically expect others to praise us because someone else has helped a person in distress, nor do we expect to feel pride if the target's distress is alleviated by a stranger, or by chance. So on the version of the empathy-specific rewards hypothesis that we are considering, we should predict that an empathically aroused agent will be pleased when he gets to help the target (either because he is feeling a jolt of pride or because he is looking forward to the rewards that others will provide), but he will not be pleased if he is unable to help the target.

For reasons that will emerge shortly, Batson distinguishes two cases in which the agent is unable to help. In the first, there is just nothing he can do to relieve the target's distress; in the second, someone (or something) else relieves the target's distress before the agent gets a chance to act. In both cases, Batson maintains, the egoistic reward-seeking agent has nothing in particular to be pleased about. Finally, Batson suggests that we can determine whether an agent is pleased by using self-report tests to assess changes in his mood— the more the mood has improved, the more pleased the agent is.

If the empathy-altruism hypothesis is correct, then agents are motivated by an ultimate desire that the target's distress be alleviated. So on this hypothesis, it shouldn't matter how the target's distress is alleviated. No matter how it is accomplished, the agent's altruistic ultimate desire will be satisfied. If we assume that people are pleased when their ultimate desires are satisfied, then the empathy-altruism hypothesis predicts that empathically aroused individuals should be pleased—and thus have elevated moods—whenever the target is helped. They should be displeased, and exhibit a lower mood, only in the case where the target's distress is not alleviated.

To see which of these predictions was correct, Batson and his associates designed an experiment in which participants were told that they would likely have the chance to perform a simple task that would reduce the number of electric shocks that a peer would receive (Batson et al. 1988, study 1). Somewhat later, half of the participants learned, by chance, that they would not be performing the helping task after all, and thus that they could not help the other student. This divided the participants into two experimental conditions, "perform" and "not perform." Subsequently, half of the participants in each condition learned that, by chance, the peer was not going to get the shocks, while the other half learned that, by chance, the peer would still have to get the shocks. This yielded two more experimental conditions, "prior relief" and "no prior relief." All participants were also asked to self-report their level of empathy for the peer, so that high- and low-empathy participants could be distinguished. To assess mood change, the moods of all participants were measured both before and after the experimental manipulation. As we saw above, the version of the empathy-specific reward hypothesis that we're considering predicts that participants in the perform + no prior relief condition should indicate an elevated mood, since they were able to help the peer; it also predicts that participants in all the other conditions should not have an elevated mood, since for one reason or another they were unable to help, and thus were ineligible for the reward. The empathy-altruism hypothesis, by contrast, predicts an elevated mood in all three conditions in which the peer escaped the shocks: perform + no prior relief, perform + prior relief, and not perform + prior relief. The only condition in which empathy-altruism predicts low mood is the one in which the peer gets the shocks: not perform + no prior relief. In fact, the results fit the pattern predicted by the empathy-altruism hypothesis, not the pattern predicted by empathy-specific reward.

We are inclined to agree with Batson that this experiment shows that the version of the empathy-specific reward hypothesis we've been considering is less plausible than the empathy-altruism hypothesis.[36] However, there's another way of elaborating the self-administered version of the empathy-specific reward hypothesis that the experiment does not address. On the version of the empathy-specific reward hypothesis we've been considering, the self-administered rewards come from something like a "jolt of pride" that the empathically aroused agent feels when he helps the target. And, as Batson rightly notes, it is unlikely that an agent would expect to get this reward if he were in no way involved in the relief of the target's distress. But the jolt of pride story is not the only one that an egoist can tell about the self-administered reward an empathically aroused agent might anticipate when confronted with an opportunity to help; another option focuses on the vicarious pleasure that empathically aroused agents might expect to feel when the target's distress is alleviated. This account, the empathic-joy hypothesis, maintains that empathically aroused individuals "help to gain the good feeling of sharing vicariously in the needy person's joy at improvement" (Batson et al. 1991, 413). On this story, the actor's ultimate goal is egoistic; the desire to help is just instrumental.

There have been a number of experiments aimed at testing the empathic-joy hypothesis. All of them rely on manipulating subjects' expectations about the sort of feedback they can expect about the condition of the target. The central idea in two of these experiments[37] was that if the empathic-joy hypothesis is correct, then high-empathy subjects should be more highly motivated to help when they expect to get feedback about the effect of their assistance on the target's well-being than when they have no expectation of learning about the effect of their assistance. In the latter ("no-feedback")

36. Batson and colleagues (Batson et al. 1988) also did a Stroop experiment aimed at testing this version of the empathy-specific reward hypothesis. But for the reasons discussed in the previous section, we don't think the Stroop procedure is useful in this context.
37. Smith et al. 1989; Batson et al. 1991, experiment 1.

condition subjects won't know if the target's situation has improved and thus they can't expect to experience vicarious joy. On the empathy-altruism hypothesis, by contrast, high-empathy subjects are motivated by an ultimate desire for the well-being of the target, so we should not expect those anticipating feedback to be more likely to help than those not anticipating feedback. In both experiments, the Stotland technique was used to manipulate empathy, and in both cases the subjects who were instructed to imagine how the target felt failed to show a higher level of helping in the feedback condition than in the no-feedback condition. This looks like bad news for the empathic-joy hypothesis, but for two reasons, the situation is less than clear-cut. First, doubts have been raised about the effectiveness of the Stotland manipulation in these experiments.[38] Second, in one experiment there was an unexpected finding: while high-empathy subjects helped more than low-empathy subjects in the no-feedback condition, they actually helped less in the feedback condition.

In an effort to buttress the case against the empathic-joy hypothesis, Batson and his colleagues designed two additional experiments in which the rationale was rather different.[39] If the empathic-joy hypothesis is true, they reasoned, then if high-empathy subjects listen to a taped interview detailing the plight of a troubled target in the recent past and are then offered a choice between getting an update on how the target is doing and hearing about another person, there should be a linear relationship between the probability that the target has improved and the likelihood of choosing to get an update on the target, since the more likely it is that the target has improved, the more likely it is that the subject will get to experience the vicarious joy that he seeks. In both experiments, subjects were given what were alleged to be experts' assessments of the likelihood that the target would improve in the time between the first and second interviews. Neither experiment showed the sort of linear relationship that the empathic-joy hypothesis predicts.

We agree with Batson and colleagues' contention that these results "cast serious doubt on the empathic-joy hypothesis" (1991, 425). But as they go on to note, the experiments were not designed to test the empathic-joy hypothesis against the empathy-altruism hypothesis, since the latter hypothesis makes no clear prediction about the scenarios in question. Therefore, Batson and colleagues (1991, 425) are appropriately cautious, observing that the experiments "did not provide unequivocal support" for empathy-altruism. The bottom line, as we see it, is that while the empathic-joy hypothesis does not look promising, more evidence is needed before coming to a final judgment.

4.7. THE SOCIAL PSYCHOLOGY OF ALTRUISM: SUMMING UP

Batson concludes that the work we have reviewed in this section gives us good reason to think that the empathy-altruism hypothesis is true.

---

38. For discussion, see Smith et al. 1989; Batson et al. 1991.

39. Batson et al. 1991, experiments 2 and 3.

Sherlock Holmes stated: "When you have eliminated the impossible, whatever remains, however improbable, must be the truth." If we apply Holmes's dictum to our attempt to answer the altruism question, then I believe we must, tentatively, accept the truth of the empathy-altruism hypothesis. It is impossible for any of the three major egoistic explanations of the empathy-helping relationship—or any combination of these—to account for the evidence reviewed.

(Batson 1991, 174)

Although we don't believe that this conclusion is justified, we think it is clear that Batson and his associates have made important progress. They have shown that one widely endorsed account of the egoistic motivation underlying helping behavior, the aversive-arousal reduction hypothesis, is very unlikely to be true in the sorts of cases used in their studies. They have also dealt a serious blow to both the socially administered empathy-specific punishment hypothesis and to several versions of the empathy-specific reward hypothesis. However, we think the jury is still out on the self-administered empathy-specific punishment hypothesis, and that the case against the empathy-specific reward hypothesis is not yet conclusive.

A worry of another sort emerges when we focus on Batson's claim that no "combination" of the three major egoistic explanations could explain the experimental data. An egoistic thesis that might be labeled disjunctive egoism maintains that when empathically aroused people try to help, they have a variety of egoistic motivations—they are sometimes motivated by the desire to reduce aversive arousal, sometimes by the desire to avoid socially or self-administered punishment and sometimes by the desire for socially or self-administered reward. Since all of Batson's experiments are designed to test empathy-altruism against one or another specific egoistic hypothesis, none of these experiments rules out this sort of disjunctive egoism. For it might be the case that in each experiment subjects are motivated by one of the egoistic goals that the experiment is not designed to rule out. We're not sure how seriously to take this concern, since it seems to require that nature is playing a shell game with the investigators, always relying on an egoistic motivation that the experiment is not designed to look for. But we do think the idea deserves more explicit attention than it has so far received in the literature.[40] Clearly, there is still much important work to be done on the social psychology of altruism.

5. Conclusion

Readers might be tempted to think, at this point, that our concluding section must be rather inconclusive. After all, we haven't claimed to have resolved the philosophically venerable egoism vs. altruism debate, and the scientific record appears somewhat equivocal,

---

40. This worry about Batson's one-at-a-time strategy was noted, albeit briefly, in Cialdini 1991. For a helpful discussion, see Oakberg (unpublished ms.).

as indeed we've been at pains to show. But before we offer refunds, we should enumerate what we think we have learned.

Our first lesson is negative: contrary to what some writers have asserted, appeal to evolutionary theory does not generate movement in the philosophical debate about altruism. This may seem disappointing, especially given the fecundity of recent explications of philosophical ethics in the light of evolutionary theory (e.g., Joyce 2006; Machery and Mallon 2010). Fortunately, our conclusions regarding the philosophical impact of experimental social psychology are rather more inspiring. Batson and associates have shown quite conclusively that the methods of experimental psychology can move the debate forward; it now looks as though certain venerable renderings of psychological egoism are not true to the contours of human psychology. Indeed, in our view, Batson and his associates have made more progress in the last three decades than philosophers using the traditional philosophical methodology of a priori arguments buttressed by anecdote and intuition have made in the previous two millennia. Their work, like other work recounted in this volume, powerfully demonstrates the utility of empirical methods in moral psychology.

REFERENCES

Aquinas, T. 1270/1917. *The Summa Theologica*. New York: Benziger Brothers.

Aubrey, J. 1949. *Aubrey's Brief Lives*. Ed. Oliver Lawson Dick. Boston: David R. Godine. Aubrey's sketch of Hobbes is available online at www.groups.dcs.stand.ac.uk/~history/Societies/Aubrey.html.

Axelrod, R., and W. D. Hamilton. 1981. The Evolution of Cooperation. *Science* 211: 1390–6.

———. 1991. *The Altruism Question: Toward a Social-Psychological Answer*. Hillsdale, NJ: Lawrence Erlbaum Associates.

Batson, C. D. 1998. Altruism and Prosocial Behavior. In D. T. Gilbert and S. T. Fiske, eds., *The Handbook of Social Psychology*, 2:282–316. Boston: McGraw-Hill.

Batson, C. D., B. Duncan, P. Ackerman, T. Buckley, and K. Birch. 1981. Is Empathic Emotion a Source of Altruistic Motivation? *Journal of Personality and Social Psychology* 40: 290–302.

Batson, C. D., K. O'Quin, J. Fultz, M. Vanderplas, and A. Isen. 1983. Self-Reported Distress and Empathy and Egoistic Versus Altruistic Motivation for Helping. *Journal of Personality and Social Psychology* 45: 706–18.

Batson, C. D., J. Dyck, R. Brandt, J. Batson, A. Powell, M. McMaster, M., and C. Griffith. 1988. Five Studies Testing Two New Egoistic Alternatives to the Empathy-Altruism Hypothesis. *Journal of Personality and Social Psychology* 55: 52–77.

Batson, C. D., G. Batson, J. Slingsby, K. Harrell, H. Peekna, and R. M. Todd. 1991. Empathic Joy and the Empathy-Altruism Hypothesis. *Journal of Personality and Social Psychology* 61: 413–26.

Beatty, J. 1992. Fitness. In E. Keller and L. Lloyd, eds., *Keywords in Evolutionary Biology*. Cambridge, MA: Harvard University Press.

Bentham, J. 1789. *An Introduction to the Principles of Morals and Legislation*. Ed. J. H. Burns and H. L. A. Hart, with a new introduction by F. Rosen. Oxford: Oxford University Press, 1996.

———. 1824. *The Book of Fallacies*. London: Hunt.

Boyd, R., and P. Richerson. 1992. Punishment Allows the Evolution of Cooperation (or Anything Else) in Sizable Groups. *Ethology and Sociobiology* 13: 171–95. Reprinted in R. Boyd and P. Richerson, *The Origin and Evolution of Cultures*. Oxford: Oxford University Press, 2005.

Bratman, M. 1987. *Intention, Plans, and Practical Reasoning*. Cambridge, MA: Harvard University Press.

Broad, C. D. 1930. *Five Types of Ethical Theory*. New York: Harcourt, Brace.

Butler, J. 1726. *Fifteen Sermons Preached at the Rolls Chapel*. Sermons I, II, III. XI, XII, reprinted in S. Darwall, ed., *Five Sermons Preached at the Rolls Chapel and a Dissertation upon the Nature of Virtue*. Indianapolis, IN: Hackett, 1983.

Carey, S., and E. Spelke. 1996. Science and Core Knowledge. *Philosophy of Science* 63, 4: 515–33.

Cialdini, R. B. 1991. Altruism or Egoism? That Is (Still) the Question. *Psychological Inquiry* 2: 124–26.

Davidson, D. 1963. Actions, Reasons, and Causes. *Journal of Philosophy* 60, 23: 685–700.

———. 1980. Agency. In *Essays on Actions and Events*. Oxford, Clarendon Press, 43–61.

Dovidio, J., J. Allen, and D. Schroeder. 1990. The Specificity of Empathy-Induced Helping: Evidence for Altruistic Motivation. *Journal of Personality and Social Psychology* 59: 249–60.

Dovidio, J., J. Piliavin, D. Schroeder, and L. Penner. 2006. *The Social Psychology of Prosocial Behavior*. Mahwah, NJ: Lawrence Erlbaum Associates.

Eisenberg, N., and P. Miller. 1987. Empathy and Prosocial Behavior. *Psychological Bulletin* 101: 91–119.

Fodor, J. 1983. *The Modularity of Mind*. Cambridge, MA: Bradford Books/MIT Press.

Fultz, J., D. Batson, V. Fortenbach, P. McCarthy, and L. Varney. 1986. Social Evaluation and the Empathy-Altruism Hypothesis. *Journal of Personality and Social Psychology* 50, 761–69.

Geller, V., and P. Shaver. 1976. Cognitive Consequences of Self-Awareness. *Journal of Experimental Social Psychology* 12: 99–108.

Ghiselin, M. 1974. *The Economy of Nature and the Evolution of Sex*. Berkeley: University of California Press.

Godfrey-Smith, P. 1996. *Complexity and the Function of Mind in Nature*. Cambridge: Cambridge University Press.

Goldman, A. 1970. *A Theory of Human Action*. Englewood-Cliffs, NJ: Prentice-Hall.

Grant, C. 1997. Altruism: A Social Science Chameleon. *Zygon* 32, 3: 321–40.

Grice, H. P. 1971. Intention and Certainty. *Proceedings of the British Academy* 57: 263–79.

Hamilton, W. D. 1963. The Evolution of Altruistic Behavior. *American Naturalist* 97: 354–56.

———. 1964a. The General Evolution of Social Behavior I. *Journal of Theoretical Biology* 7: 1–16.

———. 1964b. The General Evolution of Social Behavior II. *Journal of Theoretical Biology* 7: 17–52.

Hobbes, T. 1981. *Leviathan*. Edited with an introduction by C. B. Macpherson. London: Penguin Books. First published 1651.

Hoffman, M. 1991. Is Empathy Altruistic? *Psychological Inquiry* 2: 131–33.

Hornstein, H. 1991. Empathic Distress and Altruism: Still Inseparable. *Psychological Inquiry* 2: 133–35.

Hume, D. 1975. *Enquiry Concerning the Principles of Morals*. 3rd ed. Ed. L. A. Selby-Bigge, rev. P. H. Nidditch. Oxford: Clarendon Press. Originally published 1751.

Joyce, R. 2006. *The Evolution of Mind*. Cambridge, MA: MIT Press.

Kant, I. 1785/1949. *Fundamental Principles of the Metaphysics of Morals*. Trans. Thomas K. Abbott. Englewood Cliffs, NJ: Prentice-Hall/Library of Liberal Arts.

Krebs, D. 1975. Empathy and Altruism. *Journal of Personality and Social Psychology* 32: 1134–46.

LaFollette, H., ed. 2000a. *The Blackwell Guide to Ethical Theory*. Oxford: Blackwell.

———. 2000b. Introduction. In LaFollette 2000a, 1–12.

La Rochefoucauld, F. 2007. *Collected Maxims and Other Reflections*. Trans. E. H. Blackmore, A. M. Blackmore, and Francine Giguere. New York: Oxford University Press. Originally published 1665.

Lewis, D. 1997. Finkish Dispositions. *Philosophical Quarterly* 47: 143–58.

MacIntyre, A. 1967. Egoism and Altruism. In P. Edwards, ed., *The Encyclopedia of Philosophy*, 2:462–66. New York: Macmillan.

Machery, E., and R. Mallon. 2010. Evolution of Morality. In John Doris and the Moral Psychology Research Group, eds., *The Moral Psychology Handbook*. New York: Oxford University Press.

Martin, C. B. 1994. Disposition and Conditionals. *Philosophical Quarterly* 44: 1–8.

Mill, J. S. 1861/2001. *Utilitarianism*. Indianapolis, IN: Hackett.

Miller, D. T. 1999. The Norm of Self-Interest. *American Psychologist* 54: 1053–60.

Nagel, T. 1970. *The Possibility of Altruism*. Oxford: Oxford University Press.

Nesse, R. 1990. Evolutionary Explanations of Emotions. *Human Nature* 1: 261–89.

Nichols, S. 2004. *Sentimental Rules: On the Natural Foundations of Moral Judgment*. Oxford: Oxford University Press.

Nietzsche, F. 1997. *Daybreak: Thoughts on the Prejudices of Morality*. Trans. R. J. Hollingsdale. Ed. M. Clark and B. Leiter. Cambridge: Cambridge University Press. Originally published 1881.

Oakberg, T. Unpublished ms. A Critical Review of Batson's Project and Related Research on Altruism.

Piliavin, J., and H. Charng. 1990. Altruism—A Review of Recent Theory and Research. *Annual Review of Sociology* 16: 27–65.

Plantinga, A. 1993. *Warrant and Proper Function*. Oxford: Oxford University Press.

Rachels, J. 1990. *Created from Animals: The Moral Implications of Darwinism*. Oxford: Oxford University Press.

Rachels, J. 2000. Naturalism. In LaFollette 2000a, 74–91.

Rousseau, J. J. 1985. *A Discourse on Inequality*. New York: Penguin. Originally published 1754.

Schroeder, D., L. Penner, J. Dovidio, and J. Piliavin. 1995. *The Psychology of Helping and Altruism*. New York: McGraw-Hill.

Schroeder, W. 2000. Continental Ethics. In LaFollette 2000a, 375–99.

Smith, A. 1853. *The Theory of Moral Sentiments*. London: Henry G. Bohn. Originally published 1759.

Smith, K., J. Keating, and E. Stotland. 1989. Altruism Revisited: The Effect of Denying Feedback on a Victim's Status to Empathic Witnesses. *Journal of Personality and Social Psychology* 57: 641–50.

Sober, E. 1994. The Adaptive Advantage of Learning and A Priori Prejudice. In *From a Biological Point of View*. Cambridge: Cambridge University Press.

Sober, E., and D. S. Wilson. 1998. *Unto Others: The Evolution and Psychology of Unselfish Behavior*. Cambridge. MA: Harvard University Press.

Spelke, E. 2000. Core Knowledge. *American Psychologist* 55: 1233–43.

———. 2003. Core Knowledge. In N. Kanwisher and J. Duncan, eds., *Attention and Performance*, vol. 20: *Functional Neuroimaging of Visual Cognition*, 29–56. Oxford: Oxford University Press.

Sripada, C. 2007. Adaptationism, Culture and the Malleability of Human Nature. In P. Carruthers, S. Laurence, and S. Stich, eds., *Innateness and the Structure of the Mind: Foundations and the Future*, 311–29. New York: Oxford University Press.

Stich, S. 1978. Beliefs and Sub-Doxastic States. *Philosophy of Science* 45, 4: 499–518.

———. 1990. *The Fragmentation of Reason*. Cambridge, MA: MIT Press.

———. 2007. Evolution, Altruism and Cognitive Architecture: A Critique of Sober and Wilson's Argument for Psychological Altruism. *Biology and Philosophy* 22, 2: 267–81.

Stocks, E., D. Lishner, and S. Decker. 2009. Altruism or Psychological Escape: Why Does Empathy Promote Prosocial Behavior? *European Journal of Social Psychology* 39: 649–65.

Stotland, E. 1969. Exploratory Studies of Empathy. In L. Berkowitz, ed., *Advances in Experimental Social Psychology*, 4:271–313. New York: Academic Press.

Toi, M., and C. D. Batson. 1982. More Evidence That Empathy Is a Source of Altruistic Motivation. *Journal of Personality and Social Psychology* 43: 281–92.

Trivers, R. 1971. The Evolution of Reciprocal Altruism. *Quarterly Review of Biology* 46: 35–57.

Velleman, D. 1989. *Practical Reflection*. Princeton, NJ: Princeton University Press.

Wilson, G. 2002. Action. In Edward N. Zalta, ed., *The Stanford Encyclopedia of Philosophy*, http://plato.stanford.edu/archives/sum2002/entries/action.

Wright, R. 1994. *The Moral Animal*. New York: Pantheon Books.

Acknowledgments

I am grateful to my co-authors and to the original publishers for granting permission
to reprint these essays. Thanks are also due to Michael Sechman for help in assembling
the volume and constructing the index. The original publication of each essay is listed below.

1. Stephen P. Stich, "The Recombinant DNA Debate," *Philosophy and Public Affairs* 7,3 (1978): 187–205.
2. Stephen P. Stich and Richard E. Nisbett, "Justification and the Psychology of Human Reasoning,"
   Philosophy of Science 47, 2 (1980): 188–202.
3. Stephen P. Stich, "Could Man Be An Irrational Animal?" *Synthese* 64, 1 (1985): 115–35.
4. Stephen P. Stich, "Reflective Equilibrium, Analytic Epistemology and the Problem of Cognitive
   Diversity," *Synthese* 74, 3 (1988): 391–413.
5. Stephen P. Stich. "Moral Philosophy and Mental Representation," in M. Hechter, L. Nadel, and R.E.
   Michod, eds., *The Origin of Values*, 215–28 (New York: Aldine de Gruyter, 1993).
6. Stephen P. Stich, "Naturalizing Epistemology: Quine, Simon and the Prospects for Pragmatism," in
   C. Hookway and D. Peterson, eds., *Philosophy and Cognitive Science*, 1–17, Royal Institute of Philosophy,
   Supplement no. 34 (Cambridge: Cambridge University Press, 1993).
7. Richard Samuels, Stephen P. Stich, and Patrice D. Tremoulet, "Rethinking Rationality: From Bleak
   Implications to Darwinian Modules," in E. LePore and Z. Pylyshyn, eds., *What Is Cognitive Science?*,
   74–120 (Oxford: Blackwells, 1999).
8. Jonathan M. Weinberg, Shaun Nichols, and Stephen Stich, "Normativity and Epistemic Intuitions,"
   Philosophical Topics 29, 1–2 (2001): 429–60.
9. Richard Samuels, Stephen Stich, and Michael Bishop, "Ending the Rationality Wars: How to Make
   Disputes About Human Rationality Disappear," in Renée Elio, ed., *Common Sense, Reasoning, and
   Rationality*, 236–68 (Oxford: Oxford University Press, 2002).
10. Shaun Nichols, Stephen Stich, and Jonathan M. Weinberg, "Meta-Skepticism: Meditations on Ethno-
    Epistemology," in S. Luper, ed., *The Skeptics*, 227–47 (Aldershot, UK: Ashgate Publishing, 2003).
11. John M. Doris and Stephen P. Stich, "As a Matter of Fact: Empirical Perspectives on Ethics," in F. Jackson
    and M. Smith, eds., *The Oxford Handbook of Contemporary Philosophy*, 114–52 (Oxford: Oxford
    University Press, 2005).
12. Chandra Sripada and Stephen Stich, "A Framework for the Psychology of Norms," in P. Carruthers,
    S. Laurence, and S. Stich, eds., *The Innate Mind*, Vol. 2: *Culture and Cognition*, 280–301 (New York:
    Oxford University Press, 2006)

13. Daniel Kelly, Stephen Stich, Kevin J. Haley, Serena J. Eng, and Daniel M.T. Fessler, "Harm, Affect and the Moral /Conventional Distinction," *Mind and Language* 22, 2 (2007): 117–31.
14. Daniel Kelly and Stephen Stich, "Two Theories About the Cognitive Architecture Underlying Morality," in P. Carruthers, S. Laurence and S. Stich, eds., *The Innate Mind*, Vol. 3: *Foundations and the Future*, 348–66 (New York: Oxford University Press, 2007).
15. Stephen Stich, John Doris, and Erica Roedder, "Altruism," in *John Doris and the Moral Psychology Research Group*, eds., *The Moral Psychology Handbook*, 147–205 (New York: Oxford University Press, 2010).

Name Index

Subject Index